Breakthroughs in Software Science and Computational Intelligence

Yingxu Wang
University of Calgary, Canada

Managing Director:	Lindsay Johnston
Senior Editorial Director:	Heather A. Probst
Book Production Manager:	Sean Woznicki
Development Manager:	Joel Gamon
Development Editor:	Heather A. Probst
Acquisitions Editor:	Erika Gallagher
Typesetter:	Russell A. Spangler
Cover Design:	Nick Newcomer, Lisandro Gonzalez

Published in the United States of America by
Information Science Reference (an imprint of IGI Global)
701 E. Chocolate Avenue
Hershey PA 17033
Tel: 717-533-8845
Fax: 717-533-8661
E-mail: cust@igi-global.com
Web site: http://www.igi-global.com

Library of Congress Cataloging-in-Publication Data

Breakthroughs in software science and computational intelligence / Yingxu Wang, editor.
     p. cm.
  Includes bibliographical references and index.
  Summary: "This book charts the new ground broken by researchers exploring software science as it interacts with computational intelligence"--Provided by publisher.
  ISBN 978-1-4666-0264-9 (hardcover) -- ISBN 978-1-4666-0265-6 (ebook) -- ISBN 978-1-4666-0266-3 (print & perpetual access) 1. Computational intelligence. 2. Computer software. I. Wang, Yingxu, 1956-
  Q342.B74 2012
  006.3--dc23
                              2011051851

British Cataloguing in Publication Data
A Cataloguing in Publication record for this book is available from the British Library.

All work contributed to this book is new, previously-unpublished material. The views expressed in this book are those of the authors, but not necessarily of the publisher.

Table of Contents

Section 1
Computational Intelligence

Yingxu Wang, University of Calgary, Canada
Witold Pedrycz, University of Alberta, Canada
George Baciu, Hong Kong Polytechnic University, China
Ping Chen, University of Houston-Downtown, USA
Guoyin Wang, Chongqing University of Posts & Telecommunications, China
Yiyu Yao, University of Regina, Canada

Witold Pedrycz, University of Alberta, Canada, and Polish Academy of Sciences, Poland

Carlos Ramirez, Tec de Monterrey, Campus Querétaro, México
Benjamin Valdes, Tec de Monterrey, Campus Querétaro, México

Yang Liu, Xi'an Jiaotong University, China
Luyang Jiao, First Affiliated Hospital of Xinxiang Medical College, China
Guohua Bai, Blekinge Institute of Technology, Sweden
Boqin Feng, Xi'an Jiaotong University, China

Section 3
Software Science

Section 4
Applications of Computational Intelligence and Cognitive Computing

Detailed Table of Contents

Section 1
Computational Intelligence

Chapter 1

Yingxu Wang, University of Calgary, Canada
Witold Pedrycz, University of Alberta, Canada
George Baciu, Hong Kong Polytechnic University, China
Ping Chen, University of Houston-Downtown, USA
Guoyin Wang, Chongqing University of Posts & Telecommunications, China
Yiyu Yao, University of Regina, Canada

Cognitive Computing (CC) is an emerging paradigm of intelligent computing theories and technologies based on cognitive informatics, which implements computational intelligence by autonomous inferences and perceptions mimicking the mechanisms of the brain. The development of Cognitive Computers (cC) is centric in cognitive computing methodologies. A cC is an intelligent computer for knowledge processing as that of a conventional von Neumann computer for data processing. This paper summarizes the presentations of a set of 6 position papers presented in the ICCI'10 Plenary Panel on Cognitive Computing and Applications contributed from invited panelists who are part of the world's renowned researchers and scholars in the field of cognitive informatics and cognitive computing.

Chapter 2

Witold Pedrycz, University of Alberta, Canada, and Polish Academy of Sciences, Poland

Information granules and ensuing Granular Computing offer interesting opportunities to endow processing with an important facet of human-centricity. This facet implies that the underlying processing supports non-numeric data inherently associated with the variable perception of humans. Systems that commonly become distributed and hierarchical, managing granular information in hierarchical and distributed architectures, is of growing interest, especially when invoking mechanisms of knowledge generation and knowledge sharing. The outstanding feature of human centricity of Granular Computing along with essential fuzzy set-based constructs constitutes the crux of this study. The author elaborates on some new directions of knowledge elicitation and quantification realized in the setting of fuzzy sets. With this regard, the paper concentrates on knowledge-based clustering. It is also emphasized that collaboration and reconciliation of locally available knowledge give rise to the concept of higher type information granules. Other interesting directions enhancing human centricity of computing with fuzzy sets deals with non-numeric semi-qualitative characterization of information granules, as well as inherent evolving capabilities of associated human-centric systems. The author discusses a suite of algorithms facilitating a qualitative assessment of fuzzy sets, formulates a series of associated optimization tasks guided by well-formulated performance indexes, and discusses the underlying essence of resulting solutions.

Chapter 3

Carlos Ramirez, Tec de Monterrey, Campus Querétaro, México
Benjamin Valdes, Tec de Monterrey, Campus Querétaro, México

A cognitive model for skills and concepts representation as well as a proposal for its computational implementation is presented in this paper. The model is intended to help bridge some of the natural problems that arise in current massive education models through the adaptation and personalization of learning environments. The model is capable of representing rich semantic knowledge, including both skills and concepts, while integrating them through a coherent network of role based associations. The associations build an ontology that integrates on itself different domain taxonomies to represent the knowledge acquired by a student keeping relevant context information. The model is based on a constructivist approach.

Chapter 4

Yang Liu, Xi'an Jiaotong University, China
Luyang Jiao, First Affiliated Hospital of Xinxiang Medical College, China
Guohua Bai, Blekinge Institute of Technology, Sweden
Boqin Feng, Xi'an Jiaotong University, China

From the perspective of cognitive informatics, cognition can be viewed as the acquisition of knowledge. In real-world applications, information systems usually contain some degree of noisy data. A new model proposed to deal with the hybrid-feature selection problem combines the neighbourhood approximation and variable precision rough set models. Then rule induction algorithm can learn from selected features in order to reduce the complexity of rule sets. Through proposed integration, the knowledge acquisition process becomes insensitive to the dimensionality of data with a pre-defined tolerance degree of noise and uncertainty for misclassification. When the authors apply the method to a Chinese diabetic diagnosis problem, the hybrid-attribute reduction method selected only five attributes from totally thirty-four measurements. Rule learner produced eight rules with average two attributes in the left part of an IF-THEN rule form, which is a manageable set of rules. The demonstrated experiment shows that the present approach is effective in handling real-world problems.

Chapter 5

Jiří Wiedermann, Academy of Sciences of the Czech Republic, Czech Republic

In this paper, the author describes a simple yet cognitively powerful architecture of an embodied conscious agent. The architecture incorporates a mechanism for mining, representing, processing and exploiting semantic knowledge. This mechanism is based on two complementary internal world models which are built automatically. One model (based on artificial mirror neurons) is used for mining and capturing the syntax of the recognized part of the environment while the second one (based on neural nets) for its semantics. Jointly, the models support algorithmic processes underlying phenomena similar in important aspects to higher cognitive functions such as imitation learning and the development of communication, language, thinking, and consciousness.

Section 2
Cognitive Computing

Chapter 6

Bernard Widrow, Stanford University, USA
Juan Carlos Aragon, Stanford University, USA

Taking inspiration from life experience, the authors have devised a new form of computer memory. Certain conjectures about human memory are keys to the central idea. This paper presents a design of a practical and useful "cognitive" memory system in which the new memory does not function like a computer memory where specific data is stored in specific numbered registers; retrieval is done by reading the contents of the specified memory register, or done by matching key words as with a document search. Incoming sensory data would be stored at the next available empty memory location and could be stored redundantly at several empty locations. The stored sensory data would neither have key words nor would it be located in known or specified memory locations. Retrieval would be initiated by a prompt signal from a current set of sensory inputs or patterns. The search would be done by a retrieval system that makes use of auto-associative artificial neural networks. In this paper, the authors present a practical application of this cognitive memory system to human facial recognition.

Chapter 7

Witold Kinsner, University of Manitoba, Canada
Hong Zhang, University of Manitoba, Canada

This paper presents estimations of multi-scale (multi-fractal) measures for feature extraction from deoxyribonucleic acid (DNA) sequences, and demonstrates the intriguing possibility of identifying biological functionality using information contained within the DNA sequence. We have developed a technique that seeks patterns or correlations in the DNA sequence at a higher level than the local base-pair structure. The technique has three main steps: (i) transforms the DNA sequence symbols into a modified Lévy walk, (ii) transforms the Lévy walk into a signal spectrum, and (iii) breaks the spectrum into sub-spectra and treats each of these as an attractor from which the multi-fractal dimension spectrum is estimated. An optimal minimum window size and volume element size are found for estimation of the multi-fractal measures. Experimental results show that DNA is multi-fractal, and that the multi-fractality changes depending upon the location (coding or non-coding region) in the sequence.

Chapter 8

Takuo Suganuma, Tohoku University, Japan
Hideyuki Takahashi, Tohoku University, Japan
Norio Shiratori, Tohoku University, Japan

In a ubiquitous computing (ubicomp) environment, system components of different types, including hardware elements, software components, and network connections, must cooperate mutually to provide services that fulfill user requirements. Consequently, advanced and flexible characteristics of software that are specialized for a ubicomp environment are needed. This paper presents a proposal of an agent-based middleware for a ubicomp environment comprising computers and home electric appliances. The middleware, called AMUSE, can take quality of service (QoS) in a ubicomp environment into consideration by coping not only with user context but also with the resource context, using agent-based computing technology. Herein, we describe the concept, design, and initial implementation of AMUSE. Simulation results of an experimental ubiquitous service using AMUSE demonstrate the effectiveness of our proposed scheme. Additionally, to confirm our scheme's feasibility and effectiveness, we describe the initial implementation of a multimedia communication application based on AMUSE.

In order to apply a powerful pattern recognition algorithm to predict functional sites in proteins, amino acids cannot be used directly as inputs since they are non-numerical variables. Therefore, they need encoding prior to input. In this regard, the bio-basis function maps a non-numerical sequence space to a numerical feature space. One of the important issues for the bio-basis function is how to select a minimum set of bio-basis strings with maximum information. In this paper, an efficient method to select bio-basis strings for the bio-basis function is described integrating the concepts of the Fisher ratio and "degree of resemblance". The integration enables the method to select a minimum set of most informative bio-basis strings. The "degree of resemblance" enables efficient selection of a set of distinct bio-basis strings. In effect, it reduces the redundant features in numerical feature space. Quantitative indices are proposed for evaluating the quality of selected bio-basis strings. The effectiveness of the proposed bio-basis string selection method, along with a comparison with existing methods, is demonstrated on different data sets.

Autonomic Computing is an emerging computing paradigm used to create computer systems capable of self-management in order to overcome the rapidly growing complexity of computing systems management. To possess self-* properties, there must be mechanisms to support self-awareness, that is an autonomic system should be able to perceive the abnormality of its components. After abnormality is checked, processes of self-healing, self-configuration, self-optimization, and self-protection must be completed to guarantee the system works correctly and continuously. In role-based collaboration (RBC), roles are the major media for interaction, coordination, and collaboration. A role can be used to check if a player behaves well or not. This paper investigates the possibility of using roles and their related mechanisms to diagnose the behavior of agents, and facilitate self-* properties of a system.

Agent and Ontology are distinct technologies that arose independent of each other, having their own standards and specifications. The semantics web is one of the popular research areas these days, and is based on the current Web, which adds more semantics to it for the purpose of building the Ontology of Web content. In this regard, application program on Web can make the purpose of cross-platform calculation come true by taking advantage of Ontology. However, agent is a theory able to enhance abstraction of software itself, and as it is know, negotiation protocol is the basic principle in the electronic commerce which has a direct impact on the efficiency of the negotiation. This study examines the communication architecture with negotiation protocol on the Semantic Web. Precisely speaking, agents make computing with Ontology, and the authors define an agent's communication ontology for this communication framework and semantic web use Ontology to describe the negotiation protocol. In this context, the buyer or seller will be able to improve semantic cognitive in process of negotiation. Also, it can provide an intelligent platform for the information exchange on the same understanding about the content of communication in the electronic negotiation service.

Section 3
Software Science

Chapter 12

Yingxu Wang, University of Calgary, Canada

Xinming Tan, Wuhan University of Technology, China

Cyprian F. Ngolah, Sentinel Trending & Diagnostics Ltd., Calgary, Canada

Real-Time Process Algebra (RTPA) is a denotational mathematics for the algebraic modeling and manipulations of software system architectures and behaviors by the Unified Data Models (UDMs) and Unified Process Models (UPMs). On the basis of the RTPA specification and refinement methodologies, automatic software code generation is enabled toward improving software development productivity. This paper examines designing and developing the RTPA-based software code generator (RTPA-CG) that transfers system models in RTPA architectures and behaviors into C++ or Java. A two-phrase strategy has been employed in the design of the code generator. The first phrase analyzes the lexical, syntactical, and type specifications of a software system modeled in RTPA, which results in a set of abstract syntax trees (ASTs). The second phrase translates the ASTs into C++ or Java based on predesigned mapping strategies and code generation rules. The toolkit of RTPA code generator encompasses an RTPA lexer, parser, type-checker, and a code builder. Experimental results show that system models in RTPA can be rigorously processed and corresponding C++/Java code can be automatically generated using the toolkit. The code generated is executable and effective under the support of an RTPA run-time library.

Chapter 13

Yingxu Wang, University of Calgary, Canada

Cyprian F. Ngolah, Sentinel Trending & Diagnostics Ltd., Canada

Guangping Zeng, University of Science and Technology, China and University of California, Berkeley, USA

Phillip C.-Y. Sheu, Wuhan University, China and University of California, Irvine, USA

C. Philip Choy, University of Calgary, Canada

Yousheng Tian, University of Calgary, Canada

A real-time operating system (RTOS) provides a platform for the design and implementation of a wide range of applications in real-time systems, embedded systems, and mission-critical systems. This paper presents a formal design model for a general RTOS known as RTOS+ that enables a specific target RTOS to be rigorously and efficiently derived in real-world applications. The methodology of a denotational mathematics, Real-Time Process Algebra (RTPA), is described for formally modeling and refining architectures, static behaviors, and dynamic behaviors of RTOS+. The conceptual model of the RTOS+ system is introduced as the initial requirements for the system. The architectural model of RTOS+ is created using RTPA architectural modeling methodologies and refined by a set of Unified Data Models (UDMs). The static behaviors of RTOS+ are specified and refined by a set of Unified Process Models (UPMs). The dynamic behaviors of the RTOS+ system are specified and refined by the real-time process scheduler and system dispatcher. This work is presented in two papers; the conceptual and architectural models of RTOS+ is described in this paper, while the static and dynamic behavioral models of RTOS+ will be elaborated in a forthcoming paper.

Chapter 14

Yingxu Wang, University of Calgary, Canada

Guangping Zeng, University of Science and Technology, China and University of California, Berkeley, USA

Cyprian F. Ngolah, Sentinel Trending & Diagnostics Ltd., Canada

Phillip C.-Y. Sheu, Wuhan University, China and University of California, Irvine, USA

C. Philip Choy, University of Calgary, Canada

Yousheng Tian, University of Calgary, Canada

A real-time operating system (RTOS) provides a platform for the design and implementation of a wide range of applications in real-time systems, embedded systems, and mission-critical systems. This paper presents a formal design model for a general RTOS known as RTOS+ that enables a specific target RTOS to be rigorously and efficiently derived in real-world applications. The methodology of a denotational mathematics, Real-Time Process Algebra (RTPA), is described for formally modeling and refining architectures, static behaviors, and dynamic behaviors of RTOS+. The conceptual model of the RTOS+ system is introduced as the initial requirements for the system. The architectural model of RTOS+ is created using RTPA architectural modeling methodologies and refined by a set of Unified Data Models (UDMs). The static behaviors of RTOS+ are specified and refined by a set of Unified Process Models (UPMs). The dynamic behaviors of the RTOS+ system are specified and refined by the real-time process scheduler and system dispatcher. This work is presented in two papers in serial due to its excessive length. The static and dynamic behavioral models of RTOS+ is described in this paper; while the conceptual and architectural models of RTOS+ has been published in IJSSCI 2(2).

Chapter 15

Yingxu Wang, University of Calgary, Canada

Yanan Zhang, University of Calgary, Canada

Phillip C.-Y. Sheu, Wuhan University, China and Univ. of California, Irvine, USA

Xuhui Li, Wuhan University, China

Hong Guo, Coventry University, UK

An Automated Teller Machine (ATM) is a safety-critical and real-time system that is highly complicated in design and implementation. This paper presents the formal design, specification, and modeling of the ATM system using a denotational mathematics known as Real-Time Process Algebra (RTPA). The conceptual model of the ATM system is introduced as the initial requirements for the system. The architectural model of the ATM system is created using RTPA architectural modeling methodologies and refined by a set of Unified Data Models (UDMs), which share a generic mathematical model of tuples. The static behaviors of the ATM system are specified and refined by a set of Unified Process Models (UPMs) for the ATM transition processing and system supporting processes. The dynamic behaviors of the ATM system are specified and refined by process priority allocation, process deployment, and process dispatch models. Based on the formal design models of the ATM system, code can be automatically generated using the RTPA Code Generator (RTPA-CG), or be seamlessly transformed into programs by programmers. The formal models of ATM may not only serve as a formal design paradigm of real-time software systems, but also a test bench for the expressive power and modeling capability of exiting formal methods in software engineering.

Chapter 16

Yingxu Wang, University of Calgary, Canada

Xinming Tan, Wuhan University of Technology, China

Cyprian F. Ngolah, Sentinel Trending & Diagnostics Ltd., Canada

Phillip C.-Y. Sheu, University of California, Irvine, USA

Type theories are fundamental for underpinning data object modeling and system architectural design in computing and software engineering. Abstract Data Types (ADTs) are a set of highly generic and rigorously modeled data structures in type theory. ADTs also play a key role in Object-Oriented (OO) technologies for software system design and implementation. This paper presents a formal modeling methodology for ADTs using the Real-Time Process Algebra (RTPA), which allows both architectural and behavioral models of ADTs and complex data objects. Formal architectures, static behaviors, and dynamic behaviors of a set of ADTs are comparatively studied. The architectural models of the ADTs are created using RTPA architectural modeling methodologies known as the Unified Data Models (UDMs). The static behaviors of the ADTs are specified and refined by a set of Unified Process Models (UPMs) of RTPA. The dynamic behaviors of the ADTs are modeled by process dispatching technologies of RTPA. This work has been applied in a number of real-time and non-real-time system designs such as a Real-Time Operating System (RTOS+), a Cognitive Learning Engine (CLE), and the automatic code generator based on RTPA.

Chapter 17

Shaohua Teng, Guangdong University of Technology, China

Wei Zhang, Guangdong University of Technology, China

Haibin Zhu, Nipissing University, Canada

Xiufen Fu, Guangdong University of Technology, China

Jiangyi Su, Guangdong University of Technology, China

Baoliang Cui, Guangdong University of Technology, China

The LLF (Least Laxity First) scheduling algorithm assigns a priority to a task according to its executing urgency. The smaller the laxity value of a task is, the sooner it needs to be executed. When two or more tasks have same or approximate laxity values, LLF scheduling algorithm leads to frequent switches among tasks, causes extra overhead in a system, and therefore, restricts its application. The least switch and laxity first scheduling algorithm is proposed in this paper by searching out an appropriate common divisor in order to improve the LLF algorithm for periodic tasks.

Section 4
Applications of Computational Intelligence and Cognitive Computing

This paper proposes semantic TFIDF, an agent-based system for retrieving location-aware information that makes use of semantic information in the data to develop smaller training sets, thereby improving the speed of retrieval while maintaining or even improving accuracy. This proposed method first assigns intelligent agents to gathering location-aware data, which they then classify, match, and organize to find a best match for a user query. This is done using semantic graphs in the WordNet English dictionary. Experiments will compare the proposed system with three other commonly used systems and show that it is significantly faster and more accurate.

This paper describes a system developed to help people explore local communities by providing navigation services in social spaces created by the community members via communication and knowledge sharing. The proposed system utilizes data of a community's social network to reconstruct the social space, which is otherwise not physically perceptible but imaginary, experiential, yet learnable. The social space is modeled with an agent network, where each agent stands for a member of the community and has knowledge about expertise and personal characteristics of some other members. An agent can gather information, using its social "connections," to find community members most suitable to communicate to in a specific situation defined by the system's user. The system then deploys its multimodal interface, which "maps" the social space onto a representation of the relevant physical space, to locate the potential interlocutors and advise the user on an efficient communication strategy for the given community.

Chapter 20

For e-Government applications, the symbiotic aspect must be taken into account at three stages: at design time in order to integrate the end-user, at delivery time when civil servants have to discover and interact with new services, at run time when ambient intelligence could help the interaction of citizens with specific services. In this paper, we focus on the first two steps. We show how interoperability issues must concern application designers. We also present how semantics can help civil servants when they have to deal with e-government service frameworks. We then describe an actual application developed during the European Terregov project where semantics is the key point for simplifying the role of citizens when requesting for health care services.

Symbiotic computing leads to a proliferation of computing devices that allow linking people, favoring the development of distributed Communities of Practice (CoPs). Their members, being dispersed geographically, have to rely strongly on technological means to interact. In this context, coordinating distributed CoPs is more challenging than coordinating their collocated counterparts. Hence, the increasing role of the coordination should be supported by an adequate set of coordination tools. In this paper, we present an approach based on multi-agent systems for coordinating distributed CoPs. It includes analyzing the exchanges among members and translating this information into a graphical format to help the coordinators to follow the evolution of the participation and the domain of the community.

This paper proposes a remote conversation support system for people with aphasia. The aim of our system is to improve the quality of lives (QoL) of people suffering cognitive disabilities. In this framework, a topic list is used as a conversation assistant in addition to the video phone. The important feature is sharing the focus of attention on the topic list between a patient and the communication partner over the network to facilitate distant communication. The results of two preliminary experiments indicate the potential of the system.

By simply attaching sensor nodes to physical objects with no information about the objects, the method proposed in this paper infers the type of the physical indoor objects and the states they are in. Assuming that an object has its own states that have transitions represented by a state transition diagram, we prepare the state transition diagrams for such indoor objects as a door, a drawer, a chair, and a locker. The method determines the presumed state transition diagram from prepared diagrams that matches sensor data collected from people's daily living for a certain period. A 2 week experiment shows that the method achieves high accuracy of inferring objects to which sensor nodes are attached. The method allows us to introduce ubiquitous sensor environments by simply attaching sensor nodes to physical objects around us.

This paper is concerned with the robust stability analysis problem for uncertain stochastic neural networks with interval time-varying delays. By utilizing a Lyapunov-Krasovskii functional and conducting stochastic analysis, the authors show that the addressed neural networks are globally, robustly, and asymptotically stable if a convex optimization problem is feasible. Some stability criteria are derived for all admissible uncertainties, and these stability criteria are formulated by means of the feasibility of a linear matrix inequality (LMI), which can be effectively solved by some standard numerical packages. Five numerical examples are given to demonstrate the usefulness of the proposed robust stability criteria.

In this paper, the OpenBiomind toolkit is used to apply GA, GP, and local search methods to analyze a large SNP dataset concerning Late-Onset Alzheimer's Disease (LOAD). Classification models identifying LOAD with statistically significant accuracy are identified as well as using ensemble-based important features analysis in order to identify brain genes related to LOAD, most notably the solute carrier gene SLC6A15. Ensemble analysis is used to identify potentially significant interactions between genes in the context of LOAD.

Preface

Software Science is a discipline that studies the theoretical framework of software as instructive and behavioral information, which can be embodied and executed by generic computers in order to create expected system behaviors and machine intelligence. *Intelligence Science* is a discipline that studies the mechanisms and theories of abstract intelligence and its paradigms such as natural, artificial, machinable, and computational intelligence. The convergence of software and intelligent sciences forms the transdisciplinary field of computational intelligence, which provides a coherent set of fundamental theories, contemporary denotational mathematics, and engineering applications.

This book entitled *Breakthroughs in Software Science and Computational Intelligence* is the second volume in the IGI Series of Advances in Software Science and Computational Intelligence. The book encompasses 25 chapters of expert contributions selected from the *International Journal of Software Science and Computational Intelligence* during 2010. The book is organized in four sections on: (1) Computational intelligence; (2) Cognitive computing; (3) Software science; and (4) Applications in computational intelligence and cognitive computing.

SECTION 1: COMPUTATIONAL INTELLIGENCE

Intelligence science studies theories and models of the brain at all levels, and the relationship between the concrete physiological brain and the abstract soft mind. Intelligence science is a new frontier with the fertilization of biology, psychology, neuroscience, cognitive science, cognitive informatics, philosophy, information science, computer science, anthropology, and linguistics. A fundamental view developed in software and intelligence sciences is known as abstract intelligence, which provides a unified foundation for the studies of all forms and paradigms of intelligence such as natural, artificial, machinable, and computational intelligence. *Abstract Intelligence* (αI) is an enquiry of both natural and artificial intelligence at the neural, cognitive, functional, and logical levels from the bottom up. In the narrow sense, αI is a human or a system ability that transforms information into behaviors. However, in the broad sense, αI is any human or system ability that autonomously transfers the forms of abstract information between *data, information, knowledge,* and *behaviors* in the brain or intelligent systems.

Computational Intelligence (CoI) is an embodying form of Abstract Intelligence (αI) that implements intelligent mechanisms and behaviors by computational methodologies and software systems, such as expert systems, fuzzy systems, cognitive computers, cognitive robots, software agent systems, genetic/evolutionary systems, and autonomous learning systems. The theoretical foundations of computational intelligence root in cognitive informatics, software science, and denotational mathematics.

This section on computational intelligence encompasses the following five chapters:

- Chapter 1: Perspectives on Cognitive Computing and Applications
- Chapter 2: Granular Computing and Human-Centricity in Computational Intelligence
- Chapter 3: A General Knowledge Representation Model for the Acquisition of Skills and Concepts
- Chapter 4: Feature Based Rule Learner in Noisy Environment Using Neighbourhood Rough Set Model
- Chapter 5: A High Level Model of a Conscious Embodied Agent

Chapter 1, "Perspectives on Cognitive Computing and Applications," by Yingxu Wang, Witold Pedrycz, George Baciu, Ping Chen, Guoyin Wang, and Yiyu Yao, presents *Cognitive Computing* (CC) as an emerging paradigm of intelligent computing theories and technologies based on cognitive informatics, which implements computational intelligence by autonomous inferences and perceptions mimicking the mechanisms of the brain. The development of *Cognitive Computers* (CogC) is centric in cognitive computing methodologies. A CogC is an intelligent computer for knowledge processing as that of a conventional von Neumann computer for data processing. This chapter summarizes the presentations of a set of 6 position chapters presented in the ICCI 2010 *Plenary Panel on Cognitive Computing and Applications* contributed from invited panelists who are part of the world's renowned researchers and scholars in the field of cognitive informatics and cognitive computing.

Chapter 2, "Granular Computing and Human-Centricity in Computational Intelligence," by Witold Pedrycz, presents information granules and the general framework of Granular Computing, which offers interesting opportunities to endow processing with an important facet of human-centricity. This facet directly implies that the underlying processing supports non-numeric data inherently associated with the variable perception of humans and generates results being seamlessly comprehended by users. Given that systems, which quite commonly become distributed and hierarchical, managing granular information in hierarchical and distributed architectures, are of growing interest, especially when invoking mechanisms of knowledge generation and knowledge sharing. The outstanding feature of human centricity of Granular Computing along with essential fuzzy set-based constructs constitutes the crux of our study. We elaborate on some new directions of knowledge elicitation and quantification realized in the setting of fuzzy sets. With this regard, we concentrate on an idea of *knowledge*-based clustering, which aims at the seamless realization of the data-expertise design of information granules. It is also emphasized that collaboration and reconciliation of locally available knowledge give rise to the concept of higher type information granules. The other interesting directions enhancing human centricity of computing with fuzzy sets, deals with non-numeric, semi-qualitative characterization of information granules (fuzzy sets), as well as inherent evolving capabilities of associated human-centric systems. We discuss a suite of algorithms facilitating a qualitative assessment of fuzzy sets, formulate a series of associated optimization tasks guided by well-formulated performance indexes, and discuss the underlying essence of the resulting solutions.

Chapter 3, "A General Knowledge Representation Model for the Acquisition of Skills and Concepts," by Carlos Ramirez and Benjamin Valdes, presents a cognitive model for skills and concepts representation as well as a proposal for its computational implementation. The model is intended to help bridge some of the natural problems that arise in current massive education models, through the adaptation and personalization of learning environments. The model is capable of representing rich semantic knowledge, including both skills and concepts, integrating them through a coherent network of role-based associations. The associations build an ontology that integrates on itself different domain taxonomies to represent the knowledge acquired by a student keeping relevant context information. The model is based on a constructivist approach.

Chapter 4, "Feature Based Rule Learner in Noisy Environment Using Neighbourhood Rough Set Model," by Yang Liu, Luyang Jiao, Guohua Bai, and Boqin Feng, presents a perspective of cognitive informatics where cognition can be viewed as the acquisition of knowledge. In real-world applications, information systems usually contain some degree of noisy data. A new model, which combines the neighbourhood approximation and variable precision rough set model, is proposed to deal with hybrid-feature selection problem. Then rule induction algorithm can learn from selected features in order to reduce the complexity of rule sets. Through proposed integration, the knowledge acquisition process becomes insensitive to the dimensionality of data with a pre-defined tolerance degree of noise and un-certainty for misclassification. When we apply the method to a Chinese diabetic diagnosis problem, the hybrid-attribute reduction method selected only five attributes from totally thirty-four measurements. Rule learner produced eight rules with average two attributes in the left part of an IF-THEN rule form, which is a manageable set of rules. The demonstrated experiment shows that the present approach is effective in handling real-world problems.

Chapter 5, "A High Level Model of a Conscious Embodied Agent," by Jiří Wiedermann, presents a schematic yet cognitively powerful architecture of an embodied conscious agent. The architecture incorporates a mechanism for mining, representing, processing, and exploiting semantic knowledge. This mechanism is based on two complementary internal world models, which are built automatically. One model (based on artificial mirror neurons) is used for mining and capturing the syntax of the rec-ognized part of the environment, while the second one (based on neural nets) is used for its semantics. Jointly, the models support algorithmic processes underlying phenomena similar in important aspects to higher cognitive functions such as imitation learning and the development of communication, language, thinking and consciousness.

SECTION 2: COGNITIVE COMPUTING

Computing systems and technologies can be classified into the categories of *imperative, autonomic,* and *cognitive* computing from the bottom up. The imperative computers are a passive system based on stored-program controlled mechanisms for data processing. The autonomic computers are goal-driven and self-decision-driven machines that do not rely on instructive and procedural information. Cogni-tive computers are more intelligent computers beyond the imperative and autonomic computers, which embody major natural intelligence behaviors of the brain such as thinking, inference, and learning. The increasing demand for non von Neumann computers for knowledge and intelligence processing in the high-tech industry and everyday lives require novel cognitive computers for providing autonomous computing power for various cognitive systems mimicking the natural intelligence of the brain.

Cognitive Computing (CC) is a novel paradigm of intelligent computing methodologies and systems based on *Cognitive Informatics* (CI), which implements computational intelligence by autonomous in-ferences and perceptions mimicking the mechanisms of the brain. CC emerged and developed based on transdisciplinary research in cognitive informatics, abstract intelligence, and *Denotational Mathematics* (DM). The latest advances in CI, CC, and DM enable a systematic solution for the future generation of intelligent computers known as *Cognitive Computers* (CogCs) that think, perceive, learn, and reason. A

CogC is an intelligent computer for knowledge processing just as a conventional von Neumann computer is for data processing. CogCs are designed to embody *machinable intelligence* such as computational inferences, causal analyses, knowledge manipulations, machine learning, and autonomous problem solving.

This section on cognitive computing encompasses the following six chapters:
- Chapter 6: Cognitive Memory: Human-Like Memory
- Chapter 7: Multi-Fractal Analysis for Feature Extraction from DNA Sequences
- Chapter 8: Agent-Based Middleware for Advanced Communication Services in a Ubiquitous Computing Environment
- Chapter 9: Relevant and Non-Redundant Amino Acid Sequence Selection for Protein Functional Site Identification
- Chapter 10: Role-Based Autonomic Systems
- Chapter 11: Combining Ontology with Intelligent Agent to Provide Negotiation Service

Chapter 6, "Cognitive Memory: Human-Like Memory," by Bernard Carlos Widrow and Juan Aragon, presents a new form of computer memory inspired from life experience. Certain conjectures about human memory are keys to the central idea. We present the design of a practical and useful "cognitive" memory system. The new memory does not function like a computer memory where specific data is stored in specific numbered registers and retrieval is done by reading the contents of the specified memory register, or done by matching key words as with a document search. Incoming sensory data would be stored at the next available empty memory location, and indeed could be stored redundantly at several empty locations. The stored sensory data would neither have key words nor would it be located in known or specified memory locations. Retrieval would be initiated by a prompt signal from a current set of sensory inputs or patterns. The search would be done by a retrieval system that makes use of auto-associative artificial neural networks. In this chapter we present a practical application of this cognitive memory system to human facial recognition.

Chapter 7, "Multi-Fractal Analysis for Feature Extraction from DNA Sequences," by Witold Kinsner and Hong Zhang, presents estimations of multiscale (multifractal) measures for feature extraction from Deoxyribonucleic Acid (DNA) sequences, and demonstrates the intriguing possibility of identifying biological functionality using information contained within the DNA sequence. We have developed a technique that seeks patterns or correlations in the DNA sequence at a higher level than the local base-pair structure. The technique has three main steps: (1) transforms the DNA sequence symbols into a modified Lévy walk, (2) transforms the Lévy walk into a signal spectrum, and (3) breaks the spectrum into subspectra and treats each of these as an attractor from which the multifractal dimension spectrum is estimated. An optimal minimum window size and volume element size are found for estimation of the multifractal measures. Experimental results show that DNA is multifractal, and that the multifractality changes depending upon the location (coding or noncoding region) in the sequence.

Chapter 8, "Agent-Based Middleware for Advanced Communication Services in a Ubiquitous Computing Environment," by Takuo Suganuma, Hideyuki Takahashi, and Norio Shiratori, presents a ubiquitous computing (ubicomp) environment where system components of different types including hardware elements, software components, and network connections must cooperate mutually to provide services that fulfill user requirements. Consequently, advanced and flexible characteristics of software that are specialized for a ubicomp environment are needed. This chapter presents a proposal of an agent-based middleware for a ubicomp environment comprising computers and home electric appliances. The middleware, called AMUSE, can take quality of service (QoS) in a ubicomp environment into consideration by coping not only with user context but also with the resource context, using agent-based computing technology. Herein, we describe the concept, design, and initial implementation of AMUSE. Simulation results of an experimental ubiquitous service using AMUSE demonstrate the effectiveness of our proposed scheme. Additionally, to confirm our scheme's feasibility and effectiveness, we describe the initial implementation of a multimedia communication application based on AMUSE.

Chapter 9, "Relevant and Non-Redundant Amino Acid Sequence Selection for Protein Functional Site Identification," by Chandra Das and Pradipta Maji, presents a pattern recognition algorithm to predict functional sites in proteins where amino acids cannot be used directly as inputs since they are nonnumerical variables. They, therefore, need encoding prior to input. In this regard, the bio-basis function maps a nonnumerical sequence space to a numerical feature space. It is designed using an amino acid mutation matrix. One of the important issues for the bio-basis function is how to select a minimum set of bio-basis strings with maximum information. In this chapter, an efficient method to select bio-basis strings for the bio-basis function is described integrating the concepts of the Fisher ratio and "degree of resemblance." The integration enables the method to select a minimum set of most informative bio-basis strings. The concept of asymmetric biological distance is introduced to compute the Fisher ratio, which is more effective for selection of most relevant bio-basis strings. The "degree of resemblance" enables efficient selection of a set of distinct bio-basis strings. In effect, it reduces the redundant features in numerical feature space. Some quantitative indices are proposed for evaluating the quality of selected bio-basis strings. The effectiveness of the proposed bio-basis string selection method, along with a comparison with existing methods, is demonstrated on different data sets.

Chapter 10, "Role-Based Autonomic Systems," by Haibin Zhu, presents autonomic computing as an emerging computing paradigm in order to create computer systems capable of self-management and overcome the rapidly growing complexity of computing systems management. To possess self-* properties, there must be mechanisms to support self-awareness, i.e., an autonomic system should be able to perceive the abnormality of its components. After abnormality is checked, processes of self-healing, self-configuration, self-optimization, and self-protection must be completed to guarantee the system works correctly and continuously. In Role-Based Collaboration (RBC), roles are the major media for interaction, coordination, and collaboration. A role can be used to check if a player behaves well or not. This chapter investigates the possibility of using roles and their related mechanisms to diagnose the behavior of agents, and facilitate self-* properties of a system. The chapter asserts that role-based systems are autonomic.

Chapter 11, "Combining Ontology with Intelligent Agent to Provide Negotiation Service," by Qiumei Pu, Yongcun Cao, Xiuqin Pan, Siyao Fu, and Zengguang Hou, presents agent and ontology as distinct technologies which arose independent of each other, having their own standards and specifications. At the same time, the semantics Web is one of the popular research areas these days. It is based on the current Web, and adds more semantics to it, for the purpose of building the Ontology of Web content. So, application programs on the Web can make the purpose of cross-platform calculation come true by taking advantage of Ontology. On the other side of the coin, agent is a theory able to enhance the abstraction of software itself. Negotiation protocol is the basic principle in the electronic commerce, this principle has a direct impact on the efficiency of the negotiation. This study brings up the communication architecture with negotiation protocol on the Semantic Web. Precisely speaking, agents make computing with Ontology, and we define an agent's communication ontology for this communication framework. Semantic Web uses Ontology to describe the negotiation protocol, which will enable an agent to gain the necessary knowledge from the market. This will give agents the ability to understand each other enough to carry out their objectives. In this way, buyer or seller is able to improve semantic cognitive in the process of negotiation. At the same time, it can provide an intelligent platform for the information exchange on the same understanding about the content of communication in the electronic negotiation service.

SECTION 3: SOFTWARE SCIENCE

Software as instructive behavioral information has been recognized as an entire range of widely and frequently used objects and phenomena in human knowledge. Software science is a theoretical inquiry of software and its constraints on the basis of empirical studies on engineering methodologies and techniques for software development and software engineering organization. In the history of science and engineering, a matured discipline always gave birth to new disciplines. For instance, theoretical physics was emerged from general and applied physics, and theoretical computing was emerged from computer engineering. So does software science that emerges from and grows in the fields of software, computer, information, knowledge, and system engineering.

Software Science (SS) is a discipline of enquiries that studies the theoretical framework of software as instructive and behavioral information, which can be embodied and executed by generic computers in order to create expected system behaviors and machine intelligence. The discipline of software science studies the common objects in the abstract world such as software, information, data, concepts, knowledge, instructions, executable behaviors, and their processing by natural and artificial intelligence. From this view, software science is theoretical software engineering; while software engineering is applied software science in order to efficiently, economically, and reliably develop large-scale software systems. The phenomena shows that almost all the fundamental problems, which could not be solved in the last four decades in software engineering, simply stemmed from the lack of coherent theories in the form of software science. The vast cumulated empirical knowledge and industrial practice in software engineering have made this possible to enable the emergence of software science.

This section on software science encompasses the following six chapters:
- ◦ Chapter 12: Design and Implementation of an Autonomic Code Generator Based on RTPA
- ◦ Chapter 13: The Formal Design Model of a Real-Time Operating System (RTOS+): Conceptual and Architectural Frameworks
- ◦ Chapter 14: The Formal Design Model of a Real-Time Operating System (RTOS+): Static and Dynamic Behaviors
- ◦ Chapter 15: The Formal Design Model of an Automatic Teller Machine (ATM)
- ◦ Chapter 16: The Formal Design Models of a Set of Abstract Data Types (ADTs)
- ◦ Chapter 17: A Least-Laxity-First Scheduling Algorithm of Variable Time Slice for Periodic Tasks

Chapter 12, "Design and Implementation of an Autonomic Code Generator Based on RTPA," by Yingxu Wang, Xinming Tan, and Cyprian F. Ngolah, presents a denotational mathematics, Real-Time Process Algebra (RTPA), for the algebraic modeling and manipulations of software system architectures and behaviors by the Unified Data Models (UDMs) and Unified Process Models (UPMs). On the basis of the RTPA specification and refinement methodologies, automatic software code generation is enabled toward improving software development productivity. This chapter presents the work on designing and developing the RTPA-Based Software Code Generator (RTPA-CG) that transfers system models in RTPA architectures and behaviors into C++ or Java. A two-phrase strategy has been employed in the design of the code generator. The first phrase analyzes the lexical, syntactical, and type specifications of a software system modeled in RTPA, which results in a set of Abstract Syntax Trees (ASTs). The second phrase translates the ASTs into C++ or Java based on predesigned mapping strategies and code generation rules. The toolkit of RTPA code generator encompasses an RTPA lexer, parser, type-checker, and a code builder. Experimental results show that system models in RTPA can be rigorously processed and corresponding C++/Java code can be automatically generated using the toolkit. The code generated is executable and effective under the support of an RTPA run-time library.

Chapter 13, "The Formal Design Model of a Real-Time Operating System (RTOS+): Conceptual and Architectural Frameworks," by Yingxu Wang, Cyprian F. Ngolah, Guangping Zeng, Philip C. Y. Sheu, C. Philip Choy, and Yousheng Tian, presents a Real-Time Operating System (RTOS+) as platform for the design and implementation of a wide range of applications in real-time systems, embedded systems, and mission-critical systems. This chapter describes a formal design model for a general RTOS known as RTOS+ that enables a specific target RTOS to be rigorously and efficiently derived in real-world applications. The methodology of a denotational mathematics, Real-Time Process Algebra (RTPA), is described for formally modeling and refining architectures, static behaviors, and dynamic behaviors of RTOS+. The conceptual model of the RTOS+ system is introduced as the initial requirements for the system. The architectural model of RTOS+ is created using RTPA architectural modeling methodologies and refined by a set of Unified Data Models (UDMs). The static behaviors of RTOS+ are specified and refined by a set of Unified Process Models (UPMs). The dynamic behaviors of the RTOS+ system are specified and refined by the real-time process scheduler and system dispatcher. This work is presented in two chapters in serial due to its excessive length. The conceptual and architectural models of RTOS+ is described in this chapter; while the static and dynamic behavioral models of RTOS+ will be elaborated in Chapter 14.

Chapter 14, "The Formal Design Model of a Real-Time Operating System (RTOS+): Static and Dynamic Behaviors," by Yingxu Wang, Guangping Zeng, Cyprian F. Ngolah, Philip C. Y. Sheu, C. Philip Choy, and Yousheng Tian, presents a Real-Time Operating System (RTOS+), which is the second part of the work succeeding Chapter 13. In this chapter, the static behaviors of RTOS+ are specified and refined by a set of Unified Process Models (UPMs). The dynamic behaviors of the RTOS+ system are specified and refined by the real-time process scheduler and system dispatcher. RTOS+ provides a platform for the design and implementation of a wide range of applications in real-time systems, embedded systems, and mission-critical systems.

Chapter 15, "The Formal Design Model of an Automatic Teller Machine (ATM)," by Yingxu Wang, Yanan Zhang, Philip C. Y. Sheu, Xuhui Li, and Hong Guo, presents an Automated Teller Machine (ATM) as a safety-critical and real-time system that is highly complicated in design and implementation. This chapter presents the formal design, specification, and modeling of the ATM system using a denotational mathematics known as Real-Time Process Algebra (RTPA). The conceptual model of the ATM system is introduced as the initial requirements for the system. The architectural model of the ATM system is created using RTPA architectural modeling methodologies and refined by a set of Unified Data Models (UDMs), which share a generic mathematical model of tuples. The static behaviors of the ATM system are specified and refined by a set of Unified Process Models (UPMs) for the ATM transition processing and system supporting processes. The dynamic behaviors of the ATM system are specified and refined by process priority allocation, process deployment, and process dispatch models. Based on the formal design models of the ATM system, code can be automatically generated using the RTPA Code Generator (RTPA-CG), or be seamlessly transformed into programs by programmers. The formal models of ATM may not only serve as a formal design paradigm of real-time software systems, but also a test bench for the expressive power and modeling capability of exiting formal methods in software engineering.

Chapter 16, "The Formal Design Models of a Set of Abstract Data Types (ADTs)," by Yingxu Wang, Xinming Tan, Cyprian F. Ngolah, and Philip Sheu, presents type theories as one of the fundamental theories underpinning data object modeling and system architectural design in computing and software engineering. Abstract Data Types (ADTs) are a set of highly generic and rigorously modeled data structures in type theory. ADTs are not only important in type modeling, but also play a key role in Object-Oriented (OO) technologies for software system design and implementation. This chapter presents a formal modeling methodology for ADTs using the Real-Time Process Algebra (RTPA), which allows both architectural and behavioral models of ADTs and complex data objects to be rigorously designed and specified in a top-down approach. Formal architectures, static behaviors, and dynamic behaviors of a set of ADTs, such as stack, queue, sequence, and record, are comparatively studied. The architectural models of the ADTs are created using RTPA architectural modeling methodologies known as the Unified Data Models (UDMs). The static behaviors of the ADTs are specified and refined by a set of Unified Process Models (UPMs) of RTPA. The dynamic behaviors of the ADTs are modeled by process dispatching technologies of RTPA. This work has been applied in a number of real-time and nonreal-time system designs such as a Real-Time Operating System (RTOS+), a Cognitive Learning Engine (CLE), an ADT library for an RTPA support tool, and the automatic code generator based on RTPA.

Chapter 17, "A Least-Laxity-First Scheduling Algorithm of Variable Time Slice for Periodic Tasks," by Shaohua Teng, Wei Zhang, Haibin Zhu, Xiufen Fu, Jiangyi Su, and Baoliang Cui, presents a Least-Laxity-First (LLF) scheduling algorithm that assigns a priority to a task according to its executing urgency. The smaller the laxity value of a task is, the sooner it needs to be executed. When two or more tasks have the same or approximative laxity values, the LLF scheduling algorithm leads to frequent switches among tasks, causes extra overhead in a system, and therefore, restricts its application. The least switch and laxity first scheduling algorithm is proposed in the chapter by searching out an appropriate common divisor in order to improve the LLF algorithm for periodic tasks.

SECTION 4: APPLICATIONS OF COMPUTATIONAL INTELLIGENCE AND COGNITIVE COMPUTING

A series of fundamental breakthroughs have been recognized and a wide range of applications has been developed in software science, abstract intelligence, cognitive computing, and computational intelligence in the last decade. Because software science and computational intelligence provide a common and general platform for the next generation of cognitive computing, some expected innovations in these fields will emerge such as cognitive computers, cognitive knowledge representation technologies, semantic searching engines, cognitive learning engines, cognitive Internet, cognitive robots, and autonomous inference machines for complex and long-series inferences, problem solving, and decision making beyond traditional logic- and rule-based technologies.

This section on applications of computational intelligence and cognitive computing encompasses the following eight chapters:

- ◦ Chapter 18: Cognitive Location-Aware Information Retrieval by Agent-Based Semantic Matching
- ◦ Chapter 19: Perceiving the Social: A Multi-Agent System to Support Human Navigation in Foreign Communities
- ◦ Chapter 20: Symbiotic Aspects in e-Government Application Development
- ◦ Chapter 21: CoPBoard: A Catalyst for Distributed Communities of Practice
- ◦ Chapter 22: Remote Conversation Support for People with Aphasia
- ◦ Chapter 23: Estimating which Object Type a Sensor Node is Attached to in Ubiquitous Sensor Environment
- ◦ Chapter 24: Delay-Range-Dependent Robust Stability for Uncertain Stochastic Neural Networks with Time-Varying Delays
- ◦ Chapter 25: Classifier Ensemble Based Analysis of a Genome-Wide SNP Dataset Concerning Late-Onset Alzheimer Disease

Chapter 18, "Cognitive Location-Aware Information Retrieval by Agent-Based Semantic Matching," by Eddie C. L. Chan, George Baciu, and S. C. Mak, presents an agent system operating in both wired and wireless networks that finds and retrieves location-aware information. Agents in the proposed system must have the full range of abilities, including perception, use of natural language, learning, and the ability to understand user queries. The speed and accuracy of retrieval and the usefulness of the retrieved data depends on a number of factors including constant or frequent changes in its content or status, the effects of environmental factors such as the weather and traffic, and the techniques that are used to categorize the relevance of the retrieved data. This chapter proposes semantic TFIDF, an agent-based system for retrieving location-aware information that makes use of semantic information in the data to develop smaller training sets, thereby improving the speed of retrieval while maintaining or even improving accuracy. This proposed method first assigns intelligent agents to gathering location-aware data, which they then classify, match, and organize to find a best match for a user query. This is done using semantic graphs in the WordNet English dictionary. Experiments will compare the proposed system with three other commonly used systems and show that it is significantly faster and more accurate.

Chapter 19, "Perceiving the Social: A Multi-Agent System to Support Human Navigation in Foreign Communities," Victor V. Kryssanov, Shizuka Kumokawa, Igor Goncharenko, and Hitoshi Ogawa, presents a system developed to help people explore local communities by providing navigation services in social spaces created by the community members via communication and knowledge sharing. The proposed system utilizes data of a community's social network to reconstruct the social space, which is otherwise not physically perceptible but imaginary, experiential, and yet learnable. The social space is modeled with an agent network, where each agent stands for a member of the community and has knowledge about expertise and personal characteristics of some other members. An agent can gather information, using its social "connections," to find community members most suitable to communicate to in a specific situation defined by the system's user. The system then deploys its multimodal interface, which operates with 3D graphics and haptic virtual environments and "maps" the social space onto a representation of the relevant physical space, to locate the potential interlocutors and advise the user on an efficient communication strategy for the given community. A prototype of the system is built and used in an experiment. The study results are discussed in a context of related work, conclusions are drawn, and implications for future research are formulated.

Chapter 20, "Symbiotic Aspects in e-Government Application Development," by Claude Moulin and Marco Luca Sbodio, presents e-Government applications where the symbiotic aspect must be taken into account at three stages: at design time in order to integrate the end-user, at delivery time when civil servants have to discover and interact with new services, and at run time when ambient intelligence could help the interaction of citizens with specific services. In this chapter, we focus on the first two steps. We show how interoperability issues must concern application designers. We also present how semantics can help civil servants when they have to deal with e-government service frameworks. We then describe an actual application developed during the European Terregov project where semantics is the key point for simplifying the role of citizens when requesting for health care services.

Chapter 21, "CoPBoard: A Catalyst for Distributed Communities of Practice," by Gilson Yukio Sato and Jean-Paul A. Barthès, presents symbiotic computing to a proliferation of computing devices that allow linking people, favoring the development of distributed Communities of Practice (CoPs). Their members, being dispersed geographically, have to rely strongly on technological means to interact. In this context, coordinating distributed CoPs is more challenging than coordinating their collocated counterparts. Hence, the increasing role of the coordination should be supported by an adequate set of coordination tools. In this chapter we present an approach based on multi-agent systems for coordinating distributed CoPs. It includes analyzing the exchanges among members and translating this information into a graphical format in order to help the coordinators to follow the evolution of the participation and the domain of the community.

Chapter 22, "Remote Conversation Support for People with Aphasia," by Nilar Aye, Takuro Ito, Fumio Hattori, Kazuhiro Kuwabara, and Kiyoshi Yasuda, presents a remote conversation support system for people with aphasia. The aim of our system is to improve the Quality of Lives (QoL) of people suffering cognitive disabilities. In this framework, a topic list is used as a conversation assistant in addition to the video phone. The important feature is sharing the focus of attention on the topic list between a patient and the communication partner over the network in order to facilitate distant communication. The results of two preliminary experiments indicate the potential of the system.

Chapter 23, "Estimating which Object Type a Sensor Node is Attached to in Ubiquitous Sensor Environment," by Takuya Maekawa, Yutaka Yanagisawa, and Takeshi Okadome, presents a method for inferring the type of the physical indoor objects and the states they are in with attached sensors. Assuming that an object has its own states that have transitions represented by a state transition diagram, we prepare the state transition diagrams in advance for such indoor objects as a door, a drawer, a chair, and a locker. The method determines the presumed state transition diagram from prepared diagrams that match sensor data collected from people's daily living for a certain period of time. A two week experiment shows that the method achieves high accuracy of inferring objects to which sensor nodes are attached. The method makes it easy for us to introduce ubiquitous sensor environments by simply attaching sensor nodes to physical objects around us.

Chapter 24, "Delay-Range-Dependent Robust Stability for Uncertain Stochastic Neural Networks with Time-Varying Delays," by Wei Feng and Haixia Wu, presents a robust stability analysis problem for uncertain stochastic neural networks with interval time-varying delays. By utilizing a Lyapunov-Krasovskii functional and conducting stochastic analysis, we show that the addressed neural networks are globally, robustly, asymptotically stable if a convex optimization problem is feasible. Some stability criteria are derived for all admissible uncertainties. And these stability criteria are formulated by means of the feasibility of a Linear Matrix Inequality (LMI), which can be effectively solved by some standard numerical packages. Five numerical examples are given to demonstrate the usefulness of the proposed robust stability criteria.

Chapter 25, "Classifier Ensemble Based Analysis of a Genome-Wide SNP Dataset Concerning Late-Onset Alzheimer Disease," by Lúcio Coelho, Ben Goertzel, Cassio Pennachin, and Chris Heward, presents the OpenBiomind toolkit that is used to apply GA, GP, and local search methods to analyze a large SNP dataset concerning Late-Onset Alzheimer's Disease (LOAD). Classification models identifying LOAD with statistically significant accuracy are identified, and ensemble-based important features analysis is used to identify brain genes related to LOAD, most notably the solute carrier gene SLC6A15. Ensemble analysis is used to identify potentially significant interactions between genes in the context of LOAD.

This book is intended for researchers, engineers, graduate students, senior-level undergraduate students, and instructors as an informative reference book in the emerging fields of software science, cognitive intelligence, and computational intelligence. The editor expects that readers of *Breakthroughs in Software Science and Computational Intelligence* will benefit from the 25 selected chapters of this book, which represents the latest advances in research in software science and computational intelligence and their engineering applications.

Yingxu Wang
University of Calgary, Canada

Acknowledgment

Many persons have contributed their dedicated work to this book and related research. The editor would like to thank all authors, the associate editors of IJSSCI, the editorial board members, and the invited reviewers for their great contributions to this book. I would also like to thank the IEEE Steering Committee and organizers of the series of IEEE International Conference on Cognitive Informatics and Cognitive Computing (ICCI*CC) in the last ten years, particularly Lotfi A. Zadeh, Witold Kinsner, Witold Pedrycz, Bo Zhang, Du Zhang, George Baciu, Phillip Sheu, Jean-Claude Latombe, James Anderson, Robert C. Berwick, and Dilip Patel. I would like to acknowledge the publisher of this book, IGI Global. I would like to thank Dr. Mehdi Khosrow-Pour, Jan Travers, Kristin M. Klinger, Erika L. Carter, and Myla Harty, for their professional editorship.

Yingxu Wang
University of Calgary, Canada

Section 1
Computational Intelligence

Chapter 1
Perspectives on Cognitive Computing and Applications

Yingxu Wang
University of Calgary, Canada

Witold Pedrycz
University of Alberta, Canada

George Baciu
Hong Kong Polytechnic University, China

Ping Chen
University of Houston-Downtown, USA

Guoyin Wang
*Chongqing University of Posts &
Telecommunications, China*

Yiyu Yao
University of Regina, Canada

ABSTRACT

Cognitive Computing (CC) is an emerging paradigm of intelligent computing theories and technologies based on cognitive informatics, which implements computational intelligence by autonomous inferences and perceptions mimicking the mechanisms of the brain. The development of Cognitive Computers (cC) is centric in cognitive computing methodologies. A cC is an intelligent computer for knowledge processing as that of a conventional von Neumann computer for data processing. This paper summarizes the presentations of a set of 6 position papers presented in the ICCI'10 Plenary Panel on Cognitive Computing and Applications contributed from invited panelists who are part of the world's renowned researchers and scholars in the field of cognitive informatics and cognitive computing.

INTRODUCTION

A wide range of international efforts has been focused on the studies of the new generation of intelligent computers known as cognitive computers, which also known as intelligent computers, brain-like computers, artificial brains, and human centric computers in related research. A *Cognitive Computer* (cC) is an intelligent computer for

DOI: 10.4018/978-1-4666-0264-9.ch001

knowledge processing as that of a conventional von Neumann computer for data processing.

The development of cC is centric in cognitive computing research. *Cognitive Computing* (CC) is an emerging paradigm of intelligent computing methodologies and systems based on cognitive informatics that implements computational intelligence by autonomous inferences and perceptions mimicking the mechanisms of the brain (Wang, 2002, 2003, 2006, 2007a, 2007b, 2009a, 2009b,2010a, 2010b, 2010c, 2010d;

Wang & Wang, 2006; Wang & Kinsner, 2006; Wang et al., 2006, 2009a). CC has been emerged and developed based on the multidisciplinary research in cognitive informatics (Wang, 2002, 2003, 2007b, 2007c; Wang et al., 2009a, 2009c), which is a transdisciplinary enquiry of computer science, information science, cognitive science, and intelligence science that investigates into the internal information processing mechanisms and processes of the brain and natural intelligence, as well as their engineering applications in cognitive computing.

This paper is a summary of the position statements of panellists presented in the *Plenary Panel on Cognitive Computing and Applications* in IEEE ICCI 2010 at Tsinghua University held in July 2010 (Sun et al., 2010). It is noteworthy that the individual statements and opinions included in this paper may not necessarily be shared by all panellists.

COGNITIVE COMPUTING: THEORIES AND APPLICATIONS

The latest advances in cognitive informatics, abstract intelligence, and denotational mathematics have led to a systematic solution for the future generation of intelligent computers known as *cognitive computers* (cCs) that think, perceive, learn, and reason (Wang, 2006, 2009a, 2009b). A cC is an intelligent computer for knowledge processing as that of a conventional von Neumann computer for data processing. cCs are designed to embody *machinable intelligence* such as computational inferences, causal analyses, knowledge manipulation, learning, and problem solving.

The term *computing* in a narrow sense is an application of computers to solve a given problem by imperative instructions; while in a broad sense, it is a process to implement the instructive intelligence by a system that transfers a set of given information or instructions into expected intelligent behaviors.

The *essences* of computing are both its *data objects* and their predefined computational *operations*. From these facets, different computing paradigms may be comparatively analyzed as follows:

(a) Conventional computing
  ◦ *Data objects*: abstract bits and structured data
  ◦ *Operations*: logic, arithmetic, and functions
(b) Cognitive computing (CC)
  ◦ *Data objects*: words, concepts, syntax, and semantics
  ◦ *Basic operations*: syntactic analyses and semantic analyses
  ◦ *Advanced operations*: concept formulation, knowledge representation, comprehension, learning, inferences, and causal analyses

The above analyses indicate that cC is an important extension of conventional computing in both data objects modeling capabilities and their advanced operations at the abstract level of concept beyond bits. Therefore, cC is an intelligent knowledge processor that is much closer to the capability of human brains thinking at the level of concepts rather than bits. It is recognized that the basic unit of human knowledge in natural language representation is a concept rather than a word (Wang, 2008b, 2010e), because the former conveys the structured semantics of a word with its intention (attributes), extension (objects), and relations to other concepts in the context of a knowledge network.

It is noteworthy that, although the semantics of words may be ambiguity, the semantics of concept is always unique and precise in CC. For example, the word, "bank", is ambiguity because it may be a notion of a financial institution, a geographic location of raised ground of a river/lake, and/or a storage of something. However, the three individual concepts derived from bank, i.e.,

Figure 1. Formal concepts derived from the word "bank"

$b_o\mathbf{ST} \triangleq (A, O, R^c, R^i, R^o)$

$= (\ b_o\mathbf{ST}.A = \{$organization, company, financial business, money, deposit, withdraw, invest, exchange$\}$,

$b_o\mathbf{ST}.O = \{$international_bank, national_bank, local_bank, investment_bank, ATM$\}$

$b_o\mathbf{ST}.R^c = O \times A$,

$b_o\mathbf{ST}.R^i = \mathcal{K} \times b_o\mathbf{ST}$,

$b_o\mathbf{ST}.R^o = b_o\mathbf{ST} \times \mathcal{K}$

$)$

$b_r\mathbf{ST} \triangleq (A, O, R^c, R^i, R^o)$

$= (\ b_r\mathbf{ST}.A = \{$sides of a river, raised ground, a pile of earth, location$\}$,

$b_r\mathbf{ST}.O = \{$river_bank, lake_bank, canal_bank$\}$

$b_r\mathbf{ST}.R^c = O \times A$,

$b_r\mathbf{ST}.R^i = \mathcal{K} \times b_r\mathbf{ST}$,

$b_r\mathbf{ST}.R^o = b_r\mathbf{ST} \times \mathcal{K}$

$)$

$b_s\mathbf{ST} \triangleq (A, O, R^c, R^i, R^o)$

$= (\ b_s\mathbf{ST}.A = \{$storage, container, place, organization$\}$,

$b_s\mathbf{ST}.O = \{$information_bank, resource_bank, blood_bank$\}$

$b_s\mathbf{ST}.R^c = O \times A$,

$b_s\mathbf{ST}.R^i = \mathcal{K} \times b_s\mathbf{ST}$,

$b_s\mathbf{ST}.R^o = b_s\mathbf{ST} \times \mathcal{K}$

$)$

b_o = bank(organization), b_r = bank(river), and b_s = bank(storage), are precisely unique, which can be formally described in concept algebra [Wang, 2008b] for CC as shown in Fig. 1. In the examples of concepts, a generic framework of a concept is represented by the following model known as an abstract concept c, i.e.:

$$c \triangleq (O, A, R^c, R^i, R^o) \qquad (1)$$

where

- O is a nonempty set of objects of the concept, $O = \{o_1, o_2, ..., o_m\} \subseteq \wp O$, where $\wp O$ denotes a power set of abstract objects in the universal discourse U., $U = (O, A, R)$.

- A is a nonempty set of attributes, $A = \{a_1, a_2, ..., a_n\} \subseteq \wp A$, where $\wp A$ denotes a power set of attributes in U.

- $R^c = O \times A$ is a set of internal relations.

- $R^i \subseteq C' \times c$ is a set of input relations, where C' is a set of external concepts in U.

- $R^o \subseteq c \times C'$ is a set of output relations.

and K represents the entire concepts existed in the analyser's knowledge.

A set of denotational mathematics for cC and CC (Wang, 2002b, 2008b, 2008c, 2008d, 2009c,

2009d, 2009e; Wang et al., 2009b), particularly *concept algebra* (Wang, 2008b), has been developed by Wang during 2000 to in 2009. CA provides a set of 8 relational and 9 compositional operations for abstract concepts. A Cognitive Learning Engine (CLE) that serves as the "CPU" of cCs is under developing on the basis of concept algebra, which implements the basic and advanced cognitive computational operations of concepts and knowledge for cCs as outlined in (b) above. The work in this area may also lead to a fundamental solution to computational linguistics, Computing with Natural Language (CNL), and Computing with Words (CWW) (Zadeh, 1975, 1999).

COGNITIVE INFORMATICS AND COGNITIVE COMPUTING VERSUS COMPUTING WITH INFORMATION GRANULES: A SYNERGISTIC PLATFORM

It becomes apparent that the majority of pursuits of information processing, which in one way or another intend to exhibit a certain facet of human centricity, dwell on manipulation of abstract conceptual entities of well-defined semantics. The inherent granularity of information manifests in a variety of constructs of Granular Computing (GC) and as such supports strong linkages with the emerging area of Cognitive Informatics (CI). It is important to emphasize that the paradigm of GC underlines the cognitive faculties of informatics and brings forward the mechanisms of managing granular information in hierarchical and distributed architectures. This is visible in the framework of knowledge generation and knowledge sharing, and knowledge management, in general. Those central issues of Granular Computing and Cognitive Informatics being a subject of this position statement will be discussed in more detail with an emphasis placed on human centricity of computing with information granules and their thorough non-numeric, semi-qualitative and hierarchical characterization.

HIGH-FREQUENCY COGNITIVE PROCESSES

One of the most talked about social networking applications on the web today is Location Awareness (LA). Until recently, almost all the content generated on the internet has been mostly in a temporal setting, i.e., time-stamped, e.g., News items, blog articles, reports, proposals, etc. Only recently, location awareness has captured the vision of social network platform developers such as Facebook, Foursquare, Twitter, QQ, and many others. It is this new wave of Internet applications that has taken the web content generation to the next level. Location awareness is now the new dimension in the global cognitive process. It is in this expanded information exchange space that common reference points are established and new self-organizing social structures emerge. In this position statement, I show that spatio-temporal referencing is primordial in high-frequency communication interactions. This leads to high-frequency cognitive processes, or HFCP. The HFCP model points to a reductionist approach through event-driven information filtering and spatio-temporal synchronization. Filtering enhances the relevance of important events. Synchronization aids in the cognitive convergence of authenticity of events.

The society is larger than the sum of its parts. As self-organizing entities, organizations, cultural groups and societies, aggregate based on information exchange between individuals and intra-cognitive processes. This is the basic premise that supports larger scale cognitive processes that cross the physical boundaries in social network platforms such as Facebook, Twitter, QQ, LinkedIn, ResearchGate, and more recently Foursquare. While Facebook focused initially on networking structures and a pseudo profile matching (similar to LinkedIn, ResearhcGate, Monster.com, and social networking and service systems), Twitter had instance success due to the refinement of time resolution and increased frequency of immediate short message passing, i.e., find out "what is happening right now." This apparent simplicity in the trivial pursuit of instantaneous feedback over the network has increased the time resolution from minutes (email, blogs and message boards, to seconds (twitting). Apparently, despite the horrendous amount of redundant information being exchanged, Twitter has become one of the most successful information exchange platforms in the recent months. This shows that the demand for high resolution time referencing plays an important role in cognitive informatics (Wang, 2003, 2011) and the convergence towards location awareness.

High-Frequency Temporal Referencing: High-frequency information exchange (HFIE) exhibits strong temporal synchronization effects. For example, most of us have experienced dynamically attempting to converge to a meeting location established by frequent mobile calls as individuals seek for each other in a crowded urban environment or large indoor complex, such a convention center. Jack Dorsey, the creator and co-founder of Twitter, in his 99% conference speech in New York, in April 2010, admits his early passion for urban flow and the rapid changes in the urban environment.

The idea of high-frequency information exchange, although painfully simplistic, was not obvious in the past in the context of social networks. However, the value of HFIE emerged as users quickly realized the temporal synchronization of possible high-impact events that could lead to critical decision making or life-threatening situations. For example, the collapse of a building in a very crowded central district near Hung Hom, in Hong Kong took less than two seconds. The event propagated through internet propagated faster than from twitter like transmissions long before the first ambulances arrived at the site. The number of subscribers to twitter alone has grown from 200,000 in May 2007 to 2 million in May 2008 and 14 million in March 2009. In

March 2010, twitter surpassed the mark of 53 million twits per day – a phenomenal amount of real-time information.

High-Frequency Spatial Referencing: The next level of high-frequency information exchange is now converging towards high-frequency location awareness. More than ever, location has become the primordial factor of spatio-temporal referencing of information exchange. It is in this domain that we attempt to advance the level of cooperative development to a new global cognitive process. The additional dimension for information exchange is now *Location Referencing*.

High-frequency Location Awareness (HFLA) automatically tracks and projects motion trajectories of individual users similar to a GPS, but at a more refined scale in indoor environments. The challenge is of course the large indoor complexes which are not directly accessible by GPS location systems. Recently, we (Sysomos, 2010; Eddie et al., 2010a, 2010b; Chan et al., 2008, 2009a, 2009b) have developed an HFLA system on a Google Android HTC Nexus smart phone, Figure 2.

HFLA is also currently under development by Foursquare, an internet development company that will provide social network application based on high density location tracking of individuals in urban environments. The idea has also been captured by Facebook (with over 400 million subscribers), Twitter, Flickr, Hiya Media, Rummble, Qype, Rally, BlockChalk, Koprol, DreamWalk and many others.

High-Frequency Cognitive Processes: High-frequency cognitive processes are currently perceived as beneficial to critical decision making and ultimately to a higher predictive power on immediate future and the impact of events in our society. Whether this is good or bad remains to be seen. However, there

Figure 2. Nexus-based indoor tracking system

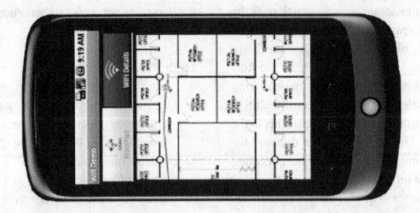

is no doubt that real-time spatio-temporal information streaming is not only highly relevant to the immediate perception of reality but provide a feedback loop on the immediate future events. Take for example the real-time submersive camera transmitting video of the deepwater horizon spill in the Gulf of Mexico, Figure 3.

In the context of natural disasters, global warming, intensified large scale events, this simple video stream significantly affects our perception of reality, from the valuation of BP by international markets to fear of excessive toxicity levels in the aquatic food chain and increased probability of cataclysmic events. (This work was partially funded by the Hong Kong RGC GRF grants PolyU 5101/07E and PolyU 5101/08E.)

IMPORTANCE OF RESEARCH ON KNOWLEDGE RESOURCES

Research of Artificial Intelligence started when modern computers were invented about sixty years ago. Many important findings have been discovered in the past six decades, from block worlds and General Problem Solver in early stages, Expert Systems in 1970's, Neural Network in 1980's, to most recent developments in Information Retrieval and Natural Language Processing. However, a clear understanding of human-level intelligence is still far from reality, and any prospect for a computer system to pass Turing's test is still remote. One critical but largely neglected area in developing high-level intelligent systems is the research and development of real-world large-scale knowledge resources, especially com-

Figure 3. Impact of high-frequency cognitive process

monsense knowledge reflecting our everyday life. Existing work in this area is scarce and often adopts manual acquisition methods, such as Cyc, WordNet, and ConceptNet. Manual approach is labor-intensive. Even with long-time efforts (both WordNet and Cyc started about twenty years ago) of many human beings (about 12,000 people contributed to ConceptNet), building a comprehensive knowledge base is still remote. Moreover, knowledge is dynamic and changes over time, so knowledge base construction requires continuous efforts on knowledge updating and collecting. Automatic approaches, such as KnowItAll, can acquire a large amount of information efficiently, but the quality of acquired knowledge is often questionable. Research in this area needs more attention and efforts from researchers of multiple areas including artificial intelligence, web mining, information retrieval, computational linguistics (Chen et al., 2009; Verma & Chen, 2007), cognitive informatics, and cognitive computing.

HUMAN FACE COGNITION: FROM 2D TO 3D

Human beings are born with a natural capacity of recovering shapes from merely a single image. However, it remains a significant challenge in cognitive computing and AI to let a computer obtain such ability. As we know, human vision system (HVS) is the key to restore 3D shape from 2D space. Simulating the underlying cognitive principle of HVS may provide a promising route for enhancements of 3D face modeling from an image. Inspired by the basic idea of 3DMM (Blanz & Vetter, 2003), to make computers recognize well about the facial shape, we propose a two-step face modeling (TSFM) scheme to make use of the prior knowledge learned from a large scale 3D face database in this paper. The main difference from 3DMM is that the 3D shape of human face is recovered from just a small number of feature points rather than optimizing on the whole im-

age. Hence, the reconstruction procedure could be finished in a matter of seconds. Further, the depth of the given features is leant from a 3D face database, which guarantees more accurate reconstructions.

Statistical linear face model construction: The core step of building a statistical linear face model is to establish a dense pixel-wise correspondence between faces. This present study proposes to solve 3D faces correspondence in 2D space, i.e., using planar templates. Texture maps of 3D models are generated at first by unwrapping 3D faces to 2D space. Then we build planar templates based on the mean shape computed by a group of annotated texture map. 34 landmarks on unwrapped texture images are located automatically by AAMs (active appearance models) and the final correspondence is finally built according to the templates.

To learn the significant components from the original data and remove the correlation between 3D faces, principal component analysis (PCA) is applied to the original data. Furthermore, to estimate the feature's depth, a sparse linear model is also built from the training set. Two-step modeling method for face reconstruction: Following observations of quantitative results of modeling accuracy, we found that the modeling precision is greatly improved by using features with 3D coordinates compared to 2D features. To compensate the defect of directly using 2D facial landmarks, a sparse linear model combining with an optimization (SLMO) process is proposed to estimate the depth of landmarks based on prior knowledge learnt from examples of 3D scans at first. Combining the known 2D coordinates with estimated depth value, Quasi-3D (Q-3D, named as their real 3D coordinates are unattainable) controls are formed. Then, we apply Q-3D controls to the deformable algorithm in recovering a person's entire 3D face. Above processes is summarized as a two-step face modeling (TSFM). In short, main contributions in 3D face modeling of TSFM are summarized as follows: a) unlike previous systems (Blanz & Vetter, 2003; Gong & Wang, 2009), Q-3D coordinates of controls are estimated before applying to modeling. We intend to show that TSFM is an algorithm free framework, i.e., it's not only suitable for the statistic methods with prior knowledge of human shape, but interpolation-based methods, such as RBFs and DFFD, can also be applied to model facial shape from a single image under TSFM; and b) Based on the framework in (Blanz & Vetter, 2003), we propose a sparse linear model combining with an optimization (SLMO) to estimate the 3D information of the 2D controls on a single image. Comparing SLMO with the technologies of best matching (BM) and interpolation fitting functions (IFF, such as RBFs and Kriging), the results show that SLMO can achieve the best accuracy in feature estimation.

GRANULAR COMPUTING AND CONCEPTUAL MODELING IN COGNITIVE COMPUTING

Conceptual modeling is an important perspective on cognitive informatics (Wang, 2002a, 2003) and cognitive computing (Wang, 2009b). Cognitive computing involves extremely complicated processes because its carrier is the brain. A suitable conceptual model enables us to focus on the main features at a more abstract level, without being overloaded with minute details and without worrying about physical or biological implementations. A number of models about the brain and cognition have been proposed and examined in philosophy, psychology, and cognitive sciences. They share some high-level similarity that supports the use of granular computing for building conceptual models of cognitive informatics, cognitive computing and the brain.

Granular computing is an emerging and fast growing field of study (Bargiela & Pedrycz, 2002; Pedrycz et al., 2008). The triarchic theory of granular computing (Yao, 2006, 2008a, 2008b) explores multilevel granular structures and consists of three perspectives, namely, granular computing as structured thinking, as structured problem solving (Zhang & Zhang, 1992), and as structured information processing (Wang, 2003). Conceptual modeling using granular structures leads to an understanding and a representation at multiple levels of granularity or abstraction. At different levels of granularity, one focuses on different issues and may use different terminology and languages.

Cognitive computing reveals some of the nature of granular computing, in which different computing modules process different types of granules. In particular, the following results are very relevant to the modeling of cognitive computing and processing based on granular computing:

- The classical work of Miller (1956) on the limited human information processing capacity and chunking, i.e., information granulation.
- The massive modularity hypothesis in evolutionary psychology (Downes, 2010).
- The Pandemonium model proposed by Selfridge (1959), consisting of demons organized into a hierarchical multilevel structure, as well as its inspired human information processing models (Lindsay & Norman, 1997).
- The simple brain model proposed by Minsky (2007), consisting of many resources.
- The hierarchical, memory based prediction framework proposed by Hawkins (Hawkins & Blakeslee, 2004).
- The layered reference model of the brain (LRMB) proposed by Wang et al. (2006).

The notions of granules, levels, and hierarchical structures may be used to suggest an expressive language for describing the above results. For instance, information chunks, information processing modules, demons, and resources are related to granules of different nature, and their hierarchical organization is related to granular structures. Therefore, granular processing may find practical applications in cognitive computing.

CONCLUSION

It has been described that Cognitive Computing (CC) is an emerging paradigm of intelligent computing methodologies and systems based on cognitive informatics that implements computational intelligence by autonomous inferences and perceptions mimicking the mechanisms of the brain. Many position papers have elaborated that the theoretical foundations underpinning cognitive computing are cognitive informatics – the science of cognitive and intelligent information and knowledge processing. This paper summarizes the presentations of a set of position papers in the IEEE ICCI'10 *Panel on Cognitive Computing and Applications* contributed from invited panelists who are part of the world's preeminent researchers and scholars in the field of cognitive informatics and cognitive computing.

REFERENCES

Anil, K., Jain, A., Ross, A., & Flynn, P. (2007). *Handbook of Biometrics*. Berlin: Springer Verlag.

Bargiela, A., & Pedrycz, W. (2002). *Granular Computing: An Introduction*. Boston: Kluwer Academic Publishers.

Blanz, V., & Vetter, T. (2002). Reconstructing the complete 3D shape of faces from partial information. *Informationsetechnik und Technische Informatik, 44*(6), 295–302.

Blanz, V., & Vetter, T. (2003). Face recognition based on fitting a 3D morphable model. *IEEE Transactions on Pattern Analysis and Machine Intelligence, 25*(9), 1063–1074. doi:10.1109/TPAMI.2003.1227983

Chan, C. L., Baciu, G., & Mak, S. (2009b). Using Wi-Fi Signal Strength to Localize in Wireless Sensor Networks. In *Proceedings of the IEEE International Conference on Communications and Mobile Computing (CMC)* (pp. 538-542).

Chan, C. L., Baciu, G., & Mak, S. C. (2008). Wireless Tracking Analysis in Location Fingerprint. In *Proceedings of the 4th IEEE Wireless and Mobile Computing, Networking and Communications (WiMOB)* (pp. 214-220).

Chan, C. L., Baciu, G., & Mak, S. C. (2009a). Using the Newton Trust-Region Method to Localize in WLAN Environment. In *Proceedings of the 5th IEEE Wireless and Mobile Computing, Networking and Communications (WiMOB)* (pp. 363-369).

Chen, P., Ding, W., Bowes, C., & Brown, D. (2009). *A Fully Unsupervised Word Sense Disambiguation Method and Its Evaluation on Coarse-grained All-words Task*. NAACL.

Downes, S. M. (2010). *Evolutionary Psychology, Stanford Encyclopedia of Philosophy*. Retrieved from http://plato.stanford.edu/entries/evolutionary-psychology/

Eddie, C. L., Chan, G. B., & Mak, S. C. (2009). Using a Cell-based WLAN Infrastructure Design for Resource-effective and Accurate Positioning. *IEEE Journal of Communications Software and Systems, 5*(4).

Eddie, C. L., Chan, G. B., & Mak, S. C. (2010a). *Newton Trust Region Method for Wi-Fi Tracking*. IEEE Transactions on Systems, Man and Cybernetics - Part A.

Eddie, C. L., Chan, G. B., & Mak, S. C. (2010b). Cognitive Location-Aware Information Retrieval by Agent-based Semantic Matching. *International Journal of Cognitive Informatics & Natural Intelligence*.

Gong, X., & Wang, G. (2009). 3D Face Deformable Model Based on Feature Points. *Journal of Software, 20*(3), 724–733. doi:10.3724/SP.J.1001.2009.03317

Hawkins, J., & Blakeslee, S. (2004). *On Intelligence.* New York: Henry Holt and Company.

Lindsay, P. H., & Norman, D. A. (1997). *An Introduction to Psychology* (2nd ed.). New York: Academic Press.

Miller, G. A. (1956). The magical number seven, plus or minus two: some limits on our capacity for processing information. *Psychological Review, 63,* 81–97. doi:10.1037/h0043158

Minsky, M. (2007). *The Emotion Machine: Commonsense Thinking, Artificial Intelligence, and the Future of the Human Mind.* New York: Simon & Schuster Paperbacks.

Pedrycz, W., Skowron, A., & Kreinovich, V. (Eds.). (2008). *Handbook of Granular Computing.* West Sussex, UK: John Wiley & Sons. doi:10.1002/9780470724163

Selfridge, O. G. (1959). Pandemonium: a paradigm for learning. In *Proceedings of the Symposium on Mechanisation of Thought Processes,* London (pp. 511-529).

Sun, Wang, Lu, Zhang, Zhang, Kinsner, & Zedah. (Eds.). (2010). In *Proceedings of the 9ᵗʰ IEEE International Conference on Cognitive Informatics (ICCI'10),* Tsinghua University, Beijing, China. Washington, DC: IEEE.

Sysomos. (2010). *Twitter and the Nine-Month Bounce.* Retrieved from http://techcrunch.com/2010/03/29/twitter-nine-month-bounce/

Verma, R., & Chen, P. (2007, April). Integrating Ontology Knowledge into a Query-based Information Summarization System. In *Proceedings of the DUC 2007,* Rochester, NY.

Wang, Y. (2002a). Keynote: On Cognitive Informatics. In *Proceedings of the 1st IEEE International Conference on Cognitive Informatics (ICCI'02),* Calgary, Canada (pp. 34-42). Washington, DC: IEEE.

Wang, Y. (2002b). The Real-Time Process Algebra (RTPA). *Annals of Software Engineering, 14,* 235–274. doi:10.1023/A:1020561826073

Wang, Y. (2003). On Cognitive Informatics. *Brain and Mind: A Transdisciplinary Journal of Neuroscience and Neurophilosophy, 4*(3), 151-167.

Wang, Y. (2006). Keynote: Cognitive Informatics - Towards the Future Generation Computers that Think and Feel. In *Proceedings of the 5th IEEE International Conference on Cognitive Informatics (ICCI'06),* Beijing, China (pp. 3-7). Washington, DC: IEEE.

Wang, Y. (2007a). *Software Engineering Foundations: A Software Science Perspective.* Boca Raton, FL: CRC.

Wang, Y. (2007b). The Theoretical Framework of Cognitive Informatics. *International Journal of Cognitive Informatics and Natural Intelligence, 1*(1), 1–27.

Wang, Y. (2007c). The OAR Model of Neural Informatics for Internal Knowledge Representation in the Brain. *International Journal of Cognitive Informatics and Natural Intelligence, 1*(3), 64–75.

Wang, Y. (2008a). On Contemporary Denotational Mathematics for Computational Intelligence. *Transactions of Computational Science, 2,* 6–29. doi:10.1007/978-3-540-87563-5_2

Wang, Y. (2008b). On Concept Algebra: A Denotational Mathematical Structure for Knowledge and Software Modeling. *International Journal of Cognitive Informatics and Natural Intelligence, 2*(2), 1–19.

Wang, Y. (2008c). On System Algebra: A Denotational Mathematical Structure for Abstract System Modeling. *International Journal of Cognitive Informatics and Natural Intelligence, 2*(2), 20–42.

Wang, Y. (2008d). RTPA: A Denotational Mathematics for Manipulating Intelligent and Computational Behaviors. *International Journal of Cognitive Informatics and Natural Intelligence, 2*(2), 44–62.

Wang, Y. (2009a). On Abstract Intelligence: Toward a Unified Theory of Natural, Artificial, Machinable, and Computational Intelligence. *International Journal of Software Science and Computational Intelligence, 1*(1), 1–18.

Wang, Y. (2009b). On Cognitive Computing. *International Journal of Software Science and Computational Intelligence, 1*(3), 1–15.

Wang, Y. (2009c). On Visual Semantic Algebra (VSA): A Denotational Mathematical Structure for Modeling and Manipulating Visual Objects and Patterns. *International Journal of Software Science and Computational Intelligence, 1*(4), 1–15.

Wang, Y. (2009d). Paradigms of Denotational Mathematics for Cognitive Informatics and Cognitive Computing. *Fundamenta Informaticae, 90*(3), 282–303.

Wang, Y. (2010a). Toward a Cognitive Behavioral Reference Model of Artificial Brains. Journal of Computational and Theoretical Nanoscience.

Wang, Y. (2010b). Abstract Intelligence and Cognitive Robots. *Journal of Behavioral Robotics, 1*(1), 66–72.

Wang, Y. (2010c). A Sociopsychological Perspective on Collective Intelligence in Metaheuristic Computing. *International Journal of Applied Metaheuristic Computing, 1*(1), 110–128.

Wang, Y. (2010d). Towards an Intelligent Behavioral Reference Model of Cognitive Robots. IEEE Robotics and Automation, 17*(4).*

Wang, Y. (2010e). On Formal and Cognitive Semantics for Semantic Computing. *International Journal of Semantic Computing, 4*(2), 83–118. doi:10.1142/S1793351X10000833

Wang, Y. (2011). *Cognitive Informatics: Foundations of Natural, Abstract, and Computational Intelligence.* Cambridge, MA: MIT Press.

Wang, Y., Baciu, G., Yao, Y., Kinsner, W., Chan, K., & Zhang, B. (2010). Perspectives on Cognitive Informatics and Cognitive Computing. *International Journal of Cognitive Informatics and Natural Intelligence, 4*(1), 1–29.

Wang, Y., & Chiew, V. (2010). On the Cognitive Process of Human Problem Solving. *Cognitive Systems Research: An International Journal, 11*(1), 81–92. doi:10.1016/j.cogsys.2008.08.003

Wang, Y., & Kinsner, W. (2006). Recent Advances in Cognitive Informatics. *IEEE Transactions on Systems, Man and Cybernetics. Part C, Applications and Reviews, 36*(2), 121–123. doi:10.1109/TSMCC.2006.871120

Wang, Y., Kinsner, W., Anderson, J. A., Zhang, D., Yao, Y., & Sheu, P. (2009c). A Doctrine of Cognitive Informatics. *Fundamenta Informaticae, 90*(3), 203–228.

Wang, Y., Kinsner, W., & Zhang, D. (2009a). Contemporary Cybernetics and its Faces of Cognitive Informatics and Computational Intelligence. *IEEE Trans. on System, Man, and Cybernetics (B), 39*(4), 1–11.

Wang, Y., & Wang, Y. (2006). Cognitive Informatics Models of the Brain. *IEEE Transactions on Systems, Man and Cybernetics. Part C, Applications and Reviews, 36*(2), 203–207. doi:10.1109/TSMCC.2006.871151

Wang, Y., Wang, Y., Patel, S., & Patel, D. (2006). A Layered Reference Model of the Brain. *IEEE Transactions on Systems, Man and Cybernetics. Part C, Applications and Reviews, 36*(2), 124–133. doi:10.1109/TSMCC.2006.871126

Wang, Y., Zhang, D., & Tsumoto, S. (2009c). Cognitive Informatics, Cognitive Computing, and Their Denotational Mathematical Foundations (I). *Fundamenta Informaticae, 90*(3), 1–7.

Wang, Y. L. (Ed.). (2009d). Special Issue on Cognitive Computing, On Abstract Intelligence. *International Journal of Software Science and Computational Intelligence, 1*(3).

Wang, Y. L., Zadeh, A., & Yao, Y. (2009b). On the System Algebra Foundations for Granular Computing. *International Journal of Software Science and Computational Intelligence, 1*(1), 1–17.

Yao, Y. (2006). Three perspectives of granular computing. *Journal of Nanchang Institute of Technology, 25,* 16–21.

Yao, Y. (2008a). A unified framework of granular computing . In Pedrycz, W., Skowron, A., & Kreinovich, V. (Eds.), *Handbook of Granular Computing* (pp. 401–410). New York: Wiley. doi:10.1002/9780470724163.ch17

Yao, Y. (2008b). Granular computing: past, present and future. In *Proceedings of the 2008 IEEE International Conference on Granular Computing* (pp. 80-85).

Zadeh, L. A. (1975). Fuzzy Logic and Approximate Reasoning. *Syntheses, 30,* 407–428. doi:10.1007/BF00485052

Zadeh, L. A. (1999). From Computing with Numbers to Computing with Words – from Manipulation of Measurements to Manipulation of Perception. *IEEE Trans. on Circuits and Systems I, 45*(1), 105–119. doi:10.1109/81.739259

Zhang, B., & Zhang, L. (1992). *Theory and Applications of Problem Solving*. Amsterdam: North-Holland.

This work was previously published in International Journal of Software Science and Computational Intelligence, Volume 2, Issue 4, edited by Yingxu Wang, pp. 32-44, copyright 2010 by IGI Publishing (an imprint of IGI Global).

Chapter 2
Granular Computing and Human–Centricity in Computational Intelligence

Witold Pedrycz
University of Alberta, Canada, and Polish Academy of Sciences, Poland

ABSTRACT

Information granules and ensuing Granular Computing offer interesting opportunities to endow processing with an important facet of human-centricity. This facet implies that the underlying processing supports non-numeric data inherently associated with the variable perception of humans. Systems that commonly become distributed and hierarchical, managing granular information in hierarchical and distributed architectures, is of growing interest, especially when invoking mechanisms of knowledge generation and knowledge sharing. The outstanding feature of human centricity of Granular Computing along with essential fuzzy set-based constructs constitutes the crux of this study. The author elaborates on some new directions of knowledge elicitation and quantification realized in the setting of fuzzy sets. With this regard, the paper concentrates on knowledge-based clustering. It is also emphasized that collaboration and reconciliation of locally available knowledge give rise to the concept of higher type information granules. Other interesting directions enhancing human centricity of computing with fuzzy sets deals with non-numeric semi-qualitative characterization of information granules, as well as inherent evolving capabilities of associated human-centric systems. The author discusses a suite of algorithms facilitating a qualitative assessment of fuzzy sets, formulates a series of associated optimization tasks guided by well-formulated performance indexes, and discusses the underlying essence of resulting solutions.

INTRODUCTION

Constructs of Computational Intelligence (CI) (Angelov et al., 2008; Crespo & Weber, 2005; Kacprzyk & Zadrozny, 2005; Kilic et al., 2007; Molina et al., 2006; Pedrycz & Gomide, 1998;

DOI: 10.4018/978-1-4666-0264-9.ch002

Pham & Castellani, 2006; Wang et al., 2009) exhibits a surprising diversity of design methodologies. The concepts and architectures of neurofuzzy systems, evolutionary fuzzy systems are becoming more visible and widespread in the literature.

In spite of this variety, there is a single very visible development aspect that cuts across the entire field of CI and fuzzy modeling, in particular.

In a nutshell, such constructs are built around a single data set. What also becomes more apparent nowadays is a tendency of modeling a variety of distributed systems or phenomena, in which there are separate data sets, quite often quite remote in terms of location or distant in time. The same complex phenomenon could be perceived and modeled using different data sets collected individually and usually not shared. The data might be expressed in different feature spaces as the views at the process could be secured from different perspectives. The models developed individually could be treated as a multitude of sources of knowledge. Along with the individual design of fuzzy models, it could be beneficial to share sources of knowledge (models), reconcile findings, collaborate with intent of forming a model, which might offer a global, unified, comprehensive and holistic view at the underlying phenomenon. Under these circumstances an effective way of knowledge sharing and reconciliation through a sound communication platform becomes of paramount relevance, see Figure 1.

A situation portrayed in Figure 1 is shown in a somewhat general way not moving into the details. It is essential to note that the mechanisms of collaboration and reconciliation are realized through passing information granules rather than detailed numeric entities.

The general category of fuzzy models under investigation embrace models described as a family of pairs $<R_i, f_i>$, i=1, 2, …,c. In essence, these pairs can be sought as concise representations of rules with R_i forming the condition part of the i-th rule and f_i standing in the corresponding conclusion part. It is beneficial to emphasize that in such rules, we admit a genuine diversity of the local models formalized by f_i. From the modeling perspective, the expression $f_i(\mathbf{x}, \mathbf{a}_i)$ could be literally *any* modeling construct, namely

- Fuzzy set,
- Linear or nonlinear regression function,
- Difference or differential equation,
- Finite state machine,
- Neural network

One can cast the fuzzy models in a certain perspective by noting that by determining a collection of information granules (fuzzy sets) R_i, one establishes a certain view at the system/phenomenon. Subsequently, the conclusion parts (f_i) are implied by the information granules and their detailed determination is realized once R_i have been fixed or further adjusted (refined).

In light of the discussion on knowledge reconciliation and mechanisms of collaboration, it becomes apparent that the interaction can focus on information granules R_i and communication schemes that invoke exchange of granules whereas conclusion parts can be adjusted accordingly once the collaborative development of information granules has been completed.

Figure 1. A General platform of knowledge reconciliation and collaboration in fuzzy modeling

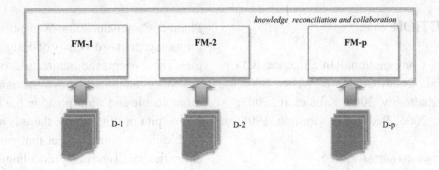

The main objectives of the study, that is reflected by the organization of the material, is to formulate and discuss a variety of collaborative models of fuzzy models as well as highlight the design principles. The constructs resulting through such collaboration give rise in one way or another to granular constructs of higher order, where the elevated level of granularity is a consequence of reconciliation of knowledge coming from the individual models. The principle of justifiable granularity is presented and shows how granularity emerges as a result of summarization of numeric information (and numeric membership values, in particular). A number of collaborative schemes are discussed where we identify main concepts and present some general ways in which such schemes can be realized. We also show how type-2 fuzzy sets (including interval-valued fuzzy sets) are formed as an immediate result of collaboration.

Throughout this study, we adhere to the standard notation. In particular information granules – fuzzy sets are denoted by capital letters. The notation and terminology is the one being in common usage in the realm of fuzzy sets.

DESIGN OF INFORMATION GRANULES

In what follows, we are concerned with a fundamental quest of forming information granules-generic entities to be used as building blocks in all pursuits of Granular Computing. To focus our attention, in what follows we will concentrate on a finite collection of numeric values (real numbers), say $X = \{x_1, x_2, ..., x_N\}$ however the proposed framework is general enough so that after some minor modifications/enhancements it could be used to deal with more general entities such as information granules (in which case a hierarchy of higher order information granules can be realized).

The three main pursuits are discussed here: (a) formation of a single information granule. In this case the principle of justifiable granularity is exploited, (b) a representation of X through a finite collection of information granules. This naturally leads to the ideas of clustering, and (c) augmentation of the techniques of clustering via incorporating of additional sources of knowledge.

THE PRINCIPLE OF JUSTIFIABLE GRANULARITY

The essence of the principle of justifiable granularity (Pedrycz, 2005) is that a meaningful representation of X can be realized as a certain information granule (Bargiela & Pedrycz, 2003, 2008; Zadeh, 1997, 2005; Wang et al., 2009) rather than a single numeric entity, no matter how such single individual has been selected. What is being done in statistics is an example of this principle that is realized in the language of *probabilistic* information granules. A sample of numeric data is represented not only by its mean or median (which is a very rough description) but also by the standard deviation. Both the mean and the standard deviation imply a realization of a certain probabilistic information granule, such as e.g., a Gaussian one. The probabilistic information granules are just one of the possibilities to construct an information granule to represent a collection of numeric data.

In case of other formalisms of information granulation, the development of the corresponding granules is guided by a certain optimization criterion. In general, in such criteria, we manage two conflicting requirements. The one is about forming an information granule of sufficiently high level of experimental evidence accumulated behind it and in this way supporting its existence. The second one is about maintaining high specificity of the resulting information granule.

We discuss several general cases to venture into more algorithmic details of the realization of information granules. We show a construction of interval-based information granules as well as information granules represented as fuzzy sets.

(a) the design of interval-based information granule of numeric data. The data are illustrated in Figure 2.

We span the numeric interval Ω (=[a, b]) in such a way that (i) the numeric evidence accumulated within the bounds of Ω is as high as possible. We quantify this requirement by counting the number of data falling within the bounds of Ω, that is card$\{ x_k \in \Omega \}$, which has to be maximized. At the same time, we require that (ii) the support of Ω is as low as possible, which makes Ω specific (detailed) enough. These two requirements are in conflict. A possible way to combine them into a single criterion is to consider the ratio

$$Q = \frac{\mathrm{card}(x_k \in \Omega)}{\mathrm{supp}(\Omega)} = \frac{\mathrm{card}(x_k \in \Omega)}{|b-a|} \qquad (1)$$

which is maximized with regard to the end-points of the interval, namely max $_{a,b}$ Q. The modified version of (1), which offers more flexibility in the development of the information granule involves a decreasing function of the length of the interval |b-a, say| f(|b-a|) which along with some parameters helps control an impact of granularity of the interval on the maximization of Q. For instance,

we consider f(|b-a|) = exp(-α|b-a|) with a being α certain parameter assuming positive values. The performance index Q reads as follows

$$Q = \mathrm{card}(x_k \in \Omega) \exp(-\alpha|b-a|) \qquad (2)$$

(b) here we design the interval information granule considering that the numeric data come with membership values, that is we are concerned with the pairs (x_k, μ_k) where μ_k stands for the k-th membership value. This specific design scenario is included in Figure 3.

The same design development as discussed in (a) applies here. As each data point comes with the associated membership value, the numeric evidence accumulated within Ω has to be computed in such a way that they are present in the calculations and contribute to the accumulated experimental evidence behind Ω. We determine the σ-sum of the evidence, that is $\sum_{x_k \in \Omega} \mu_k$. This observation leads us to the maximization of the following performance index

$$Q = \frac{\sum_{x_k \in \Omega} \mu_k}{\mathrm{supp}(\Omega)} \qquad (3)$$

Figure 3. Realization of the principle of justifiable granularity for numeric data with membership-graded (weighted numeric data) and the use of interval form of information granules

Figure 2. Realization of the principle of justifiable granularity for numeric data and interval form of information granules

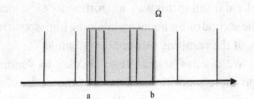

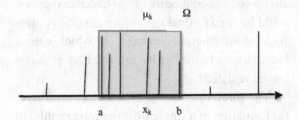

Alternatively, we can focus on the formation of the information granule Ω, which leads to the minimum of changes of the membership grades of the corresponding data. To admit x_k with membership μ_k to Ω, we need to change (elevate) the membership grade and this change is equal to $1-\mu_k$. Similarly, if we exclude x_k from Ω, the corresponding change (suppression) in membership value is equal to μ_k. Refer to Figure 4. The criterion of interest is that of the sum of all possible changes made to the membership grades. We construct Ω in such a way that the changes in membership values are as low as possible. Formally, the performance index is expressed as

$$Q = \sum_{x_k \in \Omega} (1 - \mu_k) + \sum_{x_k \notin \Omega} \mu_k \qquad (4)$$

and its minimization leads to the interval-type of information granule,

$$\text{Min}_{a,b:\, a<b} Q \qquad (5)$$

If the constructed information granule of interest is a fuzzy set rather than the interval, the above considerations are slightly revisited to account for membership degrees of the information granule A. An example of this type of optimization is illustrated in Figure 5.

The position of the modal value of A is determined by taking the numeric representative of the data (say, mean or median). Typically, to arrive at semantically meaningful A, we require that the

Figure 4. The design of interval information granule realized through the minimization of the criterion of modification of membership grades

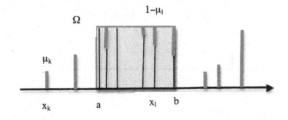

Figure 5. Realization of the principle of justifiable granularity for numeric data and fuzzy sets treated as information granules

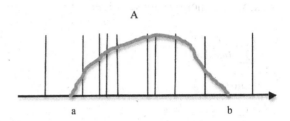

membership function A is unimodal. Given some type of the fuzzy set (say, triangular, parabolic, etc), the optimization of the spreads of the fuzzy set is realized independently for the left- and right-hand spread. The performance index considered here is a slightly modified version of (1), that is

$$Q = \frac{\sum_{k=1}^{N} A(x_k)}{\text{supp}(A)} \qquad (6)$$

Considering the fixed form of the membership functions, here are two optimization problems of parametric character: $\text{Min}_a Q$ and $\text{Min}_b Q$.

Some further flexibility can be added to the problem by introducing a parameter-enhanced version of Q, which reads as follows:

$$Q = \frac{\sum_{k=1}^{N} A^{\gamma}(x_k)}{\text{supp}(A)} \qquad (7)$$

where $\gamma > 0$. For $\gamma \in [0,1]$ there is less emphasis is placed on the membership values in the sense these values are "inflated". Note that if $\gamma \rightarrow 0$ then (6) reduces to the previous interval type of information granule. In a more general setting one can consider any continuous and increasing function g_1 of $\sum_{k=1}^{N} A(x_k)$, that is $g_1\left(\sum_{k=1}^{N} A(x_k)\right)$ and a decreasing function g_2 of supp(A) that is $g_2(\text{supp}(A))$.

In case, the numeric data are associated with some membership values (μ_k), those are taken into account in the modified version of the performance index, which includes these values

$$Q = \frac{\sum_{k=1}^{N} \mu_k A(x_k)}{\text{supp}(A)} \qquad (8)$$

All the algorithms realizing the principle of justifiable granularity produce an information granule (either an interval or a fuzzy set) based on a collection of numeric data. The nature of the numeric data themselves can be quite different. Two design situations are worth highlighting here:

(a) The numeric data could result from measuring some variables present in the system. In this case, information granules are treated as non-numeric data, which can be then used in the design of the model and highlight the structure of a large number of numeric data.

(b) The numeric data are membership values of some fuzzy sets reported for a certain point of the universe of discourse. The granular representation resulting from the discussed construct gives rise to the information granule of higher type, fuzzy set of type-2, to be more specific. Depending on the nature of the information granule formed here, we arrive at interval-valued type-2 fuzzy sets or just type-2 fuzzy sets.

The principle of justifiable granularity can be used in case of functions, which are then made granular. Given the pairs of input-output data $(\mathbf{x}_k, y_k)$, k=1, 2,…, N and having the best numeric mapping "f" we realize its granular mapping, say interval-like format (f_-, f_+). The level of granularity expressed here as the integral of difference between the bounds. The objective is to make the value of the integral as low as possible while "covering" as many output data as possible, see Figure 6.

INFORMATION GRANULES AS RESULTS OF CLUSTERING

Information granules are also results of applying clustering techniques to the data set *X*. When dealing with a broad class of objective function based clustering, the results are conveyed in the form of a partition matrix U and a finite number of "c" prototypes $\mathbf{v}_1, \mathbf{v}_2, …, \mathbf{v}_c$. Quite commonly, $\mathbf{v}_i$ are weighted means or medoids (depending upon the nature of the clustering algorithm). Depending upon the nature of the particular algorithm, we end up with information granules realized as sets, fuzzy sets, rough sets and alike. In the first case, the algorithm of K-Means is commonly used. In case of information granules represented as fuzzy sets, Fuzzy C-Means (FCM, for brief) is one of the commonly used machinery of fuzzy clustering (Bezdek, 1982; Pedrycz, 2005). Let us offer a brief summary of the essence of the method itself. Given a collection of n-dimensional data set *X*, the task of determining its structure – a collection of "c" clusters, is expressed as a minimization of the following objective function (performance index) Q being regarded as a sum of the squared distances between data and their representatives (prototypes)

$$Q = \sum_{i=1}^{c} \sum_{k=1}^{N} u_{ik}^{m} \|\mathbf{x}_k - \mathbf{v}_i\|^2 \qquad (9)$$

Figure 6. Realization of the principle of justifiable granularity in the development of granular mappings

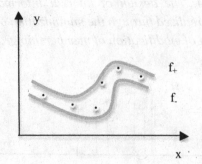

Here $\mathbf{v}_i$ s are n-dimensional prototypes of the clusters, i=1, 2,..,c and U = $[u_{ik}]$ stands for a partition matrix expressing a way of allocation of the data to the corresponding clusters; u_{ik} is the membership degree of data $\mathbf{x}_k$ in the i-th cluster. The distance between the data $\mathbf{x}_k$ and prototype $\mathbf{v}_i$ is denoted by ‖.‖. The fuzzification coefficient m (>1.0) expresses the impact of the membership grades on the individual clusters. It implies as certain geometry of fuzzy sets (membership functions).

A partition matrix satisfies two important and intuitively appealing properties

(a) $0 < \sum_{k=1}^{N} u_{ik} < N, \quad i = 1,2,...,c$

(b) $\sum_{i=1}^{c} u_{ik} = 1, \quad k = 1,2,..., N$ (10)

Let us denote by **U** a family of matrices satisfying (a)-(b). The first requirement states that each cluster has to be nonempty and different from the entire set. The second requirement states that the sum of the membership grades should be confined to 1.

The minimization of Q completed with respect to U ∈ **U** and the prototypes $\mathbf{v}_i$ of V = {$\mathbf{v}_1$, $\mathbf{v}_2$, ...$\mathbf{v}_c$} of the clusters. More explicitly, we write this down as follows

min Q with respect to U ∈ **U**, $\mathbf{v}_1$, $\mathbf{v}_2$, ..., $\mathbf{v}_c$ ∈ $\mathbf{R}^n$ (11)

DESIGN OF INFORMATION GRANULES WITH KNOWLEDGE HINTS

As it is well-known, clustering and supervised pattern recognition (classification) are the two opposite poles of the learning paradigm. In reality, there is no "pure" unsupervised learning. There is no fully supervised learning as some labels might not be completely reliable (as those encountered in case of learning with probabilistic teacher).

There is some domain knowledge and it has to be carefully incorporated into the generic clustering procedure. Knowledge hints can be conveniently captured and formalized in terms of fuzzy sets. Altogether with the underlying clustering algorithms, they give rise to the concept of knowledge-based clustering - a unified framework in which data and knowledge are processed together in a uniform fashion.

We discuss some of the typical design scenarios of knowledge-based clustering and show how the domain knowledge can be effectively incorporated into the fabric of the original data-driven only clustering techniques.

We can distinguish several interesting and practically viable ways in which domain knowledge is taken into consideration:

A subset of labeled patterns. The knowledge hints are provided in the form of a small subset of labeled patterns **K** ⊂ **N**. (Pedrycz & Waletzky, 1997(a), 1997(b)); For each of them we have a vector of membership grades f_k, k ∈ **K** which consists of degrees of membership the pattern is assigned to the corresponding clusters. As usual, we have f_{ik} ∈ [0, 1] and $\sum_{i=1}^{c} f_{ik} = 1$.

Proximity-based clustering Here we are provided a collection of pairs of patterns (Loia et al., 2003) with specified levels of closeness (resemblance) which are quantified in terms of proximity, prox (k, l) expressed for $\mathbf{x}_k$ and $\mathbf{x}_l$. The proximity offers a very general quantification scheme of resemblance: we require reflexivity and symmetry, that is prox(k, k)=1 and prox(k, l)= prox(l, k); however no transitivity requirement has to be satisfied.

"belong" and "not-belong" Boolean relationships between patterns These two Boolean relationships stress that two patterns should

belong to the same clusters, $R(\mathbf{x}_k, \mathbf{x}_l) = 1$ or they should be placed apart in two different clusters, $R(\mathbf{x}_k, \mathbf{x}_l) = 0$. These two requirements could be relaxed by requiring that these two relationships return values close to one or zero.

Uncertainty of labeling/allocation of patterns. We may consider that some patterns are "easy" to assign to clusters while some others are inherently difficult to deal with meaning that their cluster allocation is associated with a significant level of uncertainty. Let $\Phi(\mathbf{x}_k)$ stands for the uncertainty measure (e.g., entropy) for $\mathbf{x}_k$ (as a matter of fact, Φ is computed for the membership degrees of $\mathbf{x}_k$ that is $\Phi(\mathbf{u}_k)$ with $\mathbf{u}_k$ being the k-th column of the partition matrix. The uncertainty hint is quantified by values close to 0 or 1 depending upon what uncertainty level a given pattern is coming from.

Depending on the character of the knowledge hints, the original clustering algorithm needs to be properly refined. In particular the underlying objective function has to be augmented to capture the knowledge-based requirements. Below shown are several examples of the extended objective functions dealing with the knowledge hints introduced above.

When dealing with some labeled patterns we consider the following augmented objective function

$$Q = \sum_{i=1}^{c} \sum_{k=1}^{N} u_{ik}^{m} \|\mathbf{x}_k - \mathbf{v}_i\|^2$$

$$+ \pm \sum_{i=1}^{c} \sum_{k=1}^{N} (u_{ik} - f_{ik} b_k)^2 \|\mathbf{x}_k - \mathbf{v}_i\|^2 \qquad (12)$$

where the second term quantifies distances between the class membership of the labeled patterns and the values of the partition matrix. The positive weight factor (α) helps set up a suitable balance between the knowledge about classes already available and the structure revealed by the clustering algorithm. The Boolean variable b_k assumes values equal to 1 when the corresponding pattern has been labeled.

The proximity constraints are accommodated as a part of the optimization problem where we minimize the distances between proximity values being provided and those generated by the partition matrix $P(k_1, k_2)$

$$Q = \sum_{i=1}^{c} \sum_{k=1}^{N} u_{ik}^{m} \|\mathbf{x}_k - \mathbf{v}_i\|^2$$

$$\|\text{prox}(k_1, k_2) - P(k_1, k_2)\| \to \text{Min}$$

$$k_1, k_2 \in \boldsymbol{K} \qquad (13)$$

with $\boldsymbol{K}$ being a pair of patterns for which the proximity level has been provided. It can be shown that given the partition matrix the expression $\sum_{i=1}^{c} \min(u_{ik1}, u_{ik2})$ generates the corresponding proximity value. For the uncertainty constraints, the minimization problem can be expressed as follows

$$Q = \sum_{i=1}^{c} \sum_{k=1}^{N} u_{ik}^{m} \|\mathbf{x}_k - \mathbf{v}_i\|^2$$

$$\|\Phi(\mathbf{u}_k) - \gamma_k\| \to \text{Min}$$

$$k \, \boldsymbol{K} \qquad (14)$$

where $\boldsymbol{K}$ stands for the set of patterns for which we are provided with the uncertainty values γ_k.

Undoubtedly the extended objective functions call for the optimization scheme that is more demanding as far as the calculations are concerned. In several cases we cannot modify the standard technique of Lagrange multipliers, which leads to an iterative scheme of successive updates of the partition matrix and the prototypes. In general, though, the knowledge hints give rise to a more complex objective function in which the iterative scheme cannot be useful in the determination of the partition matrix and the prototypes. Alluding to the generic FCM scheme, we observe that the calculations of the prototypes in the iterative loop are doable in case of the Euclidean distance. Even the Hamming or Tchebyshev distance brings a great deal of complexity. Likewise, the knowledge hints lead to the increased complexity: the prototypes cannot be computed in a straightforward way and one has to resort himself to more advanced optimization techniques. Evolutionary computing arises here as an appealing alternative. We may consider any of the options available there including genetic algorithms, particle swarm optimization, ant colonies, to name some of them. The general scheme can be schematically structured as follows:

- repeat { EC (prototypes); compute partition matrix U;}

KNOWLEDGE RECONCILIATION: SEVERAL MECHANISMS OF COLLABORATION

The collaboration in the formation of fuzzy models is mostly focused on the collaborative formation of information granules as they form a backbone of fuzzy models. The conclusion parts are mostly realized based on the locally available data and they are constructed once the information granules have been established.

Here there are a number of possible mechanisms of interaction between the individual models when exchanging the findings about the structure of information granules. In contrast to the hierarchical mode of collaboration (to be discussed in Section 4), the mechanisms presented here can be referred to as a one-level collaboration. The form of interaction depends on the level of compatibility considering available spaces of data and spaces of

features (inputs) and commonalities among them. Refer to Figure 7.

The findings of the corresponding character are exchanged (communicated among the models) and actively used when carrying out information granulation at the level of the individually available data sets. In what follows, we elaborate on the main aspects of the collaboration modes referring the reader to the literature on their algorithmic details (Pedrycz, 2005; Pedrycz & Rai, 2008). The taxonomy provided here is based on the commonalities encountered throughout the individual data sources. Those could be present in terms of the same feature space or the same data being expressed in different feature spaces.

Collaboration through exchange of prototypes
    Here, as shown in Figure 8, the data are described in the same feature space and an interaction is realized through prototypes produced locally.
Collaboration through exchange of partition matrices Here the data are described in different feature spaces (they might overlap but are not the same). The data in each data set are the same but described in different feature spaces. The exchange of findings and collaboration is realized through interaction at the level of partition matrices. Note that these

Figure 7. Collaboration among fuzzy models realized through communication at the level of information granules

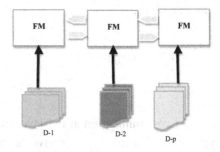

matrices abstract from the feature spaces (the spaces do not appear there in an explicit way) but the corresponding rows of the partition matrices have to coincide meaning that we are concerned with the same data).

Formally the underlying optimization problem can be expressed by an augmented objective function, which is composed of two components

$$Q = Q(D - ii) + \alpha \sum_{\substack{jj=1, \\ jj \neq ii}}^{p} ||\mathbf{G}(ii) - \mathbf{G}(jj)||^2 \quad (15)$$

The first one, Q(D-ii) is focused on the optimization of the structure based on the locally available data (so the structure one is looking for based on D-ii). The second one is concerned with achieving consistency between the granular structure $\mathbf{G}(ii)$ and the structure revealed based on other data. The positive weight (α) is used to set up a certain balance between these two components of the augmented objective function (local structure and consistency among the local structures). The notation $\mathbf{G}(ii)$ is used to concisely denote a collection of information granule obtained there, say $\mathbf{G}(ii) = \{ G_1[ii], G_2[ii], \ldots, G_c[ii] \}$. As mentioned, such granules could be represented (described) by their prototypes or partition matrices.

If we consider the FCM-like optimization (Bezdek, 1981), the objective function can be written down in a more explicit fashion as follows

$$Q = \sum_{i=1}^{c} \sum_{\substack{k=1 \\ \mathbf{x}_k \in D-ii}}^{N} u_{ik}^{m} ||\mathbf{x}_k - \mathbf{v}_i[ii]||^2$$

$$+ \alpha \sum_{\substack{jj=1, \\ jj \neq ii}}^{p} ||\mathbf{G}(ii) - \mathbf{G}(jj)||^2 \quad (16)$$

In case of communication at the level of the prototypes, Figure 8 (a), the objective function

becomes refined and its term guiding the collaboration effect arises in the form

$$\sum_{\substack{jj=1, \\ jj \neq ii}}^{p} ||\mathbf{G}(ii) - \mathbf{G}(jj)||^2 = \sum_{i=1}^{c} \sum_{\substack{jj=1, \\ jj \neq ii}}^{p} ||\mathbf{v}_i[ii] - \mathbf{v}_i[jj]||^2$$

$$(17)$$

For the communication with the aid of partition matrices, Figure 8 (b) the detailed expression for the objective function reads as follows

$$\sum_{\substack{jj=1, \\ jj \neq ii}}^{p} ||\mathbf{G}(ii) - \mathbf{G}(jj)||^2 =$$

$$(18)$$

$$\sum_{i=1}^{c} \sum_{k=1}^{N} \sum_{\substack{jj=1, \\ jj \neq ii}}^{p} (u_{ik}[ii] - u_{ik}[jj])^2 ||\mathbf{v}_i[ii] - \mathbf{v}_j[jj]||^2$$

Figure 8. A schematic view at collaboration realized through exchange of prototypes (a), and (b) sharing partition matrices

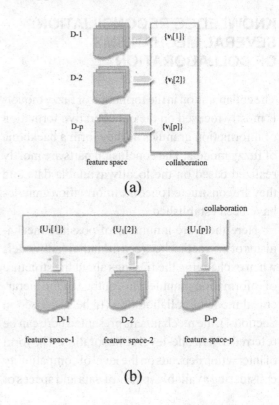

It could be noted that there is a certain direct correspondence between the prototypes and the partition matrix in the sense that each of one could be inferred given that the other one has been provided. More specifically, we envision the following pair of mappings supplying equivalence transformations,

$$\{U, D\} \rightarrow V = \{v_1, v_2, ..., v_c\}$$

$$\{V, D\} \rightarrow U \tag{19}$$

This transformation can bring a certain unified perspective at the mechanisms of exchange of information granules. For instance, one can convey a collection of the prototypes and they can induce a partition matrix over any data set.

Knowledge Reconciliation: A Hierarchy of Fuzzy Models

The overall schematic view of the hierarchical knowledge reconciliation is presented in Figure 9. The knowledge acquired at the level of the models FM-1, FM-2... FM-p is concisely arranged in a certain knowledge signature that is a collection of information granules and the associated local models. To emphasize their origin, let us use an extra index in squared brackets. For instance, the knowledge signature coming from the ii-th location is denoted as $\{ <R_i[ii], f_i[ii]> \}$.

In the hierarchical reconciliation of knowledge, we distinguish two general approaches, which depend on a way in which the knowledge is being utilized. The corresponding visualization of the essence of this mechanism is presented in Figure 9.

Passive approach In this approach, we are provided with the knowledge signature, mainly the information granules Ri[ii], which are reconciled at the higher level of the hierarchy.

The prototypes obtained at the lower level are available at the higher level of hierarchy. Here two main directions are sought:

(a) We choose a subset of prototypes, which are the most representative (in terms of a certain criterion) of all $R_i[ii]$s, i=1, 2, ..., c_{ii}, ii=1, 2, ..., P. Some reconstruction criterion can be involved here using which we express to which extent Ri[ii] are "reconstructed" by the most representative subset of the prototypes. The problem formulated in this way is of combinatorial nature and may invoke the use of methods of evolutionary optimization through which an optimal subset of the prototypes can be established.

(b) The reconciliation of knowledge is realized through clustering of these prototypes, which results in a family of high-level prototypes (and information granules) over which a fuzzy model is constructed. The associated local models are formed on a basis of some data available at the lower level. The approach is called *passive* as the formation of the model at the higher level does not impact (adjust) in any way the local knowledge (models) available at the lower level.

Figure 9. Passive and active modes of hierarchical knowledge reconciliation

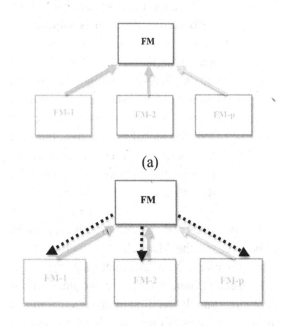

Active approach In contrast to the passive approach, here we allow for some mechanisms of interaction. The results of clustering of the prototypes realized at the higher level of the hierarchy are used to assess the quality of the information granules of the models present at the lower level. For instance, one determines how well a certain information granule is expressed (reconstructed) by the information granules developed at the higher level of the hierarchy. This feedback signal, shown in Figure 9 (b) by a dotted line, is sent back to the lower level where the formation of information granules is guided by the quality of the clusters quantified by the feedback message. The clustering mechanism applied at the lower level is updated and the clusters, which were deemed the least fit are adjusted to become more in line with the findings produced at the higher level of the hierarchy. To accommodate this feedback, the modification of the clustering method can be realized by incorporating the changes to the objective function. For instance, in the FCM, the objective function is adjusted as follows where γ_i is a certain function quantifying the quality of the i-th cluster and supplied from the higher level of the hierarchy. For instance, if this cluster is evaluated there as being irrelevant from the global perspective, then the low values of γ_i used in the objective function discounts the relevance of the i-th cluster at the lower level.

Irrespectively of the passive or active approach, in both cases the hierarchical structure gives rise to the hierarchy of information granules. As visualized in Figure 9, there are two stages of information granulation: first information granules are built on basis of data (and those are used in

forming fuzzy models at the lower level) and then they are reconciled.

The term information granules of type-2 has to be referred to the original data, so type-1 granulation pertains to the process involving original data whereas the type-2 constructs pertain to information granules built on a basis of prototypes of the information granules at the lower level; in this sense these could be sought of type-2 vis-à-vis original data. Again, here we can distinguish between two ways of forming information granules of higher type, that is (a) selection, and (b) successive granulation. In the selection mode, we choose the most representative subset of information granules from each of the models. As such, this is a combinatorial optimization problem. In the method of successive granulation, the prototypes of information granules produced at the lower level are the objects to be clustered.

It is worth noting that one could have a combination of the hierarchical as well as one-level collaboration mechanisms (Figure 10).

THE DEVELOPMENT OF GRANULAR MODELS OF TYPE-2

The hierarchical way of knowledge reconciliation outlined in Section 4, not matter whether being realized in a passive or active way, leads to fuzzy models, which are inherently associated with information granules and directly engage the principle of justifiable granularity. Let us elaborate on two general cases, which illustrate a way in which granulation of information comes to the picture.

Fuzzy models with granular outputs. The prototypes (or *metaprototypes*, being more descriptive) developed at the higher level are associated with the corresponding outputs. Consider a certain prototype, $\mathbf{v}_i$. We determine the outputs of the fuzzy models present at the lower level, that is FM-1($\mathbf{v}_i$), FM-2($\mathbf{v}_i$), and FM-p($\mathbf{v}_i$). We repeat the same calculations for all other prototypes. Apparently, the mapping from the set of prototypes

Figure 10. From data to information granules of type-1 and type-2: 9a) selection, and (b) successive granulation

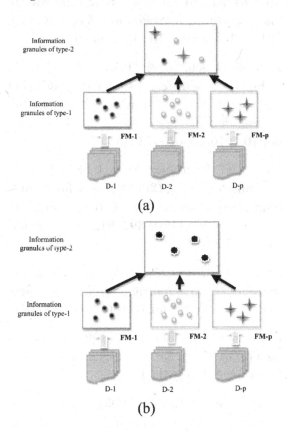

(a)

(b)

to the output space is one-to-many as for each input v_i we typically encounter several different numeric outputs. Through the use of any of the technique of granulation (see Section 2), we arrive at a collection of numeric inputs-granular output pairs of the form

$$\{ (\mathbf{v}_1, G(FM\text{-}1(\mathbf{v}_1), FM\text{-}2(\mathbf{v}_1), .., FM\text{-}p(\mathbf{v}_1))),$$

$$(\mathbf{v}_2, G(FM\text{-}1(\mathbf{v}_2), FM\text{-}2(\mathbf{v}_2), ..., FM\text{-}p(\mathbf{v}_2))), ...$$

$$(\mathbf{v}_i, G(FM\text{-}1(\mathbf{v}_i), FM\text{-}2(\mathbf{v}_i), ..., FM\text{-}p(\mathbf{vi}_1))), ...$$

$$(\mathbf{v}_c, G(FM\text{-}1(\mathbf{v}_c), FM\text{-}2(\mathbf{v}_c), ..., FM\text{-}p(\mathbf{v}_c))) \} \quad (20)$$

where $G(FM\text{-}1(\mathbf{v}_i), FM\text{-}2(\mathbf{v}_i)$, and $FM\text{-}p(\mathbf{v}_i))$ is a result of granulation of the corresponding set of numeric outputs of the fuzzy models. Considering the data set (20) visualized schematically in Figure 11, a fuzzy model can be built in different ways, say a collection of rules, neural network with granular outputs, schemes of case-based reasoning (CBR) or fuzzy regression.

CONCLUSION

The study has focused on the new category of collaborative fuzzy modeling, which has emerged when dealing with numerous sources of knowledge (local fuzzy models build on a basis of locally accessible data).

Granularity of information plays a pivotal role in fuzzy modeling: while type-1 information granules are the building blocks of fuzzy models, information granules of higher type are essential to formalize and quantify the effect of collaboration and reconciliation of knowledge, which inherently has to quantify a variety of sources of knowledge coming from individual fuzzy models. The passive and active modes of collaboration help reach a significant level of consensus and, what is equally essential, quantify the level through higher type of information granules. The detailed algorithmic aspects can be realized in different ways and those topics could be a subject of further studies.

Figure 11. The formation of granular outputs and a realization of granular models through CBR mechanisms

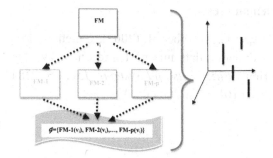

The principle of justifiable granularity in application to granular mappings can be exploited in the design of granular models such as granular neural networks, type-2 rule-based systems, or granular regression. In particular, one can consider an admissible level of granularity (treated as a knowledge representation resource), which has to be distributed in an optimal fashion so that the highest level of coverage of numeric data can be achieved. In the formulation of the problem done in this way, one can envision the use of methods of evolutionary optimization as a vehicle to allocate optimal levels of granularity to the individual parameters of the model (say, connections of the neural network or parameters of regression models).

REFERENCES

Angelov, P., Lughofer, E., & Zhou, X. (2008). Evolving fuzzy classifiers using different model architectures. *Fuzzy Sets and Systems, 159*(23), 3160–3182. doi:10.1016/j.fss.2008.06.019

Bargiela, A., & Pedrycz, W. (2003). *Granular Computing: An Introduction*. Dordrecht, The Netherlands: Kluwer Academic Publishers.

Bargiela, A., & Pedrycz, W. (2008). Toward a theory of Granular Computing for human-centered information processing. *IEEE Transactions on Fuzzy Systems, 16*(2), 320–330. doi:10.1109/TFUZZ.2007.905912

Bezdek, J. C. (1981). *Pattern Recognition with Fuzzy Objective Function Algorithms*. New York: Plenum Press.

Crespo, F., & Weber, R. (2005). A methodology for dynamic data mining based on fuzzy clustering. *Fuzzy Sets and Systems, 150*, 267–284. doi:10.1016/j.fss.2004.03.028

Kacprzyk, J., & Zadrozny, S. (2005). Linguistic database summaries and their protoforms: towards natural language based knowledge discovery tools. *Information Sciences, 173*(4), 281–304. doi:10.1016/j.ins.2005.03.002

Kiliç, K., Uncu, O., & Türksen, I. B. (2007). Comparison of different strategies of utilizing fuzzy clustering in structure identification. *Information Sciences, 177*(23), 5153–5162. doi:10.1016/j.ins.2007.06.030

Molina, C., Rodríguez-Ariza, L., Sánchez, D., & Amparo Vila, M. (2006). A new fuzzy multidimensional model. *IEEE Transactions on Fuzzy Systems, 14*(6), 897–912. doi:10.1109/TFUZZ.2006.879984

Pedrycz, W. (2005). *Knowledge-Based Clustering: From Data to Information Granules*. New York: John Wiley. doi:10.1002/0471708607

Pedrycz, W., & Gomide, F. (1998). *An Introduction to Fuzzy Sets: Analysis and Design*. Cambridge, MA: MIT Press.

Pedrycz, W., & Rai, P. (2008). Collaborative clustering with the use of Fuzzy C-Means and its quantification. *Fuzzy Sets and Systems, 159*(18), 2399–2427. doi:10.1016/j.fss.2007.12.030

Pham, D. T., & Castellani, M. (2006). Evolutionary learning of fuzzy models. *Engineering Applications of Artificial Intelligence, 19*(6), 583–592. doi:10.1016/j.engappai.2006.01.007

Wang, Y., Kinsner, W., & Zhang, D. (2009). Contemporary Cybernetics and its faces of Cognitive Informatics and Computational Intelligence. *IEEE Trans. on System, Man, and Cybernetics–Part B, 39*(4), 1–11.

Wang, Y., Zadeh, L. A., & Yao, Y. Y. (2009). On the system algebra foundations for Granular Computing. *International Journal of Software Science and Computational Intelligence, 1*(1), 1–17.

Zadeh, L. A. (1997). Towards a theory of fuzzy information granulation and its centrality in human reasoning and fuzzy logic. *Fuzzy Sets and Systems, 90*, 111–117. doi:10.1016/S0165-0114(97)00077-8

Zadeh, L. A. (2005). Toward a generalized theory of uncertainty (GTU)—an outline. *Information Sciences, 172*, 1–40. doi:10.1016/j.ins.2005.01.017

This work was previously published in International Journal of Software Science and Computational Intelligence, Volume 2, Issue 4, edited by Yingxu Wang, pp. 16-31, copyright 2010 by IGI Publishing (an imprint of IGI Global).

Chapter 3
A General Knowledge Representation Model for the Acquisition of Skills and Concepts

Carlos Ramirez
Tec de Monterrey, Campus Querétaro, México

Benjamin Valdes
Tec de Monterrey, Campus Querétaro, México

ABSTRACT

A cognitive model for skills and concepts representation as well as a proposal for its computational implementation is presented in this paper. The model is intended to help bridge some of the natural problems that arise in current massive education models through the adaptation and personalization of learning environments. The model is capable of representing rich semantic knowledge, including both skills and concepts, while integrating them through a coherent network of role based associations. The associations build an ontology that integrates on itself different domain taxonomies to represent the knowledge acquired by a student keeping relevant context information. The model is based on a constructivist approach.

I. INTRODUCTION

The study of Cognitive Informatics (CI) (Wang, 2002a, 2007), focuses on information processing mechanisms and cognition; within this discipline, knowledge is a fundamental part for cognition.

DOI: 10.4018/978-1-4666-0264-9.ch003

In this work, a model for knowledge and skills representation, called Memory Map (MM), which has a precedent in the Episodic Memory Model of Ramirez and Cooley (1997), is presented; the model presents similarities with the Object Attribute Relation OAR model (Wang, 2006), both store the concepts acquired during a learning process in a structured and flexible way: however, our model proposes a more flexible alternative as to some of the components of the CI framework, but it keeps the same approach of personalization derived from a unique perception as established in the fundamental theories of CI (Wang, 2007).

The model for the representation of concepts and skills presented here was originally created having in mind the development of Virtual Learning Environment Technology able to advance the current educational practices of instruction. The problem with current educational practices is rooted in historical reasons: since the beginning of the industrialization age till now, many voices have risen against the process of massive education without significant success, e.g., (Kilpatric, 1925; Lave & Wenger, 1990; Piaget & Inhelder, 1958; Vygotsky, 1986). Most of today's modern educational systems have significant deficiencies that hinder the natural development of concepts and skills, giving as a result the development of poor quality knowledge, focused mainly on concept memorization, mainly due to the lack of personalization of the instructional practices. Evidence of this can be observed in average students that memorize concepts, but remain unable to perform efficiently in real life situations, because of poor development of the skills necessary to apply such concepts on different contexts. What is even worse, a large amount of memorized concepts will to be forgotten shortly unless deeply understood and frequently used. It is therefore important to enrich the educational process, taking advantage of modern technological tools, to facilitate the acquisition of concepts and the development of skills.

It must be understood that learning is an individual process; as such, an educational model oriented to standardization, i.e., teaching the same content with the same methods, and at the same rate to every student, is inadequate. An individual learning process denotes a unique way of perceiving reality or the concrete world, people learn differently because they perceive the world in different ways. Unique perception of the world

by each individual is one of the cornerstones of modern thinking, which is stated in fields such as biology (Maturana, 1980), education (Harel, 1991), psychology (DeVries et al., 2002), cognitive sciences (Winograd & Flores, 1987) and cognitive informatics (Wang, 2007) among many others.

There is a latent necessity for technology that supports educational models that are not basically focused on the acquisition of concepts and memorization skills, but also on the development and frequent usage of generic skills, including those for long life learning. To successfully implement such educational model, at least the following components are required:

- A computational representation of the student's knowledge and skills, and an algorithm for the process of acquisition, which should be compatible with complex and evolving learning theories such as Constructivism (Piaget & Inhelder, 1958; Vygotsky, 1986; De-Vries, 2002), Constructionism (Harel, 1991) and Transformational Learning (Mezirow, 1981) among others. Useful elements for both representation and acquisition algorithms are found in the CI theoretical framework of Wang (2007), specifically in the OAR model and concept algebra.
- A virtual learning environment (Dillenbourg, 2002) with adaptive capabilities, such as presented in (Torres et al., 2009), where personalization of learning resources is the main concern. The learning environment ought to be based upon pervasive computing (Hanssman et al., 2003) where workbenches, which are currently being developed (Ramirez, 2010), and regular accessories: earrings, wristbands, caps, among others, are used as non-intrusive sensors to provide feedback on the users physical and emotional condition used to personalize the environment.

- A definition of processes including rules and algorithms that allows a rich and flexible interaction between the elements of the computational representation of concepts and skill, and the virtual learning environment. The CI theoretical framework provides interesting proposals through its real time process algebra and it layered reference model of the brain.

In this work, the first requirement is addressed in section 2 through the presentation of the MM; in sections 3 and 4 it is explained the cognitive and computational processes through which knowledge is acquired; in section 5, a list of the properties of the MM is presented; in section 6, the model it is shown as part of a larger project, and in section 7, conclusions and future work are presented.

II. A MODEL FOR KNOWLEDGE AND SKILLS REPRESENTATION

According to Newell (1994), semantic, episodic and procedural knowledge must be encoded into the same memory structure at least on a basic level. It is in the memory where developed skills and acquired knowledge are kept. Concepts and skills are seen as interconnected units, semantic knowledge is associated to units and to groups of units, in a flexible way. Our model supports the main cognitive processes of learning, understanding and reasoning. The structure where skills and knowledge are kept is the MM. Concepts and skills interact through associations in a special way, the interaction itself represents context and therefore generates semantic knowledge. Semantic knowledge is the key to performing order presentation adaptation in an adaptive Learning Environment (Torres et al., 2009) Algorithms use semantic knowledge to decide which kinds of adaptations are to be performed on learning resources such as Learning Objects and Learning Services, in order to create an Adaptive Learning Environment (ALE). Vygostky's (1986) constructivist paradigm is used for ALE and for the MM, enabling the model to emulate the cognitive processes that take place within the mind; this simplifies the creation of adaptive environments where active learning, simulations, group activities, different learning styles and atmospheres of uniqueness and respect, as defined by DeVries et al. (2002), can be achieved.

Since different individuals organize knowledge in different ways, a structure flexible enough to store each individual organization of concepts and skills is needed. Such organization does not always follow an ordered hierarchical structure such as the taxonomy since the hierarchy is usually defined by a dynamic criterion, which means that a more flexible structure is needed, such structure is the ontology. Ontologies have been used as extremely rich and flexible structures to represent reality. Such flexibility is provided by the describable relationships between the objects of the ontology; a detailed explanation of ontologies and their properties in Artificial Intelligence systems is presented in (Grubber, 1993).

The MM is the ontology of the student's knowledge; its knowledge domain encompasses every concept and skill the student learns. The student takes the role of expert and constructs his own MM through his activities and decisions. Gilbert Paquette (2007a, 2007b) presents a similar approach using ontologies to model competencies which he defines as a the applications of skills to concepts; The MM ontology is implemented as a directional graph where concepts and skills are the objects of the ontology and the nodes in the graph; associations are the relationships in the ontology, and therefore the arcs in the graph.

Concepts and skills have an open granularity subject to the modeler's criteria; an arbitrary level of atomicity can be specified for each node, allowing communication between different levels of granularity. Each time the student learns a new concept or develops a new skill, a new node is integrated into the graph by associating it to a previous concept or skill. Wang et al. (2003) developed similar ideas in the framework of Layered Reference Model of the Brain, where the learning cognitive processes occur when information passes from Short Term Memory to Long Term Memory using the OAR model, where concepts are represented in a network with attributes with a three layer approach. In the MM, each node can be associated to any other node within one main layer, although the configuration of concepts and skills is different; temporal layer separation is generated only at the time of retrieval, since context of the required knowledge is usually determined at that time. In the MM skills and concepts are stored in different units of representation which can be associated between each other or among the same types of representation units. Each association keeps its own information for human and computer description, which can alter the semantics of a concept and the interpretation of a skill. Albert et al. (2007) uses a cognitive structural approach to represent skills through actions and concepts in Anderson's ACT-R (Anderson, 1990) production model, his approach is well structured but less flexible than the model presented in this work. Albert suggests the use of procedural knowledge or teacher expertise like Bloom's taxonomy for skill structure. An issue on those approaches is that they are hierarchical in nature, and restrict possible cognitive associations through hierarchies. As long as there is one main or single unchanging hierarchy used for skill organization, the restriction of possible cognitive associations will persist, each hierarchy is subject to a particular criterion, and criteria usually depends on context; therefore, if the context changes, so should the criteria. Another important difference is that they lack to acknowledge that a single skill can have different levels of expertise as shown in Figure 2. Although implementations that model different expertise levels within a skill exist, they differ in the approach used to determine such levels, for instance CORE (Tollinger et al., 2005) requires a

field expert to set the expertise value, whereas our model determines the level of expertise through the usage of associations. It should be noted that even though the associations can be used to determine the level of expertise, they cannot by themselves create a new concepts or skills. The integration of new concepts or skills require external inputs which are obtained through psychometric evaluations, observation tools, expert assessments, sensing technology and regular academic tests.

Concerning the retrieval of skills and concepts, Calegari & Farina (2006) propose a Fuzzy Concept Network to find correlations between concepts and instantiations in queries, which are used to obtain relevance values and optimize searches; this approach is similar to the one taken in the MM.

A. Model Components

There are three main components in the MM: Concepts which are referred to as Concept Representation Units (CRU), Skills which are referred to as Skill Representation Units (SRU) and Associations between the members of CRUs, between the members of SRUs and associations among CRUs and SRUs. To explain how the MM works, a brief explanation of each of the components is presented below.

B. Concepts as CRUs

Two definitions are given to understand the function of concepts in the MM:

- The Representational Theory of the Mind RTM (Hobbes, 2006) states concepts and ideas as mental objects with mental properties. RTM is the concept's definition most broadly used.
- The Language of Thought LOT (Fodor, 2004) states that thoughts are represented in a language which is supported by the principles of symbolic logic and comput-

Figure 2. The amount of associations is proportional to the expertise

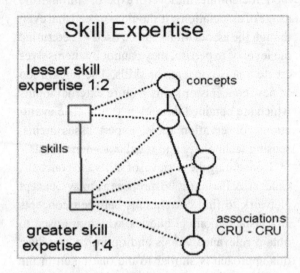

ability. Reasoning can be formalized into symbols and characters; hence it can be described and mechanized.

RTM states that concepts exist as mental objects with attributes, while LOT states that concepts are not images but words in a specific language of the mind subject to a unique syntax. The definition of concept used in the MM is influenced by those two aspects, as follows: A concept is considered as the representation of a mental object and a set of attributes, expressed through a specific language of the mind which lets it be represented through symbols, in order to be computable. Such approach defines concepts as objects formed by a set of attributes, in the same way the Classic Theory of Concept Representation (Osherson & Smith, 1981) does, which can be treated in an atomic way; but also considers descriptive capabilities of the role of a concept, in the same way that Concepts as Theory Dependent does (Carey, 1985; Murphy & Medin, 1985; Keil, 1987), embedded into symbols for computable purpose. At the same time, the model supports the representation of multiple instances of a concept, such as described by the Theory of Exemplars

(Brooks, 1978). Each concept is enclosed in its particular CRU which has associations to other SRU's or CRU's. The attributes of concepts and skills together with their associations define their semantics, therefore any skill of concept is described and defined by the associations ti has with other skills and concepts. Attributes allow grouping and therefore integration in to taxonomies and other categorization structures.

A concept is therefore

$$C (N, A) \qquad (2.1)$$

Where N is the name of the concept C, the key by which it is identified and A is a non-empty set of attributes a

$$A=\{a1,a3,a4,a5, ... an\}$$

Where a is an attribute represented by an association @ to another concept, within the group of concepts selected by Criteria Crit.

The concepts knowledge is defined by the recursive function 3.1 shown in 2.D.

C. Skills as SRUs

Skills represent a very important part of the knowledge of an individual; a system that attempts to model learning without contemplating them is incomplete. Knowledge cannot be acquired without the execution of the corresponding cognitive process, such as understanding and reasoning. Skills among other things are responsible for those processes.

In Thought and Language, Vygostky (1986) explains several processes used to learn and create ideas. Ideas stated as concepts and skills are dynamic in nature, and behave as processes in continual development which go through three evolution stages that range from syncretism heaps, i.e., loosely coupled ideas through mental images, to formal abstract stable ideas, i.e., fully developed concepts and skills manifested in language.

Benjamin Bloom (1956) developed a taxonomy for skills with a very practical approach, in which three domains are specified: cognitive, affective, and psychomotor. Each domain contains different layers depending on the complexity of the particular skill. Bloom's taxonomy is widely used, however, as with any other taxonomy, some criticisms have been raised; Spencer Kagan (2008) made the following observations:

- A given skill can have different degrees of complexity; hence a layer model might not provide an adequate representation.
- Skill integration in complexity order does not always keep true.

In CI, skills Wang (2002b) defines as processes, specifically as computer programs located in the action buffer, such processes are composed by sub-processes and are described using Real Time Process Algebra (RTPA) and are a fundamental part of the CI theoretical framework.

Taking into account such observations along through a constructivist perspective, in this work, a skill is considered as: A cognitive process that interacts with one or more concepts and other skills, usually through application, which has a specific purpose and produces a result, be it internal or external. Skills have different degrees of complexity and may be integrated with other skills. In contrast with concepts which static entities by nature, skills are process oriented, they are application/action related by nature and it is not uncommon to describe them using verbs.

Skills in the MM are enclosed in Skill Representation Units as described above, and though they coexist in the same structure associated with the CRUs, they have an independent organization structure. SRUs and CRUs have a knowledge level which can represent how evolved or deep is the understanding of a SRU or a CRU.

A skill is defined as

$$S\ (N,\ A) \tag{2.2}$$

where S is a skill who's procedural knowledge is also given by the recursive function 2.3, N is the name of the skill and A is set of attributes a

$$A=\{a_1, a_3, a_4, a_5, \dots a_n\}$$

where a is an attribute represented by an association @ to another skill, within the group of skills selected by Criteria *Crit*.

A skill shares traits with concepts, their main difference lies within their organization structure, although SRUs also have a set of associations the same way CRUs do.

D. Skills and Concepts

Skills and concepts are different in nature, procedural knowledge and declarative knowledge (Tennyson & Rasch, 1988), however, they can be present and they can interact between them in the same structure.

The MM is entirely composed by both, CRUs and SRUs. Each unit has a set of associations which provide the semantics for the knowledge and allow the appropriate use of skills, according to a given domain and a certain role. The structure of the MM can be described by the following recursive function:

$$f((C|S)_i(N, A), Crit(r_j, d_k)) = f((C|S)_{i+1}(N, A), Crit(r_{j+1}, d_{k+1}))$$

$$i = 1, 2, \dots, n$$

$$j = 1, 2, \dots, m$$

$$k = 1, 2, \dots, l \tag{2.3}$$

where n is the number of existing concepts in each domain and m is the number of existing roles and k is the number of existing domains. *Crit* is the criteria used to determine the context, *Crit* receives a set of domains D and roles R, with

$R = \{r_1, r_2, ..., r_m\}$, and

$D = \{ d_1, d_2, ..., d_l\}$

If the recursion is performed in a exhaustive way, i.e., the iterators reach n, m, and l, the entire MM will be returned; if only i is iterated until it reaches n, the entire chain of concept associations for domain k and role j will be returned; if only j is iterated until it reaches m, every role for a concept i of domain k is returned will be; and if only k is iterated until it reaches l, all domains where concept i is involved through role j will be returned.

An example of another system that integrates procedural knowledge and declarative knowledge that can interact between them in the same ontology, in a successful way, is the TELOS system (Paquette, 2007a). TELOS allows learning designers to create personalized courses and scenarios. The system is built upon ontologies integrated by concepts, skills and principles which work together to model competencies and create a student profile, which is used to personalize the student's activities. TELOS uses a graphical modeling language called MOT to create its concept-skill-principle ontologies.

In the MM, the difference between C and S lies in their organization, specifically in the roles r, that their associations @ can have. There are 2 types of roles, roles for definition and roles for appliancation/action. Definition role represent those relationship of form and composition of a declarative nature, such as the 8 types of associations in concept algebra of Wang (2006). Appliancation roles imply an action that affects the units involved in the association. Table 1 shows the types of defined roles, though this are just exemplary roles, apart from this basic roles other may be integrated into the model as long as the difference between definition and appliance is respected.

E. Associations

The purpose of the associations is to know how concepts and skills relate to each other, in order

Table 1. Association groups and their roles

Roles r	Associations @		
	R_c	R_s	
	$C - C$	$S - S$	$C - S$
Inheritance	X	X	
Extension	X	X	
Tailoring	X	X	
Substitute	X	X	
Composition	X	X	
Decomposition	X	X	
Aggregation	X	X	
Specification	X	X	
Use			X
Appliance			X

to generate knowledge. Knowledge is not only a group of memorized concepts, but the whole structure of associations between concepts and skills. This approach has its antecedents in the Theory of Episodic Memory (Ramírez & Cooley, 1997).

An association @ is defined as a relationship between two units predecessor *pre* and successor *suc* which may be either CRU or SRU, containing specific information that describes the nature of the relationship and the roles it has regarding the units involved in a domain D as follows: for associations between concepts

@ (Cpre,Csuc, r, D, dir)

for associations between skills

@ (Spre,Ssuc, r, D, dir)

for associations between Concepts and skills

$$@\ (C, S, r, D, dir) \tag{2.4}$$

where r is the role that specifies the type of association that belongs to set R_c or R_s with

$$R_c \subseteq R_s \tag{2.5}$$

where R_s is the set of every possible r and R_c is a subset of the roles allowed for C.

D is a non-empty set of domains d

$$D= \{d_1, d_2, ... d_n\}$$

where n is number of domains that exist in the structure, and *dir* is the directionality of the association.

Associations are created between a temporal parent and a child, the directionality is determined by the role of the association. A role is the type of relationship which can be used for context generation; roles can include most types of associations created in previous works such as inheritance, extension, tailoring, substitute, composition, decomposition, aggregation as specification as specified by Wang (2006) in Concept Algebra.

The chosen roles are independent of the model; a MM can be implemented with any given roles, as long as they enable the user to perform context rich queries. Two units can have several associations between them, each association with its own role and directionality, which can be assigned or reassigned during runtime using the *Crit* function. Two examples are presented in Figure 1, where different criteria for categorization use different types of roles for their respective associations, by changing the direction and hierarchy of the relationships between units. This approach enables several taxonomies or concept organizational structures to coexist within the MM, because each taxonomy or structure will have its own roles and therefore its own directionality. There is no restriction to the size or content of a taxonomy, as long as it maintains its own hierarchical structure, and no two associations exists between the two same nodes with the same role and opposite directionality in the same domain.

Associations are always connected in both ends, they may only be created from existing units and need to be associated to other existing units, In the event of the creation of a new unit, should be immediately followed by its associations.

Figure 1. Associations may take several roles depending of the context

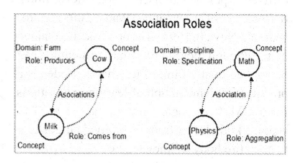

In Figure 2 it is shown, that the density of associations linked to a specific unit, along with the knowledge level of the SRUs and CRUs, and the membership value of each association, determine the level of expertise a learner has over a given concept or skill with in that domain. A greater amount of associations along with higher association values indicate a better ability for understanding and applying a concept or skill in a greater number of contexts. However as stated previously, associations between concepts and skills don´t create concepts or skills by themselves, they require further information which is obtained through user perception.

III. COGNITIVE PROCESSES

Understanding, Learning and Reasoning are closely interrelated processes that can be carried out from the MM. In order for the MM to grow, learning must take place, and in order to learn, understanding and possibly a form of reasoning must also take place at about the same time; those three main cognitive processes are intertwined and cannot be taken apart (Ramírez & Cooley, 1997). These processes are not part of the MM per se, but the model supports its operation. In this work only the learning process is presented, the processes of understanding and reasoning are the subject of further work.

Learning processes have been presented for different types of memory, be it episodic (Ramírez & Cooley, 1997), semantic (Wang, 2003) or procedural, (Newell, 1994). The process as explained here, although focused on semantic memory, can be applied to any form of it; what is needed is a practical implementation of learning algorithms for the MM; as such, learning can be used to acquire knowledge from an individual concept to an entire body of knowledge.

Learning, the fundamental cognitive process for the acquisition of knowledge and skills (Rumelhart & Norman, 1981), can be organized into five stages according to our studies, which are described below. The stages of the learning process can be applied to concepts and skills, the learning of a structure a concept would be the equivalent to the construction of a taxonomy or concept organizational structure in the MM. The approach presented here is expected to evolve in order to cope with new cognitive theories or be replaced by other approaches of learning to be used to feed the MM.

A. First Stage: Observation

The learning process starts when any form of information is perceived or some form of reasoning is carried out, in both cases obtaining a mental image a concept, either a natural or an artificial concept; later, data elements of the concept, i.e., features, are distinguished according to the observer's criteria, which is determined by the previously acquired knowledge of the individual, which enables the extraction of abstract elements that integrate the observed object, as shown in Figure 3. Several observations and element extractions may occur at the same time, since observation processes are executed in parallel, meaning that elements A, B, F, C, D and E may all be distinguished at the same time. The word by which the observed object is identified is used as the main base element, such word is the elements name. If the observed object doesn't have a name, a search using the

Figure 3. Observation of an object

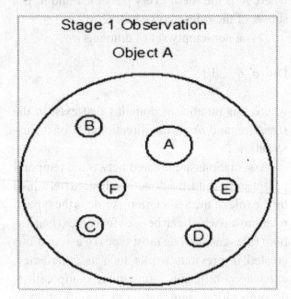

distinctions previously obtained, which can be associations, is conducted in stage two to find the object in the MM.

B. Second Stage: Search

Once an element of the object has been distinguished, a search in the MM is carried out to identify such element as a concept by itself, or as part of an existing concept, as shown in Figure 4. There are three possible outcomes of a search: A) The element is located in the MM and it is associated to another element or to a neighbor of an element extracted from the same object. B) The element is located in the MM but is not associated to any element or neighbor of an element extracted from the same object. C) The element is not found in the MM.

C. Third Stage: Micro-Model Construction

Depending on the outcome of the search different micro-models are created. A micro-model is a grouping of neighboring elements associated to the element found in the MM, which is grouped into the same micro-model. Elements that are not associated form different models. Unidentified elements are put aside in this part of the process; the built model can be seen in Figure 5. The Reasoning process is involved in the last three stages, and will be described in detail in future works.

D. Fourth Stage: Concept Model Selection

The concept models that were found and reconstructed en the previous stage are reviewed and compared in terms of similarity, the one that shows more relevant associated elements is chosen as the concept best match, if differences against the perceived concept is minimal then it is recognized as an instance of such concept already learned. However, if the differences are relevant, it means that the concept does not exist in the MM, and if there are no possible analogical substitutes, i.e., there are no other similar objects, then the object is not recognized. Relevance can be measured through several heuristics, for example by the distance between two concepts or skills, age of the concept and associations, domains related, number of associations, or the roles of their associations, among others (Figure 6).

E. Fifth Stage: Learning

After the match between the models of the concept, the element information extracted from the original concept is integrated to the MM by possibly acquiring some new elements to the object selected and by generating new associations among concepts, enriching the knowledge. When the object is not recognized, the MM acquires new knowledge; however, a new concept is added only if one of its related elements was recognized previously during the search of a concept in the MM. After the object has been added as a concept, the related elements that were not recognized will be created and associated to the concept, as shown in Figure 7.

Figure 4. Search in the MM for elements

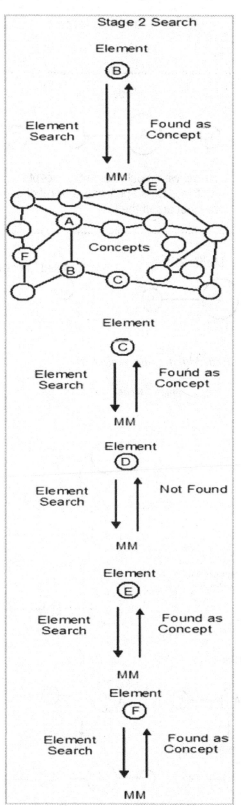

Figure 5. Choosing the model

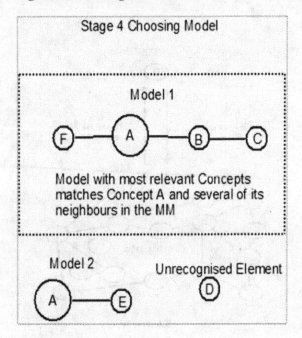

Figure 6. Making micro-model

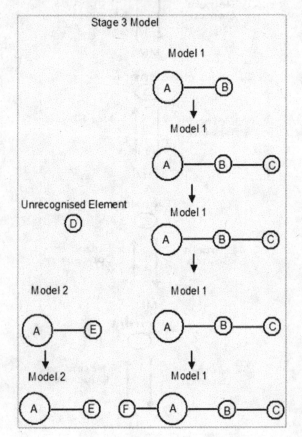

Figure 7. Learning

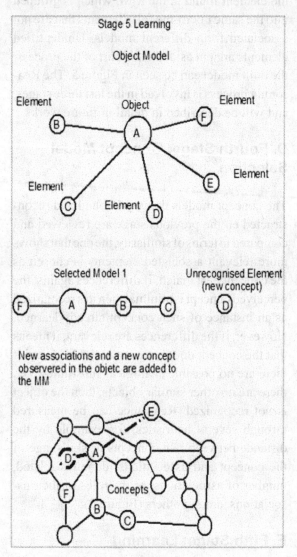

IV. INTEGRATION OF NEW CONCEPTS AND SKILLS, UPDATING THE MM

After explaining the main components of the MM, an example can be given: A student applies to a set of tests such as SAT, SOI, AVAST, TERMAN or any other skill and knowledge measurement tool, a discussion of such tests as well as their main detection capabilities and possible uses in adaptation can be found in (Torres et al., 2009). As an alternative to tests or as complementary actions, valuable information from the learner may be recollected during the interaction of the learner with diverse computer applications and gadgets. With all the collected information a MM is created for and individual, the creation must start with a node then its arcs linking to another node, for example a CRU and then its association to en existing CRU or SRU, in that specific order to avoid secluded units as shown in Figure 8. Once the basic MM structure is complete, the system gathers information from the students learning environment using tests and interaction tools to keep the MM updated with the learner's current knowledge. For instance in a course of Arithmetic there are a number of concepts such as addition, subtraction, division and multiplication as in Figure 9; each of these concepts are related by more primitive concepts such as symbols, numbers and quantity. In the student's MM each of these concepts is individually associated to other relevant concepts in terms of the learning subject. In the case of arithmetic, the use of a concept's taxonomy is important because it contains a desired group of basic concepts which serve as common ground for further learning. Another issue is the simplification of the process of planning for the student

desired knowledge. Instead of choosing concept by concept, activities can be design as to plan the acquisition of entire taxonomies, in terms of a learning path of concepts for construction of the intended knowledge of a certain subject.

V. MODEL PROPERTIES

The integration of the components described above produces the following properties:

- **Open/Unlimited Granularity:** Any user, preferably a learning designer, a professor or field expert, can determine the level of granularity specification for any unit.
- **Hierarchy:** Concept Units and Skill Units can be integrated into proper hierarchies through roles; a unit can be placed in several taxonomies. This enables the use of semantic information implied by the nature of the taxonomy when in context.

Figure 9. Memory map of a student

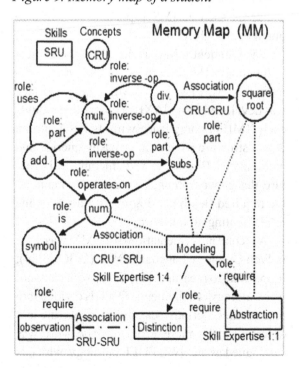

Figure 8. Integration of new concepts and skills

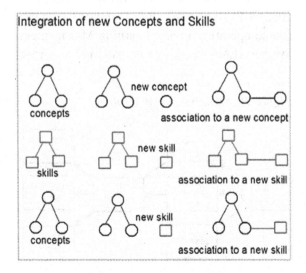

- **Economy of Knowledge:** The structure is developed in a way to avoid information redundancy, i.e. the same nodes are used for different taxonomies.
- **Informativeness Capability:** there is no limit to the amount of CRU or SRU in the structure, nor is there a limit for their attributes and associations.
- **Flexibility:** The structure can create associations between any CRU and SRU, and each association can have several roles each offering a unique behavior.
- **Representative Capability:** The degree of flexibility of the structure allows greater representation capabilities.

VI. IMPLEMENTATION

Although the MM could be implemented as a relational DB to ensure efficiency, it was implemented as an XML Schema XSD to achieve compliance with learning education standards. XSD files are the set of syntactic rules for XML files. This will ease and allow future integration with other web standards such as IMS E-portfolio which also operate through XMLs.

Each student's MM is an XML file subject to the main MM XSD rules. To edit each of the individual MM i.e., each XML, a java interface was developed using JAXB, a library that mounts each XML in compliance with its XSD into an object structure which can be easily queried and manipulated. Because of XML hierarchical structure, design workarounds were made to maintain the required flexibility. Figure 10 illustrates the implementing architecture.

A second implementation of the MM was done in Web Ontology Language OWL (W3C, 2004); it was done to measure compliance with standard web ontology requirements. OWL is divided into three main descriptive capability levels, the less descriptive the more efficient. The MM was catalogued as an OWL FULL ontology, which is

the most descriptive and expensive type of ontology that can be expressed in OWL. It was learned from this second implementation that though the MM is compliant with the standards of OWL's highest level, it is significantly harder to model in such language since the MM requires a level of freedom of associations that OWL doesn't provide naturally.

VII. CONCEPT LEARNING PATH

The MM as described above is used to configure a learning environment in order to achieve a high level of personalization. The main idea is as follows, a Concept Learning Path (CLP) is a group of concepts, skills and associations programmed to be acquired by a learner. The group of concepts can come, for example, from an academic program, a training course or any learning activity. The CLP is the product of the planning itself, it can be seen as the sketching of what a learner's MM should resemble. Due to differences in the learning abilities, knowledge, learning styles and personal goals of each learner, as explained at the beginning of this work, a general planning cannot fit every learner's profile, and the cost to create a personalized CLP for each student is prohibitive; therefore, the instructor creates only a generic CLP for a given course, as it is done traditionally; so far, a CLP is the same as the planning of a regular course operating in any Learning Management Systems (LMS), making a transition between the

Figure 10. Observation of an object

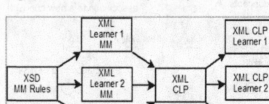

two a short and easy process. This is important because a great amount of on-line content is already present with in LMS courses; reusing this content is only reasonable.

The distinction between any regular course planning and the CLP, is that the CLP expresses in a standard way what CRUs, SRUs or associations will be developed in the MM. For example if a lab activity in a geology course explains the relationship between a drought and water tables, the activity must be specific about it, stating that "water tables" is a CRU, "drought" another CRU and the relationship between them the association. Most of this data can be found in the learning activities objectives of LO and LS, though, stronger standardization is required to automate the process of communication between a CLP and a MM. Standardization can be achieved through IMS Learning Content Package or SCORM, where specific metadata tags for objectives are defined.

Once the CLP is formatted, the personalization of CLPs can be carried out by using the information in the MM. The general CLP is given many shapes, each for every learner, by applying the appropriated adaptive algorithms, producing this way, a group of personalized CLPs, which will be used during the whole course, although dynamic adaptation may be carried out lately. A practical example of this process is as follows: Assume Peter, Ed and Jan both take a basic compiler course; one of the main topics of course is lexical analysis which requires understanding of recursion and induction. These requirements are stated in the general CLP. This general CLP is compared to the Peter's MM and discovers that the concepts of recursion is hardly developed, but that his induction concept is above average –this is computed as explained in section III.D --, as a result, Peter's personalized CLP will be modified to include an activity to develop the concept of recursion before providing more advanced content, and activities to develop math induction will be reduced or removed. On other hand, Ed's MM indicates he lacks a sufficient understanding of

induction, so his CLP would require adaptation in this direction. Then comes Jan, who already has a deep understanding of lexical analysis, Jan's personalized CLP should present her only reinforcement activities or more advanced content of lexical analysis, such as regular expressions or so, according to the politics of the instructor. Peter, Ed and Jan should develop similar CRUs, SKUs and associations regarding the basic common ground contents, yet they would differ in more advanced content, reflecting, not only different degrees of understanding, but different understanding itself.

Initially adaptation should be performed at the start of a course, but as Learning Management Systems progress and obtain real time learning process modification capabilities, the adaptations could be performed in real time, in a dynamic way, thus becoming more flexible to react to a wide variety of factors, both human and technological, such as changes in the availability of information, resources, and social events, among others. The two main challenges to achieve a fully adaptive environment are the ability to detect and understand the learning that is taking place, and the ability to modify the teaching structure accordingly.

VIII. DISCUSSION: THE MEMORY MAP IN AN INTELLIGENT ADAPTIVE LEARNING ENVIRONMENT

Although the MM has strong representation capabilities, in practice, these depend directly on the modeler, whom can be a field expert if the modeling is done manually, or an automatic heuristic to generate and approximation that can be reviewed lately. Also, the context or the particular domain or taxonomy to be modeled can significantly increase the number of associations created between the SRUs and the CRUs. Because the MM is more expressive it can also be a more complex task to model and visualize than with other representations such as OAR (Wang, 2006) or the works of Ramírez and Cooley (1997) on episodic memory.

The need for personalization of learning is one of the priorities of this work; the MM is a part of a framework designed to accomplish such task, Figure 8 shows a general pictures of the framework. The model presented in this work is the knowledge structure from which algorithms will decide what adaptation of resources is required at a given time, for a specific learner. Besides the algorithms, LCP and the MM, there are other elements necessary for the integration of an intelligent adaptive learning environment (Figure 11): information about the students learning style, an emotional architecture, an E-portfolio to store learning evidence and tools for the detection of student's reactions in a class room, all of which are also components of the student profile. Adaptations oriented to hypermedia (Brusilovsky, 2001) can be used for content presentation to different learning styles. Hernández (2007) studies provide a good starting point towards understanding the relationship between emotional conditions to the learning process. Student reactions and emotional conditions can be detected through non invasive sensors integrated into workbenches and cameras. Currently a prototype workbench is also being de-

veloped to detect emotional conditions on students through heart beat, posture and face expressions. These components interact with the MM to create new types of adaptation, for instance the emotional architecture can be combined with the workbench and the MM to detect what condition causes what emotion on a particular student, and take an integral approach to adapt the content or the environment to alter his emotional condition into a more appropriate one for learning (Csikszentmihalyi, 1991).

IX. CONCLUSION AND FUTURE WORK

A comprehensive knowledge and skills representation model was presented. One of the main contributions of the model is due to the computational properties obtained through the integrated view of all of its components, another contribution is the way concepts and skills are defined which allows an accurate representation of knowledge, such representation is directly linked to an organization of the learning process in five stage. On the application side, the model is used to perform

Figure 11. Adaptive learning environment

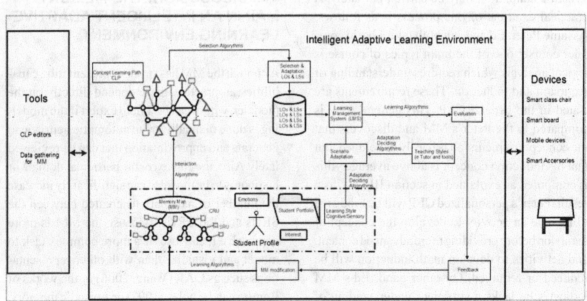

adaptations on learning resources, which take part in several aspects of a virtual adaptive learning environment, some in the presentation of content, some others in the content itself.

The context learning path of each course represents a set of concepts and skills to be learned through programmed activities. Algorithms are used to determine which new concepts are the most important to provide to a student during a learning activity, and keep them from being taught if already know. Finally the memory map has been contextualized as part of an adaptive learning environment, which seeks to provide a complete infrastructure and a computational set of tools to allow the improvement of the current educational process through personalization.

ACKNOWLEDGMENT

The authors, members of DASL4LTD research group at the Tec of Monterrey Institute thank the ITESM RZC for their financial support.

REFERENCES

Albert, D., Hockemeyer, C., Mayer, B., & Steiner, C. M. (2007). Cognitive Structural Modeling of Skills for Technology-Enhanced Learning. In *Proceedings of the Seventh IEEE International Conference on Advanced Learning Technologies (ICALT 2007)*.

Anderson, J. R. (1990). *The Adaptive Character of Thought (Studies in Cognition Series)* (p. 304). London: Psychology Press.

Bloom, B. (1956). *Taxonomy of Educational Objectives, Handbook I: The Cognitive Domain*. New York: David McKay Co Inc.

Brooks, L. R. (1978). Nonanalytic concept formtaion and memory for instances . In Rosch, E., & Loyd, B. B. (Eds.), *Cognition and Categorization* (pp. 169–215). Hillsdale, NJ: Erlbaum Associates.

Brusilovsky, P. (2001). Adaptive Hypermedia. *User Modeling and User-Adapted Interaction, 11*, 87–110. doi:10.1023/A:1011143116306

Calegari, S., & Farina, F. (2006). Fuzzy Ontologies and Scale-free Networks Analysis. *International Journal of Computer Science & Applications, 4*, 125–144.

Carey, S. (1985). *Conceptual Change in Childhood*. Cambridge, MA: MIT Press.

Csikszentmihalyi, M. (1991). *Flow: The Psychology of Optimal Experience*. New York: Harper Perennial. Retrieved from http://www.amazon.com/Flow-Psychology-Experience-Mihaly-Csikszentmihalyi/dp/0060920432

DeVries, R. (2002). *What Is Constructivist about Constructivist Education? (Freeburg Early Childhood Program)* (pp. 1–20). Iowa City, Iowa: University of Iowa.

Dillenbourg, P., Schneider, D., Synteta, P., Dillenbourg, P., Schneider, D., Synteta, P., et al. (2002). Virtual Learning Environments. *Communication*, 3-18.

Fodors, J. A. (1975). *The Language of Thought* (p. 214). Cambridge, MA: Harvard University Press.

Gruber, T. R. (1993). Toward Principles for the Design of Ontologies Used for Knowledge Sharing. *International Journal of Human-Computer Studies, 43*, 907–928. doi:10.1006/ijhc.1995.1081

Hansmann, U., Merk, L., Nicklous, M. S., & Stober, T. (2003). *Pervasive Computing: The Mobile World* (Springer Professional Computing). New York: Springer. Retrieved from http://www.amazon.com/Pervasive-Computing-Mobile-Springer-Professional/dp/3540002189

Hernández, P., & Yasmín, M. (2007). *Modelo de Comportamiento Afectivo para Sistemas Tutores Inteligentes (Tech. Rep.)*. Cuernavaca, Mexico: Instituto Tecnológico y de Estudios Superiores de Monterrey Campus Cuernavaca.

Hobbes, T. (1969). *Elements of Law, Natural and Political* (p. 186). New York: Routledge. Retrieved from http://www.amazon.com/Elements-Natural-Political-Thomas-Hobbes/dp/071462540X

Kagan, S. (2008). *Rethinking Thinking Does Bloom's Taxonomy Align with Brain Science?* Spencers Thinkpad.

Keil, F. C. (1979). *Semantic and Conceptual development: An Ontological perspective.* Cambridge, MA: Harvard University Press.

Kilpatrick, W. H. (1925). Syllabus in the philosophy of education; questions for discussion, with reading references and topics for papers. *Education*, 203–204.

Lave, & Wenge. (1990). *Situated Learning: Legitimate Periperal Participation.* Cambridge, UK: Cambridge University Press.

Maturana, H. R., & Varela, F. J. (1980). *Autopoiesis and Cognition the realization of living.* London: D. Reidel pub.

Mezirow, J. (1981). A Critical Theory of Adult Learning and Education. *Adult Education Quarterly, 32*(1), 3–24. doi:10.1177/074171368103200101

Murphy, G. L., & Medin, D. L. (1985). The role of Theories in conceptual coherence. *Psychological Review, 92,* 289–316. doi:10.1037/0033-295X.92.3.289

Newell, A. (1994). *Unified Theories of Cognition.* Cambridge, MA: Harvard University Press.

Osherson, D., & Smith, E. (1981). On the adequacy of prototype theory as a theory of concepts. *Cognition, 9*(1), 35–58. Retrieved from http://www.mendeley.com/research/on-the-adequacy-of-prototype-theory-as-a-theory-of-concepts/. doi:10.1016/0010-0277(81)90013-5

Paquette, G. (2007). An Ontology and a Software Framework for Competency Modeling and Management Competency in an Instructional Engineering Method (MISA). *Journal of Educational Technology & Society, 10,* 1–21.

Paquette, G. (2007). Graphical Ontology Modeling Language for Learning Environments. *Technology, Instruction., Cognition and Learning, 5,* 133-168. Retrieved from http://ares.licef.teluq.uqam.ca/Portals/29/docs/pub/modelisation/TICL 133-168pp. Paquette.pdf

Piaget, J., & Inhelder, B. (1958). *The Growth of Logical Thinking from Childhood to Adolescence.* New York: Basic Books.

Ramirez, C., Concha, C., & Valdes, B. (2010). Cardiac Pulse Detection in BCG Signals Implemented on a Regular Classroom Chair Integrated to an Emotional and Learning Model for Personalization of Learning Resources. In L. G. Richards & K. Curry, *Proceedings of the 40th Annual Frontiers in Education (FIE) Conference*, Arlington, VA. Washington, DC: IEEE.

Ramírez, C., & Cooley, R. (1997). A Theory of the Acquisition of Episodic Memory. In *Proceedings of the ECML-97: Case-Based Reasoning Workshop*, Prague, Czech Republic (pp. 48-55). New York: Springer Verlag.

Rumelhart, D. E., & Norman, D. A. (1981). *Cognitive Skills and their acquisition.* New York: Lawrence Earlbaum.

Tennyson, R., & Rasch, M. (1988). Linking cognitive learning theory to instructional prescriptions. *Instructional Science, 17*(167), 369–385. doi:10.1007/BF00056222

Tollinger, I., Lewis, R. L., McCurdy, M., Tollinger, P., Vera, A., Howes, A., & Pelton, L. J. (2005). *Supporting Efficient Development of Cognitive Models at Multiple Skill Levels: Exploring Recent Advances in Constraint-based Modeling.*

Torres, J., Doredo, J. M., Ramírez, C., Valdes, B., & Lugo, A. (2009). Adaptive Learning Scenarios Based on Student Profile . In de Yucatan, U. A. (Ed.), *Recursos Digitales para el Aprendizaje* (pp. 348–359). Mérida, Mexico: U. A. de Yucatan.

Torres, J., Juarez, E., Dodero, J. M., & Aedo, I. (2009). Advanced Transactional Models for Complex Learning Processes. In U.A de Yucatan (Ed.), *Recursos Digitales para el Aprendizaje* (pp. 360-368). Mérida, Mexico: U. A. de Yucatan.

Vygotsky, L. (1986). *Thought and Language.* Cambridge, MA: MIT Press.

Wang, Y. (2002). On Cognitive Informatics (Keynote Speech). In *Proceedings of the 1st IEEE International Conference on Cognitive Informatics (ICCI'02)*, Calgary, Canada (pp. 34-42). Washington, DC: IEEE.

Wang, Y. (2002). The Real-Time Process Algebra (RTPA). *Annals of Software Engineering, 14*(1). Retrieved from http://portal.acm.org/citation.cfm?id=590763.

Wang, Y. (2006). On Concept Algebra and Knowledge Representation. In *Proceedings of the 5th IEEE International Conference on Cognitive Informatic* (pp. 320-331).

Wang, Y. (2007). The Theoretical Framework and Cognitive Process of Learning. In *Proceedings of the 6th IEEE ICC I* (pp. 470-479). Washington, DC: IEEE.

Wang, Y., Wang, Y., Patel, S., & Patel, D. (2006). A Layered Reference Model of the Brain (LRMB). *IEEE Transactions on Systems, Man and Cybernetics. Part C, Applications and Reviews, 36*(2), 124–133. doi:10.1109/TSMCC.2006.871126

Winograd, T., & Flores, F. (1987). *Understanding Computers and Cognition.* Norwood, NJ: Ablex Publishing.

This work was previously published in International Journal of Software Science and Computational Intelligence, Volume 2, Issue 3, edited by Yingxu Wang, pp. 1-20, copyright 2010 by IGI Publishing (an imprint of IGI Global).

Chapter 4
Feature Based Rule Learner in Noisy Environment Using Neighbourhood Rough Set Model

Yang Liu
Xi'an Jiaotong University, China

Luyang Jiao
First Affiliated Hospital of Xinxiang Medical College, China

Guohua Bai
Blekinge Institute of Technology, Sweden

Boqin Feng
Xi'an Jiaotong University, China

ABSTRACT

From the perspective of cognitive informatics, cognition can be viewed as the acquisition of knowledge. In real-world applications, information systems usually contain some degree of noisy data. A new model proposed to deal with the hybrid-feature selection problem combines the neighbourhood approximation and variable precision rough set models. Then rule induction algorithm can learn from selected features in order to reduce the complexity of rule sets. Through proposed integration, the knowledge acquisition process becomes insensitive to the dimensionality of data with a pre-defined tolerance degree of noise and uncertainty for misclassification. When the authors apply the method to a Chinese diabetic diagnosis problem, the hybrid-attribute reduction method selected only five attributes from totally thirty-four measurements. Rule learner produced eight rules with average two attributes in the left part of an IF-THEN rule form, which is a manageable set of rules. The demonstrated experiment shows that the present approach is effective in handling real-world problems.

DOI: 10.4018/978-1-4666-0264-9.ch004

INTRODUCTION

Cognitive informatics is a study of information processing in humans, computers and in abstract (Wang, 2007a, 2007c; Yao, 2004). From the perspective of cognitive informatics, the cognition can be viewed as the acquisition of knowledge (Wang, 2007b). The study of knowledge discovery aims at building machine intelligence that facilitates human ways of thinking and understanding (Wang, 2009; Wang & Chiew, 2008). Many approaches have been implemented to improve the value of discovered knowledge intelligence (Chiew, 2002; Pazzani & Kibler, 1992; Wu, Bell, & David, 2003). The findings and in-depth understanding of knowledge discovery would have a significant impact on the advancement of cognitive informatics.

Knowledge acquisition system is the main implementation of knowledge discovery task. There have been many successful applications in real-world areas (Grzymala-Busse, 1988). However, complex application problems, such as reliable monitoring and diagnosis of diabetic patients, have emphasised the issue of knowledge acquisition and modelling. These problems are likely to present large number of features, not all of which will be essential for the task (Shen & Chouchoulas, 2002). Noisy and uncertain data cannot be ruled out. Furthermore, such applications typically require easily understood forms of knowledge that underlies data (Kurgan, 2004). Therefore, a method to allow automated generation of human comprehensible knowledge models with clear semantics in noisy environment is highly desirable (Kurgan & Musilek, 2006).

There are two most commonly used methods to generate expressive and human readable knowledge, i.e., decision trees and rule induction algorithms. Decision tree methods have drawn significant attention over the last several years, and incorporate various advanced speed, memory, and pruning optimization techniques (Quinlan, 1986). However, rule induction algorithms also exhibit a lot of desirable properties (Tsumoto,

2004). As reported by some problems (Cios & Kurgan, 2004), rule learner methods were found to outperform decision tree methods since the production of rule sets in expert system appears to be more human-comprehensible than decision trees (Michalski, 1983). In addition, rule set can be post-processed and analyzed in modality, which is very important when a decision maker needs to understand and validate the generated results, such as in medicine (Kurgan, Cios, & Dick, 2006).

LERS (Learning from examples based on rough sets) system is one of the most frequently used rough set based rule induction systems (Grzymala-Busse, 1992; Grzymala-Busse, Grzymala-Busse, & Hippe, 2001), which can handle inconsistencies using rough set theory, introduced by (Pawlak, 1982). Two algorithms LEM2 and MLEM2 are extensively used in LERS system since they perform better in applications in medicine (Grzymala-Busse, 2002). LERS system aims at optimizing the predictive performance on domain data. However, it does not meet the requirement of comprehensibility, such as the small size of rule set and the simple representation of rule forms (Liu, Bai, & Feng, 2008a). CompactLEM2 method was proposed to cope with large amounts of data and generate knowledge with simple representation (Liu, Bai, & Feng, 2008b). This method mainly measures the comprehensibility of rule set using two main factors: the number of rules, and the average length per rule. This strategy can reduce the complexity of rule set and extract compact knowledge, which in turn uses the small size of rule set and short rule forms to maintain high classification accuracy and imply useful information in datasets.

However, the real-world data sets are always not very well structured, and they tend to have high amounts of redundant attributes, which brings great difficulty in rule induction process (Guyon & Elisseeff, 2003). As nowadays thousands of attributes are stored in databases in some real-world applications, it is possible to remove irrelevant attributes to maintain the same classification accuracy of subsequent classifiers (Yu & Liu, 2004). A great number of feature selection algorithms have been developed in recent years. We can group these algorithms into quantitative and qualitative feature selection methods. In fact, data usually comes with mixed formats in real-world applications, such as medical records and marketing prediction (Hu, Liu, & Yu, 2008). As to the mixed features, neighbourhood rough set model is usually regarded as a powerful pre-processing technique for subsequent learning process (Hu, Yu, & Xie, 2006). In such cases, learning approaches can avoid curse of dimensionality and enhance learning efficiency.

Noise in training data is also an important factor degrading the performance of these methods (Wang, 2005). The number of attribute subset selected by attribute reduction algorithm is sensitive to noise: a small change of a single value in an object may significantly influence the outcome of attribute reduction algorithm (Cornelis & Jensen, n.d.). To reduce the impact of noise, the original rough set approach has been adapted by using variable precision rough set (VPRS) approximations (Ziarko, 1993). The generalized VPRS model can relax the tight definition of lower approximation into a smoother definition of tolerance towards noisy and uncertain degree so that it broadens the application of rough set approaches.

The work aims to induce low-dimensionality rule sets from real-life domains that may contain noisy data. In particular, a hybrid-attribute reduction method is proposed to act as a pre-processing procedure. This process will select a set of important features with a pre-defined tolerance to noise. It should be noted that the flexibility of the algorithm discussed here allows incorporating with any other noise-sensible rule learners. The current used CompactLEM2 rule learner provided a set of discretized feature values, exhibits log-linear computational complexity to generate classification rules that partition the feature patterns into underlying classes (Liu et al., 2008b, 2008a).

The remainder of this paper is organized as follows. First, the neighbourhood approximation spaces and variable precision rough set model are combined, and a hybrid-attribute reduction method in noisy environment is proposed in Section 2. In Section 3, we describe the algorithm CompactLEM2, and show characteristics of this log-linear rule learner. Section 4 provides the results of applying feature based rule learner to discover classification rule sets for a diabetic diagnosis problem, supported by comparison to the application of C4.5 to the same domain. In Section 5, we present the experimental results showing that the robustness of our method in noisy environment. Finally, Section 6 concludes this paper and potential work is given.

NOISE-TOLERANT HYBRID ATTRIBUTE REDUCTION

Formally, the structural data for knowledge acquisition task can be written as a tuple $IS = <U, A, V, f>$, where U is a nonempty set of universe, A is a nonempty set of attribute sets, V is the domain of attribute values and f is an information function. Specially, $<U, A, V, f>$ is also called a *decision table* if $A = C \cup D$, where C is a set of conditional attributes, D is a set of decision attributes.

Preliminary of Pawlak's Rough Set

The original Pawlak's rough set model only works in qualitative cases, i.e., assuming that all attributes in A are nominal. Let $B \subseteq C$ be a set of attributes, B induces an equivalence relation on U named as $IND(B)$, which is shown as:

$$\{(x, y) \in U \times U \mid \forall a \in B, f(x, a) = f(y, a)\}.$$

The equivalence relation $IND(B)$ is also called as the *discernibility* relation, which means the objects cannot be classified using the attribute set B. The family of all equivalence classes of $IND(B)$ partitioned by B can be denoted as

$$\prod_B = U \, / \, B = \{[x]_B \mid x \in U\}$$

Pawlak's rough set approximation using two key concepts to characterize the roughness of a set X, called as the *lower and upper approximation* respectively, which are denote as follows

$$\underline{B}X = \cup\{[x]_B \mid [x]_B \subseteq X\},$$

$$\overline{B}X = \cup\{[x]_B \mid [x]_B \cap X \neq \varnothing\}.$$

The lower approximation $\underline{B}X$ is a set of samples that can be certainly classified to X using knowledge granule B, while the upper approximation $\overline{B}X$ is the set of all samples that can be possibly classified to X using knowledge granule B. The *boundary region* $BN_B(X) = \overline{B}X - \underline{B}X$ reflects the roughness of the set X. X is a rough set if and only if $BN_B(X) \neq \varnothing$.

The union of the lower approximation of all decision classes is called as *positive region* of classification $U \, / \, D$ with respect to C, which is formulated as

$$POS_C(D) = \bigcup_{X \in U/D} \underline{C}X.$$

Real-life information systems always contain redundant attributes. In rough set theory, an attribute $a \in B$ is *redundant* in B with respect to decision attribute set D if $POS_B(D) = POS_{B-\{a\}}(D)$. A *reduct* is a set of attributes that has not any redundant attribute, which can preserve the discernibility relation induced by all attributes. The algorithm aiming to find reducts is called as an *attribute reduction* algorithm. Obviously, attribute reduction algo-

rithm is a feature-subset selection process, where the selected feature subset not only retains the representation power, but also has minimal redundancy (Pawlak & Skowron, 2007).

Neighborhood-Based Rough Set Model

Neighbourhood relations are a class of important concepts in topology. Neighbourhood space, as a more general topological space, was investigated and introduced neighbourhood relations into rough set methodology by (Lin, 1988). And then properties of neighbourhood spaces were discussed and a set of powerful tools to attribute reduction, feature selection, rule extraction and reasoning with numeric attribute values in decision table were proposed by (Q. Hu, D. Yu, J. Liu, & C. Wu, 2008; Yao, 1999).

Fuzzy-rough set based hybrid-attribute reduction methods need quadratic time and space complexity to generate a fuzzy equivalence relation from numerical attributes (Hu, Xie, & Yu, 2007). Therefore, the neighbourhood rough set based hybrid-attribute reduction methods have advantages in time and space complexity (Hu et al., 2008), which may speed up the whole computation in feature selection.

However, few applications of the model were designed to deal with noisy information system. In fact, regardless of qualitative or quantitative data are concerned, noise is an important factor degrading the performance of attribute reduction, feature selection and rule induction. To reduce the impact of noise, the neighbourhood approximation approach has been adapted by using variable precision rough set model. In this section, by relaxing the tight definition of lower approximation we introduce a noise-tolerant parameter into the lower approximation definition to allow it tolerate specific classification error.

Definition 1. Given a decision table IS, $x \in U$, $B \subseteq C$, the neighbourhood of x in B is defined as

$$\delta_B(x) = \{y \mid y \in U, \Delta_B(x, y) \leq \delta\}, \qquad (1)$$

where Δ_B is a metric function, $\forall x, y, z \in U$, it satisfies

(1) $\Delta_B(x, y) \geq 0,$

(2) $\Delta_B(x, x) = 0,$

(3) $\Delta_B(x, y) = \Delta_B(y, x),$ *and*

(4) $\Delta_B(x, z) \leq \Delta_B(x, y) + \Delta_B(y, z).$

Some metric functions are widely used according to (Hu et al., 2008). Consider that x_1 and x_2 are two objects in U, the *Minkowsky* distance is defined as

$$\Delta_P(x_1, x_2) = \left(\sum_{i=1}^{m} \mid f(x_1, a_i) - f(x_2, a_i) \mid^P \right)^{1/P}$$

where (1) if $P = 1$, it is called *Manhattan* distance (1-norm); (2) if $P = 2$, it is called *Euclidean* distance (2-norm); (3) if $P = \infty$, it is called *Chebychev* distance (∞-norm). A detail survey on distance function can be seen in (Wilson & Martinez, 1997).

However, there usually is some noise in real-world data sets. In original neighbourhood approximation model, an object belongs to lower approximation of X a set only if all the objects in its neighbourhood are included in X. However, this definition is sensitive in noisy environment. We will present an extended model to deal with this problem based on the majority inclusion operator. Given δ, $X \subseteq U$, $y \in U$, $B \subseteq C$, the majority inclusion operator in neighbourhood spaces is defined as

$$c^{\delta_B}(y, X) = 1 - \frac{Card(\delta_B(y) \bigcap X)}{Card(\delta_B(y))}. \qquad (2)$$

We say that the δ neighbourhood of y is included in X with an admissible classification

error u with respect to B if and only if $c^{\delta_B}(y, X) \leq u$. Appling this concept to neighbourhood spaces, the u variable precision based lower and upper approximation can be defined.

Definition 2. Given a decision table *IS*, $X \subseteq U$ and $B \subseteq C$, the u variable precision based lower approximation and upper approximation in δ neighbourhood spaces are defined as

$$\overline{B}_{u_1}^{\delta} X = \{y \mid c^{\delta_B}(y, X) \leq u\}, \qquad (3)$$

$$\overline{B}_{u}^{\delta} X = \{y \mid c^{\delta_B}(y, X) \leq 1 - u\}. \qquad (4)$$

Example 1. Figure 1 shows an example of binary classification in 2-D space, where the objects in positive class d_1 are labelled with "*" and the objects in negative class d_2 are labelled with "+". Consider samples x_1, x_2, x_3 and a noisy data n_1, we assign the δ neighbourhood circle to the three samples. Given noise-tolerant parameter $u = 0.25$,

Figure 1. An example with two classes

$c^{\delta_B}(x_1, d_1) = 1/6$, $c^{\delta_B}(x_2, d_1) = 3/4$, and $c^{\delta_B}(x_3, d_2) = 1/5$. According to the above definitions, $x_1 \in \underline{R}_u^{\delta} d_1$, $x_2 \notin \underline{R}_u^{\delta} d_1$, $x_3 \in \underline{R}_u^{\delta} d_2$. Assuming that n_1 is a noisy object, even if n_1 is in the neighbourhood of x_3, x_3 is still correctly classified into the variable precision lower approximation set of d_2.

Theorem 1. Given a decision table IS, δ, $B \subseteq C$, $X \subseteq U$, $0 \le u_1 \le u_2 \le 1$, we have

$$\underline{B}_{u_1}^{\delta} X \subseteq \underline{B}_{u_2}^{\delta} X \text{ and } \overline{B}_{u_1}^{\delta} X \supseteq \overline{B}_{u_2}^{\delta} X.$$

The boundary region of X in the u neighbourhood spaces is formulated as

$$BN_{u,B}^{\delta} = \overline{B}_u^{\delta} X - \underline{B}_u^{\delta} X. \tag{5}$$

The boundary region reflects the degree of roughness of the set X. Assuming that X is the subset of training data within a same decision class, the set is as more precise as possible if the boundary region of X is small. The size of the boundary region depends on parameters δ and u. Parameter δ is responsible to define the neighbourhood relation between objects, and u is a measurement that can pre-define a noise-tolerant degree (Yao, 1999).

Based on the results of neighbourhood rough set model (Hu et al., 2008), we can also get the properties of varied precision neighbourhood based rough set model.

Theorem 2. Given a decision table IS, δ, $B \subseteq C$, $X \subseteq U$, $0 \le u_1 \le u_2 \le 1$, we have

$$BN_{u_1}^{\delta} X \supseteq BN_{u_2}^{\delta} X.$$

From Theorem 2, we can easily know that if u is decreased, the noise tolerance ability will be degraded. In addition, the lower approximation of the decision, also called positive region is formulated as

$$POS_{u,B}^{\delta}(D) = \bigcup_{X \subseteq U/D} \underline{B}_u^{\delta} X. \tag{6}$$

Definition 3. Given a decision table IS, δ, $B \subseteq C, D$, the dependency degree of B to D is defined as

$$\gamma_{u,B}^{\delta}(D) = \frac{Card(POS_{u,B}^{\delta}(D))}{Card(U)}. \tag{7}$$

Figure 2. Algorithm 1. Hybrid-attribute reduction algorithm

Data: A decision table $\langle U, C \cup D, V, f \rangle$, noise-tolerant parameter u, neighborhood parameter δ.

Result: A relative reduct RED.

```
 1  RED ⇐ ∅;
 2  while True do
 3      for ∀a ∈ C \ RED do
 4          SIG(a, B, D) ⇐ γ_{u,B∪{a}}^δ(D) − γ_{u,B}^δ(D);
 5      end
 6      a_k = arg max_a SIG(a, B, D);
 7      if SIG(a_k, B, D) > 0 then
 8          RED ⇐ RED ∪ {a_k};
 9      else
10          return RED;
11      end
12  end
```

Theorem 3. Given a decision table IS, δ, u, $B_1 \subseteq B_2 \subseteq C$, D, we have

$$POS^\delta_{u,B_1}(D) \subseteq POS^\delta_{u,B_2}(D), \tag{1}$$

$$\gamma^\delta_{u,B_1}(D) \leq \gamma^\delta_{u,B_2}(D). \tag{2}$$

Proof. Assume that $\forall y \in POS^\delta_{u,B_1}(D)$, according to definition we have $y \in \underline{B}^\delta_u X$, where X is an element in is U / D. From definition of inclusion operator, we have $c^\delta_{B_1}(y, X) \leq u$. At the same time $\forall x \in U, \delta_{B_1}(x) \supseteq \delta_{B_2}(x)$ holds if $B_1 \subseteq B_2$. Accordingly, $c^\delta_{B_2}(y, X) \leq c^\delta_{B_1}(y, X)$, i.e. $c^\delta_{B_2}(y, X) \leq u$. Therefore, $y \in POS^\delta_{u,B_2}(D)$, i.e., $POS^\delta_{u,B_1}(D) \subseteq POS^\delta_{u,B_2}(D)$. According to definition, we have $\gamma^\delta_{u,B_1}(D) \leq \gamma^\delta_{u,B_2}(D)$.

Definition 4. Given a decision table IS, δ, u, $B \subseteq C, D$, B is a relative reduction of C to D if and only if

$$\gamma^\delta_{u,B}(D) = \gamma^\delta_{u,C}(D), \text{ and} \tag{1}$$

$$\forall a \in B, \gamma^\delta_{u,B}(D) > \gamma^\delta_{u,B-\{a\}}(D). \tag{2}$$

Hybrid-Attribute Reduction Algorithm

Reduct is an important concept in rough set theory and attribute reduction is a main application of rough set theory in machine learning and data mining. A number of algorithms have been established for attribute reduction (Beynon, 2001; Hu & Cercone, 1999; Mi, Wu, & Zhang, 2004). In this section, we propose a heuristic hybrid-attribute reduction algorithm based on neighbourhood approximation and variable precision rough set model.

Definition 5. Given a decision table IS, δ, u, $a \in B \subseteq C$, D, we define the significance of the attribute a in B related to D as

$$SIG(a, B, D) = \gamma^\delta_{u,B \cup \{a\}}(D) - \gamma^\delta_{u,B}(D). \tag{8}$$

Definition 5 computes the increment of discernibility power related to the decision attributes introducing by the attribute a. It is used as a supervised measurement for greedy reduction algorithm.

Here, the Algorithm 1 adds an candidate attribute with the greatest increment of dependence into the partial reduct in each time until the dependence does not increase any more, i.e., adding a new attribute will not increase the dependence of conditional attributes related to decisional attributes. The time complexity of the algorithm is $O(m^2)$, where m is the number of conditional attributes. The u is called as a noise-tolerant pre-defined tuning parameter. In fact, VPRS uses only the intermediate results from an earlier model known as the decision-theoretic rough set (DTRS) model (Greco, Slowinski, & Yao, 2007). In DTRS, the well-established Bayesian decision procedure is used to derive the required parameter. For experimental purpose, the value of u is just set to be 0.20 as default value.

The most important problem in neighbourhood spaces based feature selection is the threshold δ, which determines the size of the neighbourhood. No object will be include in the neighbourhood if δ is too small; on the other hand, the neighbourhood cannot reflect the discernibility if δ is set to be too big. In our system, the numeric attributes are first normalized to $[0, 1]$ interval, and δ is set to be 0.125 as default value for easily use purpose.

It is notable that neighbourhood feature selection is independent of the subsequent rule acquisition algorithm. Therefore, the output of neighbourhood-based feature selection is also applicable to other rule learners that are sensitive to the redundant attributes, such as KNN (Yao, 1999) and SVM (Neumann, Schnörr, & Steidl, 2005).

ROUGH SET BASED RULE LEARNER

The complexity of knowledge plays an important role in the success of any types of knowledge acquisition algorithms performing on large and possibly noisy database. LERS (Learning from examples based on rough sets) system is a rule based knowledge acquisition system that is characterized by excellent accuracy, but the complexity of generated rule set is neglected. This may cause interpretation problems for human and the classification knowledge may overfit inconsistent or noisy data. We will first briefly describe the preliminary notion in LERS system, and then introduce the main characteristics of CompactLEM2 algorithm.

LERS System Preliminary

LERS is a rough set based data mining system. The lower and upper approximations of a concept are used as input sets, which resolves the conflicting problems in training data. Algorithm LEM2 explores search space of attribute-value pairs from an input set, and consequently computes a local covering that can be converts into a rule set. The algorithm MLEM2 is a modified version of LEM2 that can handle numerical and missing values. We firstly quote a few definitions to describe main ideas of algorithm LEM2.

The main notion of algorithm LEM2 is the *block* of an attribute-value pair. For an attribute-value pair $t = (c, v), c \in C, v \in V$, a *block* of t, denoted by $[t]$, is a set of examples from U such that $\{x \mid x \in U, f(x,c) = v\}$. Let B be a nonempty lower or upper approximation of a concept

Figure 3. Algorithm 2. CompactLEM2 rule learner

Data: A non-empty lower or upper approximation set of a concept B, a set of conditional attributes C.
Result: A local covering τ.

```
1   G ← DataOpt(B, | C |);
2   τ ← ∅;
3   while G ≠ ∅ do
4       T ← ∅, TmpG = G;
5       while T = ∅ or [T] ⊄ B do
6           t ← arg max_{(a,v)∉T} Score_G(a, v);
7           T ← T ∪ {t};
8           G ← {g ∈ G | Cons_C(g, T))};
9       end
10      for ∀t ∈ T do
11          if [T \ {t}] ⊆ B and T \ {t} ≠ ∅ then
12              T ← T \ {t};
13          end
14      end
15      τ ← τ ∪ {T};
16      G ← TmpG \ {g ∈ TmpG | Cons_C(g, T))};
17  end
18  for ∀T ∈ τ do
19      if ∪_{S∈τ\{T}}[S] = B then
20          τ ← τ \ {T};
21      end
22  end
23  return τ;
```

and T be a set of attribute-value pairs, set B depends on T if and only if $\varnothing \neq [T] = \bigcap_{t \in T}[t] \subseteq B$. Set T is called as a *minimal complex* of B if and only if B depends on T and no proper subset T' of T exists such that B depends on T. Let Γ be a nonempty sets of minimal complex, Γ is a *local covering* of B if and only if

(1) $\cup_{T \in \Gamma}[T] = B$,

(2) Γ is minimal, i.e., there exists no proper subset $\Gamma' \subseteq \Gamma$ satisfy condition (1).

In order to select an appropriate attribute-value pair t, algorithm LEM2 uses a priority-based strategy. It searches for an attribute-pair t with high priority, and then adds to partial minimal complex. When a local covering is found, it is converted to a rule set for classifying new examples.

CompactLEM2 Rule Learner

There are many known rule extraction algorithm inspired by rough set theory, and LEM2 algorithm proposed by (Grzymala-Busse & Lakshmanan, 1996) is one of the most widely used algorithms for real-world applications. In this section, we propose a revised version of LEM2, which named CompactLEM2. It is proposed as a robust rule learner for knowledge acquisition task. It can generate a small size of rule set with short rule forms based on the selected feature subset, without sacrificing classification accuracy over test data set. The main reason for choosing CompactLEM2 as a back-end knowledge acquisition task is its high efficiency, and it can produce compact rule set that fully or approximately describes classifications of given examples.

Algorithm CompactLEM2 is based on algorithm LEM2 in LERS system, which improves its ability to handle large-scale problems and produce compact rule sets. The algorithm targets at finding an approximate local covering on a reduced set. Therefore, the searching space of attribute-value pair consequently shrinks to the optimized set and attribute-value pairs are selected according to their distribution. The pseudocode of CompactLEM2 is presented in Algorithm 2.

1. The *DataOpt* Procedure: The input sets are optimized by a data reduction method before searching for a local covering. It is uses the similar idea of. The procedure is a data reduction method with linear time complexity, which is used to reduce searching space in the process of finding attribute-value pairs.

The reduced set characterizes the common attribute-value information in original input set, and it additionally records the number of cases it generalized. Thus, the reduced set is called as a *generalized set* and elements in this set are called as *generalized cases*. In our algorithm, we use this procedure as the pre-processing step of input sets.

2. The *CompactLEM2* Procedure: The *CompactLEM2* procedure uses a different heuristic method for selecting candidate attribute-value pairs compared with algorithm LEM2. We introduce a *consistent check function*, which is a boolean function that checks if a given generalized case is consistent with a given block set.

Definition 6. Let T be a block set, C be an attribute set and $g \in G$ be a generalized case. The *consistent check function* is a boolean function that determines if g is consistent with T.

Definition 7. Let $a \in C$ be an attribute, $g \in G$ be an attribute value and $|V_a|$ be the total number of values of the attribute a. The score of an attribute-value pair related to a set of generalized cases G is defined in as:

$$Score_G(a, v) = \sum_{g \in G, g_a = v} g_{num} * |V_a|. \tag{10}$$

For each attribute-value pair, the score function is used to evaluate its distribution in search space. The pair with the maximal score is selected into the partial minimal complex. We note that the maximal depth of a minimal complex is equal to the number of conditional attributes.

$$Cons_C(g, T) = \begin{cases} false & \begin{aligned} & (\exists x \in T)(\exists c \in C) \\ & (x_c \neq ? \wedge g_c \neq ? \wedge x_c \neq g_c), \end{aligned} \\ true & otherwise. \end{cases} \tag{9}$$

The generalized case that is consistent with local covering will be removed from G in LINE 8, and the construction process of a minima complex T is repeated in LINE 3-17.

Let *n* be the size of input set, *m* be the number of conditional attributes. The expected running time of algorithm CompactLEM2 is $O(mn \log n)$.

CompactLEM2 can handle data with missing values. The learner uses all available information while ignoring missing values, i.e., they are handled as "do not care" values. The characteristic set (Grzymala-Busse, 2004) is used to deal with missing values and compute the lower or upper approximation set of each concept as an input of *CompactLEM2* procedure.

Discretization research shows that some machine learning algorithms can handle continuous attributes themselves, such as MLEM2 (J. W. Grzymala-Busse, 2002). It can handle continuous attributes on its own but still perform better. Algorithm CompactLEM2, as opposite to MLEM2, can only handle nominal values. The CompactLEM2 has a build-in front-end discretization algorithm CAIM (Kurgan & Cios, 2004), as this algorithm is a high quality discretization algorithm, which can subsequently improve accuracy of the rule acquisition algorithms.

CompactLEM2 learner uses one threshold to reinforce the stopping condition in the *CompactLEM2* procedure. The default value for the threshold is set to 0.125, unless a user specifies alternative values. The threshold is used to prune minimal complex for producing very specific or complex rule forms. Local covering construction process gradually selects the maximal score values and removes generalized cases covered by current partial minimal complex, and terminates if the max score value is equal or smaller than the value of the threshold. For easily scalable purpose, the threshold value is specified as the percentage of the size of input cases. The parameter has the advantage of filtering out outliers and robustness to data containing overlapping

class. It should normally be set to small values near zero.

CompactLEM2 generates a separate set of rules for each decision class. Due to the rule generation mechanism of CompactLEM2, conflicts in the rule set are possible. In general, a test case may match multiple rules in different decision classes, or matched none of rule set.

Definition 8. Let $r = B \xrightarrow{\quad x \quad} D$ be a decision rule, the *factor* of r is expressed as:

$$Factor(r) = \frac{\mid B(x) \cap D(x) \mid^2}{\mid B(x) \mid * \mid D(x) \mid}. \qquad (11)$$

The rule evaluation process investigates how well a rule will function on a test case. A simple strategy has been adopted in CompactLEM2. To classify a test case and resolve conflicts, CompactLEM2 employs a *matching factor* based procedure to classify new objects. The factor of a rule is used only when a test case is totally matched the rule. For a given test case, the sum of factors of rules that totally match this case within each concept is computed. The concept with the greatest value wins as target for classification of the test case. The reason for this choice is to avoid overlapping the classification of rule sets so that we can investigate more clearly the effect of our rule learner has on the accuracy of classifying module in noisy information systems. In experimental sections, we present *score* of a rule as 100 multiplying matching factor of the rule. We note that all unclassified cases are categorized as incorrect classifications since they are not covered by any model. In this case, these incorrect classified cases will decrease the classification accuracy of CompactLEM2.

PROBLEM CASE

To emphasize the generality of the presented methodology and its feasibility to specific application domains, one case study will be given. We first provide a brief description of the application problem, and then present the experimental results and analysis.

The Chinese Diabetes Mellitus Diagnosis Problem

Diabetes Mellitus is a major chronic disease in China, affecting about 5% of the population. Diabetes Mellitus is characterized by an alteration of the glucose metabolism due to a decreased endogenous production of insulin, the main glucoregolatory hormone (Huang, McCullagh, Black, & Harper, 2007). Patients must take treatment in order to prevent extremely high blood glucose levels (hyperglycemias), glycosuria (glucose in the urine), ketonuria (ketons in the urine), ketoacydosys and death. Diabetes Mellitus causes long-term complications, such as retinopathy, nephropathy, neuropathy and cardiovascular disease (Giardina, Azuaje, McCullagh, & Harper, 2006). Since the onset and development of diabetic complications is strictly related to the degree of metabolic control that can be achieved, the accuracy of rough set based diagnosing methods is aroused much attention (Breault, Goodall, & Fos, 2002; Stepaniuk, 1999). Recent studies show that an early treatment can significantly delay or prevent the development of long-term complications (Bellazzi, Larizza, Magni, Montani, & Stefanelli, 2000; Lutes & Baggili, 2006; Salzsieder et al., 1995). Unfortunately, the traditional diagnosis criteria are not fully undertaken by elderly people in China due to financial costs, and this leads to an increase in the probability of diabetic complications event. In some provinces in China, such as Henan, governments have invested a lot of money in general health check-ups for elderly people. Because it is a public welfare, the participation rate in check-up events is almost 87%. Since the physical check-up events for elderly are not designed to diagnosis of Diabetes Mellitus, some new diagnosis schema for Diabetes Mellitus must be acquired based on the information in check-up events.

The goal is to implement a knowledge acquisition system that, given a data set of historical measurements and without the help of an expert in this field, will produce valuable domain classification knowledge.

Data Set Description

The First Affiliated hospital of Xin Xiang Medical College has collected public's medical examination data from the year 2007 to present in P. R. China. The data was stored in a commercial clinical information system. The existing database contains 1097 subjects; each case contains 34 measurements on testing subjects, including both quantitative and qualitative attributes, such as *Gender*, *Age*, *Glucose*, *Cholesterol*, etc. The subjects' age ranged from 18 to 86, with 585 subjects younger than 50. The mean value of the subjects' age is 48. There are 468 males and 629 females in this data set. Therefore, the work concentrates on both the young and old groups of patients. The decision attribute is whether the patient needs to be treated in hospital.

Experiment and Results

As a real-world database, it is inevitable that there will be inconsistent, noisy and incomplete components. Because of the medical examination is for general purpose, the domain has numerous superfluous measurements for diagnosing Diabetes Mellitus. Some noisy data also existed due to typing errors. In such cases, it is necessary to get the most important feature set and perform knowledge acquisition tasks on it. Therefore, a pre-processing step is a very important step. The pre-processing procedure in this experiment consists of data transformation and data reduction.

In the data transformation step, the quantitative attributes are normalized first. Missing values are filled with mean values for quantitative attributes and majority values for qualitative attributes.

There are two objectives to conduct the experiments. The first one is to find optimal parameters u and δ to get the most important features in data set. We conduct a series of experiments to find optimal parameter u and δ used to deal with the diabetic data set and obtain a reduced feature space. The second one is to get classification rules from rule learner and evaluate classification performance of acquired results.

Table 1 shows the number of selected features based on 1-norm, 2-norm and ∞-norm neighbourhood spaces based variable precision attribute reduction by tuning different parameters u and δ. We can see that most of the candidate attributes are deleted when u is set greater than zero. In addition, with the same u and δ values, 1-norm based attribute reduction gets the least features, while ∞-norm based algorithm get the most ones. However, if we change δ value from 0.125 to 0.25, the numbers of selected features based on 1-norm is comparable with that based on 2-norm

algorithm with δ value being 0.125. The similar case occurs as to 2-norm and ∞-norm based feature selection. Therefore, by specifying different δ values, we can obtain similar results with different norm based feature selection algorithms.

Table 2 presents the acquired rule set by CompactLEM2 rule learner based on reduced attribute subset with five features: i.e., *GLU, AGE, GENDER, ALP* and *A/G*. We set the threshold to 0.25. The rules with scores higher than 0.01 are selected to the final rule set. In this experiment, eight rules are extracted with average two attributes in the left part of an IF-THEN rule. This rule set maintains the accuracy 75.6% in ten-fold cross validation.

For comparison purpose, C4.5 is employed as a comparison method. C4.5 is a widely accepted

Table 1. Number of selected features

	1-Norm		2-Norm		∞-Norm	
	δ=0.125	δ=0.25	δ=0.125	δ=0.25	δ=0.125	δ=0.25
u=0.00	11	26	17	29	19	33
u=0.10	7	13	9	14	10	21
u=0.15	4	8	6	9	8	15
u=0.20	4	5	4	7	6	11
u=0.25	4	5	4	5	5	8
Average	5.8	11.4	8	12.8	9.6	17.6

Table 2. Extracted rule set by ten-fold cross validation of CompactLEM2 rule learner

Rules	Score
IF GLU in (6.1, +∞] **THEN** D is 1	**21.8**
IF GLU in (6.1, +∞] and ALP in (80, +∞] **THEN** D is 1	**2.3**
IF GLU in (6.1, +∞] and AGE in (36, +∞] and GENDER=1 and A/G in (1.73, +∞]**THEN** D is 1	**0.7**
IF GLU in (6.1, +∞] and AGE in (36, +∞] and GENDER=2 and A/G in (-∞, 1.73]**THEN** D is 1	**0.9**
IF GLU in (-∞, 6.1] and ALP in (80, +∞] **THEN** D is 0	**38**
IF GLU in (-∞, 6.1] and AGE in (-∞, 36] **THEN** D is 0	**0.5**
IF GLU in (-∞, 6.1] and AGE in (36, +∞] and GENDER=1 and A/G in (-∞, 1.73]**THEN** D is 0	**1.6**
IF GLU in (-∞, 6.1] and AGE in (36, +∞] and GENDER=2 and A/G in (1.73, +∞]**THEN** D is 0	**3.6**

Note: *GLU* is glucose, *ALP* is alkaline phosphatase, *AGE* is the age, *GENDER* is gender, in which 1 represents male, 2 represents female, *A/G* is the proportion of albumin and globulin, and *D* is decision attribute.

decision tree approach, which provides a good machine learning benchmark (Quinlan, 1993). The generated decision trees can be interpreted as IF-THEN rules. Algorithms C4.5 and CompactLEM2 are conducted on a set of extracted feature subsets to learn knowledge model and perform classification task of ten-fold cross validation on data set.

The comparing accuracies and area under ROC curves (AUC) are presented in Table 3. From the table, we can find that before and after feature selection, C4.5 always had good performance for classification task. In comparison, CompactLEM2 is sensitive to feature subset, and performs comparable classification accuracies when based on smaller set of features. On average, C4.5 obtains an accuracy of around 84.8% on testing data set, while CompactLEM2 is 75.2%.

Figure 4 shows the tendency of classification accuracies with respect to different numbers of selected features. Based on a small set of features, CompactLEM2 exhibits the same performance as C4.5. However, when redundant attributes and noise occurs in data set, the performance of CompactLEM2 draws dramatically.

SCALABILITY TEST

The scalability test is conducted according to two design factors: the noise-tolerant value (with u

Figure 4. Comparison accuracy with different number of features

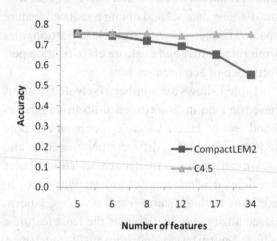

=0, 0.05, 0.10, 0.15, and 0.20 respectively), and the proportion of noise in data set β (with β =0, 5, 10, 15, and 20% respectively). The threshold of rule learner is also set to value u. Three real-life data sets with both quantitative and qualitative attributes are applied so that we can focus on the effect of rule learning algorithms without considering the complex pre-processing feature selection tasks. The characteristics of the databases are summarized in Table 4. These databases are all available from UCI Repository (Blake & Merz, 1998). Each data set is divided into two parts with 90% of the data used for training, and the remaining 10% for testing. We use 1-norm neighbourhood

Table 3. Ten-fold cross validation results between C4.5 and CompactLEM2

	Accuracy		AUC	
# Features	CompactLEM2	C4.5	CompactLEM2	C4.5
5	0.756	0.760	0.720	0.721
6	0.746	0.755	0.713	0.742
8	0.718	0.756	0.708	0.741
12	0.693	0.743	0.681	0.742
17	0.650	0.752	0.649	0.734
34	0.551	0.752	0.513	0.734
Average	0.686	0.753	0.664	0.736

model in attribute reduction step, and set δ to be 0.125. The algorithm repeats 10-fold cross validation on each data set. Besides, to test the robustness of the rule induction system, noise data of 5%, 10%, 15% and 20% of the original database size are randomly generated and added to the database, and the same experiment is conducted on these noisy data sets.

Table 5 to Table 7 show the average predictions over the three testing databases with different experimental settings u (noise-tolerant rate) and β (noisy rate). In order to evaluate the prediction accuracy, we average the classification accuracies over testing samples in ten-fold cross-validation experiments and reports the mean values.

In databases *ion*, when there is no noise proportion in data set (in the clean situation β=0), algorithm with u=0 setting exhibits the highest accuracy, which means that there may be no noise in original data set. Nevertheless, the results become worse when β increases. For example, in the first column, the accuracy value drops dramatically. Hence, the attribute reduction algorithm without noise-tolerant setting tends to be sensitive to noisy environment. Furthermore, as the environment gets more and more noisy, the value of u increases the accuracy on testing data and the algorithm obtains the highest one on some u values.

In database *wbc*, on the other hand, algorithm with u=0.05 obtains the highest accuracy in the clean situation, which shows that a proper tolerant level could also improve the system's accuracy even in a clean environment. Hence, it shows that the tolerant attribute reduction enables the rough set based rule induction algorithm to generate more noise-insensible rule sets. When the information system gets more and more noisy, the obtained highest accuracies always attained at a specific noise-tolerant degree of the system. This in turn shows that providing a proper tolerant degree might be effective in generating more noise-insensible and accurate rule sets for highly noisy information systems.

In database *win*, in all situations, increasing the tolerant degree to a proper value generally helps improve the prediction performance of knowledge acquisition system. These results show that the tolerant degree enables the knowledge acquisition system to generate noise-insensible rule sets in medium-scaled complete databases. It can be seen that results of algorithms with u=0.15 and u=0.20 are comparable to each other in all noisy environments.

As a brief summary, our rule induction system can obtain satisfactory classification accuracy by specifying proper value of u. Even in the clean environment, the noise-tolerant degree can also improve the classification performance on test data set. Furthermore, we can see that setting the tolerant degree parameter u to 0.15 or 0.20 helps improve the validation effectiveness of the rule learner in all cases. On the contrary, the non-noise tolerant rule induction system, which reported by setting u=0.0 in the system, always lose to get the highest accuracy in noisy environment. These results show that noise-tolerant degree parameter provide a flexible way to tune the rule induction system so that it can be adapted to various real-life data sets.

CONCLUSION AND FUTURE WORKS

Feature based rule learner offer an expressive and human readable form of knowledge acquisition framework. Automated generation of such rule sets is essential to the practical success of application to any domain areas. This paper has presented an approach that integrates a potentially powerful feature selection tool with a rough set based rule learner. The front-end feature selection tool maintains the underlying semantics of the feature set even in noisy environment. This is very important to ensure the resulting models are comprehensible by the users and the experts. Through the integration, the original rule induction algorithm becomes robustness to noise environment.

Neighbourhood relations provide a possible tool for hybrid-feature selection. In this paper, we combine neighbourhood approximation spaces and variable precision rough set model, and introduce a noise-tolerant attribute reduction algorithm, which is robust in noisy environment. It is a conceptually simple and easy to implement method, which can be constructed as a powerful front-end feature selection tool.

Feature based rule induction methodology take the benefits of noise tolerant characteristics. The proposed algorithm CompactLEM2 is based on a reduced feature space. It can generate general, strong rule set thanks to its mechanism of heuristic information for attribute-value pair selection, and it is faster because of working on a reduced input set. In addition, because it is targets at finding approximate minimal complex, it is robust to large-scale dataset with noise, and it can generate compact rule set efficiently.

The work has been applied to a real-world problem-solving task. Aiming at acquiring diagnosis rule set of Diabetes Mellitus, where the initial settings of the data set were not pre-processed by any method, this paper has provided the results of utilising the proposed rule induction system.

Table 5. Testing average accuracy (%) for rule learner on ion data set with various values of β and u

β value	u value				
	0.00	0.05	0.10	0.15	0.20
0% noise	89.2	85.7	80.1	81.5	82.9
5% noise	80.3	84.5	86.2	81.2	83.8
10% noise	78.0	81.3	81.4	82.5	80.2
15% noise	73.9	76.8	78.2	78.8	77.3
20% noise	67.2	69.4	69.8	71.3	72.5

Table 6. Testing average accuracy (%) for rule learner on wbc data set with various values of β and u

β value	u value				
	0.00	0.05	0.10	0.15	0.20
0% noise	88.7	89.2	85.5	82.3	80.3
5% noise	84.0	84.7	85.6	83.1	82.6
10% noise	76.5	78.0	81.5	81.3	80.8
15% noise	75.2	77.5	78.2	78.8	78.0
20% noise	70.5	72.6	74.7	76.9	76.5

Table 7. Testing average accuracy (%) for rule learner on win data set with various values of β and u

β value	u value				
	0.00	0.05	0.10	0.15	0.20
0% noise	90.3	91.6	88.8	87.2	85.3
5% noise	90.7	91.3	92.0	90.5	89.4
10% noise	85.8	88.7	86.5	87.0	86.9
15% noise	82.6	84.7	85.0	85.6	85.2
20% noise	76.4	80.2	82.7	83.0	82.6

Although the application problems encountered are complex, which includes inconsistent and noisy data and superfluous attributes, the resulting rule sets are manageable and the classification accuracy over test data set is comparable to state-of-the-art method. This methodology presents a great improvement of CompactLEM2 rule learner and makes it is possible to facilitate the hybrid-attribute reduction algorithm as a front-end feature selection tool for noise-sensible rule learners to cope with real-world applications with inconsistent and noisy data.

The robustness of our methodology is also shown in experiments. Empirical evidences show that no universally good algorithms on all data set. Nevertheless, the proposed noise-tolerant rule induction methodology did show its potentiality of being more noise-insensible, more accurate and more effective than the CompactLEM2 rule learner is. In some cases, the proposed system even possesses higher classification accuracy than C4.5 algorithm. Through setting the different values of δ and u, the rule induction system can easily adapted to real-world database.

An on-going research will be on developing an approach for automatically tuning the value of δ and u in finding good rule sets to describe the real-life problem. On the other hand, other heuristics, such as information measures and weightiness can also be combined with the noise-tolerant hybrid-attribute reduction algorithm in order to investigate the effectiveness of knowledge acquisition systems. Some more extensive diabetic data sets will be investigated. For example, if the data set can contain the diabetes' life style and real-time information, some more interesting knowledge can be extracted, which may let our method to make more contributions to domain applications.

ACKNOWLEDGMENT

The authors would like to thank Prof. Yingxu Wang, and the anonymous reviewers for their valuable suggestions and comments that have greatly improved the quality of the final version of this article. The authors would also like to thank to Dr. Jianjun Guo for his valuable comments to this research work. This work is partly supported by National Basic Research Program of China (973 Program) under Grant 2006AA012210.

REFERENCES

Bellazzi, R., Larizza, C., Magni, P., Montani, S., & Stefanelli, M. (2000). Intelligent analysis of clinical time series: an application in the diabetes mellitus domain. *Artificial Intelligence in Medicine*, *20*(1), 37–57. doi:10.1016/S0933-3657(00)00052-X

Beynon, M. (2001). Reducts within the variable precision rough sets model: A further investigation. *European Journal of Operational Research*, *134*(3), 592–605. doi:10.1016/S0377-2217(00)00280-0

Blake, E. K. C., & Merz, C. J. (1998). *UCI Repository of machine learning databases* (Tech. Rep.). Irvine, California: University of California, Irvine, Dept. of Information and Computer Sciences. Retrieved from http://www.ics.uci.edu/$\sim$mlearn/MLRepository.html

Breault, J. L., Goodall, C. R., & Fos, P. J. (2002). Data mining a diabetic data warehouse. *Artificial Intelligence in Medicine*, *26*(1-2), 37–54. doi:10.1016/S0933-3657(02)00051-9

Chiew, V. (2002). A Software Engineering Cognitive Knowledge Discovery Framework. *Proceedings of the IEEE, ICCI*, 163–174.

Cios, K. J., & Kurgan, L. A. (2004). CLIP4: Hybrid inductive machine learning algorithm that generates inequality rules. *Inf. Sci, 163*(1-3), 37–83. doi:10.1016/j.ins.2003.03.015

Cornelis, C., & Jensen, R. (n.d.). *A Noise-tolerant Approach to Fuzzy-Rough Feature Selection.* Retrieved from http://hdl.handle.net/2160/581

Giardina, M., Azuaje, F., McCullagh, P. J., & Harper, R. (2006). A Supervised Learning Approach to Predicting Coronary Heart Disease Complications in Type 2 Diabetes Mellitus Patients. In *Proceedings of BIBE* (pp. 325-331).

Greco, S., Slowinski, R., & Yao, Y. Y. (2007). Bayesian decision theory for dominance-based rough set approach. In *Proceedings of the Second International Conference on Rough Sets and Knowledge Technology (RSKT'07)* (pp. 134-141).

Grzymala-Busse, J. W. (1988). Knowledge Acquisition under Uncertainty - A Rough Set Approach. *J. Intel. Rob. Syst., 1*, 3–16. doi:10.1007/BF00437317

Grzymala-Busse, J. W. (1992). LERS - A system for learning from examples based on rough sets . In Slowinski, R. (Ed.), *Intelligent Decision Support: Handbook of Applications and Advances of the Rough Sets Theory* (pp. 3–18). Dordrecht, The Netherlands: Kluwer Academic Publishers.

Grzymala-Busse, J. W. (2002). MLEM2: A new algorithm for rule induction from imperfect data. In *Proceedings of the 9th International Conference on Information Processing and Management of Uncertainty in Knowledge-Based Systems (IPMU 2002)*, Annecy, France (pp. 243-250).

Grzymala-Busse, J. W. (2004). Data with missing attribute values: Generalization of idiscernibility relation and rule induction. *Transactions on Rough Sets, 1*, 78–95.

Grzymala-Busse, J. W., & Lakshmanan, A. (1996). LEM2 with interval extension: An induction algorithm for numerical attributes. In *Proceedings of the Fourth International Workshop on Rough Sets, Fuzzy Sets, and Machine Discovery*, Tokyo (pp. 67 - 73).

Grzymala-Busse, P., Grzymala-Busse, J. W., & Hippe, Z. S. (2001). Melanoma prediction using data mining system LERS. In *Proceedings of the 25th Annual International Computer Software and Applications Conference (COMPSAC 2001)* (pp. 615-620).

Guyon, I., & Elisseeff, A. (2003). An Introduction to Variable and Feature Selection. *Journal of Machine Learning Research, 3*, 1157–1182. doi:10.1162/153244303322753616

Hu, Q., Liu, J., & Yu, D. (2008). Mixed feature selection based on granulation and approximation. *Knowledge-Based Systems, 21*(4), 294–304. doi:10.1016/j.knosys.2007.07.001

Hu, Q., Xie, Z., & Yu, D. (2007). Hybrid attribute reduction based on a novel fuzzy-rough model and information granulation. *Pattern Recognition, 40*(12), 3509–3521. doi:10.1016/j.patcog.2007.03.017

Hu, Q., Yu, D., Liu, J., & Wu, C. (2008). Neighborhood rough set based heterogeneous feature subset selection. *Inf. Sci., 178*(18), 3577–3594. doi:10.1016/j.ins.2008.05.024

Hu, Q., Yu, D., & Xie, Z. (2006). Information-preserving hybrid data reduction based on fuzzy-rough techniques. *Pattern Recognition Letters, 27*(5), 414–423. doi:10.1016/j.patrec.2005.09.004

Hu, X., & Cercone, N. (1999). Data Mining via Discretization, Generalization and Rough Set Feature Selection. *Knowledge and Information Systems, 1*(1), 33–60.

Huang, Y., McCullagh, P. J., Black, N. D., & Harper, R. (2007). Feature selection and classification model construction on type 2 diabetic patients' data. *Artificial Intelligence in Medicine, 41*(3), 251–262. doi:10.1016/j.artmed.2007.07.002

Kurgan, L. A. (2004). Reducing Complexity of Rule Based Models via Meta Mining. In *Proceedings of the International Conference on Machine Learning and Applications* (pp. 242- 249).

Kurgan, L. A., & Cios, K. J. (2004). CAIM Discretization Algorithm. *IEEE Transactions on Data and Knowldge Engineering, 16*(2), 145–153. doi:10.1109/TKDE.2004.1269594

Kurgan, L. A., Cios, K. J., & Dick, S. (2006). Highly scalable and robust rule learner: Performance evaluation and comparison. *IEEE Transactions on Systems, Man, and Cybernetics, 36*, 32–53. doi:10.1109/TSMCB.2005.852983

Kurgan, L. A., & Musilek, P. (2006). A survey of Knowledge Discovery and Data Mining process models. *The Knowledge Engineering Review, 21*(1), 1–24. doi:10.1017/S0269888906000737

Lin, T. Y. (1988). Neighborhood systems and relational databases. In *Proceedings of the 1988 ACM sixteenth annual conference on Computer science (CSC '88)* (p. 725). New York: ACM. Retrieved from http://doi.acm.org/10.1145/322609.323183

Liu, Y., Bai, G., & Feng, B. (2008a). On Mining Rules that Involve Inequalities from Decision Table. In D. Zhang, Y. Wang, & W. Kinsner (Eds.), *Proceedings of the 7th IEEE International Conference on Cognitive Informatics (ICCI 2008)* (pp. 255–260). doi: 10.1109/COGINF.2008.4639176

Liu, Y., Bai, G., & Feng, B. (2008b, August 14-16). CompactLEM2: A Scalable Rough Set based Knowledge Acquisition Method that Generates Small Number of Short Rules. In D. Zhang, Y. Wang, & W. Kinsner (Eds.), *Proceedings of the Seven IEEE International Conference on Cognitive Informatics (ICCI 2008),* Stanford University, CA (pp. 215-223). Washington, DC: IEEE.

Lutes, K. D., & Baggili, I. M. (2006). Diabetic e-Management System (DEMS). In *Proceedings of ITNG* (p. 619-624). Washington, DC: IEEE Computer Society. Retrieved from http://doi.ieeecomputersociety.org/10.1109/ITNG.2006.53

Mi, J., Wu, W., & Zhang, W. (2004). Approaches to knowledge reduction based on variable precision rough set model. *Inf. Sci, 159*(2), 255–272. doi:10.1016/j.ins.2003.07.004

Michalski, R. S. (1983). A Theory and Methodology of Inductive Learning. *Artificial Intelligence, 20*(2), 111–161. doi:10.1016/0004-3702(83)90016-4

Neumann, J., Schnörr, C., & Steidl, G. (2005). Combined SVM-Based Feature Selection and Classification. *Machine Learning, 61*(1-3), 129–150. doi:10.1007/s10994-005-1505-9

Pawlak, Z. (1982). Rough Sets. *International Journal of Computer and Information Sciences,* 341-356.

Pawlak, Z., & Skowron, A. (2007). Rudiments of rough sets. *Inf. Sci, 177*(1), 3–27. doi:10.1016/j.ins.2006.06.003

Pazzani, M., & Kibler, D. (1992). The Utility of Knowledge in Inductive Learning. *Machine Learning, 9*, 57–94. doi:10.1007/BF00993254

Quinlan, J. (1986). Induction of Decision Trees. *Machine Learning, 1*, 81–106. doi:10.1007/BF00116251

Quinlan, J. R. (1993). C4.5: Programs for Machine Learning.

Salzsieder, E., Fischer, U., Hierle, A., Oppel, U., Rutscher, A., & Sell, C. (1995). Knowledge-Based Education Tool to Improve Quality in Diabetes Care. In *Proceedings of the AIME* (pp. 417-418).

Shen, Q., & Chouchoulas, A. (2002). A rough-fuzzy approach for generating classification rules. *Pattern Recognition, 35*(11), 2425–2438. doi:10.1016/S0031-3203(01)00229-1

Stepaniuk. (1999). Rough Set Data Mining of Diabetes Data. In *Proceedings of the 11th International Symposium on Foundations of Intelligent Systems (ISMIS '99)* (pp. 457–465). London: Springer Verlag.

Tsumoto, S. (2004). Mining diagnostic rules from clinical databases using rough sets and medical diagnostic model. *Inf. Sci.*, *162*(2), 65–80. Retrieved from http://dx.doi.org/10.1016/j.ins.2004.03.002. doi:10.1016/j.ins.2004.03.002

Wang, F. (2005). On acquiring classification knowledge from noisy data based on rough set. *Expert Systems with Applications*, *29*(1), 49–64. doi:10.1016/j.eswa.2005.01.005

Wang, Y. (2007a). The Theoretical Framework of Cognitive Informatics. *International Journal of Cognitive Informatics and Natural Intelligence*, *1*(1), 1–27.

Wang, Y. (2007b). The OAR Model of Neural Informatics for Internal Knowledge Representation in the Brain. *International Journal of Cognitive Informatics and Natural Intelligence*, *1*(3), 66–77.

Wang, Y. (2007c). The Theoretical Framework and Cognitive Process of Learning. In *Proceedings of the 6th IEEE International Conference on Cognitive Informatics* (pp. 470-479). doi: 10.1109/COGINF.2007.4341926

Wang, Y. (2009). On Abstract Intelligence: Toward a Unifying Theory of Natural, Artificial, Machinable, and Computational Intelligence. *International Journal of Software Science and Computational Intelligence*, *1*(1), 1–17.

Wang, Y., & Chiew, V. (2008). On the cognitive process of human problem solving. *Cognitive Systems Research*. doi:.doi:10.1016/j.cogsys.2008.08.003

Wilson, D. R., & Martinez, T. R. (1997). Improved Heterogeneous Distance Functions. [JAIR]. *Journal of Artificial Intelligence Research*, *6*, 1–34.

Wu, Q., & Bell, D. (2003). Multi-knowledge extraction and application (LNCS 2639, pp. 274-278).

Yao, Y. Y. (1999). Granular computing using neighborhood systems. In *Proceedings of the Advances in Soft Computing: Engineering Design and Manufacturing* (pp. 539-553). New York: Springer-Verlag.

Yao, Y. Y. (2004). Concept formation and learning: a cognitive informatics perspective. In *Proceedings of the Third IEEE International Conference on Cognitive Informatics, 2004* (pp. 42-51). doi: 10.1109/COGINF.2004.1327458.

Yu, L., & Liu, H. (2004). Efficient Feature Selection via Analysis of Relevance and Redundancy. *Journal of Machine Learning Research*, *5*, 1205–1224.

Ziarko, W. (1993). Variable Precision Rough Set Model. *Journal of Computer and System Sciences*, *46*(1), 39–59. doi:10.1016/0022-0000(93)90048-2

This work was previously published in International Journal of Software Science and Computational Intelligence, Volume 2, Issue 2, edited by Yingxu Wang, pp. 68-87, copyright 2010 by IGI Publishing (an imprint of IGI Global).

Chapter 5
A High Level Model of a Conscious Embodied Agent

Jiří Wiedermann
Academy of Sciences of the Czech Republic, Czech Republic

ABSTRACT

In this paper, the author describes a simple yet cognitively powerful architecture of an embodied conscious agent. The architecture incorporates a mechanism for mining, representing, processing and exploiting semantic knowledge. This mechanism is based on two complementary internal world models which are built automatically. One model (based on artificial mirror neurons) is used for mining and capturing the syntax of the recognized part of the environment while the second one (based on neural nets) for its semantics. Jointly, the models support algorithmic processes underlying phenomena similar in important aspects to higher cognitive functions such as imitation learning and the development of communication, language, thinking, and consciousness.

INTRODUCTION

Hyakujo wished to send a monk to open a new monastery. He told his pupils that whoever answered a question most ably would be appointed. Placing a water vase on the ground, he asked: "Who can say what this is without calling its name?" The chief monk said: "No one can call it a wooden shoe." Isan, the cooking monk, tipped over the vase with his foot and went out. Hyakujo smiled and said: "The chief monk loses." And Isan became the master of the new monastery.

The introductory quotation related to the life of Hyakujo Ekai (also known as Baizhang Huaihai in China) (720-814) indicates that the masters of the Zen philosophy knew the key to the problem known in the artificial intelligence as the *symbol grounding problem*. This problem is related to

DOI: 10.4018/978-1-4666-0264-9.ch005

the question of how words get their meanings, and of what meanings are (Harnad, 1990). Artificial intelligence started to be interested in this problem especially in nineteen eighties when this problem has become popularized as the Chinese room thought experiment designed by philosopher John Searle (1980). This experiment pointed to the problem whether a computer can understand the words (i.e., the symbols) by which it communicates with people. Searle highlighted the fact that with the symbols a computer cannot do anything else than, following some rules, to transform them into other symbols, eventually into sequences of zeros and ones whose semantic a computer cannot know either. Henceforth, this cannot be the way for computers to get the meaning of words, or "semantic knowledge". This thought experiment has started an ongoing discussion which has (among other things) lead to the development of theories claiming that in order the AI systems to "understand" their actions they need to have a body – they need to be "embodied". It is the body, usually in the interaction with the environment, which gives these systems a facility for understanding their own actions and those of other embodied agents, and for communicating with each other one. By the way, this was the facility used by Isan, the cooking monk from our quotation: not having a body and there not being a real water vase, Isan could not kick the vase with his foot, the vase would not tip over, it would not emit the corresponding characteristic sound and the monks could not see this event. All this, perceived by the sensors of all participants, would not invoke in their minds the set of corresponding memory and sensory associations which all together represent the semantics of the word "vase". Saying it poetically, Isan stroke a chord in the minds of bystanders as the unspoken world "vase" would do.

Returning to the Searle's Chinese room experiment we see that, in order to communicate "intelligently" with people, the computer should obviously have information how the people's

world looks like, what could be the abilities of people under various circumstance, etc. In short, Searle's computer should have possessed a kind of internal model of the external world (inclusively that of the self), represented in whatever useful way. This model should represent a part of rules by which the computer communicated with people.

The idea that non-trivial cognitive systems should build and exploit some form of internal world models has been around practically since the dawn of AI. However, efforts for controlling behavior by formal reasoning over symbolic internal world models have failed. Consequently, during nineteen nineties the mainstream research turned towards biology inspired behavior-based designs of cognitive systems. The respective approach has stressed the necessity of embodiment and situatedness used in sensorily driven control of behavior of simple robots, cf., Brooks (1991). This paradigm worked well with so–called subsumption architecture using incrementally upgraded layers of behavior realized by a task specific robot programming, cf., Pfeifer et al. (1999). Nevertheless, after a series of promising successes, mostly in building various reaction–driven robots, it has appeared that such a framework has its limits. Especially in humanoid robotics a further progress towards higher levels of intelligence turned out to be impossible without introducing further innovations into the basic architecture of cognitive systems with machine consciousness being the ultimate goal, cf., Holland (2003).

Nowadays, it is generally believed that in order to open the road towards higher brain functions we need automatic mechanisms that will augment the previously acquired semantic knowledge. These mechanisms often make use of internal world models. Presently, prevailing trends seem to prefer other than symbolic representation of the internal worlds, in most cases variants of neural nets. For an overview of the recent state-of-the-art and a discussion on internal world models, cf., Holland et al. (2003) or Cruse (2003).

In Holland et al. (2003) the authors argue in favor of an internal world model consisting of two separated, but interacting parts: the agent-model and the environment-model. Recently, within the theoretical computer science a similar model has also been used by Blum et al. (2005) in their quest for a formal definition of consciousness. In their work all the previously mentioned authors claim that a key to consciousness may be rooted in the formation and (co)operation of the two parts of their world models. Cruse (2003) arrives at a similar conclusion when considering an internal world model capturing the system's own body.

Our cognitive architecture makes use of two cooperating internal world models. The first model is a so-called mirror net which learns frequently occurring "perception-behavioral units". These units are represented by multimodal information which is a fusion of sensory and motor information pertinent to a single "unit" of a situation. The design of a mirror net, which is responsible for the agent's situatedness in its environment, has been inspired by the assumed properties of mirror neurons, cf., Rizzolatti et al. (1996) or Ramachandran (2000) and by the recent neurophysiological evidence (cf., Galese, 2007) that mirror neurons represent the cognitive mechanism for understanding actions, intentions and emotions which is invoked by sensory inputs. In some sense, the mirror net represents both the environment and the agent; it captures both the syntax and semantics of a correct behavior. In the corresponding multimodal information the world is represented by sensory inputs while the corresponding agent's action by motor instructions and agent's "feelings" by proprioceptive feedback from the agent's internal sensors. Thus, on one hand, the mirror net captures similar information like the assumed internal world model (in fact, a neural net) featuring agent's body in the Cruse's (2003) theory or the agent-model in the Holland and Goodman's paper (Holland et al., 2003). On the other hand, since there are also environmental elements represented by the sensory information

in the mirror net, in a certain fragmented way the mirror net also represents the environment (on a sub-symbolical level), like Holland and Goodman's environment-model (Holland et al., 2003).

The second part of our model is the agent's control unit. This unit receives multimodal information which is continuously delivered by the mirror net. The task of the control unit is to mine the ("semantic") knowledge from the flow of multimodal information. In the control unit the knowledge is represented by a (recurrent) network of concepts. The basic concepts (also called *embodied concepts* in the sequel) correspond to units of multimodal information. However, the control unit also automatically computes the derived concepts which do not correspond to any existing multimodal information. These derived concepts (also called *abstract concepts* hereafter) correspond to the knowledge abstracted from the basic concepts. The control unit discovers, by statistical rules, the frequently occurring patterns in the flow of basic concepts, forms more abstract concepts and learns their time and space contiguity. The underlying network of concepts enables learning various patterns of behavior. Based on the current situation the control unit then determines the next action of the agent. The control unit can be implemented by an artificial recurrent neural network. Obviously, the control unit captures the dynamic aspects of the agent's interaction with its environment and has no counterpart in either of the previously mentioned models by other authors.

The main contribution of our model is its relatively simple and coherent framework enabling a plausible explanation of computational mechanisms underlying phenomena similar to higher brain functions inclusively that of consciousness. In our model, machine consciousness is a final phase of a sequence of increasingly more involved system's abilities in an increasingly stimulating environment. The respective chain of abilities starts with the ability to learn by imitation, goes through body, gesture and articulated communication among conspecifics and proceeds further via speaking to oneself until thinking ability is reached. Eventually, the previous development leads to a state that an entity possesses an ability to comment (or think of), in an abstract higher level language, any internal or external event, any past, present or expected phenomenon ("to try on any 'story' for size", as Blum et al. [2005] have put it aptly), to simulate any observed action of another entity and to "replay" an action given its description in a high-level language. In our model, this state is considered to be a hallmark of consciousness. This also corresponds well to Minsky's (1995) remark that "consciousness is a big suitcase" carrying many mental abilities. The plausibility of our model is further supported, e.g., by the fact that is conformed with the seven principles for conscious embodied agents proposed recently by Sanz et al. (2007). Last but not least, there also is neurophysiological evidence that the mirror neurons, the integral part of our model, present the key for the development of higher cognitive functions (cf., Gallese et al., 2007).

The idea that the mirror neurons are at the heart of imitation learning ability and that they may play an important role in the development of the language has been around since the beginning of this century, cf., Arbib (2005), Hurford (2002), and Ramachandran (2000). One of the first computational models based on artificial mirror neurons has been described by the present author in (Wiedermann, 2003). In the present paper the idea of seeing mirror neurons as an internal, "syntactical" world model is further elaborated. Jointly with the internal semantic model both internal models represent a mechanism for automatic creation and utilization of semantic knowledge. Our results show how the cooperation of these two models solves the symbol grounding problem and give further algorithmic support to the intuition of the former researchers that suitable internal world models indeed form the basis for the evolution of higher mental functions, inclusively those invoking consciousness.

In fact, in recent years we have seen a number of proposals of cognitive systems architectures, cf., Anderson et al. (2004), Langley (2005), Shanahan (2005), Valiant (1994), or Wang (2009) to name a few of them. All these proposals have aimed if not towards implementation, then at least towards modeling and explanation of selected subsets of higher mental functions. Essentially, most of them were meant as proposals of experimental architectures with the goal to verify their viability in solving basic learning cognitive tasks, only seldom reaching the higher cognitive functions. Some of these models have been quite complex, inspired by the brain architecture (in some cases, only by an assumed one), often with "modules" responsible for realization of certain tasks (like "anticipation", "motivation", "planning", "action selection", etc.), and with only vague ideas about the corresponding algorithmic mechanisms. None of the lastly mentioned models includes the mirror neurons.

Our proposal differs from the previously mentioned works from both the methodological viewpoint and the viewpoint of its contents. From the methodological point of view, our modeling makes use of an approach used in software engineering in the design of large software systems. The resulting high-level functional system specifications are supported by the corresponding architecture of a cognitive system that is relatively simple (as compared with other approaches), concise and coherent; yet the specifications span the whole spectrum of cognitive abilities, building one upon the other, starting from imitation learning and ending with (artificial) consciousness. This gives our approach quite a unique place among the other models of cognitive agents described in the literature. Moreover, the basic features of our model, the design of its algorithmic mechanisms and their effect on the cognitive abilities of the model are underpinned by the recent accomplishments in neurobiology, cognitive psychology, language evolution theory, and other fields of cognitive science. In fact, our approach represents a method typical for cognitive informatics that studies the natural intelligence and internal information processing mechanisms of the brain, as well as the processes involved in perception and cognition (cf., Wang, 2002).

We start by sketching the architecture of our cognitive system and give an informal specification of its basic modules. This means that we define the type of data and data flow among the individual modules as well as the task of these modules in processing the data. Then we give plausible arguments why we believe that the resulting computational model will support the realization of processes which mimic higher cognitive tasks such as imitation learning and development of communication, language, thinking and consciousness. We also point to the corresponding neurophysiological evidence supporting our model.

The structure of the paper is as follows. First, the model is presented in more detail. Its functionality is then described leading, eventually, to the emergence of computational consciousness. A more detailed view of the development of mental abilities according to the model is given. Finally, in order to further stress the soundness of the model, the model is shown to correspond to the principles for consciousness recently formulated by Sanz et al. (2007).

Before continuing a word of caution is necessary: when speaking about cognitive functions and the respective algorithmic mechanisms, we always refer to our model which is inspired by our ideas how biological minds (could) work, though, but by no means it is intended as a realistic model of biological minds (although some parts of it might appear so).

The Model of a Cognitive Agent

The internal structure of our model is depicted in Figure 1. It consists of four main parts: there are sensorimotor units, the sensorimotor world model represented by a mirror net, the control unit, and the body. Arrows depict the data flow between these parts. Next, we specify the actions performed by the model's individual parts. All data transferred along the arrows are of digital nature.

The *sensorimotor units* receive so-called *motor instructions* from the control unit. These are not only instructions for locomotive organs of the agent, but also instructions for pointing the sensors in a certain direction, for changing their settings, etc. At the same time, these instructions flow into the mirror net. The sensorimotor units deliver two kinds of data back to the mirror net.

The first kind of data is *exteroceptory data* that deliver information from the sensory units scanning the agent's environment. In this case, the sensory units act as a transformer of registered physical inputs (electromagnetic waves, sounds, pressure, etc.) into the digital form. In general, this transformation cannot be described mathematically since it depends on the physical/technical characteristics of the sensory units. The second kind of data is *proprioceptory data* delivering information from the internal sensors placed within the sensorimotor units or within the agent's body. For instance, this can be information about the current settings of the units or current conditions of the unit.

The next part of the model is the *mirror net*. It is a network of artificial mirror neurons which act analogously to (our ideas on) real mirror neurons. In each unit of this net (which might consists of several neurons), the exteroceptory and proprioceptory data from sensorimotor units (denoted as 'perception' in Figure 1) meet with the motor instructions from the control unit and their conjunction—called 'units of S-M information' in Figure 1—is computed. This joint information is called *multimodal information*. The task of the mirror net is threefold:

Learning: the net learns frequently occurring multimodal information and stores its representation;

Figure 1. The structure of a cognitive agent

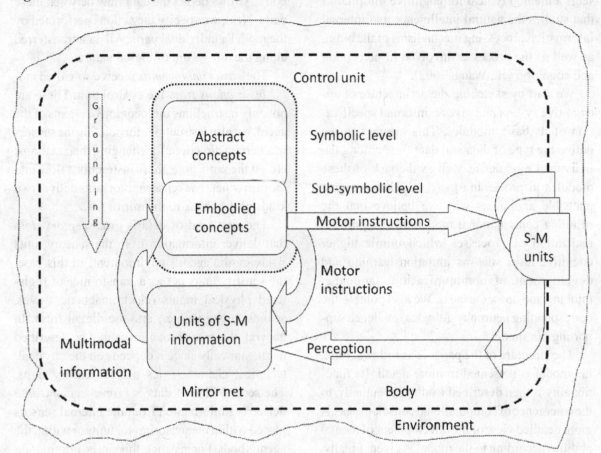

Identification: the net finds multimodal information already stored in the net which is "most similar" to the incoming information;

Associative retrieval: given only partial multimodal information in which the inputs from some sensorimotor units are missing, the net finds the entire multimodal informatik of which the partial information is available.

In order to work in this way, we must establish that there is only a finite amount of "important" multimodal information stored in the mirror net. This can be achieved, e.g., by parameterizing motor instructions by a finite set of values and preprocessing the perceptory data by extracting the key features from it. For such a purpose fuzzy techniques leading to a rough classification of

multimodal data into clusters of similar information can be used. The next requirement concerns the components of the multimodal information. In order that the associative recall can work well, the entire multimodal information must be uniquely determined by any of its significant components. For reasons that will be explained in the next section—namely in order the thinking mechanism to work—we assume that if there is a motor component in multimodal information, then this component alone determines the rest of multimodal information.

Each part of the mirror net specializes in learning and recognizing specific multimodal information corresponding to one "sensory-behavioral unit". Learning is done perpetually when complete multimodal information appears at the input to the mirror net. Such circumstance is called *standard learning mode.* Learning proceeds by Hebbian principles, i.e., by strengthening the weights of neurons representing the respective multimodal information each time when it is recognized.

Thus, in any case, irrespectively whether all parts or only a (significant) part of the multimodal information enters the net, the net outputs complete multimodal information which proceeds into the control unit. In the context of the control unit, the representations of multimodal information are called the *concepts.* The task of the control unit is, given the current multimodal information represented by the active concepts plus the incoming stream from the mirror net, to produce a new set of active concepts. The motor part of multimodal information corresponding to these concepts is sent both to the sensorimotor units and to the mirror net. Clearly, the control unit determines the next action of an agent.

Within the control unit there are so-called *embodied concepts* corresponding to each occurrence of multimodal information in the mirror net. Moreover, new, so-called *abstract concepts* are formed from the existing (mainly embodied) concepts within the control unit. Associations of various strengths connect the concepts within it. The concepts and the associations among them are all stored in the control unit and form the agent's memory. The rules of forming new concepts and strengthening the associations among them are based on the following principles; the first three of them have been already identified by the 18th century Scottish philosopher D. Hume (2003):

Contiguity in space: two concepts get associated (or the respective association gets strengthened) if they frequently occur simultaneously; also, a new koncept corresponding to the union of the two concepts gets formed;

Contiguity in time: two concepts get associated (or the respective association gets strengthened) if they frequently occur one after the other;

Similarity: a concept gets associated with another concept if the former is similar to the latter and vice versa; the notion of similarity must be appropriately defined (e.g., by requiring a sufficient overlap in multimodal information);

Abstraction: the common part of two "sufficiently" similar concepts forms an abstraction of the two; the respective "abstract" concept is added to the concepts represented in the control unit.

The control unit should work according to the following rules. At each time, some concepts in it should be in active state. These concepts represent the current *"mental state"* of the agent. When new multimodal information enters the control unit it activates a new set of concepts. Based on the current mental state and the set of newly activated concepts a new set of concepts is activated. This set represents the new mental state of the agent and determines the next motor action of the unit.

Note that the new mental state is computed from an old one and from the new input. This mechanism reminds much the control mechanism in the finite automata. The idea is that the new mental state should be computable via associations stored among the concepts. In detail, the currently and newly activated concepts jointly excite, via the associations, a set of passive concepts. This excitation strengthens all the respective associations by a little amount. At the same time, small amount weakens the remaining associations. This models the process of forgetting. From among the set of all excited concepts, the set of the most excited concepts gets activated and the previously active concepts are deactivated. The set of currently active concepts is also strengthened. This set then represents the current mental state. The set of currently active concepts can be seen as the *short-term (operational) memory* of the agent. The set of all concepts with all settings of associations and weights can be seen as a *long-term memory* of the agent. Obviously, the control unit can also be implemented by an artificial neural net.

Based on the before mentioned principles the control unit is capable of solving simple cognitive tasks: learning *simultaneous occurrence* of concepts (by contiguity in space), their sequence, so-called *simple conditioning* (by contiguity in time), *similarity based behavior* and computing their *abstractions*. In fact, these are the unit's basic operations. The mechanism is also capable to realize *Pavlovian conditioning* (cf., Valiant, 1974, p. 217), in which the control unit can be conditioned to produce a response to an apparently unrelated stimulus.

If one wants to go farther in the realization of the cognitive tasks, one should consider special concepts called *affects*. The affects come in two forms: positive and negative ones. The basic affects are activated directly from the sensors. The ones corresponding to the positive feelings are positive whereas the ones corresponding to the negative feelings are negative. The associations can also arise among affects and concepts. The role of the affects is to modulate the excitation mechanism. With the help of affects, one can simulate the reinforcement learning (also called operant conditioning) and the delayed reinforcement learning. Pavlovian conditioning, reinforcement learning and delayed reinforcement learning seems to be a minimal test, which a cognitive system aspiring to produce a non-trivial behavior should pass.

In a stimulating environment during an agent's interaction with its environment concepts within the control unit start to self–organize, via property of similarity, into *clusters* whose centers are formed by abstract concepts. Moreover, by properties of time contiguity, chains of concepts, called *habits*, linked by associations start to emerge. The habits correspond to often performed activities. The behavior of agents governed by habits starts to prevail. In most cases such a behavior unfolds effortlessly. Only at the "crossings" of some habits an additional multimodal information from the mirror net (in an on–line or off–line mode—see the next section) is required directing the subsequent behavior. For more details concerning the work and cognitive abilities of the control unit, see the author's earlier paper (Wiedermann, 1998) (and the references mentioned therein) where the control unit under the name "cogitoid" has been described.

The last component of our model is its body. Its purpose is to support the agent's sensorimotor units and to enclose all its parts into one protective envelope.

Now let us return to the question of internal models. Obviously, the mirror net can be seen as a specific kind of a static world model. In this model the world is represented in the way as it is cognised by an agent's sensory and motor actions, i.e., by an agent's interaction with its environment. It can be termed as a *sensorimotor* model describing the "syntax" of the world. In the mirror net, the combinations of the exteroceptory and proprioceptory inputs jointly with motor actions fitting together, which "make sense", are stored. Note that since the proprioceptory information is always a part of multimodal information, also elements of an agent's own model are in fact available in the mirror net.

On the other hand, the control unit is a specific model of the world capturing the "semantics" of the world. In this model the relations among concepts are stored which, obviously, correspond to real relations among real objects and phenomena observed or generated by the agent during its existence. Similar relations are also maintained among the representations of these objects and phenomena. All this information represents a kind of a dynamic internal world model. One can also see this model as a depository of the "patterns of behavior which make sense in a given situation."

In the next section we describe how the interaction of both models leads to a more complex behavior.

Towards Higher Level Cognitive Functions *B*

First we describe the mechanism of imitation learning which is a starting point for higher mental abilities, cf., Arbib (2005), Hurford (2002). Imagine the following situation: agent *A* observes agent *B* performing a certain well distinguishable task. If *A* has in its repository of behavioral units multimodal information, which matches well the situation mediated by its sensors (which, by itself, is a difficult robotic task), then *A*'s mirror net will identify the entire corresponding multimodal information (by virtue of associativity). At the same time, it will complement it by the flag saying *"this is not my own experience"* (because the proprioceptory part of information must have been filled in when completing the entire multimodal information) and deliver it to the central unit where it will be processed adequately. Thus, *A* has information to its disposal what *B* is about to do, and hence, it can forecast the future actions of *B*. "Forecasting" is done by following the associations in the control unit starting in the current mental state. Agent *A* can even reconstruct the "feelings" of *B* (via affects) since they are parts of the retrieved multimodal information. This might be called *empathy* in our model. Moreover, if we endow our agent by the ability to memorize short recent sequences of its mental states, than *A* can repeat the observed actions of *B*. This, of course, is called *imitation*.

The same mechanism helps to form a more detailed *model of the self*. Namely, observing the activities of a similar agent from a distance helps the observer to "fill in" the gaps in its own dynamic internal world model (i.e., in the control unit), since from the beginning an observer only knows "what it feels like" if it perceives its own part of the body while doing the actions at hand. At this stage, we are close to *primitive communication* done with the help of *gestures*. Indicating some action via a characteristic gesture, an agent "broadcasts" visual information that is completed by the observer's associative memory mechanism to the complete multimodal information. That is, with the help of a single gesture complex information can be mediated. A gesture acts like an element of a higher-level (proto) language. By the way, here *computational emotions* can enter

the game as a component of the communication. Their purpose is to modulate the agent's behavior. Of course, for such a purpose the agents must be appropriately equipped (e.g., by specific mimics, possibility of color changes, etc.). Once we have articulating agents, it is possible to complement and subsequently even substitute gestures by *articulated sounds*. It is the birth of a spoken language. At about this time the process of a stratification of abstract concepts from the embodied ones begins thanks to the abstraction potential of the control unit (cf. the rules of forming new concepts in the control unit). Namely, the agents "understand" their gestures (language), defined in terms of abstract concepts, via empathy in terms of their embodiment or grounding, in the same sensorimotorics and proprioception (i.e., in the same embodied concepts) (Feldman, 2006; Harnad, 1990), and in a more involved case, in the same patterns of behavior (habits). Without having a body an agent could not understand its communication (Pfeifer et al., 2006).

Returning to the previously mentioned process of concept stratification, the respective two classes of concepts can be seen as concepts on a symbolic and sub–symbolic level, respectively. This view offers an answer to an often mentioned problem, namely whether the mind works with the former or the latter class of concepts. Our model works with both classes of concepts by continuously passing from one class to the other class. The sub-symbolic level is necessary for understanding certain abstract concepts, especially those related to perception or to sensorimotor activities. The language is in fact a superstructure over the embodied concepts. There is one more aspect to be mentioned here: the abstract concepts at the symbolic level need not be grounded directly in the embodied concepts, at a sub-symbolic level. Rather, they can be "*tethered*" (this term has been coined in (Sloman, 2007) to other abstract concepts to which they are related by associations arising in the control unit. The network of certain abstract concepts can thus represent a "theory" within which an agent can "think" (see in the sequel) or act. In the case of artificial agents such a net can be prepared in the control unit prior to an agent's first activation. That is, the respective behavior need not be learned from scratch by the agent, it can be, so to speak, "innate". This mechanism would simulate the result of a development that in living creatures has been reached by evolution. For similar ideas, cf., Sloman (2007).

The transition from gestures or body language to articulation does not only mean that gestures get associated with the respective sounds but, above all, with the movements of speaking organs. In the further development this facilitates a still "speaking to oneself" and later on, the transition towards thinking (see in the sequel).

The structure and functionality of the control unit and the mirror net and their cooperation realize, in fact, the solution to the symbol grounding problem in a similar spirit as described in Steels et al. (2007). The above described sketch of higher cognitive learning is also in a good correspondence with the theory of so-called intentional attunement theory claiming that the shared neural activation pattern and the accompanying embodied simulation constitute a fundamental biological basis for understanding another's mind (Galese et al., 2007).

Having communication ability, an agent is close to thinking. In our model, *thinking means communication with oneself*, similarly as in cf., Dennett (1991). By communicating with oneself, an agent triggers the mechanism of discriminating between the external stimuli (I listen what I am talking) and the internal ones. This mechanism may be termed as *self-awareness* in our model. By a small modification (from the viewpoint of the agent's designer), one can achieve that the still self-communication can be arranged without the involvement of speaking organs at all. In this case, the respective instructions will not reach these organs; the instructions will merely proceed to the mirror net (see Figure 1). (Note that some people still move their speaking organs while intensively thinking.) Here they will invoke the

same multimodal information as in the case when an agent directly hears the spoken language or perceives its gestures via proprioception (here we make use of our assumption that a motor part of multimodal information is sufficient to determine its rest). Obviously, in the thinking mode an agent "switches off" any interaction with the external world (i.e., both perception and motor actions). Thus, in Figure 1 do the dark parts of the schema depict an agent in a *thinking mode;* this is captured by the cycle from the control unit to the mirror net and back to the control unit. In such a case, from the viewpoint of its internal mechanisms an agent operates as in the case of standard learning mode, i.e., when it receives the "real" perceptory information and executes all motor instructions. In the thinking mode, the same processes go on, but this time they are based on the virtual, rather than real, information mediated by the mirror net. One can say that in the thinking mode an agent works off-line, while in the standard mode it works on-line. Note that once an agent has the power of shutting itself of from the external world in the thinking mode, then this agent in fact distinguishes between a thought and reality and this is considered to be the hallmark of the consciousness (Smee, 1849).

In our model, we will informally define consciousness much in the spirit of Minsky's idea (Minsky, 1998) that *"consciousness is a big suitcase",* carrying many different mental abilities. In fact, in our case we should rather speak about quasi-consciousness, or artificial or computational consciousness, but for brevity we shall use the world "consciousness". A prologue to consciousness is communication and thinking. The following informal definition of consciousness assumes that the agents are able to communicate in a higher-level language. A *higher-level language* is an abstract language in which a relatively complex action (corresponding to a sequence of mental states) or an abstract concept is substituted by a word expression or a gesture. A language level is the higher the richer the language is, i.e., the greater and more abstract is a set of things about which one can communicate. The agents can be thought of as being conscious, as long as their language ability has reached such a level that they are able to fable on a given theme (note the similarity with [Blum et al.05]). More precisely, the conscious agents are able:

- To speak about, think of, and explain, from the first and the third person viewpoint, their past, present and future experience, feelings, intentions and observed objects, actions, and phenomena;
- To imitate the observed (or more generally: perceived, by whatever senses) activities of other agents, to describe them verbally, and vice versa, to perform activities given their description in a higher level language;
- Extend their higher level language by new words or to learn a new language.

Note that such a state of matters cannot be achieved without agents having an internal world model to their disposal along with the knowledge of the world's functioning and that of their own functioning within this world; to that end the agents must be constructed so that they can learn. A prerequisite for consciousness to emerge is a social interaction among agents in a higher-level language with the same or similar semantics. Obviously, consciousness is not a property, which an entity does possess, or not. Rather, it is a continuous quality which ranges from rudimentary forms towards higher ones.

An agent can posses this quality in a various degree. For instance, from the previous requirements it follows that a conscious agent should recognize itself in a mirror. A more conscious agent should be able to tell apart lies from truth. For instance, it can understand fairy tales and should „know" that these are fanciful stories. An even more conscious agent should be able to lie (not merely by the help of, e.g., mimic coloring, but in a higher language) and should still be aware of its lying.

And how do we know that a conscious agent "understands" its actions and its world? Well—we simply ask it: the ability to answer such questions is the very idea of our approach to consciousness.

The above described notion of consciousness can be seen as a test to be applied by an entity to another entity in order to determine whether the other entity is conscious according to that definition. In such a case also men proceed in accordance with such a definition. The difference with the Turing test (Turing, 1950) is that while the classical Turing test calls for judging the communication skills of an unseen entity merely by exchanging messages with it, on our case we test the cognitive abilities and imitating skills of an embodied observable entity with which we can interact in whatever reasonable way. In this respect our test is similar to the so-called total Turing test by Harnad (1991) which also involves successful performance of both linguistic and robotic behavior. However, comparing our test with the total Turing test is difficult since the latter is defined in more general terms than the ours.

As a final remark, it is interesting to observe how our model deals with so-called *symbol detachment problem* investigated in Pezzuolo et al. (2007). This is a problem of how and why do the situated agents develop representations that are *detached* from their current sensorimotor interaction, but nevertheless preserve grounding and aboutness. Our model of an evolutionary path leading from the imitation learning capabilities through thinking up to the born of consciousness offers a plausible explanation of the mechanisms and representations underlying the symbol detachment problem (cf., the emergence of the abstract concepts from the embodied concepts in the control unit) and stresses their role for the development of complex cognitive capabilities.

A Sketch of an Evolutionary Development of the Agent's Mind

Now we will summarize in a concise manner the previous ideas leading to the evolution of higher cognitive abilities within an intelligent agent according to our model. Such an evolution can be seen from two different viewpoints. First, it can be seen as a process of a development of an agent (e.g., of a human child) already possessing the respective mechanisms, in the course of agent's growing up and its education. Second, it can be seen as a stepwise 'upgrading' process over an evolutionary sequence of agents, each one of them possessing more advanced mechanisms and embodiments for managing more demanding cognitive skills than those obeyed by its predecessors.

We will describe a hypothetical evolutionary development of a cognitive agent culminating in formation of its control abilities resembling the mind. Doing so it is natural to assume a development passing through a number of evolutionary stages in which mechanisms taking care of the agents' activities aiming at its survival in a corresponding ecological niche will be formed. Clearly, an agents' physical development should go hand in hand with its mental development and both developments should correspond to possible changes in the agent's living environment. Hence both developments must be in *ecological balance*: it does not make sense for an agent to have sensorimotor units delivering more information than its brain can handle, or vice versa, to have a more efficient brain than the one that is sufficient to process the data delivered by the agents' sensorimotor units (cf., Pfeifer, 1999).

The basic assumption of cognition (cf., Harnad, 1990) is an agent's grounding in its environment. This means that an agent must have information available how to handle the environment by means of its actions; this information is obtained via its sensorimotor units. Technically, this information is represented as multimodal information stored in the agent's mirror neural net. Grounding thus takes care about agent's elementary understanding the world. Note that at the level of elementary actions an agent cannot do anything but meaningful actions, because, thanks to the control unit mechanism of concepts' and excitations' strengthening, other actions than the purposeful ones are not

acquired by the agent and therefore are not a part of its repertoire.

For its further development an agent needs a faculty of imitation learning described in the beginning of the previous section. Obviously, this developmental stage differs from the previous one since there are creatures not possessing even rudimentary imitation abilities (e.g., consider creatures lacking visual organs which seem to be necessary in order to mirror the movements of other creatures). The ability of mirroring leads to the emergence of the self-concept. This concept is necessary in order to distinguish between the actions perceived by the agent's internal and external sensors on its own body and the actions of other agents, and also to a development of a rudimentary empathy, as explained in Section 3.

What develops next is the ability to learn sequences of actions, still with the help of imitation. It is the control unit (Figure 1) and its capability to perform operations over the concepts that takes care of these and other abilities, such as learning by analogy, Pavlovian reflexes, operant conditioning, emotion processing, etc. Note that the control unit is not directly connected to any peripheral input device – in fact the control unit is a classical information processing device that has been considered in the computational paradigm of the classical AI. The input into a control unit is formed by a stream of preprocessed, corrected or completed multimodal information streaming from a mirror neural net. This data reflects the outer world and causes that the control unit is specialized solely to processing of situated data. Technically, what thea control unit does is computing the ''next move" (or transition) function, given the current state of mind and incoming multimodal information. As stressed in Section 2, the control unit is designed so as to be able to learn from experience, in various modes (in a supervised or unsupervised mode, by trial and error, positive or negative reinforcement, etc.) and their combinations. In its most developed form a control unit operates with the help of thinking – by ``mentally" simulating possible scenarios of future situation development based on experience. This simulation consists of steps, each step performing one transition which in our model is realized as one circulation of multimodal information between the mirror net and the control unit.

Going hand in hand with the evolution of learning mechanisms is the development of communication abilities and empathy. Initially, communication is very simple, based on visual signaling via gestures, in some cases perhaps based on olfactory signals and is related to specific proprioceptory signals (feelings, emotion?) and a specific communication context. The signaling repertoire gradually builds up and new communication channels, especially the acoustic ones, enter the game. By this the limbs used for gestures are freed again to other bodily activities. A multimodal combination of all signals is always built with the key role played by the motor activities. The importance of visual communication decays and the main role is taken over by a vocal communication. The role of motor activities shifts from the gesture and body language towards the organs of speech (cf., Corballis, 2002). The vocabulary of notions keeps developing along with their grounding in the sensorimotor multimodal information. The notions (concepts) and emotions can also be activated acoustically, by hearing the corresponding word(s), via associative abilities of the mirror net. It could be the case that also proprioception is caused by word activation and that this proprioception gets associated with further multimodal information related to the words.

The spoken language enables a further discrimination of objects, a further structuring of the world since an agent distinguishes more object categories. It is as though the perception organs started to deliver more distinguishable information then before making use of the same channels. What follows is a further evolution of the brain that has to cope with this blow up of information. Agents are now able to communicate among themselves and also one with itself by speaking to oneself. An agent speaking to itself starts to ``think loudly".

In the further evolution the vocalization accompanying thinking is slowly losing its importance, the movements of the speech organs decay until only motor signals (especially those for the speech organs) prevail that, however, are no longer realized but are still associated with perceptive and proprioceptive information in which the motoric has been grounded. From the viewpoint of its perception an agent finds itself in a virtual environment mediated this time not by its senses but by its completion mechanism (which was formed by the agents' senses in the standard mode). The agent has to its disposal information on its virtual situatedness and then it can happen that the agent becomes a subject of its own observation: the agent is informed about its being in a thinking mode. Could it be the case that the respective proprioceptive information could give rise to the agent's feeling of consciousness?

The evolution of an agent's mental abilities sketched above roughly corresponds to similar ideas of other authors, especially those of philosophers of mind (cf., Dennett, 1991; Minsky, 1998). The difference is that in our case our ideas are supported by concrete mechanisms that are taking care of individual evolutionary stages of the mental development of cognitive agents within our model.

An evolutionary development of an agent's mental abilities is depicted in Figure 2. Note the prominent role of mirror neurons in the above schema—starting with the second item it is difficult to see how to cope with the corresponding cognitive tasks without having the mirror neurons and, indeed, the internal world model incorporated in the agent's model.

To close this section few words on a possible agents' realization are in order. Except of very trivial cases, aiming at modeling of simple organisms such as bacteria, a realization of a cognitive agent with rich cognitive abilities would require an extensive use of the most advanced computing

Figure 2. A sketch of the evolutionary development of mental abilities of an agent

- Grounding of elementary actions in sensory-motor coordination
- Formation of the ``self'' concept, imitation of elementary actions
- Imitation of sequences of actions with the help of learning
- Communication via gestures, sign language, ``mind reading'' (i.e., intention discovering by observation), empathy
- Adding vocalization to gestures and its association with gesture motor system instructions, later with speech organs instructions
- Development of the ``vocabulary of understanding'' belonging to gestures and words and a development of the respective access mechanism by means of words; development of the corresponding proprioception
- Keeping of evolutionary balance between the increase of a number of word stimuli and the size of the brain
- Direct concept activation via words, development of abstract concepts
- The dawn of thinking: starting with a laud speaking to oneself, later gradually replacing speaking by mere movements of speech organs; when thinking the vocalization is subsequently also losing its merit; speech instructions are associated directly with the "meaning" of words
- Subjective experience as a proprioception of abstract concept activation
- Thinking as virtually situated damped sensory-motor actions
- Emergence of mental activities attributed to consciousness

technologies. As we have seen we have been able to infer a rough structure of an agent's architecture. That is, we were able to approximately specify individual components of an agent and their functionality that would be necessary in order to achieve the required behavior. We have also arrived at certain ideas concerning the development of the underlying mechanisms. From these considerations it appears that, unfortunately, there is no other way of constructing (read: developing) real physical agents than that via artificial evolution. The problem with this approach seems to be that a computational evolution alone would not suffice for the task. This is because from a modeling point of view our model of a cognitive agent captures two different tasks. The first task, done by the agent's computational units, is a computational task of internal mediation between the agent's perceptive and motor components. The second task, performed by the sensorimotor units, is realization of mappings from the real world to their internal representations. While it is relatively easy to model an evolution of an agent's finite control, it is probably very difficult to computationally model the evolution of sensorimotor units which are, in fact, pieces of dedicated, specialized hardware translating (the perception of) the real world into a digital or analog form.. Thus, what one would need are evolvable sensorimoter units (or, putting it in terms of the embodied cognition, an evolvable embodiment) which so far seems to be beyond our modeling abilities.

Nevertheless, there is one interesting case where we could avoid the necessity of a hardware evolution in hoping for a fully computational evolution of the respective agents: it is the case of artificial agents living in artificial formal worlds. This seems to be the field in which we could expect a tremendous development in the near future.

ADDRESSING THE PRINCIPLES FOR CONSCIOUSNESS

In their recent paper Sanz et al. (2007) have formulated seven general principles that a complex cognitive system incorporating consciousness abilities has to obey. In what follows we will briefly analyze our model in the context of these principles.

Principle 1. *(Model based cognition). A system is said to be cognitive if it exploits models of other systems in their interaction with them.*

Obviously, this also is the case of our model which makes use of the internal world models.

Principle 2. *(Model isomorphism). An embodied, situated cognitive system is as good as its internalized models are.*

No doubt that our model is embodied and situated. Moreover, it possesses mechanisms that build and continuously update its internal world models. These mechanisms maintain the mappings from/to reality to/from the world models and the quality of these mappings and their scope determines the efficiency of the respective agent's behavior.

Principle 3. *(Anticipatory Behavior). Except in degenerate cases, maximal timely performance can only be achieved using predictive models.*

The model's control unit also behaves as a predictive unit. This is due to the mechanism of concept formation and concept chaining. In fact, the concepts are chained by links whose emergence and strength depends on the past experience. These links are exploited to predict a most probable

course of the actions in the given situation, as perceived by the agent, and to guide its reactions.

Principle 4. *(Unified Cognitive Action Generation). Generating action based on an unified model of task, environment and self is the way for performance maximization.*

The two complementary internal world models and their coordinated actions represent a unified model of task, environment and the self. Note that the last three items—task, environment and the self—are unified, indeed, in the sense that none of these items can be singled out of the agent's structure.

Principle 5. *(Model-driven Perception). Perception is the continuous update of the integrated models used by the agent in u model-based cognitive control architecture by means of real-time sensorial information.*

As seen from the description of our model's functionality in Section 2, the previous principle is but an alternative, concise way to capture the actions of our model.

Principle 6. *(System Awareness). A system is aware if it is continuously perceiving and generating meaning from the continuously update models.*

Our model continuously processes both its external and internal sensory inputs and updates the respective parts of its internal models introducing thus the respective semantic knowledge into its structures. This can also be seen as a "meaning generation" from the sensory flow.

Principle 7. *(System Self-awareness/Consciousness). A system is conscious if it is continuously generating meanings from continuously updated self-models in a model-bases control architecture.*

Obviously, in our model both internal world models (which, unavoidably, also include the self—cf., Principle 4) are continuously updated and (hence) continuously generate meanings creating thus the basis of model's self-awareness and consciousness (cf. Section 3).

In the spirit of our methodological approach (viz. specification of complex software systems) mentioned in the Introduction the seven principles for consciousness can naturally be seen as a still higher specification of a conscious cognitive system. In this framework, our model's subsidiarity to the seven principles stated above gives additional evidence on the soundness of our model. Note that in the same time our model refers to algorithmic mechanisms that can support Sanz's et al. (2007) principles for consciousness. In this sense our model can also be seen as a further elaboration of the respective principles towards their computational realization.

CONCLUSION

In our quest for an algorithmic model of an embodied agent we have reached more than a mere definition of computational consciousness. We have brought arguments that a cognitive agent, designed in accordance with the proposed architecture, in principle could be conscious according to our informal definition of consciousness. From the functional and structural viewpoint, such an agent fulfills all assumptions needed for consciousness (in our sense) to emerge. It is a matter of an agent's proper embodiment, of appropriate technical parameters (memory capacity, operational speed, properties of sensorimotor units, etc.) of its modules, and of its suitable "education", whether in the agent consciousness will develop or not. The situation here is somewhat analogical to that in computing: any properly designed computer (a Turing machine, or a computer obeying von Neumann architecture, say) is, in principle, a universal computer, but in order to do useful

things it must be properly engineered and properly programmed. The same holds for our model with respect to thinking and consciousness. A similar idea that "it is only through an assessment and analysis of the mechanism of the organism that we can conclude whether such mechanism can support consciousness or not within that organism" has been mentioned, e.g., in Aleksander et al. (2003), but the respective mechanism has not been indicated. We believe that by our proposal we have made the first steps towards determining cognitive potential of a system not by testing the respective device but by inspecting its architecture.

In its entirety, our model offers a coherent high–level specification of the architecture—a generic architecture—of an embodied cognitive agent. It is well suited for explanatory purposes as well as the first non-trivial approximation of architecture of a cognitive system supporting high-level cognitive functions. Only the future will show to what extend this model can serve as a basis for the design and realization of artificial cognitive agents.

ACKNOWLEDGMENT

This research was partially supported by grant No. 1ET100300517 and the institutional research plan AV0Z10300504.

REFERENCES

Aleksander, I., & Dummall, B. (2003). Axioms and Tests for the Presence of Minimal Consciousness in Agents. *Journal of Consciousness Studies*, *10*(4-5).

Anderson, M., Bothell, M., Byrne, D., Douglass, S., Lebiere, C., & Qin, Y. (2004). An integrated theory of the mind. *Psychological Review*, *111*(4), 1036–1060. doi:10.1037/0033-295X.111.4.1036

Arbib, M. A. (2005). The Mirror System Hypothesis: How did protolanguage evolve? In Tallerman, M. (Ed.), *Language Origins: Perspectives on Evolution*. Oxford, UK: Oxford University Press.

Blum, M., Williams, R., Juba, B., & Humphrey, M. (2005, June). Toward a High-level Definition of Consciousness. In *Proceedings of the Annual IEEE Computational Complexity Conference*, San Jose, CA.

Brooks, R. A. (1991). Intelligence without reason. In *Proceedings of the 12th Intl. Conference on Artificial Intelligence (IJCAI-91)*.

Corballis, M. C. (2002). *From Hand to Mouth: the origins of language*. Princeton, NJ: Princeton University Press.

Cruse, H. (2003). The evolution of cognition—a hypothesis. *Cognitive Science, 27*(1).

Dennett, D. (1991). *Consciousness Explained*. New York: The Penguin Press.

Feldman, J. (2006). *From Molecule to Metaphor*. Cambridge, MA: MIT Press.

Gallese, V., Eagle, M. E., & Migone, P. (2007). Intentional attunement: mirror neurons and the neural underpinnings of interpersonal relations. *Journal of the American Psychoanalytic Association, 55*, 131–176.

Harnad, S. (1990). The Symbol Grounding Problem. *Physica D. Nonlinear Phenomena, 42*, 335–346. doi:10.1016/0167-2789(90)90087-6

Harnad, S. (1991). Other bodies, other minds: a machine incarnation of an old philosophical problem. *Minds and Machines*, (1): 43–54.

Holland, O. (Ed.). (2003)...*Journal of Consciousness Studies, 10*(4-5).

Holland, O., & Goodman, R. (2003). Robots With Internal Models: A Route to Machine Consciousness? *Journal of Consciousness Studies, 10*(4-5).

Hume, D. (1975). Enquiry Concerning Human Understanding. In L. A. Selby-Bigge (Ed.), *Enquiries concerning Human Understanding and concerning the Principles of Morals* (3rd ed., revised by P. H. Nidditch). Oxford, UK: Clarendon Press.

Hurford, J. R. (2002). Language beyond our grasp: what mirror neurons can, and cannot, do for language evolution . In Kimbrough, O., Griebel, U., & Plunkett, K. (Eds.), *The Evolution of Communication systems: A Comparative Approach*. Cambridge, MA: MIT Press.

Langley, P. (2005). An adaptive architecture for physical agents. In *Proceedings of the 2005 IEEE/WIC/ACM International Conference on Intelligent Agent Technology*, Compiegne, France (pp. 18-25). Washington, DC: IEEE.

Minsky, M. (1998). Consciousness is a big suitcase. *EDGE*. Retrieved from http://www.edge.org/3rd/culture/minsky/minsky/p2.html

Pezzulo, G., & Castelfranchi, C. (2007). The symbol detachment problem. *Cognitive Processing, 8*, 115–131. doi:10.1007/s10339-007-0164-0

Pfeifer, R., & Bongard, J. (2006). *How the body shapes the way we think: a new view of intelligence*. Cambridge, MA: MIT Press.

Pfeifer, R., & Scheier, C. (1999). *Understanding Intelligence*. Cambridge, MA: MIT Press.

Ramachandran, V. S. (2000). Mirror neurons and imitation as the driving force behind "the great leap forward" in human evolution. *EDGE: The third culture*. Retrieved from http://www.edge.org/3rd_culture/ramachandran/ ramachandran_p1.html

Rizzolatti, G., Fadiga, L., Gallese, V., & Fogassi, I. (1996). Premotor cortex and the recognition of motor actions. *Brain Research. Cognitive Brain Research, 3*, 131–141. doi:10.1016/0926-6410(95)00038-0

Sanz, R., López, I., Rodriguez, M., & Hernández, C. (2007). Principles for consciousness in integrated cognitive control. *Neural Networks, 20*, 938–946. doi:10.1016/j.neunet.2007.09.012

Searle, J. R. (1980). Minds, brains, and programs. *The Behavioral and Brain Sciences, 3*(3), 169–225. doi:10.1017/S0140525X00005756

Shanahan, M. P. (2005). Consciousness, emotion, and imagination: a brain-inspired architecture for cognitive robotics. In *Proceedings AISB 2005 Symposium on Next Generation Approaches to Machine Consciousness* (pp. 26-35).

Sloman, A. (2007). *Why symbol-grounding is both impossible and unnecessary, and why theory-tethering is more powerful anyway.* Retrieved from http://www.cs.bham.ac.uk/research/projects/cogaff/talks/models.pdf

Smee, A. (1849). *Principles of the Human Mind Deduced from Physical Laws.*

Steels, L., Loetzsch, M., & Spranger, M. S. (2007). *Semiotic dynamics solves the symbol grounding problem.* Retrieved from http://hdl.nature.com/10101/npre.2007.1234.1

Turing, A. (1950). Computing Machinery and Intelligence. *Mind, 9*(236), 433–460. doi:10.1093/mind/LIX.236.433

Valiant, L. G. (1994). *Circuits of the Mind.* New York: Oxford University Press.

Wang, Y. (2002). On cognitive informatics. In *Proceedings of the First IEEE International Conference on Cognitive Informatics (ICCI'02)* (pp. 34-42).

Wang, Y. (2009). A cognitive informatics reference model of autonomous agent systems. *International Journal of Cognitive Informatics and Natural Intelligence, 3*(1), 1–16.

Wiedermann, J. (1998). Towards Algorithmic Explanation of Mind Evolution and Functioning (Invited Talk). In L. Brim, J. Gruska, & J. Zlatuška (Eds.), *Proceedings of the 23rd International Symposium on Mathematical Foundations of Computer Science (MFCS'98)* (LNCS 1450). Berlin: Springer Verlag.

Wiedermann, J. (2003). Mirror Neurons, Embodied Cognitive Agents and Imitation Learning. In *Computing and Informatics, 22*(6).

This work was previously published in International Journal of Software Science and Computational Intelligence, Volume 2, Issue 3, edited by Yingxu Wang, pp. 62-78, copyright 2010 by IGI Publishing (an imprint of IGI Global).

Section 2
Cognitive Computing

Chapter 6
Cognitive Memory:
Human Like Memory

Bernard Widrow
Stanford University, USA

Juan Carlos Aragon
Stanford University, USA

ABSTRACT

Taking inspiration from life experience, the authors have devised a new form of computer memory. Certain conjectures about human memory are keys to the central idea. This paper presents a design of a practical and useful "cognitive" memory system in which the new memory does not function like a computer memory where specific data is stored in specific numbered registers; retrieval is done by reading the contents of the specified memory register, or done by matching key words as with a document search. Incoming sensory data would be stored at the next available empty memory location and could be stored redundantly at several empty locations. The stored sensory data would neither have key words nor would it be located in known or specified memory locations. Retrieval would be initiated by a prompt signal from a current set of sensory inputs or patterns. The search would be done by a retrieval system that makes use of auto-associative artificial neural networks. In this paper, the authors present a practical application of this cognitive memory system to human facial recognition.

INTRODUCTION

Pattern recognition remains an elusive art, even after decades of work by thousands of people in the field worldwide. Some progress has been made. You can now phone an airline company, talk to

DOI: 10.4018/978-1-4666-0264-9.ch006

a computer, and make a flight reservation. There are other examples of practical applications of current methodology, but they all exhibit far from human-like capability. What is it about humans and animals that give them such an amazing ability to recognize objects and patterns? Why after all these years are we not able to approximate animal capability for pattern recognition by artificial means? Is there something magical or supernatural about humans and animals? Or are they simply machines of great complexity? What is it?

We believe that humans and animals are superbly capable complex machines, not possessing supernatural powers. Believing that, we try to understand the mechanism, the action that takes place when we are seeing and hearing, and in particular, how we recognize patterns. Fundamentally, human and animal pattern recognition involves matching an unknown incoming pattern with a pattern seen before and currently stored in memory. Not everyone will accept this, but this is what we believe.

During a visit when an interesting subject is being discussed, the "mental tape recorder" is recording in memory the sights, sounds, etc. of the visit. In a half hour of discussion, perhaps 100,000 images of the visitor's face are recorded. These images are retinal views that capture the visitor's face with different translations, rotations, light levels, perspectives, etc. These images are stored permanently in memory, wherever there is an empty place. Unlike a digital computer with numbered memory registers where data storage locations are program controlled, and data is retrieved when needed by calling for it by register number, human memory has no numbered registers. Data is stored in human memory wherever there is an empty place and once stored, the memory has no idea where the data has been stored.

We contemplate a memory of enormous, almost unbelievable capacity, enough to hold many lifetimes of stored visual, auditory, tactile, olfactory, vestibular, etc. patterns of interest. Data and patterns are retrieved in response to an input pattern, whether visual, auditory, tactile, etc. or a combination. The input pattern serves as a prompt to initiate retrieval of data patterns related to the prompt, if they are stored in the memory. If data patterns are retrieved and if they contain an identification, the input pattern is thereby identified.

It is surprising that many aspects of human mental activity can be explained by such a simple idea of memory. Some of these aspects will be described below. On the engineering side, we will introduce new approaches to computer memory, to pattern recognition, and to control systems.

Pattern matching is complicated by the fact that unknown incoming prompt patterns may be different from stored patterns in perspective, translation, rotation, scale, etc. Simple pattern matching may not be adequate, but this will be addressed.

The memory capacity must be enormous, and it should be implemented with a parallel architecture so that search time would be independent of memory size. There are many ways to structure a content-addressable memory. The "cognitive memory" proposed herein is of a unique design that could be physically built to give a computer a "human-like" memory, and furthermore, it is intended to serve as a behavioral model for human and animal memory.

A simplified block diagram of a cognitive memory system is shown in Figure 1. The memory of Figure 1 is divided into segments. Each segment has a set of memory folders capable of storing visual auditory, tactile, olfactory, etc. patterns and if the system were artificial, it could store radar, sonar, and other sensory patterns. Each segment has its own autoassociative neural network.

During a visit, images of the visitor's face, voice sounds, tactile images, olfactory patterns, etc. are stored together in one of the empty folders. These patterns arrive on the memory input line of Figure 1. They come from visual, auditory, etc. sensors, having gone through the visual, auditory, etc. cortexes respectively.

The various sensory patterns, having been recorded simultaneously in the same folder, are permanently associated with each other. The result is that, when the contents of a folder are retrieved in response to a visual prompt which may be the image of a singer, in one's mind, the sound of the person singing can be "heard." If the prompt is the sound of singing, the image of the singer's face can be "seen" in one's mind. If the prompt

Figure 1. Cognitive memory system

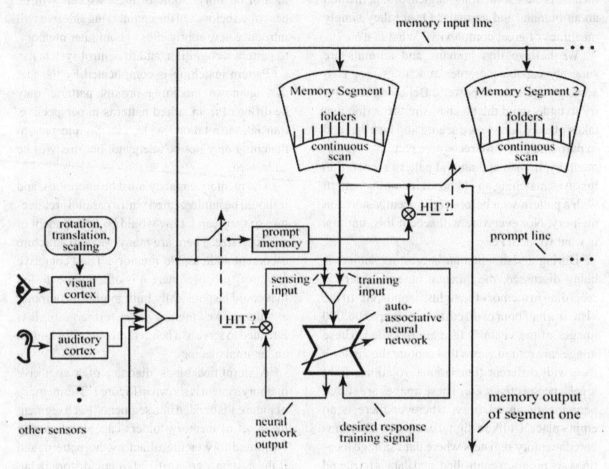

is a certain smell of cooking, the image of the kitchen or restaurant can be "seen" in one's mind.

Since the various sensory input patterns are stored together, it is likely that they are not stored in separate cortexes. The likely purpose of the cortexes is preprocessing the sensory inputs before they are sent to the storage folders. When we computer simulate the cognitive memory system, pre-processing is done with the input patterns. For example, a photograph of a person's face is rotated, translated, scaled, etc. Hundreds of images are made from a single photograph. In a paper by Widrow and Winter (1988), it is shown how neural networks can perform this kind of pre-processing in a parallel operation, resembling the processing done in living cortexes.

Offline, when the memory system is idle, the autoassociative neural networks in all the segments are trained. For humans and animals, offline training occurs during non-REM sleep. In the simulated system, a continuous scanning process extracts all the patterns one-by-one from all the folders in a segment, and trains these patterns into the segment's autoassociative neural network. This occurs simultaneously and separately in all the segments.

In the simulated system, the autoassociative neural networks were three-layer perceptrons. The backpropagation algorithm (Werbos, 1974) was used for training. Input patterns came from the memory folders. For each training pattern, the desired response pattern was identical to the training pattern. After training, unknown prompt patterns were presented to the neural networks via the prompt line. If a prompt pattern were identical or close to identical to one of the patterns in one of the folders, the output pattern from the corresponding neural network would match the prompt pattern. This is determined by subtracting the output pattern from the prompt pattern. The difference is the error pattern. The mean square error (MSE), the normalized square of the magnitude of the error pattern, was measured. If the MSE was below a set threshold, there was a "hit." This indicated that there is a pattern in one or more of the folders that matches the prompt pattern. Now knowing exactly what to look for, an exhaustive search is made, checking the hit prompt against all of the patterns in the folders. The contents of the "hit folder," the folder containing the pattern that matches the "hit prompt," are delivered as the memory output. The hit folder would deliver everything recorded in it, visual auditory, tactile, etc. as outputs.

When a prompt input pattern does not have a hit, all other versions of the pattern serve as prompts that try to make a hit with a neural network. With visual patterns, rotated, translated, scaled, etc. versions are tried. If there is no hit, the prompt fails and the memory delivers no output.

The neural networks are not trained to identify a prompt pattern, only to say hit or no hit, i.e., "I have seen that pattern before, or not." Deja vu, yes or no? Use of the neural network speeds-up the search process. Every pattern in every folder does not need to be tested against every variation of the prompt pattern. The number of combinations would be horrendous. Every pattern in every folder only needs to be tested against a single "hit prompt pattern". Hits can be determined very quickly by the parallel neural networks.

In our simulations, the neural networks were trained by backpropagation, a supervised learning algorithm. However, since the desired response patterns were in fact the same as the training patterns, the training process was not supervised learning. There was no external supervisor, and the cognitive memory system was completely self organizing!

One day while walking down the street, you see a familiar face at a great distance. You know that you know this person. Deja vu! You come closer and start a nice conversation. But you keep asking yourself, what is his name? What is his name? You keep talking and looking for ten minutes or so, when suddenly his name, Jim Jones, pops into your head and you say to him, "well Jim..." He thinks that all the while you knew his name. What happened? How did this work?

You have many Jim Jones folders in various memory segments, recorded from a number of Jim Jones visits. The folders contain many images of his face, recordings of two-way conversations, etc. One of the folders has a recording of your first meeting with him when he was introduced by a mutual friend, who said "this is Jim Jones." When you first saw him at a distance, the contents of one of the Jim Jones folders was retrieved, but that folder did not contain the sound of his name. The facial images and voice sounds of that folder are used in turn as prompt patterns. This causes more Jim Jones folders to be tapped. This works like feedback. Also, the images of his face and sounds of his voice from the current conversation act as further prompts. You keep pulling more Jim Jones folders until you come upon the one containing his name. Bingo!

Salient Features of Cognitive Memory

The cognitive memory system stores in a unified electronic memory system visual inputs (pictures and sequences of pictures), auditory inputs (acoustic patterns and sequences of patterns), tactile inputs, inputs from other kinds of sensors such as radar, sonar, etc., and retrieves stored content as required.

Incoming sensory data is stored at the next available empty memory location, and indeed could be stored redundantly at several empty locations. In any event, the location of any specific piece of recorded data would be unknown. Another feature of the system is that it stores simultaneously sensed input patterns in the same folder (e.g., simultaneous visual and auditory patterns are stored together).

Data retrieval is initiated by a "prompt" input pattern (e.g., a visual or auditory input pattern would trigger recall). A search through the memory is made to locate stored data that correlates with or relates to the present prompt input pattern. The search is done by a retrieval system that makes use of autoassociative artificial neural networks.

Application of Cognitive Memory to Face Detection and Recognition

Detection of human faces in a complicated scene is done by scanning with a low-resolution 20x20 pixel window over the scene. Different window sizes, window rotations, and various brightness and contrasts were used to create images of different rotations, translations, scale, brightness, and contrast. These images or patterns were fed to a 20x20 input autoassociative neural network. The network was trained on many versions (rotated, translated, scaled, etc.) of an arbitrary person's face. When there is a hit, a face is detected.

Once a face is detected, the system switches to a high resolution (50x50 pixels) window. The window's images were fed to a 50x50 input autoassociative neural network. This high resolution network was trained with 50x50 pixel facial images of many people. Each person had a separate folder, and the folders contained hundreds of images of the individual with different perspectives, rotations, translations, etc., plus the person's name. When the unknown 50x50 pixel images were fed to the autoassociative network, if there were a hit, the unknown hit image must be stored in one of the folders. Making an exhaustive search, the folder is found and the hit face is identified.

The whole process can be subdivided in four major components that will be described below.

A. Face Detection Training

One image of a person's face was trained in. Several training patterns were generated from this image by performing rotation at 2° increments, over 7 angles, translation (left/right, up/down, 1 pixel increments, 9 positions) and brightness variations (5 levels of intensity). The combinations of these adjustments generated a total number of 315 training patterns. The total training time was 10 minutes on an Intel 64 bit computer for 0.25% MSE. The autoassociative neural network used for this training had a total of 1100 neurons distributed over 3 layers.

We call this a low-resolution network. The network structure is presented in Table 1.

B. Face Detection Sensing

In this part the sensing of the scene is performed with the low-resolution network. Each input pattern was adjusted by scaling (6 window sizes) and translation (90 pixel increments). In this case errors with the background were about 8 times greater than with a person's face. We run 600 patterns per second through the low-resolution neural network.

C. Face Recognition Training

Three images of Widrow's face were trained in. Hundreds of patterns were generated from each training image by performing rotation (2° incre-

Table 1. Low-resolution network structure

	Number of Neurons per Layer	Number of Weights per Neuron
First Layer	400	400
Second Layer	300	400
Third Layer	400	300

ments, 7 angles), translation (left/right, up/down, 1 pixel increments, 25 positions) and scaling (3 window sizes). The total number of patterns in this case was 1575. The total training time was 2 hours on an Intel 64 bit CPU for 0.25% MSE. The autoassociative neural network had a total of 5800 neurons, and 10,950,000 weights. We call this a high-resolution network and its structure is presented in Table 2.

D. Face Recognition Sensing

When the system switched to high-resolution each input pattern was adjusted by brightness (6 levels of intensity), translation (2 pixel increments, 25 positions) and scaling (6 window sizes). In this case optimization was done for each detected face with the objective of finding the input pattern that would generate the minimum MSE. After optimization was completed we checked if the minimum MSE was below a pre-determined threshold, in which case we had a hit, otherwise we regarded the detected face as an "unknown" person. After the hit was obtained the optimized pattern (i.e., "hit prompt" pattern) was compared with the patterns stored in the folders in order to obtain the person's identification. Errors with unidentified faces were about 4 times greater than with Widrow's face. We run 5 patterns per second through the high-resolution Autoassociative neural network.

Figure 2 shows the three photos of B. Widrow that were trained into the 50x50 input autoassociative neural network. The photo of Aragon, Eliashberg, and Widrow was scanned with the

Table 2. High-resolution network structure

	Number of Neurons per Layer	Number of Weights per Neuron
First Layer	1800	2500
Second Layer	1500	1800
Third Layer	2500	1500

20x20 window and the faces were detected. The faces were checked with the 50x50 network, and the faces of Aragon and Eliashberg were called "unknown," and the face of Widrow was identified as "Dr. Widrow."

Cognitive Memory Challenged

The cognitive memory system for face recognition was tested with a larger problem. A set of facial photos were made available from NIST, their Face Recognition Grand Challenge Version 1. Facial Photos of a larger number of individuals were downloaded, and there were two different photos of each individual. All the photos were with faces forward, but there were differences in the lighting, distance to the camera, etc. Single photos of 75 individuals were selected randomly, and they were used to train a 100x100 input three layer autoassociative neural network. A window was placed manually on each photo, and then altered by translation, rotation, scale change, lighting variation, and contrast variation. A large number of training patterns were obtained for each individual. The training patterns were recorded in each individual's folder, and each folder was labeled with the person number (names of the people were not available). After training the system was tested with 375 photos that were not seen before, 75 photos of the selected individuals, and 300 photos of individuals that were not selected. The system correctly identified all 75 of the previously selected people, and rejected all 300 people that were not previously selected.

THE BIOLOGICAL VIEW

Observations from everyday life have given us insight into the workings and the behavior of human memory. Knowledge of electronics and computer memory also colors our view. We present

Figure 2. a) Photographs of Bernard Widrow used for Training b) Photos of Aragon, Eliashberg and Widrow used for Sensing

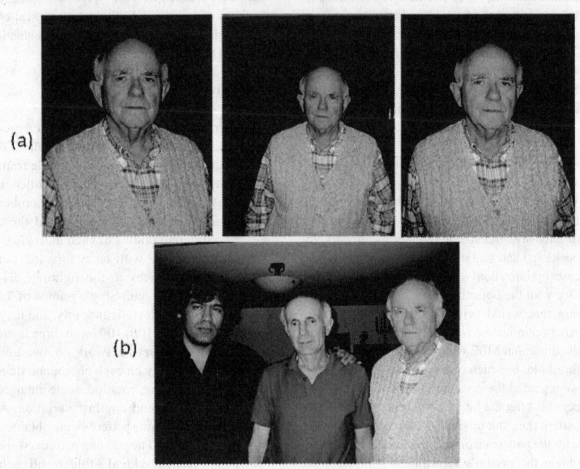

below a group of observations, conjectures and theorizations about human memory.

A. Memory Patterns are Probably Not Stored in the Brain's Synapses. Why?

We recognize that synapses do have memory capability, but this is analog memory. For stability, long-term memory requires digital memory. On the other hand, when we consider the physical aspects of neurons, dendrites, and synapses we realize that they change over time as circuitry is added during childhood brain growth, and later, circuitry dies out with aging

and disease. This continuous change demands constant training of the brain's neural networks in order to maintain stability of response. Any neural network training process requires storage of the training patterns somewhere. The situation at this point begs the following question: Why would nature provide storage for training patterns in order to train neural networks to store the training patterns? It doesn't make sense. It is a "Catch 22". It seems unlikely that memory patterns are stored in the brain's neural networks.

We theorize that neurons, dendrites, and synapses are used in the data retrieval process, not in the data storage process. They are associated with memory loss as their numbers decrease and the neural networks deteriorate.

B. Human Memory is Capable of Storing Patterns in Great Detail

Thirty or so years ago, Bela Julesz, who at that time was a researcher on 3-dimensional vision at Bell Telephone Laboratories, gave a fascinating lecture at Stanford on his research on what he called random-dot stereograms. Computer-generated random dot patterns were presented to the eyes from which 3-dimensional objects could be perceived. Using polarized light projected on a screen, the left pattern was addressed to the left eye, and the right pattern was addressed to the right eye. Looking with one eye, one sees random dots. Looking with both eyes, dramatic 3-dimensional objects emerged. He wrote a book on this subject (Julez, 1971).

Dr. Julesz described memory experiments that he did with an eidetic subject, a woman with a "photographic" memory. In the lab one day, he covered her right eye and let her stare at the left-eye random dot pattern. A week later, she returned to the lab where he covered her left eye and let her stare at the right-eye pattern. All she was seeing with her right eye was a page of random dots, but she was able to perceive the embossed characters and she read: "now is the time for all good men to come to the aid of the party."

She was able to remember in exquisite detail the left-eye pattern and compare it with what she was seeing with her right eye to get the 3-D effect.

He gave her a book to read. A week later she returned the book. He opened it at random to one of the pages, say page 373. He said to her, what do you see on page 373? She was able to tell him exactly what was on that page, word for word. He said that she was very bright, but a very unhappy person. He said that the number of people with this kind of memory would probably be several in a billion. He was asked if she had a head as big as North America. He said no, she looks like a normal young woman.

If this young woman could have such a memory, it is reasonable to assume that everyone has such a memory capability but nature somehow protects us from it. She wasn't so lucky.

C. Sensory Input Pattern Storage

Sensory patterns that are "interesting" are stored in longterm memory. They are stored in short-term memory for a long enough time to decide if they are interesting or not. They are presented on the sensory input line like prompt patterns, and if they make hits with any of the autoassociative neural networks in any of the memory segments, they relate to contents of the memory and they cause the memory's "tape recorder" to turn on, i.e., to cause the memory to start permanent recording of all sensory inputs and thus to add new patterns to the database. New data is learned, and knowledge is expanded when something familiar is observed. The following are some features of the memory system.

(a) Sensory input patterns come from eyes, ears, tactile, olfactory, vestibular and other sensors.

(b) Incoming patterns are stored in empty folders, wherever they are located.

(c) Sequences of patterns, like videos are stored in the same folder.

(d) Visual, auditory, and other sensory patterns that were received at the same time are stored in the same folder.

(e) Only "interesting" input patterns are stored in the memory. They remain for the rest of one's life. An eidetic stores everything, interesting or not.

(f) Sensory input patterns go to short term memory and, if interesting, are transferred to main memory and recorded for life.

(g) Short term memory (of the order of a few seconds) is used in the determination of what is interesting. The problem solver can also decide what is interesting.

(h)   Autoassociative neural networks are used in the pattern retrieval process.

(i)   Pattern retrieval occurs in response to prompt patterns.

(j)   Prompt patterns may come from sensory inputs.

(k)   The memory is organized in the form of independent segments to make possible a very large storage capacity.

Figure 3 is a block diagram of the sensory input pattern system. Notice the block called "problem solver." This is envisioned to embody a deductive reasoning process, perhaps modeled after the checker playing algorithms developed long ago by Arthur Samuel (Samuel, 1959). The problem solver makes use of data drawn from long-term memory, and is the "customer" for memory output. The problem solver could also turn on the memory's "tape recorder" if a loud sound or a bright light or a bright color is seen, or if something about the sensory input excites it. The problem solver is central to the reasoning process. It is not part of this memory study, however.

Figure 3. Sensory input pattern storage

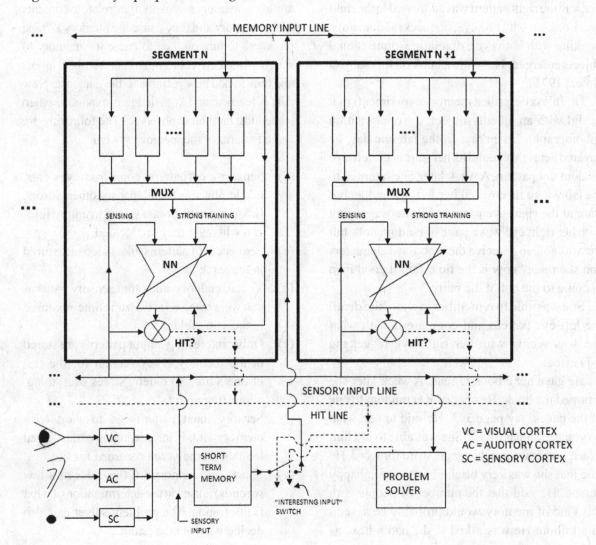

D. Innate Memory

Inborn knowledge is stored in long-term memory. We believe that inborn knowledge in the form of patterns is preloaded in the developing brain's memory and remains intact throughout one's lifetime. The following are examples of inborn knowledge:

(a) A bird building a nest involves complex construction in "safe" places such as roof tops, tree tops, telephone poles, etc.

(b) Baby horse walking and finding lunch within minutes of birth.

(c) Human baby sucking, crying, peeing and pooping.

It is conjectured that the memory storage means for inborn knowledge is the same as for sensory knowledge gained during a lifetime. Similarly, it is also conjectured that the memory retrieval means for inborn data is the same as for sensory input data. We could say (using the cognitive memory system described in this paper as an illustration) that inborn patterns are stored in folders in "memory segment 0" or in other words the "initial" memory segment.

Figure 4 is a block diagram for innate memory. This memory is like the memory for sensory input patterns.

E. Activity of a Baby's Memory

A newborn baby starts with innate knowledge in its memory and builds a database from there as it learns. Sensory inputs that correspond to items in memory create curiosity and cause the "tape recorder" to load new inputs into long-term memory. The combination of new memory patterns and innate memory patterns comprise a database for comparison with sensed objects in the real world. The bigger the database, the greater the curiosity and the faster will subsequent learning take place.

There is evidence that newborns have the ability to detect a human face in a complex scene (Morton et al., 1991). The earliest faces detected are that of hospital staff and the parents. Seeing each person turns on the tape recorder and the baby records thousands of images of each person's face. If the baby is breastfed, the folders containing images of the mother's face also contain all the sensory pleasures of being fed. Thus, mother is something special, different from everyone else.

It is believed that human memory is a self-organizing system and its learning is unsupervised. Innate knowledge, the "initial conditions," and real-world exposure seem to determine one's direction in life.

F. Pattern Retrieval System

Sensory input patterns, thought patterns, and patterns of innate knowledge are all retrieved by the same mechanism, some of whose properties are listed as follows.

(a) Patterns stored in memory can be retrieved without knowledge of their storage location.

(b) Autoassociative neural networks are part of the retrieval mechanism.

(c) Autoassociative neural networks are trained by using their input patterns as both input and desired response patterns. They are trained to produce outputs that are reproductions of their inputs.

(d) Once trained, autoassociative networks produce small input/output differences when presented with patterns that were trained in, but large differences when presented with patterns that were not trained in. Deja Vu ? Hit or no hit?

(e) Autoassociative networks are trained with all the patterns stored in the connected memory folders.

(f) The autoassociative networks are prompted with sensory input patterns or thought pat-

Figure 4. Inborn pattern storage

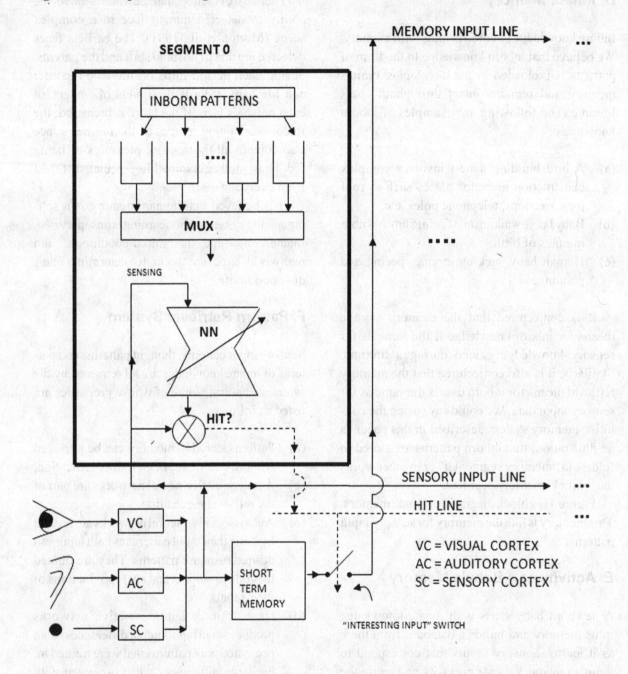

terns. Visual input patterns for example are rotated, translated, scaled, brightened, contrasted, etc. by the "visual cortex" (labeled as "VC" in Figure 5) while attempting to make a hit. If there is a hit, the hit pattern is saved and compared with the contents of all the connected memory folders. The patterns

of the folder containing the hit pattern are retrieved and sent to the memory output.

(g) These patterns in turn may be used as prompts to retrieve other folders. This type of feedback could cause a "chain reaction" resulting in the retrieval of many interrelated folders. (I have been speaking with someone for ten minutes but what is his name? Oh, now I remember. It's Jim Jones.)

A block diagram for the pattern retrieval system is shown in Figure 5.

G. Training During Non-REM Sleep

It is speculated that the autoassociative neural networks are trained during non-REM sleep. The block diagram in Figure 6 shows the training process. In this figure the Multiplexers (MUX) sense the memory folders, sequentially feeding the

pattern contents to the autoassociative networks for training. Once the brain is in "sleep mode" the training process initiates automatically and continues throughout the night during periods of non-REM sleep. Thus the autoassociative neural network in each memory segment is trained on all the patterns in all of that segment's folders.

H. Memory Activity During REM Sleep

During non-REM sleep as well as during REM sleep, input sensors such as eyes, ears, tactile, ol-

Figure 5. Pattern retrieval system

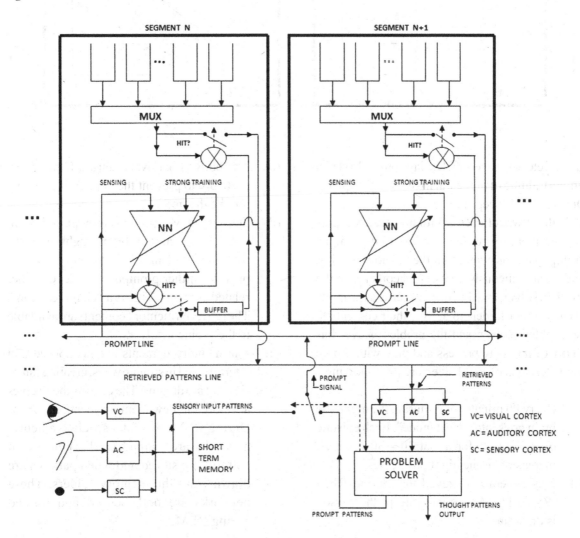

Figure 6. Training during non-rem sleep

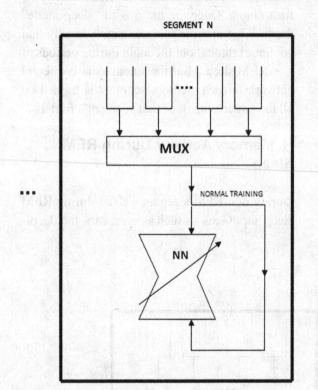

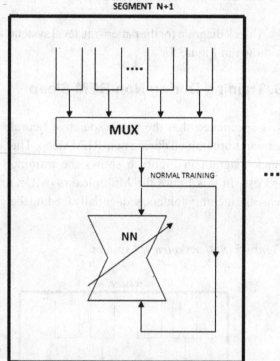

factory, etc. are turned off. During non-REM sleep, simple training of the neural networks takes place. During REM sleep, the brain is active, almost like during wakefulness. With the sensory inputs off, the memory receives no external prompts. Prompt patterns come from the memory itself. A folder spontaneously delivers its contents to the problem solver, and the contents serve as prompts to cause other folders to deliver their contents to the problem solver, and the problem solver has plenty of inputs to process and play with. Some characteristics of REM sleep are the following:

(a) Every 90 minutes or so during the night, the brain goes into "REM mode". Each episode of REM lasts for about 20 - 30 minutes, increasing as the night progresses.

(b) It is generally believed that during REM (Rapid Eye Movement) sleep, the person is dreaming.

(c) The body is paralyzed during REM sleep, probably to prevent the person from acting out the dream.

(d) During REM, contents are pulled from memory prompted by thought patterns from the problem solver. Memory contents provide further prompts to retrieve further related contents. This is a "chain reaction". The retrieved memory contents are available to the problem solver.

(e) The memory contents are juxtaposed and intermingled in strange ways, creating fantasies that are dreams. The dreams themselves are stored in new memory locations.

(f) During REM, the autoassociative neural networks are trained hard when dream patterns are stored and when patterns are drawn from the memory folders. These networks are both sensed and trained during REM.

(g) Brain activity during REM is similar to that of wide-awake consciousness, according to EEG and FMRI. The difference is that during REM, the sensory inputs from the eyes, ears, etc. are shut off.

I. Speculation about the REM State

It is speculated that the purpose of REM sleep is problem solving. Uninhibited thought can be highly creative. During a night's sleep, episodes of REM take place about every 90 minutes or so. Upon awaking one is generally unaware of having dreamt unless waking in the middle of a dream. To retrieve an unaware dream from memory, one needs an appropriate prompt. This is the function of psychoanalysis, on the couch, talking.

One manifestation of the REM state can be observed in cases of schizophrenia. It is speculated that this is an abnormal condition under which the subject is awake and conscious and in REM sleep at the same time, with fantasized images superposed on top of real-time visual, auditory, etc. inputs. This is hallucination. The fantasized images are drawn from memory spontaneously, without prompting.

J. Speculation about Seeing, Hearing, Walking, Etc.

Vision and memory are intertwined. The activity of seeing involves processing and recording new visual images and making associations with prerecorded images stored in memory. Similarly, we believe that hearing and speech understanding and memory are intertwined. In this case hearing and understanding speech involves processing and recording new auditory images and making associations with pre-recorded auditory images stored in memory.

Memory is also involved in muscle control. An example of this can be observed in the activity of walking. In this case sensory signals from all over the body deliver to the brain information about the mechanical state of the body. These sensory signals act as prompts to the memory that, in turn, provides muscle control signals that enable walking. This works like a lookup table. In other words muscle control signals are not computed in real time but are pulled from memory. Another example is observed in the process of speaking. In this case muscle control of the vocal tract is pulled from memory in response to prompts. The brain does not compute these control signals in real time.

K. Speculation about Feature Detection

Hubel and Wiesel's discovery of cat cortical cells that respond to vertical and horizontal lines suggest importance of feature detection. On the other hand, Julesz's work with random dot stereograms and experiments with an eidetic subject suggest that the visual process involves the total image in full detail (not just features) and that pattern association is critical.

L. Speculation about Learning

Human learning involves storing patterns in memory. Thus memory is a critical learning component. Supervised learning, unsupervised learning, learning with a critic, Bayesian learning are all useful concepts but probably have little to do with human learning.

M. Speculation about Memory Failure

Ageing causes memory failure through the slow death of neurons and of the dendritic tree, with insufficient rate of replacement. This affects memory retrieval as it becomes more difficult to continue training the brain's neural networks. Old data and newly recorded data gradually become inaccessible. Old data lasts the longest.

Another way to experience memory failure is through Alzheimer's disease. In this case the disease associated plaques and tangles in the neurons and the dendritic tree has an effect like accelerated ageing of these brain structures. This makes neural training more difficult, gradually becoming impossible, thereby making old and new memories but especially new memories more and more inaccessible.

Brain injury of the kind presented in the movie 'Memento' cuts the link to the "memory input line" and prevents the formation of new memories. Short-term memory still works. Recall of old memories still works, and neural training still works. Everything works except no new memories.

N. Speculation about the Mechanisms of Storage and Retrieval

At the moment of conception, DNA is taken from the mother and father to form a new cell. That is the start of a new living animal. The DNA of the new cell contains the information (the "blue print") needed to construct the body and the internal organs, including the brain. The DNA also contains the inborn information, necessary for survival, which will be pre-loaded in the developing brain (i.e., initial software). Inborn information is stored in DNA.

The mechanism for storage and retrieval of the information gained during a lifetime is the same as that for storage and retrieval of inborn information.

O. Wild Guesses

All information stored in memory is stored in DNA. The DNA that stores this information may be located in the glial cells of the brain or perhaps elsewhere. We postulate that information is not stored in the neurons and the dendritic tree. The neurons and the dendritic tree play a key role in association and retrieval of stored information.

Some Interesting Questions

(a) Why do new-born babies sleep so much, and a lot less when they become kids?

(b) Why do babies cry so much, and less as they grow older? Why do adults cry so little?

(c) Memory of children and young people is great. Why can't we remember life events that happened in the first few years?

(d) What is the connection between schizophrenia and sleep walking?

(e) What did Sigmund Freud do that was right?

(f) Why does one often not remember performing acts of habit?

(g) What are habits? How are they related to addiction?

(h) How are they related to speech and locomotion? How can you change or break habits?

(i) What causes subject wandering in the middle of a conversation?

CONCLUSION

The purpose of this paper has been to describe the design of a memory system intended to be as simple as possible, yet able to behave like and emulate certain aspects of human memory. One of our goals was to develop a new kind of memory for computers, adjunct to existing forms of memory, to facilitate solutions to problems in artificial intelligence, pattern recognition, speech recognition, control systems, etc. A second goal was to advance cognitive science with new insight into the working of human memory. We are hoping to give engineers and biologists some new thinking on subjects of great mutual interest.

REFERENCES

Julesz, B. (1971, December). *Foundations of cyclopean perception*. Chicago: University of Chicago Press.

Morton, J., & Johnson, M. (1991). CONSPEC and CONLERN: A Two-Process Theory of Infant Face Recognition. *Psychological Review, 98*(2), 164–181. doi:10.1037/0033-295X.98.2.164

Samuel, A. L. (1959). Some studies in machine learning using the game of checkers. *IBM Journal of Research and Development, 3*(3), 210–229. doi:10.1147/rd.33.0210

Werbos, P. J. (1974, August). *Beyond Regression: New Tools for Prediction and Analysis in the Behavioral Sciences*. Unpublished doctoral dissertation, Harvard University, Cambridge, MA.

Widrow, B., & Winter, R. (1988). Neural nets for adaptive filtering and adaptive pattern recognition. *Computer, 21*(3), 25–39. doi:10.1109/2.29

This work was previously published in International Journal of Software Science and Computational Intelligence, Volume 2, Issue 4, edited by Yingxu Wang, pp. 1-15, copyright 2010 by IGI Publishing (an imprint of IGI Global).

Chapter 7
Multi–Fractal Analysis for Feature Extraction from DNA Sequences

Witold Kinsner
University of Manitoba, Canada

Hong Zhang
University of Manitoba, Canada

ABSTRACT

This paper presents estimations of multi-scale (multi-fractal) measures for feature extraction from deoxy-ribonucleic acid (DNA) sequences, and demonstrates the intriguing possibility of identifying biological functionality using information contained within the DNA sequence. We have developed a technique that seeks patterns or correlations in the DNA sequence at a higher level than the local base-pair structure. The technique has three main steps: (i) transforms the DNA sequence symbols into a modified Lévy walk, (ii) transforms the Lévy walk into a signal spectrum, and (iii) breaks the spectrum into sub-spectra and treats each of these as an attractor from which the multi-fractal dimension spectrum is estimated. An optimal minimum window size and volume element size are found for estimation of the multi-fractal measures. Experimental results show that DNA is multi-fractal, and that the multi-fractality changes depending upon the location (coding or non-coding region) in the sequence.

INTRODUCTION

Deoxyribonucleic acid (DNA) has become one of the most examined molecules on the planet. Scientist around the world have been trying to unravel its secrets for many purposes. Genetic information is currently used to raise better plants and animals, create enhanced pharmaceuticals for humans, and for gene therapy in medicine, as well as for a plethora of other possible applications. Of particular interest is carbon-based DNA computing (e.g., Paum, Rozenberg, & Salomaa, 1998; Lipton & Baum, 1995; Bell & Marr, 1990). Science, as a whole, has benefited from the study

DOI: 10.4018/978-1-4666-0264-9.ch007

of genetics because of the increased understanding of biological processes that all organisms share.

In recent decades, a significant amount of research has been directed towards **sequencing and understanding** the entire human genome through the Human Genome Project (HGP) launched in 1986. The goal of the HGP was to find the location of the approximately 1×10^5 human genes, and to read the entire sequence of the human genome (about 3×10^9 base pairs, bp). An exponential grow rate of that research has resulted in reaching the goal in 2003, 50 years after the formulation of the double helix (e.g., Kieleczawa, 2008; Clayton & Dennis, 2003; França, Carrilho, & Kist, 2002). Many other genomes have also been sequenced since. For example, the rice and the mouse genomes were completed in 2002, followed by the genomes of the rat and chicken in 2004. A year later, the genomes of the chimpanzee and the dog were completed. The Cancer Genome Atlas (TCGA) pilot project started in 2005, and was escalated to a large-scale project in 2009. Modern high-throughput genome analysis techniques have accelerated considerably the rate not only of sequencing, but also of arriving at significant results and insights (e.g., Defense TechBriefs, 2009; TCGARN, 2008; Mitchelson, 2007).

On the other hand, the traditional DNA analysis methods of finding genes and their location at chromatosomes through testing their biological function have been inherently slow. Although numerous faster techniques have been developed, there is still a need to augment them with new approaches. Therefore, robust computational solutions to the gene-finding problem could provide a valuable resource for the HGP and for the molecular-biology community (e.g., Datta & Dougherty, 2006; Nunnally, 2005).

Today, we can already spell out the entire alphabet in the entire genomes of a variety of organisms. We have also learned many individual "words" (genes) in the DNA sequence. To follow the analogy of a language, this could represent a written language. How is this written language expressed (spoken)? We have learned that the three-character codons are like phonemes in the spoken language, with several codons producing the same results (protein). We have also learned a number of regulatory elements in the sequence that could signify the punctuation in the written language, and intonation in the spoken language. Unfortunately, we can comprehend just a few words in that language. We still must learn how to interpret those instructions in a more comprehensive manner. What is the Rosetta stone for DNA? This paper is intended to be a step towards this solution.

Most of the current research in the deciphering the meaning of DNA sequences is approached from the lowest base-pair level. Its main objective is to search for patterns or correlations existing in the DNA sequence related to codons, amino acids, and proteins. A number of gene-finding systems have been developed in recent decades. These systems use a variety of sophisticated computational data-mining techniques, including neural networks (Uberbacher & Mural, 1991), dynamic programming (Snyder & Stormo, 1993), rule-based methods (Solovyev, Salamov, & Lawrence, 1994), decision trees (Hutchinson & Hayden, 1992), probability reasoning (Guigo, Knudsen, Drake, & Smith, 1992), and hidden Markov chains (Henderson, Salzberg, & Fasman, 1997), and other machine-learning schemes such as genetic programming, and support vector machines (e.g., Baldi & Brunak, 1998). Most of the approaches are based on **local** measures only. In addition, many of the techniques rely on the statistical qualities of exons in the gene, thus using only the *known* gene pool as a training set for their classification. Although the model-driven techniques have demonstrated some success, improved techniques should be developed.

An approach to finding such improved techniques is to consider long-range relations (in addition to short-range relations) in the DNA sequence, spanning 10^4 nucleotides, (Voss, 1992; Karlin & Brendel, 1993; Borovik, Grosberg, & Frank-

Kamenetskii, 1994). If we had a good technique to measure such long-range relations, we would be able to estimate the fractality of any DNA sequence, without any a priori assumptions about its structure. This would be a *data-driven approach*, rather than the common model-driven approach.

Along those lines, Bains (1993) reported a local self-similarity with a 180 bp periodicity in mammalian nuclear DNA sequences. Other publications have provided evidence that the long-range fractal correlations appear in DNA sequences with different values in different regions of the sequence (Bernaola-Galvan, Roman-Roldan, & Oliver, 1996; Xiao, Chen, Shen, Sun, & Xu, 1995; Larhammar & Chatzidimitriou-Dreismann, 1993).

In this paper, we will introduce an algorithm based on a multi-fractal analysis, and will demonstrate that multi-fractal estimates can be used to characterize DNA sequences (Kinsner, 1994; Rifaat & Kinsner, 1999; Zhang, 2001).

It should be clear that the DNA sequencing and gene finding techniques constitute a subset of **bioinformatics**, the science of using information to understand biology, with its numerous tools (e.g., Dale & von Schantz, 2002; Gibas & Jambeck, 2001; Burset & Guigo, 1996). In turn, bioinformatics is a subset of **computational biology** (e.g., Murray, 2002a; Murray, 2002b) which is the application of quantitative analytical techniques in modelling biological systems. Very often, for structural biologists, DNA is not just a sequence of symbols, but implies 3D structures, molecular shapes and conformational changes, active sites, chemical reactions, and intermolecular interactions, each with a hierarchy of importance (e.g., Lodish, Berk, Matsudaira, Kaiser, Krieger, Scott, Zipursky, & Darnell, 2004; Campbell & Reece, 2002; Dale & von Schantz, 2002; Gibas & Jambeck, 2001). What might be missing from this web of various approaches to solving life-related problems through DNA analysis is **cognitive informatics** with its new approaches (Wang, 2002, 2007) and **multi-scale analytical tools** (Kinsner, 2007; Kinsner, 2008).

BACKGROUND AND METHODS

DNA and Genetic Information

DNA Structure

DNA contains the specific genetic information which directs a set of cells of living organism in their forming, running, and maintenance. This information is stored in such a way that it carries the genetic inheritance of that organism. Where is that information stored? As established by Phoebus Levene prior to the formulation of the double helix by Francis Crick and James Watson, DNA consists of complementary sequences of four nucleotide bases: *adenine* (A), *guanine* (G), *cytosine* (C), and *thymine* (T). Although four possible pairings are feasible, only the G-C (3 hydrogen bonds) and A-T (2 hydrogen bonds) are found in the DNA. Adenine and guanine (A/G) are double-ringed *purines*, while cytosine and thymine (C/T) are single-ringed *pyrimidines*. These bases are attached to the DNA sugar-phosphate backbone. Furthermore, in 1949, Erwin Chargaff had also shown that the amount of adenine (A) in DNA equals approximately the amount of thymine (T), and the amount of cytosine (C) equals approximately the amount of guanine (G). In fact, human DNA has A = 30.9% and T = 29.4%; G = 19.9% and C = 19.8%, with the amount of G-C slightly smaller than A-T also in other species.

Armed with this and other knowledge, Crick and Watson concluded in 1953 that DNA is a double stranded helix, thus containing base pairs, in which A matches T and G matches C (the classical Watson-Crick pairing) to form the most energetically stable DNA configuration. Each pair is separated from its neighbour by approximately 3.4 angstroms (Å), or 0.34 nanometres (nm). The double helix can fold into six possible 3D structures, each with a different diameter (approximately 2 nm or 20 Å) and different number of base pairs per turn (with an average just over 10 or 3.57 nm). The helix structures are mostly

Figure 1. A structure of a DNA sequence

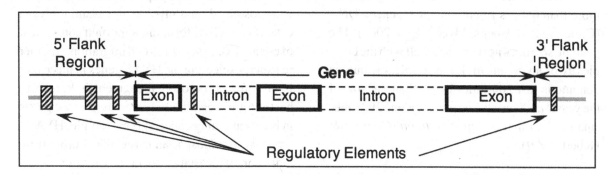

right-handed. The upstream end of DNA chain is called the 5' end in the chain, while the downstream end is called the 3' end. A good overview of DNA is provided in the *Primer on Genetics* (DOE Human Genome Program, 1992) and many other sources (e.g., Lodish, Berk, Matsudaira, Kaiser, Krieger, Scott, Zipursky, & Darnell, 2004; Campbell & Reece, 2002; Fairbanks & Andersen 1999; Thomson, Hellack, Braver, & Durica, 1997; Strachan & Read, 1996; Wolfe, 1993; Branden & Tooze, 1991; Darnell, Lodish, & Baltimore, 1990).

Genes

A *gene* is a segment of a DNA sequence, with *exons* (the coding regions) and *introns* (the non-coding regions) in higher eukaryotic organisms, as shown in Figure 1. Exons are called the coding regions because they contain 3-symbol *codons* to make proteins. They are relatively short (145 bp in humans). The introns (much longer, with 3365 for humans), together with the intergenic regions are called non-coding because they contain no in-

formation for making proteins. These non-coding regions are removed when DNA is translated into the *messenger ribonucleic acid* (mRNA).

Genes vary in length. For humans, the average gene size is about 27.9 kilobases (kb) long, with an average of 8.8 exons. Most of the regulatory elements of a gene are located in its 5' flank region. For humans, the largest gene found has a length of 2.4 magabases (Mb), the largest number of exons is 178, and the longest single exon is approximately 17 kb (e.g., Lander et at., 2001; Venter, Adams, Myers, & Li, 2001).

Genome

A *genome* refers to the complete collection of the genetic material in an organism, with its sequence of genes and the inter-genetic material, as illustrated in Figure 2. The size of genomes vary over a large range. For example, the genome sizes for *Escherichia coli*, yeast, fly, **human**, and some amphibians are around 4.6×10^6, 1.2×10^7, 1×10^8, $\mathbf{3 \times 10^9}$, and 8×10^{11}, respectively. In humans, only

Figure 2. In a genome, the genetic coding material is interspersed with different types of inter-genetic non-coding material

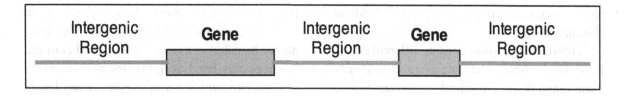

2% of the genome constitutes coding regions, and more than 64% is filled with inter-genetic DNA (Craig, Venter, Adams, Myers, & Li, 2001). The genome size does not correlate well with the complexity of an organism. For example, the human genome is just 200 times larger than the size of the yeast *Saccharomyces cerevisae*, and 200 times smaller than that of *Amoeba dubia* (Gregory & Hebert, 1999).

Chromosomes

A genome is packaged in *chromosomes*. Humans have 22 pairs of *autosomes* and one pair of sex chromosomes (XX for a female and XY for a male). Each pair of the autosomes looks like an offset character X. The point where the autosomes touch is called *centromere*, and the shorter arms are denoted by *p*, while the longer arms are denoted by *q*. All the 46 autosomes are stored in the nucleus of almost each cell.

The number of chromosomes varies between organisms: from a single chromosome in a bacterium, to 6 for a mosquito, 34 for a sunflower, 38 for a domestic cat and a domestic pig, 48 for gorillas and chimpanzees, 78 for a dog, 100 to 104 for a goldfish, and 132 for a kingfisher. These chromosomes are located in the nucleus of almost each cell in humans and other *eukaryotes* (such as plants, yeast and animals whose cells have nuclei, as opposed to *prokaryotes* whose cells have no defined nucleus).

Each chromosome contains a single DNA strand with an average of 134 Mb in humans. As mentioned already, the total number of base pairs in the human chromosomes is just over 3 gigabases (Gb). The distribution of the base pairs in the chromosomes in not uniform, from the smallest number of approximately 47 Mb in chromosome 21, to the largest of over 247 Mb in chromosome 1.

Different chromosomes carry different genes. For example, the HYAL1 (*hyalurono-glucosaminidase* 1) and HYAL2 (hyaluronoglucosaminidase 2) genes (used in this paper) are located only in chromosome 3, and involve glycosaminoglycan catabolism (GAG forms an important component of connective tissues) and cell migration. Another reason for selecting the HYAL genes in this paper is that this chromosomal segment is known to host multiple candidate tumor suppressor genes in breast and lung cancers. For example, HYAL1 type *hyaluronidase* is an independent prognostic indicator of prostate cancer progression and a biomarker for bladder cancer. In addition, there is much research interest in this chromosomal segment at our university and elsewhere (e.g., Atmuri, Martin, Hemming, Gutsol, Byers, Sahebjam, Thliveris, Mort, Carmona, Anderson, Dakshinamurti, & Triggs-Raine, 2008; Triggs-Raine, Salo, Zhang, Wicklow, & Natowicz, 1999). The total number of genes in the human genome is 32,185, with an average of 1,399 per chromosome. The distribution of genes in the human chromosomes is also non-uniform. Chromosome 11 has the lowest number of genes (379), while chromosome 1 has the highest number of genes (4,220). When chemically stained (marked) and viewed in the visible light, the brighter bands in the chromosomes have a higher content of genes than the darker stripes.

Since the location of the genes in chromosomes is of great importance, several mapping systems have been developed. One of the systems is called cytogenetic because it is based on a distinctive pattern of the stained bands, as shown in Figure 3. In this system, each gene has an address. The **first** number in the address represents the chromosome where the gene resides. For example, the numbers for humans are 1 to 22, and are substituted by a letter *X* or *Y* for the sex chromosomes. The **second** part of the address signifies the arms where the gene is located: either *p* (the shorter arms) or *q* (the longer). For example, 3*p* signifies that the gene is in chromosome 3, in the *p*-arms. The **third** part of the address has a two-digit number of the bright or dark band, with the first digit denoting a region number in an arm, and the second denot-

Figure 3. The cytogenetic addresses and relative addresses of genes in a chromosome. The diagram of chromosome 3 in the upper part of this figure is after Database of Human Genes (GeneCards, 2009).

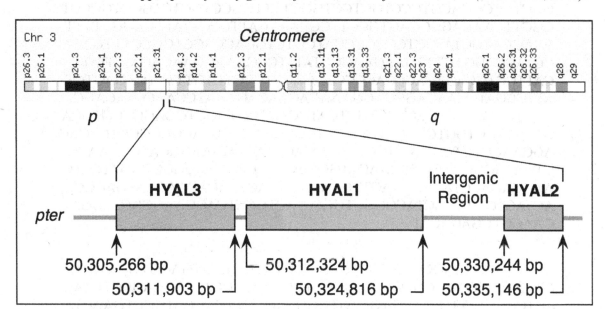

ing the actual band number . For example, 3*p*21 represents region 2 and the first band in the *p* arm of chromosome 3. The two digits can be further expanded to include a sub-band (within the bright or dark band) denoted by a period and another digit. If the sub-band has other sub-sub-bands, another digit is added. For example, 3*p*21.31 denotes the third sub-bad and the first sub-sub-band in 3*p*21. In fact this is the cygenetic address of the HYAL genes used in this paper. Notice that all the digits increase with respect to the centromere.

The above cytogenetic address locates the gene quickly, but is not precise. Precision can be achieved by providing the location of the gene in terms of the number of base pairs from the terminal points (called *telomeres*) on the arms of the X-shaped chromosome. For example (as shown in Figure 3), HYAL3 starts 50,305,266 bp from *pter*, where *p* signifies the *p*-arm, and "ter" stands for *terminus*, or the terminal point of the corresponding *telomere* of the chromosome.

For completeness, the following data describe the HYAL genes. HYAL3 ends at 50,311,903 bp from *pter*, and is 6,638 bp long, with 4 exons.

HYAL1 is separated from HYAL3 by 420 bp. It starts at 50,312,324 bp, ends at 50,324,816 bp, and is 12,493 bp long with 3 exons (almost twice the size of HYAL3). Finally, HYAL2 is separated from HYAL1 by 5,417 bp. It starts at 50,330,244 bp, ends at 50,335,146 bp, and is 4,903 bp long (shorter than HYAL1 and HYAL3), with 4 exons.

DNA Information Representations and Measures

What is the best model of DNA for the purpose of its analysis and characterization? To illustrate the difficulty of the problem, let us list a part of HYAL2 with its coding DNA (Figure 4a) and non-coding DNA (Figure 4b), as found in chromosome 3. They both look similar from the perspective of the necleotide "alphabet" (lowest level), though their functionalities are fundamentally different. Where are the genetic "words," the "punctuation," the "intonation," the "thesaurus," and other parts of the genetic language?

The sequence of nucleotides of Figure 4 can be evaluated directly, without any further translation.

Figure 4. (a) Coding HYAL2 sequence. (b) Non-coding HYAL2 sequence

GGCTCCCGGACGTCCCTGCTCCTGGCTTTTGGCCTGCTCTGCCTGCCCT
GGCTTCAAGAGGGCAGTGCCTTCCCAACCATTCCCTTATCCAGGCTTTT
TGACAACGCTATGCTCGCGCCCATCGTCTGCACCAGCTGGCCTTTGACA
CCTACCAGGAGTTTGAAGAAGCCTATATCCCAAAGGAACAGAAGTATT
CATTCCTGCAGACACCCACCCCCAGACCTCCCTCTGTTTCTCAGAGTCT
ATTCCGATCCAACAGGGAGGAAACACAACAGAAATCCAACCTAGAGC
TGCTCCGCATCTCCCTGCTGCTCATCCAGTCGTGGCTGGAGCCCGTGCA
GTTCCTCCTGGTCAGGAGTGTCTTCGCCAACAGGTACGGCGCCTCTGAC
AGCAACGTCTATGACCTCCTAAAGGACCTAGAGGAAGGCATCCAAACG
CTGATGGGGAGGCTGGAAGATGGCAGCCCCCGGACTGGGCAGATCTTC
AAGCAGACCTACAGCAAGTTCGACACAAACTCACACAACGATGACGC
ACTACTCAAGAACTACGGGCTGCTCTACTGCTTCAGGAAGGACATGGA
CAAGGTCGAGACAT

(a)

GACATCAGAAAGCCCAGTCCTAGCTTGTGTGAACATGAGGTGCTAGTC
TTCTCTGGGGAGGGTCTGCTGGCTTGGCCATCCCTTCTGCAGCCTGTAC
ACTCCCCTTTTGCCCCTTGCAGTGGGACGCCTTCAGCATGCCTGAACTA
CATAACTTCCTACGTATCCTGCAGCGGGAGGAG GAGGAGCACCTCCGC
CAGATCCTGCAGAAGTACTCCTATTGCCGCCAGAAGATCCAAGAGGCC
CTGCACGCCTGCCCCCTTGGGTGACCTCTTGTACCCCCAGGTGGAAGGC
AGACAGCAGGCAGCGCCAAGTGCGTGCCGTGTGAGTGTGACAGGGCC
AGTGGGGCCTGTGGAATGAGTGTGCATGGAGGCCCTCCTGTGCTGGGG
GAATGAGCCCAGAGAACAGCGAAGTAGCTTGCTCCCTGTGTCCACCTG
TGGGTGTAGCCAGGTATGGCTCTGCACCCCTCTGCCCTCATTACTGGGC
CTTAGTGGGCCAGGGCTGCCCTGAGAAGCTGCTCCAGGCCTGCAGCAG
GAGTGGTGC

(b)

This approach could identify the inherent structure of the code, find all its codons, code modifications, regulatory elements, boundaries between the coding and non-coding regions, regularity of the sub-regions, and any other pattern of interest. Correlations can also be computed to find any repeated patterns. Frequency of occurrence of each nucleotide can also be computed directly. However, for other analyses (e.g., spectral, or cepstral, or wavelet analysis), the nucleotide symbols must be translated into other representations.

Many attempts have been made to characterize and visualize the DNA genetic information (e.g., Jeffry, 1990; Silverman & Linsker, 1986; Hamori,

1985; Peng, Buldyrev, Goldberger, Havlin, Sciortino, Simmons, & Stanley, 1992; Voss, 1993). Those early approaches were based on translating the DNA sequence into another representation such as a multidimensional random walk, or a correlation function. The random walk or the correlation function is then transformed into the frequency domain using a fast Fourier transform (FFT). The slope of the power spectrum density is a measure of the complexity of the sequence.

The random-walk is obtained by mapping the individual bases into displacements along a direction assigned to each base. If the embedding dimension D_E is smaller than the number of bases, artificial correlations may be introduced between the bases (Silverman & Linsker, 1986). Nevertheless, such studies have shown a long-range fractal correlations (e.g., Peng, Buldyrev, Goldberger, Havlin, Sciortino, Simmons, & Stanley, 1992). Voss (1993) used the pair correlations function to eliminate the artifact in his study of DNA of primates, invertebrates, plants and others (see the previous section: *DNA and Correlation Function*). Yu et al. (2001) (Yu, Anh, & Wang, 2001; Yu & Anh, 2001) proposed a time series model based on the global structure of the complete genome, and demonstrated long-range correlations in the bacteria DNA sequences. Audit et al. (2001) (Audit, Thermes, Vaillant, d'Aubenton-Carafa, Muzy, & Arneodo, 2001) suggested that the long-range correlations observed in both coding and non-coding regions are the signatures of the higher-order structural organization of chromatin. The presence of small-range correlations (only in eukaryotic genomes) may be due to the machinery underlying the wrapping of DNA in the nucleosomal structure.

Still another measure of the complexity of a DNA sequence is based on entropy, conditional entropy, generalized entropy, and mutual information. Embeling et al. (2002) (Ebeling, Molgedey, Kurths, & Schwarz, 2002) reports that correlations on many scales, particularly long-range, can be found in DNA sequences. Using the *average mutual information* (AMI), Grosse et al. (2000) (Grosse, Herzel, Buldyrev, & Stanley, 2000) have demonstrated that the probability distribution function of the AMI are significantly different in coding and non-coding regions of DNA sequences, and that there are persistent period-three oscillations of AMI functions for the coding sequences.

A major limitation of this entropy-based approach is that it can reveal only a single long-range dependence in the nucleotides. Kinsner (1994) has proposed using **generalized entropies** to find more than one dependence in a sequence. This data-driven approach can reveal a spectrum of such dependencies, if they exist in the sequence.

If all the long-range dependencies are the same, the sequence is called *self-affine* (mono-fractal), and if they are not the same, the sequence is called *multi-fractal* (a mixture of mono-fractals). Consequently, this approach provides a natural detector of multi-fractality. Rifaat and Kinsner (Rifaat & Kinsner, 1999) used the Rényi fractal dimension spectrum to show (arguably for the first time) that the DNA sequences are multi-fractal. Another multi-fractal approach based on the wavelet transform modulus maxima (WTMM) algorithm to extract the Hölder exponent spectrum has been described by Arneodo et al. (2002) (Arneodo, Audit, Decoster, Muzy, & Vaillant, 2002). One of the most accurate and efficient wavelet techniques for the Hölder exponent spectrum has also been presented by Potter and Kinsner (2007).

DNA as 2D and 3D Random Walks

One of the approaches to DNA translation into a signal is the formation of a random walk. To map a DNA sequence using the Lévy walk model, a walker either descends or ascends one step at the position j along the DNA sequence, depending on the presence of the pyrimidine (C/T) or purine (A/G), respectively (Peng, Buldyrev, Goldberger, Havlin, Sciortino, Simmons, & Stanley, 1992). This is a two-dimensional (2D) walk. A modification of the Lévy walk algorithm (e.g., Bernaola-Galvan, Roman-Roldan, & Oliver, 1996), is used in our paper for the mapping the DNA sequence into a 3D representation. A walker either descends or rises one step in x direction when there is an 'A' or 'T', respectively (i.e., $u(j) = -1$ or $+1$) and descends or rises one step in y direction when there is a 'G' or 'C' ($v(j) = -1$ or $+1$), respectively. The displacement of the walk after N steps is defined as a vectorial sum

$$\mathbf{s}(N) = \mathbf{s}_x(N) + \mathbf{s}_y(N) \qquad (1)$$

where the x and y displacements are

Figure 5. DNA signal of ph-20 (human genomic DNA) as a Lévy walk in 3D

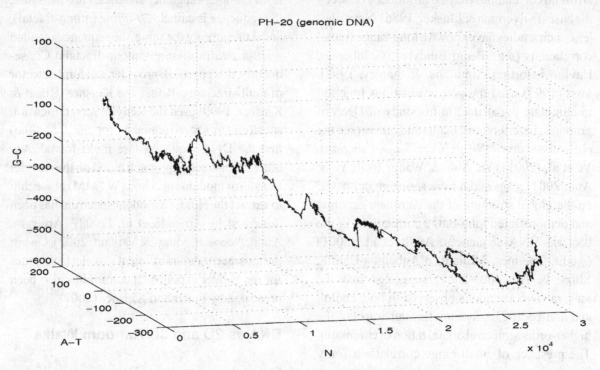

PH-20 (genomic DNA)

$$\mathbf{s}_x(N) = \left(\sum_{j=1}^{N} u(j) \right) \mathbf{1}_x \qquad (2a)$$

and

$$\mathbf{s}_y(N) = \left(\sum_{j=1}^{N} v(j) \right) \mathbf{1}_y \qquad (2b)$$

where $\mathbf{1}_x$ and $\mathbf{1}_y$ are unit vectors along the x and y directions, respectively.

Notice that the above translation produces a sequence with many interesting properties. The sequence $\{\mathbf{s}(N)\}$ can be interpreted as a discrete signal (see Figure 5 as an illustration of this DNA walk). It cannot be a random Gaussian white process because the DNA sequence is correlated. The correlation of the sequence does not drop off very rapidly; in fact long-range dependencies can be found in the sequence. The spectrum of the sequence is not narrow-band. The purpose of the

3D translation is to establish a basis for a study of all those properties, and is used in this paper. Finally, notice that there are many other translation schemes from A, G, C, and T base pairs to the corresponding signal representation.

DNA and Power Spectrum

Although the DNA signal can be analyzed directly in the space domain, if is also very useful to analyze it in the frequency domain by taking its Fourier transform. Let us abstract the DNA sequence to a continuous random variable $B(t)$, where t represents either time or space. A Fourier coefficient $B(f)$ at frequency f represents $B(t)$, because

$$B(f) \propto \int B(t) e^{2\pi i f t} dt \qquad (3)$$

Each Fourier coefficient has its magnitude $|B(f)|$ and a phase ϕ. The power spectrum density $P(f)$ of the DNA signals is then calculated by taking the squared magnitude of its Fourier coefficients

$$P_B(f) = \frac{|B(f)|^2}{\Delta f} \tag{4}$$

where Δf is the effective bandwidth of the Fourier integral. If the power spectrum density is narrowband, long-range dependencies in the original signal are unlikely. However, if the spectrum is broadband (as it is for the DNA Lévy walk), long-range correlations may exist.

If the signal has long-range dependencies, a power-law may hold in the following form (Kinsner, 1994; Larhammar & Chatzidimitriou-Dreismann, 1993)

$$P_B(f) = cf^\beta \quad \text{for} \quad f_{\min} < f < f_{\max} \tag{5}$$

where c is a constant, and $f_{\min}$ and $f_{\max}$ denote the range of frequencies $\delta f = f_{\max} - f_{\min}$ where the power-law holds. Within the range where $B(t)$ satisfies the power law in the $\log[P(f)]$ against $\log(f)$ plot, the power spectrum density could be fitted with a straight line, and the exponent β can be obtained from

$$\beta = \frac{\log P_B(\delta f)}{\log \delta f} \tag{6}$$

When it happens, the signal is called self affine (fractal). A fractal signal has no characteristic scale. Since the spectrum involves a broad range of frequencies, the spectrum is called broadband. A white noise has $\beta = 0$, the pink noise has a $\beta = -1$, the brown noise, $\beta = -2$, and a black noise is for $\beta < -2$. Notice that although we considered integer exponents, the exponent can take any real value, and may also be positive for blue noise. This exponent is also related to the spectral fractal dimension, as discussed in section entitled *DNA and Multi-fractality*.

If the fitted line is not straight, then the power law either does not apply, or the object is a multi-fractal (a mixture of mono-fractals).

DNA and Correlation Function

As mentioned in the previous section (*DNA Information Representation and Measures*), random walk modelling of a DNA sequence may introduce artificial dependencies between the bases. This problem can be minimized by either modifying the Lévy walk (see the previous section: *DNA as 2D and 3D Random Walks*), or translating the DNA sequence into a pair-correlation function (also known as the autocorrelation function) which measures the correlation between the fluctuations of $B(t)$ at points separated by a displacement τ. The function is given by

$$C_B(\tau) = \langle B(t) \times B(t + \tau) \rangle \tag{7}$$

where the brackets $\langle \bullet \rangle$ denote an ensemble average, and $\times$ denotes the correlation multiplication.

The importance of the correlation function is that it is related to the power spectrum density through the following Wiener-Khinchin relationship

$$P_B(f) \propto \int C_B(\tau) \cos(2\pi\tau) d\tau \tag{8a}$$

and

$$C_B(\tau) \propto \int P_B(f) \cos(2\pi f) df \tag{8b}$$

Thus, the power spectrum density can be obtained indirectly through the correlation function, and used to extract the β exponent (see the previous section: *DNA and Power Spectrum*).

In order to compute the correlation function on the 4-valued DNA sequences efficiently, a number of simplifying functions were introduced by Voss (1993). He also studied the power spectrum for large f (small displacements τ) and for small f (large τ). He found that the slope has increased and decreased with respect to evolutionary categories. For example, the smallest slope $\beta = 0.64$ occurred for the eukaryotic organelle, then the slope increased to $\beta = 0.82$ for a virus, to $\beta = 0.66$ for a plant, and to $\beta = 1$ for invertebrates (exact pink noise). This was followed by a decrease to $\beta = 0.87, 0.84, 0.81$, and 0.77 for vertebrates, mammals, rodents, and primates, respectively. A phage and a bacterium have a more correlated behaviour, with $\beta = 1.02$ and 1.16, respectively. All these results indicate that the DNA is pinkish and broadband. No distinction between coding and non-coding regions has been made in the literature, however.

DNA and Multi-Fractality

Fractals have been studied extensively in mathematics, physics, chemistry, geology, biology, medicine, engineering, economy, and social sciences (e.g., Peitgen, Jürgens, & Saupe, 2004; Turcotte, 1997; Kinsner, 1994; Schroeder, 1991; Mandelbrot, 1977; Voss & Clarke, 1975). In general, fractal analysis can benefit the study of nonlinear dynamical systems (e.g., Strogatz, 2000; Alligood, Sauer, & Yorke, 1996). Fractal objects are non-differentiable (non-smooth) entities whose shape or probability distributions are governed by power laws. Mathematical fractals may have those power laws without limits, while physical fractal objects may exhibit the power law over a limited range. Fractals may be deterministic or stochastic.

How can fractals be described? One of the fundamental measures is its dimension. In Euclidean geometry, a point has its topological dimension $D_T = 0$ in an embedding dimension of $D_E = 1$, a line has $D_T = 1$ in $D_E = 2$, a surface $D_T = 2$ in $D_E = 3$, and so on. Such idealized (Platonic) objects are largely smooth, with a finite number of singularities (i.e., the regions where derivatives are not defined). Since a fractal object may be nowhere differentiable, its standard measures diverge. An exponent that makes the measure of a fractal

constant is called a fractal dimension. Thus, a fractal dimension does not have to be integer. Consequently, the fractal dimension represents the degree of complexity of a fractal object (i.e., its roughness, brokenness, and irregularity) (Kinsner, 1994; Kinsner, 2007).

If a fractal object has a single fractal dimension, it is called a mono-fractal. However, if it has several dimensions, it is called a multi-fractal. Multi-fractality may occur in space, or time, or both. Some DNA signal sequences have been demonstrated to be multi-fractal (Rifaat & Kinsner, 1999; Arneodo, Audit, Decoster, Muzy, & Vaillant, 2002).

There are many definitions of fractal dimensions, including Hausdorff (or box-counting) dimension D_H, information dimension D_I, correlation dimension D_C, variance fractal dimension D_σ and spectral fractal dimension D_β. All those definitions can be unified under the umbrella of the Rényi fractal dimension spectrum D_q defined by Kinsner (1994) as

$$D_q = \lim_{Nr \to \infty} \lim_{r \to 0} \frac{1}{1-q} \frac{\log \sum_{j=1}^{Nr} p_j^q}{\log(1/r)} \text{ for } -\infty \leq q \leq \infty$$

(9)

where r is the reduction of a volume element (vel) size; Nr is the number of vels for a given vel size and a given cover of the fractal object, and pj denotes the frequency of occurrence that the fractal object intersects the jth vel, and q is the moment order. It can be shown that for q = 0, the Rényi fractal dimension is the same as the Hausdorff dimension D0 = DH. Furthermore, for q = 1, it reduces to the information dimension D1 = DI, while for q = 2, it becomes the correlation dimension D2 = DC, and so on. Thus, the Rényi dimension Dq gives a spectrum of dimensions for different moment orders q.

The Rényi fractal dimension spectrum is important for a number of reasons. First, it provides a common approach to computing the spectrum of fractal dimensions, without the differences in implementations of the individual fractal dimensions. This is important because it leads to accurate comparisons of the fractal dimensions. If all the dimensions are equal numerically, the fractal object is a mono-fractal. However, when the spectrum is not uniform, the object is a multi-fractal. Thus, the Rényi fractal dimension spectrum can be used as a detector of multi-fractality, without any assumptions in this data-driven analysis. Another reason for the usefulness of D_q is that its Legendre transform produces the Hölder exponent spectrum that is compactly supported, a feature highly desirable in pattern classification.

It should be stressed that there are many practical computational issues that must be resolved in order to obtain robust results for D_q (Kinsner, 2007; Kinsner, 1994).

NUMERICAL RESULTS AND DISCUSSION

This section presents a fractal analysis of sample sequences taken from ph-20, the human genomic DNA and complementary DNA (cDNA). The DNA sequence contains the two genes HYAL1 and HYAL2. On the other hand, hyal1 and hyal2 are the cDNAs versions. The intron selected for this study is the sequence between exon1 and exon2 of the HYAL2 gene. The hyal2-exon1 and hyal2-exon3 are the exon1 and exon3 of the HYAL2 gene. Non-coding 5' and non-coding 3' are the sequences of non-coding regions located at the HYAL2 gene flanking regions of the 5' and 3' ends, respectively. The actual locations and sizes of the genes are given in the previous subsection (*Chromosomes*).

DNA Signal

Using the technique of DNA 3D random walk described in the previous section (*DNA as 2D and 3D Random Walks*), the DNA sequence of ph-20 is transformed into DNA numerical signals. Figure 5 shows the relationship $\mathbf{s}(j)$ and the number of base-pairs N in the sequence. The sequence is 3×10^4 bp long. As expected, the structure of DNA signal is not random, and implies self-affinity of the DNA sequence. Therefore, a fractal analysis is a suitable method for the study of DNA structure.

Power Spectrum of DNA Signal

Let us calculate the power spectrum density for a piece of a human genome with $N = 8192$ bp from ph-20, as described in the previous section (*DNA and Power Spectrum*). Figure 6 shows its power spectrum as plotted in a log-log scale. Notice a typical variability in the spectrum called the "Spanish moss." The variability appears to be asymmetrical, i.e., the variability is smaller above than it is below an imaginary mid-line. This is due to the logarithmic scale of the plot. For low frequencies, the spectrum departs from the line, and should be rejected there. Similarly, the departure at the higher frequencies should also be rejected because it is due to an artifact introduced by the transformation into the Lévy walk; i.e., since the DNA is a discrete sequence, the corresponding Lévy walk is also a discrete boxcar analog signal (with finite singularities), rather than a continuously differentiable analog signal.

A standard least squares regression is used to determine the slope of the spectrum. The β value of DNA sequence is between -1 (denoted by the upper dashed line) and -2 (the lower dashed line). Recall that $\beta = -1$ correspond to pink noise, while $\beta = -2$ correspond to brown noise.

Figure 7 shows four slopes obtained from the least-squares regression of the power spectrum for the coding regions (hyal1-exon1, hyal2-exon1, and hyal2-exon3) and three non-coding regions. The lowest line (denoted by ×) is for hyal2-exon1. The next line up (denoted by o) is for hyal1-exon1. The

Figure 6. Power spectrum of a DNA signa, consisting of a DNA sample sequence of 8192 bp taken from the ph-20, a segment of human genomic DNA

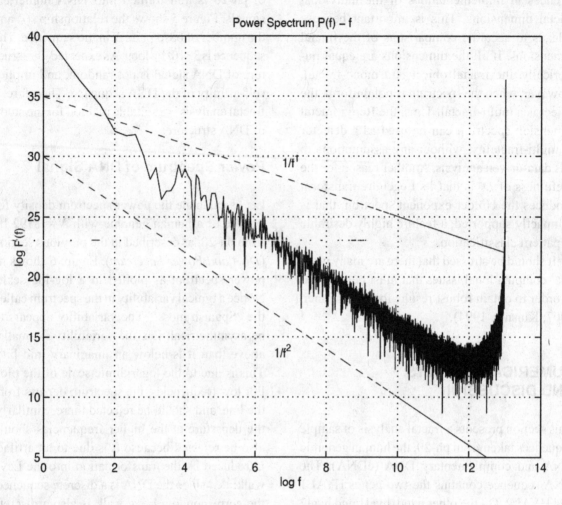

Power Spectrum P(f) – f

line consisting of dots (•) represents hyal2-exon3. The three solid lines above the previous three are all for the non-coding regions.

It is seen that there are significant differences between the coding and non-coding regions. The first difference is in the actual larger values of the power spectrum for the non-coding regions than for the coding regions. The second difference is in the slope which is smaller for the non-coding regions than it is for the coding regions. This implies that the coding regions are more correlated than the non-coding regions. Although the magnitudes of the power spectrum for hyal1-exon1 and hyal2-exon3 are almost the same, their slopes

differ (a steeper slope for hyal1-exon1). The β value of these DNA sequences is around −1 (pinkish noise). Consequently, since there are measurable differences in the slope and magnitude between all the DNA segments studied, they can be used as features for DNA segment classification.

Multi-Fractality of DNA Signals

The multi-fractality of gene segments is evaluated based on the Rényi fractal dimension spectrum, as described in the previous section (*DNA and Multi-fractality*). The segments include the entire ph-20 (29314 bp), hyal1 (2507) and hyal2 (1850),

Figure 7. The power-spectrum regression of DNA in coding and non-coding regions for hyal1 and hyal2

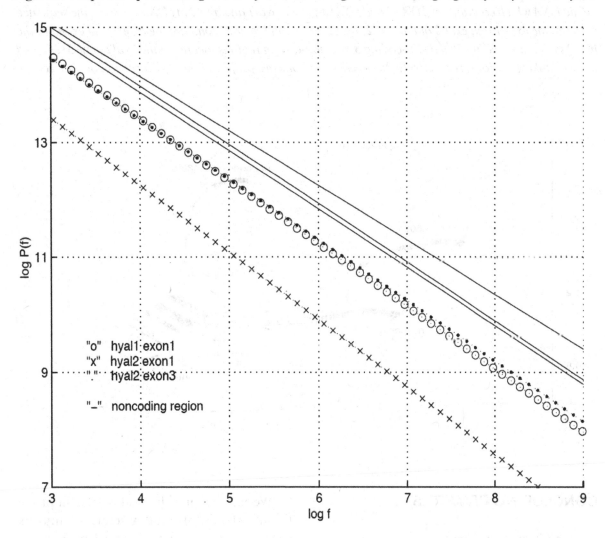

hyal2-exon1 (1057) and hyal2-exon3 (736), intron (560), as well as non-coding regions 5' (1540) and 3' (1330). The results are shown in Figure 8 as a 3D graph. For a given moment order q, a point is calculated on the fractal-dimension plane (D_x, D_y, q). The parameter q varies from -40 to +40 (notice that this range could be reduced to $q = \pm 10$ in order to reduce computational time). For positive values of q, the larger values of probabilities dominate, while for negative q, the smaller values dominate. These results indicate clearly that all the DNA segments studied are multi-fractal.

Once again, there are difference between the coding region and non-coding region. There are distinct differences between the intergenic regions (the flank regions in the HYAL2 gene) and the intragenic regions (which include exons and introns in the HYAL2). Notice that the Rényi dimension spectra vary in values between 0 and 40 due to the length of the different sequences. Consequently, since there are measurable differences in the shapes between all the DNA segments studied, the spectra can also be used as features for DNA segment classification.

Figure 8. Multi-fractal analysis of DNA sequence in three dimensions. Shown are: ph-20 –the human genomic DNA which contains the HYAL2 and HYAL1 genes; hyal1 and hyal2 in cDNAs; intron, the sequence between the exon1 and exon2 of the hyal2; hyal2-exon1 and hyal2-exon3 are the exon1 and exon3 of the hyal2 gene; non-coding 5' and non-coding 3' are non-coding regions located at the hyal2 gene 5' end and 3' end flanking regions, respectively. Non-coding regions are projected along x-direction or y-direction.

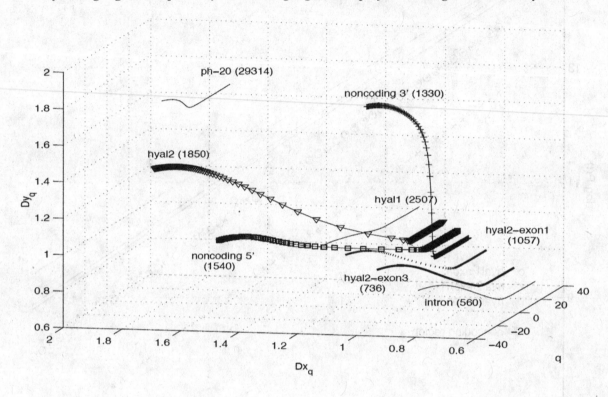

CONCLUDING REMARKS

Our algorithm shows that DNA sequences have a fractal structure due to their power-law relationship, implying long-range correlations in DNA. The linear regression analysis of the power-spectrum density shows that the slope (β) value of all the DNA sequences studied is around –1. It also shows differences in both the value of β and the magnitude (energy) of the power-spectrum density for each segment of the DNA sequence studied. Moreover, all the DNA sequences studied exhibit multi-fractality. Therefore, a new possibility opens up in the study of the functional structure DNA sequences since there is a difference between coding region and non-coding region in the DNA sequences according to this multi-fractal analysis.

We carried out additional work to improve the translation of a DNA sequence into its suitable representation for further analysis, based on a new mapping related to the organism's codon usage. In addition to the Rényi fractal dimension spectrum, we also extracted the Mandelbrot singularity spectrum, also known as the Hölder exponent spectrum. Due to space limitation, the results are not presented here.

ACKNOWLEDGMENT

This work was supported in part through a research grant from the Natural Sciences and Engineering Research Council (NSERC) of Canada.

REFERENCES

Alligood, K. T., Sauer, T. D., & Yorke, J. A. (1996). *Chaos: An Introduction to Dynamical Systems.* New York: Springer Verlag.

Arneodo, A., Audit, B., Decoster, N., Muzy, J.-F., & Vaillant, C. (2002). Wavelet based multifractal formalism: Applications to DNA sequences, satellite images of the cloud structure, and stock market data . In Bunde, A., Kropp, J., & Schellnhuber, H. J. (Eds.), *The Science of Disasters: Climate Disruptions, Heart Attacks, and Market Crashes* (pp. 27–104). Berlin: Springer Verlag.

Atmuri, V., Martin, D. C., Hemming, R., Gutsol, A., Byers, S., & Sahebjam, S. (2008, October). Hyaluronidase 3 (HYAL3) knockout mice do not display evidence of hyaluronan accumulation. *Matrix Biology, 27*(8), 653–660. doi:10.1016/j.matbio.2008.07.006

Audit, B., Thermes, C., Vaillant, C., d'Aubenton-Carafa, Y., Muzy, J.-F., & Arneodo, A. (2001). Long-range correlations in genomic DNA: A signature of the nuclosomal structure. *Physical Review Letters, 86,* 2471–2474. doi:10.1103/PhysRevLett.86.2471

Bains, W. (1993). Local self-similarity of sequence in mammalian nuclear DNA is modulated by a 180 bp periodicity. *Journal of Theoretical Biology, 161,* 137–143. doi:10.1006/jtbi.1993.1046

Baldi, P., & Brunak, S. (1998). *Bioinformatics: The Machine Learning Approach.* Cambridge, MA: MIT Press.

Bell, B. I., & Marr, T. G. (Eds.). (1990). *Computers and DNA.* Redwood City, CA: Addison-Wesley.

Bernaola-Galvan, P., Roman-Roldan, R., & Oliver, J. L. (1996). Compositional segmentation and long-range fractal correlations in DNA sequences. *Physical Review E: Statistical Physics, Plasmas, Fluids, and Related Interdisciplinary Topics, 53,* 5181–5189. doi:10.1103/PhysRevE.53.5181

Borovik, A. S., Grosberg, A. Y., & Frank-Kamenetskii, M. D. (1994). Fractality of DNA texts. *Journal of Biomolecular Structure & Dynamics, 12,* 655–669.

Branden, C., & Tooze, J. (1991). *Introduction to Protein Structure.* New York: Garland Publishing.

Burset, M., & Guigo, R. (1996). Evaluation of gene structure prediction programs. *Genomics, 34,* 353–367. doi:10.1006/geno.1996.0298

Campbell, N. A., & Reece, J. B. (2002). *Biology* (6th ed.). San Francisco, CA: Benjamin Cummings.

Clayton, J., & Dennis, C. (2003). *50 Years of DNA.* New York: Nature/Palgrave Macmillan.

Dale, J. W., & von Schantz, M. (2002). *From Genes to Genomes: Concepts and Applications of DNA Technology.* New York: Wiley. doi:10.1002/0470856912

Darnell, J., Lodish, H., & Baltimore, D. (1990). *Molecular Cell Biology* (2nd ed.). New York: W. H. Freeman.

Datta, A., & Dougherty, E. R. (2006). *Introduction to Genomic Signal Processing with Control.* Boca Raton, FL: CRC. doi:10.1201/9781420006674

Defense TechBriefs. (2009, February 1). *DNA sequencing technique can produce a genome in less than a minute.* Retrieved December 10, 2009, from http://www.defensetechbriefs.com/component/content/article/4967

DOE Human Genome Program. (1992, June). *Primer on Molecular Genetics.* Washington, DC: US Department of Energy, Office of Health and Environmental Research.

Ebeling, W., Molgedey, L., Kurths, J., & Schwarz, U. (2002). Entropy, complexity, predictability and data analysis of time series and letter sequences . In Bunde, A., Kropp, J., & Schellnhuber, H. J. (Eds.), *The Science of Disasters: Climate Disruptions, Heart Attacks, and Market Crashes* (pp. 2–25). Berlin: Springer Verlag.

Fairbanks, D. J., & Andersen, W. R. (1999). *Genetics: The Continuity of Life*. Pacific Grove, CA: Brooks/Cole.

França, L. T. C., Carrilho, E., & Kist, T. B. L. (2002). A review of DNA sequencing techniques. *Quarterly Reviews of Biophysics*, *35*(2), 169–200. doi:10.1017/S0033583502003797

GeneCards. (2009). Database of Human Genes. *Crown Human Genome Center & Weizmann Institute of Science*. Retrieved December 2009, from http://www.genecards.org/cgi-bin/carddisp.pl?gene=Hyal1

Gibas, C., & Jambeck, P. (2001). *Bioinformatics: Computer Skills*. Sebastopol, CA: O'Reilly and Associates.

Gregory, T. R., & Hebert, P. D. (1999). The modulation of DNA content: Proximate causes and ultimate consequences. *Genome Research*, *9*, 317–324.

Grosse, I., Herzel, H., Buldyrev, S. V., & Stanley, H. E. (2000). Species independence of mutual information in coding and noncoding DNA. *Physical Review E: Statistical Physics, Plasmas, Fluids, and Related Interdisciplinary Topics*, *61*, 5624–5629. doi:10.1103/PhysRevE.61.5624

Guigo, R., Knudsen, S., Drake, N., & Smith, T. (1992). Prediction of gene structure. *Journal of Molecular Biology*, *226*, 141–157. doi:10.1016/0022-2836(92)90130-C

Hamori, E. (1985). Novel DNA sequence representations. *Nature*, *314*, 585–586. doi:10.1038/314585a0

Henderson, J., Salzberg, S., & Fasman, K. H. (1997). Finding genes in DNA with a hidden Markov model. *Journal of Computational Biology*, *4*, 127–141. doi:10.1089/cmb.1997.4.127

Hutchinson, G., & Hayden, M. (1992). The prediction of exons through an analysis of spliceable open reading frames. *Nucleic Acids Research*, *20*, 3453–3462. doi:10.1093/nar/20.13.3453

Jeffry, H. J. (1990). Chaos game representation of gene structure. *Nucleic Acids Research*, *18*, 2163–2170. doi:10.1093/nar/18.8.2163

Karlin, S., & Brendel, V. (1993). Patchiness and correlations in DNA sequences. *Science*, *259*(5095), 677–680. doi:10.1126/science.8430316

Kieleczawa, J. (Ed.). (2008). *DNA Sequencing III: Dealing with Difficult Templates*. Boston, MA: Jones & Bartlett.

Kinsner, W. (1994, May). *Fractal dimensions: Morphological, entropy, spectra, and variance classes* (Tech. Rep. No. DEL94-4). Winnipeg, Manitoba, Canada: University of Manitoba, Department of Electrical & Computer Engineering.

Kinsner, W. (2007, October-December). A unified approach to fractal dimensions. *International Journal of Cognitive Informatics and Natural Intelligence*, *1*(4), 26–46.

Kinsner, W. (2008, August 14-16). Complexity and its measures in cognitive and other complex systems. In *Proceedings of the IEEE 7th Intern. Conf. Cognitive Informatics (ICCI08)*, Stanford University, Palo Alto, CA (pp. 13-29).

Kinsner, W., & Zhang, H. (2009, June 15-17). Multifractal analysis and feature extraction of DNA sequences. In *Proceedings of the IEEE 8th Intern. Conf. Cognitive Informatics (ICCI09)*, Hong Kong, China (pp. 29-37). ISBN 1-4244-4642-1

Lander, E. S., Linton, L. M., Birren, B., & Nusbaum, C. (2001). Initial sequencing and analysis of the human genome . *Nature*, *409*, 860–921. doi:10.1038/35057062

Larhammar, D., & Chatzidimitriou-Dreismann, C. A. (1993). Biological origins of long-range correlations and compositional variations in DNA. *Nucleic Acids Research*, *21*, 5167–5170. doi:10.1093/nar/21.22.5167

Lipton, R. J., & Baum, E. B. (Eds.). (1995). *DNA Based Computers*. Providence, RI: American Mathematical Society.

Lodish, H., Berk, A., Matsudaira, P., Kaiser, C. A., Krieger, M., & Scott, M. P. (2004). *Molecular Cell Biology* (5th ed.). New York: W. H. Freeman and Company.

Mandelbrot, B. B. (1977). *The Fractal Geometry of Nature*. New York: W. H. Freeman and Company.

Mitchelson, K. R. (Ed.). (2007). *New High Throughput Technologies for DNA Sequencing and Genomics*. Maryland Heights, MO: Elsevier.

Murray, J. D. (2002). *Mathematical Biology: An Introduction* (3rd ed.). New York: Springer Verlag.

Murray, J. D. (2002). *Mathematical Biology: Spatial Models and Biomedical Applications* (3rd ed.). New York: Springer Verlag.

Nunnally, B. K. (Ed.). (2005). *Analytical Techniques in DNA Sequencing*. Boca Raton, FL: CRC. doi:10.1201/9781420029086

Paum, G., Rozenberg, G., & Salomaa, A. (1998). *DNA Computing: New Computing Paradigm*. New York: Springer.

Peitgen, H.-O., Jürgens, H., & Saupe, D. (2004). *Chaos and Fractals* (2nd ed.). New York: Springer Verlag.

Peng, C.-K., Buldyrev, S. V., Goldberger, A. L., Havlin, S., Sciortino, F., Simmons, M., & Stanley, H. E. (1992). Long-range correlations in nucleotide sequences. *Nature, 356*, 168–170. doi:10.1038/356168a0

Potter, M., & Kinsner, W. (2007, April 15-20). Direct calculation of the f(α) fractal dimension spectrum from high-dimensional correlation-integral partitions. In Proceedings of the IEEE 2007 Intern. Conf. Acoustics, Speech, Signal Processing (ICASSP07), Honolulu, USA (vol. III, pp. 989-992). ISBN 1-4244-0728-1

Rifaat, R., & Kinsner, W. (1999, May 10-12). Multi-fractal analysis of DNA sequences. In *Proceedings of the IEEE Can. Conf. Electrical and Computer Eng. (CCECE'99)*, Edmonton, AB (pp. 801-804).

Schroeder, M. (1991). *Fractals, Chaos, Power Laws: Minutes from an Infinite Paradise*. New York: W. H. Freeman.

Silverman, D. D., & Linsker, R. (1986). A measure of DNA periodicity. *Journal of Theoretical Biology, 118*, 295–300. doi:10.1016/S0022-5193(86)80060-1

Snyder, E. E., & Stormo, G. D. (1993). Identification of coding regions in genomic DNA sequences: An application of dynamic programming and neural networks. *Nucleic Acids Research, 21*, 607–613. doi:10.1093/nar/21.3.607

Solovyev, V., Salamov, A., & Lawrence, C. (1994). Predicting internal exons by oligonucleotide composition and discriminant analysis of spliceable open reading frames. *Nucleic Acids Research, 22*, 5156–5163. doi:10.1093/nar/22.24.5156

Strachan, T., & Read, A. P. (1996). *Human Molecular Genetics*. New York: Wiley-Liss.

Strogatz, S. H. (2000). *Nonlinear Dynamics and Chaos*. Cambridge, MA: Westview/Perseus.

TCGARN: The Cancer Genome Atlas Research Network. (2008, October 23). Comprehensive genomic characterization defines human glioblastoma genes and core pathways. *Nature, 455*, 1061–1068. doi:10.1038/nature07385

Thomson, J. N. Jr, Hellack, J. J., Braver, G., & Durica, D. S. (1997). *Primer of Genetic Analysis: A Problem Approach* (2nd ed.). Cambridge, UK: Cambridge University Press.

Triggs-Raine, B., Salo, T. J., Zhang, H., Wicklow, B. A., & Natowicz, M. R. (1999, May 25). Mutations in HYAL1, a member of a tandemly distributed multigene family encoding disparate hyaluronidase activities, cause a newly described lysosomal disorder, Mucopolysaccharidosis IX. *Proceedings of the National Academy of Sciences of the United States of America, 96*(11), 6296–6300. doi:10.1073/pnas.96.11.6296

Turcotte, D. L. (1997). *Fractals and Chaos in Geology and Geophysics* (2nd ed.). New York: Springer Verlag.

Uberbacher, E., & Mural, R. (1991). Locating protein-coding regions in human DNA sequences by a multiple sensor-neural network approach. *Proceedings of the National Academy of Sciences of the United States of America, 88,* 11261–11265. doi:10.1073/pnas.88.24.11261

Venter, C. J., Adams, M. D., Myers, E. W., & Li, P. W. (2001, February 16). The sequence of the human genome. *Science, 291*(5507), 1304–1351. doi:10.1126/science.1058040

Voss, R. F. (1992). Evolution of long-range fractal correlations and 1/f noise in DNA base sequences. *Physical Review Letters, 68,* 3805–3808. doi:10.1103/PhysRevLett.68.3805

Voss, R. F. (1993). 1/f noise and fractals in DNA base sequences . In Crilly, A. J., Earnshaw, R. A., & Jones, H. (Eds.), *Applications of Fractals and Chaos: The Shape of Things* (pp. 7–20). New York: Springer Verlag.

Voss, R. F., & Clarke, J. (1975). 1/f noise in music and speech. *Nature, 258,* 317–318. doi:10.1038/258317a0

Wang, Y. (2002, August 19-20). Keynote, On cognitive informatics. In *Proceedings of the 1st IEEE Intern. Conf. Cognitive Informatics,* Calgary, AB (pp. 34-42).

Wang, Y. (2007). The Theoretical Framework of Cognitive Informatics. *International Journal of Cognitive Informatics and Natural Intelligence, 1*(1), 1–27.

Wolfe, S. L. (1993). *Molecular and Cellular Biology.* Belmont, CA: Wadsworth Publishing.

Xiao, Y., Chen, R., Shen, R., Sun, J., & Xu, J. (1995). Fractal dimension of exon and intron sequences. *Journal of Theoretical Biology, 175,* 23–26. doi:10.1006/jtbi.1995.0117

Yu, Z., & Anh, V. V. (2001). Time series model based on global structure of the complete genome. *Chaos, Solitons, and Fractals, 12,* 1827–1834. doi:10.1016/S0960-0779(00)00147-8

Yu, Z., Anh, V. V., & Wang, B. (2001). Correlation property of length sequences based on global structure of the complete genome. *Physical Review E: Statistical, Nonlinear, and Soft Matter Physics, 63,* 1–8.

Zhang, H. (2001). *Compositional Complexity Measures of DNA Sequence Using Multi-fractal Techniques.* Master's thesis, Winnipeg, Manitoba, Canada, University of Manitoba.

This work was previously published in International Journal of Software Science and Computational Intelligence, Volume 2, Issue 2, edited by Yingxu Wang, pp. 1-18, copyright 2010 by IGI Publishing (an imprint of IGI Global).

Chapter 8
Agent–Based Middleware for Advanced Communication Services in a Ubiquitous Computing Environment

Takuo Suganuma
Tohoku University, Japan

Hideyuki Takahashi
Tohoku University, Japan

Norio Shiratori
Tohoku University, Japan

ABSTRACT

In a ubiquitous computing (ubicomp) environment, system components of different types, including hardware elements, software components, and network connections, must cooperate mutually to provide services that fulfill user requirements. Consequently, advanced and flexible characteristics of software that are specialized for a ubicomp environment are needed. This paper presents a proposal of an agent-based middleware for a ubicomp environment comprising computers and home electric appliances. The middleware, called AMUSE, can take quality of service (QoS) in a ubicomp environment into consideration by coping not only with user context but also with the resource context, using agent-based computing technology. Herein, we describe the concept, design, and initial implementation of AMUSE. Simulation results of an experimental ubiquitous service using AMUSE demonstrate the effectiveness of our proposed scheme. Additionally, to confirm our scheme's feasibility and effectiveness, we describe the initial implementation of a multimedia communication application based on AMUSE.

DOI: 10.4018/978-1-4666-0264-9.ch008

INTRODUCTION

In recent years, studies of ubiquitous computing (ubicomp) (Weiser, 1991) environments and service provision in such environments have increased quickly. Two mainstreams exist in studies of ubiquitous services: research into user contexts in the environment, and service construction schemes. User context studies mainly investigate advanced methods for obtaining a user's physical location and determine appropriate services from location information and user profiles (Bellavista, 2003). In contrast, studies of service construction propose superior frameworks and schemes designed for dynamic cooperation among system components of many kinds—entities in a ubiquitous environment—to provide user-oriented services (Itao, 2002; Minoh, 2001; Iwamoto, 2003; Minami, 2003; Nakazawa, 2001; Gribble, 2001).

Discussions of actual applications of ubiquitous services have mainly addressed remote control of home electronics appliances from portable devices and information delivery systems based on a user's location information. Users' future demands on these ubiquitous services are expected to move into much richer applications such as multimedia communication services. Consequently, we are promoting research and development of fundamental technologies aimed at post-ubiquitous computing environments, including multimedia service provision through cooperative use of audio-visual home electronics appliances. We are targeting services such as video streaming and videoconferencing constructed through coordination of available computers, portable devices and home appliances, as portrayed in Figure 1.

To provide necessary and sufficient QoS that satisfies user requirements is an intrinsic problem to realize such ubiquitous services. To address this, we must consider not only the user context, but also the resource context of hardware, network, and software. This is true because resource availability tends to be poor and unstable in a ubiquitous environment. Furthermore, multiple users would be given ubiquitous services simultaneously; for that reason, problems of effective resource sharing and assignment should be addressed.

As described in this paper, we are aiming at investigating ubiquitous service construction scheme to provide QoS-aware and stable services against changes of resource status and the user's situation. We proposed a unique idea of effective handling of multiple contexts including the user context and resource contexts. To accomplish the

Figure 1. Application of ubiquitous service provided by multimedia home electric appliances

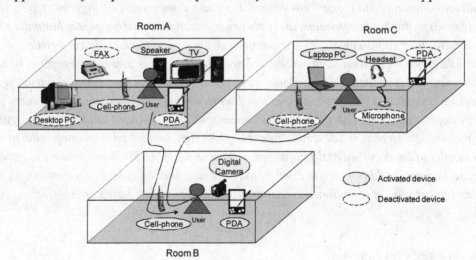

objective, we apply an agent-based middleware approach.

The remarkable feature of this approach is the agentification of each entity in the overall ubiquitous environment. We embed context management ability and cooperation ability for conflict resolution on multiple contexts to each agent. Furthermore, we provide a maintenance mechanism for the long-term context to accumulate and reuse the history and experiences of past cooperation among agents. The agents' individual and cooperative behaviors enable QoS-aware service provision. The primary contribution of our work is that it enables provision of rich services, such as multimedia communication services, anytime and at any place with comfortable quality.

As described in this paper, we propose multiagent-based middleware for ubiquitous computing environments, called Agent-based Middleware for Ubiquitous Service Environment (AMUSE). Moreover, we describe the AMUSE design, particularly addressing the service construction scheme for QoS-aware service provision considering multiple contexts. We evaluate our proposal based on results of simulation experiments. Furthermore, we present the initial implementation of multimedia communication application based on AMUSE to confirm the feasibility and effectiveness of our scheme.

The remainder of this paper is organized as follows. In section 2, we present the AMUSE motivation and concept. In section 3, a service construction scheme in AMUSE is described. The simulation results are presented in section 4. Moreover, an application of AMUSE is presented in section 5. Finally, we conclude this paper in section 6.

CONCEPT OF AMUSE

Related Works

Our work on context-aware middleware is related to those of many other studies in this field. CAR-MAN (Bellavista, 2003) is a Mobile News Service (MNS) for mobile users. It provides service based on user mobility, the device's performance and a user's preferences. When the service is provided by a single mobile device, the device performance is most important for the service. Therefore, works of various kinds examine provision of a high quality of web service within the limits of a device's performance (Lum, 2003). These works particularly address provision of individual user-centered services using a single mobile device. To provide multimedia services using available resources, it will be more efficient if many devices around the user were useful at the same time, instead of only a single mobile device.

In similar works, service is provided through coordination with devices around a user. For example, frameworks like STONE (Minami, 2003) and Ninja (Gribble, 2001) construct service based on a service template, which is requested by a user. They seek an appropriate function for requests and forge cooperation among various devices. Another framework, that of Ja-Net (Itao, 2002), specifically provides emergent services based on user preferences.

The purpose of these works is the same as that of our proposed work in terms of providing service through coordination of heterogeneous entities. Moreover, these works provide superior mechanisms of useful naming systems, service description languages, and service emergence.

However, we presume that existing service construction schemes are based only on user contexts and functional components. The schemes are designed to facilitate and safeguard coordination and operation or standardization of specifications. It is necessary for a ubiquitous environment to satisfy a particular requirement and limitation including network and computer resources. Regarding rich service provision such as multimedia communication services in a ubiquitous environment, we presume that it is much more important to consider QoS. For instance, ever-changing situations such as those of user mobility, performance of devices near users, and resource conditions exist. Therefore, the possibility exists that devices that are physically very close to the user cannot provide services because of a lack of resources, even if the devices potentially offer good performance. Moreover, it is necessary to provide a service considering cooperation difficulties posed by unexpected devices, software, and networks.

Analyses of these earlier works underscore the necessity of achieving a service construction scheme that considers not only the user context but also other contexts in an effective and integrated manner.

Target Issues

The following three technical issues must be addressed to provide QoS-aware services in a ubiquitous computing environment consisting of computers and audio-visual home electric appliances.

(P1) Resource context maintenance

Here we define "context" as a situation of a target entity at time t and temporal changes of the situation after/before time t. The target entity situation is represented as an internal representation model of the entity. Previous works for context awareness have mainly addressed user context acquisition schemes including the user's location information. However, in terms of its presence in the framework as a resource entity, it was treated only as a value of the target resource parameter at time t, not as a "context". In a ubiquitous environment consisting of various entities with different levels of functionality and performance, it is important to consider the resource context efficiently as well for proper QoS control.

(P2) Multiple context coordination

In a ubiquitous environment including many heterogeneous entities, QoS should be maintained in the range of entity level to overall system level. To do so, we must consider not only the input–output specification of the entity, but also multiple context coordination including the user context and resource context.

(P3) Non-deterministic property of service construction

Another problem must be addressed: mutual dependence and interoperability among entities that are not resolved deterministically from analyses of static specifications of entities. Each entity is fundamentally designed to function independently—not cooperatively—with other entities. Consequently, services constructed from the entities would not function properly in accordance with specifications.

AMUSE Framework

In AMUSE, we solve technical issues P1–P3, described in the previous section, using the following two approaches.

(R1) Agentification of respective entities

"Agentification" is a process of making a target entity workable as an agent by adding a knowledge-processing mechanism to the entity. In our proposal, we agentify each entity. Furthermore, we add context management ability and cooperation ability to resolve context conflict to the agents. Moreover, we embed long-term-context maintenance ability to agents to accumulate cooperation history and experiences. Consequently, we can overcome issues related to P1.

(R2) Multi-context-based Service Construction scheme

To realize QoS-aware ubiquitous service construction considering multiple contexts, we propose a contract-based service construction scheme of

Figure 2. AMUSE framework

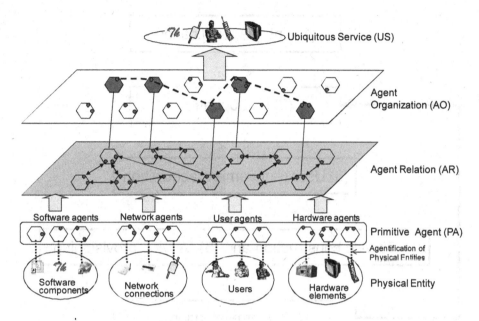

agents to solve the problem of P2. Agents produce an organization based on Contract Net Protocol (CNP (Smith, 1980)). Moreover, we model heuristics and dependency information related to the past cooperation history among agents as a long-term context among agents. Contexts of this kind are also managed by the agent. Using this context, agents can construct more advanced services using lessons that have been learned earlier. This would be a solution to P3.

The fundamental framework of AMUSE is presented in Figure 2. It consists of four layers based on concepts of symbiotic computing (Sugawara, 2002): the Primitive Agent layer (PA), Agent Relation layer (AR), Agent Organization layer (AO), and Ubiquitous Service layer (US). The first, PA, renders physical entities as agents in the system. Through the use of PA, the context of each entity is managed as a corresponding agent. In AR, inter-agent relations are created and maintained based on the long-term context among agents. In AO, agent organization is constructed based on the context in PA and AR, when user requirements are issued to a specific service. On the top layer, US, actual ubiquitous service is provided to users.

Service Provisioning Process in AMUSE

The service provision process in the AMUSE framework is portrayed in Figure 3. This process comprises the following six steps.

1.   Entity agentification

Each entity is rebuilt as an agent by adding a domain-oriented knowledge representation model that is suitable for classification of the entity. Details of the agentification mechanism are presented in section 2.5.

2.   IAR updating

We define the long-term context among agents as the Inter-agent Relation (IAR). Each agent has different IARs from those of all other agents with which it has cooperated in the past. Each agent updates its IAR after its service provision by itself or through cooperation with other agents. Details of IAR are described further in section 3.2.

3.   User requirement acquisition

Figure 3. Service provisioning process based on the AMUSE framework

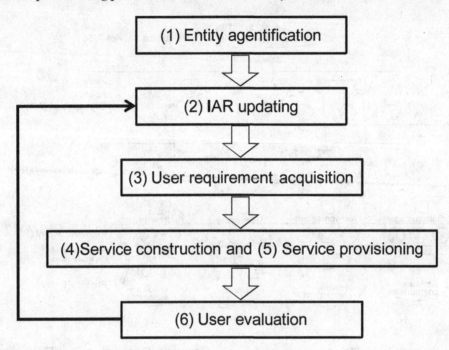

The agent acquires user requirements and analyzes requirements from the user's profile, locating information, and behavior in the ubiquitous environment. An agent must choose the most suitable manner to get the requirement because useful input devices might not be available everywhere. This remains as an open problem. It is not treated in this paper.

4.   Service construction and
5.   Service provision

After user requirements are acquired, agents construct its organization using CNP to provide service. In this scheme, we apply hierarchical CNP: task announcements are propagated in order of hardware agents, software agents, and network agents. The agent organization is created based on the context managed by each agent; actual service is constructed and provided with a combination of entities controlled by agents. Details are discussed in section 3.

6.   User evaluation

When service provision is finished, the agent organization receives a user's feedback related to the quality of the provided service. To measure the evaluation, we introduce us-effectivity (E) referring to Ja-Net (Itao, 2002). In AMUSE, when the E value changes, each agent informs all other related agents of the update: the evaluation result is propagated to all related agents; it subsequently affects service construction. Details are presented in section 3.3.

Agent Architecture for AMUSE

The basic architecture of agents in AMUSE is depicted in Figure 4. Here, the Cooperation Mechanism (CM) is a mechanism for exchanging messages among agents. Domain Knowledge (DK) is a knowledge-base system that stores and activates various domain knowledge related to the target entity. Based on that knowledge, the agent monitors and controls the target entity and performs actions to other agents. Entity Processing Mechanism (EPM) is an interface between DK

Figure 4. Basic agent architecture

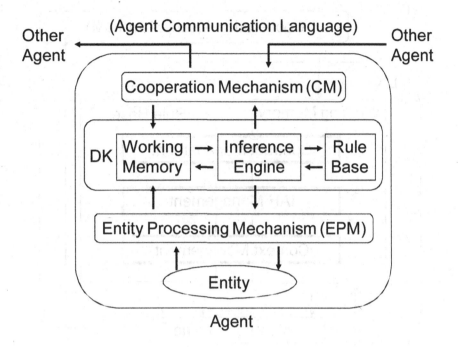

and the target entity. It passes events from entity to DK such as exceptions and directs control instructions from DK to the entity.

In fact, DK consists of three subsystems: Working Memory, an Inference Engine, and a Rule Base. The Working Memory and Rule Base respectively store sets of Facts and Rules. The Inference Engine refers to the Rules and Facts and functions as a production system. Using this inference mechanism, the agent performs interaction with other agents and controls the target entity.

Figure 5 portrays management functions used for service construction in AMUSE. These functions are implemented as a Rule set and related Facts in DK. The IAR Management is a module for maintenance of IAR such as creating, updating and deleting of it. Context Management is a module designed for monitoring and recognizing the context of the entity. Moreover, Contract Management is a module to maintain contract conditions and contract status in cases where a contract relation is created with other agents.

SERVICE CONSTRUCTION SCHEME IN AMUSE

Creation of IAR

Actually, IAR consists of relations of three kinds, as shown in Figure 6: Tight Relation (TR), Group Relation (GR), and Competing Relation (CR).

a.   Tight Relation (TR)

A TR is designated among agents that provide some service by constructing an organization of agents. Using this relation, it is possible for the agent to have past cases of success and failure in cooperation.

b.   Group Relation (GR)

A GR is assigned to groups of agents that have some potential dependencies. For instance, there is GR among hardware entities such as desktop PC, speakers, and PC displays. Using GR, it is possible

Figure 5. Management modules in DK for AMUSE

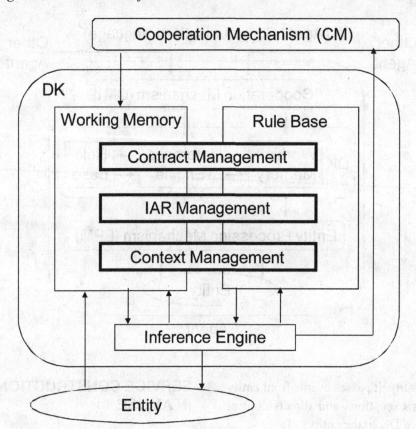

Figure 6. Creation of inter-agent relations

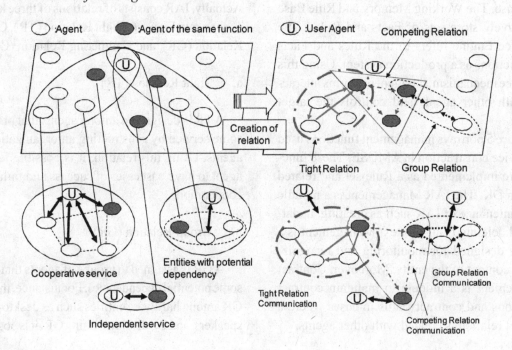

for an agent to inform group agents frequently of changes in states.

c. Competing Relation (CR)

A CR is formed among agents that have the same function. This relation is introduced because these agents would compete when a task announcement of the function is issued. Using CR, the competing agents routinely mutually inform others of their status. Thereby, they can produce a good organization when CNP-based negotiation runs.

Knowledge Representation of IAR

Figure 7 portrays a knowledge representation of IAR. The IAR is represented in sets of iar, which is an individual relation. An iar consists of id, name, func, relation, state, availability, and shared_values. The id is an integer value identifying each agent. The name is a name of agent against which the iar points. The func is an expression of functionality of the entity such as specification of I/O. It is a set of type. The type represents each function. For instance, an agent that has an I/O function of the voice has audio output and audio input in type variables. The relation indicates the relation of type: TR, GR,

or CR. The state indicates the present state of the agent. Here, running means the state of service is being provided, online means a state of standby; offline means that the state of service cannot be provided. Availability represents the degree of effectiveness of the agent. It consists of acceptability, us-effectivity, etc. The acceptability (*A*) denotes the acceptance ratio to the task announcement or bid of the agent.

In that equation, *b1* is the number of times that an agent has received a bid, *t* is number of times that an agent has sent a task, *a* is the number of times that an agent has received an award and *b2* is the number of times that an agent has sent a bid. The us-effectivity (*E*) is a metric of evaluation that an agent receives after providing a user with service.

$$E = p / n$$

Here, *p* is the total number of times of good evaluation; *n* is the total number of times of good and bad evaluation based on strength value of Ja-Net (Itao, 2002). The initial values of *p*, *n*, and *E* are set to 1. The shared_values are referred as a common index used by each agent. For instance, the operating_rate (*O*) indicates how often an agent is usually used.

$$O = u / l$$

Figure 7. Knowledge representation of IAR

```
IAR = {iar}*
iar = < id, name, func, relation, state, availability,
        shared_values >
id = int
name = string
func = {type}*
type = audio-output | audio-input | image-output |
       image-input | ...
relation =  TR | GR | CR
state = running | online | offline
availability = < acceptability, us-effectivity, ... >
shared_values = < operating_rate, ...>
```

Figure 8. Characteristic of CNP by IAR

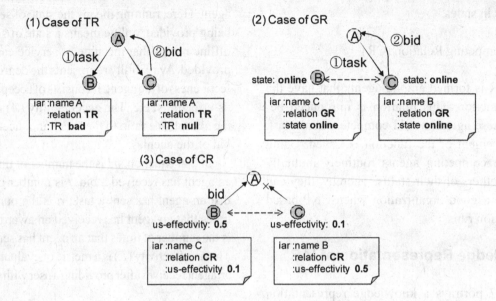

Here, *u* is the number of times which it is used. The *l* is fixed period decided by a user. It is useful to understand the trend of changes in the preference of the user according to shared_values.

CNP-based Service Construction with IAR

Our scheme, which is based on CNP, builds an agent organization using relations of three kinds. The CNP is a mechanism to produce a contract relation among agents by exchanging messages such as task announcements, bids, and awards, as presented in Figure 8. Here, we explain features of the service construction scheme with IAR.

1.   Case of Tight Relation (TR)

As shown in Figure 8(1), we assume that agent A has a relation of type TR with both agent B and agent C, although no relation exists between B and C. In fact, TR between A and B reflects that trouble occurred when they cooperated in the past; TR between A and C indicates no trouble in the past. When B and C receive a task announcement from A, they refer to each IAR. Here, B does

not send a bid because the TR against A is bad. Therefore, trouble in cooperation would occur this time too. On the other hand, C sends a bid because C judges from TR that it would contribute to the announced task. In fact, it is possible to reduce trouble in cooperation by an agent considering a coordinated relation in the past.

2.   Case of Group Relation (GR)

In Figure 8(2), we assume that agent A has no relation with either agent B or agent C, although a relation of type GR exists between B and C. Here, C recognizes that GR against B exists when C judges the task announcement from A. Then C sends a bid if C judges that B can provide a service by referring to the state in IAR. On the other hand, C ignores the task announcement if B cannot provide a service. Actually, it is possible to reduce trouble in cooperation by agents through consideration of the agents' dependency.

3.   Case of Competing Relation (CR)

As shown in Figure 8(3), we assume that a relation of type CR exists between agent B and agent C, whereas agent A has no relation with either B or C: B and C receive the task announcement. Each agent checks the IAR of type CR if it can process the task. When an agent has CR, it refers to the state of the CR. For instance, B sends a bid in the case where B judges the value of us-effectivity on this task is higher than that of C. On the other hand, C ignores the task announcement in the case in which it judged us-effectivity of B is higher than C. In fact, it is possible to construct a service efficiently through consideration of the state of the same function agent.

SIMULATION

Implementation

We implemented agents based on AMUSE to perform simulation. In the implementation, we employed the agent-based programming environment DASH (Sugawara, 2002) is based on the multiagent programming framework ADIPS

(Fujita, 1998). We also performed the simulation using IDEA (Takagaki, 2003), which is the interactive design environment for the Agent system. We used the DASH programming environment because the agent developed for the simulation can be reused later when we build a real-world system.

Evaluation Method

We simulated system behavior based on AMUSE. In this simulation, the QoS awareness of the system is measured. We investigate how much the QoS awareness is improved by the introduction of AMUSE. To measure the QoS awareness, we apply the User Request Achievement (*URA*) level. Using these metrics, we can measure the degree to which the user requirement is fulfilled with the provided quality of service by the system. Details of *URA* are described later.

Figure 9 depicts the behavioral situation representation of the system. Here, three entities—a hardware entity, a software entity, and a network entity—constitute the organization. They provide

Figure 9. Behavioral situation representation of the system

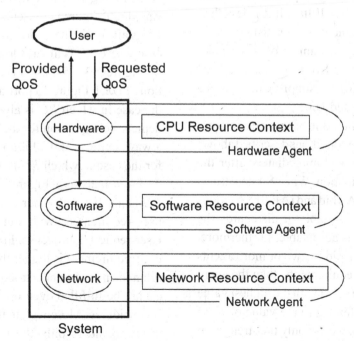

service to a User. The user issues a "User Request QoS"; then the system provides service with the "Provided QoS". The Hardware Agent (HA) monitors the CPU resource context and the Network Agent (NA) monitors the bandwidth resource context. The Software Agent (SA) has knowledge related to mapping from resource availability onto the actual user-level QoS.

The QoS evaluation of service is based on the *URA*. The *URA* is calculated by comparison between the User Request QoS *RU* and Provided QoS *SV* . We defined the range of *URA* as -1 to 1. Here, ru_i is an element of *RU* ; it represents the User Request QoS on service element *i*. In addition, sv_i is an element of *SV* ; it represents the Provided QoS on service element i. The value of ru_i and sv_i is 1–10. Here, *URA* on service element *i*, i.e. URA_i, is represented as shown below.

$$SV = \{ sv_1, sv_2, ... \}$$

$$RU = \{ ru_1, ru_2, ... \}$$

$$URAi = (sv_i - ru_i) / 10$$

Therefore, if URA_i is greater than zero, then the user requirement is fulfilled; if it is less than zero, then the requirement is not satisfied.

In this evaluation, the number of service elements is assumed to be two (*i* =1, 2) and *URA* signifies the total *URA* for simplification: it is a mean value of URA_1 and URA_2.

We performed simulation of service construction 500 times with the conditions described above. The agent constructs CR immediately after the beginning of the simulation. When SA constructs service, it refers to NA's bid and IAR. If SA judges that another agent is suitable, it disregards the task even if the task is acceptable. Furthermore, if the agent receives a bid by two or more agents that can fulfill user requirements, then the agent sends an award to the agent with the highest value of *E* of IAR after referring to the value of *E*. In the actual simulation, we use only the strength of

Ja-Net for the value of *E*. The simulation receives an assumed user evaluation each time of service construction. The user evaluation is reflected to *E*. User evaluation is assumed to be good if sv_i is within 120–100% when ru_i is regarded as 100%. In this case, value *E* is set to 1. It is assumed to be bad in case that sv_i exceeds 120% or is less than 80%, and the value is set to -1. Otherwise, it is regarded as usual, and the value is set to 0.

We compare three patterns of agent behaviors, i.e., our proposal (IAR-based approach), the case considering only the user context (User-request approach), and the case considering only the maximum QoS value of agent for QoS without consideration of resource context (Maximum approach). For the simulation, resources of HA and NA are assigned random values in every service construction. Additionally, we assign tendencies of user requests according to three patterns: high quality (7–10), middle quality (4–7), and low quality (1–4).

Simulation Results and Evaluation

Figures 10–12 portray variation of the value of *URA*. Figure 10 is a comparison where *RU* is always high. Figure 11 presents a comparison where *RU* is always in the middle. Figure 12 depicts the case where *RU* is always low.

Figures 13–15 present the frequency distribution of *URA*. Figure 13 portrays a comparison for the case in which *RU* is always high. Figure 14 depicts a comparison for the case in which *RU* is always in the middle. Figure 15 is a comparison for the case in which *RU* is always low.

From analysis of Figure 13—the case in which *RU* is always high—our approach achieved the user requirement with higher frequency than User-request approaches. From this result, if the user requirement is higher than the service environment, it can be understood that the requirement cannot be fulfilled even if only the user context is considered. Moreover, in the case in which the agent considers only the user request and the

Figure 10. Variation of value of URA where RU is always high

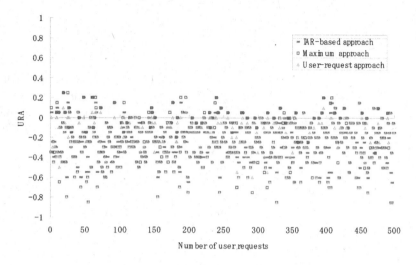

Figure 12. Variation of value of URA where RU is always low

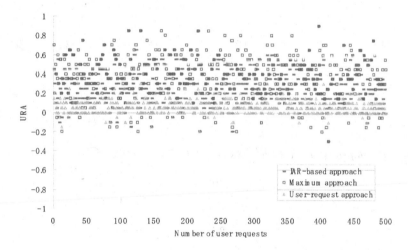

Figure 11. Variation of Value of URA where RU is always in the middle

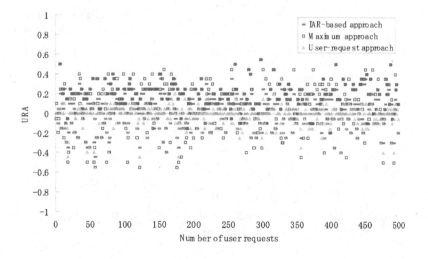

Figure 13. Results of comparison where RU is always high

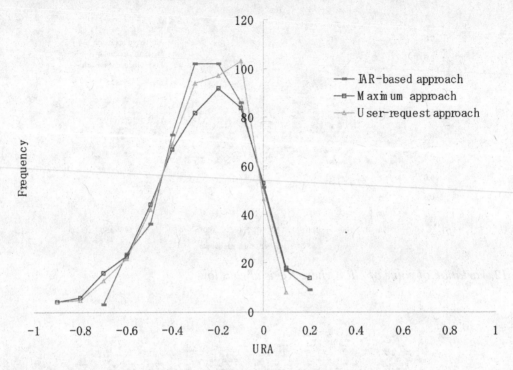

Figure 14. Results of comparison where RU is always in the middle

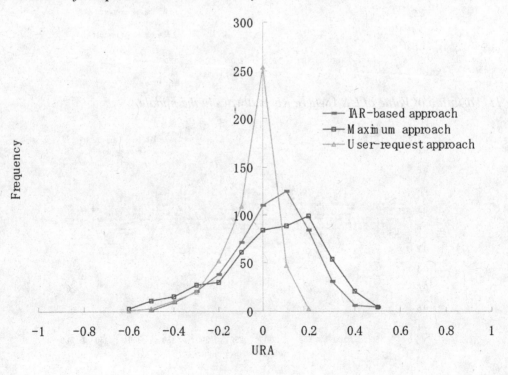

Figure 15. Results of comparison where RU is always low

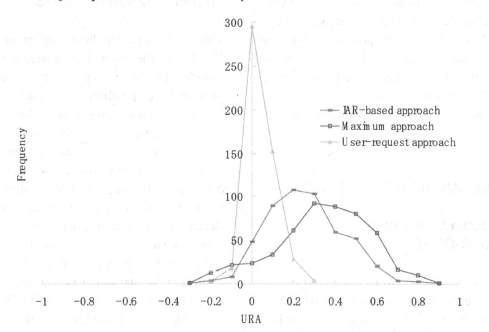

maximum value that can be selected, the *URA* is generally lower than our approach, when the user requirement is not fulfilled. It is understood that some conflicts on the resource context occurred. Additionally, it is understood that our approach decreases bad service construction by considering IAR. This is true because IAR decreases the resource context conflict. Based on these results, our approach is rather effective in such cases.

From observation of Figure 14, which shows cases in which *RU* is always in the middle, the *URA* of the User-request approach closes to zero many more times than other approaches do. On the other hand, compared to the User-request approach, the IAR-based approach was able to fulfill the user requirements more frequently. Moreover, cases in which the *URA* of our approach is higher than that of the Maximum approach are few. Consequently, we conclude that our approach can provide a slightly better service than the original user requirement if resources are available. It is also understood that our approach reduces bad service construction considerably compared to other approaches such as those depicted in Figure 13.

By analyzing Figure 15, where *RU* is always low, the *URA* of the User-request approach is extremely close to zero more frequently than other approaches. In our approach and the Maximum approach, the cases in which the *URA* approaches zero are not frequent. Nevertheless, our approach approaches zero many more times than the Maximum approach does. Moreover, our approach and the User-request approach reach much closer to zero than the Maximum approach does. Consequently, we infer that the agents construct an organization considering user requirements and the IAR. However, in this case, our approach is thought to be a meddlesome service for users who do not want excessive quality.

These simulation results clarify that our approach is most effective under an unstable environment with high-level user requirements. Furthermore, it should be considered whether user requirements or relations among agents which have a higher priority, when agents construct services: user requirements can be fulfilled mainly by considering IAR rather than user requirements in an environment with high user requirements and unstable resources. However, in an environment with suitable user requirements and stable resources, user requirements should be mainly considered rather than IAR. Therefore, we presume that it is necessary to consider the top priority between user requirements and IAR so that it matches the situation in which services are constructed in a ubiquitous environment.

C-QUSE: AN AMUSE APPLICATION

Multimedia Communication System C-QUSE

To evaluate the feasibility and effectiveness of our scheme, we implemented an application of a multimedia communication system based on AMUSE: Context and QoS-Aware Ubiquitous Service Environment (C-QUSE). Multimedia communication is a resource-sensitive application domain. Consequently, it presents a good example to confirm the effectiveness of AMUSE. In fact, C-QUSE can consider multiple contexts and provide QoS-aware multimedia communication services. This system can provide users with live streaming services—video stream or videoconferencing—whenever I/O devices such as PCs, televisions, and audio systems are available near the user. Moreover, this service can control user requests and quality according to the user's circumstances, including the user's physical position. Users can be furnished with a live video stream of distant places anywhere and at any time. This system has widely various applications. Especially, support of tele-work, teleconferencing, and content delivery for amusement, which includes music, movie, sportscasts, home movies, etc., are promising applications of this system. We are targeting services that remain close to a user's movement and provide live contents. Therefore, we presume that it is most important that the system provide such services extemporaneously in an ad hoc manner using available devices at that location.

Implementation of C-QUSE

This application has been implemented using IDEA, with the reuse of some agents developed for the simulation experiments described in Section 4. The positional information of a user, which is one user context, is tracked by IS-600 (InterSense, n.d.). We use Java Communications API to acquire the positional information from IS-600 into a Java environment. We connected a DV camera and a USB Web camera to the PC that serves as live streaming server. The streaming server agent, residing in the server, manages the streaming service. It can provide different qualities of service based on the agent request if the streaming server agent receives another agent's request. We use DVTS (Ogawa, 2000) and Java Media Framework (JMF) (Sun Developer Network, n.d.) for sending streams of different quality. As home electrical appliances, we used a television set. We converted digital DV streams to an analog signal using a DV converter.

Empirical Study with C-QUSE

In this experiment, we evaluate the feasibility and effectiveness of AMUSE particularly addressing its ability of multiple context management. This experiment consists of the following three scenarios. We observed the system behavior according to some scenarios.

1. User-location-oriented behavior

    Here, we check that our system based on AMUSE can provide location-oriented service to the user similarly to existing ubiquitous services.

2. User-request-oriented behavior

    In this case, we confirm that our system can provide the service based on user requests. From this scenario, we prove that AMUSE can provide the service considering not only the user location but also user requests.

3.   Multiple-context-oriented behavior

In this case, we confirm that our system can provide context-aware services considering QoS through cooperation among agents. From this case, we prove that our framework has a potential and beneficial effect on ubiquitous multimedia communication services.

Figure 16 presents the user-location-oriented service provision of C-QUSE. In this case, we used a position sensor (Soni-Disc, Intersense IS-600 Mark 2) attached to a cellular telephone to track the user's positional information. A laptop PC, which can provide I/O of video services, is managed by an agent. When a user approaches the laptop PC (Figure 16 (step 1)), the agent recognizes the user and starts the service. Managing the laptop PC, the agent checks the available software for receiving the video stream and the required streaming server agent of the video stream using JMF. The streaming server agent receives the request; then it delivers the video stream to a laptop PC (Figure 16 (step 2)). From this case, we can confirm that our system based on AMUSE can provide service as in the case of the existing user-location-oriented ubiquitous services. However, QoS is not considered in this case; thereby a comfortable service that satisfies the user requirement cannot be available.

Figure 17 presents behavior in the case of user-request-oriented service provision. In this

Figure 16. User-location-oriented service provisioning by C-QUSE

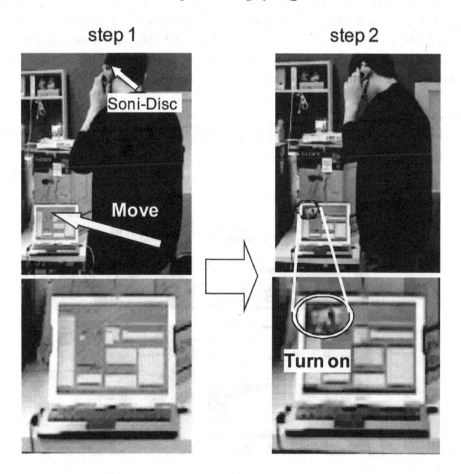

case, we employed a position sensor (Soni-Disc) attached to a cellular telephone, as portrayed in Figure 16. We used television and desktop PCs to provide video service I/O. These hardware devices are managed, respectively, by a TV agent and Desktop PC agent. When the user approaches the television and the desktop PC, these agents referred to the user request of quality from user contexts. Regarding Figure 17 (scenario 1), the user requested only video stream service with no requirement of quality. Then, the Desktop PC agent required the streaming server agent of the video stream using JMF. This stream does not consume large amounts of network resources. Regarding Figure 17 (scenario 2), the user requested high-quality service. Then, the TV agent required the streaming server agent of the video stream using DVTS; the TV agent provided high-quality video stream service. From this case, we confirmed that our system can provide users with service based on user request information other than the user location.

Figure 18 depicts behavior in cases of multiple-context-oriented service provision. In this case, we used three hardware devices for providing I/O of video services: a television, a desktop PC, and a laptop PC. For this simulation, we assume that a user brings a portable terminal device such as a PDA and has a position sensor (Soni-Disc) attached to a laptop PC. The user moves with the laptop PC and the user request is high quality. These hardware devices are managed, respectively, by the TV agent, the Desktop PC agent, and the Laptop PC agent.

In step 1 shown in Figure 18, the laptop PC is the only device that can provide a user with service from the location of user contexts and hardware contexts. Therefore, the laptop PC agent provides users with the stream using JMF because the laptop PC agent infers the available function as a maximum quality. In step 2 shown in Figure 18, the TV agent and the Desktop PC agent recognized that a user is approaching their range of service area. They referred to the user requests from contexts and other agents' contexts from their own IAR. They knew the Laptop PC agent was providing the user with the service. They compared the available quality with the laptop PC agent

Figure 17. User-request-oriented service provisioning by C-QUSE

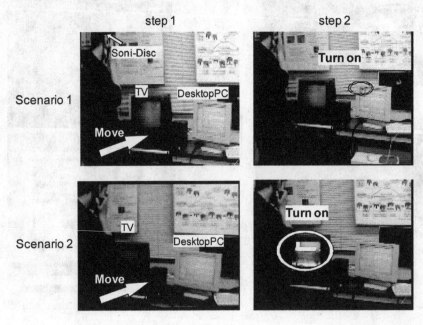

Figure 18. Multiple-context-oriented service provisioning using C-QUSE

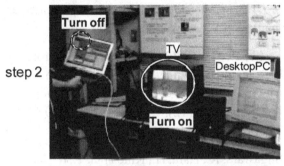

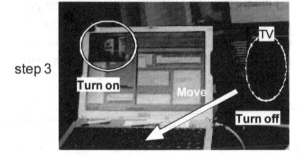

because user requests of quality were high. The TV agent made the judgment that it is possible to provide much higher quality than anyone else, and requested stopping of the service with the Laptop PC agent. Then, the TV agent required the streaming server agent of the video stream using DVTS after the Laptop PC agent accepted the TV agent request. In step 3 of Figure 18, when a user moved away from the TV that was providing the service and the Desktop PC, the TV agent stopped the service with other agents. Furthermore, the Laptop PC agent started the service for the nearest device from the user. From this case, we

can verify that individual agents based on AMUSE can provide service while controlling quality by considering other agents' contexts.

From these three experiments, we have confirmed the remarkable features of our scheme compared to the traditional ubiquitous system. Agents that have competing functions can cooperate mutually through effective use of IAR. For instance, when streaming server's resources are low, the streaming server bogs down if any agent requests DVTS and JMF solely by considering user contexts.

CONCLUSION

As described in this paper, we proposed AMUSE: multiagent-based middleware for Context-aware ubiquitous service. We described the AMUSE design, particularly addressing the service construction scheme for QoS-aware service provision considering multiple contexts. We also evaluated our scheme through simulation experiments and confirmed its remarkable usefulness in a ubiquitous environment, particularly for multimedia services. Moreover, we implemented an application as a first step towards practical use of AMUSE and performed some empirical studies with a prototype system concentrating on evaluation of the effectiveness of multiple context management.

Future efforts will be undertaken to evaluate the prototype system using various actual hardware devices such as PCs and home electrical appliances to confirm the feasibility, effectiveness, and basic performance in a real-world environment. As a future goal of our research, we shall consider various agent statuses more dynamically to improve the updating and deletion mechanism of IAR with more extensive simulation.

ACKNOWLEDGMENT

This work was partially supported by Japan Society for the Promotion of Science Grants-in-Aid for Scientific Research, 19200005 and 20500060.

REFERENCES

Bellavista, P., Corradi, A., Montanari, R., & Stefanelli, C. (2003). Context-Aware Middleware for Resource Management in the Wireless Internet. *IEEE Transactions on Software Engineering, 29*(12), 1086–1099. doi:10.1109/TSE.2003.1265523

Fujita, S., Hara, H., Sugawara, K., Kinoshita, T., & Shiratori, N. (1998). Agent-based design model of adaptive distributed systems. *The International Journal of Artificial Intelligence . Neural Networks and Complex Problem-Solving Technologies, 9*(1), 57–70.

Gribble, S., Welsh, M., Behren, R., Brewer, E., Culler, D., Borisov, N., et al. (2001). The Ninja architecture for robust Internet-scale systems and services. *Special Issue of Computer Networks on Pervasive Computing, 35*(4). InterSense. (n.d.). *IS600: IS-600 Mark 2 Precision Motion Tracker*. Retrieved from http://www.isense.com/

Itao, T., Nakamura, T., Matsuo, M., Suda, T., & Aoyama, T. (2002). Adaptive creation of network applications in the jack-in-the-net architecture. In *Proceedings of IFIP Networking* (pp. 129-140).

Iwamoto, T., & Tokuda, H. (2003). PMAA: Media access architecture for ubiquitous computing. *Journal of IPSJ, 44*(3), 848–856.

Lum, W. Y., & Lau, F. C. M. (2003). User-centric content negotiation for effective adaptation service in mobile computing. *IEEE Transactions on Software Engineering, 29*(12), 1100–1111. doi:10.1109/TSE.2003.1265524

Minami, M., Morikawa, H., & Aoyama, T. (2003). The design and evaluation of an interface-based naming system for supporting service synthesis in ubiquitous computing environment. *IEICE Transactions, J86-B*(5), 777-789.

Minoh, M., & Kamae, T. (2001). Networked appliance and their peer-to-peer srchitecture AMIDEN. *IEEE Communications Magazine, 39*(10), 80–84. doi:10.1109/35.956117

Nakazawa, J., Tobe, Y., & Tokuda, H. (2001). On dynamic service integration in VNA architecture. *IEICE Transactions . E (Norwalk, Conn.), 84-A*(7), 1624–1635.

Ogawa, A., Kobayashi, K., Sugiura, K., Nakamura, O., & Murai, J. (2000). *Design and implementation of DV based video over RTP*. Paper presented at the Packet Video Workshop 2000.

Smith, R. G. (1980). The contract net protocol high-level communication and control in a distributed problem solver. *IEEE Transactions on Computers, 29*(12), 1104–1113. doi:10.1109/TC.1980.1675516

Sugawara, K., Hara, H., Kinoshita, T., & Uchiya, T. (2002). Flexible distributed agent system programmed by a rule-based language. In *Proceedings of the Sixth IASTED International Conference of Artificial Intelligence and Soft Computing* (pp. 7-12).

Sugawara, K., Shiratori, N., & Kinoshita, T. (2003). Toward post ubiquitous computing–symbiotic computing. *IEICE Technical Report, 103*(244), 43–46.

Sun Developer Network. (n.d.). *JMF: Java media framework*. Retrieved from http://java.sun.com/products/java-media/jmf/

Takagaki, A., Uchiya, T., Hara, H., Abe, T., & Kinoshita, T. (2003). Interactive development support environment for agent systems. *Information Technology Letters, 2*, 143–144.

Weiser, M. (1991). The computer for the twenty-first century. *Scientific American, 265*(3), 94–104.

This work was previously published in International Journal of Software Science and Computational Intelligence, Volume 2, Issue 1, edited by Yingxu Wang, pp. 1-23, copyright 2010 by IGI Publishing (an imprint of IGI Global).

Chapter 9
Relevant and Non–Redundant Amino Acid Sequence Selection for Protein Functional Site Identification

Chandra Das
West Bengal University of Technology, India

Pradipta Maji
Indian Statistical Institute, India

ABSTRACT

In order to apply a powerful pattern recognition algorithm to predict functional sites in proteins, amino acids cannot be used directly as inputs since they are non-numerical variables. Therefore, they need encoding prior to input. In this regard, the bio-basis function maps a non-numerical sequence space to a numerical feature space. One of the important issues for the bio-basis function is how to select a minimum set of bio-basis strings with maximum information. In this paper, an efficient method to select bio-basis strings for the bio-basis function is described integrating the concepts of the Fisher ratio and "degree of resemblance". The integration enables the method to select a minimum set of most informative bio-basis strings. The "degree of resemblance" enables efficient selection of a set of distinct bio-basis strings. In effect, it reduces the redundant features in numerical feature space. Quantitative indices are proposed for evaluating the quality of selected bio-basis strings. The effectiveness of the proposed bio-basis string selection method, along with a comparison with existing methods, is demonstrated on different data sets.

DOI: 10.4018/978-1-4666-0264-9.ch009

INTRODUCTION

Cognitive informatics is the cross fertilization between computer science, artificial intelligence, systems science, cognitive science, neuropsychology, life science, and so forth (Wang, 2009a; Wang, 2009b; Wang et al., 2006b). It investigates the internal information processing mechanisms and processes of natural intelligence, and forges links between a number of natural science and life science disciplines with informatics and computing science (Wang et al., 2006a; Wang et al., 2006b).

The fundamental methodology of cognitive informatics uses informatics and computing techniques to investigate cognitive science problems such as memory, learning, and reasoning in one direction, although it is bidirectional and comparative in nature (Wang, 2009a; Wang, 2009b; Wang et al., 2006a; Wang et al., 2009; Wang et al., 2006b). In this paper, a new learning algorithm is presented to select a set of relevant and non-redundant amino acid sequences for identification of protein functional sites.

Recent advancement and wide use of high-throughput technology for biological research are producing enormous size of biological data. The successful analysis of biological data has become critical. Although laboratory experiment is the most effective method to analyze the biological data, it is very financially expensive and labor intensive. Pattern recognition techniques and machine learning methods provide useful tools for analyzing the biological data (Arrigo et al., 1991; Ferran et al., 1991; Cai et al., 1998; Baldi et al., 1995).

The prediction of functional sites in proteins is an important issue in protein function studies and hence, drug design. As a result, most researchers use protein sequences for the analysis or the prediction of protein functions in various ways (Baldi et al., 1998; Yang, 2004). Thus, one of the major tasks in bioinformatics is the classification and prediction of protein sequences. There are two types of analysis of protein sequences. The first is to analyze whole sequences aiming to annotate novel proteins or classify proteins. In this method the protein function is annotated through aligning a novel protein sequence with a known protein sequence. If the similarity between a novel sequence and a known sequence is very high, the novel protein is believed to have the same or similar function as the known protein. The second is to recognize functional sites within a sequence. The latter normally deals with subsequences (Yang, 2004).

The problem of functional sites prediction deals with the subsequences; each subsequence is obtained through moving a fixed length sliding window residue by residue. The residues within a scan form a subsequence. If there is a functional site within a subsequence, the subsequence is labeled as functional; otherwise it is labeled as non-functional. Therefore, protein subsequence analysis problem is to classify a subsequence whether it is functional or non-functional (Yang, 2004). The major objective in classification analysis is to train a classification model based on labeled data. The trained model is then used for classifying novel data. Classification analysis requires two descriptions of an object: one is the set of features that are used as inputs to train the model and the other is referred to as the class label. Classification analysis aims to find a mapping function from the features to the class label.

Many powerful pattern recognition algorithms like back-propagation neural networks (Cai et al., 1998; Qian et al., 1988; Narayanan et al., 2002), Kohonen's self-organising map (Arrigo et al., 1991), feed-forward and recurrent neural networks (Baldi et al., 1995; Baldi et al., 1998), bio-basis function neural networks (Thomson et al., 2003; Berry et al., 2004; Yang et al., 2005a; Yang, 2005b; Yang et al., 2005b; Yang et al., 2004), and support vector machines (Yang, 2004; Cai, 2002; Minakuchi, 2002), have been used to predict different functional sites in proteins such as protease cleavage sites of HIV (human immunodeficiency virus) and Hepatitis C Virus, linkage sites of glycoprotein, enzyme active sites, post-translational phosphorylation sites, immunological domains, Trypsin cleavage sites, protein-protein interaction sites, etc. Most of these algorithms work with numerical inputs. Hence, the biological data cannot be used as direct inputs for these algorithms since they are nonnumeric variables (features). In order to apply a powerful pattern recognition algorithm to predict functional sites in proteins, the biological data, therefore, have to be encoded prior to input. The objective of coding biological information in sequences is to provide a method for converting non-numerical attributes in sequences to numerical attributes. There are two main methods for coding a subsequence, distributed encoding technique (Qian et al., 1988) and bio-basis function method (Thomson, 2003; Berry, 2004; Yang et al., 2005a). The most commonly used method in subsequence analysis is distributed encoding, which encodes each of 20 amino acids using a 20-bit binary vector (Qian et al., 1988). In this method, the input space for modeling is expanded unnecessarily. Also, the ratio of the number of parameters in a model is significantly decreased, which degenerates the statistical significance of the available data for modeling. Moreover, the use of the Euclidean distance may not be able to encode biological content in sequences efficiently.

In this background, Thomson et al., Berry et al., and Yang and Thomson (Thomson et al., 2003; Berry et al., 2004; Yang et al., 2005a) proposed the concept of bio-basis function for analyzing biological subsequences. It uses a kernel function to transform biological sequences to the feature vectors directly. The bio-basis strings are the sections of biological sequences that code for features of interest in the study, and are responsible for the transformation of biological data to high dimensional feature space. Transformation of input data to high dimensional feature space is performed based on the similarity of an input subsequence to a bio-basis string with reference to a biological similarity matrix. The use of similarity matrices

to map features allows the bio-basis function to analyze biological sequences without the need for encoding. The concept of bio-basis function has been successfully applied to predict different functional sites in proteins (Thomson et al., 2003; Berry et al., 2004; Yang et al., 2005a; Yang, 2005b; Yang et al., 2004; Yang et al., 2005b).

The most important issue for bio-basis function is how to select a minimum set of bio-basis strings with maximum information. Berry et al. (Berry et al., 2004) used the Fisher ratio for selection of bio-basis strings. Yang and Thomson (Yang et al., 2005a] proposed a method to select bio-basis strings using mutual information. In principle, the bio-basis strings in non-numerical sequence space should be such that the degree of resemblance between pairs of bio-basis strings would be as minimum as possible. Each of them would then represent a unique feature in numerical feature space. However, the methods proposed in (Berry et al., 2004) and (Yang et al., 2005a) have not adequately addressed this problem. Also, it has not been paid much attention earlier.

In this paper, we propose an efficient method, integrating the Fisher ratio and the concept of "degree of resemblance", to select most informative and distinct bio-basis strings for the kernel function. Instead of using symmetric similarity measure, the asymmetric biological distance is used to calculate the Fisher ratio, which is more effective for selection of most informative bio-basis strings. The biological distance is measured using an amino acid mutation matrix. The "degree of resemblance" enables efficient selection of a set of distinct bio-basis strings. In effect, it reduces the redundant features in numerical feature space. Some quantitative measures are introduced to evaluate the quality of selected bio-basis strings. The effectiveness of the proposed bio-basis string selection method, along with a comparison with existing methods, is demonstrated on different protein data sets.

The structure of the rest of this paper is as follows: Section 2 briefly introduces necessary notions of bio-basis function, and the bio-basis string selection methods proposed by Berry et al. (2004) and Yang and Thomson (2005a). In Section 3, the concept of asymmetricity of biological distance is introduced. In Section 4, an efficient bio-basis string selection method is proposed based on the Fisher ratio and the "degree of resemblance". Some quantitative performance measures are presented in Section 5 to evaluate the quality of selected bio-basis strings. A few case studies and a comparison with existing methods are presented in Section 6. Concluding remarks are given in Section 7.

BIO-BASIS FUNCTION AND STRING SELECTION METHODS

In this section, the basic notion in the theory of bio-basis function is reported, along with the bio-basis string selection methods proposed by Yang and Thomson (2005a) and Berry et al. (2004).

Bio-Basis Function

A widely used method in sequence analysis is the sequence alignment (Altschul et al., 1990; Altschul et al., 1994). An alignment of nucleotide or amino acid sequences represents a hypothesis about the evolutionary path by which the two subsequences diverged from a common ancestor. Pair-wise comparison is a fundamental task in sequence analysis, which seeks to determine whether sequences are significantly similar, and hence whether or not they are likely to be homologous (sequences, that share a common ancestor). If the alignment between a novel sequence and a known sequence gives a very high homology score, the novel sequence is believed to have the same or similar function as the known sequence. In pair-wise homology alignment method, an amino acid mutation matrix is commonly used. Each mutation matrix has 20 columns and 20 rows. A value at the nth row and mth column is a probability or a

likelihood value that the nth amino acid mutates to the mth amino acid after a particular evolutionary time (Henrikoff, 1992; Johnson, 1993). The mutation probabilities as similarities among amino acids are, therefore, metrics. The Dayhoff matrix (Figure 1) was the first mutation matrix developed in 1978 (Dayhoff, 1978) and many new mutation matrices were developed later on, for instance, the Blosum62 matrix (Henrikoff, 1992). However, the above method may not be useful directly for subsequence analysis. This is because a subsequence may not contain enough information for conventional homology alignment. A high homology alignment score between a novel subsequence and a known subsequence cannot assert that two subsequences have the same (proteolytic) function.

To alleviate this problem, the concept of bio-basis function is introduced in (Thomson et al., 2003; Berry et al., 2004; Yang et al., 2005a) for subsequence analysis, which is based on the principle of conventional alignment technique. Using a table look-up technique, a homology score as a similarity value can be obtained for a pair of subsequences. The non-gapped pair-wise alignment technique is used to calculate this similarity value, where no deletion or insertion is used to align two subsequences (Thomson et al., 2003; Berry et al., 2004; Yang et al., 2005a). For ease of discussions, in rest of the paper, the following terminologies are used.

- $A = \{ A, C, \ldots\ldots, W, Y\}$ be the set of 20 amino acids.
- $X = \{ x_{1, \ldots\ldots,} x_{j,} \ldots\ldots,x_{n} \}$ be the set of n subsequences with m residues, $x_j \in A^m$, $\forall_j^n = 1$

$$\overline{\sigma}_{A_i}^2 = \frac{1}{n_1} \sum \{d^2(x_j,x_i) - \overline{U}_{A_i}\}^2; x_j \in \Omega_A; \overline{\sigma}_{B_i}^2$$

$$= \frac{1}{n_2} \sum \{d^2(x_k,x_i) - \overline{U}_{B_i}\}^2; x_k \in \Omega_B$$

- c represents the total number of bio-basis strings.

Figure 1. Dayhoff mutation matrix

	A	C	D	E	F	G	H	I	K	L	M	N	P	Q	R	S	T	V	W	Y
A	40	24	32	32	16	36	28	28	28	24	28	32	36	32	24	36	36	32	8	20
C	24	80	12	12	16	20	20	24	12	8	12	16	20	12	16	32	24	24	0	32
D	32	12	48	44	8	36	36	24	32	16	20	40	28	40	28	32	32	24	4	16
E	32	12	44	48	12	32	36	24	32	20	24	36	28	40	28	32	32	24	4	16
F	16	16	8	12	68	12	24	36	12	40	32	16	12	12	16	20	20	28	32	60
G	36	20	36	32	12	52	24	20	24	16	20	32	28	28	20	36	32	28	4	12
H	28	20	36	36	24	24	56	24	32	24	24	40	32	44	40	28	28	24	20	32
I	28	24	24	24	36	20	24	52	24	40	40	24	24	24	28	28	32	48	12	28
K	28	12	32	32	12	24	32	24	52	20	32	36	28	36	44	32	32	24	20	16
L	24	8	16	20	40	16	24	40	20	56	48	20	20	24	20	20	24	40	24	28
M	28	12	20	24	32	20	24	40	32	48	56	24	24	28	32	24	28	40	16	24
N	32	16	40	36	16	32	40	24	36	20	24	40	28	36	32	36	32	24	16	24
P	36	20	28	28	12	28	32	24	28	20	24	28	56	32	32	36	28	28	8	12
Q	32	12	40	40	12	28	44	24	36	24	28	36	32	48	36	28	28	24	12	16
R	24	16	28	28	16	20	40	24	44	20	32	32	32	36	56	32	28	24	40	16
S	36	32	32	32	20	36	28	28	32	20	24	36	36	28	32	40	36	28	24	20
T	36	24	32	32	20	32	28	32	32	24	28	32	32	28	28	36	44	32	12	20
V	32	24	24	24	28	28	48	24	40	40	24	28	24	24	32	28	32	48	8	24
W	8	0	4	4	32	4	20	12	20	24	16	16	8	12	40	24	12	8	100	32
Y	20	32	16	16	60	12	32	28	16	28	24	24	12	16	16	20	20	24	32	72

- $V = \{ v_1, ..., v_i, ..., v_c \}$ be the set of c bio-basis strings, $v_i \in X$ and $v_i \in A^m$, $\forall_i^c - 1$
- $x_{jk} \in A$, $v_{ik} \in A$, $\forall_k^m = 1$

The definition of bio-basis function is as follows: (Thomson et al., 2003; Yang et al., 2005a):

$$f(x_j, v_i) = \exp\left\{ \gamma_b \frac{h(x_j, v_i) - h(v_i, v_i)}{h(v_i, v_i)} \right\} \quad (1)$$

- $h(x_j, v_i)$ is the homology score between a subsequence between a subsequence x_j and a bio-basis string v_i calculated using an amino acid mutation matrix [Thomson et al.03; Berry et al.04; Yang et al.05a] ;
- $h(v_i, v_i)$ denotes the maximum homology score of the ith bio-basis string v_i ; and
- γ_b is a constant and typically chosen to be 1.

Suppose both x_j and v_i have m residues, the homology score between x_j and v_i is then defined as:

$$h(x_j, v_i) = \sum_{k=1}^{m} M(x_{jk}, v_{ik}) \quad (2)$$

where $M(x_{jk}, v_{ik})$ can be obtained from an amino acid mutation matrix through a table look-up method. Note that $x_{jk}, v_{ik} \in A$ and A is a set of 20 amino acids (Table 1).

Consider two bio-basis strings v_1=KPRT and v_2=YKAE, and a subsequence x_1=IPRS having m = 4 residues. The non-gapped pair-wise homology score is calculated between the subsequence x_1 and each bio-basis string considering the mutation probabilities as in Table 1. For the first bio-basis string v_1, four mutation probabilities are

$$M(x_{11}, v_{11}) = M(I, K) = 24; M(x_{12}v_{12}) = M(P, P) = 56$$

$$M(x_{13}, v_{13}) = M(R, R) = 56; M(x_{14}v_{14}) = M(S, T) = 36$$

Hence, the homology score between the subsequence x_1 and the bio-basis string v_1 is given by

$$h(x_1, v_1) = \sum_{k=1}^{4} M(x_{1k}, v_{1k}) = 172$$

Similarly, for the second bio-basis string v_2, four mutation probabilities are 28, 28, 24, and 32. Thus, the value of $h(x_1, v_2)$ between the subsequence x_1 and the bio-basis string v_2 is as follows:

$$h(x_1, v_2) = \sum_{k=1}^{4} M(x_{1k}, v_{2k}) = 112$$

The maximum homology scores of two bio-basis strings v_1 and v_2 are given by

$$h(v_1, v_1) = 208 \text{ and } h(v_2, v_2) = 212$$

Considering the value of $\gamma_b = 1$

$$f(x_1, v_1) = \exp\left\{\gamma_b \frac{h(x_1, v_1) - h(v_1, v_1)}{h(v_1, v_1)}\right\} = 0.633334$$

$$f(v_1, v_1) = \exp\left\{\gamma_b \frac{h(v_1, v_1) - h(v_1, v_1)}{h(v_1, v_1)}\right\} = 1.000000$$

$$f(x_1, v_2) = \exp\left\{\gamma_b \frac{h(x_1, v_2) - h(v_2, v_2)}{h(v_2, v_2)}\right\} = 0.287988$$

$$f(v_2, v_2) = \exp\left\{\gamma_b \frac{h(v_2, v_2) - h(v_2, v_2)}{h(v_2, v_2)}\right\} = 1.000000$$

Hence, the value of bio-basis function $f(x_i, x_j)$ is high if two subsequences x_i and x_j are similar or close to each other. The function value is one if two subsequences are identical, and small if they are distinct. The function needs a subsequence as a support (bio-basis string). Each bio-basis string is a feature dimension in a numerical feature space. If A is used to denote a collection of 20 amino acids, an input space of all potential subsequences with m residues is A^m. Then, a collection of c bio-basis strings formulates a numerical feature space R^c, to which a non-numerical sequence space A^m is mapped for analysis. More importantly, the bio-basis function can transform various homology scores to a real number as a similarity within the interval [0, 1], that is,

$$0 \leq f(x_j, v_i) \leq 1 \tag{3}$$

After the mapping using bio-basis strings, a non-numerical subsequence space A^m will be mapped to a c-dimensional numerical feature space R^c, that is, $A^m \rightarrow R^c$.

Selection of Bio-Basis Strings Using Mutual Information

In (Yang et al., 2005a), Yang and Thomson proposed a method for bio-basis string selection using mutual information (Shannon et al., 1964). In principle, the mutual information is used to quantify the information shared by two objects. If two independent objects do not share much information, the mutual information value between them is small. While two highly nonlinearly correlated objects will demonstrate a high mutual information value (Shannon et al., 1964). The objects can be the class label and the bio-basis strings. The necessity for a bio-basis string to be an independent and informative feature can, therefore, be determined by the shared information between the bio-basis string and the rest as well as the shared information between the bio-basis string and class label (Yang et al., 2005a).

The mutual information is quantified as the difference between the initial uncertainty and the conditional uncertainty. Let $\phi = \{v_i\}$ be a set of selected bio-basis strings, $\theta = \{v_k\}$, a set of candidate bio-basis strings. $\phi = \Phi$ (empty) at the beginning. A prior probability of a bio-basis string v_k is referred as $p(v_k)$. The initial uncertainty of v_k is defined as

$$H(v_k) = -p(v_k) \ln p(v_k) \tag{4}$$

Similarly, the joint probability of two bio-basis strings v_k and v_i is given by

$$H(v_k, v_i) = -p(v_k, v_i) \ln p(v_k, v_i) \tag{5}$$

where $v_i \in \phi$ and $v_k \in \theta$. The mutual information between v_k and v_i is, therefore, given by

$$\begin{aligned} I(v_k, v_i) &= H(v_k) + H(v_i) - H(v_k, v_i) \\ &= -p(v_k) \ln p(v_k) - p(v_i) \ln p(v_i) \\ &\quad + p(v_k, v_i) \ln p(v_k, v_i) \end{aligned} \tag{6}$$

Hence, the mutual information of v_k with respect to all the bio-basis strings in ϕ is

$$I(v_k, \Phi) = \sum_{v_i \in \Phi} I(v_k, v_i) \qquad (7)$$

Combining (6) and (7), we get [36]

$$I(v_k, \Phi) = \sum_{v_i \in \Phi} p(v_k, v_i) \ln \left\{ \frac{p(v_k, v_i)}{p(v_k)p(v_i)} \right\} \qquad (8)$$

Replacing ϕ with the class label $\Omega = \{\Omega_1, \ldots, \Omega_j, \ldots, \Omega_M\}$, the mutual information measures the mutual relationship between v_k and Ω. A bio-basis string whose $I(v_k, \Omega)$ value is the largest will be selected as v_k and will make the largest contribution to modeling (discrimination using Ω) among all the remaining bio-basis strings in θ. Therefore, there are two mutual information measurements for v_k, the mutual information between v_k and Ω ($I(v_k, \Omega)$) and the mutual information between v_k and ϕ($I(v_k, \phi)$). In this method, the following criterion is used for the selection of bio-basis strings (Yang et al., 2005a; Yang, 2005a)

$$I(v_k, \Omega) = \sum_{\Omega_j \in \Omega} p(v_k, \Omega_j) \ln \left\{ \frac{p(v_k, \Omega_j)}{p(v_k)p(\Omega_j)} \right\} \qquad (9)$$

$$J(v_k) = \alpha_{YT} I(v_k, \Omega) - (1 - \alpha_{YT}) I(v_k, \Phi) \qquad (10)$$

where α_{YT} is a constant. In the current study, the value of α_{YT} is set at 0.7 to give more weight-age in discrimination (Yang et al., 2005a; Yang, 2005a). Two major drawbacks of the method proposed by Yang and Thomson (Yang et al., 2005a) are as follows:

1. A huge number of prior and joint probabilities are to be calculated, which makes the method computationally expensive.
2. Also, this method does not incorporate the biological content of sequences.

Selection of Bio-Basis Strings Using Fisher Ratio

In (Berry et al., 2004), Berry et al. (2004) proposed a method to select a set of c bio-basis strings from the whole set of n subsequences based on their discriminant capability. The discriminant capability of each subsequence is calculated using the Fisher ratio (Duda, 2001). Since the n subsequences would have different compositions of amino acids, they should have different pair-wise alignment scores with the remaining training subsequences. As the class properties of the training subsequences are known, these similarity values can be subdivided into two groups or classes (functional and non-functional), which are denoted as $\Omega_A \in \Omega$ and $\Omega_B \in \Omega$. Denoting the similarity between two subsequences x_i and x_j as $h(x_j, x_i)$, the mean and standard deviation values for these two groups with respect to the subsequence x_i are as follows:

$$U_{A_i} = E_A[h(x_j, x_i)] = \frac{1}{n_1} \sum h(x_j, x_i) \forall_{x_j} \in \Omega_A \qquad (11)$$

$$U_{B_i} = E_B[h(x_k, x_i)] = \frac{1}{n_2} \sum h(x_k, x_i) \forall_{x_k} \in \Omega_B \qquad (12)$$

$$\sigma_{A_i}^2 = E_A[h^2(x_j, x_i)] - [E_A[h(x_j, x_i)]]^2 = \frac{1}{n_1} \sum \{h(x_j, x_i) - U_{A_i}\}^2; x_j \in \Omega_A \qquad (13)$$

$$\sigma_{B_i}^2 = E_B[h^2(x_k, x_i)] - [E_B[h(x_k, x_i)]]^2 = \frac{1}{n_2} \sum \{h(x_k, x_i) - U_{B_i}\}^2; x_k \in \Omega_B \qquad (14)$$

where n_1 and n_2 are the number of subsequences in Ω_A and Ω_B, respectively. $E_A[h(x_j, x_i)]$ and $E_B[h^2(x_k, x_i)]$ represent the mean or expectation of first and second order similarity, that is, expectation of $h(x_j, x_i)$ and $h^2(x_j, x_i)$ respectively.

Based on these four quantities, the discriminant capability of each subsequence can be measured using the Fisher ratio

$$F(x_i) = \frac{|U_{A_i} - U_{B_i}|}{\sqrt{\sigma_{A_i}^2 + \sigma_{B_i}^2}} \qquad (15)$$

$$\left|U_{A_i} - U_{B_i}\right| = \left|E_A[h-(x_j, x_i)] - E_B[h(x_k, x_i)]\right| \qquad (16)$$

$$\sigma_{A_i}^2 + \sigma_{B_i}^2 = \{E_A[h^2(x_j, x_i)] + E_B[h^2(x_k, x_i)]\}$$
$$- \{[E_A[h(x_j, x_i)]]^2 + [E_B[h(x_k, x_i)]]^2\} \qquad (17)$$

The larger the Fisher ratio value, the larger the discriminant capability of the subsequence. Based on the values of the Fisher ratio, n subsequences can be ranked from the strongest discriminant capability to the weakest one. The method yields a set of c subsequences as the bio-basis strings which possess good discriminant capability between the two classes, having evolved from the original data set.

However, the bio-basis strings in non-numerical sequence space should be such that the similarity between pairs of bio-basis strings would be as minimum as possible. Each of them would then represent a unique feature in numerical feature space. The methods proposed in (Berry et al., 2004) and (Yang et al., 2005a) have not adequately addressed this problem. Also, not much attention has been paid to it earlier.

ASYMMETRICITY OF BIOLOGICAL DISTANCE

In this section, the concept of asymmetricity of biological distance is presented. Here, we define two asymmetric distances between two subsequences x_i and x_j as follows:

$$d_{x_i} \rightarrow x_j = d(x_j, x_i) = \{h(x_i, x_i) - h(x_j, x_i)\}$$
$$d_{xj} \rightarrow x_i = d(x_i, x_j) = \{h(x_j, x_j) - h(x_i, x_j)\} \qquad (18)$$

Where $dx_i \rightarrow x_j$ denotes the distance of subsequence x_j from the subsequence x_i and $h(x_i, x_j)$ $(=h(x_j, x_i))$ is the non-gapped homology score between two subsequences x_i and x_j.

Consider two subsequences x_i = KPRT and x_j = YKAE with 4 residues. According to the Dayhoff mutation matrix ([Dayhoff et al.78], Table 1), the non-gapped pair-wise homology score between two subsequences x_i and x_j is, therefore, $h(x_i, x_j)$ = $h(x_j, x_i)$ = 100, while the maximum homology scores of two subsequences x_i and x_j are given by $h(x_i, x_j)$ = 208 and $h(x_j, x_i)$ = 212, respectively. Hence, the distance of subsequence x_j from the subsequence x_i is given by

$$d(x_j, x_i) = \{h(x_i, x_i) - h(x_j, x_i)\} = 208 - 100 = 108$$

Where as the distance of x_i from x_j is as follows:

$$d(x_i, x_j) = \{h(x_j, x_j) - h(x_i, x_j)\} = 212 - 100 = 112$$

Thus, the distance is asymmetric in nature, that is,

$$d(x_j, x_i) \neq d(x_i, x_j) \qquad (19)$$

It should be noted that the term "distance" is used as a matter of convenience, though the distance should be symmetric in general. The asymmetricity reflects domain organizations of two subsequences x_i and x_j. When two subsequences x_i and x_j consist of the same single domain, $d(x_j, x_i)$ and $d(x_i, x_j)$ will be similar small values. However, suppose that x_i has one extra domain, then $d(x_j, x_i)$ becomes large even if $d(x_i, x_j)$ is small. These distances may be used for clustering of protein sequences or subsequences so that domain organizations are well reflected. The asymmetric property of the biological distance was also observed by Stojmirovic (2004) and Itoh et al. (2005). The asymmetric distance might be a powerful tool to cluster sequences and to explore the gene/protein universe.

PROPOSED BIO-BASIS STRING SELECTION METHOD

One of the main problems in bio-basis function is how to select a set of most informative bio-basis strings. Each bio-basis string is a biological subsequence that represents a feature of interest and transforms biological data to numerical feature space. Hence, the problem of selecting a set $V = \{v_1, \cdots, v_p, \cdots, v_c\}$ of c subsequences as the bio-basis strings from the whole set $X = \{x_1, \cdots, x_j, \cdots, x_n\}$ of n subsequences, where $V \subset X$, is a feature selection problem.

In real biological data analysis, the data set may contain a number of similar or redundant subsequences with low discriminant capability or relevance to the classes. The selection of such similar and non-relevant subsequences as the bio-basis strings may lead to a reduction in the useful information in numerical feature space. Ideally, the selected bio-basis strings should have high discriminant capability with the classes while the similarity among them would be as low as possible. The subsequences with high discriminant capability are expected to be able to predict the classes of the subsequences. However, the prediction capability may be reduced if many similar subsequences are selected as the bio-basis strings. In contrast, a data set that contains subsequences not only with high relevance with respect to the classes but with low mutual redundancy is more effective in its prediction capability. Hence, to assess the effectiveness of the subsequences as the bio-basis strings, both the relevance and the redundancy (similarity) need to be measured quantitatively. The proposed bio-basis string selection method addresses the above issues through following three phases:

1. Computation of the discriminant capability or relevance of each subsequence;
2. Determination of the non-relevant subsequences; and
3. Computation of the similarity or redundancy among subsequences.

An asymmetric biological distance based Fisher ratio is chosen here to compute the discriminant capability or relevance of each subsequence to the classes, while a novel concept of the "degree of resemblance" is used to calculate the mutual redundancy (similarity) among subsequences. The non-relevant subsequences are discarded using a nearest mean classifier. Prior to describe the proposed method for selecting bio-basis strings, next we provide the calculation of the Fisher ratio using asymmetric biological distance along with the principle of nearest mean classifier and the concept of "degree of resemblance".

Fisher Ratio Using Asymmetric Biological Distance

In the proposed method, the Fisher ratio [Duda01] is used to measure the discriminant capability or relevance of each subsequence. The Fisher ratio is calculated based on the asymmetric biological distance that is as follows:

$$\overline{\mathbb{F}}(x_i) = \frac{\left| U_{A_i} - U_{B_i} \right|}{\sqrt{\overline{\sigma}_{A_i}^2 + \overline{\sigma}_{B_i}^2}} \qquad (20)$$

where U_{A_i}, U_{B_i}, σ_{A_i} and σ_{B_i} represent the mean and standard deviation values of the subsequence x_i for two groups Ω_A and Ω_B, respectively. These four quantities are calculated based on the square of asymmetric biological distance with respect to the subsequence x_i and are as follows:

$$U_{A_i} = \frac{1}{n_1}\sum d^2(x_j, x_i); x_j \in \Omega_A \text{ and } |\Omega_A| = n_1$$

$$(21)$$

$$U_{B_i} = \frac{1}{n_1}\sum d^2(x_k, x_i); x_k \in \Omega_B \text{ and } |\Omega_B| = n_2$$

$$(22)$$

$$\overline{\sigma}^2_{A_i} = \frac{1}{n_1}\sum \{d^2(x_j, x_i) - \overline{U}_{A_i}\}^2; x_j \in \Omega_A; \overline{\sigma}^2_{B_i}$$

$$= \frac{1}{n_2}\sum \{d^2(x_k, x_i) - \overline{U}_{B_i}\}^2; x_k \in \Omega_B$$

$$(23)$$

Let $\kappa_i = h(x_i, x_i)$ represents the maximum homology score of the subsequence x_i. The above four quantities can be written using κ_i as

$$\overline{U}_{A_i} = \{k_i^2 + E_A[h^2(x_j, x_i)] - 2k_i E_A[h(x_j, x_i)]\}$$

$$\overline{U}_{B_i} = \{k_i^2 + E_B[h^2(x_k, x_i)] - 2k_i E_B[h(x_k, x_i)]\}$$

$$\overline{\sigma}^2_{A_i} = \{4k_i^2(E_A[h^2(x_j, x_i)] - [E_A[h(x_j, x_i)]]^2)$$

$$\frac{TP}{TP + FP}; TP_f = \frac{TP}{TP + FN}; TN_f \frac{TN}{TN + FP}$$

$$-[E_A[h^2(x_j, x_i)]]^2 + E_A[h^4(x_j, x_i)]\}$$

And

$$\overline{\sigma}^2_{B_i} = \{4k_i^2(E_B[h^2(x_k, x_i)] - [E_B[h(x_k, x_i)]]^2)$$

$$-4k_i(E_B[h^3(x_k, x_i)] - E_B[h(x_k, x_i)]E_B[h^2(x_k, x_i)])$$

$$-[E_B[h^2(x_k, x_i)]]^2 + E_B[h^4(x_k, x_i)]\}$$

where $E[h^r(x_j, x_i)]$ represents the mean or expectation of the rth order similarity $h(x_j, x_i)$ of two subsequences x_i and x_j. Now, the numerator of (20) is given by

$$\left|\overline{U}_{A_i} - \overline{U}_{B_i}\right| = \left|\{E_A[h^2(x_j, x_i)] - E_B[h^2(x_k, x_i)]\}\right.$$

$$\left. - 2_{k_i}\{E_A[h(x_j, x_i)] - E_B[h(x_k, x_i)]\}\right|$$

$$(24)$$

Hence, the numerator of (20) not only depends on the difference of expectation of first order similarity of two groups as in (15), it also takes into account the difference of expectation of second order similarity as well as the maximum homology score of the subsequence x_i. That is, the numerator of (20) depends on following three factors:

- Difference of expectation of similarity of two groups, $\{E_A[h(x_j, x_i)] - E_B[h(x_k, x_i)]\}$;
- Difference of expectation of second order similarity of two groups, $\{E_A[h^2(x_j, x_i)] - E_B[h^2(x_k, x_i)]\}$;
- Maximum homology score of the subsequence x_i, that is, $\kappa_i = h(x_i, x_i)$.

Similarly, the denominator of (20) contains the following terms:

$$\overline{\sigma}^2_{A_i} + \overline{\sigma}^2_{B_i} = [4k_i^2\{E_A[h^2(x_j, x_i)] + E_B[h^2(x_k, x_i)]\}$$

$$(25)$$

Hence, the denominator of (20) considers expectation of higher order (upto fourth order) similarity of two groups as well as the maximum homology score of the subsequence x_i while that of (15) only takes into account the expectation of first and second order similarity of two groups and does not consider the maximum homology score of the subsequence x_i. In effect, (20) calculates the discriminant capability of each subsequence x_i more accurately.

Nearest Mean Classifier

After computing the discriminant capability or relevance $F(x_i)$ of each subsequence x_i according to (20), the non-relevant subsequences are discarded using a nearest mean classifier (Duda, 2001). If the discriminant capability $F(x_t)$ of the subsequence x_t is the maximum, then x_t is declared to be the first bio-basis string. In order to find other candidate bio-basis strings, the subsequence x_t and those have the discriminant capability less than $F(x_t)/10$ are removed. The mean (**M**) of the discriminant capability of the remaining subsequences is then calculated. Finally, the minimum mean distance is calculated as follows:

$$D(x_\delta) = \min \left| \overline{\overline{\mathbb{F}}}(x_i) - M \right| : 1 < i < n \qquad (26)$$

where the discriminant capability $F(x_s)$ of the subsequence x_s has the minimum distance with **M**. The subsequences those have the discriminant capability larger than or equal to the threshold value δ are also declared to be the candidate bio-basis strings, where

$$\delta = \overline{\overline{\mathbb{F}}}(x_\delta) \qquad (27)$$

After eliminating non-relevant subsequences using the principle of nearest mean classifier, the redundancy among existing subsequences (candidate bio-basis strings) is calculated in terms of non-gapped homology score. A quantitative measure is introduced next to compute the similarity (redundancy) between two subsequences.

Degree of Resemblance

The "degree of resemblance" of the subsequence x_j with respect to the subsequence x_i is defined as

$$DOR(x_j, x_i) = \frac{h(x_j, x_i)}{h(x_i, x_i)} \qquad (28)$$

It is the ratio between the non-gapped pairwise homology score of two input subsequences x_i and x_j to the maximum homology score of the subsequence x_i. It is used to quantify the similarity in terms of homology score between pairs of subsequences. Combining (18) and (28), the relation between the "degree of resemblance" and the asymmetric distance of the subsequence x_j with respect to the subsequence x_i is

$$d(x_j, x_i) = h(x_i, x_i)[1 - DOR(x_j, x_i)] \qquad (29)$$

Let us consider two subsequences x_i = KPRT and x_j = YKAE with 4 residues. The non-gapped homology score between x_i and x_j is given by $h(x_i, x_j) = h(x_j, x_i) = 100$, while the maximum homology scores of two subsequences x_i and x_j are given by $h(x_i, x_i) = 208$ and $h(x_j, x_j) = 212$,

$$DOR(x_j, x_i) = \frac{h(x_j, x_i)}{h(x_i, x_i)} = \frac{100}{208} = 0.480769,$$

while that of x_i with respect to x_j is as follows:

$$DOR(x_j, x_i) = \frac{h(x_i, x_j)}{h(x_j, x_j)} = \frac{100}{212} = 0.471698,$$

The "degree of resemblance" is asymmetric in nature, that is,

$$DOR(x_i, x_j) \neq DOR(x_j, x_i) \qquad (30)$$

Hence, if two subsequences are different in nature, the "degree of resemblance" between them is small. A high value of $DOR(x_i, x_j)$ between two subsequences x_i and x_j asserts that the similarity between them is high. If two subsequences are same, the "degree of resemblance" between them is maximum, that is, 1. Thus,

$$0 < DOR(x_i, x_j) \leq 1 \qquad (31)$$

Details of the Algorithm

While the concept of the Fisher ratio is used to calculate the discriminant capability or relevance

---

Algorithm 1. Selection of Bio-Bases
- Input: $X = \{x_1, \cdots, x_i, \cdots, x_n\}$ be the set of n subsequences with m residues, where $x_{jk} \in A$
and $A = \{A, C, \cdots, W, Y\}$ be the set of 20 amino acids.
- Output: $V = \{v_1, \cdots, v_i, \cdots, v_c\}$ be the set of c bio-basis strings with m residues, where $v_i \in X$
and $v_{ik} \in A$.
begin:
1. Initialize $V \leftarrow X$, $\overline{V} \leftarrow \varnothing$, and $c \leftarrow 0$.
2. For each subsequence $x_i \in V$, calculate the discriminant capability F(x_i) using the concept of
Fisher ratio based on asymmetricity of biological distance as in (20).
3. Compute the threshold value δ using (27).

4. Eliminate the subsequence x_i if F (x_i) < δ. In effect, $V = V \setminus x_i$ and $n \leftarrow n - 1$.

5. Repeat step (4) for all the remaining subsequences of V.

6. Select subsequence x_i as the candidate bio-basis string from V that has the highest discriminant

Capability F (x_i). In effect, $x_i \in \overline{V}$, $c \leftarrow c + 1$, $V = V \setminus x_i$, and $n \leftarrow n - 1$.

7. For the selected subsequence x_i, calculate DOR(x_i, x_j) between itself and the subsequence $x_j \in V$ as in (28).
8. If DOR(x_i, x_j) > ξ, then x_j cannot be considered as a bio-basis string, resulting in a reduced set of

subsequences to be considered for bio-basis strings. In effect, $x_j \notin V$, $V = V \setminus x_j$, and $n \leftarrow n - 1$.

9. Repeat steps (7) and (8) for all the remaining subsequences of V.

10. Repeat steps (6) to (9) for all the remaining subsequences of V.
11. Stop.

---

of each subsequence, the "degree of resemblance" takes into account the similarity or redundancy between two subsequences. Based on the concepts of the "degree of resemblance" as in (28) and the Fisher ratio as in (20), the method for selecting a set of most informative bio-basis strings is described next. The algorithm proceeds as follows:

Note that the main motive of introducing the "degree of resemblance" and the nearest mean classifier lies in reducing the number of bio-basis strings. That is, both attempt to eliminate non-relevant and redundant bio-basis strings from the whole subsequences. The whole approach is therefore data dependent.

QUANTITATIVE MEASURE

In this section we propose some quantitative indices to evaluate the quality of selected bio-basis strings incorporating the concept of asymmetric biological distance. Based on this concept, next we introduce three indices -- α, β, and γ for

evaluating quantitatively the quality of selected bio-basis strings.

α **Index:** It is defined as

$$\alpha = \frac{1}{c} \sum_{i=1}^{c} \frac{1}{n_i} \sum_{x_j} (h(v_i, v_i) - h(x_j, v_i)) \quad (32)$$

where n_i is the total number of subsequences having minimum distance from the ith bio-basis string v_i among all the bio-basis strings and $\{h(v_i, v_i) - h(x_j, v_i)\}$ is the asymmetric distance from the bio-basis string v_i to the subsequence x_j obtained using an amino acid mutation matrix. The α index represents the average asymmetric distance of the input subsequences from their corresponding bio-basis strings. In other words, the value of α measures the compactness of input subsequences with make all input subsequences as close to their bio-basis strings as possible. The α index increases with the increase in asymmetric distance of all the subsequences from their corresponding bio-basis string. Therefore, for a given data set and c value, the lower the average asymmetric distance, the lower would be the α value. The α value decreases with the increase of compactness of subsequences with respect to their corresponding bio-basis strings.

β Index: The β index maximizes asymmetric distance between two bio-basis strings. It can be defined as

$$\beta = \min_{i,j} \frac{1}{2}\{d(v_j, v_i) + d(v_i, v_j)\}$$
$$= \min_{i,j} \frac{1}{2}\{h(v_i, v_i) + h(v_j, v_j) - 2h(v_j, v_i)\} \tag{33}$$

A good bio-basis string selection procedure should make the asymmetric distance between all bio-basis strings as high as possible. Actually, the β index measures how the bio-basis strings are separated from each other. The β index increases with the increase of asymmetric distance between bio-basis strings.

γ Index: It can be defined as

$$\gamma = \min_i \{\acute{U}_{A_i} - \acute{U}_{B_i}\} \tag{34}$$

where $\acute{U}_{A_i}$ and $\acute{U}_{B_i}$ are the average distances of the ith bio-basis string v_i from all bio-basis strings of two classes Ω_A and Ω_B, respectively and are as follows:

$$\acute{U}_{A_i} = \frac{1}{C_1}\sum_{i=1}^{C_1} d(v_j, v_i); \acute{U}_{B_i} = \frac{1}{C_2}\sum_{k=1}^{C_2} d(v_k, v_i)$$

where $\forall v_j \in \Omega_A; \forall v_k \in \Omega_B$; and $c_1 + c_2 = c$

The γ index maximizes the difference between asymmetric distances of two different classes bio-basis strings. A good bio-basis string selection procedure should make the asymmetric distance between two different class bio-basis strings as high as possible. Actually, the γ index measures how much two different class bio-basis strings are

separated. The γ index increases with the increase of separation between the bio-basis strings of two different classes.

EXPERIMENTAL RESULTS

The performance of the proposed "FRDistance+DOR" based bio-basis string selection method (using the concepts of asymmetric distance based Fisher ratio, nearest mean classifier, and "degree of resemblance", Algorithm 1) is compared extensively with that of various other related ones. These involve different combinations of the individual components of the proposed hybrid scheme, as well as other related schemes. The algorithms compared are

1. "MInformation": the mutual information based method as in (10) introduced by Yang and Thomson [Yang et al.05a],
2. "FRSimilarity": using the similarity based Fisher ratio as in (15) proposed by Berry et al. [Berry et al.04],
3. "FRDistance": using the asymmetric distance based Fisher ratio as in (20), and
4. "FRSimilarity+DOR": integration of the FRSimilarity [Berry et al.04] and the concepts of nearest mean classifier and "degree of resemblance".

All the algorithms are implemented in C language and run in LINUX environment having machine configuration Pentium IV, 3.2 GHz, 1 MB cache, and 1 GB RAM. To compare the performance of bio-basis string selection methods, α, β, and γ indices are used. The Dayhoff amino acid mutation matrix is used to calculate the non-gapped pairwise homology score between two subsequences [Henrikoff92; Johnson93; Dayhoff78]. The performance is also evaluated based on the prediction accuracy of support vector machines (SVMs). The source code of the SVMs is obtained from http://

svmlight.joachims.org/. Details of the SVMs and the prediction accuracy are reported next.

Support Vector Machines

The essence in classification is to minimize the probability of error in using the trained classifier, which is refereed to as the structural risk. It has been shown that the SVMs (Vapnik, 1995) are able to minimize the structural risk through finding a unique hyper-plane with maximum margin to separate data from two classes. Because of this, the SVMs provide best generalization ability on unseen data compared with the other classifiers.

A classification algorithm aims to find a mapping function between input features x and a class membership $t \in -1, 1 : \Gamma = f(x, w)$, where w is the parameter vector, $f(x, w)$ the mapping function and Γ the output. With other classification algorithms, the Euclidean distance (error) between Γ and t is minimized to optimize w. This can lead to a biased hyper-plane for discrimination.

In searching for the best hyper-plane, the SVMs find a set of data points that are most difficult training points to classify. These data points are referred to as support vectors. In constructing an SVM classifier, the support vectors are closed in the hyper-plane and are located on the boundaries of the margin between two classes. The advantage of using SVMs is that the hyper-plane is searched through maximizing the margin. Because of this, the SVM classifier is the most robust, and hence has the best generalization ability. The trained SVM classifier is a linear combination of the similarity between an input and the support vectors. The similarity between an input and the support vectors is quantified by a kernel function defined as: $\psi(x, v_i)$, where v_i is the ith support vector. The decision is made using the following equation:

$$\Gamma = sign \sum a_i t_i \psi(x, v_i) \qquad (35)$$

where t_i is the class label of the ith support vector and a_i is the positive parameter of the ith support vector determined by an SVM algorithm.

However, the kernel function must be specially designed to deal with a data set having non-numerical attributes such as protein or DNA sequences. In this paper, the bio-basis function is used in the SVM for handling biological subsequences. The performance of the string kernel function is compared by measuring the classification accuracy of the SVMs. Four parameters used for this comparison are total accuracy, sensitivity, true positive fraction (TP_f), and true negative fraction (TN_f) as follows:

$$Total\ Accuracy = \frac{TP + TN}{TP + FP + TN + FN}$$

$$Sensitivity=$$
$$\frac{TP}{TP + FP} ; TP_f = \frac{TP}{TP + FN} ; TN_f \frac{TN}{TN + FP}$$

where TP is the number of true positive predictions, TN is the number of true negative predictions, FP is the number of false positive predictions and FN is the number of false negative predictions. Hence, the values of TP_f and TN_f represent the precision measures of the positive class and negative class, respectively. To compute the classification accuracy, sensitivity, TP_f, and TN_f of the SVM, the leave one-cross-validation is performed.

Description of Data Set

To analyze the performance of the proposed bio-basis string selection method, we have used the data sets of five whole HIV protein sequences, Cai-Chou HIV data set (Cai et al., 1998), and caspase cleavage protein sequences.

FiveWhole HIV Protein Sequences

The HIV protease belongs to the family of aspartyl proteases, which have been well-characterized as proteolytic enzymes. The catalytic component is composed of carboxyl groups from two aspartyl residues located in both NH_2- and COOH-terminal halves of the enzyme molecule in HIV protease (Pearl et al., 1987). They are strongly substrate-selective and cleavage-specific demonstrating their capability of cleaving large, virus specific polypeptides called polyproteins between a specific pair of amino acids. Miller et al. showed that the cleavage sites in HIV polyprotein can extend to an octapeptide region (Miller et al., 1989). The amino acid residues within this octapeptide region are represented by P_4-P_3-P_2-P_1-$P_{1'}$-$P_{2'}$-$P_{3'}$-$P_{4'}$, where P_4-P_3-P_2-P_1 is the NH_2-terminal half and $P_{1'}$-$P_{2'}$-$P_{3'}$-$P_{4'}$ the COOH-terminal half. Their counterparts in the HIV protease are represented by S_4-S_3-S_2-S_1-$S_{1'}$-$S_{2'}$-$S_{3'}$-$S_{4'}$ (Chou, 1993). The HIV protease cleavage site is exactly between P_1 and $P_{1'}$.

The five whole HIV protein sequences have been downloaded from the NCBI (National Center for Biotechnology Information, http://www.ncbi.nlm.nih.gov). The accession numbers are AAC82593, AAG42635, AAO40777, NP057849, and NP 057850. Details of these five sequences are included in Figure 2. Note that MA, CA, NC, TF, PR, RT, RH, and IN are matrix protein, capsid protein, nucleocapsid core protein, trans-frame peptide, protease, reverse transcriptase, RNAse, and integrase, respectively. They are all cleavage products of the HIV protease. p1, p2, and p6 are also cleavage products (Chou, 1993). For instance, 132 (MA/CA) means that the cleavage site is between the residues 132 (P_1) and 133 ($P_{1'}$) and the cleavage split the poly-protein producing two functional proteins, the matrix protein and the capsid protein. The subsequences from each of five whole protein sequences are obtained through moving a sliding window with 8 residues. Once a subsequence is produced, it is considered as functional if there is a cleavage site between P_1-$P_{1'}$, otherwise it is labeled as non-functional. The total number of subsequences with 8 residues in AAC82593, AAG42635, AAO40777, NP057849,

and NP 057850 are 493, 491, 493, 1428, and 493, respectively.

Cai-Chou HIV Data Set

In (Cai et al., 1998), Cai and Chou have described a benchmark data set of the HIV. It consists of 114 positive oligopeptides and 248 negative oligopeptides, in total 362 subsequences with 8 residues. The data set has been collected from the University of Exeter, UK.

Caspase Cleavage Data Set

The programmed cell death, also known as apoptosis, is a gene-directed mechanism, which serves to regulate and control both cell death and tissue homeostasis during the development and the maturation of cells. The importance of apoptosis study is that many diseases such as cancer, ischemic damage, etc., result from apoptosis malfunction. A family of cysteine proteases called caspases that are expressed initially in the cell as proenzymes is the key to apoptosis (Rohn et al., 2004). As caspase cleavage is the key to programmed cell death, the study of caspase inhibitors could represent effective drugs against some disease where blocking apoptosis is desirable. Without a careful study of caspase cleavage specificity effective drug design could be difficult.

The 13 protein sequences containing various experimentally determined caspase cleavage sites have been downloaded from the NCBI (http://www.ncbi.nih.gov). Figure 3 represents the information of these sequences. C_i depicts the ith caspase. The total number of non-cleaved subsequences is about 8340, while the number of cleaved subsequences is only 18. In total, there are 8358 subsequences with 8 residues.

Example

Consider the data set AAG42635 with sequence length 498. The number of subsequences obtained

Figure 2. Five whole HIV protein sequences from the NCBI

Accession No	Length	Cleavage Sites at P_1
AAC82593	500	132(MA/CA), 363(CA/p2), 377(p2/NC), 432(NC/p1), 448(p1/p6)
AAG42635	498	132(MA/CA), 363(CA/p2), 376(p2/NC), 430(NC/p1), 446(p1/p6)
AAO40777	500	132(MA/CA), 363(CA/p2), 377(p2/NC), 432(NC/p1), 448(p1/p6)
NP_057849	1435	488(TF/PR), 587(PR/RT), 1027(RT/RH), 1147(RH/IN)
NP_057850	500	132(MA/CA), 363(CA/p2), 377(p2/NC), 432(NC/p1), 448(p1/p6)

Figure 3. Thirteen caspase cleavage proteins from the NCBI

Proteins	Gene	Length	Cleavage sites
O00273	DFFA	331	117(C3), 224(C3)
Q07817	BCL2L1	233	61(C1)
P11862	GAS2	314	279(C1)
P08592	APP	770	672(C6)
P05067	APP	770	672(C6), 739(C3/C6/C8/C9)
Q9JJV8	BCL2	236	64(C3 and C9)
P10415	BCL2	239	34(C3)
O43903	GAS2	313	278(C)
Q12772	SREBF2	1141	468(C3 and C7)
Q13546	RIPK1	671	324(C8)
Q08378	GOLGA3	1498	59(C2), 139(C3), 311(C7)
O60216	RAD21	631	279(C3/C7)
O95155	UBE4B	1302	109(C3/C7), 123(C6)

through moving a sliding window with 8 residues is 491. The parameters used as well as generated in the proposed FRDistance+DOR based method for selection of bio-basis strings are shown in Table 4 only for AAG42635 data, as an example.

In the proposed FRDistance+DOR based method, the discriminant capability of each subsequence in original set is calculated in terms of the Fisher ratio as in (20). The Fisher ratio of each subsequence in original set and reduced set is shown in Fig. 5 for the proposed method. While Fig. 5(a) represents the Fisher ratio of the subsequences in original set, Fig. 5(c) shows the same in reduced set considering the values of $\delta = 0.135$ and $\xi = 0.75$. The value of δ is calculated using (27). The 86 subsequences present in the reduced set are considered as the bio-basis strings in the proposed FRDistance+DOR based method. For the purpose of comparison, the 86 subsequences with maximum discriminant capability are selected from the original 491 subsequences of Fig. 5(a) considering the values of $\delta = 0.00$ and $\xi = 1.00$. These subsequences are the bio-basis strings for the FRDistance based method and shown in Fig. 5(b). Similarly, the 86 bio-basis strings are selected using the methods proposed by Berry et al. (2004) (FRSimilarity) (Berry et al., 2004) and Yang and Thomson (2005a) (MInformation) (Yang et al., 2005a), and the FRSimilarity+DOR based method. In the FRSimilarity (Berry et al., 2004) based method, the Fisher ratio of each subsequence in original set is calculated using (15). Fig. 6(a) represents the Fisher ratio of the subsequences in original set, while the bio-basis strings corresponding to the FRSimilarity based method are shown in Fig. 6(b). In this case, the 86 subsequences are selected from the original set of Fig. 6(a) as the bio-basis strings which possess strongest discriminant capability. Fig. 6(c) represents the results related to the FRSimilarity+DOR, that is, if the concepts of nearest mean classifier and "degree of resemblance" are incorporated in the existing method FRSimilarity (Berry et al., 2004). In this case, the value of $\delta = 0.035$ computed using (27) and $\xi = 0.75$.

The performance of the FRDistance+DOR based method is shown in Figure 4, along with the results obtained using the existing FRSimilarity [Berry et al.04] and MInformation (Yang et al., 2005a) based bio-basis string selection methods, and the FRDistance and FRSimilarity+DOR based methods. All the results reported in Figure 4, Figure 5, and Figure 6, establish the superiority of the proposed FRDistance+DOR based bio-basis string selection method over the existing bio-basis string selection methods reported in [Berry et al.04; Yang et al.05a] in terms of the proposed (e.g., α, β, and γ) indices.

Performance of Proposed Bio-Basis String Selection Method

The performance of the proposed FRDistance+DOR based bio-basis string selection method, along with a comparison with related algorithms, is demonstrated in Figures 7-11. Subsequent discussions analyze the results presented in these figures with respect to α, β, γ, prediction accuracy, and execution time.

Optimum Value of ξ

The threshold ξ in Algorithm 1 has an influence on the performance of the proposed bio-basis string selection method. It controls the degree of non-redundancy between two subsequences. To find out the optimum value of ξ, extensive experiments are carried out for different values of ξ. It may be also noted that the optimum choice of c (the number of bio-basis strings) is a function of ξ. Figure 7 represents the values of α, β, and γ along with the number of bio-basis strings c obtained using the proposed FRDistance+DOR based method for all the data sets reported in Section 6.2. Results are reported for different values of ξ. It is seen from the results of Figure 7 that as the value of ξ increases, the FRDistance+DOR based method consistently achieves better performance. That is, the value of α decreases, and the values of β and γ increase with the increase in ξ. The best performance with respect to α, β, and γ is achieved with $\xi = 0.75$. However, for $\xi > 0.75$, the performance decreases with the increase in ξ. That is the best performance of the FRDistance + DOR based bio-basis string selection method is obtained when one subsequence x_j is considered to contain redundant information of another subsequence x_i if the homology score between them is greater than or equal to the 75% of the maximum homology score of x_i. Hence, to achieve best performance using the proposed bio-basis string selection method, the subsequence x_j is considered as a redundant one of the subsequence

Figure 4. Comparative analysis of different methods for AAG42635

Sequence length = 498; Number of subsequences, $n = 491$
Value of $\xi = 0.75$; Value of $\delta = 0.135$; Number of bio-basis strings, $c = 86$

Quantitative Measures
MInformation [36]: $\alpha = 67.03$; $\beta = 317.66$; $\gamma = 48.49$
FRSimilarity [6]: $\alpha = 68.85$; $\beta = 314.00$; $\gamma = 46.37$
FRDistance: $\alpha = 67.39$; $\beta = 314.00$; $\gamma = 46.42$
FRSimilarity+DOR: $\alpha = 60.81$; $\beta = 350.00$; $\gamma = 45.60$
FRDistance+DOR: $\alpha = 54.11$; $\beta = 366.00$; $\gamma = 57.33$

Figure 5. Discriminate capability of subsequences in FRDistance and FRDistance+DOR based methods

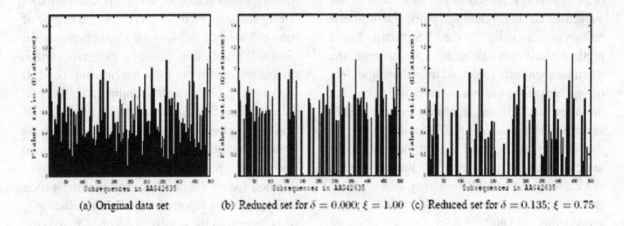

(a) Original data set   (b) Reduced set for $\delta = 0.000$; $\xi = 1.00$ (c) Reduced set for $\delta = 0.135$; $\xi = 0.75$

Figure 6. Discriminant capability of subsequences in FRSimilarity [6] and FRSimilarity+DOR based methods

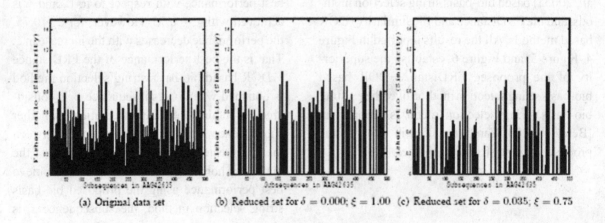

(a) Original data set   (b) Reduced set for $\delta = 0.000$; $\xi = 1.00$ (c) Reduced set for $\delta = 0.035$; $\xi = 0.75$

Figure 7. Performace of FRDistance+DOR based method for different values of ξ

Value of ξ	Different Indices	Description of Different Data Sets						
		AAC82593	AAG42635	AAO40777	NP_057849	NP_057850	Cai-Chou	Caps. Cleav.
0.60	e	14	11	16	22	14	14	37
	α	105.96	86.96	113.53	122.51	105.97	110.63	105.56
	β	352.00	310.00	352.00	350.00	352.00	292.00	380.00
	γ	193.54	92.00	193.00	119.80	193.54	84.26	155.56
0.65	e	34	28	33	56	34	32	75
	α	93.68	82.60	93.14	95.98	93.68	91.95	93.20
	β	332.00	398.00	324.00	384.00	332.00	332.00	346.00
	γ	80.86	89.00	79.59	110.96	80.86	69.28	142.86
0.70	e	58	42	59	101	58	36	166
	α	72.52	66.23	70.03	77.42	72.53	98.50	76.11
	β	350.00	354.00	350.00	362.00	350.00	326.00	354.00
	γ	70.51	74.66	67.67	127.95	70.518	68.79	137.45
0.75	e	88	86	93	211	88	58	393
	α	52.23	54.11	52.61	51.61	53.23	67.89	46.20
	β	350.00	366.00	360.00	370.00	350.00	320.00	376.10
	γ	61.57	57.33	62.80	128.01	61.57	58.68	85.03
0.80	e	97	86	97	278	97	30	863
	α	53.43	54.83	53.43	51.90	53.44	75.49	46.25
	β	318.00	328.00	322.00	322.00	318.00	268.00	376.00
	γ	60.49	56.197	61.49	90.97	60.49	58.66	54.98
0.85	e	40	34	46	146	40	15	1628
	α	59.289	61.76	55.93	55.68	105.97	67.37	33.65
	β	286.00	286.00	322.00	350.00	300.00	266.00	376.00
	γ	69.48	60.96	61.49	119.80	88.61	78.80	48.87

x_i if $h(x_j, x_i) \geq 0.75 \times h(x_i, x_i)$, where $h(x_j, x_i)$ and $h(x_i, x_i)$ represent the homology score between x_j and x_i, and the maximum homology score of x_i, respectively. In other words, the. "degree of resemblance" between two subsequences selected as two non-redundant bio-basis strings must be less than 0.75.

6.4.2. Degree of Resemblance and Nearest Mean Classifier

The main objective of introducing the concepts of "degree of resemblance" and nearest mean classifier in the proposed bio-basis string selection method is to reduce the number of bio-basis strings from the whole set of subsequences. While the "degree of resemblance" eliminates the redundant subsequences, the principle of nearest mean classifier is used to discard the non-relevant subsequences. In effect, the proposed FRDistance+DOR based bio-basis string selection method selects a set of relevant and non-redundant bio-basis strings.

In order to establish the importance of both the "degree of resemblance" and the nearest mean classifier, extensive experiments are carried out. Figure 8 provides comparative results of the bio-basis string selection methods with and without considering the above two concepts. The discriminant capability of each subsequence in both cases (FRDistance+DOR and FRDistance) is calculated using the Fisher ratio as in (20), while the value of ξ is set to 0.75 and the value of δ is computed according to (27) for the FRDistance+DOR based method. The proposed FRDistance+DOR based method is found to improve the performance of the FRDistance based method in terms of α, β, and γ. Although the execution time required for the FRDistance+DOR based method is slightly higher compared to that of the FRDistance based based method, FRDistance+DOR based method selects the bio-basis strings that are more informative (relevant) and distinct (nonredundant). Hence, to improve the performance of the FRDistance based method by eliminating similar and non-relevant bio-basis strings, the "degree of resemblance" and the nearest mean classifier should be incorporated with the FRDistance based method. In effect, the FRDistance+DOR based method selects an effective reduced set of bio-basis strings and efficiently generates distinct features in numerical feature space.

Importance of Asymmetricity of Biological Distance

The proposed FRDistance+DOR based method calculates the relevance or discriminant capability of each subsequence using the principle of asymmetric biological distance as in (20), while the existing method FRSimilarity considers the similarity to compute the discriminant capability using (15). As a result, the FRDistance+DOR based method takes into account the expectation of higher order similarity (upto forth order) as well as the maximum homology score of the subsequence, while the existing FRSimilarity based method does not consider the maximum homology score and considers the expectation upto second order only. In effect, the proposed method selects the relevant bio-basis strings more accurately compared to the existing FRSimilarity based method.

In order to establish the importance of asymmetric biological distance over symmetric biological similarity, extensive experiments are carried out. Figure 9 provides comparative results of the

FRDistance+DOR and FRSimilarity+DOR based bio-basis string selection methods considering $\xi = 0.75$.

The asymmetric distance based method is found to improve the performance in terms of α, β, and γ with comparable time. Only, in case of Cai-Chou HIV data set, the value of α is better in similarity based approach, while the values of β and γ are higher in distance based approach.

Comparative Analysis of Different Methods

Finally, Figure 10 provides the comparative results of different algorithms for the protein sequences reported in Section 6.2. It is seen that the FRDistance+DOR based method produces bio-basis strings having the lowest α value and highest β and γ values for all the cases. Figure 10 also reports execution time (in ms) of different algorithms for all protein data sets. The execution time required for the FRDistance+DOR based method is comparable to the existing methods. For the FRSimilarity, although the execution time is less, the performance is significantly poorer than that of the MInformation, FRDistance.

Prediction Accuracy Assessment

The performance of the proposed method is also compared with the existing methods with respect to the prediction accuracy of the SVMs (support vector machines). The bio-basis function is used in the SVM for handling biological subsequences. Figure 11 provides the results for the Cai-Chou HIV data set.

To compute the classification accuracy, sensitivity, TP_f, and TN_f of the SVM, the leave-one-out cross-validation is performed. From the results reported in Figure 11, it is seen that the bio-basis function transforms non-numerical sequence space to numerical feature space accurately when the bio-basis strings are generated using the pro-

Figure 8. Comparative analysis of FRDistance and FRDistance+DOR

Data Sets	Methods	α	β	γ	Time
AAC8	FRDistance+DOR	52.23	350.00	61.57	2732
2593	FRDistance	66.68	318.00	52.70	2378
AAG4	FRDistance+DOR	54.11	366.00	57.33	2724
2635	FRDistance	67.39	314.00	46.42	2335
AAO4	FRDistance+DOR	52.61	360.00	62.80	2768
0777	FRDistance	64.86	348.00	53.80	2389
NP_05	FRDistance+DOR	51.61	370.00	128.01	7749
7849	FRDistance	67.90	368.00	97.00	7425
NP_O5	FRDistance+DOR	53.23	350.00	61.57	2778
7850	FRDistance	66.57	310.80	52.75	2356
Cai-Chou	FRDistance+DOR	67.89	320.00	58.68	2487
HIV Data	FRDistance	77.89	300.00	48.74	2172
Capsage	FRDistance+DOR	46.20	376.10	85.03	48529
Cleavage	FRDistance	58.09	376.00	84.00	43819

Figure 9. Comparison of biological similarity and distance

Data Sets	Fisher Ratio	α	β	γ	Time
AAC8	FRDistance+DOR	52.23	350.00	61.57	2732
2593	FRSimilarity+DOR	60.00	340.00	54.89	2721
AAG4	FRDistance+DOR	54.11	366.00	57.33	2724
2635	FRSimilarity+DOR	60.81	350.00	45.60	2711
AAO4	FRDistance+DOR	52.61	360.00	62.80	2768
0777	FRSimilarity+DOR	60.00	354.00	60.00	2745
NP_05	FRDistance+DOR	51.61	370.00	128.01	7749
7849	FRSimilarity+DOR	55.48	342.00	98.38	7689
NP_O5	FRDistance+DOR	53.23	350.00	61.57	2778
7850	FRSimilarity+DOR	60.20	341.23	55.68	2756
Cai-Chou	FRDistance+DOR	67.89	320.00	58.68	2487
HIV Data	FRSimilarity+DOR	60.46	286.78	50.67	2429
Capsage	FRDistance+DOR	46.20	376.10	85.03	48529
Cleavage	FRSimilarity+DOR	58.09	290.00	79.08	46537

posed FRDistance+DOR based method. The following conclusions can be drawn from the results reported in Figures 7-11: although the execution time is less, the performance is significantly poorer than that of the MInformation, FRDistance, FRSimilarity+DOR, and FRDistance+DOR .

1. It is seen that the proposed FRDistance+DOR based bio-basis string selection method, us-

Figure 10. Comparative performance of different methods

Data Sets	Methods	α	β	γ	Time
AAC8 2593	FRDistance+DOR	52.23	350.00	61.57	2732
	FRSimilarity+DOR	60.00	340.00	54.89	2721
	FRDistance	66.68	318.00	52.70	2378
	FRSimilarity	67.13	312.68	52.70	2217
	MInformation	62.18	322.60	52.81	2561
AAG4 2635	FRDistance+DOR	54.11	366.00	57.33	2724
	FRSimilarity+DOR	60.81	350.00	45.60	2711
	FRDistance	67.39	314.00	46.42	2335
	FRSimilarity	68.85	314.00	46.37	2192
	MInformation	67.03	317.66	48.49	2568
AAO4 0777	FRDistance+DOR	52.61	360.00	62.80	2768
	FRSimilarity+DOR	60.00	354.00	60.00	2745
	FRDistance	64.86	348.00	53.80	2389
	FRSimilarity	65.17	328.10	52.33	2120
	MInformation	63.19	351.30	54.10	2412
NP_O5 7849	FRDistance+DOR	51.61	370.00	128.01	7749
	FRSimilarity+DOR	55.48	342.00	98.38	7689
	FRDistance	67.90	368.00	97.00	7425
	FRSimilarity	70.12	317.50	93.70	7108
	MInformation	64.18	332.70	98.30	7468
NP_O5 7850	FRDistance+DOR	53.23	350.00	61.57	2778
	FRSimilarity+DOR	60.20	341.23	55.68	2756
	FRDistance	66.57	310.80	52.75	2356
	FRSimilarity	68.13	304.84	52.75	2071
	MInformation	62.75	337.10	55.11	2683
Cai-Chou HIV Data	FRDistance+DOR	67.89	320.00	58.68	2487
	FRSimilarity+DOR	60.46	286.78	50.67	2429
	FRDistance	77.89	300.00	48.74	2172
	FRSimilarity	77.17	285.90	48.60	2026
	MInformation	71.63	306.10	50.65	2216
Capsage Cleavage	FRDistance+DOR	46.20	376.10	85.03	48529
	FRSimilarity+DOR	58.09	290.00	79.08	46537
	FRDistance	58.09	376.00	84.00	43819
	FRSimilarity	61.08	288.50	78.06	40173
	MInformation	57.10	328.40	80.33	46119

Figure 11. Prediction accuracy assessment using SVMs

Data Sets	Methods	TN_f	TP_f	Sensitivity	Accuracy
Cai-Chou HIV Data	FRDistance+DOR	0.87 (215)	0.90 (103)	0.76	0.88 (318)
	FRSimilarity+DOR	0.81 (201)	0.87 (99)	0.68	0.83 (300)
	FRDistance	0.80 (198)	0.84 (96)	0.66	0.81 (294)
	FRSimilarity	0.79 (195)	0.84 (96)	0.64	0.80 (291)
	MInformation	0.78 (195)	0.85 (97)	0.65	0.81 (292)

ing asymmetric biological distance, nearest mean classifier, and "degree of resemblance", is superior to the existing FRSimilarity [Berry et al.04] and MInformation (Yang et al., 2005a) based methods. However, the FRSimilarity and MInformation methods require slightly lesser time compared to that of the FRDistance+DOR based method. But, the performance of existing methods is significantly poorer than the proposed method.

2. The FRDistance+DOR based method is found to improve the values of α, β, γ, and prediction accuracy substantially.

3. It is observed that the proposed FRDistance+DOR based algorithm requires significantly less time compared to FRSimilarity having comparable performance. Reduction in time is achieved due to the concepts of nearest mean classifier and "degree of resemblance". In effect, the bio-basis function transforms non-numerical sequence space to numerical feature space more accurately.

The best performance of the proposed method in terms of α, β, γ, and prediction accuracy is achieved due to the following reasons:

1. The asymmetricity of biological distance in calculating the Fisher ratio is more effective for selection of most informative (relevant) bio-basis strings compared to the symmetric similarity measure.

2. The principle of nearest mean classifier and the concept of "degree of resemblance" enable efficient selection of relevant and distinct bio-basis strings. As a result, it minimizes the non-relevant and redundant features in numerical feature space.

In effect, a minimum set of bio-basis strings having maximum information is obtained using the proposed bio-basis string selection method. Hence, the best prediction accuracy of support vector machine is achieved using proposed bio-basis string selection method.

CONCLUSION

The major contributions of the paper are as follows:

1. The development of an efficient method for selection of most informative and minimum set of bio-basis strings based on the principle of asymmetricity of biological distance;

2. Defining new measures based on non-gapped homology score to evaluate the quality of selected bio-basis strings; and

3. Demonstrating the effectiveness of the proposed bio-basis string selection method, along with a comparison with existing methods, on different protein data sets.

The asymmetric biological distance is effective in transforming non-numerical sequence space to numerical feature space. Also, the asymmetricity of distance makes the proposed iscriminant analysis scheme using the Fisher ratio more effective. The principle of nearest mean classifier and the concept of "degree of resemblance" are found to be successful in efficient selection of a minimum set of most informative bio-basis strings compared to the existing methods.

Some of the indices (e.g., α, β, and γ) used for evaluating the quality of selected bio-basis strings may be used in a suitable combination to act as the objective function of an evolutionary algorithm, for generating a minimum set of bio-basis strings with maximum information. This formulation is geared towards maximizing the utility of the biological content with respect to bio-basis string selection task.

REFERENCES

Altschul, S. F., Boguski, M. S., Gish, W., & Wootton, J. C. (1994). Issues in Searching Molecular Sequence Databases. *Nature Genetics, 6,* 119–129. doi:10.1038/ng0294-119

Altschul, S. F., Gish, W., Miller, W., Myers, E., & Lipman, D. J. (1990). Basic Local Alignment Search Tool. *Journal of Molecular Biology, 215,* 403–410.

Arrigo, P., Giuliano, F., & Damiani, G. (1991). Identification of A New Motif on Nucleic Acid Sequence Data Using Kohonen's Self-Organising Map. *CABIOS, 7,* 353–357.

Baldi, P., & Brunak, S. (1998). *Bioinformatics: The Machine Learning Approach.* Cambridge, MA: The MIT Press.

Baldi, P., Pollastri, G., Anderson, C. A., & Brunak, S. (1995). Matching Protein Beta-Sheet Partners by Feedforward and Recurrent Neural Networks. In [ISMB]. *Proceedings of the International Conference on Intelligent Systems for Molecular Biology, 8,* 25–36.

Berry, E. A., Dalby, A. R., & Yang, Z. R. (2004). Reduced Bio-Basis Function Neural Network for Identification of Protein Phosphorylation Sites: Comparison with Pattern Recognition Algorithms. *Computational Biology and Chemistry, 28,* 75–85. doi:10.1016/j.compbiolchem.2003.11.005

Cai, Y. D., & Chou, K. C. (1998). Artificial Neural Network Model for Predicting HIV Protease Cleavage Sites in Protein. *Advances in Engineering Software, 29*(2), 119–128. doi:10.1016/S0965-9978(98)00046-5

Cai, Y. D., Liu, X. J., Xu, X. B., & Chou, K. C. (2002). Support Vector Machines for Predicting the Specificity of GalNAc-transferase. *Peptides, 23,* 205–208. doi:10.1016/S0196-9781(01)00597-6

Chou, K. C. (1993). A Vectorised Sequence-Coupling Model for Predicting HIV Protease Cleavage Sites in Proteins. *The Journal of Biological Chemistry, 268*(23), 16938–16948.

Chou, K. C. (1996). Prediction of Human Immunodeficiency Virus Protease Cleavage Sites in Proteins. *Analytical Biochemistry, 233*(1), 1–14. doi:10.1006/abio.1996.0001

Dayhoff, M. O., Schwartz, R. M., & Orcutt, B. C. (1978). A Model of Evolutionary Change in Proteins. Matrices for Detecting Distant Relationships. *Atlas of Protein Sequence and Structure, 5,* 345-358.

Duda, R. O., Hart, P. E., & Stork, D. G. (2001). *Pattern Classification.* New York: John Wiley & Sons.

Ferran, E. A., & Ferrara, P. (1991). Topological Maps of Protein Sequences. *Biological Cybernetics, 65,* 451–458. doi:10.1007/BF00204658

Henikoff, S., & Henikoff, J. G. (1992). Amino Acid Substitution Matrices from Protein Blocks. *PNSA, 89,* 10915–10919. doi:10.1073/pnas.89.22.10915

Itoh, M., Goto, S., Akutsu, T., & Kanehisa, M. (2005). Fast and Accurate Database Homology Search Using Upper Bounds of Local Alignment Scores. *Bioinformatics (Oxford, England), 21*(7), 912–921. doi:10.1093/bioinformatics/bti076

Johnson, M. S., & Overington, J. P. (1993). A Structural Basis for Sequence Comparisons. An Evaluation of Scoring Methodologies. *Journal of Molecular Biology, 233*, 716–738. doi:10.1006/jmbi.1993.1548

Miller, M., Schneider, J., Sathayanarayana, B. K., Toth, M. V., Marshall, G. R., & Clawson, L. (1989). Structure of Complex of Synthetic HIV-1 Protease with Substrate-Based Inhibitor at at 2.3 Resolution. *Science, 246*, 1149–1152. doi:10.1126/science.2686029

Minakuchi, Y., Satou, K., & Konagaya, A. (2002). Prediction of Protein-Protein Interaction Sites Using Support Vector Machines. *Genome Informatics, 13*, 322–323.

Narayanan, A., Wu, X. K., & Yang, Z. R. (2002). Mining Viral Protease Data to Extract Cleavage Knowledge. *Bioinformatics (Oxford, England), 18*, 5–13.

Pearl, L. H., & Taylor, W. R. (1987). A Structural Model for the Retroviral Proteases. *Nature, 329*, 351–354. doi:10.1038/329351a0

Qian, N., & Sejnowski, T. J. (1988). Predicting the Secondary Structure of Globular Proteins Using Neural Network Models. *Journal of Molecular Biology, 202*, 865–884. doi:10.1016/0022-2836(88)90564-5

Rohn, T. T., Cusack, S. M., Kessinger, S. R., & Oxford, J. T. (2004). Caspase Activaion Independent of Cell Death is Required for Proper Cell Dispersal and Correct Morphology in PC12 Cells. *Experimental Cell Research, 293*, 215–225. doi:10.1016/j.yexcr.2003.12.029

Shannon, C., & Weaver, W. (1964). *The Mathematical Theory of Communication*. Chicago: University of Illinois Press.

Stojmirovic, A. (2004). Quasi-Metric Spaces With Measure. *Topology Proceedings, 28*(2), 655–671.

Thomson, R., Hodgman, C., Yang, Z. R., & Doyle, A. K. (2003). Characterising Proteolytic Cleavage Site Activity Using Bio-Basis Function Neural Network. *Bioinformatics (Oxford, England), 19*(14), 1741–1747. doi:10.1093/bioinformatics/btg237

Vapnik, V. (1995). *The Nature of Statistical Learning Theory*. New York: Springer Verlag.

Wang, Y. (2009). On Cognitive Computing. *International Journal of Software Science and Computational Intelligence, 1*(3), 1–15.

Wang, Y. (2009). Paradigms of Denotational Mathematics for Cognitive Informatics and Cognitive Computing. *Fundamenta Informaticae, 90*(3), 282–303.

Wang, Y., & Kinsner, W. (2006). Recent Advances in Cognitive Informatics. *IEEE Transactions on Systems, Man, and Cybernetics . Part C, 36*(2), 121–123.

Wang, Y., Kinsner, W., & Zhang, D. (2009). Contemporary Cybernetics and its Faces of Cognitive Informatics and Computational Intelligence. *IEEE Transactions on Systems, Man, and Cybernetics. Part B, Cybernetics, 39*(4), 1–11.

Wang, Y., & Wang, Y. (2006). Cognitive Informatics Models of the Brain. *IEEE Transactions on Systems, Man, and Cybernetics . Part C, 36*(2), 203–207.

Yang, Z. R. (2004). Biological Application of Support Vector Machines. *Briefings in Bioinformatics, 5*(4), 328–338. doi:10.1093/bib/5.4.328

Yang, Z. R. (2005). Orthogonal Kernel Machine for the Prediction of Functional Sites in Proteins. *IEEE Transactions on Systems, Man, and Cybernetics. Part B, Cybernetics, 35*(1), 100–106. doi:10.1109/TSMCB.2004.840723

Yang, Z. R. (2005). Prediction of Caspase Cleavage Sites Using Bayesian Bio-Basis Function Neural Networks. *Bioinformatics (Oxford, England)*, *21*(9), 1831–1837. doi:10.1093/bioinformatics/bti281

Yang, Z. R., & Chou, K. C. (2004). Predicting the Linkage Sites in Glycoproteins Using Bio-Basis Function Neural Networks. *Bioinformatics (Oxford, England)*, *20*(6), 903–908. doi:10.1093/bioinformatics/bth001

Yang, Z. R., & Thomson, R. (2005). Bio-Basis Function Neural Network for Prediction of Protease Cleavage Sites in Proteins. *IEEE Transactions on Neural Networks*, *16*(1), 263–274. doi:10.1109/TNN.2004.836196

Yang, Z. R., Thomson, R., McNeil, P., & Esnouf, R. (2005). RONN: Use of the Bio-Basis Function Neural Network Technique for the Detection of Natively Disordered Regions in Proteins. *Bioinformatics (Oxford, England)*, *21*(16), 3369–3376. doi:10.1093/bioinformatics/bti534

This work was previously published in International Journal of Software Science and Computational Intelligence, Volume 2, Issue 2, edited by Yingxu Wang, pp. 19-43, copyright 2010 by IGI Publishing (an imprint of IGI Global).

Chapter 10
Role–Based Autonomic Systems

Haibin Zhu
Nipissing University, Canada

ABSTRACT

Autonomic Computing is an emerging computing paradigm used to create computer systems capable of self-management in order to overcome the rapidly growing complexity of computing systems management. To possess self-* properties, there must be mechanisms to support self-awareness, that is an autonomic system should be able to perceive the abnormality of its components. After abnormality is checked, processes of self-healing, self-configuration, self-optimization, and self-protection must be completed to guarantee the system works correctly and continuously. In role-based collaboration (RBC), roles are the major media for interaction, coordination, and collaboration. A role can be used to check if a player behaves well or not. This paper investigates the possibility of using roles and their related mechanisms to diagnose the behavior of agents, and facilitate self-* properties of a system.

INTRODUCTION

Cognitive Informatics (CI) is an interdisciplinary study into the internal information processing mechanisms and processes of the Natural Intelligence (NI) (Wang, 2007a). Autonomic computing is one of the fundamental technologies of for intelligent agents, which are a simulation of the natural intelligence possessed by human brains with computers (Wang, 2009).

DOI: 10.4018/978-1-4666-0264-9.ch010

Traditional computer systems management is often centralized and hierarchical. Current computing systems are physically scattered in different places, and functionally distributed with increasingly complex connections and interactions. This situation makes centralized management schemes much more difficult and even infeasible (Samimi et al., 2006; Tesauro et al., 2004). The autonomic computing paradigm is proposed to deal with the increasing complexity in computer-based systems, and the shortage of skilled human manpower to advance the related technological developments and innovations (Wang, 2007b). Compared with traditional systems, autonomic and autonomous management is required to guarantee that the overall computing system operates properly. Autonomic systems should be capable of managing themselves. These properties make autonomic computing more advanced and challenging.

Autonomic computing is to simulate the natural neural system of human bodies to possess autonomic properties, i.e., self-* properties (Horn 2001; Kephart, 2005; Muller et al., 2006): **self-awareness:** an autonomic system should "know itself" and be aware of its state and behaviors; **self-configuring:** an autonomic application should be able to configure and reconfigure itself under varying and unpredictable conditions; **self-optimizing:** an autonomic system should be able to detect suboptimal behaviors and optimize itself to improve its execution; **self-healing:** an autonomic system should be able to detect and recover from potential problems and continue to function smoothly; and **self-protection:** an autonomic system should be capable of detecting and protecting its resources from both internal and external attack and maintaining overall system security and integrity.

Three basic ways are used to make a system autonomic (Lapouchnian, 2006): building an isomorphic space of possible system configurations; designing planned capabilities and social skills to delegate tasks to components; and evolutionary approaches such as making components as biological cells. Role-based approaches belong to the second category.

In fact, a human body is composed of numerous cells and cell groups. All the cells and cell groups collaborate and accomplish different tasks to provide the functions of their host - the human body (Wang, 2003). Because a human body is in a micro-world, it is easier to understand the autonomic properties of a system with a human society in a macro-world.

A person is social. Without a society, a person never shows and requires his or her sociability.

Without the requirement of sociability, one does not need to present their autonomy and autonomicity, because they coexist with the sociability. In a society, people work, interact, and collaborate with each other directly and roles are abstract regulations for them to collaborate and coordinate. In such situations, roles are abstract and implicit tools to evaluate people's performance in completing tasks. This kind of evaluation is ambiguous and qualitative most of the time. Therefore, it is difficult to operate role-based evaluations in the social world. However, roles can be made into easily managed mechanisms to evaluate agents' performances in computer-based systems (Zhu, 2007, 2008; Zhu & Zhu, 2003, 2006, 2008a, 2008b, 2008c).

In a multi-agent system, there are two kinds of "selves": one is the system itself and the other is an agent itself. To efficiently present the autonomic properties of the system self, we must fully develop the autonomic properties of the agent self. To present the system self, there must be task distributions, coordination and collaboration among agents. To make agents autonomic, they must be made be aware of their environments, respond to these environments, and be self-regulating.

The self-management of a society comes from a good central government and the active participation of their members. The self-management of a networked computer system also requires a central management and the participations of their component computers. From the viewpoint of multi-agent systems, an autonomic system is composed of a central manager and many autonomous and autonomic agents.

Role-Based Collaboration (RBC) is a computational thinking methodology that mainly uses roles as underlying mechanisms to facilitate abstraction, classification, separation of concern, dynamics, interactions and collaboration. Based on roles, RBC is such an emerging methodology designed to facilitate an organizational structure, provide orderly system behavior, and consolidate system security for both human and non-human entities that collaborate and coordinate their activities with or within systems. RBC is an appropriate approach to building autonomic systems.

This paper is arranged as follows. Section 2 restates and revises the definitions of roles and agents of our previously proposed model E-CARGO; Section 3 specifies the relations among roles in role-based systems (RBS); Section 4 investigates autonomic elements in RBS; Section 5 demonstrates how roles help a system possess the property of self-awareness; Section 6 discusses the self-healing and self-configuration properties of a role-based system; Section 7 discusses self-protection; Section 8 presents the self-optimization property; Section 9 discusses related work; and Section 10 concludes this paper and proposes future work.

1. THE REVISED E-CARGO MODEL AND ROLE-BASED SYSTEMS

With the E-CARGO model (Zhu & Zhou, 2006, 2008c), collaboration is based on roles. In E-CARGO, a system $\sum$ can be described as a 9-tuple $\sum ::= <C, O, A, M, R, E, G, s_0, H>$, where C is a set of classes, O is a set of objects, A is a set of agents, M is a set of messages, R is a set of roles, E is a set of environments, G is a set of groups, s_0 is the initial state of a collaborative system, and H is a set of users. In such a system, A and H, E and G are tightly-coupled sets. In role-based collaboration, a human user and his/her agent play a role together. Every group should work within an environment. An environment regulates a group. With this tight coupling, a role-based collaborative system is composed of both computers and human beings. With the participation of people H, such as joining in a team $\sum$, accessing objects of the team, sending messages through roles, forming a group in an environment, $\sum$ evolves, develops and functions. The results of the team work are a new state of $\sum$ that is expressed by the values of C, O, A, M,

E, G, and H. To apply role-based collaboration methodologies into autonomic computing, agents A will be incorporated with some functions of human beings H.

In this paper, roles, agents and environments are major mechanisms to support autonomic properties. Roles are considered abstract interface specifications as proposed in the E-CARGO model. The process meanings of roles (Zhu & Zhou, 2008b) are not applied. Agents are role players. The definitions of an agent and role are carefully revised based on the requirements of autonomic properties (to form the necessary structures for autonomic computing), where, if x is a set, | x | is its cardinality; a.b means b of a or a's b; "a=b" means a is equivalent to b; "a:= b" means that a is assigned with b; and "a::= b" means that a is defined as b. In E-CARGO, agents are considered to have only one central processing unit and they can only play one role and process the related messages at one time.

Definition 1: *role.* A role is defined as r::= <n, I, s, α, β, A_c, A_p, A_o, R_r, O_r > where,

- n is the identification of the role;
- I::= < M_{in}, M_{out} > denotes a set of messages, where M_{in} expresses the incoming messages to the relevant agents, and M_{out} expresses a set of outgoing messages or message templates to roles, i.e., M_{in}, M_{out} ⊂ M;
- s is the qualification (or called credit) requirement for an agent to play this role;
- α is the time limit for an agent to play this role;
- β is the space limit for an agent to play this role.
- A_c is a set of agents who are currently playing this role;
- A_p is a set of agents who are qualified to play this role;
- A_o is a set of agents who used to play this role; and

○ O_r is a set of objects that can be accessed by the agents playing this role;

Definition 2: *agent*. An agent is defined as $a ::= <n, c_a, s_a, V_a, \alpha_a, \beta_a, r_c, R_p, R_o, N_g>$, where

○ n is the identification of the agent;

○ c_a is a special class that describes the common properties of users;

○ s_a is the qualification (or credit) vaule of the agent;

○ V_a is a set of services provided by the agent;

○ α_a is the time requirement of the agent;

○ β_a is the memory space requirement of the agent;

○ r_c means a role that the agent is currently playing. If it is empty, then this agent is free;

○ R_p means a set of roles that the agent is potentially to play ($r_c \notin a.R_p$);

○ R_o means a set of roles that the agent played before; and

○ N_g means a set of groups that the agent belongs to.

All the current role and the potential roles of agent *a* (i.e., $a.R_p \sqcup \{a.r_c\}$) form its repository role set, denoted as R_r.

Definition 3: *message*. $m ::= <n, v, l, p, f, \alpha_m, \beta_m, \delta>$ where

○ n is the identification of the message including its sender (a role) and the host's address of its sender;

○ v is the receiver of the message expressed by an identification of a role;

○ l is the pattern of a message, specifying the types, sequence and number of parameters;

○ p is a complex object taken as the parameters with the message pattern l;

○ f is a flag that expresses any, some or all-message;

○ α_m is the time limit for this message to be processed;

○ β_m is the space limit for this message to be processed; and

○ δ is a pubishment value to the agent that process this message.

Definition 4: *environment*. $e ::= <n, B, R_x>$ where

○ n is the identification of the environment; and

○ $B = \{< r, q, o_s>\}$ is a set of tuples of role (or more exactly, a role class), role range and a shared object, where, the cardinality range q tells how many agents may play this role in this environment and is expressed by [l, u]; and

○ R_x is a set of role relations between roles specified by B (See Section 2).

For example, q might be [1, 1], [2, 2], [1, 10], [3, 50], … . It states that how many agents may play the same role r in the group. The object o_s expresses the object accessed (or shared) by all the agents that play the role r.

Definition 5: *group*. $g = <n, e, J>$ where

○ n is the identification of the group;

○ e is an environment for the group to work; and

○ J is a set of tuples of identifications of an agent and role, i.e., $J = \{< a, r>| \exists q \in Q, o_s \in O \ni (<r, q, o_s> \in e.B)\}$, where, Q is used to express the whole set of pairs of positive integers, such as, [l, u].

When an agent joins a group, it must play a role and is attached with (put aside a part of its memory for) a role instance.

E, C, A, R, G, O and M are used to express the whole set of environments, classes, agents, roles, groups, objects and messages. With the E-CARGO model, a role engine can be designed to support RBC in the way stated by Shakespeare: All the world is a stage (E, C, O), and all the men and women merely players (A); they all have their exits and entrances (G); and one man in his time plays many parts (R) (As You Like It, Act II, Scene 7). Role-based approaches are good candidates to build autonomic computing systems, because "autonomic computing technology must work in real world scenarios (Lightstone, 2007)."

In the following discussions, "T" is used to express true and "F" false.

Definition 6: *workable role.* A role r is workable in an environment e if it is assigned enough agents to currently play it, i.e., $\exists q \in Q$, $o_s \in O \ni (<r, q, o_s> \in e.B) \wedge (|r.A_c| \geq q.l)$. This is denoted as *workable*(r) = T.

Definition 7: *workable group.* A group g is workable if all its roles are workable, i.e., $\forall r \in R$ ($\exists q \in Q$, $o_s \in O \ni <r, q, o_s> \in g.e.B \rightarrow$ (*workable*(r) = T)).

With E-CARGO, a role-based system is composed of *groups* of *agents* playing *roles* situated in an *environment* to access *classes* of *objects* (Figure 1).

With role-based approaches, a role engine is implemented on an operating system. The role engine manages roles and agents. From this viewpoint, a process is composed of an agent and its current role. When a process is scheduled, an agent and its current role (r_c) and potential roles (A_p) are loaded into the memory space of this process and then the code segment of the agent is executed on the CPU.

In this view, context switch has two levels: one is agent switch and the other is role switch. Agents are scheduled first, followed by roles. Agent switch is similar to the heavy-weight process switch and role switch is similar to the light-weight process (thread) switch.

Roles are different from threads. Roles are interfaces and objects accessed by the agents. A role switch makes an agent execute different code segments originally stored in the memory space of an agent. A role is mainly used to regulate the behaviors and check the performance of an agent. The accessibility of an agent is restricted by its current role.

In a role-based distributed computer system (Figure 2), roles are designed and stored in different computers including the hardware and Operating System (OS). Roles are the medium for inter-computer communications through their message exchanges. An environment can be organized with roles without considering their locations. This establishes distributed groups.

Agents are designed and stored in the peripheral memories of different computers. Agents are assigned with both current and potential roles. Running agents are loaded into the main memory and scheduled for processing on the CPUs. Agents transfer their roles based on the commands of role engine. After agents are assigned with roles

Figure 1. A role-based system

Agents
Groups
Environments
Roles
Role Engine (New OS facilities)
Classes and Objects (Operating Systems(OS))
Hardware(CPU + Memory + Network Interface)

Figure 2. A role-based distributed system

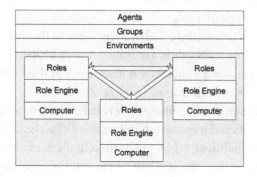

located on various computers in an environment, a distributed group is established and agents may be mobile. The workability of a group is dependent upon the workability of its roles.

2. RELATIONS AMONG ROLES

To possess the autonomic properties, the relationships among system components must be carefully built. With role-based approaches, the role engine specifies the relations among roles and the regulations, rules and policies of role playing (Zhu, 2008), such as, role transfer and role promotion. The role engine is to maintain and keep the system sufficient, necessary and consistent with the specification of environments, i.e., e:

- Every request has a service;
- Every service has a request;
- Every role is workable; and
- There is no circulation among the role relations such as inheritance, request, report-to, and promotion.

The role relation set R_x in an environment e are composed of the following kinds of relations.

2.1 Role Classes and Instances

To specify role relations, it is required to specify what a role is. When roles are discussed, arguments about roles always occur. What are roles? Are roles classes? Are roles instances? What is a message to a role?

In role-based collaboration, we state that roles are instances of r in Definition 1 with properties of classes. r is actually a meta-class in the view of object-orientation (Zhu & Zhou, 2003). On the aspect of an instance, a role has its concrete agents and messages. On the aspect of a class, its cardinalities ($|A_c|$, $|A_p|$, $|A_o|$) are actually to express how many instances can be created for agents to play it. To classify this, we define role classes and role instances.

Definition 7: *role class*. Role classes are instances of r.

Definition 8: *role instance*. A role instance is an instance of a role class.

In the definition of role of the revised E-CARGO model, role *r* is in fact a meta-class (Zhu & Zhou, 2003) for all role classes. When a new role class is defined, it is actually an instance of *r*. When an agent plays a role, it plays a role instance that belongs to an instance of *r*. In RBC and E-CARGO, a concrete role instance only shows the concrete values for O_r, where O_r is a class in a role class. A role instance and its player together form the dynamic status of an agent. Role instances can also be implemented by agents playing a role class (Zhu & Zhou, 2008a). The number of role instances is restricted by the cardinalities of a role in an environment. In the following discussions, the relations at the level of role classes are concentrated on. In RBC, a message is at first sent to a role class. The role class dispatches the message to agents that are players of the role class.

2.2 Inheritance Relation

Roles themselves can be a classification tool. They are related in a classification hierarchy.

Definition 9: *inheritance relation, super roles and sub roles*. Role r_j is a *super role* of role r_i if r_i possesses all the properties of r_j. Vise versa, r_i is a *sub role* of r_j. An *inheritance relation* denoted as Ω is a set of tuples of roles <r_i, r_j>, where, r_j is a super role of r_i and r_i is a sub role of r_j. Here, "inheritance" is similar to the inheritance concept of object-orientation (Zhu & Zhou, 2003).

Figure 3 shows the inheritance relations among a group of role classes.

Figure 3. Super roles and sub-roles

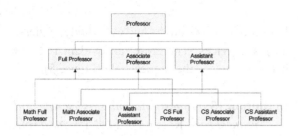

Definition 10: *root role and leaf role*. Role r_i is called a root role if it has no super roles. Role r_i is called a leaf role if it has no sub roles.

In Figure 3, *Professor* is a super role of roles *Full Professor, Associate Professor, and Assistant Professor. Professor* is a root role, and *Math Full Professor, Math Associate Professor, ...,* and *CS Assistant Professor* are leaf roles. In such a hierarchy, it is needed to clarify that an agent should be assigned with a leaf role, because leaf roles are concrete and executable by agents.

Note: CS means Computer Science

Definition 11: *message types*. In RBC, a message can be three types: *any, all, and some*. Suppose r is a non leaf role, $r_0, r_1, ...,$ and r_{n-1} are leaf roles whose super role is r *Any-messages* to r should be sent to an agent that plays $r_0, r_1, ...,$ or r_{n-1}. *All-messages* should be sent to all the agents that play $r_0, r_1, ...,$ and r_{n-1}. *Some-messages* should be sent to some (>1) agents that play $r_0, r_1, ...,$ or r_{n-1}.

Definition 12: *successful message sending*. When a message is sent to a role, it is *successful* if the role covers the message pattern and it finally finds its receivers, i.e., agents.

It is needed to check if this message is included in the role's service set or in the role's sub roles' service sets. If the message is in the sets and the required agents are ready to respond to this message, the message sending is successful. In role-based systems, a role (or more exactly role class) accepts and dispatches messages and agents playing this role respond to messages while accessing its role instance. A role cannot respond to messages directly.

2.3 Promotion Relations

In a well-designed community, there are pre-designed role promotion relations. This relation encourages the members in the community to work hard to contribute. It means that an agent could play an upper level role only when it has played the lower level role before (Zhu & Zhou, 2008a).

Definition 13: *role promotion, lower role and upper role*. Role r_j is an *upper role* of role r_i if r_i must be played by agent a before r_j is assigned to a. Vise versa, r_i is called a *lower role* of r_j. A *promotion relation* denoted as Λ is a set of tuples of roles $<r_i, r_j>$, where r_i is a lower role of r_j and r_j an upper role of r_i.

Role promotion is not natural but man-made. It is set in a role engine in order to be fair in role assignment (or re-assignment) of potential roles. It is set during the initialization and may be adjusted during collaboration.

Figure 4 gives two examples of promotion relations in the education and information technology fields.

Figure 4. Examples of promotion relations

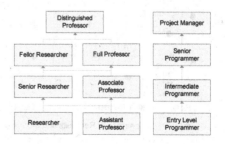

2.4 Report-to Relations

A role provides many services. However, not all other roles can request its services and obtain instant responses. Some regulations are introduced to control the accessibilities of the services. For example, a team leader can tell a team member to complete a task but a team member cannot tell a team leader what to do (Colman & Han, 2007). This leads to a report-to relation.

Definition 14: *report-to relation, supervisor role and supervisee role.* Role r_j is a *supervisor role* of role r_i if role r_i must respond to the requests from role r_j in a time limit set by r_j. Vise versa, r_i is a *supervisee role* of r_j. A *report-to relation* denoted as Δ is a set of tuples of roles $<r_i, r_j>$, where, r_i is a supervisee role of r_j and r_j is a supervisor role of r_i.

From this definition, a rule can be designed in a role engine: an agent playing a supervisee role obtains punishments if it does not respond to its supervisor's requests on time, i.e., the qualification value s_a of the agent is decreased (See rule (9) in Section 6).

A report-to relation is different from a promotion relation in that an agent plays a supervisee role may be impossible to be promoted to its supervisor role and a lower role may not be supervised by its upper role.

Figure 5. A request relation

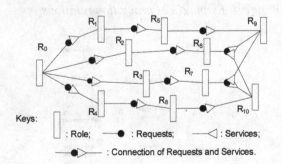

2.5 Request Relations

Everybody serves others and everybody requests others' services. Therefore, an evident relation between roles is the request role (Figure 5).

Definition 15: *request relation, service role and request role.* Role r_i is called a *request role* of role r_j if r_j provides the services requested by r_i, i.e., $r_i.I.M_{out} \subset r_j.I.M_{in}$. Vise versa, r_j is called a *service role* of r_i. A *request relation* denoted as Θ is a set of tuples $<r_i, r_j>$, where r_i is a request role of r_j and r_j is a service role of r_i, i.e., $<r_i, r_j> \in \Theta$ if $r_i.I.M_{out} \subset r_j.I.M_{in}$.

The request relation also holds the irreflexive property. This property guarantees a role does not issue a request itself in order to save the offset of message passing. Note that, we include those roles requesting part of other roles' services in the request relation.

2.6 Derived Relations

The following relations are derived from the above basic relations. They are not independent.

Definition 16: *competition relation and competitor role.* Role r_i is called a *competitor role* of role r_j if roles r_i and r_j have the same request role or the same upper role. A *competition relation* denoted as $€$ is a set of tuples of roles $<r_i, r_j>$, where, r_i and r_j are competitor roles of each other. More exactly, $<r_i, r_j> \in €$ if $\exists r_k \ni (<r_k, r_i> \in \Theta \wedge <r_k, r_j> \in \Theta) \vee (<r_i, r_k> \in \Lambda \wedge <r_j, r_k> \in \Lambda))$.

For examples, roles *software consultant* and *software developers* are competitor roles because they provide same services, i.e., in software development, role *client* may request the same services from them; in Figure 4, roles *researcher* and *assistant professor* are competitor roles but roles *programmer* and *researcher* are not competitor roles. The competition relations are used to establish regulations for assigning roles and dispatching messages.

Definition 17: *peer relation and peer role*. Role r_i is a *peer role* of role r_j if r_i and r_j have the same supervisor role. A *peer relation* denoted as $\Diamond$ is a set of tuples of roles $<r_i, r_j>$, where, r_i and r_j are peer roles of each other. More exactly, $<r_i, r_j> \in \Diamond$ if $\exists \ r_k \ni (<r_i, r_k> \in \Delta \wedge <r_j, r_k> \in \Delta)$.

2.7 Conflict Relations

In role-based access control (RBAC), Nyanchama and Osborn (1999) point out that there are many conflicts when authorization of roles is concerned: user-user/group-group/user-group conflicts; role-role conflicts; privilege-privilege conflicts; user-role assignment conflicts; and role-privilege assignment conflicts. From the viewpoint of RBC, roles may be conflict when they are assigned to agents.

Definition 18: *conflict relation, conflict roles.* Roles r_i and r_j are conflict if one agent cannot play them together. r_i is called a conflict role of r_j and vise versa. A *conflict relation* denoted as Ξ is a set of tuples $<r_i, r_j>$, where r_i, r_j are conflict roles of each other. More exactly, $<r_i, r_j> \in \Xi \rightarrow \forall \ a \in A, r_i, r_j \in R \ (\neg (r_i \in a.R_r \wedge r_j \in a.R_r))$.

In a role-based system, the conflict relation is actually pre-defined in order to protect conflict roles from being assigned to the same agent.

2.8 Summary of Role Relations

As a summary, Γ is used to express all the relations among roles in an RBC system. Suppose r_i, $r_j \in R$ and $r_i \neq r_j$, $\Gamma ::= <\Omega, \Lambda, \Delta, \Theta, \Epsilon, \Diamond, \Xi>$, where,

- Ω: an inheritance relation. $<r_i, r_j> \in \Omega$ if r_i inherits from r_j.
- Λ: a promotion relation. $<r_i, r_j> \in \Lambda$ if r_i is a lower role of r_j and r_j is a upper role of r_i.
- Δ: a report-to relations. $<r_i, r_j> \in \Delta$ if is a supervisee role of r_j and r_j is a supervisor role of r_i.
- Θ: a request relation. $<r_i, r_j> \in \Theta$ if $r_i.I.M_{out} \subset r_j.I.M_{in}$.
- $\Epsilon$: a competition relation. $<r_i, r_j> \in \Epsilon$ if $\exists \ r_k \ni (<r_k, r_i> \in \Theta \wedge <r_k, r_j> \in \Theta) \vee (<r_i, r_k> \in \Lambda \wedge <r_j, r_k> \in \Lambda))$.
- $\Diamond$: a peer relation. $<r_i, r_j> \in \Diamond$ if $\exists \ r_k \ni (<r_i, r_k> \in \Delta \wedge <r_j, r_k> \in \Delta)$.
- Ξ: a conflict relation. $<r_i, r_j> \in \Xi$ if r_i and r_j are conflict.

The following properties should be kept in a role-based system.

Property 1: *irreflexive*. $\forall \ r_i \in R(<r_i, r_i> \notin \Omega) \wedge (<r_i, r_i> \notin \Delta) \wedge (<r_i, r_i> \notin \Lambda) \wedge (<r_i, r_i> \notin \Theta) \wedge (<r_i, r_i> \notin \Epsilon) \wedge (<r_i, r_i> \notin \Diamond) \wedge (<r_i, r_i> \notin \Xi)$.

Property 2: *transitive*.
- $\forall \ r_i, r_j, r_k \in R(<r_i, r_j> \in \Omega \wedge <r_j, r_k> \in \Omega \rightarrow <r_i, r_k> \in \Omega)$;
- $\forall \ r_i, r_j, r_k \in R(<r_i, r_j> \in \Lambda \wedge <r_j, r_k> \in \Lambda \rightarrow <r_i, r_k> \in \Lambda)$;
- $\forall \ r_i, r_j, r_k \in R(<r_i, r_j> \in \Delta \wedge <r_j, r_k> \in \Delta \rightarrow <r_i, r_k> \in \Delta)$;
- $\forall \ r_i, r_j, r_k \in R(<r_i, r_j> \in \Epsilon \wedge <r_j, r_k> \in \Epsilon \rightarrow <r_i, r_k> \in \Epsilon)$; and
- $\forall \ r_i, r_j, r_k \in R(<r_i, r_j> \in \Diamond \wedge <r_j, r_k> \in \Diamond \rightarrow <r_i, r_k> \in \Diamond)$.

Property 3: *symmetrical*.
- $\forall \ r_i, r_j \in R(<r_i, r_j> \in \Epsilon) \rightarrow (<r_j, r_i> \in \Epsilon)$;
- $\forall \ r_i, r_j \in R(<r_i, r_j> \in \Diamond) \rightarrow (<r_j, r_i> \in \Diamond)$; and
- $\forall \ r_i, r_j \in R(<r_i, r_j> \in \Xi) \rightarrow (<r_j, r_i> \in \Xi)$.

Property 4: *noncircular*. There are not circles in inheritance, request, promotion, and report-to relations, i.e., $\neg \; \exists \, r_0, \; r_1, \; r_2, \; ..., \; r_n \in R$, $<r_i, \; r_{i+1}>(r_i \neq r_{i+1}) \in X(X = \Omega, \Lambda, \Delta \text{ or } \Theta)$ (i = 0, 1, ..., n-1) $\ni (r_n = r_0)$.

Definition 19: *role graph.* A role net is a directed graph (Skiena, 1990) formed by all the relations of Γ, denoted as $\Gamma.G$, i.e., $\Gamma.G ::= < R, \Gamma >$, where, R are the node set and Γ are the edge set.

Definition 20: *interrelated roles.* Roles r_i and r_j are interrelated if $<r_i, r_j>$ belongs to the role graph, i.e. $<r_i, r_j> \in (\Omega \cup \Lambda \cup \Delta \cup \Theta \cup \in \cup \Diamond \cup \Xi)$.

3. AUTONOMIC ELEMENTS

An autonomic element manages its own internal state and interactions with its environment (i.e., other autonomic elements) (Muller et al., 2006). It consists of a managed component and an autonomic manager (Parashar & Hariri, 2005; Sterritt & Hinchey, 2005a, 2005b). An element's internal behavior and its relationships with other elements are driven by the goals and policies the designers have built into the system. Control loops with sensors and effectors together with system knowledge and planning/adapting policies allow the autonomic elements to be self-aware and self-management.

An autonomic element consists of one autonomic manager and one or more managed elements. At the core of an autonomic element is a control loop that integrates the manager with the managed element. The autonomic manager consists of sensors, effectors, and a five-component engine including a monitor, an analysis engine, a planning engine, an execution engine and a knowledge base (Muller et al., 2006).

An autonomic manager must be armed with tools for monitoring the elements managed by it (Lapouchnian et al., 2006). It needs to analyze the collected data to determine whether the elements behave as expected, to plan a series of actions if a problem is detected, and to tune the parameters of the elements. With role-based approaches, the role engine (denoted as Π) and roles take the role of the autonomic manger and agents are managed elements (Figure 1 and Figure 2). The regular tasks of a role engine are as follows (Zhu, 2008):

- *qualification(a)*: return the qualification value of agent a.
- *set-qualification(a, s):* set the qualification value of agent a as s, i.e., $a.s_a := s$.
- *qualified-for(a, r)*: return T if agent a is qualified to play role r else F.
- *apply-for(a, r)*: deal with an application for role r from agent a.
- *approve(a, r)*: check if agent a is appropriate to play role r.
- *disapprove(a, r)*: deprive agent a's right to play role r.
- *workable(r)*: return T if role r is workable else F.
- *workable(g)*: return T if role g is workable else F.
- *misbehaving(a)*: check agent a's current working state. It returns T if a does not behave well else F.
- *transfer(r, a)*: transfer role r's current agent to another one *a*. It returns T if successful else F.
- *sender (m)*: return the role that sends message m.
- *address(m)*: return the host address of the sender of message m. Note that the identification of a message includes the host address, such as, the port number and the Internet Protocol (IP) address.
- *accept(r, m)*: let role r accept message m. It returns T if successful else F.
- *dispatch(r, a, m, t_d)*: dispatch message m received by role r to agent a at t_d. It returns T if successful else F.
- *reply(a, r, m, p, t_r, c)*: return the result object p produced by agent a to role r with respect to message m at t_r with the space

c accessed by a. It returns T if successful else F.

Roles are added to a role engine based on the requirement of an environment of a system. When a role is added, there are vacant positions (the cardinality range of the role) for agents.

With E-CARGO, an agent is an instance of the agent class *Agent* defined in the model. Agents are created and added to a role engine based on the requirements of newly added roles (Zhu, 2007). Agents are made simpler because the role engine takes many controlling responsibilities from agents. The goal for an agent is to collect as many credits as possible. It needs to work hard: try to play roles, try to serve as many messages as possible, and try to play upper roles. An agent checks the vacant positions from an environment, checks if it is qualified to play the roles with vacant positions; then bids for the positions with other agents.

Definition 21: *qualified agent.* Agent a is qualified to play role r if a's qualifications cover the qualification requirement of r, i.e., $\forall$ r $\in$ R, a $\in$ A$((r.I.M_{in} \subset a.V_d) \wedge (a.s_a \geq r.s)) \rightarrow (\Pi.qualified\text{-}for(a, r) = T))$.

Agents are required to adjust their time and memory parameters α_a and β_a timely to reflect its current performances. Suppose there is a method defined in a subclass of a corresponding to message m. Agent a (*this* in the pseudo-code) is an instance of a subclass of the following Java-like class specification *Agent*, its major loop is shown in *run()*, where, *thread* is a Java class, and *sleep()* is a method of class thread used to set a thread to an inactive state.

In the above specification, a sleeping agent may be awaken when a role has a vacancy, it is approved the role it has applied for, or a message comes.

In the following sections 5-8, rules to present the autonomicity of a system are introduced. Some rules are used to tell the system how to operate and some rules to tell what the status the system should keep.

4. SELF-AWARENESS

Self-awareness refers to the ability to perceive internal environment, motivation, willingness, and desire, and goals of the whole system. With these abilities, self-diagnosis can be implemented. A person's body possesses such an ability because of a well-established neural system. People will wish to see a doctor when they do not feel well. There is then a need to express the nature of the malady. Therefore, a feeling or perception of some abnormality is the first step in seeking treatment by a doctor. If a person cannot sense evidence of an illness, there would be no obvious need to obtain a doctors' assistance in seeking a cure for his/her medical problem. Autonomic systems have similar requirements. Self-diagnosis is the

```
abstract class Agent extends thread {
void run(){
 while (true){
 while ( ∀ e∈ E, r∈ R, q∈ Q, oᵣ∈ O ∋ ((<r, q, oᵣ> ∈ e.B) ∧ (|r.Aᶜ |=q.u)) this.sleep();
 if (Π.qulified-for(this, r) = T) Π.apply-for (this, r);
 while (!Π.approve (this, r)) this.sleep();
 while (!Π.dispatch(r, this, m, t_a)) this.sleep();
 Π.reply(this, r, m, this.m(), t, c);
 }
 }
}
```

first step for autonomic computing to become a reality. "Problem localization and/or determination, the challenges become especially interesting (Kephart, 2005)." How is agent behavior to be evaluated? A typical traditional way is to probe failures, i.e., to issue a ping command to a component. If the responses are out of the time limit, it can be taken as a possible indication of a bad component (Kephart, 2005).

Roles provide new mechanisms to meet this requirement. In human societies, people (detectives and police persons) detect the abnormal behavior of some possible criminals by comparing their behaviors with the required behaviors by their declared roles. In computer-based systems, roles can also perform similar tasks. Roles are templates to regulate software agents' behavior and the interactions among agents. In a multi-agent system, agents are composed of qualifications and abilities. They behave based on their pre-programmed processes. An agent behaves abnormally when its pre-programmed processes are infected by malicious attacks. These kinds of agents are called **infected agents**.

The basic assumption is that an infected agent cannot complete routine tasks in the required time and within a preset space specified in its current role. It must take extra time and extra space to do some other jobs that are unrelated with its required tasks. For example, if a criminal wants to do some bad things, s/he must pretend to do the regular routine tasks. S/he must take more time than regular time consumption and perform activities in more places than the regular ones. Criminals may lie to find some excuses in social life to avoid penalty. However, such lies can be easily checked in computer-based systems because the CPU cycles used by an agent are definite, exactly measured and recorded.

When an infected agent is running, it actually takes extra CPU time and memory space to behave according to as its affected code. The role engine has a time slot to run to check every agent's performances and report if an agent is ill.

A role's main content is composed of messages. There is no code in a role. Therefore, it is not easy for a role to be affected by malicious intruders. The role engine can compare the parameters specified in the role and the actual performance parameters of the agent to report if it is affected.

Rules (1-4) show the conditions for finding a misbehaving agent, i.e., (1) if the message is not correctly processed and replied; (2) if the message is processed in a too long period; (3) if the message is processed with a too large space; (4) if the collected space and time is over the limit; then the agent misbehaves. Rule (5) is to set the qualification value of the misbehaving agent as zero. It is reasonable to set the fourth rule to check if an agent is infected because each message process may not be significantly enough to express the agent's wrong behavior. At the role level, it is easier to check the agent's state by accumulating its tiny bad behaviors.

$$\forall\, a \in A(\exists\, m \in M, \exists\, r \in R(\Pi.\mathit{dispatch}(r, a, m, t_d)=$$

$$T) \wedge (\Pi.\mathit{reply}(a, r, m, p, t_r, c)=F)) \rightarrow (\Pi.\mathit{misbehaving}(a)=T)$$
$$(1)$$

$$\forall\, a \in A(\exists\, m \in M, \exists\, r \in R(\Pi.\mathit{dispatch}(r, a, m, t_d)=T) \wedge$$

$$(\Pi.\mathit{reply}(a, r, m, p, t_r, c)=T) \wedge (t_r\text{-}t_d > m.\alpha_m)) \rightarrow (\Pi.\mathit{misbehaving}(a)=T)$$
$$(2)$$

$$\forall\, a \in A(\exists\, m \in M, \exists\, r \in R((\Pi.\mathit{reply}(a, r, m, p, t_r, c)=T)$$

$$\wedge (c > m.\beta_m)) \rightarrow (\Pi.\mathit{misbehaving}(a)=T) \qquad (3)$$

$$\forall\, a \in A(a.\alpha_a \geq a.r_c.\alpha) \vee (a.\beta_a \geq a.r_c.\beta) \rightarrow (\Pi.\mathit{misbehaving}(a)=T)$$
$$(4)$$

$$\forall\, a \in A\,(\Pi.\mathit{misbehaving}(a)=T) \rightarrow (\Pi.\mathit{set\text{-}qualification}\,(a,0))$$
$$(5)$$

There may be an argument that fake infection reports are possible for rules (3) and (4) because a message m may have a large parameter p. This can be overcome by special design considerations, i.e., the space used for processing the message and that for the parameter p are separate and checked with different standards.

5. SELF-HEALING AND SELF-CONFIGURATION

When abnormality is found, it should be reported or recorded by a manager of the system. The manager is called role engine in a role-based system. The role engine will respond to the report and take action to cure the abnormality. The misbehaving agent should be stopped and replaced in a limited time. The major curing method is to transfer the role currently played by the infected agent to another qualified and uninfected agent. In fact, the situation is to replace the current abnormal agent by a normal qualified agent.

With E-CARGO, qualified agents are actually those agents belonging to its repository role set, i.e., A_r. A_r and related algorithms reflect the ability of a system to recover. A benefit of role-based systems is that once an agent is evaluated to be an infected one, it will never be assigned opportunities to run until it is cleaned or cured, because it cannot pass the qualification checking of the role. Rule (6) invokes a role transfer (Zhu & Zhou, 2008c), i.e., if there is a qualified agent a' for role r, the current role of agent a will be currently played by agent a' and the current role of a is deprived.

$$\exists a \in A \ \exists a' \in A \ ((a.s_a = 0) \wedge \Pi.\textit{qualified-for}$$
$$(a', a.r_c) \rightarrow \Pi.\textit{transfer}(a.r_c, a') \wedge$$
$$\Pi.\textit{disapprove}(a, a.r_c)) \ ---- \tag{6}$$

To have the ability of self-configuration (Bulusu et al., 2004; Parashar & Hariri, 2005), finding qualified agents instantly are required. This is when there are not enough role pre-assignments, i.e., there exists not a successful role transfer (Zhu et al., 2007; Zhu & Zhou, 2008c).

To meet this requirement, the role engine should actively search from all the available agents. Therefore, a new operation should be added to the role engine:

- *search-for-instantly(a, r)*: find an qualified agent a for role r in the agent set and assign it to role r, i.e., $a.r_c = r \wedge a \in r.A_c$
- *search-for (a, r)*: find a qualified agent a for role r in the agent set and put it into the set of qualified agents of role r, i.e., $(a.R_p := a.R_p \cup \{r\}) \wedge (r.A_p := r.A_p \cup \{a\})$.

For instant self-configuration, rule (7) is applied. It tells that an instant replacement of current agent a for role r is required.

$$\forall a, a' \in A \ ((\Pi.\textit{transfer}(a.r_c, a') = F \rightarrow$$
$$\Pi.\textit{search-for-instantly}(a', a.r_c)) \ ---- \tag{7}$$

For a system expressed by g to re-configurate before an instant searching is required, rule (8) is applied.

$$\forall r \in R \ ((\exists q \in Q, o_r \in O \ni \ <r, q, o_r> \in g.e.B)$$
$$\wedge \ (|r.A_c| < q.u) \rightarrow \Pi.\textit{search-for}(a, r)) \ ---- \tag{8}$$

Rule (8) tells us that the reconfiguration occurs when there are vacancies for role r.

Rule (2) can be tuned to new rules (9) and (10) based on the report-to relation Δ.

$$\forall a \in A(\exists m \in M, \exists r \in R(\Pi.\textit{dispatch}(r, a, m,$$
$$t_d) = T) \wedge \ (\Pi.\textit{reply}(a, r, m, p, t_r, c) = T) \wedge (t_r - t_d > m.$$
$$\alpha_m) \wedge (< \Pi.\textit{sender} (m), r> \in \Delta) \rightarrow \ a.s_a := a.s_a$$
$$- m.\delta) \ ---- \tag{9}$$

$$\forall r \in R \ (\forall a \in r.A_r) \rightarrow (\Pi.\textit{qualified-for}(a, r) = T) \ ---- \tag{10}$$

Further more, the role engine check timely the system with the properties 1-4 to guarantee the consistences of the system. The role engine can also take actions based on checking the status of roles (rule1 (11) and (12)).

$$\forall\, r \in R \; \exists\, q \in Q, o_s \in O \ni (<r, q, o_s> \in e.B) \wedge (|r. A_c | < q.l) \rightarrow (workable(r) = F) \text{ ----} \qquad (11)$$

$$\forall\, r \in R \; (workable(r) = F) \rightarrow \Pi.search\text{-}for\text{-}instantly(a, r)) \text{ ----} \qquad (12)$$

6. SELF-PROTECTION

In Role-Based Access Control (RBAC), roles possess the following characteristics which are beneficial to self-protection (Bertino et al., 2005; Covington et al., 2000; Ferraiolo et al., 2001; Joshi et al., 2005; Nyanchama & Osborn, 1999; Sandhu et al., 1999; Simon & Zurke, 1997):

- Least Privilege: It requires that outsider agents be given no more privileges than necessary to perform their job function.
- Separation of concerns: (1) a role can be associated with an operation of a business function only if the role is an authorized role for the subject and the role was not be assigned previously to all of the other operations; (2) an outside agent is authorized as a member of a role only if that role is not mutually exclusive with any of the other roles for which the agent already possesses membership; and (3) a subject can become active in a new role only if the proposed role is not mutually exclusive with any of the roles in which the subject is currently active.
- Cardinality: The capacity of a role cannot be exceeded by an additional role member.
- Dependency constraints: There is a hierarchy or a relationship among roles such as contains, *excludes* and *transfers*.

With these properties, roles can help a system effectively protect outside malicious messages from intruding the system.

In the current architecture of distributed systems, a computer affects other computers by issuing messages through the network interface. Other computers are affected through their network interfaces. The protection should be activated when a message is received. That is why a fire-wall is used. If the messages pass the checking of the fire-wall, the malicious codes in the messages still affect the target machines.

Under a RBAC system permissions are associated with roles (Bertino et al., 2001). Bertino et al. (2001) proposes an ID system to determine role intruders to database systems, that is, individuals that while holding a specific role, have a behavior different from the normal behavior of the role. They emphasize that RBAC mechanisms can be used to protect against insider threats.

In autonomic computing, a distributed system should be self-managing. A manager component should be able to detect exceptions at its network interface by checking the incoming messages including the packaged data and the message type.

From the message definition of E-CARGO, hacker messages basically simulate the regular or legal message pattern l and hide malicious code in the parameter object p. To check whether a message has such malicious code is a typical task for protection mechanisms to accomplish. Traditional methods mainly involve using firewalls and anti-virus software. Firewalls are set up on an operating system and check the sending addresses of the incoming packages and block those packages from those addresses not allowed. Anti-virus software searches the files on the disks and checks the feature codes of viruses in files to state if a file has been infected by viruses.

Roles are good mechanisms for protecting the agent and the system from intrusion. With role-based approaches, an agent sends a message through its current role and then the message is dispatched by the role engine. In this situation, a malicious message can only be sent out by an agent with malicious aims.

Let us analyze the possible way to send out a malicious message to role-based systems. A hacker must pretend to issue a regular message m directing to a role r and put the malicious code into the parameter object p. Suppose that a role engine receives a message m from the hacker machine. It is the role r (m.v) that decides the final destination of the message. The hacker will not be able to send its malicious code to a specific destination. As stated before, role r is not easily infected because it has no code in it. Therefore, a hacker faces greater difficulty in attacking a role-based system versus traditional systems.

Furthermore, the role engine at the receiver side can check the message. This protection occurs when a message is received, dispatched and executed.

At time when the message is received: A firewall like mechanism $(\Pi.l_m)$ can be set in the role engine to check the source address of the message to protect messages from those malicious or unintended message senders.

$$\forall \, m \in M \, ((\Pi.address(m) \in \Pi.l_m) \rightarrow \Pi.accept(m.v, m)) \text{ ----} \tag{13}$$

If the message passes the first protect line - rule (13). Note that *m.v* is a role that receives the message *m*. It is still controlled and scrutinized.

At the second protection line, i.e., the time when the message is dispatched: It is the role that receives the message and dispatches its message to an agent. This dispatch is totally irrelevant to the message senders. The simplest way is to choose the first qualified agent: rule (14).

$$\forall \, a \in A \, (\Pi.accept(m.v, m) \wedge (\Pi.qualified\text{-}for \, (a, \\ m.v)=T)) \rightarrow \Pi.dispatch(m.v, a, m, t_d)) \text{ ----} \tag{14}$$

At the time when the message is executed: The activities of the agent are confined and restricted by the role. The accessible objects are regulated by the role and its environment.

Therefore, the malicious code cannot be executed without any restrictions.

With role-based approaches, agents are set with a credit in a role engine to keep track of the agent's trust. If its trust cannot meet the requirement, no message will be dispatched to it and its role will be disapproved – rule (15). If the malicious code wants to activate when the agent is scheduled to run, the roles could find the irregular behaviors of the agent and quickly tag it as an infected agent through rules (1-5).

$$\forall \, a \in A \, ((a.s_a \geq m.v.s) \rightarrow (\Pi.qualified\text{-}for \, (a, m.v)=T)) \text{ ----} \tag{15}$$

7. SELF-OPTIMIZATION

Optimization is often associated with space and time efficiencies. Optimizing a system infrastructure according to such specific objectives is complicated, because it is unclear at the beginning how to set relevant parameters which affect business objectives (Aiber et al., 2004). Moreover, optimizing the infrastructure is continuous effort, as there may be changes which occur in the environment of the infrastructure, i.e., optimization must be dynamic and instant.

In a role-based system, different agents play different roles. The agents possess attributes related to space and time. Optimization jobs are activated when some qualified agents for a role are not best suited to play the current role. These agents may require additional space and time to complete tasks or services required by the role. The role engine could use idle times to instantly evaluate the performance of agents and transfer agents' roles to optimize the whole system. Assignment of potential agents to roles is a fundamental for dynamic optimization in role-based systems. The following rules (17-22) are used to help a role-based system do self-optimization. Note that, rule (16) holds in the role engine for roles (17-22).

$$\forall\, r \in R\, ((a \in A_p) \to (\Pi.qualified\text{-}for\ (a, m.v) = T))\ \text{----} \tag{16}$$

For computation extensive systems,

$$\forall\, a \in A, r \in R\, (a.r_c \in r.A_c) \to \neg\, (\exists\, a' \in r.A_p \to a'.\alpha_a < a.\alpha_a)\ \text{---} \tag{17}$$

For memory extensive systems,

$$\forall\, a \in A, r \in R\, (a.r_c \in r.A_c) \to \neg\, (\exists\, a' \in r.A_p \to a'.\beta_a < a.\beta_a)\ \text{---} \tag{18}$$

For systems with balanced memory or computation requirement,

$$\forall\, a \in A,\ r \in R\, (a.r_c \in r.A_c) \to \neg\, (\exists\, a' \in r.A_p \to (a'.\alpha_a + a'.\beta_a) < (a.\alpha_a + a.\beta_a))\ \text{----} \tag{19}$$

Based on the above rules, the role engine does optimization in idle times.

$$(\exists\, a' \in r.A_p \wedge a'.\alpha_a < a.\alpha_a) \to \Pi.transfer\ (a.r_c,\ a')\ \text{----} \tag{20}$$

$$(\exists\, a' \in r.A_p \wedge a'.\beta_a < a.\beta_a) \to \Pi.transfer\ (a.r_c,\ a')\ \text{----} \tag{21}$$

$$(\exists\, a' \in r.A_p \wedge (a'.\alpha_a + a'.\beta_a) < (a.\alpha_a + a.\beta_a)) \to \Pi.transfer\ (a.r_c,\ a')\ \text{----} \tag{22}$$

8. RELATED WORK

Applying roles to offer autonomic properties is an exciting idea. However, very few writings mention such a topic. Some related articles discussed the adaptability of a system with the support of roles.

Colman and Han (2007) discuss some ideas on applying roles into adaptive software development by elaborating how contracts can be used to monitor, regulate and configure the interactions between clusters of software entities called roles. By their method, abstract management contracts regulate the flow of control through the roles and provide monitoring interception points. Concrete contracts are domain specific and allow the specification of performance conditions. These contracts bind clusters of roles into self-managed composites—each composite with its own organizer role. The organizer roles can control, create, abrogate and reassign contracts. Adaptive systems are built from a recursive structure of such self-managed composites.

Tamai et al. (2005) propose to realize object adaptation to environments with the support of a role-based model Epsilon and a language EpsilonJ. In Epsilon, an environment is defined as a field of collaboration between roles and an object adapts to the environment assuming one of the roles. Objects can freely enter or leave environments and belong to multiple environments at a time so that dynamic adaptation or evolution of objects is realized. Environments and roles are the first class constructs at runtime as well as at model description time so that separation of concerns is not only materialized as a static structure but also observed as behaviors. Environments encapsulating collaboration are independent reuse components to be deployed separately from objects.

Ren et al. (2007) present a coordination model, i.e., the Actor, Role and Coordinator (ARC) model. Roles are taken as a key thrust in the ARC model and this is similar to the role dynamics in (Zhu, 2007). In their model, behaviors of actors, roles and coordinators are formally defined and applied into supporting the re-configurability and fault localization for open distributed embedded software systems. The specified behaviors regulate some policies and regulations of agents' behaviors in a system, such as, memberships and configurations.

The followings are some contributions mentioning role relations. Marwell and Hage (1970) present 100 role relationships in different societies including economic, political, health and welfare, science and education, family, religion, art and leisure sectors. Each role-relationship involves occupants, activities, locations and occurrences.

All the relationships are classified in the senses of sociology, i.e., *gemeizsclzaft* and *gesellschaft*. Their analysis lacks abstraction in the sense of collaboration, management and systems and is not very useful in such fields.

In RBAC, Simon and Zurko (1997) mention the role conflict relations when they discuss conflicts of interests relevant to complex tasks in a workflow management system. Conflicts are common in business transactions that require two signatures before a check is issued and processes to avoid fraud. Nyanchama and Osborn (1999) discuss the role-role conflict relations by role graphs. A role-role conflict means that the two roles should never appear together. This implies they should never be assigned to a single user, which is checked on user-role assignment. Their discussion concentrates on the conflict of permission authorizations to access system resources.

Skarmeas (1995) proposes a role model to deal with the tree hierarchy of roles in organizations. Roles may contain other roles and/or elementary roles. In their proposed tree structures, elementary roles are leaves. In describing organizational relations, he introduces virtual roles to deal with the supervision relations among roles. Virtual roles are used to assign roles supervised by them to individuals. He mentions the role consistency problem mainly when role transfers occur. However, tasks of a role and roles themselves are not clearly separated.

Olarnsakul and Batanov (2004) emphasize that roles have relationships (i.e., interactions and dependencies) with one another in order to fulfill assigned responsibilities. They present that roles and relationships are the building blocks of the organizational structure. In their model, a role relationship is a set of protocols that represent collaboration tasks or business processes.

Odell et al. (2005) describe a metamodel for agents, roles, and groups which are incorporated with Unified Modelling Language (UML) notations. They believe that roles provide the building blocks for agent social systems. Roles meet the requirements of describing interactions among agents. They use associations to describe the relationships among roles. Classifier classes are introduced to illustrate the relationships among agents and roles. Their metamodel is a good reference to analyze and design systems with roles.

Wang (2007b) explores the theoretical foundations and technical paradigms of autonomic computing. He reviews the historical development that leads to the transition from imperative computing to autonomic computing, investigates the interdisciplinary theoretical foundations from behaviorism, cognitive informatics, denotational mathematics, and intelligent science, and proposes a coherent model of autonomic computing. This model is an inspiring model from the viewpoint of Role-Based Collaboration. The E-CARGO model discussed in this paper may be improved by introducing the denotation semantics of Wang's (2007b) model.

9. CONCLUSION

Self-* properties are pursued by the researchers of autonomic computing. Self-awareness, self-healing self-protection, and self-optimization are mainly discussed in this paper. More specifically, roles are taken as the fundamental mechanisms to facilitate self-* properties. The significant contributions of this paper include: specifying the infrastructure of role-based systems at the viewpoint of autonomic computing; building relationships among roles in role based systems; and asserting that roles are good mechanisms to facilitate self-* properties by formalizations.

Newly introduced role-based mechanisms come at the cost of increased overhead in a system's performance. Accurate performance analyses are required to determine whether the benefits obtained by role-based approaches are worth the overhead introduced by role-based mechanisms. More future work includes formally proving the least complete set of the component definitions of the E-CARGO model; complete case studies of the proposed method; and prototype implementation.

ACKNOWLEDGMENT

This research is in part supported by National Scientific and Engineering Research Council, Canada (NSERC: 262075-06) and IBM Eclipse Innovation Grant. Thanks go to Mike Brewes of Nipissing University for his assistance in proofreading this article.

REFERENCES

Aiber, S., Gilat, D., Landau, A., Razinkov, N., Sela, A., & Wasserkrug, S. (2004, May). Autonomic self-optimization according to business objectives. In *Proceedings of the International Conference on Autonomic Computing*, New York (pp. 206- 213).

Bertino, E., Bonatti, P. A., & Ferrari, E. (2001, August). TRBAC: A Temporal Role-Based Access Control Model. *ACM Transactions on Information and System Security, 4*(3), 191–223. doi:10.1145/501978.501979

Bertino, E., Terzi, E., Kamra, A., & Vakali, A. (2005, December). Intrusion detection in RBAC-administered databases. In *Proceedings of the 21st Annual Computer Security Applications Conference*, Tucson, AZ (pp. 170-182).

Bulusu, N., Heidemann, J., Estrin, D., & Tran, T. (2004, February). Self-configuring localization systems: Design and Experimental Evaluation. [TECS]. *ACM Transactions on Embedded Computing Systems, 3*(1), 24–60. doi:10.1145/972627.972630

Colman, A., & Han, J. (2007). Using role-based coordination to achieve software adaptability. *Science of Computer Programming, 64*, 223–245. doi:10.1016/j.scico.2006.06.006

Covington, M. J., Moyer, M. J., & Ahamad, M. (2000). Generalized Role-Based Access Control for Securing Future Applications. In *Proceedings of the 23rd National Information Systems Security Conference*. Retrieved October 20, 2008, from http://smartech.gatech.edu/dspace/bitstream/1853/6580/1/GIT-CC-00-02.pdf

Ferraiolo, D. F., Sandhu, R., Gavrila, S., Kuhn, D. R., & Chandramouli, R. (2001, August). Proposed NIST Standard: Role-Based Access Control. *ACM Transactions on Information and System Security, 4*(2), 224–274. doi:10.1145/501978.501980

Horn, P. (2001, October). *Autonomic Computing: IBM's perspective on the State of Information Technology*. IBM. Retrieved October 20, 2008, from http://www.research.ibm.com/autonomic/

Joshi, J. B. D., Bertino, E., Latif, U., & Ghafoor, A. (2005, January). Generalized Temporal Role Based Access Control Model. *IEEE Transactions on Knowledge and Data Engineering, 7*(1), 4–23. doi:10.1109/TKDE.2005.1

Kephart, J. O. (2005, May). Research Challenges of Autonomic Computing. In *Proceedings of the International Conference on Software Engineering (ICSE'05)*, St. Louis, MO (pp. 15-22).

Lapouchnian, A., Yu, Y., Liaskos, S., & Mylopoulos, J. (2006, October). Requirements-Driven Design of Autonomic Application Software. In *Proceedings of the conference of the Center for Advanced Studies on Collaborative Research*, Toronto, Canada.

Lightstone, S. (2007, March). Foundations of Autonomic Computing Development. In *Proceedings of the 4th IEEE International Workshop on Engineering of Autonomic and Autonomous Systems (EASe '07)*, Tucson, AZ (pp. 163-171).

Marwell, G., & Hage, J. (1970). The Organization of Role-Relationships: A Systematic Description. *American Sociological Review, 35*(5), 884–900. doi:10.2307/2093299

Müller, H., O'Brien, L., Klein, M., & Wood, B. (2006). *Autonomic Computing* (Technical Note CMU/SEI-2006-TN-006). Pittsburgh, PA: Carnegie Mellon University. Retrieved October 20, 2008, from http://www.sei.cmu.cdu/pub/documents/06.reports/pdf/06tn006.pdf

Nyanchama, M., & Osborn, S. (1999). The Role Graph Model and Conflict of Interest. *ACM Transactions on Information and System Security, 2*(1), 3–33. doi:10.1145/300830.300832

Odell, J., Nodine, M., & Levy, R. (2005). A Metamodel for Agents, Roles, and Groups. In J. Odell, P. Giorgini, & J. Müller (Eds.), *Agent-Oriented Software Engineering (AOSE)* (LNCS 3382, pp. 78-92). Berlin: Springer.

Olarnsakul, M., & Batanov, D. N. (2004). Customizing Component-Based Software Using Component Coordination Model. *International Journal of Software Engineering and Knowledge Engineering, 14*(2), 103–140. doi:10.1142/S0218194004001622

Parashar, M., & Hariri, S. (2005). Autonomic Computing: An Overview. In J. P. Banâtre (Eds.), *Proceedings of UPP 2004* (LNCS 3566, pp. 247-259). Berlin: Springer Verlag.

Ren, S., Yu, Y., Chen, N., Tsai, J. J.-P., & Kwiat, K. (2007, September). The role of roles in supporting re-configurability and fault localizations for open distributed and embedded systems. *ACM Trans. Autonomic & Adaptive Sys., 2*(3), 1–27.

Samimi, F. A., McKinley, P. K., & Masoud Sadjadi, S. M. (2006). Mobile Service Clouds: A Self-managing Infrastructure for Autonomic Mobile Computing Services. In A. Keller & J.-P. Martin-Flatin (Eds.), *Proceedings of SelfMan 2006* (LNCS 3996, pp. 130-141). Berlin: Springer Verlag.

Sandhu, R., Bhamidipati, V., & Munawer, O. (1999, February). The ARBAC97 Model for Role-Based Administration of Roles. *ACM Transactions on Information and System Security, 2*(1), 105–135. doi:10.1145/300830.300839

Simon, R., & Zurko, M. E. (1997, June). Separation of duty in role based access control environments. In *Proceedings of the 10th IEEE Workshop on Computer Security Foundations*, Rockport, MA (pp. 183-194).

Skarmeas, N. (1995, January). Organizations through Roles and Agents. In *Proceedings of the Int'l Workshop on the Design of Cooperative Systems*, Antibes-Juan-Les-Pins, France. Retrieved October 20, 2008, from http://citeseer.ist.psu.edu/174774.html

Skiena, S. (1990). *Implementing Discrete Mathematics: Combinatorics and Graph Theory with Mathematica*. Reading, MA: Addison-Wesley.

Sterritt, R., & Hinchey, M. (2004, April). Apoptosis and Self-Destruct: A Contribution to Autonomic Agents? In *Proceedings of the 3rd NASA/IEEE Workshop on Formal Approaches to Agent-Based Systems*, Greenbelt, MD (pp. 262-270).

Sterritt, R., & Hinchey, M. (2005, April). Engineering ultimate self-protection in autonomic agents for space exploration missions. In *Proceedings of the 12th IEEE International Conference and Workshops on the Engineering of Computer-Based Systems*, Greenbelt, MD (pp. 506-511).

Tamai, T., Ubayashi, N., & Ichiyama, R. (2005, May). An Adaptive Object Model with Dynamic Role Binding. In *Proceedings of the Int'l Conf. of Software Engineering*, St. Louis, MO (pp. 166-175).

Tesauro, G., Chess, D. M., Walsh, W. E., Das, R., Segal, A., Whalley, I., et al. (2004, July). A Multi-Agent Systems Approach to Autonomic Computing. In *Proceedings of the Third Int'l Joint Conf. on Autonomous Agents and Multiagent Systems,* New York (Vol. 1, pp. 464-471).

Wang, J. F. (2003). *Cell Biology.* Beijing, China: Science Press.

Wang, Y. (2007a, January). The Theoretical Framework of Cognitive Informatics. *International Journal of Cognitive Informatics and Natural Intelligence, 1*(1), 1–27.

Wang, Y. (2007b, July). Toward Theoretical Foundations of Autonomic Computing. *International Journal of Cognitive Informatics and Natural Intelligence, 1*(3), 1–16.

Wang, Y. (2009, January). A Cognitive Informatics Reference Model of Autonomous Agent Systems (AAS). *International Journal of Cognitive Informatics and Natural Intelligence, 3*(1), 1–16.

Zhu, H. (2007, July). Role as Dynamics of Agents in Multi-Agent Systems. *System and Informatics Science Notes, 1*(2), 165–171.

Zhu, H. (2008, May). Fundamental Issues in the Design of a Role Engine. In *Proceedings of the 5th Int'l Symp. on Collaborative. Systems and Technologies,* San Diego, CA (pp. 399-407).

Zhu, H., Grenier, M., Alkins, R., Lacarte, J., & Hoskins, J. (2008, May). A Visualized Tool for Role Transfer. In *Proceedings of the 6th Int'l Conf. on Infor. Sys. for Crisis Response and Management,* Washington, DC (pp. 2225-2230).

Zhu, H., & Zhou, M. C. (2003, October). Methodology First and Language Second: A Way to Teach Object-Oriented Programming. In *Proceedings of the 2003 Educator's Symposium on Object-Oriented Programming, Systems, Languages and Applications (OOPSLA'03)* (pp. 140-147).

Zhu, H., & Zhou, M. C. (2006, July). Role-Based Collaboration and its Kernel Mechanisms. *IEEE Trans. on Systems, Man and Cybernetics, Part C, 36*(4), 578-589. Zhu, H., & Zhou, M. C. (2008, June). New Java Mechanism for Role-Based Information System Development. *International Journal of Intelligent Control and Systems, 13*(2), 97–108.

Zhu, H., & Zhou, M. C. (2008, May). Role Mechanisms in Information Systems - A Survey. *IEEE Trans. on Systems, Man and Cybernetics . Part C, 38*(6), 377–396.

Zhu, H., & Zhou, M. C. (2008, November). Role Transfer Problems and their Algorithms. *IEEE Trans. on Systems, Man and Cybernetics . Part A, 38*(6), 1442–1450.

This work was previously published in International Journal of Software Science and Computational Intelligence, Volume 2, Issue 3, edited by Yingxu Wang, pp. 32-51, copyright 2010 by IGI Publishing (an imprint of IGI Global).

Chapter 11
Combining Ontology with Intelligent Agent to Provide Negotiation Service

Qiumei Pu
MINZU University of China, China

Yongcun Cao
MINZU University of China, China

Xiuqin Pan
MINZU University of China, China

Siyao Fu
MINZU University of China, China

Zengguang Hou
MINZU University of China, China

ABSTRACT

Agent and Ontology are distinct technologies that arose independent of each other, having their own standards and specifications. The semantics web is one of the popular research areas these days, and is based on the current Web, which adds more semantics to it for the purpose of building the Ontology of Web content. In this regard, application program on Web can make the purpose of cross-platform calculation come true by taking advantage of Ontology. However, agent is a theory able to enhance abstraction of software itself, and as it is know, negotiation protocol is the basic principle in the electronic commerce which has a direct impact on the efficiency of the negotiation. This study examines the communication architecture with negotiation protocol on the Semantic Web. Precisely speaking, agents make computing with Ontology, and the authors define an agent's communication ontology for this communication framework and semantic web use Ontology to describe the negotiation protocol. In this context, the buyer or seller will be able to improve semantic cognitive in process of negotiation. Also, it can provide an intelligent platform for the information exchange on the same understanding about the content of communication in the electronic negotiation service.

DOI: 10.4018/978-1-4666-0264-9.ch011

Agent-mediated negotiation is one of new technology that now plays an increasing role in electronic commerce application. With the increasing automation of e-commerce applications, we will see the use of software agents that cooperate to perform business transactions.

MAS is a powerful paradigm in nowadays distributed systems such as negotiation system, however its disadvantage is that it lacks the interconnection with semantic web standards such as OWL. OWL was developed as a W3C Web Ontology Language, which is used to describe the ontology semantics. Semantic web is a recent and promising research area, the application of ontology-based modeling and reasoning to semantic web, which is these days often realized using intelligent architectures.

The principle of cognitive science is intelligent entity on the interaction with their environment. This theory makes software shift from object paradigm to intelligence agent paradigm, and thus constructs the software into an object with mental model.

In related research we often take interaction of agents as methods to resolve business problems. But in the process of the interaction of multi-agent, agent must take the same communication language and use common understanding about the content of communication. But in the open environment, the object that agent communicate with is different time by time and every agent may have different understanding about the same thing. Multi-agent system will become complicate when the interaction among agents get more times. With the technology of agent and semantic web gradually in-depth development, agent and multi-agent systems has been applied on semantic web technology. A lot of theory about agent issues needs further study. Such as agent should have what kind of structure, capacity constraints, it can be interacting with other agent on open and dynamic semantic web or intelligent Web environment.

Cooperative transactions require peer-to-peer protocols which based on inter-agent communica-

tion. This paper proposes a novel approach to negotiation, in which the negotiation protocol to adopt is not coded within the agents but it is expressed in terms of a common shared ontology that is shared by the agents in order to participate to a negotiation session. The negotiation ontology is defined in a way general enough to support a wide variety of market mechanisms, thus being particularly suitable for flexible applications such as electronic commerce. The paper describes the negotiation process and provides a prototype system that implements this vision using JADE agent platform.

The purpose of our study is to apply agent technique to semantics web, and our method is to make application program of semantic web be able to make intelligent computing by utilizing agents. Moreover, agents can realize the information integration among platforms of agents by making capital of Ontology on Semantics Web.

The rest of the document is organized as follows. First, we resume the related work and summarize the software framework for automated negotiations introduced in and show how it fits into our e-commerce model. Then we describe the negotiation service and present the process of negotiation server in negotiation environment. Next, we describe the communicative act ontology with owl and present the results of experiments. Finally, we present conclusions and put forward future work.

SweetDeal (Grosof, 2004) is a rule-based approach to representation of business contracts that enables software agents to create, evaluate, negotiate, and execute contracts with substantial automation. The contract rules are represented in the Situated Courteous Logic Programs knowledge representation encoded in RuleML, the leading approach to Semantic Web rules. The system of SweetDeal is the first to combine emerging Semantic Web standards for knowledge representation of rules (RuleML) with ontologies (DAML+OIL/OWL) with each other, and moreover for a practical e-business application domain, and further to do so with process knowledge.

Literature (Benyoucef, 2001) build negotiating agents called INfraStructure for RULE-driven (INSULA), INSULA contain a variety of negotiation patterns, such as multi-attribute, multi-output, multi-copy and combined negotiations, it use if-then rules to describe the strategy of negotiation. This paper believe that the rules is a highly abstract and easily understood by human beings, the negotiation agent can show a more abundant capacity through the expansion of rule engine.

Literature (Pokraev, 2004) propose software architecture to help enterprises alliance traders to automate negotiation, the authors put forward the following response to cognitive semantic research questions: two sides of the format and semantic information inconsistent; the two sides on how to automate negotiation by lack of consistent cognitive consensus.

From the above research, agent will not only be given the knowledge and act according to their own tasks or goals. A great deal agents also can communicate with each other through the same communication language and common knowledge. Although the agent can interact each other through information communication, but the interaction between multi-agents has also led to new problems, because the interaction between many agents processes, not only have the same communication language, for communication have a common understanding of things. Agent must also be between the same interactions rules in accordance with the rules of communication. The interaction rules will be clear that agent take what action in the process of negotiation at every stage according to different circumstances (Pokraev, 2004; Tamma, 2005).

Ontology and Concept algebra can abstract the essence of the domain of interest and helps to catalogue and distinguish various types of objects in the domain, their properties and relationships (see, Bartolini, 2002; Wang, 2008). An agent can use such a vocabulary to express its beliefs and actions, and so communicate about them in the context of cognitive informatics (Wang, 2003, 2007).

1. SYSTEM DESCRIPTION

1.1 Negotiation Service

According with the relevant discussion of MAS, a separate agent generally is able to complete a simple task through the implementation of a simple activity. Federal agent can use one of a special agent to implement a complex activity (Agent collaboration by other members) to achieve a relatively complex task. In this paper, we abstract this method which put a single agent or federal agent to finish the mission as a service.

Service refers to an entity (individual or business) that can finish a mission, this mission not only can be executed by agent owned by entities, but also achieve through the general processes (such as production) and can be provided to another entity through negotiation.

A service consists of three elements: service provider, service demand and service implementation (Figure 1).

Service demand side: it need other agent to assist the implementation of an event and look for provide services (the implementation of this activity) of the agent. It can send task to the agent which has the capacity to provide the service.

Service provider: it has ability to perform certain activities (services).

Service implementation: it executes a (simple or complex) by the agent or provided through the general processes (such as production, sales).

Figure 1. Three elements of service

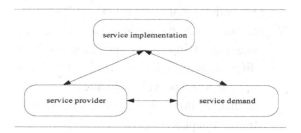

In this paper, we put forward the negotiation framework which consists of three parts: buyer, seller, negotiation server.

Seller (Service provider): It will be able to provide products or services information related to negotiation and publishes it to the negotiation server.

Buyer (Service demand): It search negotiation server to get product or service information.

Negotiation server (Service implementation): It is a platform to provide various negotiation approaches.

1.2 Process of Negotiation Server

Our environment acts as a distributed marketplace that e-shops and allows buyer and seller to visit them and purchase products in semantic network. We provide semantic web service interface to interact with negotiation server. Agent can visit interface and get negotiation mechanism from server. The detailed design of negotiation server as shown in Figure 2:

Let us now describe each part of the system in upper figure and their respective functionalities.

Seller: In the process of negotiation, he is to provide products and services side. Find a suitable buyer, the seller must be able to carry out negotiation, therefore, the buyer and the seller is a necessary condition in negotiation.

Buyer: he wants the buyer will receive the product or service. At the same time through negotiation, he can be the initiator of negotiation, the addresser of negotiation.

Negotiation server: it contains different types of negotiation approach to meet the needs of different users of the negotiation, at the same time, it is also provide semantic interface to exchange information especially in negotiation protocol.

1.1 Negotiation Ontology

Negotiation protocol is the basic principle of e-commerce, this principle have a direct impact on the efficiency of the negotiation. Semantic web use Ontology to describe the protocol, which will enable agent gain the necessary knowledge of the protocol from the market.

In this paper we use negotiation protocol as necessary knowledge to agent in the negotiation activities. Agent participated in negotiation must have the same cognitive for the knowledge. Here we assumption that each agent have its own strategies. Ontology can be use specific areas of expertise to the abstract way to express, through the concept of separation of entities and the logic of justice to allow the agent communicate with non-specific targets of negotiation, both parties can determine whether the contents of the communication have the same semantic cognition. The definition of negotiation ontology is as followed:

Concept= {Thing, NegotiationActivity, Negotiation Protocol, Negotiation Strategy, Negotiation State, Communicative Acts, InteractionProtocol, Party, Initiator, Participator, Accept, Reject, Recommendation, Begin, End, Ongoing, ContractNet, Accept Propose, Agree, Call for proposal, Cancel, Conform, Failure}

Attribute= {hasNegotiationState, hasInteractionProtocol, hasParty, hasEvent, hasAction, hasNegotiationProtocol, hasNegotiationObject}

We give negotiation ontology by the reference of e-commerce negotiation service. This paper rebuilds some core concepts, examples and related relations to establishment an ontology model. We use Protégé to edit this negotiation ontology and its concept hierarchy is illustrated in Figure 3:

At the same time, we know contract net is one sort of negotiation protocols (FIPA Contract Net Interaction Protocol Specification, 2006). For

Figure 2. Process of negotiation service

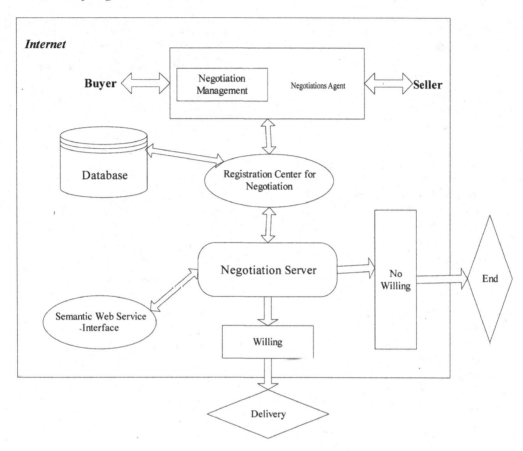

example, in multi-agents cooperation such as Contract Net Protocol, the number of participant(s) is greater than or equal to one. Additionally, a participant also can play an initiator to start another protocol in the course of interaction.

As the reference of Contract Net Protocol process in this paper, Agent can be taken at every stage of action as well as their judgments based on agreement by consensus in the development of ontology concepts and attributes to describe the interaction rules (Tu, 2000).

Agent must be for different objects using different interaction rules in order to make the agent to be more flexible. At the beginning of negotiation, negotiation initiator must inform all interactive rules to all those involved in negotiation agent, so that all participants will be loaded to the rules of interaction rules engine, according

to the interaction rules to carry out negotiation. And participants only need to have the negotiation ontology.

Because the description of interaction rules is agreement by consensus in the development of ontology concepts and attributes for the source, so as long as the agent to reach agreement as different interactive ontology shared cognitive rules, you can understand the description of interaction rules and the rules engine through the negotiation activities to learn at every stage can take.

For example, the concept of a description of the rules is that when the Contract Net interaction rules for the state to begin negotiate, the action of initiator is taken include require participants to carry out the proposal, the rules of design concepts can be expressed as follows:

Figure 3. Negotiation ontology

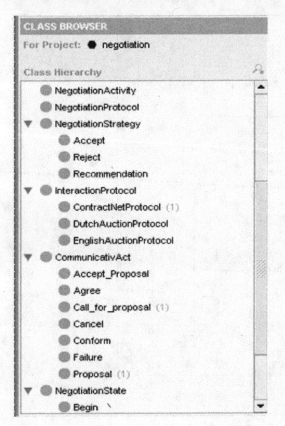

```
If(NegotiationActivity.hasParty =
Initiator) and
(NegotiationActivity.hasNegotiation-
State = Begin) and
(NegotiationProtocol .hasInteraction-
Protocol =
ContractNetInteractionProtocol)
```

Then

```
(NegotiationProtocol .hasAction =
CallForProposal)
```

In one word, we use Ontology to model the negotiation protocol, which represent the relevant knowledge in the negotiation process [12]. So in the process of negotiation, agent only requires the knowledge of negotiation protocol, it is able to negotiation with the non-specific object.

2. IMPLEMENTATION AND EXPERIMENTS

The current implementation of the proposed environment has been made within the JADE (Java Agent Development Framework), it is a FIPA specifications with the Multi-Agent System middleware platform [8]. This platform provides a flexible and configurable architecture that matches well with our requirements. Negotiations between seller and buyer agents take place in JADE containers.

In our system, agent communication is implemented using FIPA ACL messages (FIPA SL Content Language Specification, 2000). FIPA ACL message defined by the Communications Message Protocol, sending agent ID, receiving agent ID, message ontology, language of message content and message content. Description of the message content of the language is very flexible, it can use SL (Semantic Language) and can also use VB, Java and other high-level programming language (FIPA SL Content Language Specification, 2000), which bring understand problem in the communication message of the different agent platform.

In this paper, we use W3C metadata modeling language OWL to improve communication between agent languages (W3C Owl Web Ontology Language Use Cases and Requirements, 2004). OWL equivalent a platform for encoding and decoding language, so agent can exchange information each other. Because OWL-DL support for reasoning, this paper can use the reasoning mechanism to define action of agent.

In the process of agent communication, this article describes the communication language using OWL language and its action, the application ontology can be formulated very good expression and reasoning without having to consider the application of the system. Communication action expressions using OWL to describe the content of language can be expressed as follows in Figure 4:

According to the above described communication language and communication actions, this paper will use OWL to describe communication act. The attribute hasSender identifies the communication action of the initiator, which included agent class. The class can be individual or a machine. This attribute of each instance there can be only one value, meaning that each communication action can be only one initiator. That is the same to the description of hasReceiver and hasContent.

```
<owl:FunctionalProperty
rdf:about="#hasSender">
<rdfs:range rdf:resource="#Agent"/>
<rdf:type rdf:resource="&owl;ObjectPr
operty"/>
<rdfs:domain rdf:resource="#Communica
tiveAct"/>
</owl:FunctionalProperty>
```

In the process of negotiation, each round of transactions recorded through the communication language including each time initiated negotiation, the proposal and counter-proposal, as well as the DF, AMS Communications.

Communication process in the form of communication language displayed to the buyers and sellers, making the two sides can understand the

Figure 4. OWL as content for FIPA ACL

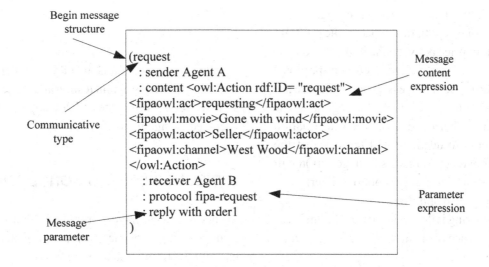

Figure 5. Communication Process with JADE agent only requires the knowledge of negotiation protocol, it is able to negotiation with the non-specific object

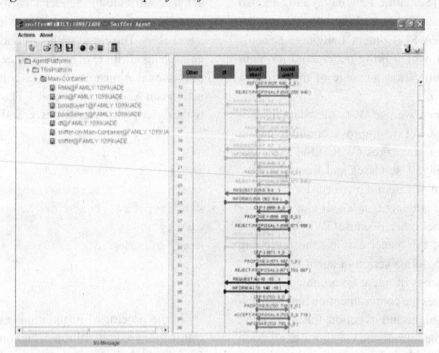

specific process of negotiation and negotiation process in this history, which is the case library for future similar negotiation carried out to study. The communication process provided by the JADE components named sniffer to monitor. The sniffer is able to provide all the AMS in the Agent platform activities and information exchange situation (Caire, 2003), with the colors of the arrows appearing in the JADE, as shown in Figure 5:

In the above negotiation process, the program gives random price between the highest and lowest prices with proposals and counter-proposal given by the random process. If both sides are not satisfied with the price, then the negotiation is over. On the other condition, when negotiation time is access to deadline, but the price of the object did not reach a consensus, negotiation will be ended. Many-to-many negotiation interface is shown in Figure 6 and Figure 7:

The following is the definition of communication in the process of the OWL language code format:

```
public static String OWL_HEAD =
"<?xml version=\"1.0\"
encoding=\"UTF-8\" ?>\n"+
"<rdf:RDF\n"+
" xmlns=\""+ Config.BASE + "#\"\n"+
" xmlns:rdf=\"" + RDF + "\"\n"+
" xmlns:rdfs=\"" + RDFS + "\"\n"+
" xmlns:owl=\"" + OWL + "\"\n"+
" xml:base=\""+ Config.BASE +
"\">\n";
```

Ontology is encoded in OWL. It describes domain knowledge of unit testing and the relationship between testing data and developer. It can be accessed by agents using JENA API.

3. DISCUSSION AND CONCLUSION

In this paper we have introduced ontology and agent based electronic negotiation system that has actually been implemented and show to fulfill

Figure 6. Seller Interface

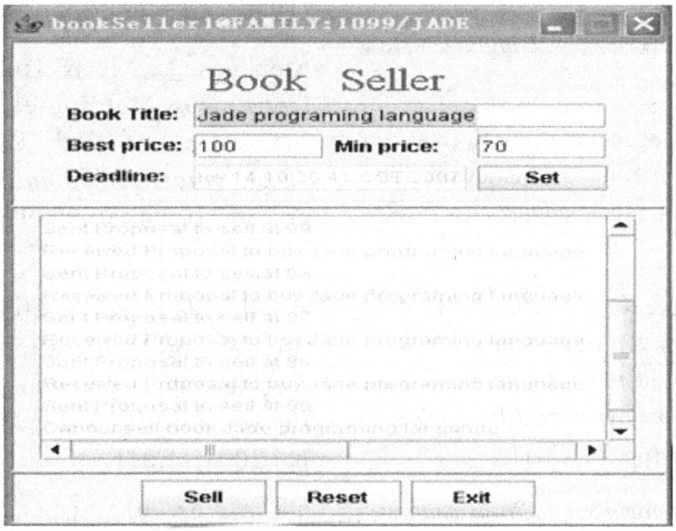

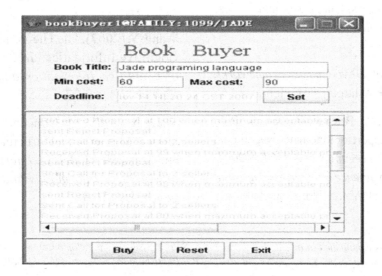

the basic function of agent system. We believe that this approach will facilitate reaching more sound and effective mutual understanding and communication in a multi-agent system. At the same time, the proposed system has a number of shortcomings that we are aware off such as reasoning is not sufficient for various existed system. So in the reasoning process, we can also combine the SWRL (Semantic Web Rule Language) and inference engine named JESS through the establishment of rules and logical reasoning (Tu, 2000: Stephens, 2001). It can effectively improve the intelligence. For example, we could represent rules in a rule engine such as JESS. But there are many related technologies need to be further research. Our approach is able to give a feasible method to communicate with agents in semantic web. Moreover, in future work we intend to investigate use of the rules engine to reach a relative intelligent system.

Figure 7. Buyer Interface

REFERENCES

W3C. (2004). *Owl Web Ontology Language Use Cases and Requirements*.

Bartolini, C., Preist, C., & Jennings, N. R. (2002). Architecting for reuse: A software framework for automated negotiation. In . *Proceedings, AOSE-02*, 87–98.

Benyoucef, M., Alj, H., & Keller, R. K. (2001). An infrastructure for rule-driven negotiating software agents. In *Proceedings of the 12th International Workshop on Database and Expert Systems Applications*, Montreal, Canada (pp. 737-741).

Caire, G. (2003). *Jade Turorial: Jade Programming for Beginners*.

FIPA. (2000). *FIPA SL Content Language Specification*.

FIPA. (2002, December 6). *Contract Net Interaction Protocol Specification*. Retrieved from http://www.fipa.org/specs/fipa00029/SC00029H.pdf

FIPA. (2002, December 6). *Iterated Contract Net Interaction Protocol Specification*. Retrieved from http://www.fipa.org/specs/fipa00030/SC00030H.pdf

Grosof, B. N., & Poon, T. C. (2004). SweetDeal: Representing Agent Contracts with Exceptions using Semantic Web Rules, Ontologies, and Process Descriptions. *Internaltional Journal of Electronic Commerce, 8*(4).

JADE. *(Java Agent DEvelopment Framework)*. (2004). Retrieved from http://jade.cselt.it/

Pokraev, S., Zlatev, Z., Brussee, R., & Eck, P. V. (2004). Semantic Support for Automated Negotiation with Alliances. In *Proceedings of the ICEIS 2004: 6th International conference on enterprise information systems*, Portugal (Vol. 5, No. 3, pp. 244-249).

Riley, E. P., Lochry, E. A., & Shapiro, N. R. (1979). *Lack of response inhibition in rats*.

Stephens, L. M., & Huhns, M. N. (2001). Consensus Ontologies. Reconciling The Semantics of Web Pages and Agents. *IEEE Internet Computing, 5*(5), 92–95. doi:10.1109/4236.957901

Tamma, V., Phelps, S., Dickinson, I., & Wooldridge, M. (2005). Ontologies for Supporting Negotiation in E-Commerce. *Engineering Applications of Artificial Intelligence, 18*(2), 223–236. doi:10.1016/j.engappai.2004.11.011

Tamma, V., Wooldridge, M., & Dickinson, I. (2002). An ontology for automated negotiation. In *Proceedings of the Workshop on Ontologies in Agent Systems*, Bologna, Italy (pp. 267-273).

Tu, M. T., Kunze, C., & Lamersdorf, W. (2000). A rule management framework for negotiating mobile agents. In *Proceedings of the 4th International Enterprise Distributed Object Computing Conference*, Makuhari, Japan (pp. 135-143).

Wang, Y. (2003). On Cognitive Informatics. *Brain and Mind: A Transdisciplinary Journal of Neuroscience and Neurophilosophy, 4*(2), 151-167.

Wang, Y. (2007). The Theoretical Framework of Cognitive Informatics. *International Journal of Cognitive Informatics and Natural Intelligence, 1*(1), 1–27.

Wang, Y. (2008). On Concept Algebra: A Denotational Mathematical Structure for Knowledge and Software Modeling. *International Journal of Cognitive Informatics and Natural Intelligence, 2*(2), 1–19.

This work was previously published in International Journal of Software Science and Computational Intelligence, Volume 2, Issue 3, edited by Yingxu Wang, pp. 52-61, copyright 2010 by IGI Publishing (an imprint of IGI Global).

Section 3
Software Science

Chapter 12
Design and Implementation of an Autonomic Code Generator Based on RTPA

Yingxu Wang
University of Calgary, Canada

Xinming Tan
Wuhan University of Technology, China

Cyprian F. Ngolah
Sentinel Trending & Diagnostics Ltd., Calgary, Canada

ABSTRACT

Real-Time Process Algebra (RTPA) is a denotational mathematics for the algebraic modeling and manipulations of software system architectures and behaviors by the Unified Data Models (UDMs) and Unified Process Models (UPMs). On the basis of the RTPA specification and refinement methodologies, automatic software code generation is enabled toward improving software development productivity. This paper examines designing and developing the RTPA-based software code generator (RTPA-CG) that transfers system models in RTPA architectures and behaviors into C++ or Java. A two-phrase strategy has been employed in the design of the code generator. The first phrase analyzes the lexical, syntactical, and type specifications of a software system modeled in RTPA, which results in a set of abstract syntax trees (ASTs). The second phrase translates the ASTs into C++ or Java based on predesigned mapping strategies and code generation rules. The toolkit of RTPA code generator encompasses an RTPA lexer, parser, type-checker, and a code builder. Experimental results show that system models in RTPA can be rigorously processed and corresponding C++/Java code can be automatically generated using the toolkit. The code generated is executable and effective under the support of an RTPA run-time library.

DOI: 10.4018/978-1-4666-0264-9.ch012

Figure 1. Program code generation based on RTPA

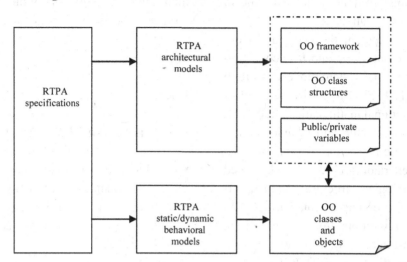

INTRODUCTION

Automatic code generation on the basis of rigorous system models and formal specifications is one of the central objectives of software engineering, which leads to the improvement of software development productivity, efficiency, and quality (McDermid, 1991; Michael & Butler, 1996; Wang, 2007). However, automatic code generation is an intricate and difficult endeavor in software engineering. Many efforts were reported on simplified system specifications and simple target languages (RAISE, 1995; Univan & Chris, 2000). It is a great challenge to design and implement a comprehensive code generator that covers the entire range of software modeling needs including real-time device drives and machine-level event/time/interrupt-driven mechanisms.

The process metaphor for software system modeling, specification, and implementation was initially proposed by Hoare and others (Hoare, 1978; Milner, 1980) that perceived a software system as the composition of a set of interacting processes.

Various algebraic approaches to describe the behaviors of communicating and concurrent systems were developed known as process algebra (Hoare, 1978, 1985; Milner, 1980), which provide a set of formal notations and rules for describing algebraic relations of software behaviors. A set of denotational mathematics was recently developed (Wang, 2008a) for rigorously modeling both architectures and behaviors of software systems. Denotational mathematics is a category of expressive mathematical structures that deal with *high-level mathematical entities* beyond numbers and sets, such as abstract objects, complex relations, perceptual information, abstract concepts, knowledge, intelligent behaviors, behavioral processes, and systems (Wang, 2009a). The paradigms of de-notational mathematics are such as concept algebra (Wang, 2008b), Real-Time Process Algebra (RTPA) (Wang, 2008c), and system algebra (Wang et al., 2008).

RTPA is a form of de-notational mathematics for formally modeling and describing architectures and behaviors of software systems (Wang, 2002, 2008c, 2008d). Based on the RTPA methodology and models, software code may be seamlessly generated as shown in Fig. 1. In the scheme of RTPA-based code generation, the RTPA architectural model for a system is used to generate the structural framework and global/local variables of classes or objects; while the RTPA behavioral model is then transferred into object methods in a target programming language.

This paper develops a methodology and a tool that facilitate automatic C++ and Java code generation based on formal system models specified and refined in RTPA. First, RTPA is briefly introduced as a denotational mathematical methodology for software architecture and behavior modeling and manipulations. Second, the RTPA-based software code generator (RTPA-CG) is described on its design strategies, structures, and support environments. Third, the implementation of RTPA-CG is presented with its lexer, parser, type checker, and run-time library, as well as their integration. Last, applications of RTPA-CG are reported with case studies and experimental results.

RTPA: A DENOTATIONAL MATHEMATICS FOR SOFTWARE SYSTEM MODELING

On the basis of the process metaphor of software systems, abstract processes can be rigorously treated as a long chain of embedded relations (Wang, 2007) beyond sets and functions. RTPA is designed as a coherent algebraic system for software system modeling, specification, refinement, and implementation. RTPA encompasses a set of meta-processes and relational process operations, which can be used to describe both logical and physical models of software and intelligent systems. Logic views of system architectures and their physical platforms can be described using the same set of notations. When system architecture is formally modeled, the static and dynamic behaviors performed on the architectural model can be specified by a three-level refinement scheme at the system, class, and object levels in a top-down approach.

Definition 1. *RTPA* is a denotational mathematical structure for algebraically modelling and manipulating system behavioural processes and their data objects and architectures by a triple, i.e.:

$$RTPA \triangleq (\mathfrak{T}, \mathfrak{P}, \mathfrak{R}) \qquad (1)$$

where

- $\mathfrak{T}$ is a set of 17 primitive types for modeling system architectures and data objects;
- $\mathfrak{P}$ a set of 17 meta-processes for modeling fundamental system behaviors;
- $\mathfrak{R}$ a set of 17 relational process operations for constructing complex system behaviors.

RTPA provides an algebraic notation system and mathematical rules for the specification and refinement of real-time/nonreal-time systems and safety-critical systems. Detailed descriptions of $\mathfrak{T}$, $\mathfrak{P}$, and $\mathfrak{R}$ in RTPA will be extended in the following subsections.

The Type System of RTPA

A type is a set in which all member data objects share a common logical property or attribute. The maximum range of values of variables in the set is the domain of a type. A type is always associated with a set of predefined or allowable operations in computing. A type can be classified as *primitive* and *derived* (complex) types. The former are the most elementary types that cannot be further divided into simpler ones; the latter are a compound form of multiple primitive types based on given type rules. In computing, most primitive types are provided by programming languages; while most user defined types are derived ones.

A *type system* specifies data object modeling and manipulation rules in computing. The set of 17 primitive types of RTPA, T, is elicited in computing and human cognitive process modeling, as summarized in Figure 2, from works in (Martin-Lof, 1975; Cardelli & Wegner, 1985; Stubbs & Webre, 1985; Mitchell, 1990; Wang,

Figure 2. RTPA Primitive Types and their Domains

No.	Type	Syntax	D_m	D_l
1	Natural number	**N**	[0, +∞]	[0, 65535]
2	Integer	**Z**	[-∞, +∞]	[-32768, +32767]
3	Real	**R**	[-∞, +∞]	[-2147483648, 2147483647]
4	String	**S**	[0, +∞]	[0, 255]
5	Boolean	**BL**	[**T, F**]	[**T, F**]
6	Byte	**B**	[0, 255]	[0, 255]
7	Hexadecimal	**H**	[0, +∞]	[0, max]
8	Pointer	**P**	[0, +∞]	[0, max]
9	Time	**TI = hh:mm:ss:ms**	**hh**: [0, 23] **mm**: [0, 59] **ss**: [0, 59] **ms**: [0, 999]	**hh**: [0, 23] **mm**: [0, 59] **ss**: [0, 59] **ms**: [0, 999]
10	Date	**D = yy:MM:dd**	**yy**: [0, 99] **MM**: [1, 12] **dd**: [1, 31}	**yy**: [0, 99] **MM**: [1, 12] **dd**: [1, 31}
11	Date/Time	**DT = yyyy:MM:dd: hh:mm:ss:ms**	**yyyy**: [0, 9999] **MM**:[1, 12] **dd**: [1, 31] **hh**: [0, 23] **mm**: [0, 59] **ss**: [0, 59] **ms**: [0, 999]	**Yyyy**: [0, 9999] **MM**:[1, 12] **dd**: [1, 31] **hh**: [0, 23] **mm**: [0, 59] **ss**: [0, 59] **ms**: [0, 999]
12	Run-time determinable type	**RT**	–	–
13	System architectural type	**ST**	–	–
14	Random event	**@eS**	[0, +∞]	[0, 255]
15	Time event	**@tTM**	[0**ms**, 9999 **yyyy**]	[0**ms**, 9999 **yyyy**]
16	Interrupt event	**@int◉**	[0, 1023]	[0, 1023]
17	Status	ⓢs**BL**	[**T, F**]	[**T, F**]

2007). In Figure 2, the first 11 primitive types are for mathematical and logical manipulations of data objects, and the remaining 6 are for system architectural modeling.

Based on Figure 2, the set of primitive types of RTPA can be summarized as follows.

Definition 2. The *RTPA type system* 𝔗 encompasses 17 primitive types of computational objects, i.e.:

$$\mathfrak{T} \triangleq \{\textbf{N, Z, R, S, BL, B, H, P, TI, D, DT, RT, ST}, @e\textbf{S}, @t\textbf{TM}, @int\odot, \textcircled{S}s\textbf{BL}\} \tag{2}$$

where the primitive types stand for *natural number, integer, real, string, Boolean, byte, hexadecimal, pointer, time, date, date/time, run-time determinable type, system architectural type, random event, time event, interrupt event,* and *system status.*

It is noteworthy that although a generic computing behavior is constrained by the *mathematical* domain D_m of types, an executable program is constrained by the *language-defined domain D_l*, and in most cases, it is further restricted by the *user-defined domain D_u*, i.e.:

$$D_u \subseteq D_l \subseteq D_m \qquad (3)$$

The Meta-Processes of RTPA

RTPA adopts foundationalism in order to elicit the most primitive computational processes known as the meta-processes. In this approach, complex processes are treated as derived processes from the meta-processes based on a set of algebraic rules for process compositions known as process relations. It is noteworthy that, although, CSP (Hoare, 1978, 1985), the Timed-CSP (Boucher & Gerth, 1987; Nicollin & Sifakis, 1991; Fecher, 2001), and other process algebra treated any computational operation as a process, RTPA distinguishes the concepts of meta-processes from those of complex and derived processes, which are composed by algebraic and relational process operations on the meta-processes.

Definition 3. A *meta-process* in RTPA is a primary computational operation that cannot be broken down to further individual actions or behaviors.

In RTPA, a set of 17 meta-processes has been elicited as shown in Figure 3, from essential and primary computational operations commonly identified in existing formal methods and modern programming languages (Higman, 1977; Aho et al., 1985; Hoare et al., 1987; Wilson & Clark, 1988; Louden, 1993; Woodcock & Davies, 1996; Lewis & Papadimitriou, 1998). Mathematical notations and syntaxes of the meta-processes are formally described in Table 2, while formal semantics of the meta-processes of RTPA may be referred to its deductive semantics (Wang, 2006, 2008e), denotational semantics (Tan & Wang,

2008), and operational semantics (Wang & Ngolah, 2008).

Definition 4. The *RTPA meta-process system* P encompasses 17 fundamental computational operations, i.e.:

$$\mathfrak{P} = \{:=, \blacklozenge, \Rightarrow, \Leftarrow, \nRightarrow, \vartriangleright, \vartriangleleft, |\vartriangleright, |\vartriangleleft, @, \triangleq, \uparrow, \downarrow, !, \otimes, \boxtimes, \S\} \qquad (4)$$

where the meta-processes of RTPA stand for *assignment, evaluation, addressing, memory allocation, memory release, read, write, input, output, timing, duration, increase, decrease, exception detection, skip, stop*, and *system*, respectively.

As shown in Definition 4 and Figure 3, each meta-process is a basic operation on one or more operands such as variables, memory elements, or I/O ports. Structures of the operands and their allowable operations are constrained by their types as described in the preceding subsection. It is noteworthy that not all generally important and fundamental computational operations, as shown in Figure 3, had been explicitly identified in conventional formal methods such as the evaluation, addressing, memory allocation/release, timing/duration, and the system processes. However, all these are found necessary and essential in modeling system architectures and behaviors.

The Relational Process Operations of RTPA

Definition 5. A *process relation* in RTPA is an algebraic operation and a compositional rule between two or more meta-processes in order to construct a complex process.

A set of 17 process relations has been elicited from fundamental algebraic and relational operations in computing in order to build and compose complex processes. Syntaxes and usages of the 17 RTPA

Figure 3. RTPA Meta-Processes

No.	Metaprocess	Notation	Syntax
1	Assignment	:=	$y\mathbb{T} := x\mathbb{T}$
2	Evaluation	◆	$◆_\mathbb{T}exp\mathbb{T} \rightarrow \mathbb{T}$
3	Addressing	⇒	$id\mathbb{T} \Rightarrow \text{MEM}[ptr\mathbb{P}]\ \mathbb{T}$
4	Memory allocation	⇐	$id\mathbb{T} \Leftarrow \text{MEM}[ptr\mathbb{P}]\ \mathbb{T}$
5	Memory release	⇍	$id\mathbb{T} ⇍ \text{MEM}[\bot]\mathbb{T}$
6	Read	>	$\text{MEM}[ptr\mathbb{P}]\mathbb{T} > x\mathbb{T}$
7	Write	<	$x\mathbb{T} < \text{MEM}[ptr\mathbb{P}]\mathbb{T}$
8	Input	|>	$\text{PORT}[ptr\mathbb{P}]\mathbb{T} \|> x\mathbb{T}$
9	Output	|<	$x\mathbb{T} \|< \text{PORT}[ptr\mathbb{P}]\mathbb{T}$
10	Timing	$\underset{=}{@}$	$@t\textbf{TM} \quad §t\textbf{TM}$ $\textbf{TM} = \textbf{yy:MM:dd}$ $\quad \| \textbf{hh:mm:ss:ms}$ $\quad \| \textbf{yy:MM:dd:hh:mm:ss:ms}$
11	Duration	≙	$@t_n\textbf{TM} \quad §t_n\textbf{TM} + \Delta n\textbf{TM}$
12	Increase	↑	$\uparrow(n\mathbb{T})$
13	Decrease	↓	$\downarrow(n\mathbb{T})$
14	Exception detection	!	$!\ (@e\textbf{S})$
15	Skip	⊗	⊗
16	Stop	⊠	⊠
17	System	§	$§(SysID\textbf{ST})$

process relations are formally described in Figure 3. Formal semantics of RTPA process relations may be referred to (Wang, 2006, 2008e; Tan & Wang, 2008; Wang & Ngolah, 2008).

Definition 6. The *RTPA process relations* R encompasses 17 fundamental algebraic and relational operations for composing complex processes in computing, i.e.:

$$\mathfrak{R} = \{\rightarrow, \curvearrowright, |, |...|..., R^*, R^+, R^i, \circlearrowleft, \rightarrowtail, \|, \oiint, \|\|, », ≮, \vdash_t, \vdash_e, \vdash_i\} \quad (5)$$

where the relational operators of RTPA stand for *sequence, jump, branch, while-loop, repeat-loop, for-loop, recursion, function call, parallel, concurrence, interleave, pipeline, interrupt, time-driven dispatch, event-driven dispatch,* and *interrupt-driven dispatch,* respectively.

The RTPA Methodology for System Modeling and Refinement

RTPA provides both a coherent notation system and a formal engineering methodology for modeling both software and intelligent systems. In the RTPA methodology, the architecture and behaviors of any software system are modeled by the unified data model and unified process model, respectively.

Definition 7. A *unified data model* (UDM) is a *generic architectural* model of a *software system* as well as its *hardware components, interfaces,* and *internal control strutures,* which can be rigorously modeled and refined in denotational mathematics as a *tuple* τ, i.e.:

$$UDM \triangleq \tau$$
$$= (\underset{i\mathbf{N}=1}{\overset{n\mathbf{N}}{R}} < S_i \mid \forall e_i \in S_i, p_i(e_i) >) \qquad (6)$$

where e_i is an arbitrary element of a given set S_i that is constrained by the same property of P_i, $1 \leq i \leq n$, and n is a natural number.

Any software system architecture, at the top level, can be specified as a list of UDMs and their relations. The counterpart computing model of tuples for UDMs is a record structure as follows:

$$UDM \triangleq UDM - ID\mathbf{S} :$$
$$\begin{aligned} &(< \text{Field}_1 : \text{type}_1 \mid \text{constraint}_1 >, \\ &< \text{Field}_2 : \text{type}_2 \mid \text{constraint}_2 >, \\ &\dots \\ &< \text{Field}_n : \text{type}_n \mid \text{constraint}_n > \\ &) \end{aligned} \qquad (7)$$

The unified process model of RTPA can be rigorously described as follows.

Definition 8. A *process P* is an embedded relation of a set of statements or processes of n meta-statements p_i and p_j, $1 \leq i < n, j = i+1$, according to certain composing relations r_{ij}, i.e.

$$P = \underset{i=1}{\overset{n-1}{R}}(p_i \ r_{ij} \ p_j), j = i+1$$
$$= (\dots(((p_1) \ r_{12} \ p_2) \ r_{23} \ p_3) \dots r_{n-1,n} \ p_n) \qquad (8)$$

where r_{ij} is a set of relations or composition rules.

Definition 9. The unified process model (UPM) of a *program* $\wp$ is a composition of a finite set of k processes according to the time-, event-, and interrupt-based process dispatching rules, i.e.:

$$\begin{aligned} \wp &= \underset{k=1}{\overset{m}{R}}(@ e_k \mathbf{S} \mapsto P_k) \\ &= \underset{k=1}{\overset{m}{R}} [@ e_k \mathbf{S} \mapsto \underset{i=1}{\overset{n-1}{R}}(s_i(k) \ r_{ij}(k) \ s_j(k))], \\ j &= i+1 \end{aligned} \qquad (9)$$

RTPA can be used to describe both *logical* and *physical* models of systems, where logic views of the architecture of a software system and its operational platform can be described using the same set of notations. When the system architecture is formally modelled, the static and dynamic behaviors that perform on the system architectural model can be specified by a three-level refinement scheme at the system, class, and object levels in a top-down approach (Wang, 2007, 2008c).

DESIGN OF THE RTPA CODE GENERATOR

The RTPA code generator (RTPA-CG) is a special compiler that transfers a mathematical model of a software system in RTPA into C++, Java, or other programming languages (with specific plug-in code builder modules). A set of semantic mapping strategies and patterns is designed to guide the processes of code generation under the support of the RTPA runtime library and the standard language libraries of C++/Java.

Figure 4. RTPA Process Relations and Algebraic Operations

No.	Process Relation	Notation	Syntax
1	Sequence	$\rightarrow$	$P \rightarrow Q$
2	Jump	$\curvearrowright$	$P \curvearrowright Q$
3	Branch	|	$\blacklozenge exp\mathbf{BL} = \mathbf{T} \rightarrow P$ $\| \blacklozenge \sim \rightarrow Q$
4	Switch	| ... |	$\blacklozenge exp\mathbb{T} =$ $i \rightarrow P_i$ $\| \sim \rightarrow \oslash$ where $\mathbb{T} \in \{\mathbf{N}, \mathbf{Z}, \mathbf{B}, \mathbf{S}\}$
5	While-loop	R^*	$\displaystyle R^{\mathbf{F}}_{exp\mathbf{BL}=\mathbf{T}} P$
6	Repeat-loop	R^+	$\displaystyle P \rightarrow R^{\mathbf{F}}_{exp\mathbf{BL}=\mathbf{T}} P$
7	For-loop	R^i	$\displaystyle R^{n\mathbf{N}}_{i\mathbf{N}=1} P(i\mathbf{M})$
8	Recursion	$\circlearrowright$	$\displaystyle R^{0}_{i\mathbf{N}=n\mathbf{N}} P^{i\mathbf{M}} \circlearrowright P^{i\mathbf{M}-1}$
9	Function call	$\rightarrowtail$	$P \rightarrowtail F$
10	Parallel	$\|$	$P \| Q$
11	Concurrence	$\oiint$	$P \oiint Q$
12	Interleave	$\|\|\|$	$P \|\|\| Q$
13	Pipeline	$\gg$	$P \gg Q$
14	Interrupt	$\lightning$	$P \lightning Q$
15	Time-driven dispatch	$\hookrightarrow_t$	$@t_i\mathbf{TM} \hookrightarrow_t P_i$
16	Event-driven dispatch	$\hookrightarrow_e$	$@e\mathbf{S} \hookrightarrow_e P_i$
17	Interrupt-driven dispatch	$\hookrightarrow_i$	$@int_j\odot \hookrightarrow_i P_j$

Design Considerations of the RTPA-CG

The challenges to automatic code generation based on RTPA specifications stem from the following issues:

a) As a denotational mathematical notation system, RTPA adopts prefix, postfix, and infix notations. Although these features of RTPA enable an excellent readability in system modeling, they are extremely difficult for machine processing.

b) Because the information about identifiers in an RTPA model is distributed throughout the specification, identifier identifications and their consistence checking become a very complicated problem in RTPA-based code generation.

c) As a general purpose process algebra, RTPA encompasses a rich set of process operations,

Figure 5. The framework of the RTPA code generator and its support environment

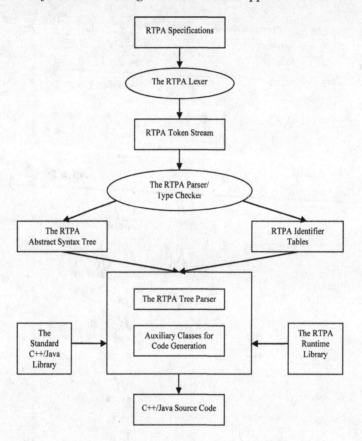

such as real-time dispatching, dynamic memory manipulations, and device input/output. These features of RTPA require the support of a real-time operating system kernel as the runtime environment.

In order to cope with the above challenges, a two-pass code generation framework is adopted. The code generator first recognizes and processes a formal system model specified in RTPA, which produces a set of uniquely identified Abstract Syntax Trees (ASTs) (Aho et al., 1985). Then, the code generator transfers the ASTs into C++/Java code based on predefined mapping strategies and patterns. The workflow of RTPA-CG is designed as follows:

a) An RTPA model of a software system is specified by system analysts and architects.

b) The RTPA specification is processed by the RTPA lexical analyzer, parser, and type checker.

c) A set of ASTs is generated after the phase of type checking.

d) Grammar and constraint information, such as process priority levels and event usages, are analyzed based on the ASTs.

e) C++/Java code is generated for the given system model specified in RTPA supported by the RTPA runtime library.

Structure of the RTPA-CG

The structure of RTPA-CG is designed as shown in Fig. 5, which encompasses the RTPA lexer, parser, type checker, code builder, and the runtime library. RTPA-CG parses a set of ASTs derived from an RTPA specification in order to generate corresponding code in C++, Java, or other programming languages. The RTPA identifier tables are used to record all related information and their cross-references. Code is generated using the RTPA-C++/Java mapping strategies and patterns supported by the RTPA runtime library.

The RTPA Code Generation Techniques

The RTPA methodology specifies a software system in three-subsystems known as its architecture, static behaviors, and dynamic behaviors (Wang, 2007) as shown in Fig. 1. Corresponding to the RTPA model of a software system, the architecture of the system in RTPA is translated into C++/Java architectural class with object declarations. The UDM schemas in RTPA are translated into member classes in the architecture class, where each field of a schema is presented by corresponding member variables and each constraint is implemented by an enumeration type in C++ or a special enumeration class in Java. The corresponding member variables are then declared using the defined classes. The UDM objects of RTPA schemas are transferred into global class constructors that act as initializations for the member classes obtained from the UDM schemas.

System static behaviors specified in RTPA are individual functions of a system and their interactions with the UDMs defined in the system architectures. Each static behavior specified in RTPA is modeled as a UPM, which is transferred into a corresponding method in C++/Java classes using a combination of meta-types, meta/complex processes, and process relations as defined in RTPA.

The dynamic behaviors of a software system describe the interactions between the defined static processes and their environment at runtime. In RTPA, the dynamic behaviors of a system are described in three refinement steps that can generally be grouped into process classification, process deployment, and process dispatch (Wang, 2007). RTPA-CG treats an RTPA process deployment and process dispatch as the main class in the target system, which implements precisely timed event/time/interrupt-driven behaviors at different priority levels of the system.

The RTPA runtime library consists of a kernel and an RTPA interface. The kernel of the RTPA runtime library provides the essential functionality of a real-time operating system kernel for multitasking and timing mechanisms. The kernel implements special RTPA processes such as parallel, concurrency, interrupt, real-time clock, and time/event driven mechanisms. The second component of the RTPA runtime library, the RTPA interface, serves port I/O, timing, and time/event-driven dispatches based on the RTPA kernel. The RTPA real-time support environment is designed based on the formal models of the Real-Time Operating Systems (RTOS+) (Wang et al., 2010) and the support of the Micro Controller Operating System II (μC/OS-II) (Labrosse, 1999).

IMPLEMENTATION OF THE RTPA CODE GENERATOR

The technical approach to implementing the RTPA-CG is shown in Fig. 6. RTPA-CG transfers a formal system model specified in RTPA into C++/Java code. The RTPA tree parser guides the code builder to generate source code under the support of the RTPA runtime library and the auxiliary identifier tables.

Based on the design of the RTPA-CG as elaborated in the preceding section, both a C++ and a Java version of RTPA-CG are developed on the platform of DOS enhanced by μC/OS-II. This section describes the implementation of key components of RTPA-CGs, as well as the configuration and integration of the system.

Figure 6. Implementation of the RTPA code generator

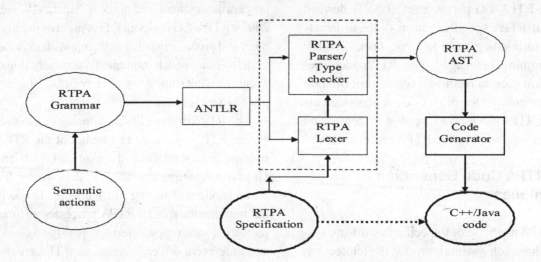

Implementation of Key Components of RTPA-CG

The key components of RTPA-CG, such as the RTPA lexer, parser, type checker, AST parser, code builder, identifier table manipulator, and runtime library, are implemented as described in the following:

a) **The RTPA Lexer:** The front-end of the code generator employs a lexical analyzer (lexer) and a parser for system specifications in RTPA. The RTPA lexer analyzes the input of a formal system model in RTPA, and produces an output of a machine recognizable token stream. The RTPA lexer is generated by ANTLR (Parr & Quong, 1995; Parr, 2000) based on LL(k) grammar (Aho, 1985; Grune et al., 2000). In the RTPA syntactic analysis, most of the grammar rules for RTPA terminal symbols can be recognized by LL(k) algorithm. However, for those exceptional non-LL(k) grammar rules of RTPA, an arbitrary-length forward pre-trial algorithm, which will not consume the tokens in the input token stream, is adopted until a determinate choice can be made.

b) **The RTPA Parser:** The parser transfers RTPA specifications into abstract syntax in the form of a set of ASTs. The ASTs are then inputted to the code generator after type checking, which creates the executable code in C++/Java. The parser is built using ANTLR based on the predefined RTPA grammar rules in LL(k) (Wang, 2007). The key syntax of RTPA is defined by a set of 280 LL(k) grammar rules in EBNF (Tan, Wang, & Ngolah, 2004). To deal with the special non-LL(k) grammar rules of RTPA, the syntactic predicates provided by ANTLR are adopted to create guarded and extended rules. The same techniques used in the lexical analysis are applied in the parsing of the RTPA specifications.

c) **The RTPA Type Checker:** The type checker is an intermediate processor between the RTPA parser and code builder. Because RTPA is strongly typed, every identifier in an RTPA specification has a type suffix and every expression is evaluated to a definite type. Therefore, only those operations among compatible types are allowed, while the operations among incompatible types are forbidden unless explicit type casting is adopted. The type checking for RTPA specifications can be classified into three categories namely: (i) identifier type compliance, (ii) expression type compliance, and (iii) process constraint consistence. The first two tasks are considered as similar to those of programming language processing, while the third task is special due to the features of RTPA as a process-based algebraic notation system.

d) **The RTPA AST Parser:** A tree parser provides the means to walk through the ASTs generated by the preceding components (a) through (c) and transform them into corresponding code in C++/Java. The tree parser scans ASTs derived from a given system model, and transfers them into corresponding code in C++ or Java. With the ANTLR tool support (Parr, 2000); the first step to build the tree parser for RTPA is to specify the structure of ASTs generated by the RTPA Lexer and Type Checker in form of a set of ANTLR tree parser rules. Directed by the passing rules, the RTPA AST parser

can be produced using the ANTLR tool automatically.

e) **The RTPA Code Builder:** The RTPA code builder is implemented based on the AST parser, which carries out corresponding semantic actions on each node of the given AST. A set of semantic actions is specified for expected functions in code generation such as RTPA identifier information manipulation and code transformation, which are implemented in the Java classes rtpaIDTable and rtpaCodeGeneration.

f) **The RTPA Runtime Library:** The RTPA runtime library encompasses the following RTPA functions: rtpaPortIn, rtpaPortOut, rtpaTiming, rtpaDuration, rtpaMakeDate-Time, rtpaCreateEvent, rtpaEventSignal, rtpaEventWait, rtpaEventGroupSignal, rtpaEventGroupWait, rtpaTimeDispatch, and rtpaStop as shown in Table 1. The RTPA kernel is implemented based on DOS with the support of μC/OS-II, where the latter embodies the concurrency, interrupt, real-time clock, and time/event driven mechanisms.

Table 1. RTPA runtime library functions

RTPA Process	Runtime Library Function	Description
Input	int rtpaPortIn (unsigned port)	Input data from a port
Output	int rtpaPortOut (unsigned port, int data)	Output data to a port
Timing	rtpaTM* rtpaTiming(rtpaTM *tm)	Take system time
Duration	rtpaTM* rtpaDuration(rtpaTM *tm, unsigned n)	Delay for *n* milliseconds
	rtpaDATETIME rtpaMakeDateTime(char *dt, int type)	Make an RTPA Date/Time form string
Event detection	rtpaEVENT rtpaCreateEvent(unsigned int count) unsigned char rtpaEventSignal(rtpaEVENT x)	Create a system event Report event x signaled
Event-driven dispatch (individual)	void rtpaEventWait(rtpaEVENT x, unsigned timeout, unsigned char *err)	Wait on an event x
Event-driven dispatch (group)	OS_FLAGS rtpaEventGroupWait((OS_FLAG_GRP *pgrp, OS_FLAGS flags, unsigned char wait_type, unsigned timeout, unsigned char *err)	Wait on an event in event group pgrp
Time-driven dispatch	rtpaTM* rtpaTimeDispatch(rtpaTM *tm)	Time-driven dispatch
Exception detection	OS_FLAGS rtpaEventGroupSignal(OS_FLAG_GRP *pgrp, OS_FLAGS flags, unsigned char opt, unsigned char *err)	Report an event in event group pgrp signaled
Stop	void rtpaStop(void)	System stop

The RTPA interface functions implement the RTPA device-drive processes such as port I/O, timing, and time/event-driven dispatch processes.

The techniques applied to build a kernel of a real-time operating system are exploited in the implementation of the key RTPA real-time processes. Real-time task scheduling and event handling mechanisms are built into the core of the RTPA runtime library. The real-time kernel of RTPA guarantees that code under generation will meet the real-time requirements of a system specification.

g) **The Identifier Table and its Manipulations:** The identifier table class provides a set of internal records of all identifiers in a given RTPA specification. It supports the following functions: a) Building and maintaining the identifier tables; b) Creating corresponding variables from RTPA identifiers and constructing their internal names and types; c) Accessing and modifying identifier attributes; and d) Handling hierarchical structures when walking through a specification. Four types of identifier tables are implemented for type-checking and code generation. They are: (i) The general RTPA identifier table that holds all identifiers specified in an RTPA model; (ii) The event table that includes all events in the RTPA specification; (iii) The event relation group table that maintains event associations in the RTPA specification; and (iv) The process table that contains all process priority information in the RTPA specification.

Configuration and Integration of the Code Generator

The configuration of RTPA-CG encompasses five Java classes such as RTPALexer, RTPATypeChecker, RTPACodeBuilder, rtpaIDTable,

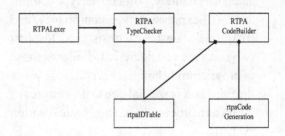

Figure 7. Structure of the RTPA code generation classes

and rtpaCodeGeneration. The relationships of the five classes can be described by a class diagram in Fig. 7.

Derived from the RTPA tree parser, RTPACodeBuilder generates code by walking through a given AST. With the guide of AST, corresponding code is automatically composed by invoking target functions provided in the classes rtpaIDTables and rtpaCodeGeneration.

The integration of RTPA-CG can be divided into the following steps as illustrated in Fig. 8:

a) Specify the rules of the RTPA tree parser;
b) Develop the five functional classes for RTPA code generation;
c) Insert ANTLR semantic actions to process a set of rules for the RTPA code builder;
d) Apply the ANTLR tool to generate the RTPA code generator class.

The automatically generated code is executable and effective under the support of the standard C++ library and the specially developed RTPA run-time library. Experimental results show that RTPA specifications can be rigorously checked and corresponding C++/Java code can be automatically generated from RTPA specifications using the toolkit.

Figure 8. Integration of the RTPA code generator

Figure 9. Structure of the RTPA code generation classes

```
public static void main (String[] args) {
    try {
        FileReader fin = new FileReader(args[0]);
        RTPALexer lexer = new RTPALexer(fin);
        RTPATypeChecker checker =
                new RTPATypeChecker(lexer);
        checker.rtpa_specification();
        AST t = checker.getAST();
        if (t==null) return;
            RTPACodeGenerator cgen =
                    new RTPACodeGenerator(checker.idt);
        cgen.rtpa_specification(t);
        cgen.cg.rtpaSaveCode(args[1], cgen.idt);
    } catch (Exception e) {
            System.err.println("exception: "+e);
        }
}
```

APPLICATIONS OF THE RTPA CODE GENERATOR

This section describes applications of the RTPA-CG toolkit. A set of case studies on RTPA-based code generation in C++ and Java is presented.

Automatic Code Generation using RTPA-CG

RTPA-CG compiles an RTPA specification into C++ or Java following the scheme as designed in Fig. 9. The program head of RTPA-CG is structured as an integration of the classes of RTPALexer, RTPATypeChecker, and RTPACodeBuilder in order to generate target code for a formal system specification modeled in RTPA.

A number of case studies on automatic code generation have been carried out using RTPA-CG. The real-world case studies cover large-scale real-time software systems such as the Telephone Switching System (TSS) (Wang, 2009b), the Lift Dispatching System (LDS) (Wang et al., 2009), the Automated Teller Machine (ATM) (Wang et al., 2010), a Real-Time Operating System (RTOS+) (Wang et al., 2010), and a number of typical computing algorithms (Wang, 2007). The

testing results demonstrate that RTPA-CG can atomically and seamlessly generate executable and effective C++ and Java code on the basis of formal system models in RTPA.

A Case Study on RTPA-Based Code Generation in Java

A case study on RTPA-based code generation in Java for the In-Between Sum (IBS) algorithm is presented in this subsection as a sample of applications of the RTPA-CG system. The IBS algorithm calculates the sum of digits between two given numbers A and B where A is the lower bound and B the upper bound. The formal model of the IBS algorithm specified in RTPA is given in Figs. 10 and 11 with both its architecture *IBSAlgorithm. Architecture***ST** and behaviours *IBSAlgorithm. StaicBehaviors***PC**, respectively.

Based on the formal models of IBS as given in Figs. 10 and 11, RTPA-CG can automatically generate source code for the IBS algorithm in Java as shown in Fig. 12 (Ngolah and Wang, 2009). In Fig. 12, the first part of the code is the

Figure 10. The architecture model of the IBS algorithm

```
IBSAlgorithm.ArchitectureST ≙
{ Input: (<LowerBound:: A: N | 0 < AN < 65535>,
          <UpperBound:: B: N | 0 < BN < 65535>,
          <Constraints:: AN < BN>)
  || <IBSum: N>
}
```

IBS structure and variable declarations; the second part of the code is the method of the IBS algorithm in Java; and the third part of the code is the corresponding dynamic behaviors of the algorithm when it is a part of another system. The Java version of RTPA-CG is implemented under the support of a real-time Java virtue machine (Bollella et al., 2002) and the Java Native Interface (JNI) (Sheng, 1999) with the plug-in modules of Java code generation classes and support libraries.

A Case Study on RTPA-Based Code Generation in C++

A case study on RTPA-based code generation in C++ for a simple real-time device driver (RTDD) is presented in this subsection as a sample of applications of the RTPA-CG system. RTDD is designed to drive a device represented by a set of six LEDs and a switch connected to the parallel port of a computer (Tan, Wang, & Ngolah, 2006). The driver turns on the LEDs using different patterns controlled by the input of the switch. The driver checks the switch's status periodically and lights the LEDs in specified patterns when a switch-on status is detected while the system handles other real-time tasks at the same time.

a) The Formal Model of RTDD in RTPA

The RTPA model of the RTDD system specifies the architecture, static behaviors, and dynamic behaviours of RTDD as given in Eq. 10, i.e.:

Figure 11. The behavior model of the IBS algorithm

```
IBSAlgorithm.StaticBehaviorsPC ({I:: AN, BN}; {O:: ⓈIBSResultBL, IBSumN}) ≙
{
    MaxN := 65535
    → ( ◆ (0 < AN < maxN) ∧ (0 < BN < maxN) ∧ (AN < BN)
            → IBSumN := ((BN - 1) * BN) / 2) - (AN * (AN + 1) / 2)
            → ⓈIBSResultBL := T
       | ◆ ~
            → ⓈIBSResultBL := F
            → ! (@'AN and/or BN out of range, or AN ≥ BN')
    )
}
```

RTDD§≙ RTDD **§** Architecture**ST**
|| RTDD **§** Static Behaviours**PG**
|| RTDD **§** Dynamic Behaviours**PC** (10)

The architecture of RTDD, RTDD**§**.Architecture**ST**, is modeled as shown in Fig. 13, which consists of two unified data models (UDMs), also known as component logical models (CLMs), and a set of events and status. The UDM of Switch**ST** specifies the input devices of RTDD such as the structure and interface of the switch with specific initial values. The UDM of LEDs**ST** models the output devices of RTDD with six LEDs as well as their shared port address and output patterns.

The static behaviors of RTDD are specified in Fig. 14 by three processes known as SystemInitial**PC**, RequestScan**PC**, and RequestHandling**PC**. As modeled in RTDD**§**.StaticBehaviors**PC**, RequestScan**PC** detects the switch status via the port interface and passes the device request to ReguesHandling**PC** via the global system status ⓈRequestIdentified**BL**. When ⓈRequestIdentified**BL** = **T** is identified, RequestHandling**PC** turns on the six LEDs in predesigned patterns.

The dynamic behaviours of RTDD, TDD**§**.DynamicBehaviors**PC**, are specified in Fig. 15. All real-time tasks of RTDD is deployed at two levels known as the base and interrupt levels. The former deals with routine and low priority tasks RequestHandling**PC**, and other processes after the system is initialized and before it is shutdown. The latter handles high priority and timing-sensitive tasks such as RequestScan**PC**, which scans

Figure 12. Code generated by RTPA-CG for the IBS algorithm in Java

---

1. Java code for the architecture of IBS

```
public class IBSAlgorithm_Architecture_ST{
Clm_ST Clm= new Clm_ST();
class Clm_ST{
    int  LowerBound_N;
    int  UpperBound_N;
    int  IBSum_N;
    }
RealTimeVirtualMachine RTVM = new RealTimeVirtualMachine();
class Result_IBS_Algorithm{          //Definition of return type class
  long IBSum_N;
  }
  //Object Initializations
  public void Clm_ST(){
  }
}
```

---

2. Java code for the static behaviors of IBS

```
public class IBSAlgorithm_StaticBehaviors_PC extends
        IBSAlgorithm_Architecture_ST {
public Result_IBS_Algorithm IBS_Algorithm (
                int LowerBound_N, int UpperBound_N)
  {
    Result_IBS_Algorithm  res = new Result_IBS_Algorithm();
    Max_N = 65535;
    If ((0)<(LowerBound_N) &&
       ((LowerBound_N)<(Max_N)) &&
       (0)<(UpperBound_N) &&
       ((UpperBound_N)<(Max_N)) &&
       (LowerBound_N)<(UpperBound_N))
       {
       res.IBSum_N = ((((UpperBound_N-1)*UpperBound_N)/2)-
                       (LowerBound_N*(LowerBound_N+1)/2));
       IBSResult_BL = true;
       } else
       {
       IBSResult_BL = false;
       }
  } return res;
  }
}
```

---

3. Java code for the dynamic behavior of IBS

```
public class IBSAlgorithm_DynamicBehaviors_PC extends
IBSAlgorithm_StaticBehaviors_ST {
    if (RTVM.eventCapture(@IBSAlgorithm_S))
    {
      IBS_Algorithm(A_N, B_N);
      System.exit(0);
    }
  public IBSAlgorithm_DynamicBehaviors_PC() {
  }
  public static void main(String[] args) {
  IBSAlgorithm_DynamicBehaviors_PC1 =
      new IBSAlgorithm_DynamicBehaviors_PC();
      ...          // Any additional processes
  }
}
```

Figure 13. The architectural model of RTDD in RTPA

```
RTDD§.ArchitectureST ≙ {  <Switch : ST | [1]>
                         || <LEDs : ST | [6]>
                         || <@Events : ST >
                         || <ⓢStatus : ST>
                        }
= { SwitchST ≙ (<InputPortAddr : H | InputPortAddrH = 0379H>;
                <KeyInput : B | KeyInputB = 0000 0111B>,
                <KeyScanStatus : B | KeyScanStatusB = 0000 0000B>
               )

  || LEDsST ≙ (<NofLEDs : B | NofLEDsNB = 6>,
               <LightPattern : B | LightPatternB = 0000 0000B>,
               <OuputPortAddr : H | OuputPortAddrH = 0378H>
               )

  || @EventST ≙ ( @SwitchOnS
                | @SwitchOffS
                | @SysClock100msInt⊙
                )

  || ⓢStatusST ≙ ( ⓢRequestIdentifiedBL
                 )
  }
```

the status of the switch device per 100 milliseconds.

b) Code Automatically Generated for the RTDD System

A set of C++ programs of RTDD generated by RTPA-GC are listed in Figs. 16 and 17. The first file presented in Fig. 16, class RTD, is the head file for the class RTDD. The RTDD class implemented in C++, RTDD::RTDD(), is shown in Fig. 17. With support of μC/OS-II and Borland C++ Compiler 5.1, the generated files were compiled under DOS larger mode. Then, the executable code for RTDD generated by RTPA-CG can be run as expected to respond to the device requests for displaying desired LED patterns and other application processes simultaneously.

The results of the sample case studies show that machine-based autonomic code generation based on formal system models in RTPA is technically feasible. As a formal notation and methodology, RTPA is not only easy to understand but also seamlessly transformable into high-level programming languages such as C++ and Java. Further case studies on RTPA methodologies and RTPA-based code generation technologies have been reported in (Wang, 2007, 2009b; Wang et al., 2009, 2010a, 2010b). The case studies demonstrate that RTPA-CGs provide a seamless transformation technology from formal system models in RTPA to executable code in C++ and Java. Applications of RTPA-CGs may greatly improve program development productivity in software engineering and in the software industry.

CONCLUSION

This paper has reported the design and implementation methodologies and techniques for the Real-Time Process Algebra (RTPA) code generators in C++ and Java. RTPA has been introduced as a denotational mathematics for the algebraic

Figure 14. The static behavioural model of RTDD

```
RTDD§.StaticBehaviorsPC ≙ ( SystemInitial(<I:: ( )>; <O:: LEDsST>)PC
                            || RequestScan(<I:: SwitchST>; <O:: ⓈRequestIdentifiedBL)PC
                            || RequestHandling(<I:: ⓈRequestIdentifiedBL>; <O:: LEDsST>)PC
                            )

SystemInitial(<I:: ( )>; <O:: LEDsST>)PC ≙
{ LEDsST.LightPatternB := 0000 0011B
  → LEDsST.LightPatternB |⋖ PORT(LEDsST.OuputPortAddrH)B
}

RequestScan(<I:: SwitchST>; <O:: ⓈRequestIdentifiedBL)PC ≙
{PORT(SwitchST.InputPortAddrH)B |> SwitchST.KeyInputB
 → ( ◆ SwitchST.KeyScanStatusB = SwitchST.KeyInputB
       → ⓈRequestIdentifiedBL := T
   | ◆ ~
       → ⓈRequestIdentifiedBL := F
   )
}

RequestHandling(<I:: ⓈRequestIdentifiedBL>; <O:: LEDsST>)PC ≙
{◆ ⓈRequestIdentifiedBL = T
    → 0000 1100B |⋖ Port (LEDsST.OuputPortAddrH)B        // Turn on LEDs 1 and 2
    → @tTM ≙ §tTM + 1000ms                               // Delay 1 second
    → 0000 0000B |⋖ Port (LEDsST.OuputPortAddrH)B        // Turn off all LEDs
    → @tTM ≙ §tTM + 1000ms
    → 0011 0000B |⋖ Port (LEDsST.OuputPortAddrH)B        // Turn on LEDs 3 and 4
    → @tTM ≙ §tTM + 1000ms
    → 0000 0000B |⋖ Port (LEDsST.OuputPortAddrH)B
    → @tTM ≙ §tTM + 1000ms
    → 1100 0000B |⋖ Port (LEDsST.OuputPortAddrH)B        // Turn on LEDs 5 and 6
    → @tTM ≙ §tTM + 1000ms
    → 0000 0000B |⋖ Port (LEDsST.OuputPortAddrH)B
}
```

Figure 15. The dynamic behavioural model of RTDD

```
RTDD§.DynamicBehaviorsPC ≙
{ // Base level processes
 @SysInitialS
   ↳ SystemInitialPC(<I:: ( )>; <O:: LEDsST>)
              T
   →          R          ( ↳ RequestHandlingPC(<I:: ⓈRequestIdentifiedBL>; <O:: LEDsST>)
     ⓈSysShutDownBL=F
                           ↳ ...                  // Other processes
                         )
   → ⊠
|| // Interrupt level processes
  @SysClock100msInt⨀
    ↗ (↳ RequestScanPC(<I:: SwitchST>; <O:: ⓈRequestIdentifiedBL)
       → @SysClock100msInt⨀ := off
      )
    ↘ ⊙
}
```

Figure 16. The head file of RTDD generated by RTPA-CG

```
#ifndef RTDD_H
#define RTDD_H
#include "rtpa_cg_cpp.h"

class RTDD
{public:
        RTDD();
        struct Type_ST {
                Type_ST *cptr;
                char *id_S;
                LEDStatusSet_BL_Type_ST  LEDStatusSet_BL;
        };
        struct Switch_ST {
                Switch_ST *cptr;
                char *id_S;
                int InputPortAddr_H;
                char KeyInput_B;
                char KeyScanStatus_B;
        };
        struct LEDs_ST {
                LEDs_ST *cptr;
                char *id_S;
                int NofLEDs_N;
                char LightPattern_B;
                int OuputPortAddr_H;
        };
        Type_ST Type_S;
        Switch_ST Switch_S;
        LED_ST LED_S;
        rtpaEVENT SwitchOn_S;
        rtpaEVENT SwitchOff_S;
        rtpaEVENT SysClock100msInt_S;
        rtpaEVENT rtpaConEvent1;
        BOOLEAN RequestIdentified_BL;
        BOOLEAN RequestServed_BL;
        void SysInitial();
        void RequestScan();
        void RequestHandling();
        void Deployment();
};
#endif
```

Figure 17. The code generated for RTDD based on the RTPA model

```
#include <includes.h>
#include "RTDD.h"
RTDD::RTDD() {
        Switch_S.InputPortAddr_H = 0x379;
        Switch_S.KeyInput_B = 1;
        Switch_S.KeyScanStatus_B = 23;
        LEDs_S.NofLEDs_N = 6;
        LEDs_S.LightPattern_B = 0;
        LEDs_S.OuputPortAddr_H = 0x378;
        // Other processes
        RequestIdentified_BL = FALSE;
        RequestServed_BL = FALSE;
}
void RTDD::SystemInitial() {
        LEDs_S.LightPattern_B = 3;
        rtpaPortOut(LEDs_S.OuputPortAddr_H, LEDs_S.LightPattern_B);
}
void RTDD::RequestScan() {
        Switch_S.KeyInput_B = rtpaPortIn(Switch_S.InputPortAddr_H);
        If  (Switch_S.KeyScanStatus_B == Switch_S.KeyInput_B)
            RequestIdentified_BL =  TRUE;
        else
            RequestIdentified_BL =  FALSE;
}
void RTDD::RequestHandling() {
        rtpaDATETIME t_TIME;
        if (RequestIdentified_BL == TRUE) {
                LEDs_S.LightPattern_B = 12;
                rtpaPortOut(LEDs_S.OuputPortAddr_H, LEDs_S.LightPattern_B);
                rtpaDuration(&t_TIME, 1000);
                LEDs_S.LightPattern_B = 0;
                rtpaPortOut(LEDs_S.OuputPortAddr_H, LEDs_S.LightPattern_B);
                rtpaDuration(&t_TIME, 1000);
                LEDs_S.LightPattern_B = 48;
                rtpaPortOut(LEDs_S.OuputPortAddr_H, LEDs_S.LightPattern_B);
                rtpaDuration(&t_TIME, 1000);
                LEDs_S.LightPattern_B = 0;
                rtpaPortOut(LEDs_S.OuputPortAddr_H, LEDs_S.LightPattern_B);
                rtpaDuration(&t_TIME, 1000);
                LEDs_S.LightPattern_B = 192;
                rtpaPortOut(LEDs_S.OuputPortAddr_H, LEDs_S.LightPattern_B);
                rtpaDuration(&t_TIME, 1000);
                LEDs_S.LightPattern_B = 0;
                rtpaPortOut(LEDs_S.OuputPortAddr_H, LEDs_S.LightPattern_B);
        }
}
void RTDD::Deployment(){
        SysInitial();
        // Other processes
}
```

modeling and manipulations of software system architectures and behaviors by the Unified Data Models (UDMs) and Unified Process Models (UPMs). The RTPA code generator (RTPA-CG) has been configured encompassing the RTPA lexer, parser, type-checker, code-builder, and the real-time runtime library. The framework for RTPA code generation has provided a great flexibility by separating RTPA code generation into two passes of specification parsing and code building. It has been demonstrated that the system is practical and efficient to generate software code in C++ and Java, as well as other target programming languages with specific plug-in supporting modules. A number of experiments on code generations using RTPA-CG have been carried out. The results have shown that the approach adopted to automatically generate program code from formally modeled system specifications is achievable and practical, which can seamlessly transfer a software system model specified in RTPA into executable and effective code.

ACKNOWLEDGMENT

The authors would like to acknowledge the Natural Science and Engineering Council of Canada (NSERC) for its partial support to this work. We would like to thank the anonymous reviewers for their valuable comments and suggestions.

REFERENCES

Aho, A. V., Sethi, R., & Ullman, J. D. (1985). *Compilers: Principles, Techniques, and Tools*. Reading, MA: Addison-Wesley.

Bollella, G., Brosgol, B., Dibble, P., Furr, S., Gosling, J., & Hardin, D. (2002). *The Real-Time Specification for Java*. Reading, MA: Addison-Wesley.

Cardelli, L., & Wegner, P. (1985). On Understanding Types, Data Abstraction and Polymorphism. *ACM Computing Surveys*, *17*(4), 471–522. doi:10.1145/6041.6042

Fecher, H. (2001). A Real-Time Process Algebra with Open Intervals and Maximal Progress. *Nordic Journal of Computing*, *8*(3), 346–360.

Grune, D., Bal, H. E., Jacobs, C. J. H., & Langendoen, K. G. (2000). *Modern Compiler Design*. New York: John Wiley & Sons.

Higman, B. (1977). *A Comparative Study of Programming Languages* (2nd ed.). Westfield, NJ: MacDonald.

Hoare, C. A. R. (1978). Communicating Sequential Processes. *Communications of the ACM*, *21*(8), 666–677. doi:10.1145/359576.359585

Hoare, C. A. R. (1985). *Communicating Sequential Processes*. London: Prentice-Hall.

Labrosse, J. J. (1999). *MicroController/OS-II, The Real-Time Kernel* (2nd ed.). Gilroy, CA: R&D Books.

Lewis, H. R., & Papadimitriou, C. H. (1998). *Elements of the Theory of Computation* (2nd ed.). Upper Saddle River, NJ: Prentice-Hall.

Louden, K. C. (1993). *Programming Languages: Principles and Practice*. Boston: PWS-Kent Publishing Co.

Martin-Lof, P. (1975). An Intuitionistic Theory of Types: Predicative Part . In Rose, H., & Shepherdson, J. C. (Eds.), *Logic Colloquium 1973*. Amsterdam, The Netherlands: North Holland. doi:10.1016/S0049-237X(08)71945-1

McDermid, J. (Ed.). (1991). *Software Engineer's Reference Book*. Oxford, UK: Butterworth Heinemann Ltd.

Michael, H. C., & Butler, R. W. (1996). Impediments to Industrial Use of Formal Method. *IEEE Computer*, *24*(9), 25–26.

Milner, R. (1980). *A Calculus of Communicating Systems* (LNCS 92). New York: Springer.

Mitchell, J. C. (1990). Type Systems for Programming Languages. In van Leeuwen, J. (Ed.), *Handbook of Theoretical Computer Science* (pp. 365–458). Amsterdam, The Netherlands: North Holland.

Ngolah, C. F., & Wang, Y. (2009). Tool Support for Software Development based on Formal Specifications in RTPA. *International Journal of Software Engineering and Its Applications, 3*(3), 71–88.

Ngolah, C. F., & Wang, Y. (2010). The Formal Design Model of a Real-Time Operating System (RTOS+). *International Journal of Software Science and Computational Intelligence, 2*(2).

Nicollin, X., & Sifakis, J. (1991). An Overview and Synthesis on Timed Process Algebras. In *Proceedings of the 3rd International Computer Aided Verification Conference* (pp. 376-398).

Parr, T. (2000). *ANTLR Reference Manual*. Retrieved from http://www.antlr.org/doc/

Parr, T. J., & Quong, R. W. (1995). ANTLR: A Predicated-LL(k) Parser Generator. *Software, Practice & Experience, 25*(7), 789–810. doi:10.1002/spe.4380250705

RAISE. (1995). *The RAISE Specification Language (BCS Practitioner Series)*. London: Prentice Hall, London.

Sheng, L. (1999). *The Java Native Interface: Programmers Guide and Specification*. Reading, MA: Addison-Wesley.

Stubbs, D. F., & Webre, N. W. (1985). *Data Structures with Abstract Data Types and Pascal*. Monterey, CA: Brooks/Cole Publishing Co.

Tan, X., & Wang, Y. (2008). A Denotational Semantics of Real-Time Process Algebra (RTPA). *International Journal of Cognitive Informatics and Natural Intelligence, 2*(3), 57–70.

Tan, X., Wang, Y., & Ngolah, C. F. (2004). Specification of the RTPA Grammar and Its Recognition. In *Proceedings of the 2004 IEEE International Conference on Cognitive Informatics (ICCI'04)*, Victoria, Canada (pp. 54-63). Washington, DC: IEEE CS Press.

Tan, X., Wang, Y., & Ngolah, C. F. (2006, May). Design and Implementation of an Automatic RTPA Code Generator. In *Proceedings of the 19th Canadian Conference on Electrical and Computer Engineering (CCECE'06)*, Ottawa, ON, Canada (pp. 1605-1608).

Univan, A., & Chris, G. (2000). C++ Translator for RAISE Specifications (Tech. Rep. No. 220). Macau: UNU-IIST.

Wang, Y. (2002). The Real-Time Process Algebra (RTPA). *Annals of Software Engineering, 14*, 235–274. doi:10.1023/A:1020561826073

Wang, Y. (2006). On the Informatics Laws and Deductive Semantics of Software. [Part C]. *IEEE Transactions on Systems, Man, and Cybernetics, 36*(2), 161–171. doi:10.1109/TSMCC.2006.871138

Wang, Y. (2007). *Software Engineering Foundations: A Software Science Perspective* (CRC Series in Software Engineering, Vol. 2). Oxford, UK: Auerbach Publications.

Wang, Y. (2008a). On Contemporary Denotational Mathematics for Computational Intelligence. *Transactions of Computational Science, 2*, 6–29. doi:10.1007/978-3-540-87563-5_2

Wang, Y. (2008b). On Concept Algebra: A Denotational Mathematical Structure for Knowledge and Software Modeling. *International Journal of Cognitive Informatics and Natural Intelligence, 2*(2), 1–19.

Wang, Y. (2008c). RTPA: A Denotational Mathematics for Manipulating Intelligent and Computational Behaviors. *International Journal of Cognitive Informatics and Natural Intelligence, 2*(2), 44–62.

Wang, Y. (2008d). Mathematical Laws of Software. *Transactions of Computational Science, 2,* 46–83. doi:10.1007/978-3-540-87563-5_4

Wang, Y. (2008e). Deductive Semantics of RTPA. *International Journal of Cognitive Informatics and Natural Intelligence, 2*(2), 95–121.

Wang, Y. (2009a). Paradigms of Denotational Mathematics for Cognitive Informatics and Cognitive Computing. *Fundamenta Informaticae, 90*(3), 282–303.

Wang, Y. (2009b). The Formal Design Model of a Telephone Switching System (TSS). *International Journal of Software Science and Computational Intelligence, 1*(3), 92–116.

Wang, Y., & Ngolah, C. F. (2008). An Operational Semantics of Real-Time Process Algebra (RTPA). *International Journal of Cognitive Informatics and Natural Intelligence, 2*(3), 71–89.

Wang, Y., Ngolah, C. F., Ahmadi, H., Sheu, P. C.-Y., & Ying, S. (2009). The Formal Design Model of a Lift Dispatching System (LDS). *International Journal of Software Science and Computational Intelligence, 1*(4), 98–122.

Wang, Y., Ngolah, C. F., Zeng, G., Sheu, P. C.-Y., Choy, C. P., & Tian, Y. (2010b). The Formal Design Models of a Real-Time Operating System (RTOS+): Conceptual and Architectural Frameworks. *International Journal of Software Science and Computational Intelligence, 2*(2).

Wang, Y., Zadeh, L. A., & Yao, Y. (2008). On the System Algebra Foundation for Granular Computing. *International Journal of Software Science and Computational Intelligence, 1*(1), 64–86.

Wang, Y., Zhang, Y., Sheu, P., Li, X., & Guo, H. (2010a). The Formal Design Models of an Automatic Teller Machine (ATM). *International Journal of Software Science and Computational Intelligence, 2*(1), 102–131.

Wilson, L. B., & Clark, R. G. (1988). *Comparative Programming Language.* Reading, MA: Addison-Wesley Publishing Co.

Woodcock, J., & Davies, J. (1996). *Using Z: Specification, Refinement, and Proof.* Upper Saddle River, NJ: Prentice Hall International.

This work was previously published in International Journal of Software Science and Computational Intelligence, Volume 2, Issue 2, edited by Yingxu Wang, pp. 44-67, copyright 2010 by IGI Publishing (an imprint of IGI Global).

Chapter 13

The Formal Design Model of a Real–Time Operating System (RTOS+):
Conceptual and Architectural Frameworks

Yingxu Wang
University of Calgary, Canada

Cyprian F. Ngolah
Sentinel Trending & Diagnostics Ltd., Canada

Guangping Zeng
University of Science and Technology, China and University of California, Berkeley, USA

Phillip C.-Y. Sheu
Wuhan University, China and University of California, Irvine, USA

C. Philip Choy
University of Calgary, Canada

Yousheng Tian
University of Calgary, Canada

ABSTRACT

A real-time operating system (RTOS) provides a platform for the design and implementation of a wide range of applications in real-time systems, embedded systems, and mission-critical systems. This paper presents a formal design model for a general RTOS known as RTOS+ that enables a specific target RTOS to be rigorously and efficiently derived in real-world applications. The methodology of a denotational mathematics, Real-Time Process Algebra (RTPA), is described for formally modeling and refining architectures, static behaviors, and dynamic behaviors of RTOS+. The conceptual model of the RTOS+ system is introduced as the initial requirements for the system. The architectural model of RTOS+ is created using RTPA architectural modeling methodologies and refined by a set of Unified Data Models (UDMs). The static behaviors of RTOS+ are specified and refined by a set of Unified Process Models (UPMs). The dynamic behaviors of the RTOS+ system are specified and refined by the real-time process scheduler and system dispatcher. This work is presented in two papers; the conceptual and architectural models of RTOS+ is described in this paper, while the static and dynamic behavioral models of RTOS+ will be elaborated in a forthcoming paper.

DOI: 10.4018/978-1-4666-0264-9.ch013

INTRODUCTION

An *operating system* is a set of integrated system software that organizes, manages, and controls the resources and computing power of a computer or a computer network. It also provides users a logical interface for accessing the physical machine in order to run applications. A general-purpose operating system may be perceived as an agent between the hardware and resources of a computer and the applications and users. An operating system may be divided into three subsystems known as those of the *kernel* or *system management*, the *resource management*, and the *process management* (Dijkstra, 1968; Brinch-Hansen, 1971; Liu & Layland, 1973; Peterson & Silberschantz, 1985; Anderson et al., 1989; McDermid, 1991; Deitel & Kogan, 1992; Tanenbaum, 1994; Viscarola & Mason, 2001; Silberschatz et al., 2003; Wang, 2004, 2007). The kernel of an operating system is a set of central components for computing, including CPU scheduling and process management. The resource management subsystem is a set of supporting functions for various system resources and user interfaces. The process management subsystem is a set of transition manipulation mechanisms for processes and threads interacting with the system kernel and resources.

A *real-time operating system* (RTOS) is an operating system that supports and guarantees timely responses to external and internal events of real-time systems (Laplante, 1977; Sha et al., 1990; ISO/IEC, 1996; Ford, 1997; Bollella et al., 2002; Kreuzinger et al., 2002; Ngolah, Wang, & Tan, 2004). An RTOS monitors, responds to, and controls an external environment, which is connected to the computer system through sensors, actuators, or other input-output (I/O) devices. In a real-time system in general and an RTOS in particular, the correctness of system behaviors depends not only on the logical results of computation but also on the time point at which the results are obtained. Real-time systems can be divided into hard and soft real-time systems. In

the former, a failure to meet timing constraints will be of serious consequences, while in the latter, a timing failure may not significantly affect the functioning of the system.

A great variety of RTOS's have been developed in the last decades (Lewis & Berg, 1998; Labrosse, 1999; Yodaiken, 1999; Rivas & Harbour, 2001; Lamie, 2008; ETTX, 2009). The existing RTOS's are characterized as target-machine-specific, implementation-dependent, and not formally modeled. Therefore, they are usually not portable as a generic real-time operating system to be seamlessly incorporated into real-time or embedded system implementations. Problems often faced by RTOS's are CPU and tasks scheduling, time/event management, and resource management. Efficient and precise methodologies and notations for describing solutions to these problems are critical in RTOS design and implementation. Generally, RTOS's require multitasking, process threads, and a sufficient number of interrupt levels to deal with the random interrupt mechanisms in real-time systems. In modern RTOS's, *multitasking* is a technique used for enabling multiple tasks to share a single processor. A *thread* is individual execution of a process in order to handle concurrent tasks. In addition, an *interrupt* is a request of an external device or internal process that causes the operating system to suspend the execution of a current low priority task, serve the interrupt, and hand control back to the interrupted process.

This paper develops a comprehensive design paradigm of the formal real-time operating system (RTOS+) in a top-down approach on the basis of the RTPA methodology. The conceptual model, architectural model, and the static/dynamic behavioral models of RTOS+ are systematically presented. In the remainder of this paper, the conceptual model of RTOS+ is described as the initial requirements for the system. The architectural model of RTOS+ is created based on the conceptual model using the RTPA architectural modeling methodologies and refined by a set of unified data models (UDMs). Then, the static

Figure 1. The architecture of RTOS+

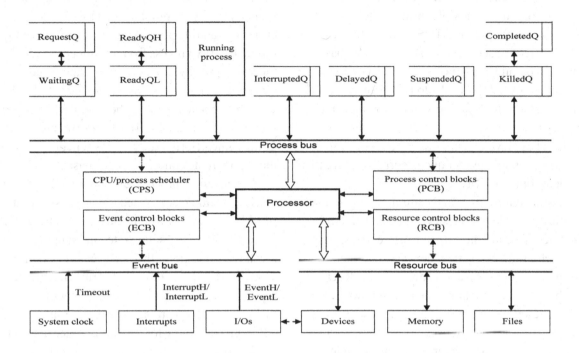

behaviors of RTOS+ are specified and refined by a set of unified process models (UPMs). The dynamic behaviors of RTOS+ are specified and refined by process priority allocation, process scheduling, and system dispatching models. Due to its excessive length and complexity, this paper presents the first part of RTOS+ on its conceptual and architectural models, followed in serial by another paper that presents the second part of this work on the static and dynamic behavioral models of RTOS+ (Wang et al., 2010c).

THE CONCEPTUAL MODEL OF RTOS+

The multi-task and multithread real-time operating system (RTOS+) is a portable and rigorous RTOS with formal architectural models and behavioral processes. As a preparation, this section presents the conceptual models of RTOS+ from the fac-

ets of its architectures, resources, and processes (tasks), as well as their interactions. The top-level framework and the process scheduling scheme of RTOS+ are informally introduced.

The Architecture of RTOS+

RTOS+ is designed for handling event-, time-, and interrupt-driven processes as a potable real-time system platform. The conceptual architecture of RTOS+ is described as shown in Figure 1, where interactions between system resources, components, and internal control models are illustrated. The conceptual architecture of RTOS+ can be divided into three subsystems: a) the processor and the CPU/process/system schedulers, b) the resource/event controllers, and c) the process control structures.

The schedulers for CPU, processes, and the entire system are the innermost operating system kernel that directly controls the CPU as well as system tasks, processes, events, and resources. The process scheduling mechanism of RTOS+ is priority-based. A flexible priority scheduling technique is adopted in RTOS+, where the priority of a given process for a task is assigned based on its type and importance when it is created. Processes are categorized into five priority levels known as the high and low periodic interrupts, device I/O interrupt, user application interrupts, and the base levels. A process, when it is created, will be put into a proper queue corresponding to its predefined priority level.

The resources of RTOS+ are modeled by the entities of memory, time, devices (ports), interrupt facilities, files, and internal control structures such as dispatching queues, system/device/event/memory, and process control blocks. The resources in RTOS+ can be classified into three categories known as the system resources (memory, device, and files), event resources (system timing events, interrupts, and I/O events), and resource control structures (running processes and tasks in other states).

Process Scheduling in RTOS+

The process scheduling of RTOS+ is priority-based and event-driven as shown in Figure 2. The process scheduler is responsible for determining which process should be executed on the processor at a given time interval of CUP time. The dynamic performance of tasks in RTOS+ is embodied by a series of coherent processes and threads. A task is created by the system (State 1) as a process in the waiting queue with an assigned priority based on its importance and timing requirement. When the required resource is available, the process pending in the waiting queue will be scheduled into a ready queue with the proper priority. The process scheduler dispatches tasks in the high ready queues before scheduling those in the low ready queue in State 2. It continuously checks the ready queues to see if there is any process ready to be run in State 3. If there are ready processes in the queue, it compares the priorities of the currently executing process and that of the first process in the queue. If the first process in the queue has a higher priority, it pre-empts the CPU from the currently running process, assigns the CPU to the higher priority process from the queue, and sends the lower priority process to the delayed queue in State 6. The delayed process is re-dispatched to the appropriate ready queue to be executed when the CPU becomes available. If there are two processes of the same priority, the process scheduler treats them on a first-come-first-serve basis.

A scheduled process executes on the CPU until it is either completed (State 4) or is suspended due to lack of a resource or pending for an event (State 7). As illustrated in Figure 2, there are three conditions that may cause a running process to be re-scheduled out of running: a) Interrupted by a process or event with higher priority; b) Timed-out for a pre-scheduled time-interval of CPU; and c) Waiting for a specific device or event. An interrupted running process is sent to the interrupted queue (State 5) and later returned to the appropriate ready queue when the interrupt service (State 9) is over. A process that has exhausted its assigned time interval must go to the delayed queue (State 6), while it can be re-scheduled back to one of the ready queues immediately for waiting for the next available CPU executing interval. However, a process that can no longer be executed due to lack of memory or resource has to be sent to the suspended queue (State 7), which may return to the appropriate ready queue when the pending resource has become available. A process interrupted, delayed, or suspended at States 5, 6, or 7, respectively, may be killed (State 8) by the process scheduler in case there is a persistent unavailability on demanded resources or CPU time.

More rigorous description of the system dispatching and process scheduling strategies and algorithms will be elaborated by the entire dynamic behaviors of RTOS+, particularly the CPUScheduler**ST** (Figure 18), ProcessSchedulerST (Figure 31), and SystemDispatcher**ST** (Fig. 30) from the bottom up.

Figure 2. State transition diagram of the process scheduler in RTOS+

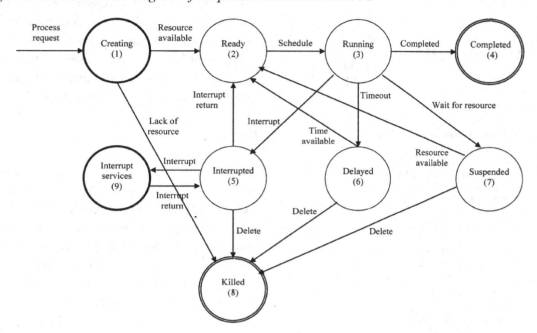

On the basis of the conceptual models of RTOS+ as described in Figs. 1 and 2, the formal design models for RTOS+ can be developed in a rigorous and systematical approach using Real-Time Process Algebra (RTPA) (Wang, 2002, 2008a, 2008c). According to the RTPA methodology for system modeling, specification, and refinement (Wang, 2007, 2008a), the top-level RTPA specification of RTOS+ is given as follows:

§(RTOS+) ≙ RTOS+§ Architecture**ST**
    || RTOS+§ StaticBehaviors**PC**
    || RTOS+§ DynamicBehaviors**PC** (1)

where || indicates that these three subsystems are related in parallel, and **§**, **ST**, and **PC** are type suffixes of *system, system structure,* and *process,* respectively.

The following sections will extend and refine the top level framework of the RTOS+**§** into a set of detailed architectural models (UDMs) and behavioral process models (UPMs).

THE ARCHITECTURAL MODEL OF THE RTOS+ SYSTEM

The architecture of a real-time system is a framework that represents the overall structure, components, processes, as well as their interrelationships and interactions. This section formally specifies the architecture of RTOS+, RTOS+**§**.Architectur-e**ST**, based on its conceptual models as provided in the preceding section (Figsures 1-2). Each of the architectural components will be modeled and refined as a UDM (also known as *component logical model (CLM)*) (Wang, 2002, 2008a).

The Architectural Framework of RTOS+

System architectures, at the top level, specify a list of identifiers of UDMs and their relations. A UDM may be regarded as a predefined class of system hardware or internal control models, which can be inherited or implemented by corresponding UDM objects as specific instances in the succeeding architectural refinement for the system.

Figure 3. The high level architecture of the RTOS+ system

```
RTOS+§.ArchitectureST ≜ { ProcessorST
                          || ResourcesST
                          || ProcessesST
                        }
= { ( <CPU : ST | [1]>
     || <SystemClock : ST | [1]>
     || <SystemControlBlock : ST | [1]>
     || <EventControlBlocks : ST | [1]>
    )
   || ( <MemoryControlBlocks : ST | [1]>
      || <DeviceControlBlocks : ST | [1]>
      || <Files : ST | [MaxFiles N]>
    )
   || ( <ProcessControlBlocks : ST | [1]>
      || <RequestQ : ST | [1]>
      || <WaitingQ : ST| [1]>
      || <ReadyQH : ST | [1]>
      || <ReadyQL : ST | [1]>
      || <CompletedQ : ST | [1]>
      || <InterruptedQ : ST | [1]>
      || <DelayedQ : ST | [1]>
      || <SuspendedQ : ST | [1]>
      || <KilledQ : ST | [1]>
    )
}
```

Corresponding to the conceptual model of RTOS+ as shown in Figures 1 and 2, the high-level specification of the architecture of RTOS+, RTOS+§.ArchitectureST, is given in Fig. 3. RTOS+§.ArchitectureST encompasses parallel structures of three architectural subsystems known as ProcessorST, ResorucesST, and ProcessesST, as well as a set of events @EventsS and a set of statuses &StatusBL. Each subsystem may be further refined by detailed UDMs as shown in Figure 3, where the numbers in the angle brackets indicate the configuration of a specific UDM in the system. Detailed UDMs for all structural components in the three subsystems will be specified and refined in the following subsections.

The Architecture of the Processor Subsystem

According to the high level architectural model of RTOS+ as given in Fig. 3, the processor subsystem of RTOS+, ProcessorST, represents an abstract model of the system kernel such as the CPUST, SystemControlBlockST, EventControlBlockST, and SystemClockST. The following subsections formally describe the architectures of the kernel components by a set of UDMs in RTPA.

The CPU

The CPU of RTOS+ is formally modeled as a set of parallel computing entities with their associated resources in a broad view. The CPU's computing capabilities are logically abstracted as a set of processes and underlying resources such as CPU time, processes, and the event-/time-/interrupt-driven dispatch mechanisms; while the computing resources are modeled by the system clock, memory, devices (ports), system variables, and system status.

An abstract model of the target CPU of RTOS+ is described as shown in Figure 4, where the CPUST is modeled as a *generic computing system* (Wang, 2007), §, which is a virtual machine of the executing platform of the processor denoted by a set of parallel computing resources and processes. The computing system § controls all computing resources of the abstract target machine and the behavioral processes embodied on them.

The System Control Block

The *system control block* (SCB) is the central and top-level control structure of the entire RTOS+. The UDM of SCB, SystemControlBlockST = SCBST, is modeled as shown in Figure 5. SCBST specifies a set of system constants such as the maximum capacities of processes (threads), memory, devices (ports), events, interrupts, and timers. Then, the current numbers of dynamic process and resource usages of system are modeled within the constraints of system capacity constants. The numbers of the current running process (PNN), event (ENN), and device (DNN) are specially modeled for system control.

Figure 4. The UDM of an abstract target machine

$$\text{CPU}\textbf{ST} \triangleq \S ::$$

$$\left\{ \ < \mathop{R}_{i\textbf{N}=0}^{n_{proc}\textbf{N}-1} P_i\textbf{ST}> \right. \qquad \text{// Processes}$$

$$\| < \mathop{R}_{addr\textbf{P}=0}^{n_{MEM}\textbf{N}-1} \text{MEM}[addr\textbf{P}]\textbf{RT}> \qquad \text{// Memory}$$

$$\| < \mathop{R}_{ptr\textbf{P}=0}^{n_{PORT}\textbf{N}-1} \text{PORT}[addr\textbf{P}]\textbf{RT}> \qquad \text{// Ports (devices)}$$

$$\| <\S t\textbf{TM}> \qquad \text{// The system clock}$$

$$\| < \mathop{R}_{k\textbf{N}=0}^{n_e\textbf{N}-1} @e_k\textbf{S} \hookrightarrow P_k> \qquad \text{// Event-driven dispatch}$$

$$\| < \mathop{R}_{k\textbf{N}=0}^{n_t\textbf{N}-1} @t_k\textbf{TM} \hookrightarrow P_k> \qquad \text{// Time-driven dispatch}$$

$$\| < \mathop{R}_{k\textbf{N}=0}^{n_{int}\textbf{N}-1} @int_k\odot \hookrightarrow P_k > \qquad \text{// Interrupt-driven dispatch}$$

$$\| < \mathop{R}_{i\textbf{N}=0}^{n_V\textbf{N}-1} V_i\textbf{RT}> \qquad \text{// System variables (events)}$$

$$\| < \mathop{R}_{i\textbf{N}=0}^{n_S\textbf{N}-1} \circledS S_i\textbf{BL}> \qquad \text{// System statuses}$$

$$\left. \right\}$$

The Event Control Blocks

An event control block (ECB) is a global control structure for system event management. The UDM of ECBs, EventControlBlock**ST** = $\mathop{R}\limits_{EN\textbf{N}=1}^{SCB\textbf{ST}.\#Events\textbf{N}}$ ECB(EN**N**)**ST**, is modeled as shown in Figure 6, which is a dynamic structure with varying number of ECBs, controlled by SCB**ST**.#Events**N**, as a series of indexed records. An ECB**ST** registers the key informant of an event in RTOS+ such as its status, type, time detected, device required, and source/target process (if any).

The System Clock

A *system clock* is a typical real-time device for event timing, process duration manipulation, and system synchronization. The UDM model of the system clock of RTOS, SysClock**ST**, is designed as given in Figure 7. SysClock**ST** provides an *absolute* (calendar) clock §t$_c$**hh:mm:ss:ms** as the logical time reference for the entire system and a *relative* clock §t$_r$**N** as a generic counter. The real-time system clock will be updated at run-time by the process SysClock**PC** as shown in Figure 15.

The Architecture of the Resources Subsystem

According to the high level architectural model of RTOS+ as given in Figure 3, the resource subsystem of RTOS+, Resources**ST**, manages system internal and external resources such as memory, devices (ports), and files. The following subsections formally describe the architectures of the resource components by a set of UDMs in RTPA.

Figure 5. The UDM of the system control block of RTOS+

SystemControlBlockST ≙ SCB**ST** ::
(// *System configurations*
  <MaxProcs : **N** | MaxProcs**N** = 100>;
  <MaxMemory : **B** | MaxMemory**B** = 200G**B**>;
  <MaxMemBlocks : **N** | MaxMemBlocks**N** = 3000>;
  <MaxMemBlockSize : **B** | MaxMemBlockSize**B** = 50k**B**>;
  <MaxPorts : **N** | MaxPorts**N** = 512>;
  <MaxDevices : **N** | MaxDevices**N** = 512>;
  <MaxEvents : **N** | MaxEvents**N** = 1024>;
  <MaxInterrupts : **N** | MaxInterrupts**N** = 512>;
  <MaxFiles : **N** | MaxFiles**N** = 1024>;
  <MaxTimers : **N** | MaxTimers**N** = 100>;

  // *System control structures*
  <#ProcRequest : **N** | 0 ≤ #ProcRequest**N** ≤ MaxProcs**N**>;
  <#ProcWaiting : **N** | 0 ≤ #ProcWaiting**N** ≤ MaxProcs**N**>;
  <#ProcReadyQH : **N** | 0 ≤ #ProcReadyH**N** ≤ 6>;
  <#ProcReadyQL : **N** | 0 ≤ #ProcReadyL**N** ≤ 4>;
  <#ProcCompleted : **N** | 0 ≤ #ProcCompleted**N** ≤ MaxProcs**N**>;
  <#ProcInterrupted : **N** | 0 ≤ #ProcInterrupted**N** ≤ MaxProcs**N**>;
  <#ProcDelayed : **N** | 0 ≤ #ProcDelayed**N** ≤ MaxProcs**N**>;
  <#ProcSuspended : **N** | 0 ≤ #ProcSuspended**N** ≤ MaxProcs**N**>;
  <#ProcKilled : **N** | 0 ≤ #ProcKiled**N** ≤ MaxProcs**N**>;
  <#MemBlocksUsed : **N** | 0 ≤ #MemBlocksUsed**N** ≤ MaxMemBlocks**N**>;
  <#Devices : **N** | 0 ≤ Devices**N** ≤ MaxDevices**N**>;
  <#Files : **N** | 0 ≤ #Files**N** ≤ MaxFiles**N**>;
  <#Procs : **N** | 0 ≤ #Procs**N** ≤ MaxProcs**N**>;
  <#Events : **N** | 0 ≤ #Events **N** ≤ MaxEvents**N**>;
  <#Interrupts : **N** | 0 ≤ #Interrupts**N** ≤ MaxInterrupts**N**>;
  <#Timers : **N** | 0 ≤ #Timers**N** ≤ MaxTimers**N**>;
  // *System control status*
  <CurrentPN : **N** | 0 ≤ CurrentPN**N** ≤ #Procs**N**>;
  <CurrentEN : **N** | 0 ≤ CurrentEN**N** ≤ #Events**N** >;
  <CurrentDN : **N** | 0 ≤ CurrentDN**N** ≤ #Devices**N**>;
  <ⓈRunEnd : **BL** | {ⓈRunEnd**BL** ={(**T**, ProcEnd), (**F**, ProcRuning)}
)

Figure 6. The UDM of the event control block of RTOS+

EventControlBlocksST ≙ $\overset{\text{SCB}\textbf{ST}.\#Events\textbf{N}}{\underset{EN\textbf{N}=1}{\textbf{R}}}$ ECB(EN**N**)**ST** ::
    (<Status : **BL** | Status**BL** = {(**T**, New), (**F**, Processed)}>;
    <Type : **N** | Type**N** = {(1, DeviceInt), (2, DeviceI/O), (3, TimerEvent)}>;
    <TimeDetected : **hh:mm:ss:ms**>;
    <DeviceReq : **N** | 1 ≤ DeviceReq**N** ≤ SCB**ST**.#MaxDevices**N**>;
    <SourceProc : **N** | 1 ≤ SourceProc**N** ≤ SCB**ST**.#MaxProc**N**>;
    <TargetProc : **N** | 1 ≤ TargetProc**N** ≤ SCB**ST**.#MaxProc**N**>
)

Figure 7. The schema and detailed UDM model of system clock

$$\textbf{SysClockST} \triangleq \ (\ <\S t_r : \textbf{N} \mid 0 \le \S t\textbf{N} \le 1{,}000{,}000>;$$
$$<\S t_c : \textbf{hh:mm:ss:ms} \mid 00{:}00{:}00 \le <\S t_c\textbf{hh:mm:ss:ms} \le 23{:}59{:}59{:}999>;$$
$$<\text{MainClockPort} : \textbf{H} \mid \text{MainClockPort}\textbf{B} = \text{FFF1}\textbf{H}>;$$
$$<\text{ClockInterval} : \textbf{N} \mid \text{ClockInterval}\textbf{N} = 1\textbf{ms}>;$$
$$\text{MaxTimers}\textbf{N}$$
$$< \quad \underset{i\textbf{N}=0}{R} \quad (<\text{Timer}(i\textbf{N})\textbf{ST}.\text{Timer}\textbf{ms}>;$$
$$<\text{Timer}(i\textbf{N})\textbf{ST}.\text{SourceProc}\textbf{N}>$$
$$)>$$
$$)$$

The Memory Control Blocks

Memory management is one of the key functions of operating systems because memory is both the working space and storage of data or files. Common memory management technologies of operating systems are contiguous allocation, paging, segmentation, and combinations of these methods (Silberschatz et al., 2003).

The abstract model of the memory system, MEM**ST**, can be described as follows:

$$\text{MEM}\textbf{ST} \triangleq [addr_1\textbf{H} \ldots addr_2\textbf{H}]\textbf{B} \qquad (2)$$

Typical memory manipulations are addressing, memory allocation, memory release, read, and write, as modeled in the RTPA meta-processes.

The *addressing* manipulation, $\Rightarrow$, is a fundamental operation of RTPA that maps a given logical *id***S** into a block of the physical memory denoted by *addr*Þ**P** accommodating n bytes of memory, i.e.:

$$id\textbf{S} \Rightarrow \text{MEM}[addr\text{Þ}\textbf{P}]\textbf{B}$$
$$\Leftrightarrow (\pi : id\textbf{S} \to addr\text{Þ}\textbf{P}$$
$$\to \text{MEM}[addr\textbf{P}, addr\textbf{P} + n\textbf{H} - 1]\textbf{B} \qquad (3)$$
$$)$$

where π: *id***S** $\to$ *addr*Þ**P** is a function that maps a given logical *id***S** into the physical memory block identified by *addr*Þ**P** in MEM[*addr***P**, *addr***P**+*n***H**-1]

B, in which n**H** is the size of the memory block and Þ**P** is a power set of **P**.

Memory allocation, $\Leftarrow$, is a fundamental computing operation that collects a unique memory block logically named *id***S** and physically located by *addr*Þ**P** accommodating n bytes of memory, i.e.:

$$id\textbf{S} \Leftarrow \text{MEM}[addr\text{Þ}\textbf{P}]\textbf{B}$$
$$\Leftrightarrow (\pi^{-1} : addr\text{Þ}\textbf{P} \to id\textbf{S}$$
$$\to id\textbf{S} = \text{MEM}[addr\textbf{P}, addr\textbf{P} + n\textbf{H} - 1]\textbf{B}$$
$$)$$

$$(4)$$

Memory allocation is a key meta-process for dynamic memory manipulation in RTOS+. The memory allocation process, *id***S** $\Leftarrow$ MEM[*addr***P**, *addr***P**+*n***H**-1]**B**, will be implemented in Figure 19.

Memory release, $\nLeftarrow$, is an inverse operation that dissociates and frees a unique block of n continuous physical memory elements denoted by *addr*Þ**P** from its logical identifier *id***S**, i.e.:

$$id\textbf{S} \nLeftarrow \text{MEM}[\bot]\textbf{B}$$
$$\Leftrightarrow (\pi : id\textbf{S} \to addr\text{Þ}\textbf{P}$$
$$\to \text{MEM}[addr\textbf{P}, addr\textbf{P} + n\textbf{H} - 1]\textbf{B} := \bot$$
$$\to addr\textbf{P} := \bot$$
$$\to id\textbf{S} := \bot$$
$$)$$

$$(5)$$

Figure 8. The UDM of the memory control block of RTOS+

$$\text{MemoryControlBlocks}\mathbf{ST} \triangleq \overset{\text{SCB}\mathbf{ST}.\#\text{MemBlocksUsed}\mathbf{N}}{\underset{MBN\mathbf{N}=1}{R}} \text{MCB(MBN}\mathbf{N})\mathbf{ST} ::$$

(<Staus : **BL** | Status**BL** = {(**T**, InUse), (**F**, Free)}>;
  <Size : **B** | Size**B** = n**N** ×10k**B**>;
  <StartingAddr : **H** | 0 ≤ StartingAddr**H** ≤ SCB**ST**.MaxMemory**B**-1>;
  <TimeAllocated : **hh:mm:ss:ms**>;
  <ReqProc : **N** | 1 ≤ ReqProc**N** ≤ SCB**ST**,#MaxProcs**N**>;
)

Memory release is a key meta-process that dissociates a given memory block from a logical identifier *id***S**, and returns the memory block to the system. The memory release process, *id***S** ⇎ MEM[⊥]**B**, will be implemented in Figure 19.

Memory read, ≻, is a meta-process of RTPA that gets data *x***B** from a given memory location MEM[*addr***P**], where *addr***P** is a pointer that identifies the physical memory address, i.e.:

$$\text{MEM}[addr\mathbf{P}]\mathbf{B} \succ x\mathbf{B} \tag{6}$$

Memory write, ≺, is a meta-process of RTPA that puts data *x***B** to a given memory location MEM[*addr***P**], where *addr***P** is a pointer that identifies the physical memory address, i.e.:

$$x\mathbf{B} \prec \text{MEM}[addr\mathbf{P}]\mathbf{B} \tag{7}$$

The memory control block (MCB) is a global control structure for system memory management. The UDM of MCBs of RTOS+,

$$\text{MemoryControlBlock}\mathbf{ST} = \overset{\text{SCB}\mathbf{ST}.\#\text{MemBlocksUsed}\mathbf{N}}{\underset{MBN\mathbf{N}=1}{R}}$$

MCB(MBN**N**)**ST**, is modeled as shown in Figure 8, which is a dynamic structure with varying number of MCBs controlled by SCB**ST**.#MemBlocksUsed**N** as a series of indexed records. An MCB(MBN**N**)**ST** registers the key information, such as its status, size in terms of a number of 10k**B**, starting address, time allocated, and required process (if any),

into the allocated memory block identified by the memory block number (MBN**N**) in RTOS+.

The Device Control Block and Ports

Devices in an operating system encompass a variety of generic and special-purpose hardware and interfaces. Typical I/O devices that an operating system deals with are those of system, storage, human interface, communication, and special devices. I/O devices are connected to the computer through buses with specific ports or I/O addresses. Usually, between an I/O device and the bus, there is a device controller and an associated device driver. The I/O management system of an operating system is designed to enable users to use and access system I/O devices seamlessly, harmoniously, and efficiently. I/O management techniques of operating systems can be described as polling, interrupt, DMA, and socket.

A general abstraction of device interfaces can be modeled by a special system architectural type known as the port. The generic *system I/O port model*, PORT**ST**, can be described as a finite linear space, i.e.:

$$\text{PORT}\mathbf{ST} \triangleq [addr_1\mathbf{H} \dots addr_2\mathbf{H}]\mathbf{B} \tag{8}$$

where *addr*$_1$**H** and *addr*$_2$**H** are the start and end addresses of the port space, and **B** is the byte type of each of the port I/O interfaces.

Figure 9. The UDM of the device control block of RTOS+

$$
\text{DeviceControlBlocks} \mathbf{ST} \triangleq \underset{DN\mathbf{N}=1}{\overset{\text{SCB}\mathbf{ST}.\#Devices\mathbf{N}}{R}} \text{DCB(DN}\mathbf{N})\mathbf{ST} ::
$$

```
(<DeviceID : S>;
 <Type : N | TypeN = {(0, Output), (1, Input), (2, I/O)}>;
 <Status : N | StatusN = {(0, Idle), (1, Seized), (2, InUse), (3, IntReq), (4, Faulty)}>;
 <InputPortAddr : N | F000 ≤ InputPortAddrN ≤ F0FFN>;
 <OutputPortAddr : N | F100 ≤ OutputPortAddrN ≤ F1FFN>;
 <IntPortAddr : N | 1000 ≤ IntPortAddrN ≤ 10FFN>;
 <TimeAllocated : hh:mm:ss:ms>;
 <ReqProc : N | 1 ≤ ReqProcN ≤ SCBST.MaxProcsN>
 <IntServiceProc : N | IntServiceProcN = DNN>
 )
```

Typical port manipulations are port input and output as modeled in the RTPA meta-processes. An *input*, denoted by $|\gg$, is a metaprocess that receives data $x\mathbf{B}$ from a given system I/O port PORT[$addr\mathbf{P}$] $\mathbf{B}$, where $addr\mathbf{P}$ is a pointer that identifies the physical address of the port interface, i.e.:

$$\text{PORT}[addr\mathbf{P}]\mathbf{B} \,|\gg\, x\mathbf{B} \tag{9}$$

An *output*, denoted by $|\ll$, is a meta-process that sends data $x\mathbf{B}$ to a given system I/O port PORT[$addr\mathbf{P}$]$\mathbf{B}$, where $addr\mathbf{P}$ is a pointer that identifies the physical address of the port interface, i.e.:

$$x\mathbf{B} \,|\ll\, \text{PORT}[addr\mathbf{P}]\mathbf{B} \tag{10}$$

The device control block (DCB) is a global control structure for system device management. The UDM of DCBs of RTOS+, Device-ControlBlocks$\mathbf{ST}$ = $\underset{DN\mathbf{N}=1}{\overset{\text{SCB}\mathbf{ST}.\#Devices\mathbf{N}}{R}}$ DCB(DN$\mathbf{N}$)$\mathbf{ST}$, is formally modeled in Figure 9, which is a dynamic structure with varying number of DCBs controlled by SCB$\mathbf{ST}$.#Devices$\mathbf{N}$ as a series of indexed records. A DCB(DN$\mathbf{N}$)$\mathbf{ST}$ registers the key informant, such as the device ID, type, status, addresses of input/output, interrupt ports, time allocated, and required process (if any), into a corresponding DCB identified by the device number (DN$\mathbf{N}$) in RTOS+.

Files

The file system is a type of abstract resources of operating systems. A *file* is a logical storage unit of data or code separated from its physical implementation and location. Types of files can be text, source code, executable code, object code, word processor formatted, or system library code. The attributes of files can be identified by name, type, location (path of directory), size, date/time, user ID, and access control information. Logical file structures can be classified as sequential and random files. The former are files that organize information as a list of ordered records; while the latter are files with fixed-length logical records accessible by its block number.

The file system of an operating system consists of a set of files and a directory structure that organizes all files and provides detailed information about them. The major function of a file management system is to map logical files onto physical storage devices such as disks or tapes. Most file systems organize files by a tree-structured directory. A file in the file system can be identified by its name and detailed attributes

Figure 10. The UDM of system files of RTOS+

$$
\begin{aligned}
\textbf{FilesST} &\triangleq \text{FileID}\textbf{ST} :: \\
&\quad (<\text{FileSize} : \mathbf{N} \mid 0 \leq \text{FileSize}\mathbf{N} \leq \text{SCB}\textbf{ST}.\text{Memory}\mathbf{B}\text{-}1>; \\
&\quad < \overset{\text{FileSize}\mathbf{N}}{\underset{i\mathbf{N}=1}{\mathrm{R}}}(<\text{Index}(i\mathbf{N})\textbf{ST}: \text{Array}\textbf{ST}>, <\text{Record}(\text{Key}\mathbf{N})\textbf{ST}: \text{Record}\textbf{ST}>)> \\
&\quad) \\[8pt]
\text{Index}(i\mathbf{N})\textbf{ST} &\triangleq (<i : \mathbf{N} \mid 0 \leq i\mathbf{N} \leq \text{FileSize}\mathbf{N}\text{-}1>; \\
&\quad\quad\quad <\text{Key} : \mathbf{N}> \\
&\quad\quad\quad) \\[8pt]
\text{Record}(\text{Key}\mathbf{N})\textbf{ST} &\triangleq (<\text{Key} : \mathbf{N} \mid 0 \leq \text{Key}\mathbf{N} \leq \text{FileSize}\mathbf{N}\text{-}1>; \\
&\quad\quad\quad\quad <\text{Data} : \mathbf{RT}> \\
&\quad\quad\quad\quad)
\end{aligned}
$$

provided by the file directory. The most frequently used method for directory management is a *hash table*. A physical file system can be implemented by contiguous, linked, and indexed allocation. Contiguous allocation can suffer from external fragmentation. Direct-access is inefficient with linked allocation. Indexed allocation may require substantial overheads for its index block. Typical file operations are reading, writing, and appending. Common file management operations are creating, deleting, opening, closing, copying, and renaming.

The file system of RTOS+, Files**ST**, is modeled using an index table and a set of records as shown in Figure 10. In the UDM of Files**ST**, each record has two components known as the Index**ST** and Record**ST**. The former uses an index $i\mathbf{N}$ in the index table to find the key, Key$\mathbf{N}$, that points to a record in Record**ST**. The latter is a set of records that holds a specific data record to Key$\mathbf{N}$. The formal model of Files**ST** supports both sequential and random access to the file system of RTOS+. Using the primary key of a record and its address, a record can be randomly accessed; while for sequential access, the entries in the index table can be sequentially accessed to locate a particular record through its address.

The Architecture of the Processes Subsystem

According to the high level architectural model of RTOS+ as given in Figure 3, the process subsystem of RTOS+, Processes**ST**, models a set of internal control UDMs and priority control queues such as the ProcessControlBlock**ST**, RequestQ**ST**, ReadyQH**ST**/ReadyQL**ST** for high/low priority processes, CompletedQ**ST**, InterruptedQ**ST**, DelayedQ**ST**, SuspendendQ**ST**, which support system state transitions in task scheduling as shown in Figures 1 and 2. The following subsections formally describe the architectures of the process control components by a set of UDMs in RTPA.

The Process Control Blocks

The UDM of the process control block in RTOS+,

$$
\text{ProcessConrolBlocks}\textbf{ST} = \overset{\text{SCB}\textbf{ST}.\#\text{Procs}\mathbf{N}}{\underset{\text{PN}\mathbf{N}=1}{\mathrm{R}}} \text{PCB}(\text{PN}\mathbf{N})
$$

ST, is specified in Figure 11. PCB**ST** models multiple tasks in RTOS+ indexed by the process number PN$\mathbf{N}$. Each task in the system is created as a process with a process number, a task priority class, status, time created, and resources required for such as memory, device, and event.

Figure 11. The UDM of process control block of RTOS+

$$
\mathbf{ProcessControlBlocksST} \triangleq \overset{SCB\mathbf{ST}.\#Procs\mathbf{N}}{\underset{PN\mathbf{N}=1}{R}} PCB(PN\mathbf{N})\mathbf{ST} ::
$$

(<TaskPriority : **N** | TaskPriority**N** = {(1, High), (2, Low)}>;
  <TaskStatus : **N** | TaskStatus**N** = {(0, Requested), (1, Created), (2, Ready), (3, Running), (4, Completed),
                         (5, Interrupted), (6, Delayed), (7, Suspended), (8, Killed), (9, IntService), (10, Free)}>;
  <TimeCreated : **hh:mm:ss:ms**>;
  <MemoryReq : **N** | 0 ≤ MemoryReq**N** ≤ SCB**ST**.MaxMemBlocks**N**>;
  <MemorySize : **B** | 0 ≤ MemorySize**B** ≤ 50kB>;
  <DeviceReq : **N** | 0 ≤ DeviceReq**N** ≤ SCB**ST**.MaxDevices**N**>;
  <DeviceID : **S**>;
  <EventReq : **N** | 0 ≤ Eventeq**N** ≤ SCB**ST**.MaxEvents**N**>;
  <TimerStatus : **BL** | TimerStatus**BL** = {(**T**, Timeout), (**F**, Timing)}>;
)

Figure 12. The schema and detailed UDM model of the system dispatching queues

$$
\mathbf{DispatchingQueuesST} \triangleq \overset{9}{\underset{i\mathbf{N}=1}{R}} Queue(i\mathbf{N})\mathbf{ST} ::
$$

(<Size : **N** | 0 ≤ Size**N** ≤ MaxProcs**N**-1>;
  <PN : **N** | 1 ≤ PN**N** ≤ SCB**ST**.MaxProcs**N**>;
  <CurrentPos : **P** | 0 ≤ CurrentPos**P** ≤ Size**N**-1>;
  <Empty : **BL** | {(**T**, Empty), (**F**, NotEmpty)}>;
  <Full : **BL** | {(**T**, Full), (**F**, NonFull)}>
)

= Queue(1)**ST** = RequestQ**ST**: (Size**N**, PN**N**, CurrentPos**P**, Empty**BL**, Full**BL**) := (1000, 0, 0, **T**, **F**)
‖ Queue(2)**ST** = WaitingQ**ST**: (Size**N**, PN**N**, CurrentPos**P**, Empty**BL**, Full**BL**) := (1000, 0, 0, **T**, **F**)
‖ Queue(3)**ST** = ReadyQH**ST**: (Size**N**, PN**N**, CurrentPos**P**, Empty**BL**, Full**BL**) := (6, 0, 0, **T**, **F**)
‖ Queue(4)**ST** = ReadyQL**ST**: (Size**N**, PN**N**, CurrentPos**P**, Empty**BL**, Full**BL**) := (4, 0, 0, **T**, **F**)
‖ Queue(5)**ST** = CompletedQ**ST**: (Size**N**, PN**N**, CurrentPos**P**, Empty**BL**, Full**BL**) := (1000, 0, 0, **T**, **F**)
‖ Queue(6)**ST** = InterruptedQ**ST**: (Size**N**, PN**N**, CurrentPos**P**, Empty**BL**, Full**BL**) := (1000, 0, 0, **T**, **F**)
‖ Queue(7)**ST** = DelayedQ**ST**: (Size**N**, PN**N**, CurrentPos**P**, Empty**BL**, Full**BL**) := (1000, 0, 0, **T**, **F**)
‖ Queue(8)**ST** = SuspendedQ**ST**: (Size**N**, PN**N**, CurrentPos**P**, Empty**BL**, Full**BL**) := (1000, 0, 0, **T**, **F**)
‖ Queue(9)**ST** = KilledQ**ST**: (Size**N**, PN**N**, CurrentPos**P**, Empty**BL**, Full**BL**) := (1000, 0, 0, **T**, **F**)

The Process Dispatching Queues

As specified in SCB**ST** as shown in Fig. 5, there are a set of nine dispatching queues adopted in RTOS+ such as RequestQ**ST**, WaitingQ**ST**, ReadyQH**ST**, ReadyQL**ST**, CompletedQ**ST**, InterruptedQ**ST**, DelayedQ**ST**, SuspendedQ**ST**, and KilledQ**ST**. A generic queue structure is modeled as shown in Fig. 12 that is shared by all system queues where the instances of the DispatchingQueues**ST** are also refined with their initial values.

The behaviors of queues can be generically modeled as *enqueue, serve, clear, empty test* and *full test* in addition to *create* and *release* of queues (Wang, 2007), i.e.:

$$
\mathbf{QueueST}.\mathbf{StaticBehaviorsPC} \triangleq \mathbf{CreatePC}
$$
$$
\begin{vmatrix} \mathbf{Enqueue\ PC} \\ \mathbf{Serve\ PC} \\ \mathbf{Clear\ PC} \\ \mathbf{EmptyTest\ PC} \\ \mathbf{FullTest\ PC} \end{vmatrix}
$$

(11)

where *enqueue* is a process that appends a process at the end of the queue; and serve is a process that fetches the front process of the queue and shifts the remainder elements toward the front of the queue by one element.

The system architectural models specified in this section provide a set of abstract object models and rigorous interfaces between system hardware and software. By reaching this point, the co-design of a real-time system can be separately carried out by separated hardware and software teams. It is recognized that system architecture specification by the means of UDMs is a fundamental and the most difficult part in software system modeling, while conventional technologies and languages hardly provide any support for this purpose. On the basis of the system architecture specification and with the work products of system architectural components or UDMs, the specification of the operational components of the RTOS+ system as behavioral processes can be carried out directly as elaborated in the second part of this work on the static and dynamic behavioral models of RTOS+ as presented in (Wang et al., 2010c).

CONCLUSION

The design of real-time operating systems has been recognized as a comprehensive and complex system design paradigm in computing, software engineering, and information system design. This paper has demonstrated that the RTOS+ system, including its architecture, static behaviors, and dynamic behaviors, can be essentially and sufficiently described by RTPA. On the basis of the formal specifications of RTOS+ by the coherent set of UDMs and UPMs in RTPA, the architectural and behavioral consistency and run-time integrity of an RTOS have been significantly enhanced. It has been identified that RTOS+ can be applied not only as a formal design paradigm of RTOS's, but also a support framework for a wide range of applications in design and implementation of

real-time and embedded systems. The RTOS+ system model may have also provided a test bench for the expressive power and modeling capability of existing formal methods in software engineering.

With a stepwise specification and refinement methodology for describing both system architectural and operational components, the formal model of the RTOS+ system has provided a foundation for implementation of a derived real-time operating system in multiple programming languages and on different operating platforms. It has also improved the controllability, reliability, maintainability, and quality of the design and implementation in real-time software engineering. The formal models of RTOS+ have been adopted as part of the supporting environment for the implementation of the RTPA-based software code generator (RTPA-CG) (Wang et al., 2010b; Ngolah & Wang, 2009). On the basis of the formal and rigorous models of the RTOS+ system, code can be automatically generated by RTPA-CG or be manually transferred from the formal models.

A series of formal design models of real-world and real-time applications in RTPA have been developed using RTPA notations and methodologies (Wang, 2002, 2007, 2008a, 2008b, 2008c, 2009a; Wang & Huang, 2008) in the formal design engineering approach, such as the telephone switching system (Wang, 2009b), the lift dispatching system (Wang et al., 2009), the automated teller machine (ATM) (Wang et al., 2010a), the real-time operating system (RTOS+), the air traffic control system (to be reported), the railway dispatching system (to be reported), and the intelligent traffic lights control system (to be reported). Further studies have demonstrated that RTPA is not only useful as a generic notation and methodology for software engineering, but also good at modeling human cognitive processes in cognitive informatics and computational intelligence as reported in (Wang, 2008d, 2009a; Wang & Ruhe, 2007; Wang & Chiew, 2010).

ACKNOWLEDGMENT

The authors would like to acknowledge the Natural Science and Engineering Council of Canada (NSERC) for its partial support to this work. We would like to thank the reviewers for their valuable comments and suggestions.

REFERENCES

Anderson, T. E., Lazowska, E. D., & Levy, H. M. (1989). The Performance Implications of Thread Management Alternatives for Shared-Memory Multiprocessors. *IEEE Transactions on Computers*, *38*(12), 1631–1644. doi:10.1109/12.40843

Bollella, G., & Brosgol, B. (2002). *The Real-Time Specification for Java*. Reading: Addison Wesley.

Brinch-Hansen, P. (1971, October). Short-Term Scheduling in Multiprogramming Systems. In *Proceedings of the Third ACM Symposium on Operating Systems Principles* (pp. 103-105).

Deitel, H. M., & Kogan, M. S. (1992). *The Design of OS/2*. Reading, MA: Addison-Wesley.

Dijkstra, E. W. (1968). The Structure of the THE Multiprogramming System. *Communications of the ACM*, *11*(5), 341–346. doi:10.1145/363095.363143

ETTX. (2009, February). In *Proceedings of the First Eueopean TinyOS Technology Exchange*, Cork, Ireland.

Ford, B., Back, G., Benson, G., Lepreau, J., Lin, A., & Shivers, O. (1997). The Flux OSKit: a Substrate for OS and Language Research. In *Proceedings of the 16th ACM Symposium on Operating Systems Principles*, Saint Malo, France.

ISO/IEC 9945-1. (1996). ISO/IEC Standard 9945-1: Information Technology-Portable Operating System Interface (POSIX) - Part 1: System Application Program Interface (API) (C Language). *ISO/IEC*.

Kreuzinger, J., Brinkschult, U. S., & Ungerer, T. (2002). *Real-Time Event Handling and Scheduling on a Multithréad Java Microntroller*. Maryland Heights, MO: Elsevier Science Publications.

Labrosse, J. J. (1999). *MicroC/OS-II, The Real-Time Kernel* (2nd ed.). Gilroy, CA: R&D Books.

Lamie, E. L. (2008). *Real-Time Embedded Multithreading using ThreadX and MIPS*. Newnes.

Laplante, P. A. (1977). *Real-Time Systems Design and Analysis* (2nd ed.). Washington, DC: IEEE Press.

Lewis, B., & Berg, D. (1998). *Multithreaded Programming with Pthreads*. Upper Saddle River, NJ: Sun Microsystems Press.

Liu, C., & Layland, J. (1973). Scheduling Algorithms for Multiprogramming in Hard-Real-Time Environments. *Journal of the Association for Computing Machinery*, *20*(1), 46–56.

McDermid, J. (Ed.). (1991). *Software Engineer's Reference Book*. Oxford, UK: Butterworth Heinemann Ltd.

Ngolah, C. F., & Wang, Y. (2009). Tool Support for Software Development based on Formal Specifications in RTPA. *International Journal of Software Engineering and Its Applications*, *3*(3), 71–88.

Ngolah, C. F., Wang, Y., & Tan, X. (2004). The Real-Time Task Scheduling Algorithm of RTOS+. *IEEE Canadian Journal of Electrical and Computer Engineering*, *29*(4), 237–243.

Peterson, J. L., & Silberschantz, A. (1985). *Operating System Concepts*. Reading, MA: Addison-Wesley.

Rivas, M. A., & Harbour, M. G. (2001, May). MaRTE OS: An Ada Kernel for Real-Time Embedded Applications. In Proceedings of Ada-Europe 2001, Leuven, Belgium.

Sha, L., Rajkumar, R., & Lehoczky, J. P. (1990, September). Priority Inheritance Protocols: An Approach to Real-Time Synchronization. *IEEE Transactions on Computers*, 1175. doi:10.1109/12.57058

Silberschatz, A., Galvin, P., & Gagne, G. (2003). *Applied Operating System Concepts* (1st ed.). New York: John Wiley & Sons, Inc.

Tanenbaum, A. S. (1994). *Distributed Operating Systems*. Upper Saddle River, NJ: Prentice Hall Inc.

Viscarola, P. G., & Mason, W. A. (2001). *Windows NT Device Driver Development*. Indianapolis, IN: Macmillan Technical Publishing.

Wang, Y. (2002). The Real-Time Process Algebra (RTPA). *Annals of Software Engineering: An International Journal*, *14*, 235–274. doi:10.1023/A:1020561826073

Wang, Y. (2004). Operating Systems . In Dorf, R. (Ed.), *The Engineering Handbook* (2nd ed.). Boca Raton, FL: CRC Press.

Wang, Y. (2007). *Software Engineering Foundations: A Software Science Perspective* (CRC Series in Software Engineering, Vol. 2). Boston: Auerbach Publications.

Wang, Y. (2008a). RTPA: A Denotational Mathematics for Manipulating Intelligent and Computational Behaviors. *International Journal of Cognitive Informatics and Natural Intelligence*, *2*(2), 44–62.

Wang, Y. (2008b). Mathematical Laws of Software. *Transactions of Computational Science*, *2*, 46–83. doi:10.1007/978-3-540-87563-5_4

Wang, Y. (2008c). Deductive Semantics of RTPA. *International Journal of Cognitive Informatics and Natural Intelligence*, *2*(2), 95–121.

Wang, Y. (2008d). On Contemporary Denotational Mathematics for Computational Intelligence. *Transactions of Computational Science*, *2*, 6–29. doi:10.1007/978-3-540-87563-5_2

Wang, Y. (2009a). Paradigms of Denotational Mathematics for Cognitive Informatics and Cognitive Computing. *Fundamenta Informaticae*, *90*(3), 282–303.

Wang, Y. (2009b). The Formal Design Model of a Telephone Switching System (TSS). *International Journal of Software Science and Computational Intelligence*, *1*(3), 92–116.

Wang, Y., & Chiew, V. (2010). On the Cognitive Process of Human Problem Solving. *Cognitive Systems Research: An International Journal*, *11*(1), 81–92. doi:10.1016/j.cogsys.2008.08.003

Wang, Y., & Huang, J. (2008). Formal Modeling and Specification of Design Patterns Using RTPA. *International Journal of Cognitive Informatics and Natural Intelligence*, *2*(1), 100–111.

Wang, Y., Ngolah, C. F., Ahmadi, H., Sheu, P. C. Y., & Ying, S. (2009). The Formal Design Model of a Lift Dispatching System (LDS). *International Journal of Software Science and Computational Intelligence*, *1*(4), 98–122.

Wang, Y., & Ruhe, G. (2007). The Cognitive Process of Decision Making. *International Journal of Cognitive Informatics and Natural Intelligence*, *1*(2), 73–85.

Wang, Y., Tan, X., & Ngolah, C. F. (2010b). Design and Implementation of an Autonomic Code Generator based on RTPA. *International Journal of Software Science and Computational Intelligence*, *2*(2)44-67.

Wang, Y., Zeng, G., Ngolah, C. F., Sheu, P. C. Y., Choy, C. P., & Tian, Y. (2010c. (in press). The Formal Design Model of a Real-Time Operating System (RTOS+): Static and Dynamic Behavior Models. *International Journal of Software Science and Computational Intelligence*.

Wang, Y., Zhang, Y., Sheu, P., Li, X., & Guo, H. (2010a). The Formal Design Models of an Automatic Teller Machine (ATM). *International Journal of Software Science and Computational Intelligence*, 2(1), 102–131.

Yodaiken, V. (1999, May). An RT-Linux Manifesto. In *Proceedings of the 5th Linux Expo*, Raleigh, NC.

Chapter 14
The Formal Design Model of a Real-Time Operating System (RTOS+):
Static and Dynamic Behaviors

Yingxu Wang
University of Calgary, Canada

Phillip C.-Y. Sheu
Wuhan University, China and University of California, Irvine, USA

Guangping Zeng
University of Science and Technology, China and University of California, Berkeley, USA

C. Philip Choy
University of Calgary, Canada

Cyprian F. Ngolah
Sentinel Trending & Diagnostics Ltd., Canada

Yousheng Tian
University of Calgary, Canada

ABSTRACT

A real-time operating system (RTOS) provides a platform for the design and implementation of a wide range of applications in real-time systems, embedded systems, and mission-critical systems. This paper presents a formal design model for a general RTOS known as RTOS+ that enables a specific target RTOS to be rigorously and efficiently derived in real-world applications. The methodology of a denotational mathematics, Real-Time Process Algebra (RTPA), is described for formally modeling and refining architectures, static behaviors, and dynamic behaviors of RTOS+. The conceptual model of the RTOS+ system is introduced as the initial requirements for the system. The architectural model of RTOS+ is created using RTPA architectural modeling methodologies and refined by a set of Unified Data Models (UDMs). The static behaviors of RTOS+ are specified and refined by a set of Unified Process Models (UPMs). The dynamic behaviors of the RTOS+ system are specified and refined by the real-time process scheduler and system dispatcher. This work is presented in two papers in serial due to its excessive length. The static and dynamic behavioral models of RTOS+ is described in this paper; while the conceptual and architectural models of RTOS+ has been published in IJSSCI 2(2).

DOI: 10.4018/978-1-4666-0264-9.ch014

INTRODUCTION

An *operating system* is a set of integrated system software that organizes, manages, and controls the resources and computing power of a computer or a computer network. It also provides users a logical interface for accessing the physical machine in order to run applications. A general-purpose operating system may be perceived as an agent between the hardware and resources of a computer and the applications and users. An operating system may be divided into three subsystems known as those of the *kernel* or *system management*, the *resource management*, and the *process management* (Dijkstra, 1968; Brinch-Hansen, 1971; Liu & Layland, 1973; Peterson & Silberschantz, 1985; Anderson et al., 1989; McDermid, 1991; Deitel & Kogan, 1992; Tanenbaum, 1994; Viscarola & Mason, 2001; Silberschatz et al., 2003; Wang, 2004, 2007). The kernel of an operating system is a set of central components for computing, including CPU scheduling and process management. The resource management subsystem is a set of supporting functions for various system resources and user interfaces. The process management subsystem is a set of transition manipulation mechanisms for processes and threads interacting with the system kernel and resources.

A *real-time operating system* (RTOS) is an operating system that supports and guarantees timely responses to external and internal events of real-time systems (Laplante, 1977; Sha et al., 1990; ISO/IEC, 1996; Ford, 1997; Bollella et al., 2002; Kreuzinger et al., 2002; Ngolah, Wang, & Tan, 2004). An RTOS monitors, responds to, and controls an external environment, which is connected to the computer system through sensors, actuators, or other input-output (I/O) devices. In a real-time system in general and an RTOS in particular, the correctness of system behaviors depends not only on the logical results of computation but also on the time point at which the results are obtained. Real-time systems can be divided into hard and soft real-time systems. In the former, a failure to meet timing constraints will be of serious consequences, while in the latter, a timing failure may not significantly affect the functioning of the system.

A great variety of RTOS's have been developed in the last decades (Lewis & Berg, 1998; Labrosse, 1999; Yodaiken, 1999; Rivas & Harbour, 2001; Lamie, 2008; ETTX, 2009). The existing RTOS's are characterized as target-machine-specific, implementation-dependent, and not formally modeled. Therefore, they are usually not portable as a generic real-time operating system to be seamlessly incorporated into real-time or embedded system implementations. Problems often faced by RTOS's are CPU and tasks scheduling, time/event management, and resource management. Efficient and precise methodologies and notations for describing solutions to these problems are critical in RTOS design and implementation. Generally, RTOS's require multitasking, process threads, and a sufficient number of interrupt levels to deal with the random interrupt mechanisms in real-time systems. In modern RTOS's, *multitasking* is a technique used for enabling multiple tasks to share a single processor. A *thread* is individual execution of a process in order to handle concurrent tasks. In addition, an *interrupt* is a request of an external device or internal process that causes the operating system to suspend the execution of a current low priority task, serve the interrupt, and hand control back to the interrupted process.

This paper develops a comprehensive design paradigm of the formal real-time operating system (RTOS+) in a top-down approach on the basis of the RTPA methodology. The conceptual model, architectural model, and the static/dynamic behavioral models of RTOS+ are systematically presented. In the remainder of this paper, the conceptual model of RTOS+ is described as the initial requirements for the system. The architectural model of RTOS+ is created based on the conceptual model using the RTPA architectural modeling methodologies and refined by a set of unified data models (UDMs). Then, the static behaviors of RTOS+ are specified and refined by a set of unified process models (UPMs). The dynamic behaviors of RTOS+ are specified and refined by process priority allocation, process scheduling, and system dispatching models. Due to its excessive length and complexity, this paper presents the second part of RTOS+ on its static and dynamic behavioral models following in serial with the conceptual and architectural models of RTOS+ published in IJSSCI 2(2) (Wang et al., 2010c).

THE STATIC BEHAVIORAL MODELS OF THE RTOS+ SYSTEM

According to the RTPA methodology, a static behavior is an encapsulated function of a given system that can be determined before run-time (Wang, 2007). On the basis of the system architecture specifications and with the UDMs of system architectural components developed in the preceding section, the operational components of the given RTOS+ system and their behaviors can be specified as a set of UPMs as behavioral processes operating on the UDMs.

The basic functions of operating systems can be classified as system management, resources management, and processes management. The high-level static behaviors of RTOS+, RTOS+**§**. StaticBehaviors**PC**, encompasses three process subsystems such as SystemManagement**PC**, ResourcesManagement**PC**, and ProcessesManagement**PC** in parallel as specified below:

$$
\begin{aligned}
\text{RTOS+}\textbf{§}.\text{StaticBehaviors}\textbf{PC} \triangleq\ &\text{SystemManagement}\textbf{PC} \\
&\|\ \text{ResourcesManagement}\textbf{PC} \\
&\|\ \text{ProcessesManagement}\textbf{PC} \quad (12)
\end{aligned}
$$

The high level specification of RTOS+**§**. StaticBehaviors**PC** as given in Eq. 12 can be further extended and refined as shown in Figure 13 by a set of UPMs. Each schema of the UPMs in Figure 13 models the input data objects (<**I**:: (..)>), output data objects (<**O**:: (..)>), and operated UDMs (<**UDM**:: (..)>) for a specific behavioral process of RTOS+. The UDMs play an important role in system architectural design as global and permanent I/O structures, which usually have a longer life-span than those of the process created or invoked them, particularly in a real-time system.

The following subsections describe how the RTOS+ static behaviors in the three subsystems as specified in Figure 13 are modeled and refined using the denotational mathematical notations and methodologies of RTPA (Wang, 2007, 2008a).

UPMs for System Management in RTOS+

According to the high level specifications of the static behaviors of RTOS+ as given in Figure 13, the *system management* subsystem of RTOS+ encompasses a set of five behavioral processes such as system initialization, system clock manipulation, system event capture, Device interrupt handling, and the CPU scheduler, i.e.: (see Exhibit 1)

Exhibit 1.

SystemManagement**PC** ≜
(SysInitial**PC**(<**I**:: ( )>; <**O**:: ( )>; <**UDM**:: SCB**ST**, PCB**ST**, DCB**ST**, ECB**ST**, MCB**ST**, SysClock**ST**>)
| SysClock**PC**(<**I**:: @1ms⊙>; <**O**:: §t**N**, §t **hh:mm:ss:ms**)>; <**UDM**:: SysClcok**ST**, SCB**ST**>)
| SysEventCapture**PC**(<**I**:: ( )>; <**O**:: RequestQ**ST**>; <**UDM**:: SCB**ST**, DCB**ST**, ECB**ST**, SysClock**ST**>)
| DeviceInterruptHandling**PC**(<**I**:: @DeviceInt⊙>; <**O**:: InterruptedQ**ST**>; <**UDM**:: SCB**ST**, DCB**ST**, ECB**ST**, MCB**ST**, CPU**ST**>)
| CPUScheduling**PC**(<**I**:: ReadyQH**ST**, ReadyQL**ST**>; <**O**:: CompletedQ**ST**, DelayedQ**ST**, InterruptedQ**ST**, SuspendedQ**ST**>;

<**UDM**:: SCB**ST**, PCB**ST**, DCB**ST**, ECB**ST**, MCB**ST**, CPU**ST**, SysClock**ST**>) (13)

Figure 13. High level specification of the static behaviors of RTOS+

```
RTOS+§.StaticBehaviorsPC ≙ {  SystemManagementPC
                              || ResourcesManagementPC
                              || ProcessesManagementPC
                              }
 = {( SysInitialPC(<I:: ( )>; <O:: ( )>; <UDM:: SCBST, PCBST, DCBST, ECBST, MCBST, SysClockST>)
    | SysClockPC(<I:: @1ms⊙>; <O:: §trN, §tchh:mm:ss:ms)>; <UDM:: SysClcokST, SCBST>)
    | SysEventCapturePC(<I:: ( )>; <O:: RequestQST>; <UDM:: SCBST, DCBST, ECBST, SysClockST>)
    | DeviceInterruptHandlingPC(<I:: @DeviceInt⊙>; <O:: InterruptedQST>; <UDM:: SCBST, DCBST, ECBST, MCBST, CPUST>)
    | CPUSchedulingPC(<I:: ReadyQHST, ReadyQLST>; <O:: CompletedQST, DelayedQST, InterruptedQST, SuspendedQST>;
                      <UDM:: SCBST, PCBST, DCBST, ECBST, MCBST, CPUST, SysClockST>)
   )
  | ( AllocateMemoryPC (<I:: PNN>; <O:: MemIDN, ⓢMemAllocatedBL>; <UDM:: SCBST, PCBST, ECBST, RCBST, MCBST>)
    | ReleaseMemory(<I:: MemIDN>; <O:: ⓢMemReleasedBL>; <UDM:: SCBST, PCBST, DCBST, ECBST, MCBST>)
    | GetDevicePC(<I:: DeviceTypeN, PNN>; <O:: DNN, ⓢDeviceAllocatedBL>; <UDM:: SCBST, DCBST, PCBST>)
    | ReleaseDevicePC(<I:: DNN>; <O:: ( )>; <UDM:: SCBST, DCBST>)
    | FileManagementPC(<I:: FileIDS>; <O:: ( )>; <UDM:: FilesST>)
   )
  | ( ProcessRequestPC(<I:: TaskPriorityN, MemoryReqB, DeviceReqN>; <O:: RequestQST>; <UDM:: SCBST, PCBST>)
    | ProcessCreationPC(<I:: RequestQST>; <O:: WaitingQST>; <UDM:: SCBST, PCBST, DCBST, ECBST, MCBST, KilledQST>)
    | ProcessReadyPC(<I:: WaitingQST>; <O:: ReadyQHST, ReadyQLST>; <UDM:: SCBST, PCBST, DCBST, ECBST, MCBST>)
    | ProcessRunningPC = CPUSchedulerPC
    | ProcessCompletedPC(<I:: CompletedQST>; <O:: ( )>; <UDM:: SCBST, PCBST, DCBST, ECBST, MCBST>)
    | ProcessInterruptedPC(<I:: InterruptQST>; <O:: ReadyQHST, ReadyQLST>;
                           <UDM:: SCBST, PCBST, DCBST, ECBST, MCBST, CPUST, KilledQST>)
    | ProcessDelayedPC(<I:: DelayedQST>; <O:: ReadyQHST, ReadyQLST>;
                       <UDM:: SCBST, PCBST, DCBST, ECBST, MCBST, KilledQST>)
    | ProcessSuspendedPC(<I:: SuspendedQST>; <O:: ReadyQHST, ReadyQLST>;
                         <UDM:: SCBST, PCBST, DCBST, ECBST, MCBST, KilledQST>)
    | ProcessKilledPC(<I:: KilledQST>; <O:: ( )>; <UDM:: SCBST, PCBST, ECBST, RCBST, MEMST, PORTST, CPUST>)
   )
}
```

The detailed UPMs of the system management processes of RTOS+ are refined and elaborated in the following subsections.

A) The System Initialization Process

The system initialization process boots the entire operating system, sets its initial environment, and pre-assigns the initial values of data objects of the system such as variables, constants, as well as architectural (hardware interface) and control (internal) UDMs. Initialization is crucially important for a real-time operating system as well as its control logic specified in the behavioral processes.

The *system initialization* process of RTOS+, SysInitial**PC**, is modeled in Figure 14, where all system architectural and control UDMs are initialized as specified in the architectural models. It also sets the predetermined initial values of internal control models, system status, and system events. The central function of SysInitial**PC** is the initialization of the global system control block SCB**ST**, which registers and monitors the system processes, resources, events, and status as well as the current sizes of all dispatching queues.

B) The System Clock Process

The *system clock* process maintains and updates an absolute (calendar) clock and a relative clock for the operating system in order to synchronize all activities, behaviors, events, and states of RTOS+.

Figure 14. The behavior model of the system initialization process

```
SysInitial(<I:: ( )>; <O:: ( )>;
            <UDM:: SCBST, PCBST, DCBST, ECBST, MCBST, SysClockST>)PC ≙
{Initial RTOS+_UDMsST                                    // Initialization of all UDMs
  → SysClockST.§t_rN := 0
  → SysClockST.§t_c hh:mm:ss:ms := CurrentTime hh:mm:ss:ms  // Set current time
  → SCBST.#ProcRequestsN := 0                             // Reset system control blocks
  → SCBST.#ProcWaitingN := 0
  → SCBST.#ProcReadyHN := 0
  → SCBST.#ProcReadyLN := 0
  → SCBST.#ProcCompletedN := 0
  → SCBST.#ProcInterruptedN := 0
  → SCBST.#ProcDelayedN := 0
  → SCBST.#ProcSuspendedN := 0
  → SCBST.#ProcKiledN := 0
  → SCBST.#MemBlocksUsedN := 0
  → SCBST.#DevicesN := 0
  → SCBST.#FilesN := 0
  → SCBST.#ProcsN := 0
  → SCBST.#EventsN := 0
  → SCBST.#InterruptsN := 0
  → SCBST.#TimersN := 0
  → SCBST.CurrentPN := 0
  → SCBST.CurrentEN := 0
  → SCBST.CurrentDN := 0
  → SCBST.Ⓢ RunEndBL := T
}
```

The system clock process of RTOS+, SysClock**PC**, is modeled in Figure 15. The source of the system clock is obtained from the 1ms time interrupt signal generated by the system hardware, by which the absolute clock with real-time millisecond, second, minute, and hour, $\S t_c$ **hh:mm:ss:ms**, are generated and periodically updated. The second clock in RTOS+ is the relative clock, $\S t_r$**N**, which is adopted for relative timing and duration manipulations. SysClock**PC** updates the relative clock $\S t_r$**N** per millisecond, and resets it to zero at midnight every day in order to prevent it from overflow.

In addition to the function of system clock maintaining, SysClock**PC** also updates all timers created by application processs by deceasing its current value by 1ms if it has not reached the timeout status, i.e., Timer(i**N**)**ms** = 0. The timeout event of a specific timer will be detected by the system in order to trigger a suitable action in a corresponding application process identified by an ECB**ST** and the event PCB(PN**N**)**ST**.TimerStatus**BL**:= **T**.

C) The System Event Capture Process

Events capture and handling are important behaviors of a real-time operating system. The event types in RTOS+ can be classified into *operational, time,* and *interrupt* events, which are identified by the common event prefix @ and the type suffixes **S**, **TM**, and ⊙, respectively, where **TM** is an abbreviation of time **TI** = **hh:mm:ss:ms**, date **D** = **yy:MM:dd**, and date-time **DT** = **yyyy:MM:dd:hh:mm:ss:ms**. Although a time event @t**TM** occurs at a given

Figure 15. The behavior model of the system clock process

$$
\begin{aligned}
&\textbf{SysClock}(<\textbf{I}:: @1ms\ >; <\textbf{O}:: §t_r\textbf{N}, §t_c\textbf{hh:mm:ss:ms}>; <\textbf{UDM}:: \text{SysClcok}\textbf{ST}, \text{SCB}\textbf{ST}>)\textbf{PC} \triangleq \\
&\{\ \uparrow(\text{SysClock}\textbf{ST}.§t_r\textbf{N}) &&\text{// Update relative clock} \\
&\quad \uparrow(\text{SysClock}\textbf{ST}.§t_c\textbf{ms}) &&\text{// Update absolute clock} \\
&\quad\quad \to \blacklozenge\ \text{SysClock}\textbf{ST}.§t_c\textbf{ms} = 1000 \\
&\quad\quad\quad \to \text{SysClock}\textbf{ST}.§t_c\textbf{ms} := 000 \\
&\quad\quad\quad \to \uparrow(\text{SysClock}\textbf{ST}.§t_c\textbf{ss}) \\
&\quad\quad\quad \to \blacklozenge\ \text{SysClock}\textbf{ST}.§t_c\textbf{ss} = 60 \\
&\quad\quad\quad\quad \to \text{SysClock}\textbf{ST}.§t_c\textbf{ss} := 00 \\
&\quad\quad\quad\quad \to \uparrow(\text{SysClock}\textbf{ST}.§t_c\textbf{mm}) \\
&\quad\quad\quad\quad \to \blacklozenge\ \text{SysClock}\textbf{ST}.§t_c\textbf{mm} = 60 \\
&\quad\quad\quad\quad\quad \to \text{SysClock}\textbf{ST}.§t_c\textbf{mm} := 00 \\
&\quad\quad\quad\quad\quad \to \uparrow(\text{SysClock}\textbf{ST}.§t_c\textbf{hh}) \\
&\quad\quad\quad\quad\quad\quad \to \blacklozenge\ \text{SysClock}\textbf{ST}.§t_c\textbf{hh} = 24 \\
&\quad\quad\quad\quad\quad\quad\quad \to \text{SysClock}\textbf{ST}.§t_c\textbf{hh} := 00 \\
&\quad\quad\quad\quad\quad\quad\quad \to \text{SysClock}\textbf{ST}.§t_r\textbf{N} := 0 &&\text{// Relative clock reset} \\
&\quad\quad\quad\quad\quad\quad\quad \to \text{SCB}\textbf{ST}.\#\text{Procs}\textbf{N} := 0 &&\text{// Update system control block} \\
&\quad\quad\quad\quad\quad\quad\quad \to \text{SCB}\textbf{ST}.\#\text{Events}\textbf{N} := 0 \\
\end{aligned}
$$

$$
\begin{aligned}
&\to\ \mathop{\textbf{R}}\limits_{i\textbf{N}=1}^{\text{SCB}\textbf{ST}.\#\text{Timers}\textbf{N}}\ (\ \blacklozenge\ \text{Timer}(i\textbf{N})\textbf{ST}.\text{Timer}\textbf{ms} \neq 0 \\
&\quad\quad\quad\quad \to \downarrow(\ \text{Timer}(i\textbf{N})\textbf{ST}.\text{Timer}\textbf{ms}) &&\text{// Update timers} \\
&\quad\quad\quad |\blacklozenge \\
&\quad\quad\quad\quad \to \uparrow(\text{SCB}\textbf{ST}.\#\text{Events}\textbf{N}) \\
&\quad\quad\quad\quad \to \text{EN}\textbf{N} := \text{SCB}\textbf{ST}.\#\text{Events}\textbf{N} \\
&\quad\quad\quad\quad \to \text{ECB}(\text{EN}\textbf{N})\textbf{ST}.\text{Status}\textbf{BL} := \textbf{T} \\
&\quad\quad\quad\quad \to \text{ECB}(\text{EN}\textbf{N})\textbf{ST}.\text{Type}\textbf{N} := 2 &&\text{// Time out event} \\
&\quad\quad\quad\quad \to \text{ECB}(\text{EN}\textbf{N})\textbf{ST}.\text{TimeDetected}\textbf{hh:mm:ss:ms} := §t_c\textbf{hh:mm:ss:ms} \\
&\quad\quad\quad\quad \to \text{ECB}(\text{EN}\textbf{N})\textbf{ST}.\text{SourceProc}\textbf{N} := \text{Timer}(i\textbf{N})\textbf{ST}.\text{SourceProc}\textbf{N} \\
&\quad\quad\quad\quad \to \text{PN}\textbf{N} := \text{Timer}(i\textbf{N})\textbf{ST}.\text{SourceProc}\textbf{N} \\
&\quad\quad\quad\quad \to \text{PCB}(\text{PN}\textbf{N})\textbf{ST}.\text{TimerStatus}\textbf{BL} := \textbf{T} \\
&\quad\quad\quad) \\
&\} \\
\end{aligned}
$$

system time point or periodically, the operational event @e$\textbf{S}$ and interrupt event @e$\odot$ may occur randomly. A special kind of operational events is the exception events, @ex$\textbf{S}$, which is detected by the system *exception detection* process !(@ex$\textbf{S}$) in order to log a detected exception event at runtime. The RTPA exception detection mechanism provides a fundamental process for safety and dependable system specification, which enables system exception detection, handling, or postmortem analysis to be implemented.

The system event capture process of RTOS+, SysEventCapture$\textbf{PC}$, is a low interrupt level pro-

cess that monitors and handles operational events (@e$\textbf{S}$) generated by a device as shown in Figure 16. SysEventCapture$\textbf{PC}$ detects any event occurred externally in order to create a corresponding event control block, ECB$\textbf{ST}$, as modeled in the UDMs of RTOS+. A detected device I/O event will be used to create a new process required by the event. Processing separately as that of external (device) events, however, the time and interrupt events will be handled by system dynamic behaviors (Figure 30) and DeviceIntteruptHandingPC (Figure 17), respectively.

Figure 16. The behavior model of the system event capture process

```
SysEventCapture(◁:: ( )>; <O:: (RequestQST)>; <UDM :: SCBST, DCBST, ECBST, SysClockST>)PC ≜
{ // External event scan
      SCBST.#DevicesN
  →        R          (◆ (DCB(iN)ST.TypeN < 1 ∨ DCB(iN)ST.TypeN = 2)
        iN=1
                   ∧ DCB(iN)ST.StatusN < 3                              // Device in use
                   → PORTST(DCB(iN)ST.InputPortAddrH)B |> EventScanB
                      → ◆ EventScanB ∧ 0000 0001B ≠ 0
                          → ↑(SCBST.#EventsN)
                          → ENN := SCBST.#EventsN
                          → ECB(ENN)ST.StatusBL := T
                          → ECB(ENN)ST.TypeN := 2                       // I/O event
                          → ECB(ENN)ST.TimeDetectedhh:mm:ss:ms := §tchh:mm:ss:ms
                          → ECB(ENN)ST.DeviceReqN := iN
                          → ECB(ENN)ST.SourceProcN := 0
                          → ECB(ENN)ST.TargetProcN := 0
                          // Create new process request by Device I/O
                          → ↑(SCBST.#ProcsN)
                          → PNN := SCBST.#ProcsN
                          → PCB(PNN)ST.TaskPriorityN := 1               // High level
                          → PCB(PNN)ST.MemorySizeB := 50kB
                          → PCB(PNN)ST.TimeCreatedhh:mm:ss:ms := §tchh:mm:ss:ms
                          → PCB(PNN)ST.DeviceIDS := DCB(iN)ST.DeviceIDS
                          → PCB(PNN)ST.TaskStatusN := 0                 // Process requested
                          ↦ EnqueuePC(◁:: PNN>; < O:: ( )>; <UDM:: RequestQST>)
                          → ↑(SCBST.#ProcRequestsN)
                   )
}
```

D) The Device Interrupt Handling Process

The interrupt mechanism enables execution priority change and control-taking-over between processes. An *interrupt*, denoted by ξ, is a parallel process relation in which a running process P is temporarily held before termination by another higher priority process Q triggered by an interrupt event $@e\odot$ at the interrupt point $\odot$. The interrupted process P will then be resumed after process Q has been completed, i.e.:

$$P \xi Q = P \parallel (@int\odot \nearrow Q \searrow \odot) \qquad (14)$$

where $\nearrow$ and $\searrow$ denote an *interrupt service* and an *interrupt return*.

Therefore, an *interrupt-driven dispatch*, denoted by $\hookmapsto$ is a process operation in which the ith process P_i is triggered by a predefined system interrupt $@int_i\odot$, i.e.:

$$@int_i\odot \hookmapsto P_i, i \in \{1, ..., n\} \qquad (15)$$

The device interrupt handling process of RTOS+, DeviceInterruptHandling**PC**, is a low-level interrupt service process that monitors and handles device interrupt events ($@int\odot$) from port interfaces of RTOS+ as shown in Figure 17. DeviceInterruptHandling**PC** detects any inter-

Figure 17. The behavior model of the device interrupt handling process

```
DeviceInterruptHandling(<I:: @DeviceInt⊙>; <O:: InterruptedQST>;
                        <UDM:: SCBST, DCBST, ECBST, MCBST, CPUST>)PC ≜
{ // Swap out current base level process
   → PORTST(IntPortAddressH)B |> IntVectorB
   → DNN := IntVectorB
   → ↑(SCBST.#InterruptsN)
   → ENN := SCBST.#InterruptsN
   → ECB(ENN)ST.StatusBL := T
   → ECB(ENN)ST.TypeN := 3                                     // Device interrupt
   → ECB(ENN)ST.TimeDetectedhh:mm:ss:ms := §tchh:mm:ss:ms
   → PNN := SCBST.CurrentPNN                                   // Find current PN
   → ECB(ENN)ST.SourceProcN := PNN
   → ECB(ENN)ST.TargetProcN := 0
   ↣ EnqueuePC(<I:: PNN>; <O:: ( )>; <UDM:: InterruptedQST>)   // Swap interrupted process
   → PCB(PNN)ST.TaskStatusN := 7                               // Interrupted
   → ↑(SCBST.#ProcInterruptedN)
  // Run int service process for the device request
   → DCB(DNN)ST.RecProcN := 0
   → DCB(DNN)ST.StatusN := 2                                   // In use
   → DCB(DNN)ST.TimeAllocatedhh:mm:ss:ms := §tchh:mm:ss:ms
   → PNN := DCB(DNN)ST.IntServiceProcN
   → PCB(PNN)ST.TaskStatusN := 3                               // Running
   → SCBST.CurrentPNN := PNN
   → SCBST.ⓈRunEndBL := F
   ↳ RunPC(<I:: PNN>; <O:: SCBST.ⓈRunEndBL>; <UDM:: SCBST, PCBST, DCBST, MCBST, CPUST>)
}
```

rupt requested by a device or system resource in order to create a corresponding event control block from the interrupt in ECB**ST** as modeled in the UDMs of RTOS+. A detected interrupt will be used to dispatch a corresponding interrupt service process after the current base level process is scheduled into the interrupted queue, InterruptedQ**ST**, by the system process scheduler (ProcessScheduler**PC**).

As illustrated in Figure 2, once a device interrupt is identified, the system control on the CPU is automatically passed to the interrupt service process, which responds to the interrupt and then returns control to the interrupted task. The interrupted task is then sent back to the *ready* state after the completion of the interrupt service. An interrupted task may be killed from the system if resources are not enough for servicing a high priority interrupt. RTOS+ allows hierarchical interrupts where a high-level interrupt may take over control from other lower-level ones.

In RTOS+, the *periodic* time interrupts, @SysClock1msInt◉ and @SysClock10msInt◉, are the highest level system interrupts in the kernel of RTOS+, which are handled differently as those of the *random* device and resource interrupts. The periodic time interrupts are detected and handled by the kernel RTOS+§.SysDispatcher**PC** directly, which will be described in Figure 30.

E) The CPU Scheduling Process

CPU scheduling is the most inner kernel process of a real-time operating system to maximize CPU utilization (Brinch-Hansen, 1971). RTOS+ adopts multiprocess and multithread techniques to keep the CPU running different processes or threads of multiple processes on a time-sharing basis with a predetermined scheduling interval. The CPU scheduler selects which process in the ready queue should be run next based on a predefined scheduling algorithm or strategy. The CPU scheduler switches control of the CPU to the process selected for a certain time interval.

In RTOS+, every ten time-intervals (10ms) forms a cycle to run all ready processes in the ReadyQHST (maximum 6) and ReadyQLST (maximum 4) as specified in the design of the system control block SCBST. The CPU scheduler process of RTOS+, CPUSchedulerPC, as shown in Figure 18, dispatches a maximum of ten processes in both ready queues ReadyQHST and ReadyQLST within a low interrupt period 10ms, where each of them will be dispatched for running for 1ms scheduled by the high interrupt period. In the peak CPU load period of RTOS+, 6 tasks from ReadyQHST and 4 from ReadyQLST will be scheduled, respectively, in a series of ten 1ms time intervals. However, during low CPU load period, any combination of high/low tasks may be scheduled including a series of multiple threads of the same process. In case there is a current task in the CPU but no other task in the ReadyQHST and ReadyQLST, the currently scheduled task may continue to run for at least another 1ms interval until the statuses of the ready queues are changed. Except the above two special conditions, the current process will

be swapped out of the CPU as a delayed process. Instead, a new qualified process in the front of ReadyQHST or ReadyQLST will be scheduled into CPU for running.

CPUSchedulerST is triggered by @SysClock-1msInt◉ per 1ms. As modeled in Figure 18, when there is no currently dispatched task in the CPU as well as in either ready queues, ReadyQHST or ReadyQLST, the scheduler does nothing but exits the current cycle of CPU scheduling.

UPMs FOR RESOURCES MANAGEMENT IN RTOS+

According to the high level specifications of the static behaviors of RTOS+ as given in Figure 13, the *resources management* subsystem of RTOS+ encompasses the behavioral processes of memory management, device (port) management, and file management, i.e.: (see Exhibit 2)

The detailed UPMs of the resource management processes of RTOS+ are refined and elaborated in the following subsections.

A) The Memory Management Process

Memory management is one of the key functions of operating systems because memory is both the working space and storage of data and files. RTOS+ adopts a flexible segmentation method

---

Exhibit 2.

ResourcesManagementPC ≙
(AllocateMemoryPC (<I:: PNN>; <O:: MemIDN, &MemAllocatedBL>;
          <UDM:: SCBST, PCBST, ECBST, RCBST, MCBST>)
| ReleaseMemory(<I:: MemIDN>; <O:: &MemReleasedBL>;
          <UDM:: SCBST, PCBST, DCBST, ECBST, MCBST>)
| GetDevicePC(<I :: DeviceType$N$, PNN>; <O:: DNN, &DeviceAllocatedBL>;
          <UDM:: SCBST, DCBST, PCBST>)
| ReleaseDevicePC(<I:: DNN>; <O:: ( )>; <UDM:: SCBST, DCBST>)
| FileManagementPC(<I:: FileIDS>; <O:: ( )>; <UDM:: FilesST>)
)

(16)

Figure 18. The behavior model of the CPU scheduling process

```
CPUScheduler(<I:: ReadyQHST, ReadyQLST>; <O:: CompletedQST, DelayedQST, InterruptedQST, SuspendedQST>;
             <UDM:: SCBST, PCBST, DCBST, ECBST, MCBST, CPUST, SysClockST>)PC ≜
{ // Triggered by @SysClock1msInt⊙
  → PNN := SCBST.CurrentPNN
  → ⓢProcSwapBL := F
  → ( ◆ SCBST.ⓢRunEndBL = T
        → PCB(PNN)ST.TaskStatusN := 4                          // Completed
        ↣ EnqueuePC(<I:: PNN>; <O:: ( )>; <UDM:: CompletedQST>)
        → ↑(SCBST.#ProcCompletedN)
        → ⓢProcSwapBL := T
    | ◆ ~
        → DNN := PCB(PNN)ST.DeviceReqN
        → ◆ DCB(DNN)ST.StatusN ≥ 2
              → PCB(PNN)ST.TaskStatusN := 7                    // Swap to SuspendedQ due to device unavailable
              ↣ EnqueuePC(<I:: PNN>; <O:: ( )>; <UDM:: SuspendedQST>)
              → ↑(SCBST.#ProcSuspendedN)
              → ⓢProcSwapBL := T
          | ◆ ~
              → ◆ SCBST.#ProcReadyQHN ≠ 0 ∨ SCBST.#ProcReadyQLN ≠ 0
                    → PCB(PNN)ST.TaskStatusN := 6              // Swap to DelayedQ due to CPU timeout
                    ↣ EnqueuePC(<I:: PNN>; <O:: ( )>; <UDM:: DelayedQST>)
                    → ↑(SCBST.#ProcDelayedN)
                    → ⓢProcSwapBL := T
    )
  // Dispatch a new task for running
  → ◆ ⓢProcSwapBL = T
      → ( ◆ SCBST.#ProcReadyHN ≠ 0                             // Dispatch a new task from ReadyQH
            ↣ ServePC(<I:: ReadyQHST>; <O:: PNN>; <UDM:: PCBST>)
            → ↓(SCBST.#ProcReadyHN)
            → PCB(PNN)ST.TaskStatusN := 3                      // Running
            → SCBST.CurrentPNN := PNN
            ↳ RunPC(<I:: PNN>; <O:: SCBST.ⓢRunEndBL>; <UDM:: SCBST, PCBST, DCBST, MCBST, CPUST>)
        | ◆ SCBST.#ProcReadyLN ≠ 0                             // Dispatch a new task from ReadyQL
            ↣ ServePC(<I:: ReadyQLST>; <O:: PNN>; <UDM:: PCBST>)
            → ↓(SCBST.#ProcReadyLN)
            → PCB(PNN)ST.TaskStatusN := 3                      // Running
            → SCBST.CurrentPNN := PNN
            → SCBST.ⓢRunEndBL := F
            ↳ RunPC(<I:: PNN>; <O:: SCBST.ⓢRunEndBL>; <UDM:: SCBST, PCBST, DCBST, MCBST, CPUST>)
        )
}
```

for system memory management with variable sizes of memory blocks for different events and processes. The memory management process of RTOS+, MemoryManagement**PC**, encompasses the AllocateMemory**PC** and ReleaseMemory**PC** processes, as shown in Figure 19. Memory-Management**PC** supports dynamic and absolute physical memory manipulations that are neces-

Figure 19. The behavior model of the memory management process

```
MemoryManagementPC ≙ {  AllocateMemoryPC
                     | ReleaseMemoryPC
                     }

AllocateMemory(<I :: PNN>; <O:: MemIDN, Ⓢ MemAllocatedBL>;
              <UDM:: SCBST, PCBST, DCBST, ECBST, MCBST>)PC ≙

{  MaxMemBlockN-1 ◆ MCB(MBNN)ST.StatusBL = F ∧
    R
  MBNN=0       MCB(MBNN)ST.SizeB = PCB(PNN)ST.MemorySizeB
              → MCB(MBNN)ST.StatusBL := T
              → MCB(MBNN)ST.ReqProcN := PNN
              → MemIDN := MBNN
              → Ⓢ MemAllocatedBL := T
          | ◆ ~
              → ! (Memory allocation for, MBNN, failed due to lack of resources.)
              → Ⓢ MemAllocatedBL := F
}

ReleaseMemory(<I:: MemIDN>; <O:: Ⓢ MemReleasedBL>;
             <UDM:: SCBST, PCBST, DCBST, ECBST, MCBST>)PC ≙
{MBNN := MemIDN
 → ◆ MCB(MBNN)ST.StatusBL = T
     → MCB(MBNN)ST.StatusBL := F
     → MCB(MBNN)ST.ReqProcN := 0
     → Ⓢ MemReleasedBL := T
  | ◆ ~
     → ! (Memory release for, MBNN, failed due to unidentified memory block.)
     → Ⓢ MemReleaseBL := F
}
```

sary for real-time operating systems and real-time applications.

The process AllocateMemory**PC** deals with dynamic memory allocations in RTOS+. When a request for memory from a process is identified by the system, AllocateMemory**PC** searches for a suitable sized memory block that is free. When a suitable memory block is identified by a given memory block number (MBN), AllocateMemory**PC** sets its status as in-use. Then, the associated process requiring the memory will be registered in the memory control block. Inversely, the number of the allocated memory block, MemID**N** = MBN**N**, will be registered to the requir-

ing process. If there is no free and suitable memory block available in the system, a feedback status, Ⓢ MemAllocated**BL**:= **F**, will be generated along with a system warning for the exception condition.

The process ReleaseMemory**PC** deals with dynamic memory release requests of the system when a process terminates and the memory allocated to it is no longer required. ReleaseMemory**PC** operates on the memory control block when it is invoked. It gets the memory block number associated to the process that requests to release the memory. Then, it sets the status of the given memory block to free and disconnects the link

Figure 20. The behavior model of the device management process

```
DeviceManagementPC ≙ { GetDevicePC
                       | ReleaseDevicePC
                       }

GetDevice(<I :: DeviceIDS, PNN>; <O:: DNN, ⓢDeviceAllocatedBL>;
          <UDM:: SCBST, DCBST, PCBST>)PC ≙

{ SCBST.#DevicesN(◆ DeviceIDS = DCB(DNN)ST.DeviceIDS ∧ DCB(DNN)ST.StatusN = 0
    R
  DNN=1            → DCB(DNN)ST.StatusN := 1                          // Seized
                   → DCB(DNN)ST.ProcReqN := PNN
                   → DCB(DNN)ST.TimeAllocatedhh:mm:ss:ms := §tchh:mm:ss:ms
                   → ↑(SCBST.#DeviceUsedN)
                   → ⓢDeviceAllocatedBL := T
             | ◆ ~
                   → ! (Device allocation for, DNN, failed due to lack of resources.)
                   → ⓢDeviceAllocatedBL := F
             )
}

ReleaseDevice(<I :: DNN>; <O:: ( )>; <UDM:: SCBST, DCBST>)PC ≙
{DCB(DNN)ST.StatusN := 0                                               // Set to idle
 → DCB(DNN)ST.UserProcN := 0                                           // Delink from process
 → ↓(SCBST.#DeviceUsedN)
}
```

between the memory block and the previously occupied process.

B) The Device Management Process

Devices as well as their I/O ports are directly manipulated by the processes DeviceManagement**PC** in RTOS+ as shown in Figure 20. DeviceManagement**PC** encompasses both GetDevice**PC** and ReleaseDevice**PC** processes. Additional plug-in device drivers may also be incorporated via the same interface mechanisms by the adding device and deleting device processes.

The process GetDevice**PC** handles device allocations in RTOS+. When a request for a device from a process is identified by the system, GetDevice**PC** searches for a suitable type of device that is free. When a suitable device is found, GetDevice**PC** sets its status as seized. Then, the associate process required the device is registered in the device control block. If there is no free and/or suitable device available in the system, a feedback status, &DeviceAllocated**BL**:= **F**, will be generated.

The process ReleaseDevice**PC** handles device release requests for the system when a process terminates the use of a device. ReleaseDevice**PC** operates on the device control block when it is invoked. It first gets the device number (DN**N**) to be released associated to the process. Then, it sets the status of the given device in DCB**ST** as free and disconnects the link between the device and the previously associated process.

C) The File Management Process

On the basis of the architectural model of the file system Files**ST** as given in Figure 10, the behaviors

Figure 21. The high-level behavioral model of file management in RTOS+

```
FileManagementPC ≜ ( FileSysAdministrationPC
                      || FileManipulationsPC
                      )
= ( CreateFile(<I:: FileIDS>; <O:: ⓈFileID.CreatedBL, ⓈFileID.ExistBL>; <UDM:: FilesST>)PC
  | OpenFile(<I:: FileIDS>; <O:: ⓈFileID.FileOpenBL>; <UDM:: FilesST>)PC
  | CloseFile(<I:: FileIDS>; <O:: ⓈFileID.FileClosedBL>; <UDM:: FilesST>)PC
  | ReadFile(<I:: FileIDS>; <O:: ⓈFileID.FileReadBL>; <UDM:: FilesST>)PC
  | SaveFile(<I:: FileIDS>; <O:: ⓈFileID.FileSavedBL>; <UDM:: FilesST>)PC
  | DeleteFile(<I:: FileIDS>; <O:: ⓈFileID.FileDeletedBL>; <UDM:: FilesST>)PC
  | FileEmptyTest(<I:: FileIDS>; <O:: ⓈFileID.EmptyBL>; <UDM:: FilesST>)PC
  | FileFullTest(<I:: FileIDS>; <O:: ⓈFileID.FullBL>; <UDM:: FilesST>)PC
  | MaintainIndex(<I:: FileIDS, IndexST>; <O:: ⓈFileID.IndexCleanedBL>; <UDM:: FilesST>)PC
  )
|| ( InsertRecord(<I:: FileIDS, KeyN, RecordST>; <O:: ⓈFileID.RecordInsertedBL>; <UDM:: FilesST>)PC
  | AppendRecord(<I:: FileIDS, KeyN, RecordST>; <O:: ⓈFileID.RecordAppendedBL>; <UDM:: FilesST>)PC
  | DeleteRecord(<I:: FileIDS, KeyN>; <O:: ⓈFileID.RecordDeletedBL>; <UDM:: FilesST>)PC
  | UpdateRecord(<I:: FileIDS, KeyN, RecordST>; <O:: ⓈFileID.FiledUpdatedBL>; (<UDM:: FilesST>)PC
  | FindRecord(<I:: FileIDS, KeyN>; <O:: ⓈFileID.RecordFoundBL>; (<UDM:: FilesST>))PC
  )
```

of the file management subsystem of RTOS+, FileManagement^{PC}, are modeled by a set of 14 behavioral processes in the categories of file system administrations and file manipulations as shown in Figure 21. Detailed RTPA models of the file management processes have been provided in (Wang, 2007).

UPMs FOR PROCESS MANAGEMENT IN RTOS+

A *process* is a basic unit of system function that represents an execution of a program on a computer under the support of an operating system. A process can be a system process or a user process. The former executes system code, and the latter runs an application. Processes may be executed sequentially or concurrently depending on the type of operating systems.

A thread is an important concept of process management in operating systems (Anderson et al., 1989; Lewis & Berg, 1998). A *thread* is a

basic unit of CPU utilization, or a flow of control within a process, supported by a PCBST, a program counter, a set of registers, and a stack. Conventional operating systems are single thread systems. Multithreaded systems enable a process to control a number of execution threads. The benefits of multithreaded operating system are responsiveness, resource sharing, implementation efficiency, and utilization of multiprocessor architectures of modern computers.

According to the high level specifications of the static behaviors of RTOS+ as given in Figure 13, the *process management* subsystem of RTOS+ encompasses a set of nine task handling processes as specified in Figure 22 through 29 corresponding to the states of behavioral processes for the entire task lifecycle of process manipulating as shown in Figure 2, i.e.: (see Exhibit 3)

The following subsections formally describe the refined UPMs of process management in RTOS+ such as those of process request, creation, ready, running, completion, interrupted, delayed,

---

Exhibit 3.

ProcesesManagementPC ≙
(ProcessRequest**PC**(<**I**:: TaskPriority**N**, MemoryReq**B**, DeviceReq**N**>; <**O**:: RequestQ**ST**>;
               <**UDM**:: SCB**ST**, PCB**ST**>)
| ProcessCreation**PC**(<**I**:: RequestQ**ST**>; <**O**:: WaitingQ**ST**>;
               <**UDM**:: SCB**ST**, PCB**ST**, DCB**ST**, ECB**ST**, MCB**ST**, KilledQ**ST**>)
| ProcessReady**PC**(<**I**:: WaitingQ**ST**>; <**O**:: ReadyQH**ST**, ReadyQL**ST**>;
               <**UDM**:: SCB**ST**, PCB**ST**, DCB**ST**, ECB**ST**, MCB**ST**>)
| ProcessRunning**PC** = CPUScheduler**PC**
| ProcessCompleted**PC**(<**I**:: CompletedQ**ST**>; <**O**:: ( )>; <**UDM**:: SCB**ST**, PCB**ST**, DCB**ST**, ECB**ST**, MCB**ST**>)
| ProcessInterrupted**PC**(<**I**:: InterruptQ**ST**>; <**O**:: ReadyQH**ST**, ReadyQL**ST**>;
               <**UDM**:: SCB**ST**, PCB**ST**, DCB**ST**, ECB**ST**, MCB**ST**, CPU**ST**, KilledQ**ST**>)
| ProcessDelayed**PC**(<**I**:: DelayedQ**ST**>; <**O**:: ReadyQH**ST**, ReadyQL**ST**>;
               <**UDM**:: SCB**ST**, PCB**ST**, DCB**ST**, ECB**ST**, MCB**ST**, KilledQ**ST**>)
| ProcessSuspended**PC**(<**I**:: SuspendedQ**ST**>; <**O**:: ReadyQH**ST**, ReadyQL**ST**>;
               <**UDM**:: SCB**ST**, PCB**ST**, DCB**ST**, ECB**ST**, MCB**ST**, KilledQ**ST**>)
| ProcessKilled**PC**(<**I**:: KilledQ**ST**>; <**O**:: ( )>; <**UDM**:: SCB**ST**, PCB**ST**, ECB**ST**, RCB**ST**, MEM**ST**, PORT**ST**, CPU**ST**>)   (17)

Figure 22. The behavior model of the request process

ProcessRequest(<**I**:: TaskPriority**N**, MemoryReq**B**, DeviceID**S**>; <**O**:: RequestQ**ST**>;
              <**UDM**:: SCB**ST**, PCB**ST**>)**PC** ≙
{ // Triggered by @UserRequestInt⊙
   → ↑(SCB**ST**.#Procs**N**)
   → PN**N** := SCB**ST**.#Procs**N**
   → PCB(PN**N**)**ST**.TaskPriority**N** := TaskPriority**N**
   → PCB(PN**N**)**ST**.MemorySize**B** := MemoryReq**B**
   → PCB(PN**N**)**ST**.TimeCreated**hh:mm:ss:ms** := §t꜀.**hh:mm:ss:ms**
   → PCB(PN**N**)**ST**.DeviceID**S** := DeviceID**S**
   → PCB(PN**N**)**ST**.TaskStatus**N** := 0   // Process requested
   ↣ Enqueue**PC**(<**I**:: PN**N**>; <**O**:: ( )>; <**UDM**:: RequestQ**ST**>)
   → ↑(SCB**ST**.#ProcRequests**N**)
}

suspended, and killed. The relationship and inter-actions of the nine task handling processes will be modeled in the dynamic behaviors of RTOS+.

A) The Request Process

The request process of RTOS+, ProcessRequest**PC**, is modeled as shown in Figure 22, which operates on the UDMs of SCB**ST**, PCB**ST**, and Request-Q**ST** as specified in the architectures of RTOS+. ProcessRequest**PC** requires RTOS+ to establish a process for a user application. It creates a new PCB in PCB**ST** with information such as TaskPriority**N**, MemoryReq**B**, and DeviceIDS in order to specify the priority of the target process and to allocate required memory and device(s). Then, it queues the process request into RequestQ**ST** for further processing by ProcessScheduler**PC**.

B) The Creation Process

The creation process of RTOS+, ProcessCre-ation**PC**, is modeled as shown in Figure 23, which operates on the UDMs of SCB**ST**, PCB**ST**, DCB**ST**, ECB**ST**, MCB**ST**, Request**ST**, WaitingQ**ST**, and KilledQ**ST** as specified in the architectures of RTOS+. For each user request in applications, ProcessCreation**PC** allocates both required memory

Figure 23. The behavior model of the creation process

```
ProcessCreation(<I:: RequestQST>; <O:: WaitingQST>;
                <UDM:: SCBST, PCBST, DCBST, ECBST, MCBST, KilledQST>)PC ≙
{ ◆ RequestQST.Empty = F
    ↦ ServePC(<I:: RequestQST>; <O:: PNN>; <UDM:: SCBST, PCBST>)
    → ↓(SCBST.#ProcRequestsN)
    ↦ AllocateMemoryPC (<I:: PNN>; <O:: MemIDN, ⓈMemAllocatedBL>;
                        <UDM:: SCBST, PCBST, DCBST, ECBST, MCBST>)
    → ( ◆ ⓈMemAllocatedBL = T
        → PCB(PNN)ST.MemoryReqN := MemIDN
        → DeviceTypeN := PCB(PNN)ST.DeviceReqN
        ↦ GetDevicePC(<I:: DeviceIDS, PNN>; <O:: DNN, ⓈDeviceAllocatedBL>;
                      <UDM:: SCBST, DCBST, PCBST>)
        → ( ◆ ⓈDeviceAllocatedBL = T
            → PCB(PNN)ST.DeviceReqN := DNN
            → PCB(PNN)ST.TaskPriorityN = 1                              // Created
            ↦ EnqueuePC(<I:: PNN>; <O:: ( )>; <UDM:: WaitingQST>)
            → ↑(SCBST.#ProcWaitingN)
          |◆ ~
            → PCB(PNN)ST.TaskStatusN := 8                               // Killed
            ↦ EnqueuePC(<I:: PNN>; <O:: ( )>; <UDM:: KilledQST>)
            → ! (Process creation for, PNN, failed due to device unavailable.)
            → ↑(SCBST.#ProcKilledN)
          )
      |◆ ~
        → PCB(PNN)ST.TaskStatusN := 8                                  // Killed
        ↦ EnqueuePC(<I:: PNN>; <O:: ( )>; <UDM:: KilledQST>)
        → ! (Process creation for, PNN, failed due to memory unavailable.)
        → ↑(SCBST.#ProcKilledN)
      )
}
```

and device for the process. Then, it completes the creation process by queuing the process into WaitingQST. For a process under creation, if there is not enough memory or the required device is busy, it will be sent into the killed queue KilledQST. In this case, a proper system exception log and related warning information will be generated.

C) The Ready Process

The ready process of RTOS+, ProcessReadyPC, is modeled as shown in Figure 24, which operates on the UDMs of SCBST, PCBST, DCBST, ECBST, MCBST, WaitingQST, ReadyQHST, and ReadyQLST as specified in the architectures of RTOS+. ProcessReadyPC first fetches the front process in the waiting queue, WaitingQST, if it is not empty. Then, the process will be dispatched to ReadyQHST or ReadyQLST depending on the specified priority of the task.

The capacity of ReadyQHST is designed for six high-priority processes and that of ReadyQLST for four low priority processes, which fit the maximum dispatching cycle of 10ms for ten 1ms executing intervals for each of these ready processes. Therefore, when either target ready queue is full, the process will be re-queued back to WaitingQST for future dispatching. A process on

Figure 24. The behavior model of the ready process

```
ProcessReady(<I:: WaitingQST>; <O:: ReadyQHST, ReadyQLST>;
              <UDM:: SCBST, PCBST, DCBST, ECBST, MCBST>)PC ≙

{ ◆ WaitingQST.EmptyBL = F
    ↣ ServePC(<I:: WaitingQST>; <O:: PNN>; <UDM:: SCBST, PCBST>)
    → ↓(SCBST.#ProcWaitingN)
    → ( ◆ PCB(PNN)ST.TaskPriorityN = 1
            → ( ◆ ReadyQHST.FullBL = F
                    ↣ EnqueuePC(<I:: PNN>; <O:: ( )>; <UDM:: ReadyQHST>)
                    → PCB(PNN)ST.TaskStatusN := 2                          // Ready
                    → ↑(SCBST.#ProcReadyHN)
                    → ( ◆ SCBST.#ProcReadyHN = 0
                            → ReadyQHST.EmptyBL := T
                        | ◆ SCBST.#ProcReadyHN = 6
                            → ReadyQHST.FullBL := T
                        )
                | ◆ ~
                    ↣ EnqueuePC(<I:: PNN>; <O:: ( )>; <UDM:: WaitingQST>)
                    → PCB(PNN)ST.TaskStatusN := 1                          // Return to WaitingQ
                    → ↑(SCBST.#ProcWaitingN)
                )
        | ◆ ~
            → ( ◆ ReadyQLST.FullBL = F
                    ↣ EnqueuePC(<I:: PNN>; <O:: ( )>; <UDM:: ReadyQLST>)
                    → PCB(PNN)ST.TaskStatusN := 2                          // Ready
                    → ↑(SCBST.#ProcReadyLN)
                    → ( ◆ SCBST.#ProcReadyLN = 0
                            → ReadyQLST.EmptyBL := T
                        | ◆ SCBST.#ProcReadyLN = 4
                            → ReadyQLST.FullBL := T
                        )
                | ◆ ~
                    ↣ EnqueuePC(<I:: PNN>; <O:: ( )>; <UDM:: WaitingQST>)
                    → PCB(PNN)ST.TaskStatusN := 1                          // Return to WaitingQ
                    → ↑(SCBST.#ProcWaitingN)
                )
        )
}
```

the scheduling states of creation, interrupted, and delayed can be scheduled into the ready queues as soon as the queues are not full. However, a suspended process may do so only when its required resource/device has become available.

D) The Running Process

It is noteworthy that the process State 3, Process-RunningPC, in the state transition diagraph as given in Figure 2 is not dispatched at the base level as other state transition processes. Due to its central role in the kernel of RTOS+, ProcessRunningPC

Figure 25. The behavior model of the completed process

```
ProcessCompleted(<I:: CompletedQST>; <O:: ( )>; <UDM:: SCBST, PCBST, DCBST, ECBST, MCBST>)PC ≜
{◆ CompletedQST.EmptyBL = F
    ↣ ServePC(<I:: CompletedQST>; <O:: PNN>; <UDM:: PCBST>)
    → ↓(SCBST.#ProcCompletedN)
    → MemIDN := PCBST(PNN).MemoryReqN                                  // Release memory
    ↣ ReleaseMemoryPC (<I :: MemIDN>; <O:: ⓈMemReleasedBL>;
                      <UDM:: SCBST, PCBST, ECBST, RCBST, MCBST>)
    → DNN := PCBST(PNN).DeviceReqN                                     // Release device
    ↣ ReleaseDevicePC(<I:: DNN>; <O:: ( )>; <UDM:: SCBST, DCBST>)
    → ECBST(EventReqN).StatusBL := F                                   // Release event
    → ECBST(EventReqN).SourceProcN := 0
    → ECBST(EventReqN).TargetProcN := 0
    → PCBST(PNN).TaskStatusN := 10                                     // Free process block
}
```

is executed at the high periodic interrupt level per 1ms known as the process CPUScheduler**PC** as specified in Figure 18.

E) The Completed Process

The completed process of RTOS+, ProcessCompleted**PC**, is modeled as shown in Figure 25, which operates on the UDMs of SCB**ST**, PCB**ST**, DCB**ST**, ECB**ST**, MCB**ST**, and CompletedQ**ST** as specified in the architectures of RTOS+. ProcessCompleted**PC** releases the front process in the CompletedQ**ST** if the queue is not empty. It first fetches the process number PN**N** by which the specific PCB in PCB**ST** is found. Then, the occupied memory, device, and event control blocks associated with the process are released. As a result, the task status of PN**N** is set as 10 to indicate a free process block in PCB**ST** for new tasks. In addition, the system control numbers of completed processes #ProcCompleted**N** is updated in SCB**ST**.

F) The Interrupted Process

The interrupted process of RTOS+, ProcessInterrupted**PC**, is modeled as shown in Figure 26, which operates on the UDMs of SCB**ST**, PCB**ST**, DCB**ST**, ECB**ST**, MCB**ST**, CPU**ST**, ReadyQH**ST**, ReadyQL**ST**, InterruptedQ**ST**, and Killed**ST** as specified in the architectures of RTOS+. ProcessInterrupted**PC** handles the process in front of InterruptedQ**ST** if it is not empty. The interrupted process caused by a device interrupt is re-enqueued into ReadyQH**ST** or ReadyQL**ST** according to its task priority. During the re-schedule of an interrupted process to the ready queues, if the target queue is full, the process will be returned to InterruptedQ**ST** if it is not full as well; Otherwise, the interrupted process will be killed due to lack of a resource. In this case, a proper system exception log and related warning information will be generated.

G) The Delayed Process

The delayed process of RTOS+, ProcessDelayed**PC**, is modeled as shown in Figure 27, which operates on the UDMs of SCB**ST**, PCB**ST**, DCB**ST**, ECB**ST**, MCB**ST**, ReadyQH**ST**, ReadyQL**ST**, and DelayedQ**ST** as specified in the architectures of RTOS+. ProcessDelayed**PC** handles the front process in a non-empty delayed queue. A high priority delayed process will be moved into ReadyQH**ST**, while a low priority delayed process

Figure 26. The behavior model of the interrupted process

```
ProcessInterrupted(<I:: InterruptQST>; <O:: ReadyQHST, ReadyQLST>;
                    <UDM:: SCBST, PCBST, DCBST, ECBST, MCBST, CPUST, KilledQST>)PC ≜
{◆ InterruptQST.EmptyBL = F
  ↣ ServePC(<I:: InterruptQST>; <O:: PNN>; <UDM:: PCBST>)
  → ↓(SCBST.#ProcInterruptedN)
  → ◆ PCBST(PNN).TaskPriorityN = 1                          // High priority task
      → ( ◆ ReadyQHST.FullBL = F                            // Less than 6 high priority procs ready
          ↣ EnqueuePC(<I:: PNN>; <O:: ( )>; <UDM:: ReadyQHST>)
          → PCB(PNN)ST.TaskStatusN := 2        // Ready
          → ↑(SCBST.#ProcReadyHN)
        |◆ ~
          → ( ◆ InterruptQST.FullBL = F                     // Return InterruptQ due to ReadyQH is full
              ↣ EnqueuePC(<I:: PNN>; <O:: ( )>; <UDM:: InterruptedQST>)
              → PCB(PNN)ST.TaskStatusN := 5       // Interrupted
              → ↑(SCBST.#ProcInterruptedN)
            |◆ ~                                             // Killed due to InterruptQ is full
              → ! (Process re-schedule for, PNN, failed due to lack of resources.)
              ↣ EnqueuePC(<I:: PNN>; <O:: ( )>; <UDM:: KilledQST>)
              → PCB(PNN)ST.TaskStatusN := 8       // Killed
              → ↑(SCBST.#ProcKilledN)
            )
        )
    |◆ ~                                                     // Low priority task
      → ( ◆ ReadyQLST.FullBL = F                            // Less than 4 low priority procs ready
          ↣ EnqueuePC(<I:: PNN>; <O:: ( )>; <UDM:: ReadyQLST>)
          → PCB(PNN)ST.TaskStatusN := 2       // Ready
          → ↑(SCBST.#ProcReadyLN)
        |◆ ~
          → ( ◆ InterruptQST.FullBL = F                     // Return InterruptQ due to ReadyQL is full
              ↣ EnqueuePC(<I:: PNN>; <O:: ( )>; <UDM:: InterruptedQST>)
              → PCB(PNN)ST.TaskStatusN := 5       // Interrupted
              → ↑(SCBST.#ProcInterruptedN)
            |◆ ~                                             // Killed due to InterruptQ is full
              → ! (Process re-schedule for, PNN, failed due to lack of resources.)
              ↣ EnqueuePC(<I:: PNN>; <O:: ( )>; <UDM:: KilledQST>)
              → PCB(PNN)ST.TaskStatusN := 8       // Killed
              → ↑(SCBST.#ProcKilledN)
            )
        )
}
```

Figure 27. The behavior model of the delayed process

```
ProcessDelayed(<I:: DelayedQST>; <O:: ReadyQHST, ReadyQLST>;
               <UDM:: SCBST, PCBST, DCBST, ECBST, MCBST, KilledQST>)PC ≙
{◆ DelayedQST.EmptyBL = F
   ⟼ ServePC(<I:: DelayedQST>; <O:: PNN>; <UDM:: PCBST>)
   → ↓(SCBST.#ProcDelayedN)
   → ◆ PCBST(PNN).TaskPriorityN = 1                          // High priority task
      → ( ◆ ReadyQHST.FullBL = F                             // Less than 6 high priority procs ready
            ⟼ EnqueuePC(<I:: PNN>; <O:: ( )>; <UDM:: ReadyQHST>)
            → PCB(PNN)ST.TaskStatusN := 2                    // Ready
            → ↑(SCBST.#ProcReadyIIN)
         | ◆ ~
            → ( ◆ DelayedQST.FullBL = F                      // Return DelayedQ due to ReadyQH is full
                  ⟼ EnqueuePC(<I:: PNN>; <O:: ( )>; <UDM:: DelayedQST>)
                  → PCB(PNN)ST.TaskStatusN := 6              // Delayed
                  → ↑(SCBST.#ProcDelayedN)
               | ◆ ~                                         // Killed due to DelayedQ is full
                  → ! (Process re-schedule for, PNN, failed due to lack of resources.)
                  ⟼ EnqueuePC(<I:: PNN>; <O:: ( )>; <UDM:: KilledQST>)
                  → PCB(PNN)ST.TaskStatusN := 8              // Killed
                  → ↑(SCBST.#ProcKilledN)
               )
         )
   | ◆ ~                                                     // Low priority task
      → ( ◆ ReadyQLST.FullBL = F                             // Less than 4 low priority procs ready
            ⟼ EnqueuePC(<I:: PNN>; <O:: ( )>; <UDM:: ReadyQLST>)
            → PCB(PNN)ST.TaskStatusN := 2                    // Ready
            → ↑(SCBST.#ProcReadyLN)
         | ◆ ~
            → ( ◆ DelayedQST.FullBL = F                      // Return DelayedQ due to ReadyQL is full
                  ⟼ EnqueuePC(<I:: PNN>; <O:: ( )>; <UDM:: DelayedQST>)
                  → PCB(PNN)ST.TaskStatusN := 6              // Delayed
                  → ↑(SCBST.#ProcDelayedN)
               | ◆ ~                                         // Killed due to DelayedQ is full
                  → ! (Process re-schedule for, PNN, failed due to lack of resources.)
                  ⟼ EnqueuePC(<I:: PNN>; <O:: ( )>; <UDM:: KilledQST>)
                  → PCB(PNN)ST.TaskStatusN := 8              // Killed
                  → ↑(SCBST.#ProcKilledN)
               )
         )
}
```

will be moved into ReadyQL**ST**, if the queues are not full limited by six high priority processes and four low priority ones, respectively. When there is no available ready queue, the delayed process is re-queued back into DelayedQ**ST** when it is not full; Otherwise, the delayed process will be killed due to lack of a resource. In this case, a

H) The Suspended Process

The suspended process of RTOS+, Process-Suspended**PC**, is modeled as shown in Figure 28, which operates on the UDMs of SCB**ST**, PCB**ST**, DCB**ST**, ECB**ST**, MCB**ST**, ReadyQH**ST**, ReadyQL**ST**, SuspendedQ**ST**, and Killed**ST** as specified in the architectures of RTOS+. Process-Suspended**PC** handles the first processes in front of SuspendedQ**ST** if it is not empty. Because the reason for a process' suspension was the non-availability of a certain device required by the process, ProcessSuspended**PC** checks if the device identified by DN**N** in DCB**ST** has become free or not. If the current status of the device remains unchanged, the suspended process is returned into SuspendedQ**ST**; Otherwise, the suspended process can be re-enqueued into ReadyQH**ST** or ReadyQL**ST** according to its task priority. During the re-schedule of a process to the ready queues, if the target queue is full, the target process will be returned to SuspendedQ**ST** when it is not full as well; Otherwise, the suspended process will be killed due to lack of a resource. In this case, a proper system exception log and related warning information will be generated.

I) The Killed Process

The killed process of RTOS+, ProcessKilled**PC**, is modeled as shown in Figure 29, which operates on the UDMs of SCB**ST**, PCB**ST**, DCB**ST**, ECB**ST**, MCB**ST**, and KilledQ**ST** as specified in the architectures of RTOS+. ProcessKilled**PC** releases the front process in the KilledQ**ST** if the queue is not empty. It fetches the process number PN**N** in order to find the specific PCB in PCB**ST**. Then, the occupied memory, device, and event control blocks associated with the process are released. As a result, the task status of PN**N** is set as 10 to indicate a free process block in PCB**ST** for new

tasks. In addition, the system control number of killed processes #ProcKilled**N** is updated in SCB**ST**.

THE DYNAMIC BEHAVIORAL MODELS OF THE RTOS+ SYSTEM

Dynamic behaviors of a system are run-time process deployment and dispatching mechanisms based on the static behaviors modeled in UPMs. The dynamic behaviors of RTOS+, as modeled by RTOS+**§**.DynamicBehaviors**PC**, integrate and interact the static behavioral processes at run-time. With the UPMs developed in the preceding section as a set of static behavioral processes of RTOS+, this section models and elaborates the dynamic behaviors of the RTOS+ system at run-time via the dynamic processes of *system dispatcher* and *process scheduler* as follows:

$$RTOS+\text{§}.\text{DynamicBehaviors}\textbf{PC} \triangleq \text{SysDispatcher}\textbf{PC}$$
$$| \ \text{ProcessScheduler}\textbf{PC} \quad (18)$$

where the former describes the time- and interrupt-driven mechanisms of the system, and the latter specifies the event-driven mechanism of RTOS+.

THE SYSTEM DISPATCHER OF RTOS+

The system dispatcher of RTOS+, RTOS+**§**.SysDispatcher**PC**, handles time- and interrupt-driven behaviors of the real-time operating system at the system level. SysDispatcher**PC** encompasses 5-level processes, as shown in Figure 30, known as the tasks at the base, high-periodic-interrupt, low-periodic-interrupt, device interrupt, and user request interrupt levels, as well as their interactions. The system dispatcher of RTOS+ runs ProcessScheduler**PC** (Figure 31) continuously at the base level, after the system is initialized, unless the system is requested to shut down. However, four kinds of interrupts may occur

Figure 28. The behavior model of the suspended process

```
ProcessSuspended(<I:: SuspendedQST>; <O:: ReadyQHST, ReadyQLST>;
                 <UDM:: SCBST, PCBST, DCBST, ECBST, MCBST, KilledQST>)PC ≙
{◆ SuspendedQST.EmptyBL = F
   ↦ ServePC(<I:: SuspendedQST>; <O:: PNN>; <UDM:: PCBST>)
   → ↓(SCBST.#ProcSuspendedN)
   → DNN := PCBST(PNN).DeviceReqN
   → ( ◆ DCBST(DNN).StatusN ≠ 0                        // Device is still unavailable
         ↦ EnqueuePC(<I:: PNN>; <O:: ( )>; <UDM:: SuspendedQST>)
         → PCB(PNN)ST.TaskStatusN := 7                 // Return SuspendedQ
         → ↑(SCBST.#ProcSuspendedN)
      |◆ ~                                             // Device available
      → DCBST(DNN).StatusN = 1                         // Seize the device
      → ◆ PCBST(PNN).TaskPriorityN = 1                 // High priority task
         → ( ◆ ReadyQHST.FullBL = F                    // Less than 6 high priority procs ready
            ↦ EnqueuePC(<I:: PNN>; <O:: ( )>; <UDM:: ReadyQHST>)
            → PCB(PNN)ST.TaskStatusN := 2              // Ready
            → ↑(SCBST.#ProcReadyHN)
         |◆ ~
            → ( ◆ SuspendedQST.FullBL = F       // Return SuspendedQ due to ReadyQH is full
               ↦ EnqueuePC(<I:: PNN>; <O:: ( )>; <UDM:: SuspendedQST>)
               → PCB(PNN)ST.TaskStatusN := 7          // Suspended
               → ↑(SCBST.#ProcSuspendedN)
            |◆ ~                                       // Killed due to SuspendedQ is full
               → ! (Process re-schedule for, PNN, failed due to lack of resources.)
               ↦ EnqueuePC(<I:: PNN>; <O:: ( )>; <UDM:: KilledQST>)
               → PCB(PNN)ST.TaskStatusN := 8          // Killed
               → ↑(SCBST.#ProcKilledN)
            )
         )
      |◆ ~                                             // Low priority task
      → ( ◆ ReadyQLST.FullBL = F                       // Less than 4 low priority procs ready
         ↦ EnqueuePC(<I:: PNN>; <O:: ( )>; <UDM:: ReadyQLST>)
         → PCB(PNN)ST.TaskStatusN := 2                 // Ready
         → ↑(SCBST.#ProcReadyLN)
      |◆ ~
         → ( ◆ SuspendedQST.FullBL = F        // Return SuspendedQ due to ReadyQL is full
            ↦ EnqueuePC(<I:: PNN>; <O:: ( )>; <UDM:: SuspendedQST>)
            → PCB(PNN)ST.TaskStatusN := 7             // Suspended
            → ↑(SCBST.#ProcSuspendedN)
         |◆ ~                                         // Killed due to SuspendedQ is full
            → ! (Process re-schedule for, PNN, failed due to lack of resources.)
            ↦ EnqueuePC(<I:: PNN>; <O:: ( )>; <UDM:: KilledQST>)
            → PCB(PNN)ST.TaskStatusN := 8             // Killed
            → ↑(SCBST.#ProcKilledN)
         )
      )
   )
}
```

Figure 29. The behavior model of the killed process

```
ProcessKilled(<I:: KilledQST>; <O:: ( )>;
                <UDM:: SCBST, PCBST, ECBST, RCBST, MEMST, PORTST, CPUST>)PC ≙
{◆ KilledQST.EmptyBL = F
    ↣ ServePC(<I:: KilledQST>; <O:: PNN>; <UDM:: PCBST>)
    → ↓(SCBST.#ProcKilledN)
    → MemIDN := PCBST(PNN).MemoryReqN                        // Release memory
    ↣ ReleaseMemoryPC (<I :: MemIDN>; <O:: ⓢMemReleasedBL>;
                       <UDM:: SCBST, PCBST, ECBST, RCBST, MCBST>)
    → DNN := PCBST(PNN).DeviceReqN                           // Release device
    ↣ ReleaseDevicePC(<I:: DNN>; <O:: ( )>; <UDM:: SCBST, DCBST>)
    → ECBST(EventReqN).StatusBL := F                         // Release event
    → ECBST(EventReqN).SourceProcN := 0
    → ECBST(EventReqN).TargetProcN := 0
    → PCBST(PNN).TaskStatusN := 10                           // Free process block
}
```

during the running of the base level processes, which are @SysClock1msInt⊙, @SysClock10msInt⊙, @DeviceInt⊙, and @UserRequestInt⊙ in descending priority. Each interrupt redirects the regular routine processes to more urgent real-time requests such as: a) System clock update (Figure 15) and CPU scheduling (Figure 18) at the high-periodic-interrupt level; b) System event capture (Figure 16) at the low-periodic-interrupt level; c) Device interrupt handling (Figure 17) at the device interrupt level; and d) User's application interrupt handling (Figure 22) at the user request interrupt level.

In RTOS+, four categories of sources, known as user applications, external events, device I/O interrupts, and system interrupts, may be identified for requesting the creation of a process. An application process is initiated by ProcessRequest**PC** via a user's system call, @UserRequestInt⊙, with request information in specific PCB**ST**. An external event process is initiated by SysEventCapture**PC** via @SysClock10msInt⊙ interrupt with request information in specific PCB**ST**. A device I/O interrupt is directly served by a predesigned process, DeviceInterruptHandling**PC**, via a corresponding call @DeviceInt⊙ with request information in specific PCB**ST**, where the device interrupt service process is application specific dependent on the function of a specific device. A system interrupt is directly handled by CPUScheduler**PC** (Figure 18) and SysClock**PC** driven by the periodic interrupt @SysClock1msInt⊙.

THE PROCESS SCHEDULER OF RTOS+

Corresponding to the conceptual state transition diagram as given in Figure 2, the process scheduler of RTOS+ is modeled as shown in Figure 31. An event-driven mechanism is adopted based on the status of a specific process. Because all task transition interfaces of RTOS+ are buffered in different queues according to the FIFO mechanism as shown in Figure 1, in each scheduling cycle, ProcessScheduler**PC** handles only one of the processes in each task state, i.e., from PCB(PN**N**)ST.TaskStatus**N** = 1 through 8 corresponding to the creation through killed processes. Each scheduled process is obtained from the front of a specific queue by using the support process Serve**PC** for

Figure 30. The dynamic process dispatching model of RTOS+

```
RTOS+§.SysDispatcherPC ≙ RTOS+§ →
{  // Base level tasks
   @SystemInitialS
     ↳ (SysInitialPC
                        T
        →               R          (↳ ProcessSchedulerPC
                 ⓈSysShutDownBL=F        )
        → ⊠
       )
 ↯ // High-periodic-interrupt level tasks
   @SysClock1msInt⊙
     ↗ (↳ SysClockPC
        ↳ CPUSchedulerPC
        → @SysClock1msInt⊙ := off
       )
     ↘ ⊙
 ↯ // Low-periodic-interrupt level tasks
   @SysClock10msInt⊙
     ↗ (↳ SysEventCapturePC
        → @SysClock1omsInt⊙ := off
       )
     ↘ ⊙
 ↯ // Device-interrupt level tasks
   @DeviceInt⊙
     ↗ (↳ DeviceInterruptHandlingPC
        → @DeviceInt⊙ := off
       )
     ↘ ⊙
 ↯ // User-interrupt level tasks
   @UserRequestInt⊙
     ↗ (↳ ProcessRequestPC
        → @UserRequestInt⊙ := off
       )
     ↘ ⊙
} → RTOS+§
```

Figure 31. The dynamic process scheduling model of RTOS+

```
ProcessScheduler(<I:: ( )>; <O:: ( )>; <UDM:: SCBST, PCBST, DCBST, ECBST, MCBST, CPUST>)PC ≙

        SCBST.#ProcsN
    {        R           (◆ PCB(PNN)ST.TaskStatusN
           PNN=1
                         | 1: ↪ ProcessCreationPC(<I:: RequestQST>; <O:: WaitingQST>;
                                          <UDM:: SCBST, PCBST, DCBST, ECBST, MCBST, KilledQST>)
                         | 2: ↪ ProcessReadyPC(<I:: WaitingQST>; <O:: ReadyQHST, ReadyQLST>;
                                          <UDM::.SCBST, PCBST, DCBST, ECBST, MCBST>)
                         | 3: → ∅               // Implemented by CPUSchedulerPC as a 1ms int process
                         | 4: ↪ ProcessCompletedPC(<I:: CompletedQST>; <O:: ( )>;
                                          <UDM:: SCBST, PCBST, DCBST, ECBST, MCBST>)
                         | 5: ↪ ProcessInterruptedPC(<I:: InterruptQST>; <O:: ReadyQHST, ReadyQLST>;
                                          <UDM:: SCBST, PCBST, DCBST, ECBST, MCBST, CPUST, KilledQST>)
                         | 6: ↪ ProcessDelayedPC(<I:: DelayedQST>; <O:: ReadyQHST, ReadyQLST>;
                                          <UDM:: SCBST, PCBST, DCBST, ECBST, MCBST, KilledQST>)
                         | 7: ↪ ProcessSuspendedPC(<I:: SuspendedQST>; <O:: ReadyQHST, ReadyQLST>;
                                          <UDM:: SCBST, PCBST, DCBST, ECBST, MCBST, KilledQST>)
                         | 8: ↪ ProcessKilledPC(<I:: KilledQST>; <O:: ( )>;
                                          <UDM:: SCBST, PCBST, ECBST, RCBST, MEMST, PORTST, CPUST>)
                         | ~ → ∅
                         )
    }
```

queue operations. Then, it returns to the base level control of the system and re-enters the system outer cycles to repeat the same routine processes.

It is noteworthy that some routine processes are not handled by ProcessSchedulerPC in process scheduling, because of their special priority allocation and timing requirements, such as CPUSchedulerPC and all periodic interrupt processes. These exceptions are indicated in Figure 31 by the skip operator (→ ∅) of RTPA.

As shown in Figure 30 and Figure 31, RTOS+ schedules all real-time tasks in the system by the most inner-loop 1ms periodic CPU scheduling, the 10ms periodic process scheduling, and the base level routine processes. SysDispatcherPC schedules the execution of each ready process for a 1ms interval within the 10ms outer loop. This dispatching mechanism guarantees any high priority process will have a chance to be executed for at least once in ten 1ms intervals. Therefore, the entire system behaviors are embodied by the CPUSchedulerPC in the kernel, the ProcessSched-ulerPC in the middle, and the SysDiapatcherPC on the top of RTOS+.

CONCLUSION

The design of real-time operating systems has been recognized as a comprehensive and complex system design paradigm in computing, software engineering, and information system design. This paper has demonstrated that the RTOS+ system, including its architecture, static behaviors, and dynamic behaviors, can be essentially and sufficiently described by RTPA. On the basis of the formal specifications of RTOS+ by the coherent set of UDMs and UPMs in RTPA, the architectural and behavioral consistency and run-time integrity of an RTOS have been significantly enhanced. It has been identified that RTOS+ can be applied not only as a formal design paradigm of RTOS's, but also a support framework for a wide range of applications in design and implementation of real-time and embedded systems. The RTOS+ system model may have also provided a test bench for the expressive power and modeling capability of existing formal methods in software engineering.

With a stepwise specification and refinement methodology for describing both system architectural and operational components, the formal model of the RTOS+ system has provided a foundation for implementation of a derived real-time operating system in multiple programming languages and on different operating platforms. It has also improved the controllability, reliability, maintainability, and quality of the design and implementation in real-time software engineering. The formal models of RTOS+ have been adopted as part of the supporting environment for the implementation of the RTPA-based software code generator (RTPA-CG) (Wang et al., 2010b; Ngolah & Wang, 2009). On the basis of the formal and rigorous models of the RTOS+ system, code can be automatically generated by RTPA-CG or be manually transferred from the formal models.

A series of formal design models of real-world and real-time applications in RTPA have been developed using RTPA notations and methodologies (Wang, 2002, 2007, 2008a, 2008b, 2008c, 2009a; Wang & Huang, 2008) in the formal design engineering approach, such as the telephone switching system (Wang, 2009b), the lift dispatching system (Wang et al., 2009), the automated teller machine (ATM) (Wang et al., 2010a), the real-time operating system (RTOS+), the air traffic control system (to be reported), the railway dispatching system (to be reported), and the intelligent traffic lights control system (to be reported). Further studies have demonstrated that RTPA is not only useful as a generic notation and methodology for software engineering, but also good at modeling human cognitive processes in cognitive informatics and computational intelligence as reported in (Wang, 2008d, 2009a; Wang & Ruhe, 2007; Wang & Chiew, 2010).

ACKNOWLEDGMENT

The authors would like to acknowledge the Natural Science and Engineering Council of Canada (NSERC) for its partial support to this work. We would like to thank the reviewers for their valuable comments and suggestions.

REFERENCES

Anderson, T. E., Lazowska, E. D., & Levy, H. M. (1989). The Performance Implications of Thread Management Alternatives for Shared-Memory Multiprocessors. *IEEE Transactions on Computers, 38*(12), 1631–1644. doi:10.1109/12.40843

Bollella, G. (2002). *The Real-Time Specification for Java*. Reading, MA: Addison Wesley.

Brinch-Hansen, P. (1971). Short-Term Scheduling in Multiprogramming Systems. In *Proceedings of the Third ACM Symposium on Operating Systems Principles* (pp. 103-105).

Deitel, H. M., & Kogan, M. S. (1992). *The Design of OS/2*. Reading, MA: Addison-Wesley.

Dijkstra, E. W. (1968). The Structure of the Multiprogramming System. *Communications of the ACM, 11*(5), 341–346. doi:10.1145/363095.363143

ETTX. (2009, February). In *Proceedings of the First Eueopean TinyOS Technology Exchange*, Cork, Ireland.

Ford, B., Back, G., Benson, G., Lepreau, J., Lin, A., & Shivers, O. (1997). The Flux OSKit: a Substrate for OS and Language Research. In *Proceedings of the 16th ACM Symposium on Operating Systems Principles*, Saint Malo, France.

ISO/IEC 9945-1. (1996). *ISO/IEC Standard 9945-1: Information Technology-Portable Operating System Interface (POSIX) - Part 1: System Application Program Interface (API) [C Language]*. Geneva, Switzerland: ISO/IEC.

Kreuzinger, J., Brinkschult, U. S., & Ungerer, T. (2002). *Real-Time Event Handling and Scheduling on a Multithread Java Microntroller*. Dordrecht, The Netherlands: Elsvier Science Publications.

Labrosse, J. J. (1999). *MicroC/OS-II, The Real-Time Kernel* (2nd ed.). Gilroy, CA: R&D Books.

Lamie, E. L. (2008). *Real-Time Embedded Multithreading using ThreadX and MIPS*.

Laplante, P. A. (1977). *Real-Time Systems Design and Analysis* (2nd ed.). Washington, DC: IEEE Press.

Lewis, B., & Berg, D. (1998). *Multithreaded Programming with Pthreads*. Upper Saddle River, NJ: Sun Microsystems Press.

Liu, C., & Layland, J. (1973). Scheduling Algorithms for Multiprogramming in Hard-Real-Time Environments. *Journal of the Association for Computing Machinery*, *20*(1), 46–56.

McDermid, J. (Ed.). (1991). *Software Engineer's Reference Book*. Oxford, UK: Butterworth Heinemann Ltd.

Ngolah, C. F., & Wang, Y. (2009). Tool Support for Software Development based on Formal Specifications in RTPA. *International Journal of Software Engineering and Its Applications*, *3*(3), 71–88.

Ngolah, C. F., Wang, Y., & Tan, X. (2004). The Real-Time Task Scheduling Algorithm of RTOS+. *IEEE Canadian Journal of Electrical and Computer Engineering*, *29*(4), 237–243.

Peterson, J. L., & Silberschantz, A. (1985). *Operating System Concepts*. Reading, MA: Addison-Wesley.

Rivas, M. A., & Harbour, M. G. (2001). MaRTE OS: An Ada Kernel for Real-Time Embedded Applications. In *Proceedings of Ada-Europe 2001*, Leuven, Belgium.

Sha, L., Rajkumar, R., & Lehoczky, J. P. (1990). Priority Inheritance Protocols: An Approach to Real-Time Synchronization. *IEEE Transactions on Computers*, 1175. doi:10.1109/12.57058

Silberschatz, A., Galvin, P., & Gagne, G. (2003). *Applied Operating System Concepts* (1st ed.). New York: John Wiley & Sons, Inc.

Tanenbaum, A. S. (1994). *Distributed Operating Systems*. Upper Saddle River, NJ: Prentice Hall Inc.

Viscarola, P. G., & Mason, W. A. (2001). *Windows NT Device Driver Development*. New York: Macmillan.

Wang, Y. (2002). The Real-Time Process Algebra (RTPA). *Annals of Software Engineering: An International Journal*, *14*, 235–274. doi:10.1023/A:1020561826073

Wang, Y. (2004). Operating Systems . In Dorf, R. (Ed.), *The Engineering Handbook* (2nd ed.). Boca Raton, FL: CRC Press.

Wang, Y. (2007). Software Engineering Foundations: A Software Science Perspective. In *Software Engineering, Vol. II*. New York: Auerbach Publications.

Wang, Y. (2008a). RTPA: A Denotational Mathematics for Manipulating Intelligent and Computational Behaviors. *International Journal of Cognitive Informatics and Natural Intelligence*, *2*(2), 44–62.

Wang, Y. (2008b). Mathematical Laws of Software. *Transactions of Computational Science*, *2*, 46–83. doi:10.1007/978-3-540-87563-5_4

Wang, Y. (2008c). Deductive Semantics of RTPA. *International Journal of Cognitive Informatics and Natural Intelligence*, *2*(2), 95–121.

Wang, Y. (2008d). On Contemporary Denotational Mathematics for Computational Intelligence. *Transactions of Computational Science*, *2*, 6–29. doi:10.1007/978-3-540-87563-5_2

Wang, Y. (2009a). Paradigms of Denotational Mathematics for Cognitive Informatics and Cognitive Computing. *Fundamenta Informaticae, 90*(3), 282–303.

Wang, Y. (2009b). The Formal Design Model of a Telephone Switching System (TSS). *International Journal of Software Science and Computational Intelligence, 1*(3), 92–116.

Wang, Y., & Chiew, V. (2010). On the Cognitive Process of Human Problem Solving. *Cognitive Systems Research: An International Journal, 11*(1), 81–92. doi:10.1016/j.cogsys.2008.08.003

Wang, Y., & Huang, J. (2008). Formal Modeling and Specification of Design Patterns Using RTPA. *International Journal of Cognitive Informatics and Natural Intelligence, 2*(1), 100–111.

Wang, Y., Ngolah, C. F., Ahmadi, H., Sheu, P. C. Y., & Ying, S. (2009). The Formal Design Model of a Lift Dispatching System (LDS). *International Journal of Software Science and Computational Intelligence, 1*(4), 98–122.

Wang, Y., Ngolah, C. F., Zeng, G., Sheu, P. C. Y., Choy, C. P., & Tian, Y. (2010c). The Formal Design Model of a Real-Time Operating System (RTOS+): Conceptual and Architectural Frameworks. *International Journal of Software Science and Computational Intelligence, 2*(2), 107–124.

Wang, Y., & Ruhe, G. (2007). The Cognitive Process of Decision Making. *International Journal of Cognitive Informatics and Natural Intelligence, 1*(2), 73–85.

Wang, Y., Tan, X., & Ngolah, C. F. (2010b). Design and Implementation of an Autonomic Code Generator based on RTPA. *International Journal of Software Science and Computational Intelligence, 2*(2), 44–67.

Wang, Y., Zhang, Y., Sheu, P., Li, X., & Guo, H. (2010a). The Formal Design Models of an Automatic Teller Machine (ATM). *International Journal of Software Science and Computational Intelligence, 2*(1), 102–131.

Yodaiken, V. (1999, May). An RT-Linux Manifesto. In *Proceedings of the 5th Linux Expo,* Raleigh, NC.

This work was previously published in International Journal of Software Science and Computational Intelligence, Volume 2, Issue 3, edited by Yingxu Wang, pp. 79-105, copyright 2010 by IGI Publishing (an imprint of IGI Global).

Chapter 15
The Formal Design Model of an Automatic Teller Machine (ATM)

Yingxu Wang
University of Calgary, Canada

Yanan Zhang
University of Calgary, Canada

Phillip C.-Y. Sheu
Wuhan University, China and University of California, Irvine, USA

Xuhui Li
Wuhan University, China

Hong Guo
Coventry University, UK

ABSTRACT

An Automated Teller Machine (ATM) is a safety-critical and real-time system that is highly complicated in design and implementation. This paper presents the formal design, specification, and modeling of the ATM system using a denotational mathematics known as Real-Time Process Algebra (RTPA). The conceptual model of the ATM system is introduced as the initial requirements for the system. The architectural model of the ATM system is created using RTPA architectural modeling methodologies and refined by a set of Unified Data Models (UDMs), which share a generic mathematical model of tuples. The static behaviors of the ATM system are specified and refined by a set of Unified Process Models (UPMs) for the ATM transition processing and system supporting processes. The dynamic behaviors of the ATM system are specified and refined by process priority allocation, process deployment, and process dispatch models. Based on the formal design models of the ATM system, code can be automatically generated using the RTPA Code Generator (RTPA-CG), or be seamlessly transformed into programs by programmers. The formal models of ATM may not only serve as a formal design paradigm of real-time software systems, but also a test bench for the expressive power and modeling capability of exiting formal methods in software engineering.

DOI: 10.4018/978-1-4666-0264-9.ch015

INTRODUCTION

The modeling and description of an Automated Teller Machine (ATM) are a typical design case in safety-critical and real-time systems (Laplante, 1977; Hayes, 1985; McDermid, 1991; Corsetti et al., 1991; Liu, 2000; Wang, 2002, 2007). As a real-time control system, the ATM system is characterized by its high degree of complexity, intricate interactions with hardware devices and users, and necessary requirements for domain knowledge. All these factors warrant the ATM system as a complex but ideal design paradigm in large-scale software system design in general and in real-time system modeling in particular.

There is a lack of systematical and detailed documentation of design knowledge and modeling prototypes of ATM systems and a formal model of them in denotational mathematics and formal notation systems (Wang, 2008a, 2008b). This paper presents the formal design, specification, and modeling of the ATM system using a denotational mathematics known as Real-Time Process Algebra (RTPA) (Wang, 2002, 2003, 2007, 2008a, 2008c, 2008d). RTPA introduces only 17 meta-processes and 17 process relations to describe software system architectures and behaviors with a stepwise refinement methodology (Wang, 2007, 2008c). According to the RTPA methodology for system modeling and refinement, a software system can be specified as a set of *architectural* and *operational components* as well as their interactions. The former is modeled by *Unified Data Models* (UDMs, also known as the component logical model (CLM)) (Wang, 2008c), which is an abstract model of system hardware interfaces, an internal logic model of hardware, and/or an internal control structure of the system. The latter is modeled by *static* and *dynamic processes* using the *Unified Process Models* (UPMs) (Hoare, 1978, 1985; Bjorner & Jones, 1982; Wang, 2007, 2008c; Wang & King, 2000).

This paper develops a formal design model of the ATM system in a top-down approach on the basis of the RTPA methodology. This work demonstrates that the ATM system can be formally modeled and described by a set of real-time processes in RTPA. In the remainder of this paper, the conceptual model of the ATM system is described as the initial requirements for the system. The architectural model of the ATM system is created based on the conceptual model using the RTPA architectural modeling methodologies and refined by a set of UDMs. Then, the static behaviors of the ATM system are specified and refined by a set of processes (UPMs). The dynamic behaviors of the ATM system are specified and refined by process priority allocation, process deployment, and process dispatching models. With the formal and rigorous models of the ATM system, code can be automatically generated by the RTPA Code Generator (RTPA-CG) (Wang, 2007), or be seamlessly transferred into program code manually. The formal models of ATM may not only serve as a formal design paradigm of real-time software systems, but also a test bench for the expressive power and modeling capability of existing formal methods in software engineering.

THE CONCEPTUAL MODEL OF THE ATM SYSTEM

An ATM system is a real-time front terminal of automatic teller services with the support of a central bank server and a centralized account database. This paper models an ATM that provides money withdraw and account balance management services. The architecture of the ATM system, as shown in Figure 1, encompasses an ATM processor, a system clock, a remote account database, and a set of peripheral devices such as the card reader, monitor, keypad, bills storage, and bills disburser.

The conceptual model of an ATM system is usually described by a Finite State Machine (FSM), which adopts a set of states and a set of state transition functions modeled by a transition dia-

Figure 1. The conceptual model of the ATM system

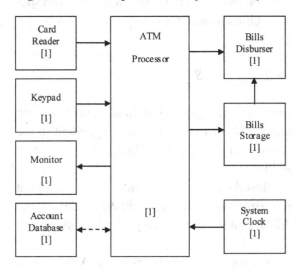

gram or a transition table to describe the basic behaviors of the ATM system. On the basis of the conceptual model of the ATM system as given in Figure 1, the top level behaviors of ATM can be modeled in a transition diagram as shown in Figure 2.

Corresponding to the transition diagram of the ATM as given in Figure 2, a formal model of the ATM system as an FSM, ATM**ST**, is defined as a 5-tuple as follows:

$$ATM\textbf{ST} \triangleq (S, \Sigma, s, F, \delta) \tag{1}$$

where

- S is a set of valid states that forms the domain of the ATM, $S = \{s_0, s_1, ..., s_7\}$ where the states are: s_0 – System, s_1 – Welcome, s_2 - Check PIN, s_3 – Input withdraw amount, s_4 - Verify balance, s_5 - Verify bills availability, s_6 - Disburse bills, and s_7 - Eject card, respectively;

- Σ is a set of events that the ATM may accept and process, $\Sigma = \{e_0, e_1, ..., e_{10}\}$ where e_0 - Start, e_1 - Insert card, e_2 - Correct PIN, e_3 - Incorrect PIN, e_4 – Request $\leq$ max, e_5 – Request > max, e_6 - Cancel transaction, e_7 - Sufficient funds, e_8 - Insufficient

Figure 2. The transition diagram of the ATM behaviors

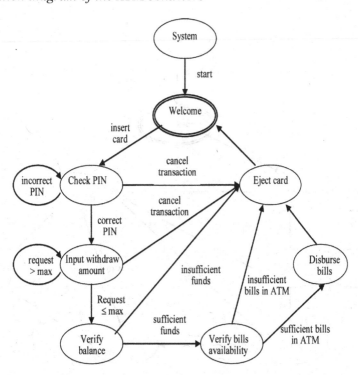

Table 1. The state transition table of the ATM

s_i	e_i	$s_{i+1} = \delta(s_i, e_i)$
s_0	e_0	s_1
s_1	e_1	s_2
s_2	e_2	s_3
s_2	e_3	s_2
s_2	e_6	s_7
s_3	e_4	s_4
s_3	e_5	s_3
s_3	e_6	s_7
s_4	e_7	s_5
s_4	e_8	s_7
s_5	e_9	s_6
s_5	e_{10}	s_7
s_6	-	s_7
s_7	-	s_1

funds, e_9 - Sufficient bills in ATM, and e_{10} - Insufficient bills in ATM;

- s is the start state of the ATM, $s = s_1$ (Welcome);
- F is a set of ending states, $F = \{s_1\}$;
- δ is the transition function of the ATM that determines the next state of the FSM, s_{i+1},

on the basis of the current state s_i and a specific incoming event e_i, i.e., $s_{i+1} = \delta(s_i, e_i)$, where

$$\delta = f: S \times \sum \rightarrow S \qquad (2)$$

which can be rigorously defined in the transition table as shown in Table 1 corresponding to the conceptual model of the ATM behaviors as shown in Figure 2.

Based on the above conceptual models and descriptions, an abstract FSM model of the ATM system can be described as shown in Figure 3.

The top level framework of the ATM system can be modeled by a set of architecture, static behaviors, and dynamic behaviors using RTPA (Wang, 2002, 2008a) as follows:

$$§(ATM) \triangleq ATM§.Architecture\textbf{ST}$$
$$\| ATM§.StaticBehaviors\textbf{PC}$$
$$\| ATM§.DynamicBehaviors\textbf{PC} \qquad (3)$$

Figure 3. The abstract FSM model of the ATM behaviors

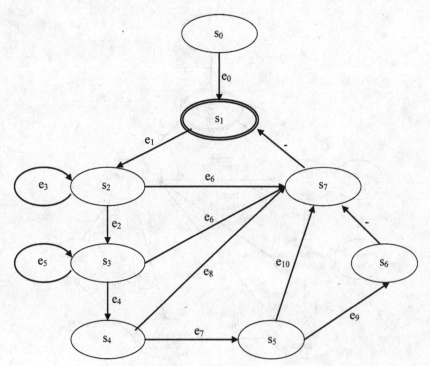

where ∥ indicates that these three subsystems related in parallel, and **§**, **ST**, and **PC** are type suffixes of *system, system structure,* and *process,* respectively.

The conceptual models of ATM as presented in Figs. 1 through 3 describe the configuration, basic behaviors, and logical relationships among components of the ATM system. According to the RTPA methodology for system modeling, specification, and refinement (Wang, 2008a, 2008b), the top level model of any system may be specified in a similar structure as given in Eq. 3. The following sections will extend and refine the top level framework of ATM§ into detailed architectural models (UDMs) and behavioral models (UPMs).

THE ARCHITECTURAL MODEL OF THE ATM SYSTEM

The architecture of a hybrid hardware/software system, particularly a real-time system, is a system framework that represents the overall structure, components, processes, and their interrelationships and interactions. This sections specifies the architecture of the ATM system, ATM**§**.Architecture**ST**, by a high-level architectural framework based on its conceptual model as provided in Figure 1. Then, each of its architectural components will be refined as a UDM (also known as *Component Logical Model* (CLM)) (Wang, 2002, 2007, 2008c).

The Architectural Framework of the ATM System

System architectures, at the top level, specify a list of structural identifiers of UDMs and their relations. A UDM may be regarded as a predefined class of system hardware or internal control models, which can be inherited or implemented by corresponding UDM objects as specific instances in the succeeding architectural refinement processes for the system.

Corresponding to the conceptual model of ATM as shown in Figs. 1 to 3, the high-level specification of the architecture of ATM, ATM**§**.Architecture**ST**, is given in Figure 4 in RTPA. ATM**§**.Architecture**ST** encompasses parallel structures of a set of UDMs such as the ATMProcessor**ST**, CardReader**ST**, Keypad**ST**, Monitor**ST**, BillStorage**ST**, BillsDisburser**ST**, AccountDatabase**ST**, and SysClock**ST**, as well as a set of system events @Events**S** and a set of statuses ⓈStatus**BL**. The numbers in the angel brackets indicate the configuration of how many data objects that share the same UDM.

The set of events of ATM are predefined global control variables of the system, as given in Eq. 4, which represent an external stimulus to a system or the occurring of an internal change of status such as an action of users, an updating of the environment, and a change of the value of a control variable. Types of general events, @Event**S**, that may trigger a behavior in a system can be classified into operational (@*e***S**), time (@*t***TM**), and interrupt (@*int*◉) events where @ is the *event prefix,* and **S**, **TM**, and ⊙ the type suffixes of string, time, and interrupt, respectively, i.e.: (see Exhibit 1)

Exhibit 1.

$$
\begin{aligned}
\text{ATM}\textbf{§}.\text{Architecture}\textbf{ST}.\text{Events}\textbf{ST} &\triangleq @\text{SysInitial}\textbf{S} \\
&\mid @t\textbf{TM} = \textbf{§}t\textbf{hh:mm:ss} \\
&\mid @\text{SysClock100msInt}\text{⊙}
\end{aligned} \tag{4}
$$

Figure 4. The architectural framework of the ATM system

ATM§.ArchitectureST ≜ <ATMProcessor : **ST** | [1]>
|| <CardReader : **ST** | [1]>
|| <Keypad : **ST** | [1]>
|| <Monitor : **ST** | [1]>
|| <BillStorage : **ST** | [1]>
|| <BillsDisburser : **ST** | [1]>
|| <SysClock : **ST** | [1]
|| <SysDatabase : **ST** | [1]>
|| <@Events**S**>
|| <ⓈStatus**BL**>

In RTPA, a status denoted by Ⓢ*s***BL** is an abstract model of system state in Boolean type with a status prefix Ⓢ, such as an operation result and an internal condition. The ATM statuses as a set of predefined global control variables are shown in Exhibit 2.

The UDM Structures of the ATM System

As modeled in Figure 4, the ATM system encompasses eight UDMs for modeling the system hardware interfaces and internal control structures. It is recognized that UDMs are a powerful modeling means in system architectural modeling (Wang, 2002, 2007, 2008c), which can be used to unify user defined complex data objects in system modeling, and to represent the abstraction and formalization of domain knowledge and structural information. The generic mathematical model of UDMs is tuples. Each of the eight UDMs of the ATM system is designed and modeled in the following subsections, except that the ATMProcessor**ST** will be embodied by its static and dynamic behavioral models (UPMs) in other sections.

a. The UDM of the Card Reader

The card reader of the ATM system, CardReader**ST**, is an architectural model of the interface device, which accepts an inserted bank card, scans predesigned identification information on the card, and returns the card to users. The UDM model of CardReader**ST** specifies seven functional fields as shown in Figure 5. The card input port is an input structure consisting of two fields known as the CardInputAddress**H** and CardInput**N**. The card insert port is an output structure consisting of two fields known as the CardInsertAddress**H** and CardInsertEngine**BL**. The card eject port is another output structure consisting of two fields known as the CardEjectAddress**H** and CardEjectEngine**BL**. There are three CardReader**ST** operating statuses modeled in the fields of CardReadStatus**BL**, CardInsertStatus**BL**, and CardEjectStatus**BL**.

b. The UDM of the Keypad

The keypad of the ATM system, Keypad**ST**, is an architectural model of the interface device for users entering required information such as the personal identification number (PIN) and withdraw amount of money. The UDM model of

Exhibit 2.

$$
\begin{aligned}
\text{ATM\S.Architecture\textbf{ST}.Status\textbf{ST}} \triangleq\ &\text{ⓈCardReadStatus\textbf{BL}}\\
|\ &\text{ⓈMonitorStatus\textbf{BL}}\\
|\ &\text{ⓈKeypadStatus\textbf{BL}}\\
|\ &\text{ⓈBillStorageStatus\textbf{BL}}\\
|\ &\text{ⓈBillsDisburserStatus\textbf{BL}}\\
|\ &\text{ⓈBillsDisburseEngineStatus\textbf{BL}}\\
|\ &\text{ⓈBillsAvailable\textbf{BL}}\\
|\ &\text{ⓈBillsDisbursed\textbf{BL}}\\
|\ &\text{ⓈCardInserted\textbf{BL}}\\
|\ &\text{ⓈCardEjected\textbf{BL}}\\
|\ &\text{ⓈCancellKeyPressed\textbf{BL}}\\
|\ &\text{ⓈEnterKeyPressed\textbf{BL}}\\
|\ &\text{ⓈDataEntered\textbf{BL}}\\
|\ &\text{ⓈTimeOut\textbf{BL}}\\
|\ &\text{ⓈServiceCompleted\textbf{BL}}\\
|\ &\text{ⓈServiceCancelled\textbf{BL}}\\
|\ &\text{ⓈSystemFailure\textbf{BL}}\\
|\ &\text{ⓈSysShutDown\textbf{BL}}\\
|\ &\text{ⓈValidAmount\textbf{BL}}\\
|\ &\text{ⓈValidBalance\textbf{BL}}\\
|\ &\text{ⓈValidCard\textbf{BL}}\\
|\ &\text{ⓈValidPIN\textbf{BL}}
\end{aligned}
\tag{5}
$$

Figure 5. The refined UDM model of the card reader

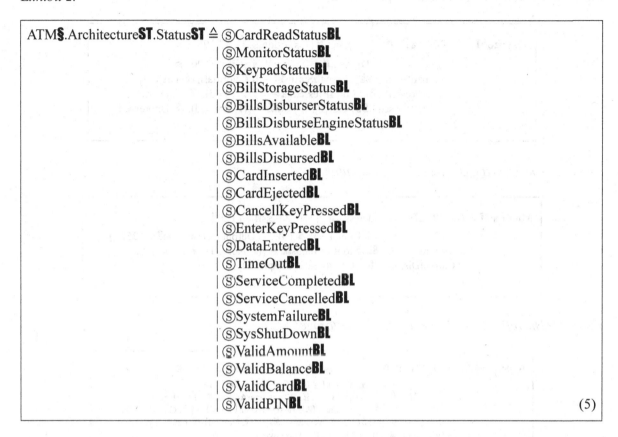

KeypadST specifies five functional fields with certain design constraints as shown in Figure 6. The field of PortAddressH represents the physical input address of the keypad. The field of Input-DigitsH represents information (≤ 4 digits) entered from the keypad. The field of KeypadStatusBL represents the working conditions of the keypad.

The fields of EnterPressedBL and CancelPressedBL represent a valid or invalid input entered by the keypad, respectively.

Figure 6. The refined UDM model of the keypad

$$
\begin{aligned}
\textbf{KeypadST} \triangleq (&<\text{PORTST}(<\text{PortAddress} : \textbf{H} \mid \text{PortAddressH} = \text{FF10H}>, \\
&\qquad <\text{InputDigits} : \textbf{N} \mid 0 \le \text{InputDigitsN} \le 1000>)>, \\
&<\text{KeypadStatus} : \textbf{BL} \mid \text{KeypadStatusBL} = \{(\textbf{T}, \text{Normal}), (\textbf{F}, \text{Faulty})\}>, \\
&<\text{EnterPressed} : \textbf{BL} \mid \text{EnterPressedBL} = \{(\textbf{T}, \text{Pressed}), (\textbf{F}, \text{Unpressed}>, \\
&<\text{CancelPressed} : \textbf{BL} \mid \text{CancelPressedBL} = \{(\textbf{T}, \text{Pressed}), (\textbf{F}, \text{Unpressed})\}> \\
&)
\end{aligned}
$$

Figure 7. The refined UDM model of the monitor

$$
\begin{aligned}
\textbf{MonitorST} \triangleq (&<\text{PORTST}(<\text{PortAddress} : \textbf{H} \mid \text{PortAddressH} = \text{FF20H}>, \\
&\qquad <\text{OutputInformation} : \textbf{S} \mid 0 < \#(\text{Output InformationS}) \le 255>)>, \\
&<\text{MonitorStatus} : \textbf{BL} \mid \text{MonitorStatusBL} = \{(\textbf{T}, \text{Normal}), (\textbf{F}, \text{Faulty})\}>, \\
&<\text{CurrentDisplay} : \textbf{S} \mid 0 \le \#(\text{CurrentDisplayS}) \le 255>)> \\
&)
\end{aligned}
$$

Figure 8. The refined UDM model of the bills storage

$$
\begin{aligned}
\textbf{BillStorageST} \triangleq (&<\text{PORTST}(<\text{BillStorageAddress} : \textbf{H} \mid \text{BillStorageAddressH} = \text{FF30H}>, \\
&\qquad <\text{BillsAmount} : \textbf{N} \mid 1 \le \text{BillsAmountN} \le 1000>)>, \\
&<\text{PORTST}(<\text{BillsDeliverAddress} : \textbf{H} \mid \text{BillsDeliverAddressH} = \text{FF31H}>, \\
&\qquad <\text{BillsDeliverEngine} : \textbf{BL} \mid \text{BillsDeliveryEngineBL} = \{(\textbf{T}, \text{On}), (\textbf{F}, \text{Off})\}>)>, \\
&<\text{BillStorageStatus} : \textbf{BL} \mid \text{BillStorageStatusBL} = \{(\textbf{T}, \text{Normal}), (\textbf{F}, \text{Faulty})\}>, \\
&<\text{BillsLevel} : \textbf{N} \mid 0 \le \text{BillsLevelN} \le \text{MaxLevelN}> \\
&)
\end{aligned}
$$

c. The UDM of the Monitor

The monitor of the ATM system, MonitorST, is an architectural model of the output device that displays system operational and status information to users. The UDM model of MonitorST specifies four functional fields with certain design constraints as shown in Figure 7. The field of PortAddressH represents the physical output address to the monitor. The field of OutputInformationS represents a string of letters (≤ 255 characters) that will be displayed on the monitor. The field of MonitorStatusBL represents the operational conditions of the monitor. The field of CurrentDisplyS is a system feedback of the latest output information on the monitor.

d. The UDM of the Bills Storage

The bills storage of the ATM system, BillStorageST, is an architectural model of the internal device that stores bills in different notes, which can be sent to the bills disburser in various combinations. The UDM model of BillStorageST specifies six functional fields with certain design constraints as shown in Figure 8. The bills storage port is an output structure consisting of two fields known as the BillStorageAddressH and BillsAmountN. The bills deliver port is an output structure consisting of two fields known as the BillsDeliverAddressH and BillsDeliverEngineBL. The field of BillStorageStatusBL represents the operational conditions of the bills storage. The

Figure 9. The refined UDM model of the bills disburser

$$
\begin{aligned}
\textbf{BillsDisburserST} \triangleq (&<\text{PORT\,ST}(<\text{DisburserDriveAddress} : \textbf{H} \mid \text{DisburserDriveAddress}\textbf{H} = \text{FF41}\textbf{H}>, \\
&<\text{DisburseEngine} : \textbf{BL} \mid \text{DisburseEngine}\textbf{BL} = \{(\textbf{T}, \text{On}), (\textbf{F}, \text{Off})\}>)>, \\
&<\text{BillsDisburserStatus} : \textbf{BL} \mid \text{BillsDisburserStatus}\textbf{BL} = \{(\textbf{T}, \text{Normal}), (\textbf{F}, \text{Faulty})\}>, \\
&<\text{AmountDisbursed} : \textbf{N} \mid 1 \leq \text{AmountDisbursed}\textbf{N} \leq 1000>)> \\
&)
\end{aligned}
$$

Figure 10. The refined UDM model of the system clock

$$
\begin{aligned}
\textbf{SysClockST} \triangleq (&<\S t : \textbf{N} \mid 0 \leq \S t\textbf{N} \leq 1{,}000{,}000>, \\
&<\text{CurrentTime} : \textbf{hh:mm:ss} \mid 00{:}00{:}00 \leq \\
&\qquad\qquad\qquad \text{CurrentTime}\textbf{hh:mm:ss} \leq 23{:}59{:}59>, \\
&<\text{MainClockPort} : \textbf{H} \mid \text{MainClockPort}\textbf{B} = \text{FFF1}\textbf{H}>, \\
&<\text{ClockInterval} : \textbf{N} \mid \text{ClockInterval}\textbf{N} = 100\textbf{ms}>, \\
&<\text{InterruptCounter} : \textbf{N} \mid 0 \leq \text{InterruptCounter}\textbf{N} \leq 9> \\
&)
\end{aligned}
$$

Figure 11. The refined UDM model of the system database

$$
\textbf{SysDatabaseST} \triangleq \mathop{R}_{i\textbf{N}=0}^{1000000} \text{SysAccount(i\textbf{N})}\textbf{ST:}
$$

$$
\begin{aligned}
(&<\text{AccountNum} : \textbf{N} \mid 0 \leq \text{AccountNum}\textbf{N} \leq 1000000>) : \\
&<\text{AccountStatus} : \textbf{BL} \mid \text{AccountStatus}\textbf{BL} = \{(\textbf{T}, \text{Active}), (\textbf{F}, \text{Inactive})\}>, \\
&<\text{PIN} : \textbf{N} \mid 0000 \leq \text{PIN}\textbf{N} \leq 9999>, \\
&<\text{CardHolder} : \textbf{S} \mid 0 < \#(\text{CardHolder}\textbf{S}) \leq 255>, \\
&<\text{Balance} : \textbf{N} \mid 0 \leq \text{Balance}\textbf{N} \leq 10000>, \\
&<\text{MaxAllowableWithdraw} : \textbf{N} \mid \text{MaxAllowableWithdraw}\textbf{N} = 1000>, \\
&<\text{CurrentWithdraw} : \textbf{N} \mid 5 \leq \text{CurrentWithdraw}\textbf{N} \leq \text{MaxAllowableWithdraw}\textbf{N}> \\
&)
\end{aligned}
$$

field of BillsLevel**N** represents the current level of bills in the bills storage.

e. The UDM of the Bills Disburser

The bills disburser of the ATM system, BillsDisburser**ST**, is an architectural model of the output device that delivers bills of requested amount from the bills storage to the customer. The UDM model of BillsDisburser**ST** specifies four functional fields with certain design constraints as shown in Figure 9. The disburser drive port is an output structure consisting of two fields known as the DisburserDriveAddress**H** and DisburseEngine**BL**.

The field of BillsDisburserStatus**BL** represents the operational conditions of the bills disburser. The field of AmountDisbursed**N** is a system feedback signal of bills disbursed to the customer in the current transaction.

f. The UDM of the System Clock

The system clock of the ATM system is an architectural model for event timing, process duration manipulation, and system synchronization. The UDM model of the system clock, SysClock**ST**, is designed as given in Figure 10. SysClock**ST** provides an *absolute* (calendar) clock CurrentTime**hh:mm:ss** as the logical time reference of the entire system and a *relative* clock §t**N** as a generic counter of the ATM system. The InterruptCounter**N** is adopted to transfer the system timing ticks at 100ms interval into the second signal. The real-time system clock is updated by the process SysClock**PC**, which will be described in the following section on system static behaviors.

g. The UDM of the System Database

The system database of the ATM system, SysDatabase**ST**, is an architectural model of the internal centralized database located in the bank`s server where the ATM connects to. The ATM uses the card number scanned from a bank card and the PIN entered from the keypad to access the system database in order to verify the validity of the card and information recorded in the corresponding account in SysDatabase**ST**, such as the card holder, current balance, and withdraw constraints.

The UDM model of SysDatabase**ST** specifies a set of accounts with seven functional fields as shown in Figure 11. The field of AccountNum**N** represents a specific account existed in the system that is corresponding to the number assigned to the bank card. The field of AccountStatus**BL** represents the current status of an account such as active or inactive in the system. The field of PIN**H** represents a user defined PIN ($\leq$ 4 digits) recorded in the system. The field of CardHolder**S** records the name of person that holds the account. The field of Balance**N** represents the current remaining money in the given account. The field of MaxAllowableWithdraw**N** represents the limit set by the bank for the given account. The field of CurrentWithdraw**N** specifies the valid user requested amount of withdraw in the current transaction.

The system architectural models specified in this section provide a set of abstract object models and clear interfaces between system hardware and software. By reaching this point, the co-design of a real-time system can be carried out in parallel by separated hardware and software teams. It is recognized that system *architecture specification* by the means of UDMs is a fundamental and difficult phase in software system modeling, while conventional formal methods hardly provide any support for this purpose. From the above examples in this subsection, it can be seen that RTPA provides a set of expressive notations for specifying system architectural structures and control models, including hardware, software, and their interactions. On the basis of the system architecture specification and with the work products of system architectural components or UDMs, specification of the operational components of the LDS system as behavioral processes can be carried out directly as elaborated in the following sections.

THE STATIC BEHAVIORAL MODEL OF THE ATM SYSTEM

A static behavior is a component-level function of a given system that can be determined before run-time. On the basis of the system architecture specifications and with the UDMs of system architectural components developed in preceding section, the operational components of the given ATM system and their behaviors can be specified as a set of UPMs as behavioral processes operating on the UDMs.

The static behaviors of the ATM system, ATM**§**.StaticBehaviors**PC**, can be described through operations on its architectural models (UDMs). ATM**§**.StaticBehaviors**PC** encompasses eight transactional processes as given in Eq. 1 and Figures 2 and 3, as well as the support processes SysInitial**PC**, SysClock**PC**, and SysDiagnosis**PC**, in parallel as specified in Exhibit 3.

The following subsections describe how the ATM static behaviors as specified in Eq. 5 are modeled and refined using the denotational mathematical notations and methodologies of RTPA in term of sets of UPMs for the ATM transaction processes and support processes, respectively.

Exhibit 3.

ATM§.StaticBehaviorsPC ≜ SysTransactionProcesses**PC**
| SysSupportProcesses**PC**
= (Welcome(<**I**:: (PN**N**)>; <**O**:: (PN**N**, AccountNum**N**, ⓢValidCard**BL**)>;
<**UDM**:: (CardReader**ST**, Monitor**ST**, SysDatabase**ST**, SysClock**ST**)>)**PC**
| CheckPIN(<**I**:: (PN**N**, AccountNum**N**)>; <**O**:: (PN**N**, ⓢValidPIN**BL**, ⓢServiceCancelled**BL**)>;
<**UDM**: (Monitor**ST**, Keypad**ST**, SysDatabase**ST**, SysClock**ST**)>)**PC**
| InputWithdrawAmount(<**I**:: (PN**N**, AccountNum**N**)>; <**O**:: (PN**N**, ⓢValidAmount**BL**, ⓢServiceCancelled**BL**)>;
<**UDM**:: (CardReader**ST**, Monitor**ST**, Keypad**ST**, SysDatabase**ST**, SysClock**ST**)>)**PC**
| VerifyBalance(<**I**:: (PN**N**, AccountNum**N**)>; <**O**:: (PN**N**, AmountToWithdraw**N**, ⓢValidBalance**BL**,
ⓢServiceCancelled**BL**)>; <**UDM**:: (Monitor**ST**, Keypad**ST**, SysDatabase**ST**, SysClock**ST**)>)**PC**
| VerifyBillsAvailability(<**I**:: (PN**N**, AccountNum**N**)>; <**O**:: (PN**N**, ⓢBillsAvailable**BL**, ⓢServiceCancelled**BL**)>;
<**UDM**::(CardReader**ST**, Monitor**ST**, Keypad**ST**, BillStorage**ST**, SysDatabase**ST**, SysClock**ST**))>)**PC**
| DisburseBills(<**I**:: (PN**N**, AccountNum**N**)>; <**O**:: (PN**N**, ⓢBillsDisbursed**BL**, ⓢServiceCompleted**BL**,
ⓢServiceCancelled**BL**)>; <**UDM**:: (CardReader**ST**, Monitor**ST**, Keypad**ST**, BillStorage**ST**,
BillsDisburser**ST**, SysDatabase**ST**, SysClock**ST**)>)**PC**
| EjectCard(<**I**:: (PN**N**)>; <**O**:: (PN**N**, ⓢCardEjected**BL**)>; <**UDM**::(CardReader**ST**, Monitor**ST**)>)**PC**
| SysFailure(<**I**:: (PN**N**)>; <**O**:: (PN**N**, ⓢSystemFailure**BL**, ⓢCardEjcted**BL**, ⓢSysShutDown**BL**)>;
<**UDM**:: (CardReader**ST**, Monitor**ST**)>)**PC**
)
| (SysInitial (<**I**:: ()>; <**O**:: (PN**N**, AccountNum**N**, ⓢCadInserted**BL**, ⓢSystemFailure**BL**)>; <**UDM**::(All_ATM_UDMs**ST**)>)**PC**)
| SysClock (<**I**:: ()>; <**O**:: ()>; <**UDM**:: (SysClock**ST**)>) **PC**
| SysDiagnosis(<**I**:: ()>; <**O**:: ()>; <**UDM**:: (All_ATM_UDMs**ST**)>)**PC**
) (6)

UPMs of the ATM State Transition Processes

The ATM system encompasses eight transaction processes as specified in Eq. 6, i.e., the Welcome**PC**, CheckPIN**PC**, InputWithdrawAmount**PC**, VerifyBalance**PC**, VerifyBillsAvailability**PC**, DisburseBills**PC**, EjectCard**PC**, and SysFailure**PC** processes. The following subsections formally describe the UPMs of the eight ATM state transition processes in RTPA.

a. The UPM of the Welcome Process

The welcome process of the ATM system, Welcome**PC**, as shown in Figure 12, is the first transition process (PN**N** = 1) that promotes system welcome information until a card is inserted. The ATM system adopts a transaction process number PN**N**, 0 ≤ PN**N** ≤ 8, as a global integer variable to represent the current system state, i.e.: (PN**N** = 0, System), (PN**N** = 1, Welcome), (PN**N** = 2, Check PIN), (PN**N** = 3, Input withdraw amount), (PN**N** = 4, Verify balance), (PN**N** = 5, Verify bills availability), (PN**N** = 6, Disburse bills), (PN**N** = 7, Eject card), and (PN**N** = 8, System failure).

Welcome**PC** reads account information stored in the card via the card reader's input port address. The obtained account number, AccountNum**N**, as a global variable of the system as that of PN**N** is used to seek if there is a corresponding account in the central database and if its status is active. If so, the card is identified as a valid one and the transaction is transferred to the next process

CheckPIN**PC** (PN**N** = 2). Otherwise, the system will terminate the transaction and eject the invalid card by transferring the current process to EjectCard**PC** (PN**N** = 7). A timer, SysClock**ST**.Timer**SS** = 10, is introduced in this process, when a valid card is identified, which requests users to enter a PIN within 10 seconds before a timeout termination is resulted in the following process.

It is noteworthy in the first part of the Welcome**PC** process that a useful safety-critical system design strategy is adopted, in which the key system devices involved are always be checked before a system function is executed. The Welcome**PC** process checks the conditions of related system devices modeled by the UDMs such as CardReader**ST** and Monitor**ST**. The functional processes may only go ahead when both of their statuses are normal. Otherwise, exceptional warring message will be generated such as ! ('Monitor fault.') and/or ! ('Card reader fault.').

b. The UPM of the Check PIN Process

The check PIN process of the ATM system, CheckPIN**PC** (PN**N** = 2), as shown in Figure 13, determines if a valid card matches its PIN. The processes first tests the conditions of related system UDMs operated in this process such as Monitor**ST** and Keypad**ST**, before the functional processes may be carried out. It also checks the 10 second timer set in the preceding process and finds out if a timeout condition has been generated when SysClock**ST**.Timer**SS** = 0, which is updated automatically by the system in the process of SysClock**PC**.

The CheckPIN**PC** process scans the PIN entered by the user via the keypad of the system. If the PIN is correct and matches the account number, the transaction is transferred to the next process InputWithdrawAmount**PC** (PN**N** = 3) after a new 10s timer is set for waiting the customer to enter the requested amount of withdraw. Otherwise, the system will allow the

user to retry PIN input up to three times before the transaction is transferred to EjectCard**PC** (PN**N** = 7). During the three time trials, if the user gives up by pressing the cancel key, i.e., Keypad**ST**.CancelPressed**BL** = **T**, the system will also transfer the transaction to EjectCard**PC** (PN**N** = 7).

c. The UPM of the Input Withdraw Amount Process

The input withdraw amount process of the ATM system, InputWithdrawAmount**PC** (PN**N**=3), as shown in Figure 14, captures the user requested amount of withdraw. The processes first tests the conditions of related system UDMs operated in this process such as Monitor**ST**, Keypad**ST**, and CardReader**ST**, before the functional processes may be carried out. It also checks the 10 second timer set in the preceding process and finds out if a timeout condition has been generated when SysClock**ST**.Timer**SS** = 0.

The InputWithdrawAmount**PC** process reads the requested amount provided by the user via the keypad of the system. If the amount to withdraw is within the predetermined maximum allowable limit for the specific account, which is set to be Account(i**N**)**ST**.MaxAllowableWithdraw**N** = \$1000 in the system database, the transaction is transferred to the next process CheckBalance**PC** (PN**N** = 4). Otherwise, the system will promote the user to reenter a valid withdraw amount. If the user presses 'Yes' (Keypad**ST**.EnterPressed**BL** = **T**) by pressing the Enter key on the keypad, the transaction will remain in the same process with a newly set 10s timer. However, if the user presses 'No' (Keypad**ST**.CancelPressed**BL** = **T**) by pressing the Enter key on the keypad, the transaction will be transferred to EjectCard**PC** (PN**N** = 7).

Figure 13. The behavior model of the check PIN process

```
CheckPIN(<I:: (PNN, AccountNumN)>; <O:: (PNN, ⓈValidPINBL, ⓈServiceCancelledBL)>;
        <UDM: (MonitorST, KeypadST, SysDatabaseST, SysClockST)>)PC ≙
{// PNN = 2
   R^T_{ⓈDataEnteredBL=F} (ⓈMonitorStatusBL := MonitorST.MonitorStatusBL
            → ⓈKeypadStatusBL := KeypadST.KeypadStatusBL
            → ( ◆ SysClockST.TimerSS ≠ 0 ∧ ⓈMonitorStatusBL = T ∧ ⓈKeypadStatusBL = T
                  → 'Enter your PIN.' |≺ PORT(MonitorST.PortAddressN)ST.OutputInformationS
                  → ⓈDataEnteredBL := KeypadST.EnterPressedBL
               | ◆ ~
                  → ( ◆ SysClockST.TimerSS = 0
                          → ⓈTimeoutBL := T
                          → ! ('Operation time out.')
                          → PNN := 7                          // To eject card
                    | ◆ ⓈMonitorStatusBL = F
                          → ! ('Monitor fault.')
                          → PNN := 8                          // To system failure
                    | ◆ ⓈKeypadStatusBL = F
                          → ! ('Keypad fault.')
                          → PNN := 8                          // To system failure
                    )
                  → ⊗
              )
          )
 → PORT(KeypadST.PortAddressN)ST.InputDigitsN |≻ PINN
 → ( ◆ PINN = SysAccount(AccountNumN)ST.PINN)
      → ⓈValidPINBL := T
      → SysClockST.TimerSS := 10                 // To wait for enter withdraw amount
      → PNN := 3                                 // To check balance
   | ◆ ~
      → ⓈValidPINBL := F
      → ↓ (PINTrialTimesN)
      → ( ◆ PINTrialTimesN > 0
            → 'Wrong PIN. Do you want to try again?' |≺ PORT(MonitorST.PortAddressN)ST.OutputInformationS
            → R^T_{ⓈTimeOutBL=F} ( ◆ ΔtN = §tN + 3                  // Delay 3s
                      → ⓈTimeOutBL := T
                    )
            → ⓈEnterKeyPresedBL := KeypadST.EnterPressedBL
            → ⓈCancelKeyPressedBL := KeypadST.CancelPressedBL
            → ( ◆ ⓈEnterKeyPressedBL = T
                  → PNN := 2                          // To retry PIN
              | ◆ ⓈCancelKeyPressedBL = T
                  → ⓈServiceCancelledBL := T
                  → PNN := 7                          // To eject card
              )
        | ◆ ~
            → 'Invalid PIN.' |≺ PORT(MonitorST.PortAddressN)ST.OutputInformationS
            → ⓈValidPINBL := F
            → PNN := 7                                // To eject card
        )
   )
}
```

d. The UPM of the Verify Balance Process

The verify balance process of the ATM system, VerifyBalance**PC** (PN**N** = 4), as shown in Figure 15, determines if the current balance of the account is enough for the withdraw request obtained in the preceding process. VerifyBalance**PC** first tests the conditions of related system UDMs operated in this process such as Monitor**ST** and Keypad**ST**, before the functional processes may be carried out.

The VerifyBalance**PC** process checks if the requested withdraw amount is less or equal to the current balance of the account maintained in the central database. If so, the transaction is transferred to the next process VerifyBillsAvail-

Figure 14. The behavior model of the input withdraw amount process

```
InputWithdrawAmount(<I:: (PNN, AccountNumN)>; <O:: (PNN, ⓈValidAmountBL, ⓈServiceCancelledBL)>;
                    <UDM:: (CardReaderST, MonitorST, KeypadST, SysDatabaseST, SysClockST)>)PC ≙
{ // PNN = 3
   R^T_{ⓈDataEnteredBL=F}  (ⓈMonitorStatusBL := MonitorST.MonitorStatusBL
         → ⓈCardReadStatusBL := CarReaderST.CardReadStatusBL
         → ( ◆ SysClockST.TimerSS ≠ 0 ∧ ⓈMonitorStatusBL = T ∧ ⓈCardReadStatusBL = T
               → 'Enter the amount you wish to withdraw ($5 … $500).' |<
                 PORT(MonitorST.PortAddressH)ST.OutputInformationS
               → ⓈDataEnteredBL := KeypadST.EnterPressedBL
            |◆ ~
               → (◆ SysClockST.TimerSS = 0
                     → ⓈTimeOutBL := T
                     → ! ('Operation time out.')
                     → PNN := 7                                  // To eject card
                  | ◆ ⓈMonitorStatusBL = F
                     → ! ('Monitor fault.')
                     → PNN := 8                                  // To system failure
                  | ◆ ⓈCardReadStatusBL = F
                     → ! ('Card reader fault.')
                     → PNN := 8                                  // To system failure
                 )
               → ⊗
           )
      )
   → PORT(KeypadST.PortAddressH)ST.InputDigitsN |> AmountToWithdrawN
   →( ◆ 5 ≤ AmountToWithdrawN ≤ SysAccount(AccountNumN)ST.MaxAllowableWithdrawN
         → ⓈValidAmountBL := T
         → SysAccount(AccountNumN)ST.CurrentWithdrawN := AmountToWithdrawN
         → PNN := 4                                     // To check balance of account
    |◆ ~
         → ⓈValidAmountBL := F
         → 'Amount required is out of range.' |< PORT(MonitorST.PortAddressH)ST.OutputInformationS
         →  R^T_{ⓈTimeOutBL=F}  (◆ ΔtN = §tN + 3                  // Delay 3s
                     → ⓈTimeOutBL := T
                  )
         → ⓈEnterKeyPresedBL := KeypadST.EnterPressedBL
         → ⓈCancelKeyPressedBL := KeypadST.CancelPressedBL
         → ( ◆ ⓈEnterKeyPressedBL = T
               → SysClockST.TimerSS := 10                     // Reset timer
               → PNN := 3                                     // To retry input
            | ◆ ⓈCancelKeyPressedBL = T
               → ⓈServiceCancelledBL := T
               → PNN := 7                                     // To eject card
           )
    )
}
```

ability**PC** (PN**N** = 5). Otherwise, the system will promote the customer to choose either to reenter a smaller amount (Keypad**ST**.EnterPressed**BL** = **T**) or give up (Keypad**ST**.CancelPressed**BL** = **T**). The former will result in the transaction being transferred to the amount reenter, i.e., PN**N** = 3, after a new timer is set for limiting the waiting time for entering the new requested amount of withdraw; However, the latter will result in the termination of the current transaction, i.e., PN**N** = 7.

Figure 15. The behavior model of the verify balance process

```
VerifyBalance(<I:: (PNN, AccountNumN)>; <O:: (PNN, AmountToWithdrawN, ⓈValidBalanceBL,
        ⓈServiceCancelledBL)>; <UDM:: (MonitorST, KeypadST, SysDatabaseST, SysClockST)>)PC ≜
{ // PNN = 4
     T
     R            (ⓈMonitorStatusBL := MonitorST.MonitorStatusBL
ⓈDataEnteredBL=F
               → ⓈKeypadStatusBL := KeypadST.KeypadStatusBL
               → ( ◆ ⓈMonitorStatusBL = F
                      → ! ('Monitor fault.')
                      → PNN := 8                              // To system failure
                      → ⊗
                 | ◆ ⓈKeypadStatusBL = F
                      → ! ('Keypad fault.')
                      → PNN := 8                              // To system failure
                      → ⊗
                 )
             )
 → AmountToWithdrawN := SysAccount(AccountNumN)ST.CurrentWithdrawN
 → ( ◆ AmountToWithdrawN = SysDatabase(AccountNumN)ST.BalanceN
       → ⓈValidBalanceBL := T
       → PNN := 5                                             // To check bills availability
   | ◆ ~
       → ⓈValidBalanceBL := F
       → 'Account balance is insufficient to withdraw. Retry a smaller amount?' |<
         PORT(MonitorST.PortAddressN)ST.OutputInformationS
                T
       →        R        (◆ ΔtN = §tN + 3                     // Delay 3s
           ⓈTimeOutBL=F
                           → ⓈTimeOutBL := T
                         )
       → ⓈEnterKeyPresedBL := KeypadST.EnterPressedBL
       → ⓈCancelKeyPressedBL := KeypadST.CancelPressedBL
       → ( ◆ ⓈEnterKeyPressedBL = T
              → SysClockST.TimerSS := 10                      // Set timer
              → PNN := 3                                      // To re-enter amount
         | ◆ ⓈCancelKeyPressedBL = T
              → ⓈServiceCancelledBL := T
              → PNN := 7                                      // To eject card
         )
   )
}
```

e. The UPM of the Verify Bills Availability Process

The verify bills availability process of the ATM system, VerifyBillsAvailability**PC** (PN**N** = 5), as shown in Figure 16, checks if the bills are available in the ATM that meet the demanded withdraw. The processes first tests the conditions of related system UDMs operated in this process such as CardReader**ST**, Monitor**ST**, Keypad**ST**, and BillStorage**ST**, before the functional processes may be carried out.

The VerifyBillsAvailability**PC** process checks the bills level in the bills storage. If the bills level is higher than the valid withdraw amount, BillStorage**ST**.BillsLevel**N** ≥ AmountToWithdraw**N**, the system will transfer the current transaction to DisburseBills**PC** (PN**N** = 6) process. Otherwise, the system will find out if the customer wishes to reenter a lower amount by promoting a system message on the monitor and wait for 3 seconds for response. When the customer selects 'Yes' by pressing the Enter key on the keypad, the system will transfer the current process

Figure 16. The behavior model of the verify bill availability process

```
VerifyBillsAvailability(<I:: (PNN, AccountNumN)>; <O:: (PNN, ⓈBillsAvailableBL, ⓈServiceCancelledBL)>;
                 <UDM::(CardReaderST, MonitorST, KeypadST, BillStorageST, SysDatabaseST,
                 SysClockST))>)PC ≜
{ // PNN = 5
  ⓈMonitorStatusBL := MonitorST.MonitorStatusBL
  → ⓈCardReadStatusBL := CarReaderST.CardReadStatusBL
  → ( ◆ ⓈMonitorStatusBL = F
        → ! ('Monitor fault.')
        → PNN := 8                                                   // To system failure
        → ⊗
     | ◆ ⓈCardReadStatusBL = F
        → ! ('Card reader fault.')
        → PNN := 8                                                   // To system failure
        → ⊗
    )
  → (◆ BillStorageST.BillStorageStatusBL) = T
        → AmountToWithdrawN := SysAccount(AccountNumN)ST.CurrentWithdrawN
        → ( ◆ BillStorageST.BillsLevelN ≥ AmountToWithdrawN
              → ⓈBillsAvailableBL := T
              → PNN := 6                                             // To disburse cash
              → ⊗
          | ◆ ~
              → ⓈBillsAvailableBL := F
              → 'No sufficient cash available in this machine. Retry a new amount?' |≺
                PORT(MonitorST.PortAddressH)ST.OutputInformationS
                    T
              →     R          (◆ ΔtN = §tN + 3                        // Delay 3s
               ⓈTimeOutBL=F
                                    → ⓈTimeOutBL := T
                               )
              → ⓈEnterKeyPressedBL := KeypadST.EnterPressedBL
              → ⓈCancelKeyPressedBL := KeypadST.CancelPressedBL
              → ( ◆ ⓈEnterKeyPressedBL = T
                    → SysClockST.TimerSS := 10                       // Set timer
                    → PNN := 3                                       // To re-enter amount
                    → ⊗
                | ◆ ⓈCancelKeyPressedBL = T ∨ (ⓈCancelKeyPressedBL = F ∧ ⓈEnterKeyPressedBL = F)
                    → ⓈServiceCancelledBL := T
                    → PNN := 7                                       // To eject card
                    → ⊗
                )
          )
    | ◆ ~
        → ⓈBillStorageStatusBL := F
        → ! ('Bills storage faulty.')
        → PNN := 8                                                   // To system failure
  )
}
```

back to InputWithdrawAmount**PC** (PN**N** = 3), in order to obtaining a new amount for withdraw. However, if the customer selects 'No' by pressing the Cancel key on the keypad or there was no action after 3 seconds, the system will terminate the transaction by transferring it to EjectCard**PC** (PN**N** = 7).

f. The UPM of the Disburse Bills Process

The disburse bills process of the ATM system, DisbureseBills**PC** (PN**N** = 6), as shown in Figure 17, delivers the requested and validated amount of bills from the bills storage to the customer. The process first tests the conditions of related system UDMs operated in this process such as Monitor**ST**, Keypad**ST**, Cardreader**ST**, BillStorage**ST**, and

BillsDisburser**ST**, before the functional processes may be carried out.

The DisbureseBills**PC** process deducts the balance in the corresponding account, updates the bills level in the bills storage, prepares the exact amount of bills as requested in the bills storage, and deliver them via the output device of the bills disburser. Then, the transaction is successfully completed and is transferred to the next process EjectCard**PC** (PN**N** = 7). When bills disburse cannot be carried out because a bill disburser malfunction, the process will promote a system failure information, and the transaction is terminated after the system is transferred to the exception state SysFailure**PC** (PN**N** = 8).

g. The UPM of the Eject Card Process

The eject card process of the ATM system, EjectCard**PC** (PN**N** = 7), as shown in Figure 18, terminates a complete or exceptional transaction, returns the inserted card, and prepares for next service. The process first tests the conditions of related system UDMs operated in this process such as Monitor**ST** and Cardreader**ST**, before the functional processes may be carried out.

There are five designated causes that drive a transaction of the ATM system into the state EjectCard**PC**, i.e., &ServiceCompleted**BL** = **T**, &ServiceCancelled**BL** = **T**, &TimeOut**BL** = **T**, &ValidCard**BL** = **F**, and &ValidPIN**BL** = **F**. Except the first condition, all other conditions are due to an operational exception. Therefore, the Eject-Card**PC** process is designed as a switch structure where a different causal event corresponding to different actions before the system returns to Welcome**PC** (PN**N** = 1). However, when an unknown cause results in transaction termination, the system will provide a warring information and transfers to SystemFailure**PC** (PN**N** = 8).

Figure 17. The behavior model of the disburse bills process

Figure 18. The behavior model of the eject card process

```
EjectCard (<I:: (PNN)>; <O:: (PNN, §CardEjectedBL)>; <UDM::(CardReaderST, MonitorST)>)PC ≙
{// PNN = 7
§MonitorStatusBL := MonitorST.MonitorStatusBL
→ §CardReadStatusBL := CarReaderST.CardReadStatusBL
→ ( ◆ §MonitorStatusBL = F
        → ! ('Monitor Fault.')
        → PNN := 8                                                      // To system failure
        → ⊗
   | ◆ §CardReadStatusBL = F
        → ! ('Card Reader Fault.')
        → PNN := 8                                                      // To system failure
        → ⊗
   )
→ ( ◆ §ServiceCompletedBL = T
        → 'Please collect your card.' |< PORT(MonitorST.PortAddressH)ST.OutputInformationS
        → EjectCardBL := T
        → EjectCardBL |< PORT(CardReaderST.CardEjectAddressH)ST.CardEjectEngineBL
        → §CardEjectedBL := T
        → PNN := 1
   | ◆ §ServiceCancelledBL = T
        → 'Please collect your card.' |< PORT(MonitorST.PortAddressH)ST.OutputInformationS
        → EjectCardBL := T
        → EjectCardBL |< PORT(CardReaderST.CardEjectAddressH)ST.CardEjectEngineBL
        → §CardEjectedBL := T
        → PNN := 1
   | ◆ §TimeOutBL = T
        → 'Service time out. Please collect your card.' |<
             PORT(MonitorST.PortAddressH)ST.OutputInformationS
        → EjectCardBL := T
        → EjectCardBL |< PORT(CardReaderST.CardEjectAddressH)ST.CardEjectEngineBL
        → §CardEjectedBL := T
        → §TimeOutBL := F
        → PNN := 1
   | ◆ §ValidCardBL = F
        → 'Invalid Card.' |< PORT(MonitorST.PortAddressH)ST.OutputInformationS
        → EjectCardBL := T
        → EjectCardBL |< PORT(CardReaderST.CardEjectAddressH)ST.CardEjectEngineBL
        → §CardEjectedBL := T
        → PNN := 1
   | ◆ §ValidPINBL = F
        → 'Invalid PIN.' |< PORT(MonitorST.PortAddressH)ST.OutputInformationS
        → EjectCardBL := T
        → EjectCardBL |< PORT(CardReaderST.CardEjectAddressH)ST.CardEjectEngineBL
        → §CardEjectedBL := T
        → PNN := 1
   | ◆ ~
        → ! ('An exceptional fault detected.')
        → PNN := 8                                                      // To system failure
   )
}
```

h. The UPM of the System Failure Process

The system failure process of the ATM system, SysFailurePC (PNN = 8), as shown in Figure 19, terminates the system in order to handle an exceptional problem by system maintainers. The SysFailurePC process ejects any card remaining in the machine, provides a warring message on the monitor, and instructs the system dispatching process as shown in Figure 24 to shut down system interactions to customers until it is recovered by maintainers.

UPMs of the ATM Support Processes

In addition to the transaction processing processes of the ATM system as modeled and described in the preceding subsections, a set of system support processes is required for ATM in order to provide

Figure 19. The behavior model of the system failure process

```
SysFailure (<I:: (PNN)>; <O:: (PNN, ⓈSystemFailureBL, ⓈCardEjctedBL, ⓈSysShutDownBL)>;
            <UDM:: (CardReaderST, MonitorST)>)PC ≜
{// PNN = 8
 ⓈSystemFailureBL := T
 → ! ('System failure.')
 → 'System failure. Please use another machine.' |< PORT(MonitorST.PortAddressH) ST.OutputInformationS
 → EjectCardBL := T
 → EjectCardBL |> PORT(CardReaderST.CardEjectAddressH)ST.CardEjectEngineBL
 → ⓈCardEjectedBL := T
 → ⓈSysShutDownBL := T
 → ⊗
}
```

necessary system functions. The support processes of the ATM system as specified in Eq. 5 encompass three UPMs such as the SysInitial**PC**, SysClock**PC**, and SysDiagnosis**PC** processes. The following subsections formally describe the refined UPMs of the ATM support processes in RTPA.

a. The UPM of the System Initialization Process

System initialization is a common process of a real-time system that boots the system, sets its initial states and environment, and preassigns the initial values of data objects of the system such as variables, constants, as well as architectural (hardware interface) and control (internal) UDMs. Initialization is crucially important for a real-time system as well as its control logic specified in the functional processes. The system initialization process of the ATM system, SysInitial**PC**, is modeled as a UPM in RTPA as shown in Figure 20, where all system architectural and control UDMs are initialized as specified in their UDMs. Then, the system clock and timing interrupt are set to

Figure 24. Dynamic process deployment of the ATM system

```
ATM§.ProcessDeploymentPC ≜ § →
{ // L1: Basic level processes
  @SystemInitialS
   ↳ (SysInitialPC
                T
      ↣        R        (ATM§.SysTransactionProcessesPC          // See Eq. 5
        @SysShutDownBL=F
                          → ◆ SysClockST.CurrentTimehh:mm:ss = xx:00:00 ∧ SysClockST.PNN = 1
                              → SysClockST.PNN := 0              // Enter system diagnosis mode
                              ↣ SysDiagniosisPC
                              → SysClockST.PNN := 1              // Exit system diagnosis mode
                        )
      → ⊠
     )
 ↯ // L3: Interrupt level processes
    @SysClock100msIntS
    ↗ SysClockPC
    ↘
} → §
```

their initial logical or calendar values. However, the system central database, SysDatabase**ST**, is initialized and maintained by the system server of the bank.

b. The UPM of the System Clock Process

The system clock process is a generic support process of a real-time system that maintains and updates an absolute (calendar) clock and a relative clock for the system. The system clock process of the ATM system, SysClock**PC**, is modeled in Figure 21. The source of the system clock is obtained from the 100ms interrupt clock signal generated by system hardware, via which the absolute clock with real-time second, minute, and hour, SysClock**ST**.CurrentTime**hh:mm:ss**, are generated and periodically updated. The second clock in a real-time system is the relative clock, SysClock**ST**.§t**N**, which is usually adopted for relative timing and duration manipulations. The relative clock is reset to zero at midnight each day in order to prevent it from overflow.

c. The UPM of the System Diagnosis Process

The system diagnosis process of the ATM system, SysDiagnosis**PC**, as shown in Figure 22 (a) and (b), is a built-in system diagnosis component that is triggered every hour on the hour when there is no current service. The dispatching mechanism of the system diagnosis process is specified at the base-level of system process deployment in Figure 24. SysDiagnosis**PC** tests all system devices such as the card reader, keypad, monitor, bills storage, and bills disburser. Testing results are diagnosed in order to update the current system operating conditions modeled by a set of global system statuses as shown as part of Eq. 5. It is noteworthy that

Figure 20. The behavior model of the system initialization process

SysInital (<**I**:: ( )>; <**O**:: (PN**N**, AccountNum**N**, ⓢCadInserted**BL**, ⓢSystemFailure**BL**)>;
<**UDM**::(All_ATM_UDMs**ST**)>)**PC**) ≙
{ Initial ATM_UDMs**ST** // Initialize all UDMs
→ CardReader**ST**.CardReadStatus**BL** := **T**
→ CardReader**ST**.CardInsertStatus**BL** := **T**
→ CardReader**ST**.CardEjectStatus**BL** := **T**
→ Keypad**ST**.KeypadStatus**BL** := **T**
→ Minitor**ST**.MonitorStatus**BL** := **T**
→ BillStorage**ST**.BillStorageStatus**BL** := **T**
→ BillsDisburser**ST**.BillsDisburserStatus**BL** := **T**
→ BillsDisburser**ST**.DisburserEngineStatus**BL** := **T**
→ SysClock**ST**.§t**N** := 0
→ SysClock**ST**.CurrentTime**hh:mm:ss** := hh:mm:ss // Set current time
→ SysClock**ST**.InterruptCounter**N** := 0
→ SysClock**ST**.Timer**N** := 0
→ ⓢCardInserted**BL** := **F**
→ ⓢSystemFailure**BL** := **F**
→ PN**N** := 1
→ AccountNum**N** := 0
→ PINTrialTimes**N** := 3
}

Figure 21. The behavior model of the system clock process

```
SysClock(<I:: ( )>; <O:: ( )>; UDM:: (SysClockST)>)PC ≜
{ ↑(SysClockST.InterruptCounterN)                          // 100ms clock interrupt
  → ◆ SysClockST.InterruptCounterN = 9                     // Set to 1 second
      (→ SysClockST.InterruptCounterN := 0
        → ↑(SysClockST.§tN)
        → ↑ (SysClockST.CurrentTimehh:mm:ss)
        → ◆ SysClockST.CurrentTimehh:mm:ss = 23:59:59
            → SysClockST.CurrentTimehh:mmss := 00:00:00
            → SysClockST.§tN := 0
        → ◆ SysClockST.TimerSS ≠ 0
            → ↓ (SysClockST.TimerSS)
      )
}
```

the built-in-tests (BITs) technology (Wang et al., 2000) adopted in the ATM system diagnosis process may be further enhanced by additional manual tests regularly conducted by maintainers because many sophisticated tests for the ATM system need interactive operations and feedback of human operators.

THE DYNAMIC BEHAVIORAL MODEL OF THE ATM SYSTEM

Dynamic behaviors of a system are run-time process deployment and dispatching mechanisms based on the static behaviors modeled in UPMs. Because the static behaviors are a set of component processes of the system, to put the static processes into a life and interacting system at run-time, the dynamic behaviors of the system in terms of process priority allocation, process deployment, and process dispatch, are yet to be specified. With the UPMs developed in the preceding section as a set of static behavioral processes of the ATM system, this section describes the dynamic behaviors of the ATM system at run-time via *process priority allocation, process deployments,* and *process dispatch.*

Process Priority Allocation of the ATM System

The process priority allocation of system dynamic behaviors is the executing and timing requirements of all static processes at run-time. In general, process priorities can be specified at 4 levels for real-time and nonreal-time systems in an increasing priority known as: L1: *base* level processes, L2: *high* level processes, L3: *low interrupt* level processes, and L4: *high interrupt* level processes. The L1 and L2 processes are system dynamic behaviors that are executable in normal sequential manner. However, the L3 and L4 processes are executable in periodical manner triggered by certain system timing interrupts. It is noteworthy that some of the priority levels may be omitted in modeling a particular system, except the base level processes. That is, any system encompasses at least a base level process, particularly for a nonreal-time or transaction processing system.

According to the RTPA system modeling and refinement methodology (Wang, 2007), the first step refinement of the dynamic behaviors of the ATM system known as process priority allocation can be specified as shown in Figure 23. It may be observed that all non-periodical

Figure 22. (a) The behavior model of the system diagnosis process (b) The behavior model of the system diagnosis process

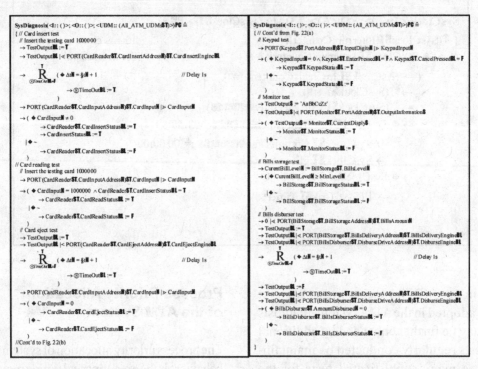

processes at run-time including SysInitial**PC**, SysDiagnosis**PC**, and the 8 transaction processes such as Welcome**PC**, CheckPIN**PC**, InputWithdrawAmount**PC**, VerifyBalance**PC**, VerifyBillsAvailability**PC**, DisburseBills**PC**, EjectCard**PC**, and SysFailure**PC**, are allocated at the base level (L1). Therefore, there is no high level process in the ATM system. However, the process with strict timing constraints, SysClock**PC**, is allocated as periodical interrupt processes at L3.

Process Deployment of the ATM System

Process deployment is a dynamic behavioral model of systems at run-time, which refines the timing relations and interactions among the system (**§**), system clock, system interrupts, and all processes at different priority levels. Process deployment is a refined model of process priority allocation for time-driven behaviors of a system. On the basis of

Figure 23. Process priority allocation of ATM dynamic behaviors

```
ATM§.DynamicBehaviorsPC ≙
{     §
  || // L1: Base level processes
  (    SysInitial PC
     | WelcomePC
     | CheckPIN PC
     | InputWithdrawAmountPC
     | VerifyBalancePC
     | VerifyBillsAvailabilityPC
     | DisburseBillsPC
     | EjectCardPC
     | SysFailurePC
     | SysDiagnosisPC
  )
  || // L3: Interrupt level processes
       SysClock PC
}
```

the process priority allocation model as developed in previous subsection in Figure 23, the ATM dynamic behaviors can be further refined with a process deployment model as shown in Figure 24, where precise timing relationships between different priority levels are specified.

The dynamic behaviors of the ATM system can be described by the interactions of parallel categories of processes at the base and interrupt levels triggered by the event @SystemInitial**S** or @SysClock100msInst⊙, respectively. The ATM system repeatedly executes the eight transaction processes at base level until the event SysShutDown**BL** = **T** is captured by the system (**§**). The system diagnosis process, SysDiagnosis**PC**, is also deployed at the base level, which is triggered every hour on the hour when the system is idle, i.e., PN**N** = 1.

When the interrupt-level process occurs per 100ms during run-time of base level processes, the system switches priority scheduling to the interrupt level process SysClock**PC**. Once it is completed, the interrupt-level process hands over control to the system in order to resume the interrupted base-level functions.

Process Dispatch of the ATM System

Process dispatch is a dynamic behavioral model of systems at run-time, which refines relations between system events and processes. Dynamic process dispatch specifies event-driven behaviors of a system. In the ATM system, the iterative transaction processing processes, ATM**§**.TransactionProcesses**PC**, are a complex process that can be further refined in a system process dispatching framework as shown in Figure 25. The ATM process dispatching model specifies that the system iteratively handles transaction processes by a switch structure. In a certain process, one of the eight possible transaction processes determined by the value of current process numbers of the system (PN**N**) is dispatched. Then, the dispatch process returns control to the system (**§**).

Figure 25. Dynamic process dispatch of the ATM system

```
ATM§.ProcessDispatchingPC ≙ § →
{ @'PNN = 0' ↳  SysDiagnosis(<I:: ()>; <O:: ( )>; <UDM:: (All_ATM_UDMsST)>)PC
 | @'PNN = 1' ↳  Welcome(<I:: (PNN)>; <O:: (PNN, AccountNumN, ⓢValidCardBL)>;
                   <UDM:: (CardReaderST, MonitorST, SysDatabaseST, SysClockST)>)PC
 | @'PNN = 2' ↳  CheckPIN(<I:: (PNN, AccountNumN)>; <O:: (PNN, ⓢValidPINBL, ⓢServiceCancelledBL)>;
                   <UDM: (MonitorST, KeypadST, SysDatabaseST, SysClockST)>)PC
 | @'PNN = 3' ↳  InputWithdrawAmount(<I:: (PNN, AccountNumN)>; <O:: (PNN, ⓢValidAmountBL,
                   ⓢServiceCancelledBL)>; <UDM:: (CardReaderST, MonitorST,
                   KeypadST, SysDatabaseST, SysClockST)>)PC
 | @'PNN = 4' ↳  VerifyBalance(<I:: (PNN, AccountNumN)>; <O:: (PNN, AmountToWithdrawN,
                   ⓢValidBalanceBL, ⓢServiceCancelledBL)>;
                   <UDM:: (MonitorST, KeypadST, SysDatabaseST, SysClockST)>)PC
 | @'PNN = 5' ↳  VerifyBillsAvailability(<I:: (PNN, AccountNumN)>; <O:: (PNN, ? BillsAvailableBL,
                   ⓢServiceCancelledBL)>; <UDM::(CardReaderST, MonitorST,
                   KeypadST, BillStorageST, SysDatabaseST, SysClockST))>)PC
 | @'PNN = 6' ↳  DisburseBills(<I:: (PNN, AccountNumN)>; <O:: (PNN, ⓢBillsDisbursedBL,
                   ⓢServiceCompletedBL, ⓢServiceCancelledBL)>; <UDM:: (CardReaderST,
                   MonitorST, KeypadST, BillStorageST, BillsDisburserST, SysDatabaseST,
                   SysClockST)>)PC
 | @'PNN = 7' ↳  EjectCard(<I:: (PNN)>; <O:: (PNN, ⓢCardEjectedBL)>;
                   <UDM::(CardReaderST, MonitorST)>)PC
 | @'PNN = 8' ↳  SysFailure(<I:: (PNN)>; <O:: (PNN, ⓢSystemFailureBL, ⓢCardEjctedBL, ⓢSysShutDownBL)>;
                   <UDM:: (CardReaderST, MonitorST)>)PC
 | ~             → ⊗
} → §
```

The formal design models of the ATM system and their refinements demonstrate a typical system modeling paradigm of the entire architectures, static behaviors, and dynamic behaviors according to the RTPA specification and refinement methodology. The practical formal engineering method of RTPA for system modeling and specification provides a coherent notation system and systematical methodology for large-scale software and hybrid system design and implementation. The final-level refinements of the ATM specifications provide a set of detailed and precise design blueprints for seamless code generation, system implementation, tests, and verifications in software engineering.

CONCLUSION

This paper has demonstrated that the ATM system, including its architecture, static behaviors, and dynamic behaviors, can be essentially and sufficiently described by RTPA. The experimental case study has shown that the formal specification and modeling of the ATM system are helpful for improving safety operations and quality services of the system. With a stepwise specification and refinement method for describing both system architectural and operational components, the formal model of the ATM system provides a foundation for implementation in multiple programming languages and on different operating platforms. It also improves the controllability, reliability, maintainability, and quality of the design and implementation in real-time software engineering.

A comprehensive set of real-world applications of RTPA for formally modeling real-time systems may be referred to (Wang, 2003, 2007, 2009b; Wang, Ngolah, Ahmadi, Sheu, & Ying, 2009; Ngolah, Wang, & Tan, 2004). Further studies have demonstrated that RTPA is not only useful as a generic notation and methodology for software engineering, but also good at modeling human cognitive processes. The applications of RTPA in modeling cognitive processes of the brain and computational intelligence may be referred to (Wang, 2009a, 2009c; Wang & Chiew, in press; Wang & Ruhe, 2007; Wang, Kinsner, & Zhang, 2009; Wang, Zadeh, & Yao, 2009).

ACKNOWLEDGMENT

The authors would like to acknowledge the partial support of Natural Science and Engineering Council of Canada (NSERC) to this work. The authors would like to thank the anonymous reviewers for their invaluable comments that have greatly improved the latest version of this paper.

REFERENCES

Bjorner, D., & Jones, C. B. (1982). *Formal specification and software development*. Upper Saddle River, NJ: Prentice Hall.

Corsetti, E., Montanari, A., & Ratto, E. (1991). Dealing with different time granularities in formal specifications of real-time systems. *Journal of Real-Time Systems*, *3*(2), 191–215. doi:10.1007/BF00365335

Hayes, I. (1985). Applying formal specifications to software development in industry. *IEEE Transactions on Software Engineering*, *11*(2), 169–178. doi:10.1109/TSE.1985.232191

Hoare, C. A. R. (1978). Communicating sequential processes. *Communications of the ACM*, *21*(8), 666–677. doi:10.1145/359576.359585

Hoare, C. A. R. (1985). *Communicating sequential processes*. Upper Saddle River, NJ: Prentice-Hall.

Laplante, P. A. (1977). *Real-time systems design and analysis* (2nd ed.). Washington, DC: IEEE Press.

Liu, J. (2000). *Real-time systems*. Upper Saddle River, NJ: Prentice-Hall.

McDermid, J. A. (Ed.). (1991). *Software engineer's reference book*. Oxford, UK: Butterworth-Heinemann.

Ngolah, C. F., Wang, Y., & Tan, X. (2004). The real-time task scheduling algorithm of RTOS+. *IEEE Canadian Journal of Electrical and Computer Engineering, 29*(4), 237–243.

Wang, Y. (2002). The real-time process algebra (RTPA). *Annals of Software Engineering, 14*, 235–274. doi:10.1023/A:1020561826073

Wang, Y. (2003). Using process algebra to describe human and software system behaviors. *Brain and Mind, 4*(2), 199–213. doi:10.1023/A:1025457612549

Wang, Y. (2007). Software engineering foundations: A software science perspective. In *CRC series in software engineering* (Vol. II). Boca Raton, FL: Auerbach Publications.

Wang, Y. (2008a). On contemporary denotational mathematics for computational intelligence. *Transactions of Computational Science, 2*, 6–29. doi:10.1007/978-3-540-87563-5_2

Wang, Y. (2008b). Mathematical laws of software. *Transactions of Computational Science, 2*, 46–83. doi:10.1007/978-3-540-87563-5_4

Wang, Y. (2008c). RTPA: A denotational mathematics for manipulating intelligent and computational behaviors. *International Journal of Cognitive Informatics and Natural Intelligence, 2*(2), 44–62.

Wang, Y. (2008d). Deductive semantics of RTPA. *International Journal of Cognitive Informatics and Natural Intelligence, 2*(2), 95–121.

Wang, Y. (2009a). On abstract intelligence: Toward a unified theory of natural, artificial, machinable, and computational intelligence. *International Journal of Software Science and Computational Intelligence, 1*(1), 1–17.

Wang, Y. (2009b). The formal design model of a telephone switching system (TSS). *International Journal of Software Science and Computational Intelligence, 1*(3), 92–116.

Wang, Y. (2009c). On cognitive computing. *International Journal of Software Science and Computational Intelligence, 1*(3), 1–15.

Wang, Y., & Chiew, V. (in press). On the cognitive process of human problem solving. *Cognitive Systems Research: An International Journal, 10*(4).

Wang, Y., & King, G. (2000). Software engineering processes: Principles and applications. In *CRC series in software engineering* (Vol. I). Boca Raton, FL: CRC Press.

Wang, Y., King, G., Fayad, M., Patel, D., Court, I., & Staples, G. (2000). On built-in tests reuse in object-oriented framework design. *ACM Journal on Computing Surveys, 32*(1), 7–12. doi:10.1145/351936.351943

Wang, Y., Kinsner, W., & Zhang, D. (2009). Contemporary cybernetics and its faces of cognitive informatics and computational intelligence. *IEEE Trans. on System, Man, and Cybernetics (B), 39*(4), 823–833. doi:10.1109/TSMCB.2009.2013721

Wang, Y., Ngolah, C. F., Ahmadi, H., Sheu, P., & Ying, S. (2009). The formal design model of a lift dispatching system (LDS). *International Journal of Software Science and Computational Intelligence, 1*(4), 98–122.

Wang, Y., & Ruhe, G. (2007). The cognitive process of decision making. *International Journal of Cognitive Informatics and Natural Intelligence, 1*(2), 73–85.

Wang, Y., Zadeh, L. A., & Yao, Y. (2009). On the system algebra foundations for granular computing. *International Journal of Software Science and Computational Intelligence, 1*(1), 64–86.

This work was previously published in International Journal of Software Science and Computational Intelligence, Volume 2, Issue 1, edited by Yingxu Wang, pp. 102-131, copyright 2010 by IGI Publishing (an imprint of IGI Global).

Chapter 16
The Formal Design Models of a Set of Abstract Data Types (ADTs)

Yingxu Wang
University of Calgary, Canada

Xinming Tan
Wuhan University of Technology, China

Cyprian F. Ngolah
Sentinel Trending & Diagnostics Ltd., Canada

Phillip C.-Y. Sheu
University of California, Irvine, USA

ABSTRACT

Type theories are fundamental for underpinning data object modeling and system architectural design in computing and software engineering. Abstract Data Types (ADTs) are a set of highly generic and rigorously modeled data structures in type theory. ADTs also play a key role in Object-Oriented (OO) technologies for software system design and implementation. This paper presents a formal modeling methodology for ADTs using the Real-Time Process Algebra (RTPA), which allows both architectural and behavioral models of ADTs and complex data objects. Formal architectures, static behaviors, and dynamic behaviors of a set of ADTs are comparatively studied. The architectural models of the ADTs are created using RTPA architectural modeling methodologies known as the Unified Data Models (UDMs). The static behaviors of the ADTs are specified and refined by a set of Unified Process Models (UPMs) of RTPA. The dynamic behaviors of the ADTs are modeled by process dispatching technologies of RTPA. This work has been applied in a number of real-time and non-real-time system designs such as a Real-Time Operating System (RTOS+), a Cognitive Learning Engine (CLE), and the automatic code generator based on RTPA.

DOI: 10.4018/978-1-4666-0264-9.ch016

INTRODUCTION

Computational operations can be classified into the categories of *data object, behavior,* and *resource* modeling and manipulations. Based on this view, programs are perceived as a coordination of the data objects and behaviors in computing. *Data object modeling* is a process to creatively extract and abstractly represent a real-world problem by data models based on the constraints of given computing resources.

Using types to model real-world entities can be traced back to the mathematical thought of Bertrand Russell (Russell, 1903) and Georg Cantor in 1932 (Lipschutz & Lipson, 1997). A type is a category of variables that share a common property such as the kind of data, domain, and allowable operations. Types are an important logical property shared by data objects in programming (Cardelli & Wegner, 1985; Mitchell, 1990). Although data in their most primitive form is a string of bits, types are found expressively convenient for data representation at the logical level in programming. Type theory can be used to prevent computational operations on incompatible operands, to help software engineers to avoid obvious and not so obvious pitfalls, and to improve regularity and orthogonality in programming language design.

Definition 1. A *data type*, shortly a *type*, is a set in which all member data objects share a common logical property or attribute.

The mathematical foundation of types is set theory. The maximum range of values that a variable can assume is a type, and a type is associated with a set of predefined or allowable operations. Methodologies of types and their properties have been defined in Real-Time Process Algebra (RTPA) (Wang, 2002, 2008a, 2008b, 2008c), where 17 primitive types in computing and software engineering have been elicited (Wang, 2007). A type can be classified as either *primitive* or *derived* (complex) types. The former is the most

elementary types that cannot further be divided into more simple ones; the latter is a compound form of multiple primitive types based on certain type rules. Most primitive types are provided by programming languages; while most user defined types are derived ones.

A *type system* specifies data object modeling and manipulation rules of a programming language, as that of a grammar system that specifies program syntaxes and composing rules of the language. Therefore, the generic complex types can be modeled by abstract data types (Guttag, 1977; Broy et al., 1984), which are a logical model of a complex and/or user defined data type with a set of predefined operations.

Definition 2. An *Abstract Data Type* (ADT) is an abstract model of data objects with a formal encapsulation of the logical architecture and valid operations of the data object.

An ADT encapsulates a data structure and presents the user with an interface through which data can be accessed. It exports a type, a set of valid operations, and any axioms and preconditions that define the application domain of the ADT. ADTs extend type construction techniques by encapsulating both data structures and functional behaviors. The interface and implementation of an ADT can be separated in design and implementation. Based on the models of ADTs as generic data structures, concrete data objects can be derived in computing.

A number of ADTs have been identified in computing and system modeling such as *stack, queue, sequence, record, array, list, tree, file,* and *graph* (Wang, 2007). A summary of the ten typical ADTs is provided in Table 1 where the structures and behaviors of the ADTs are described. ADTs possess the following properties: (i) An extension of type constructions by integrating both data structures and functional behaviors; (ii) A hybrid data object modeling technique that *encapsulates* both user defined data structures (types) and allowable operations on them; (iii) The interface

Table 1. Summary of typical ADTs in software system modeling

No.	ADT	Structure	Behaviors
1	Stack	Stack**ST**	Stack**ST**.{Create, Push, Pop, Clear, EmptyTest, FullTest, Release}
2	Queue	Queue**ST**	Queue**ST**.{Create, Enqueue, Serve, Clear, EmptTest, FullTest, Release}
3	Sequence	Sequence**ST**	Sequence**ST**.{Create, Append, FindElement, Retrieve, Clear, EmptyTest, FullTest, Release}
4	Record	Record**ST**	Record**ST**.{Create, Initialization, UpdateField, UpdateRecord, RetrieveField, RetrieveRecord, Release}
5	Array	Array**ST**	Array**ST**.{Create, Update, Retrieve, Initialization, Clear, Release}
6	List	List**ST**	List**ST**.{Create, FindNext, FindPrior, FindIth, FindKey, Retrieve, Update, InsertAfter, InsertBefore, Delete, CurrentPos, FullTest, EmptyTest, GetSize, Clear, Release}
7	Binary Tree	B-Tree**ST**	B-Tree**ST**.{Create, Traverse, Insert, DeleteSub, Update, Retrieve, Find, Characteristics, EmptyTest, Clear, Release}
8	File (Sequential)	SeqFile**ST**	SeqFile**ST**.{Create, Open, Reset, Save, Close, Delete} ∪ {Read, Append, EmptyTest, FullTest}
9	File (Random)	RandFile**ST**	RandFile**ST**.{Create, Open, Reset, Save, Close, Delete} ∪ {ReadRec, InsertRec, UpdateRec, DeleteRec, EmptyTest, FullTest}
10	Diagraph	Digrapg**ST**	Digrapg**ST**.{Create, InsertNode, InsertEdge, DeleteNode, DeleteEdge, Retrieve, Update, FindNode, FindEdge, CurrentNode, CurrentEdge, Release}

and implementation of an ADT are separated. Detailed implementation of the ADT is hidden to applications that invoke the ADT and its pre-defined operations.

There are a number of approaches to the specification of ADTs. Mathematically, the main approaches are of logical and algebraic, as well as their combinations. Although each of these approaches has its advantages, there are gaps when applying them to solve real-world problems. The logical approach is good at specifying high-level static behaviors of ADTs in forms of their preconditions and post-conditions of operations. For instance, a specification of *queue* as an ADT in predicate logic is shown in Figure 1 (Stubbs & Webre, 1985). However, the logic-based approach is not suitable for behavioral refinement and the modeling of dynamic behaviors of ADTs.

Another approach to ADT specification is the algebraic methods, which treat an ADT as an algebraic structure of sorts and operations on the sorts (McDermid, 1991). An algebraic model of

an ADT, stack, is illustrated in Figure 2 (Louden, 1993). The advantage of algebraic models of ADTs is its abstraction and elegance. However, it is often too abstract for system implementers and users, especially for dealing with some non-trivial ADTs.

In order to enhance the algebraic methods and reduce their complexity, RTPA is introduced (Wang, 2007). The RTPA methodology provides an explicit and easy-to-use algebraic approach for ADT and system modeling. RTPA reveals two fundamental technologies for ADT system modeling and refinement known as the unified data model and the unified process model (Wang, 2007).

Definition 3. A *Unified Data Model* (UDM) is a *generic architectural* model of a software system as well as its hardware components, interfaces, and internal control structures, which can be rigorously modeled and refined in denotational mathematics as a tuple, i.e.:

Figure 1. A logical model of the ADT queue (adapted from Stubbs & Webre, 1985)

```
Elements:  e, f, g, … of type stdelement
Structure: Queue Q = {<e, tₑ>, <f, tբ>, <g, t_g>, …}, where tₓ is the time of insertion
           of <x, tₓ> into Q(<x, tₓ>, <y, tᵧ> ∈ S | x ◇ y → tₓ ◇ tᵧ )
Domain:    0 ≤ #Q ≤ maxsize
Operations:
  enqueue(e: stdelement)
           pre:    ∃Q ∧ #Q ≠ maxsize
           post:   Q = Q' ∪ {<e, tₑ>}
  serve(var e: stdelement)
           pre:    ∃Q ∧ Q ◇ {}
           Post:   Q = Q' - {<e, tₑ>}|(∀<x, tₓ> ∈ Q, tₑ < tₓ)
  empty: boolean
           pre:    ∃Q
           post:   empty = (#Q = 0)
  full: boolean
           pre:    ∃Q
           post:   full = (#Q = maxsize)
  clear
           pre:    ∃Q
           post:   Q = {}
  create
           pre:    true
           Post:   ∃Q ∧ Q = {}
```

$$UDM \triangleq (\mathop{R}_{i=1}^{n} < S_i \,|\, \forall e_i \in S_i, p(e_i) >) \qquad (1)$$

Definition 4. The *Unified Process Model (UPM)* of a *program* $\wp$ is a composition of a finite set of k processes according to the time-, event-, and interrupt-based process dispatching rules, i.e.:

Figure 2. An algebraic model of the ADT stack (adapted from Louden, 1993)

```
ADT Stack (element : RT) : ST

operations:
        create:   → stack
        push:     stack × element → stack
        pop:      stack → element
        empty:    stack → Boolean
variables:
        s: stack;
        e: element
axioms:
        create (s) = s
        push (s, e) = ê ŝ
        pop (create (s)) = error
        pop (push (s, e)) = e
        empty (create (s)) = T
        empty (push (s, e)) = F
```

$$\wp = \mathop{R}_{k=1}^{m}(@e_k\mathbf{S} \hookrightarrow P_k)$$

$$= \mathop{R}_{k=1}^{m} [@e_k\mathbf{S} \hookrightarrow \mathop{R}_{i=1}^{n-1}(s_i(k)\ r_{ij}(k)\ s_j(k))], j = i+1 \qquad (2)$$

This paper presents a formal algebraic modeling methodology for ADTs using a denotational mathematics, RTPA, which allows both architectural and behavioral models of ADTs and complex data objects to be rigorously designed and implemented in a top-down approach. The methodology of a denotational mathematics based on RTPA is introduced to formally model and refine architectures, static behaviors, and dynamic behaviors of a set of ADTs. Stacks, queues, sequences, and records are chosen to comparatively elaborate the proposed RTPA-based ADT modeling methodologies. The architectural models of ATDs are created using the RTPA methodology known as UDMs. The static behaviors of ADTs are specified and refined by the RTPA methodology known as UPMs. The dynamic behaviors of ADTs are modeled by the RTPA methodology known as the event-driven process dispatching models.

THE FORMAL MODEL OF ADT1 – STACKS

A stack is a typical data structure for modeling the Last-In-First-Out (LIFO) mechanism of an ADT with a set of elements in the same type. The conceptual model of stacks and its key control variables are introduced in this section. Based on it, formal models of the stack ADT in terms of its architectural and static/dynamic behavioral models are rigorously developed in RTPA.

The Conceptual Model of Stacks

The stack as a common data structure is described as shown in Figure 3. The protocol of stacks is LIFO, which implies that the I/O operations of stacks must be on its top or most recent elements as identified by the pointer of the current position. In the stack model, Stack**ST**, each Element**RT** shares the same type where **RT** represents the run-time type in RTPA. Two of the key control variables of the stack are Size**N** denoting the maximum capacity of the stack and CurrentPos**P** denoting the current top position of the stack. The addresses of elements grow from the bottom up with the relative base address at 0**H**.

Figure 3. The conceptual model of stacks

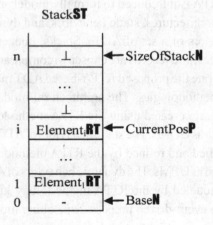

The top-level ADT model of the stack, Stack**ST**, encompassing its architecture, static behaviors, and dynamic behaviors, can be specified in RTPA as follows:

$$ADT\S.Stack\textbf{ST} \triangleq Stack\textbf{ST}.Architecture\textbf{ST}$$
$$\| \ Stack\textbf{ST}.StaticBehaviors\textbf{PC}$$
$$\| \ Stack\textbf{ST}.DynamicBehaviors\textbf{PC}$$

$$(3)$$

According to the RTPA methodology for system modeling, specification, and refinement (Wang, 2007, 2008a), the following subsections will refine the top level framework of Stack**ST** into detailed architectural models (UDMs) and behavioral models (UPMs).

The Architectural Model of Stacks

The architecture of Stack**ST** can be rigorously modeled using the UDM technology of RTPA, which is a predefined class of system hardware or internal control models that can be inherited or implemented by corresponding UDM objects as specific instances in the succeeding architectural refinement for the system. The UDM model of the stack ADT, Stack**ST**.Architecture**ST**, as shown in Figure 4 provides a generic architectural model for any concrete stack in applications with three key fields, i.e., Element**RT**, Size**N**, and CurrentPos**P**, where the constraints of each field are given in the right-hand side of the vertical bar. Supplement to the key architectural attributes, there is a set of status fields in the stack, which models the current operational status of the stack in Boolean type such as Created**BL**, Pushed**BL**, Popped**BL**, Cleared**BL**, Empty**BL**, Full**BL**, and Released**BL**. It is noteworthy that the type of the data elements in an abstract stack is specified in the run-time type **RT**, i.e., **RT** ∈ {**S**, **N**, **R**, **ST**, ...}, for design flexibility. However, the data elements in a concrete stack must be in the same type once it is chosen at run-time for a specific implementation of an instance of the generic abstract stack.

Figure 4. The UDM model of the stack ADT

> Stack**ST**.Architecture**ST** $\triangleq$ StackID**ST** ::
>   (<Element : **RT** | Element**RT** $\in$ {**S, N, R, ST**, ...}>,
>   <Size : **N** | 0 $\leq$ Size**N** $\leq$ MaxSize**N**>,
>   <CurrentPos : **P** | 0 $\leq$ CurrentPos**P** $\leq$ SizeOfStack**N**-1>,
>   <Created : **BL** | Created**BL** = {(**T**, Yes), (**F**, No)}>,
>   <Pushed : **BL** | Pushed**BL** = {(**T**, Yes), (**F**, No)}>,
>   <Popped : **BL** | Popped**BL** = {(**T**, Yes), (**F**, No)}>,
>   <Cleared : **BL** | Cleared**BL** = {(**T**, Yes), (**F**, No)}>,
>   <Empty : **BL** | Empt**BL** = {(**T**, Yes), (**F**, No)}>,
>   <Full : **BL** | Full**BL** = {(**T**, Yes), (**F**, No)}>,
>   <Released : **BL** | Released **BL** = {(**T**, Yes), (**F**, No)}>
>   )

Exhibit 1.

> Stack**ST**.StaticBehaviors**PC** $\triangleq$
>   (CreateStack**PC**(<**I**:: StackID**S**, Size**N**, Element**RT**>;
>   <**O**:: StackID**ST**.Crated**BL**>; <**UDM**:: StackID**ST**>)
> | Push**PC**(<**I**:: StackID**S**, Element**RT**>; < **O**:: StackID**ST**.Pushed**BL**>; <**UDM**:: StackID**ST**>)
> | Pop**PC**(<**I**:: StackID**S**>; < **O**:: StackID**ST**.Popped**BL**, Element**RT**>; <**UDM**:: StackID**ST**>)
> | Clear**PC**(<**I**:: StackID**S**>; < **O**:: StackID**ST**.Cleared**BL**>; <**UDM**:: StackID**ST**>)
> | EmptyTest (<**I**:: StackID**S**>; < **O**:: StackID**ST**.Empty**BL**>; <**UDM**:: StackID**ST**>)
> | FullTest (<**I**:: StackID**S**>; < **O**:: StackID**ST**.Full**BL**>; <**UDM**:: StackID**ST**>)
> | ReleaseStack**PC**(<**I**:: StackID**S**>; < **O**:: StackID**ST**.Released**BL**>; <**UDM**:: StackID**ST**>)
>   )
>   (4)

The Static Behavioral Model of Stacks

A static behavior is an encapsulated function of a given system that can be determined before run-time (Wang, 2007). On the basis of the UDM model of Stack**ST** developed in the preceding subsection, the behaviors of the stack can be modeled as a set of UPMs operating on the UDMs and related input variables. The high-level behavioral model of the stack ADT is modeled by Stack**ST**.StaticBehaviors**PC** as shown in Eq. 4. It can be further refined by a set of UPMs for each of the behavioral processes. The schemas of the UPMs in Eq. 4 model the input data objects (<**I**:: (...)>),

output data objects (<**O**:: (...)>), and operated UDMs (<**UDM**:: (...)>) for each specific process of Stack**ST**. The UDMs play an important role in system architectural design as global and permanent I/O structures, which usually have a longer life-span than those of the process(es) that created and/or invoked them, particularly in a real-time system. (see Exhibit 1)

The following subsections describe how each of the seven behavioral processes of ADT Stack**ST** as specified in Eq. 4 are modeled and refined using the denotational mathematical notations and methodologies of RTPA.

a) The Process of Stack Creation

The *stack creation* process of Stack**ST**, CreateStack**PC**, is formally modeled as shown in Figure 5, which establishes a new stack in system memory and links it to a specified logical ID. The input arguments of the process are the given name of the stack as well as its size and the type of element. The output result and status are the creation of the stack as well as the settings of related initial values in the UDM of StackID**ST**.Architecture**ST**. In order to create a physical stack and link it to the logical name of StackID**ST**, the process calls a system support process, AllocateObject**PC**, for dynamic memory manipulation for ADTs as illustrated in Figure 12. When the given stack has already existed or cannot be established due to memory availability, CreateStack**PC** results in a specific error message and sets StackID**ST**. Created**BL** = **F**.

b) The Process of Stack Push

The *push* process of Stack**ST**, Push**PC**, is formally modeled as shown in Figure 6, which puts a given element onto the top of the stack. The input arguments of the process are the target stack ID and the given element. The output is the status of the push operation. Push**PC** writes the given element onto the top of the current stack contents, after checking that the stack is not full and the CurrentPos**P** has been updated. When the given stack has already been full or does not exist, Push**PC** generates a specific error message and sets StackID**ST**.Pushed**BL** = **F**.

c) The Process of Stack Pop

The *pop* process of Stack**ST**, Pop**PC**, is formally modeled as shown in Figure 7, which elicits the top element of the stack. The input argument of

Figure 5. The UPM model of the stack creation process

```
CreateStackPC(<I:: StackIDS, SizeN, ElementRT>;
              <O:: StackIDST.CreatedBL>; <UDM:: StackIDST>) ≜
{
  → ( ◆ StackIDST.ExistedBL = F
        → ObjectIDS := StackIDS
        → #ElementsN := StackIDST. SizeN
        → ElementTypeRT := ElementRT
        ↦ AllocateObjectPC(<I:: ObjectIDS, #ElementsN, ElementTypeRT)>;
                          <O:: ObjectAllocatedBL>; <UDM:: MEMST>)
        → ( ◆ ObjectAllocatedBL = T
              → StackIDS ⇐ MEM(PhysicalStackST)
              → StackIDST.SizeN := SizeN
              → StackIDST.CurrentPosP := 0
              → StackIDST.EmptyBL := T
              → StackIDST.FullBL := F
              → StackIDST.CreatedBL := T
            | ◆~
              → StackIDST.CreatedBL := F
              → ! (" 'StackIDST' creation is failed.")
          )
      | ◆~
        → StackIDST.CreatedBL := F
        → ! (" 'StackIDST' has already been existed.")
    )
}
```

Figure 12. The UPM model of the allocate object process

```
AllocateObjectPC(<I:: ObjectIDS, #ElementsN, ElementTypeRT>;
                    <O:: ObjectIDST.ExistedBL>, <UDM:: ObjectIDST, MemoryST>) ≜
{
 nN := #ElementsN

       nN
  →    R    New (ObjectID(iN)ST : ElementTypeRT)
      iN=1
  → (  ◆ ObjectAllocatedBL = T
         → ObjectIDS ⇐ MEM(ObjectIDST)ST
         → ObjectIDST.ExistedBL := T
      | ◆ ~
         → ObjectIDST.ExistedBL := F
    )
}
```

the process is the target stack ID. Its outputs are the top element obtained and the status of the pop operation. When the target stack is not empty, PopPC does not only read the current top element of the stack, but also remove it from the stack. As a result, PopPC reduces the current pointer by one after the pop operation. When the given stack has already been empty or does not exist, PopPC generates a specific error message and sets StackIDST.PoppedBL = F.

d) The Process of Clear Stack

The *clear* process of StackST, ClearPC, is formally modeled as shown in Figure 8, which logically sets all elements of the stack as empty. The input argument of the process is the given stack ID. Its output is the status of the clear operation. ClearStackPC only logically sets the pointer StackIDST.CurrentPosP = 0 in order to denote the stack has been cleaned, rather than to remove all data elements of the stack. It is noteworthy that ClearStackPC is different from ReleaseStackPC, where the former

Figure 6. The UPM model of the stack push process

```
PushPC(<I:: StackIDS, ElementRT>; <O:: StackIDST.PushedBL>; <UDM:: StackIDST>) ≜
{
  → (  ◆ StackIDST.CreatedBL = T
        → (  ◆ StackIDST.CurrentPosP < StackIDST.SizeN
              → ↑ (StackIDST.CurrentPosP)
              → ElementRT ⋖ StackID(CurrentPosP)ST.ElementRT
              → StackIDST.PushedBL := T
          | ◆~
              → StackIDST.PushedBL := F
              → StackIDST.FullBL := T
              → ! (" 'StackIDST' is full.")
          )
     | ◆~
        → StackIDST.PushedBL := F
        → ! (" 'StackIDST' does not exist.")
    )
}
```

Figure 7. The UPM model of the stack pop process

```
PopPC(<I:: StackIDS>; <O:: StackIDST.PoppedBL, ElementRT>; <UDM:: StackIDST>) ≜
{
  → ( ◆ StackIDST.CreatedBL = T
        → ( ◆ StackIDST.CurrentPosP > 0
              → StackID(CurrentPosP)ST.ElementRT > ElementRT
              → ↓ (StackIDST.CurrentPosP)
              → StackIDST.PoppedBL := T
          | ◆~
              → StackIDST.PoppedBL := F
              → StackIDST.EmptyBL := T
              → ! (" 'StackIDST' is empty.")
          )
    | ◆~
        → StackIDST.PoppedBL := F
        → ! (" 'StackIDST' does not exist.")
    )
}
```

logically declares the given stack as empty, while the latter physically removes the target stack as well as its contents from the memory. If the given stack does not exist, ClearStackPC generates a specific error message.

e) The Process of Stack Empty Test

The *empty test* process of StackST, EmptyTestPC, is formally modeled as shown in Figure 9, which detects whether a given stack is empty. The input argument of the process is the target stack ID. Its output is the status of the stack as being empty or not. The status of an empty stack is characterized by StackIDST.CurrentPosP = 0. Therefore, EmptyTestPC verifies if the logical top pointer StackIDST.CurrentPosP points at the relative base address of the stack in order to determine whether the stack is empty or not. When the target stack does not exist, EmptyTestPC generates a specific error message.

f) The Process of Stack Full Test

The *full test* process of StackST, FullTestPC, is formally modeled as shown in Figure 10, which detects whether a given stack is full. The input argument of the process is the target stack ID. Its output is the status of the stack as being full or not. The status of a full stack is characterized by StackIDST.CurrentPosP = StackIDST.SizeN. Therefore, FullTestPC verifies if the logical top pointer StackIDST.CurrentPosP is equal to the physical size of the stack StackIDST.SizeN in order to determine whether the stack is full or not. When the given stack does not exist, FullTestPC generates a specific error message.

g) The Process of Stack Release

The *stack release* process, ReleaseStackPC, is formally modeled as shown in Figure 11, which physically removes a given stack and related memory with the contents. The input argument of the process is the given stack ID. Its output is the status of the release operation. ReleaseStackPC disconnects the physical stack and its logical name. Then, the memory space of the physical stack is returned to the system by calling a system support process, ReleaseObjectPC, for dynamic memory manipulation for ADTs as illustrated in Figure 13. If the given stack does not exist logically or

Figure 8. The UPM model of the stack clear process

```
ClearPC(<I:: StackIDS>; <O:: StackIDST.ClearedBL>; <UDM:: StackIDST>) ≜
{
 → ( ◆ StackIDST.CreatedBL = T
        → StackIDST.CurrentPosP := 0
        → StackIDST.ClearedBL := T
        → StackIDST.EmptyBL := T
    | ◆~
        → StackIDST.ClearedBL := F
        → ! (" 'StackIDST' does not exist.")
    )
}
```

Figure 9. The UPM model of the stack empty test process

```
EmptyTestPC(<I:: StackIDS>; <O:: StackIDST.EmptyBL>; <UDM:: StackIDST>) ≜
{
 → ( ◆ StackIDST.CreatedBL = T
        → ( ◆ StackIDST.CurrentPosP = 0
              → StackIDST.EmptyBL := T
              → StackIDST.FullBL := F
          | ◆~
              → StackIDST.EmptyBL := F
          )
    | ◆~
        → StackIDST.EmptyBL := F
        → ! (" 'StackIDST' does not exist.")
    )
}
```

Figure 10. The UPM model of the stack full test process

```
FullTestPC(<I:: StackIDS>; <O:: StackIDST.FullBL>; <UDM:: StackIDST>) ≜
{
 → ( ◆ StackIDST.CreatedBL = T
        → ( ◆ StackIDST.CurrentPosP = StackIDST.SizeN
              → StackIDST.FullBL := T
              → StackIDST.EmptyBL := F
          | ◆~
              → StackIDST.FullBL := F
          )
    | ◆~
        → StackIDST.FullBL := F
        → ! (" 'StackIDST' does not exist.")
    )
}
```

Figure 11. The UPM model of the release stack process

```
ReleaseStackPC(<I:: StackIDS>; <O:: StackIDST.ReleasedBL>; <UDM:: StackIDST>) ≜
{
  → ( ◆ StackIDST.CreatedBL = T
        → ObjectIDS := StackIDS
        ⟼ ReleaseObjectPC(<I:: ObjectIDS>; <O:: ObjectReleasedBL>; <UDM:: MEMST>)
        → ( ◆ ObjectReleasedBL = T
              → StackIDS ⇍ MEM(PhysicalStackST)
              → StackIDST.ReleasedBL := T
          | ◆~
              → StackIDST.ReleasedBL := F
              → ! (Target memory for 'StackIDST' is not found.)
          )
    | ◆~
        → StackIDST.DeletedBL := F
        → ! ('StackIDST' does not existed.)
    )
}
```

physically, ReleaseStackPC produces a specific error message and sets StackIDST.ReleasedBL = F.

h) Associate Processes of Dynamic Memory Manipulations for ADTs

There are two support processes, AllocateObjectPC and ReleaseObjectPC, for dynamic memory allocation and the management of ADT creation and release manipulations. The AllocateObjectPC

process as shown in Fig. 12 finds out a suitable block of available memory for the required ObjectST, whose size is determined by: #ElementsN × Byte(ElementTypeRT)N bytes. AllocateObjectPC repetitively requests a unit of suitable bytes for each element of ObjectST. Then, it links the logical ID of the object to the allocated memory block. If memory allocation is failed, AllocateObjectPC feeds back an error message ObjectIDST.ExistedBL = F.

Figure 12.

```
AllocateObjectPC(<I:: ObjectIDS, #ElementsN, ElementTypeRT>;
                 <O:: ObjectIDST.ExistedBL>, <UDM:: ObjectIDST, MemoryST>) ≜
{
  nN := #ElementsN
        nN
  →    R    New (ObjectID(iN)ST : ElementTypeRT)
       iN=1
  → ( ◆ ObjectAllocatedBL = T
        → ObjectIDS ⇐ MEM(ObjectIDST)ST
        → ObjectIDST.ExistedBL := T
    | ◆ ~
        → ObjectIDST.ExistedBL := F
    )
}
```

Figure 13. The UPM model of the release object process

```
ReleaseObjectPC(<I:: ObjectIDS>; <O:: ObjectIDST.ReleasedBL>; <UDM:: ObjectIDST, MemoryST>) ≙
{
  → ObjectIDS ⇍ MEM(ObjectST)ST
  → ReleasePC(<I:: MEM(ObjectST)>; <O:: ⓢMemoryReleasedBL>; <UDM:: MemoryST>)
  → ObjectIDS := ⊥
  → ( ◆ MemoryReleasedBL = T
        → ObjectIDST.ReleasedBL := T
     | ◆ ~
        → ObjectIDST.ReleasedBL := F
    )
}
```

The ReleaseObject**PC** process is a support process as shown in Figure 13, which is invoked by an ADT release process such as ReleaseStack**PC**. The ReleaseObject**PC** process identifies an associate memory block of a given ObjectID**S** and disconnects the object from the memory. After the release operation, the object is set to be undefined, i.e., ObjectID**S**:= ⊥. If memory release is failed, ReleaseObject**PC** feeds back an error message ObjectID**ST**.Released**BL** = **F**.

The Dynamic Behavior Model of Stacks

Dynamic behaviors of a system are run-time process deployment and dispatching mechanisms based on the static behaviors. Because system static behaviors are a set of component processes of the system, to put the static processes into an interacting system at run-time, the dynamic behaviors of the system in terms of process dispatching are yet to be specified. With the work products, Stack**ST**.StaticBehaviors**PC**, developed in the preceding section as a set of static behavioral processes, this subsection describes the dynamic behaviors of Stack**ST** at run-time using the RTPA process dispatching methodology. Stack**ST**.DynamicBehaviors**PC** as shown in Figure 14 models the event-driven behaviors of Stack**ST**, which establishes the relations between system events and the stack behavioral processes. The event-driven dispatching mechanisms also put Stack**ST** into the context of applications.

Figures 3 through 14 describe a typical ADT model, Stack**ST**, in a coherent design and using an unified formal notation. With the RTPA

Figure 14. The dynamic behavioral model of the stack ADT

```
StackST.DynamicBehaviorsPC ≙
{ § →
  ( @CreateStackS    ↳ CreateStackPC(<I:: StackIDS, SizeN, ElementRT>; <O:: StackIDST.CreatedBL>;
                                     <UDM:: StackIDST>)
  | @PushS           ↳ PushPC(<I:: StackIDS, ElementRT>; <O:: StackIDST.PushedBL>; <UDM:: StackIDST>)
  | @PopS            ↳ PopPC(<I:: StackIDS>; <O:: StackIDST.PoppedBL, ElementRT>; <UDM:: StackIDST>)
  | @ClearS          ↳ ClearPC(<I:: StackIDS>; <O:: StackIDST.ClearedBL>; <UDM:: StackIDST>)
  | @EmptyTestS      ↳ EmptyTestPC(<I:: StackIDS>; <O:: StackIDST.EmptyBL>; <UDM:: StackIDST>)
  | @FullTestS       ↳ FullTestPC(<I:: StackIDS>; <O:: StackIDST.FullBL>; <UDM:: StackIDST>)
  | @ReleaseStackS   ↳ ReleaseStackPC(<I:: StackIDS>; <O:: StackIDST.ReleasedBL>; <UDM:: StackIDST>)
  ) → §
}
```

specification and refinement methodology, the mechanisms, architectures, and behaviors of Stack**ST** are rigorously and precisely modeled.

THE FORMAL MODEL OF ADT2 – QUEUES

A queue is a typical data structure for modeling the First-In-First-Out (FIFO) mechanism of an ADT with a set of elements in the same type. The conceptual model of queues and its key control variables are introduced in this section. Based on it, formal models of the queue ADT in terms of its architectural and static/dynamic behavioral models are rigorously developed in RTPA.

The Conceptual Model of Queues

The queue as a common data structure is described as shown in Figure 15. The protocol of queues is FIFO, which implies that the I/O operations of queues must be at both its tail and head, respectively. In the queue model, Queue**ST**, each element**RT** share the same type **RT**. Two of the key control variables of the queue are SizeOfQueue**N** denoting the maximum capacity of the queue and CurrentPos**P** denoting the current tail position of the queue. The address of an element is growing from head to tail with the relative base address

reserved at 0**H**. The head or the front element of the queue, Element₁**RT**, is always located at address 1**H** based on the relative base address of the queue Base**N**.

The top-level ADT model of queue, Queue**ST**, encompassing its architecture, static behaviors, and dynamic behaviors, can be specified in RTPA as follows:

ADT**§**.Queue**ST** ≜ Queue**ST**.Architecture**ST**
|| Queue**ST**.StaticBehaviors**PC**
|| Queue**ST**.DynamicBehaviors**PC**
(5)

According to the RTPA methodology for system modeling, specification, and refinement (Wang, 2007, 2008a), the following subsections will refine the top level framework of Queue**ST** into detailed architectural models (UDMs) and behavioral models (UPMs).

The Architectural Model of Queues

The architecture of Queue**ST** can be rigorously modeled using the UDM technology of RTPA. The UDM model of the queue ADT, Queue**ST**.Architecture**ST**, as shown in Figure 16 provides a generic architectural model for any concrete queue in applications with three key fields, i.e., Element**RT**, Size**N**, and CurrentPos**P**, where the

Figure 16. The UDM model of the queue ADT

```
Queue**ST**.Architecture**ST** ≜ QueueID**ST** ::
    (<Element : **RT** | Element**RT** ∈ {**S, N, R, ST**, …}>,
    <Size : **N** | 0 ≤ Size**N** ≤ MaxSize**N**>,
    <CurrentPos : **P** | 0 ≤ CurrentPos**P** ≤ SizeOfQueue**N**-1>,
    <Created : **BL** | Created**BL** = {(**T**, Yes), (**F**, No)}>,
    <Enqueued : **BL** | Enqueued**BL** = {(**T**, Yes), (**F**, No)}>,
    <Served : **BL** | Served**BL** = {(**T**, Yes), (**F**, No)}>,
    <Cleared : **BL** | Cleared**BL** = {(**T**, Yes), (**F**, No)}>,
    <Empty : **BL** | Empt**BL** = {(**T**, Yes), (**F**, No)}>,
    <Full : **BL** | Full**BL** = {(**T**, Yes), (**F**, No)}>,
    <Released : **BL** | Released **BL** = {(**T**, Yes), (**F**, No)}>
    )
```

Exhibit 2.

QueueST.StaticBehaviorsPC ≜
 (CreateQueuePC(<I:: QueueIDS, SizeN, ElementRT>;
        <O:: QueueIDST.CreatedBL>; <UDM:: QueueIDST>)
 | EnqueuPC(<I:: QueueIDS, ElementRT>; < O:: QueueIDST.EnqueuedBL>;
        <UDM:: QueueIDST>)
 |ServePC(<I:: QueueIDS>; < O:: QueueIDST.ServedBL, ElementRT>; <UDM:: QueueIDST>)
 | ClearPC(<I:: QueueIDS>; < O:: QueueIDST.ClearedBL>; <UDM:: QueueIDST>)
 | EmptyTest (<I:: QueueIDS>; < O:: QueueIDST.EmptyBL>; <UDM:: QueueIDST>)
 | FullTest (<I:: QueueIDS>; < O:: QueueIDST.FullBL>; <UDM:: QueueIDST>)
 | ReleaseQueuePC(<I:: QueueIDS>; < O:: QueueIDST.ReleasedBL>; <UDM:: QueueIDST>)
)

(6)

constraints of each field are given in the right-hand side of the vertical bar. Supplement to the key architectural attributes, there is a set of status fields in the queue, which models the current operational status of the queue in Boolean type such as CreatedBL, EnqueuedBL, ServedBL, ClearedBL, EmptyBL, FullBL, and ReleasedBL.

The Behavioral Model of Queues

On the basis of the UDM model of QueueST developed in the preceding subsection, the behaviors of the queue can be modeled as a set of UPMs operating on the UDMs and related input variables. The high level behavioral model of the queue ADT is modeled by QueueST.StaticBehaviorsPC as shown in Eq. 6. The schemas of the queue can be further refined by a set of UPMs for each of the behavioral processes. (see Exhibit 2)

A set of seven behavioral processes such as *create, enqueue, serve, clear, empty test, full test, and release* is designed in QueueST.StaticBehaviorsPC. The following subsections describe how the static behaviors of QueueST as specified in Eq. 6 are modeled and refined using the denotational mathematical notations and methodologies of RTPA. Because of the similarity of the ADT manipulation processes between QueueST and StackST as described in Eq. 4, only two key pro-

cesses, EnqueuePC and ServePC, of QueueST will be formally modeled in the following subsections.

a) The Process of Enqueue

The *enqueue* process of QueueST, EnqueuePC, is formally modeled as shown in Figure 17, which puts a given element at the tail of the queue. The input arguments of the process are the target queue ID and a given element. Its output is the status of the enqueue operation. EnqueuePC checks if the given queue is not full and shifts CurrentPosP to the next position of the current tail, before the given element is appended into the queue. As a consequence, CurrentPosP of the queue is increased by one. When the given queue has already been full or does not exist, EnqueuePC generates a specific error message and sets QueueIDST.EnqueueBL=F.

b) The Process of Serve Queue

The *serve* process of QueueST, ServePC, is formally modeled as shown in Figure 18, which obtains the element in the front of the queue. The input argument of the process is the target queue. Its outputs are the front element of the queue and the status of the serve operation. The serve operation may be carried out when the given queue is not empty. Once the front element is elicited, ServePC has to update

Figure 17. The UPM model of the enqueue process

```
EnqueuPC(<I:: QueueIDS, ElementRT>; <O:: QueueIDST.EnqueuedBL>; <UDM:: QueueIDST>) ≙
{
  → ( ◆ QueueIDST.CreatedBL = T
        → ( ◆ QueueIDST.CurrenpPosP < QueueIDST.SizeN
              → ↑ (QueueIDST.CurrentPosP)
              → ElementRT <QueueID(CurrentPosP)ST.ElementRT
              → QueueIDST.EnqueuedBL := T
            | ◆~
              → QueueIDST.EnqueuedBL := F
              → QueueIDST.FullBL := T
              → ! (" 'QueueIDST' is full.")
          )
      | ◆~
          → QueueIDST.EnqueuedBL := F
          → ! (" 'QueueIDST' does not exist.")
    )
}
```

Figure 18. The UPM model of the serve queue process

```
ServePC(<I:: QueueIDS>; < O:: QueueIDST.ServedBL, ElementRT>; <UDM:: QueueIDST>) ≙
{
  → ( ◆ QueueIDST.CreatedBL = T
        → ( ◆ QueueIDST.CurrentPosP > 0
              → QueueID(1)ST.ElementRT > ElementRT
                    CurrentPosP
              →      R            QueueID(iN))ST.ElementRT >QueueID(iN-1)ST.ElementRT
                    iN=2
              → ↓ (QueueIDST.CurrentPosP)
              → QueueIDST.ServedBL := T
            | ◆~
              → QueueIDST.ServedBL := F
              → QueueIDST.EmptyBL := T
              → ! (" 'QueueIDST' is empty.")
          )
      | ◆~
          → QueueIDST.ServedBL := F
          → ! (" 'QueueIDST' does not exist.")
    )
}
```

Figure 19. The dynamic behavioral model of the queue ADT

```
QueueST.DynamicBehaviorsPC ≙
{ § →
  ( @CreateQueueS ↦ CreateQueuePC(<I:: QueueIDS, SizeN, ElementRT>; <O:: QueueIDST.CreatedBL>;
                                    <UDM:: QueueIDST>)
  | @EnqueueS      ↦ EnqueuePC(<I:: QueueIDS, ElementRT>; <O:: QueueIDST.EnqueuedBL>; <UDM:: QueueIDST>)
  | @ServeS        ↦ ServePC(<I:: QueueIDS>; <O:: QueueIDST.ServedBL, ElementRT>; <UDM:: QueueIDST>)
  | @ClearS        ↦ ClearPC(<I:: QueueIDS>; <O:: QueueIDST.ClearedBL>; <UDM:: QueueIDST>)
  | @EmptyTestS    ↦ EmptyTestPC(<I:: QueueIDS>; <O:: QueueIDST.EmptyBL>; <UDM:: QueueIDST>)
  | @FullTestS     ↦ FullTestPC(<I:: QueueIDS>; <O:: QueueIDST.FullBL>; <UDM:: QueueIDST>)
  | @ReleaseQueueS ↦ ReleaseQueuePC(<I:: QueueIDS>; <O:: QueueIDST.ReleasedBL>; <UDM:: QueueIDST>)
  ) → §
}
```

the queue by shifting all other elements that follow the currently removed front element by one place towards the front of the queue. As a consequence, CurrentPos**P** of the queue is decreased by one. When the given queue has already been empty or does not exist, Serve**PC** generates a specific error message and sets QueueID**ST**.Served**BL** = **F**.

Contrasting the behavioral models of Queue**ST**. Behaviors**PC** in RTPA as developed in this section and that of predicate logic as shown in Figure 1, advances of the RTPA method and notations are well demonstrated. Among them, the most important merit is that an ADT model in RTPA can be seamlessly transformed into code in any programming language when the formal models are designed and refined systematically.

The Dynamic Behavior Model of Queues

On the basis of the work products, Queue**ST**. StaticBehaviors**PC**, developed in the preceding subsection as a set of static behavioral processes, this subsection describes the dynamic behaviors of Queue**ST** at run-time using the RTPA process dispatching methodology. Queue**ST**.DynamicBehaviors**PC** as shown in Figure 19 models the event-driven behaviors of Queue**ST**, which establishes the relations between system events and the stack behavioral processes. The event-driven dispatching mechanisms also put Queue**ST** into the context of applications.

Figures 15 through 19 describe a typical ADT model, Queue**ST**, in a coherent design and using a unified formal notation. With the RTPA specification and refinement methodology, the mechanisms, architectures, and behaviors of Queue**ST** are rigorously and precisely modeled.

Figure 20. The conceptual model of sequences

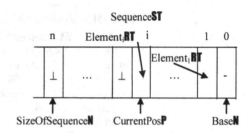

THE FORMAL MODEL OF ADT3 – SEQUENCES

A sequence is a typical data structure for modeling an ADT with a series of elements in the same type where their order information is important. The conceptual model of sequences and its key control variables are introduced in this section. Based on it, formal models of the sequence ADT in terms of its architectural and static/dynamic behavioral models are rigorously developed in RTPA.

The Conceptual Model of Sequences

The sequence as a common data structure is described as shown in Figure 20. The protocol of sequence is FIFO, which implies that the I/O operations of sequence must be at its tail and head, respectively. In the sequence model, Sequence**ST**, each Element**RT** share the same type **RT**. Two of the key control variables of the sequence are Size**N** denoting the maximum capacity of the sequence and CurrentPos**P** denoting the current tail position of the sequence. The addresses of elements grow from the head to the tail with the relative base address reserved at 0**H**. The head or the front element of the sequence, Element$_i$**RT**, is always located at address 1**H** based on the relative base address of the sequence Base**N**.

The top-level ADT model of sequence, Sequence**ST**, encompassing its architecture, static behaviors, and dynamic behaviors, can be modeled in RTPA as follows:

Figure 21. The UDM model of the sequence ADT

```
Sequence𝐒𝐓.Architecture𝐒𝐓 ≜ SequenceID𝐒𝐓 ::
    (<Element : 𝐑𝐓 | Element𝐑𝐓 ∈ {𝐒, 𝐍, 𝐑, 𝐒𝐓, …}>,
     <Size : 𝐍 | 0 ≤ Size𝐍 ≤ MaxSize𝐍>,
     <CurrentPos : 𝐏 | 0 ≤ CurrentPos𝐏 ≤ SizeOfSequence𝐍-1>,
     <Created : 𝐁𝐋 | Created𝐁𝐋 = {(𝐓, Yes), (𝐅, No)}>,
     <Appended : 𝐁𝐋 | Appended𝐁𝐋 = {(𝐓, Yes), (𝐅, No)}>,
     <ElementFound : 𝐁𝐋 | ElementFound𝐁𝐋 = {(𝐓, Yes), (𝐅, No)}>,
     <Retrieved : 𝐁𝐋 | Retrieved𝐁𝐋 = {(𝐓, Yes), (𝐅, No)}>,
     <Cleared : 𝐁𝐋 | Cleared𝐁𝐋 = {(𝐓, Yes), (𝐅, No)}>,
     <Empty : 𝐁𝐋 | Empt𝐁𝐋 = {(𝐓, Yes), (𝐅, No)}>,
     <Full : 𝐁𝐋 | Full𝐁𝐋 = {(𝐓, Yes), (𝐅, No)}>,
     <Released : 𝐁𝐋 | Released 𝐁𝐋 = {(𝐓, Yes), (𝐅, No)}>
    )
```

$$
\begin{aligned}
\text{ADT𝐒.Sequence𝐒𝐓} \triangleq\ & \text{Sequence𝐒𝐓.Architecture𝐒𝐓} \\
& \| \ \text{Sequence𝐒𝐓.StaticBehaviors𝐏𝐂} \\
& \| \ \text{Sequence𝐒𝐓.DynamicBehaviors𝐏𝐂}
\end{aligned}
$$

(7)

According to the RTPA methodology for system modeling, specification, and refinement (Wang, 2007, 2008a), the following subsections will refine the top level framework of Sequence𝐒𝐓 into detailed architectural models (UDMs) and behavioral models (UPMs).

The Architectural Model of Sequences

The architecture of Sequence𝐒𝐓 can be rigorously modeled using the UDM technology of RTPA. The UDM model of the sequence ADT, Sequence𝐒𝐓.Architecture𝐒𝐓, as shown in Figure 21 provides a generic architectural model for any concrete sequence in applications with three key fields, i.e., Element𝐑𝐓, Size𝐍, and CurrentPos𝐏, where the constraints of each field are given in the right-hand side of the vertical bar. Supplement to the key architectural attributes, there is a set of status fields in the sequence, which models the current operational status of the sequence in Boolean type such as Created𝐁𝐋, Appended𝐁𝐋, FirstFound𝐁𝐋, LastFound𝐁𝐋, Retrieved𝐁𝐋, Cleared𝐁𝐋, Empty𝐁𝐋, Full𝐁𝐋, and Released𝐁𝐋.

The Behavioral Model of Sequences

On the basis of the UDM model of Sequence𝐒𝐓 developed in the preceding subsection, the behaviors of the sequence can be modeled as a set of UPMs operating on the UDMs and related input variables. The high level behavioral model of the sequence ADT is modeled by Sequence𝐒𝐓.StaticBehaviors𝐏𝐂 as shown in Eq. 8. The schemas of the sequence can be further refined by a set of UPMs for each of the behavioral processes.

A set of eight behavioral processes such as *create, append, find element, retrieve, clear, empty test, full test, and release* is designed in Sequence𝐒𝐓.StaticBehaviors𝐏𝐂. The following subsections describe how the static behaviors of Sequence𝐒𝐓 as specified in Eq. 8 are modeled and refined using the denotational mathematical notations and methodologies of RTPA. Because of the similarity of ADT manipulation processes between Sequence𝐒𝐓 and Stack𝐒𝐓 as described in Eq. 4, only key processes, Append𝐏𝐂, FindElement𝐏𝐂, and Retrieve𝐏𝐂, of Sequence𝐒𝐓 will be formally modeled in the following subsections. (see Exhibit 3)

Exhibit 3.

Sequence**ST**.StaticBehaviors**PC** ≜
  (CreateSequence**PC**(<**I**:: SequenceID**S**, Size**N**, Element**RT**>;
                     <**O**:: SequenceID**ST**.Crated**BL**>; <**UDM**:: SequenceID**ST**>)
  | Append**PC**(<**I**:: SequenceID**S**, Element**RT**>; < **O**:: SequenceID**ST**.Appended**BL**>;
             <**UDM**:: SequenceID**ST**>)
  | FindElement**PC**(<**I**:: SequenceID**S**, Element**RT**>; < **O**:: SequenceID**ST**.ElementFound**BL**,
           ElementPositon**P**>; <**UDM**:: SequenceID**ST**>)
  | Retrieve**PC**(<**I**:: SequenceID**S**, i**N**>; < **O**:: SequenceID**ST**.Retrieved**BL**, Element**RT**>;
             <**UDM**:: SequenceID**ST**>)
  | Clear**PC**(<**I**:: SequenceID**S**>; < **O**:: SequenceID**ST**.Cleared**BL**>; <**UDM**:: SequenceID**ST**>)
  | EmptyTest (<**I**:: SequenceID**S**>; < **O**:: SequenceID**ST**.Empty**BL**>; <**UDM**:: SequenceID**ST**>)
  | FullTest (<**I**:: SequenceID**S**>; < **O**:: SequenceID**ST**.Full**BL**>; <**UDM**:: SequenceID**ST**>)
  | ReleaseSequence**PC**(<**I**:: SequenceID**S**>; < **O**:: SequenceID**ST**.Released**BL**>; <**UDM**:: SequenceID**ST**>)
)
                                                                       (8)

a) The Process of Sequence Append

The *append* process of Sequence**ST**, Append**PC**, is formally modeled as shown in Figure 22, which puts an element at the current end of the sequence. The input arguments of the process are the target sequence ID and the given element. Its output is the status of the append operation. Append**PC** writes the given element at the end of the sequence after checking that the sequence is not full and CurrentPos**P** is shifted to the address of the next element of the current tail. When the given sequence has already been full or does not exist, Append**PC** generates a specific error message and sets SequenceID**ST**.Appended**BL** = **F**.

b) The Process of Find Element in a Sequence

The *find element* process of Sequence**ST**, FindElement**PC**, is formally modeled as shown in Figure 23, which finds out the position of a given element in the sequence. The input arguments of the process are the target sequence ID and the given element. Its outputs are the position of the element in the sequence, if found, and the status of the search operation. FindElement**PC** is a read-only operation that reports the position of the given element in a sequence, but does not change the structure and contents of the sequence. When the given sequence does not exist or is empty, FindElement**PC** generates a specific error message and sets SequenceID**ST**. ElementFound**BL** = **F**.

c) The Process of Sequence Retrieve

The *retrieve* process of Sequence**ST**, Retrieve**PC**, is formally modeled as shown in Figure 24, which reads the *i*th element in the sequence. The input arguments of the process are the target sequence ID and a given position in the sequence. Its outputs are the element at the given position, if any, and the status of the retrieve operation. Retrieve**PC** is a read-only operation to find out the content at a certain position of the sequence, after conforming that the sequence is not empty. When the given sequence is empty or does not exist, Retrieve**PC** generates a specific error message and sets SequenceID**ST**.Retrieved**BL** = **F**.

Figure 22. The UPM model of the sequence append process

```
AppendPC(<I:: SequenceIDS, ElementRT>; <O:: SequenceIDST.AppendedBL>; <UDM:: SequenceIDST>) ≙
{
  → ( ◆ SequenceIDST.CreatedBL = T
        → ( ◆ SequenceIDST.CurrentPosP < SequenceIDST.SizeN
              → ↑(SequenceIDST.CurrentPosP)
              → ElementRT > (SequenceIDST.Element(CurrentPosP))RT
              → SequenceIDST.AppendedBL := T
          | ◆~
              → SequenceIDST.AppendedBL := F
              → SequenceIDST.FullBL := T
              → ! (" 'SequenceIDST' is full.")
          )
    | ◆~
        → SequenceIDST.AppendedBL := F
        → ! (" 'SequenceIDST' does not exist. ")
    )
}
```

Figure 23. The UPM model of the find element process

```
FindElementPC(<I:: SequenceIDS, ElementRT>; <O:: SequenceIDST.ElementFoundBL,
              ElementPositonP>; <UDM:: SequenceIDST>) A
{
  → ( ν SequenceIDST.CreatedBL = T ∧ SequenceIDST.CurentPosP ≠ 0
                SizeOfSequenceN
      →        R           ( ν SequenceIDST.Element(iN))RT = ElementRT
               iN=1
                            → ElementPositonP := iN
                            → SequenceIDST. ElementFoundBL := T
                            → ⊗
                        | ν~
                            → SequenceIDST. ElementFoundBL := F
                        )
    | ν~
        → SequenceIDST.ElementFoundBL := F
        → ! (" 'SequenceIDST' does not exist or is empty. ")
    )
}
```

Figure 24. The UPM model of the sequence retrieve process

```
RetrievePC(<I:: SequenceIDS, iN>; <O:: SequenceIDST.RetrievedBL, ElementRT>; <UDM:: SequenceIDST>) ≙
{
  → ( ◆ SequenceIDST.CreatedBL = T ∧ SequenceIDST.CurrentPosP ≠ 0
        → ( ◆ 0 < iN ≤ SequenceST.CurrentPosP
              → SequenceIDST.Element(iN)RT ◁ ElementRT
              → SequenceIDST. RetrievedBL := T
          | ◆~
              → SequenceIDST.RetrievedBL := F
              → ! ("Given index is out of range.")
          )
    | ◆~
        → SequenceIDST.RetrievedBL := F
        → ! (" 'SequenceIDST' does not exist or is empty. ")
    )
}
```

Figure 25. The dynamic behavioral model of the sequence ADT

```
SequenceST.DynamicBehaviorsPC ≜
{ § →
  ( @CreateSequenceS      ↪ CreateSequencePC(<I:: SequenceIDS, SizeN, ElementRT>;
                                               <O:: SequenceIDST.CreatedBL>; <UDM:: SequenceIDST>)
  | @AppendS              ↪ AppendPC(<I:: SequenceIDS, ElementRT>; <O:: SequenceIDST.AppendedBL>;
                                               <UDM:: SequenceIDST>)
  | @FindElementS         ↪ FindElementPC(<I:: SequenceIDS, ElementRT>; <O:: SequenceIDST.ElementFoundBL,
                                               ElementPositionP>; <UDM:: SequenceIDST>)
  | @RetrieveS            ↪ RetrievePC(<I:: SequenceIDS>; <O:: SequenceIDST.RetrievedBL, ElementRT>;
                                               <UDM:: SequenceIDST>)
  | @ClearS               ↪ ClearPC(<I:: SequenceIDS>; <O:: SequenceIDST.ClearedBL>; <UDM:: SequenceIDST>)
  | @EmptyTestS           ↪ EmptyTestPC(<I:: SequenceIDS>; <O:: SequenceIDST.EmptyBL>;
                                               <UDM:: SequenceIDST>)
  | @FullTestS            ↪ FullTestPC(<I:: SequenceIDS>; <O:: SequenceIDST.FullBL>; <UDM:: SequenceIDST>)
  | @ReleaseSequenceS     ↪ ReleaseSequencePC(<I:: SequenceIDS>; <O:: SequenceIDST.ReleasedBL>;
                                               <UDM:: SequenceIDST>)
  ) → §
}
```

The Dynamic Behavior Model of Sequences

On the basis of the work products, SequenceST. StaticBehaviorsPC, developed in the preceding subsection as a set of static behavioral processes, this subsection describes the dynamic behaviors of SequenceST at run-time using the RTPA process dispatching methodology. SequenceST.DynamicBehaviorsPC as shown in Figure 25 models the event-driven behaviors of SequenceST, which establishes the relations between system events and the stack behavioral processes. The event-driven dispatching mechanisms also put SequenceST into the context of applications.

Figures 20 through 25 describe a typical ADT model, SequenceST, in a coherent design and using a unified formal notation. With the RTPA specification and refinement methodology, the mechanisms, architectures, and behaviors of SequenceST are rigorously and precisely modeled.

THE FORMAL MODEL OF ADT4 – RECORDS

A record is a typical data structure for modeling an ADT with a set of fields configured in different types. The conceptual model of record and its key control variables are introduced in this section. Based on it, formal models of the record ADT in terms of its architectural and static/dynamic behavioral models are rigorously developed in RTPA. It is recognized that record is one of the most powerful and widely used ADTs and data structures, because it allows flexible field structures and data types. The mathematical model of

Figure 26. The conceptual model of records

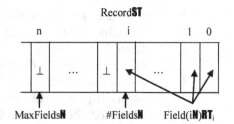

a record is a tuple, which forms a fundamental architectural modeling means in ADT and software system modeling.

The Conceptual Model of Records

The record as a common data structure is described as shown in Figure 26. The protocol of record is the direct accessibility to its fields, which implies that the I/O operations of records may be directly (randomly) conducted in any field of the record. In the record model, Record**ST**, the element in each field, Field(i**N**)**RT**$_i$ is allowed in different types. Two of the key control variables of the record ADT are MaxFields**N** and #Fields**N**. The former denotes the maximum allowable fields of the record; and the latter denotes the current position of the last field in the record. The addresses and the order of all fields are parallel and arbitrary. The constraints on each field of Record**ST** may be explicitly specified in the architectural model of the record.

The top-level ADT model of the record, Record**ST**, encompassing its architecture, static behaviors, and dynamic behaviors, can be modeled in RTPA as follows:

$$ADT\S.Record\mathbf{ST} \triangleq Record\mathbf{ST}.Architecture\mathbf{ST}$$
$$\| Record\mathbf{ST}.StaticBehaviors\mathbf{PC}$$
$$\| Record\mathbf{ST}.DynamicBehaviors\mathbf{PC}$$

(9)

According to the RTPA methodology for system modeling, specification, and refinement (Wang, 2007, 2008a), the following subsections will refine the top level framework of Record**ST** into detailed architectural models (UDMs) and behavioral models (UPMs).

The Architectural Model of Records

The architecture of Record**ST** can be rigorously modeled using the UDM technology of RTPA. The UDM model of the record ADT, Record**ST**.Architecture**ST**, as shown in Figure 27 provides a generic architectural model for any concrete record in applications with two key parameters, i.e., #Fields**N** and FiledType(i**N**)**RT**, where the constraints on each field are given in the right-hand side of the vertical bar. Supplement to the key architectural attributes, there is a set of status fields in the record, which models the current operational status of the record in Boolean

Figure 27. The UDM model of the record ADT

$$Record\mathbf{ST}.Architecture\mathbf{ST} \triangleq RecordID\mathbf{ST} ::$$
$$(<\#Fields : \mathbf{N} \mid 1 \le \#Fields\mathbf{N} \le MaxFields\mathbf{N}>,$$
$$\mathop{R}_{i\mathbf{N}=0}^{\#Fields\mathbf{N}-1} <FieldType(i\mathbf{N}) : \mathbf{RT} \mid FieldType(i\mathbf{N})\mathbf{RT} \in \{\mathbf{S, N, R, ST}, ...\}>$$
$$<Created : \mathbf{BL} \mid Created\mathbf{BL} = \{(\mathbf{T}, Yes), (\mathbf{F}, No)\}>,$$
$$<Initialized : \mathbf{BL} \mid Initialized\mathbf{BL} = \{(\mathbf{T}, Yes), (\mathbf{F}, No)\}>,$$
$$<FieldRetrieved : \mathbf{BL} \mid FieldRetrieved\mathbf{BL} = \{(\mathbf{T}, Yes), (\mathbf{F}, No)\}>,$$
$$<RecordRetrieved : \mathbf{BL} \mid RecordRetrieved\mathbf{BL} = \{(\mathbf{T}, Yes), (\mathbf{F}, No)\}>,$$
$$<FieldUpdated : \mathbf{BL} \mid FieldUpdated\mathbf{BL} = \{(\mathbf{T}, Yes), (\mathbf{F}, No)\}>,$$
$$<RecordUpdated : \mathbf{BL} \mid RecordUpdated\mathbf{BL} = \{(\mathbf{T}, Yes), (\mathbf{F}, No)\}>,$$
$$<Released : \mathbf{BL} \mid Released\mathbf{BL} = \{(\mathbf{T}, Yes), (\mathbf{F}, No)\}>$$
$$)$$

Exhibit 4.

$\text{Record}\textbf{ST}.\text{StaticBehaviors}\textbf{PC} \triangleq$

$\{ \text{ CreateRecord}\textbf{PC}(<\textbf{I}:: \text{RecordID}\textbf{S}, \#\text{Fields}\textbf{N}, \displaystyle\mathop{R}_{i\textbf{N}=0}^{\#\text{Fields}\textbf{N}-1} \text{Field}(i\textbf{N})\textbf{RT}>;$

$\qquad\qquad <\textbf{O}:: \text{RecordID}\textbf{ST}.\text{Created}\textbf{BL}>; <\textbf{UDM}:: \text{Record}\textbf{ST}>)$

$| \text{ InitializeRecord}\textbf{PC}(<\textbf{I}:: \text{RecordID}\textbf{S}, \text{InitialValue}\textbf{RT}>; <\textbf{O}:: \text{RecordID}\textbf{ST}.\text{Initialized}\textbf{BL}>; <\textbf{UDM}:: \text{Record}\textbf{ST}>)$

$| \text{ RetrieveField}\textbf{PC}(<\textbf{I}:: \text{RecordID}\textbf{S}, i\textbf{N}>; <\textbf{O}:: \text{RecordID}\textbf{ST}.\text{FieldRetrieved}\textbf{BL}, \text{Field}(i\textbf{N})\textbf{RT}>; <\textbf{UDM}:: \text{Record}\textbf{ST}>)$

$| \text{ RetrieveRecord}\textbf{PC}(<\textbf{I}:: \text{RecordID}\textbf{S}>; <\textbf{O}:: \text{RecordID}\textbf{ST}.\text{RecordRetrieved}\textbf{BL},$

$\qquad\qquad \displaystyle\mathop{R}_{i\textbf{N}=0}^{\#\text{Fields}\textbf{N}-1} \text{Field}(i\textbf{N})\textbf{RT}>; <\textbf{UDM}:: \text{Record}\textbf{ST}>)$

$| \text{ UpdateField}\textbf{PC}(<\textbf{I}:: \text{RecordID}\textbf{S}, \text{Field}(i\textbf{N})\textbf{RT}>; <\textbf{O}:: \text{RecordID}\textbf{ST}.\text{FieldUpdated}\textbf{BL}>; <\textbf{UDM}:: \text{Record}\textbf{ST}>)$

$| \text{ UpdateRecord}\textbf{PC}(<\textbf{I}:: \text{RecordID}\textbf{S}, \#\text{Fields}\textbf{N}, \displaystyle\mathop{R}_{i\textbf{N}=0}^{\#\text{Fields}\textbf{N}-1} \text{Field}(i\textbf{N})\textbf{RT}>;$

$\qquad\qquad <\textbf{O}:: \text{RecordID}\textbf{ST}.\text{RecordUpdated}\textbf{BL}>; <\textbf{UDM}:: \text{Record}\textbf{ST}>)$

$| \text{ ReleaseRecord}\textbf{PC}(<\textbf{I}:: \text{RecordID}\textbf{S}>; <\textbf{O}:: \text{RecordID}\textbf{ST}.\text{Released}\textbf{BL}>; <\textbf{UDM}:: \text{Record}\textbf{ST}>)$

$\}$

(10)

type such as Created**BL**, Initialized**BL**, FieldRetrieved**BL**, RecordRetrieved**BL**, FieldUpdated**BL**, RecordUpdated**BL**, Cleared**BL**, Empty**BL**, Full**BL**, and Released**BL**.

The Behavioral Model of Records

On the basis of the UDM model of Record**ST** developed in the preceding subsection, the behaviors of the record can be modeled as a set of UPMs operating on the UDMs and related input variables. The high level behavioral model of the record ADT is modeled by Record**ST**.StaticBehaviors**PC** as shown in Eq. 10. The schemas of the record can be further refined by a set of UPMs for each of the behavioral processes. (see Exhibit 4)

A set of seven behavioral processes such as *create, initialize record, retrieve field, retrieve record, update field, update record,* and *release* is designed in Record**ST**.StaticBehaviors**PC**. The following subsections describe how the static behaviors of Record**ST** as specified in Eq. 10 are modeled and refined using the denotational mathematical notations and methodologies of RTPA. Because of the similarity of ADT manipulation processes between Record**ST** and Stack**ST** as described in

Figure 28. The UPM model of the record initialization process

$\text{InitializeRecord}\textbf{PC}(<\textbf{I}:: \text{RecordID }\textbf{S}, \text{InitialValue }\textbf{RT}>; <\textbf{O}:: \text{RecordID }\textbf{ST}.\text{Initialized}\textbf{BL}>; <\textbf{UDM}:: \text{Record}\textbf{ST}>) \triangleq$

$\{$

$\rightarrow (\text{ } \vee \text{ RecordID}\textbf{ST}.\text{Created}\textbf{BL} = \textbf{T} \wedge \text{RecordID}\textbf{ST}.\#\text{Fields}\textbf{N} \neq 0$

$\qquad \rightarrow \displaystyle\mathop{R}_{i\textbf{N}=0}^{\#\text{Fields}\textbf{N}-1} \text{RecordID}\textbf{ST}.\text{Field}(i\textbf{N})\textbf{RT} := \text{InitialValue}\textbf{RT}$

$\qquad \rightarrow \text{RecordID}\textbf{ST}.\text{Initialized}\textbf{BL} := \textbf{T}$

$| \vee\sim$

$\qquad \rightarrow \text{RecordID}\textbf{ST}.\text{Initialized}\textbf{BL} := \textbf{F}$

$\qquad \rightarrow ! (\text{“ 'RecordID}\textbf{ST}\text{' does not exist or is empty.''})$

$\text{ })$

$\}$

Figure 29. The UPM model of the retrieve field process

```
RetrieveFieldPC(<I:: RecordIDS, iN>; <O:: RecordIDST.FieldRetrievedBL, Field(iN)RT>; <UDM:: RecordST>) ≜
{
 → ( ◆ RecordIDST.CreatedBL = T ∧ RecordIDST.#FieldsN ≠ 0
        → ( ◆ 0 ≤ iN ≤ RecordIDST.#FieldsN
              → RecordIDST.Field(iN)RT ▷ Field(iN)RT
              → RecordIDST.FieldRetrievedBL := T
          | ◆~
              → RecordIDST.RetrievedBL := F
              → ! ("Field index is out of range.")
          )
   | ◆~
        → RecordIDST.RetrievedBL := F
        → ! (" 'RecordIDST' does not exist or is empty. ")
   )
}
```

Eq. 4, only key processes, InitializeRecord**PC**, RetrieveField**PC**, RetrieveRecord**PC**, Update-Field**PC**, and UpdateRecord**PC**, of Record**ST** will be formally modeled in the following subsections.

a) The Process of Record Initialization

The *record initializing* process of Record**ST**, InitializeRecord**PC**, is formally modeled as shown in Figure 28, which sets each element of the record with the same given initial value. The input arguments of the process are the target record ID and the given initial value. Its output is the status of the initialization operation. InitializeRecord**PC** puts the initial value into each element of the record, after checking that the record exists and is not empty. When the given record is empty or does not exist, InitializeRecord**PC** generates a specific error message and sets RecordID**ST**.Initialized**BL** = **F**.

b) The Process of Record Field Retrieve

The *record field retrieve* process of Record**ST**, RetrieveField**PC**, is formally modeled as shown in Figure 29, which reads the contents of a given field of the record. The input arguments of the process are the target record ID and the number of the expected field. Its outputs are the contents of the given field in the record and the status of the retrieve operation. RetrieveField**PC** is a read-only operation to report the contents of a specific field in the record. Before the retrieve is conducted, the given number of the field must be validated and the record must not be empty. When the given record is empty or does not exist, RetrieveField**PC** generates a specific error message and sets RecordID**ST**.Fieldretrieved**BL** = **F**.

c) The Process of Record Retrieve

The *record retrieve* process of Record**ST**, RetrieveRecord**PC**, is formally modeled as shown in Figure 30, which reads the contents of all fields from the given record. The input argument of the process is the target record ID. Its outputs are the contents of each fields of the record and the status of the retrieve operation. RetrieveRecord**PC** is a read-only operation to repetitively report the contents of all fields in the record. When the given record is empty or does not exist, RetrieveRecord**PC** generates a specific error message and sets RecordID**ST**.RecordRetrieved**BL** = **F**.

Figure 30. The UPM model of the record retrieve process

$$
\begin{aligned}
&\text{RetrieveRecord}\mathbf{PC}(<\mathbf{I}::\text{RecordID}\mathbf{S}>; <\mathbf{O}::\text{RecordID}\mathbf{ST}.\text{RecordRetrieved}\mathbf{BL}, \\
&\qquad\qquad R_{iN=0}^{\#Fields\mathbf{N}} \text{FieldID}(i\mathbf{N})\mathbf{RT}>; <\mathbf{UDM}::\text{Record}\mathbf{ST}>) \triangleq
\end{aligned}
$$

{
→ (◆ RecordID**ST**.Created**BL** = **T** ∧ RecordID**ST**.#Fields**N** ≠ 0

    → (◆ #Fields**N** = RecordID**ST**.#Field**N**

$$
\qquad\qquad \rightarrow R_{iN=0}^{\#Fields\mathbf{N}-1} \text{RecordID}\mathbf{ST}.\text{Field}(i\mathbf{N})\mathbf{RT} > \text{FieldID}(i\mathbf{N})\mathbf{RT}
$$

        → RecordID**ST**.RecordRetrieved**BL** := **T**

    | ◆~

        → RecordID**ST**.RecordRetrieved**BL** := **F**

        → ! ("Input field number does not match 'RecordID**ST**'.")

)

| ◆~

    → RecordID**ST**.RecordRetrieved**BL** := **F**

    → ! (" 'RecordID**ST**' does not exist or is empty.")

)

}

Figure 31. The UPM model of the record field update process

$$
\text{UpdateField}\mathbf{PC}(<\mathbf{I}::\text{RecordID}\mathbf{S}, \text{Field}(i\mathbf{N})\mathbf{RT}>; <\mathbf{O}::\text{RecordID}\mathbf{ST}.\text{FieldUpdated}\mathbf{BL}>; <\mathbf{UDM}::\text{Record}\mathbf{ST}>) \triangleq
$$

{
→ (◆ RecordID**ST**.Created**BL** = **T** ∧ RecordID**ST**.#Fields**N** ≠ 0

    → (◆ 0 ≤ i**N** ≤ RecordID**ST**.#Fields**N**

        → RecordID**ST**.Field(i**N**)**RT** := Field(i**N**)**RT**

        → RecordID**ST**.FieldUpdated**BL** := **T**

    | ◆~

        → RecordID**ST**.Created**BL** := **F**

        → ! ("Field index is out of range.")

)

| ◆~

    → RecordID**ST**.Created**BL** := **F**

    → ! (" 'RecordID**ST**' does not exist or is empty. ")

)

}

d) The Process of Update Record Field

The *update record field* process of Record**ST**, UpdateField**PC**, is formally modeled as shown in Figure 31, which writes a given value onto the specific field of the record. The input arguments of the process are the target record ID and the data for the given field. Its output is the status of the field update operation. UpdateField**PC** is an inverse operation of RetrieveField**PC**. Before the operation is carried out, the number of the filed must be validated and the record must be nonempty. When the given record is empty

Figure 32. The UPM model of the record update process

$$
\begin{aligned}
&\text{UpdateRecord}\textbf{PC}(<\textbf{I}:: \text{RecordID}\textbf{S}, \#\text{Fields}\textbf{N}, \underset{i\textbf{N}=0}{\overset{\#\text{Fields}\textbf{N}-1}{R}} \text{FieldID}(i\textbf{N})\textbf{RT}>; \\
&\qquad\qquad <\textbf{O}:: \text{RecordID}\textbf{ST}.\text{RecordUpdated}\textbf{BL}>; <\textbf{UDM}:: \text{Record}\textbf{ST}>) \triangleq \\
&\{ \\
&\quad \to (\ \blacklozenge\ \text{RecordID}\textbf{ST}.\text{Created}\textbf{BL} = \textbf{T} \wedge \text{RecordID}\textbf{ST}.\#\text{Fields}\textbf{N} \neq 0 \\
&\qquad\quad \to (\ \blacklozenge\ \#\text{Fields}\textbf{N} = \text{RecordID}\textbf{ST}.\#\text{Field}\textbf{N} \\
&\qquad\qquad \to \underset{i\textbf{N}=0}{\overset{\#\text{Fields}\textbf{N}-1}{R}} \text{RecordID}\textbf{ST}.\text{Field}(i\textbf{N})\textbf{RT} := \text{Field}(i\textbf{N})\textbf{RT} \\
&\qquad\qquad \to \text{RecordID}\textbf{ST}.\text{RecordUpdated}\textbf{BL} := \textbf{T} \\
&\qquad\quad |\ \blacklozenge\sim \\
&\qquad\qquad \to \text{RecordID}\textbf{ST}.\ \text{RecordUpdated}\textbf{BL} := \textbf{F} \\
&\qquad\qquad \to !\ (\text{``Input field number does not match `RecordID}\textbf{ST}\text{'."}) \\
&\qquad\quad) \\
&\quad |\ \blacklozenge\sim \\
&\qquad\quad \to \text{RecordID}\textbf{ST}.\ \text{RecordUpdated}\textbf{BL} := \textbf{F} \\
&\qquad\quad \to !\ (\text{`` `RecordID}\textbf{ST}\text{' does not exist or is empty. ''}) \\
&\quad) \\
&\}
\end{aligned}
$$

or does not exist, UpdateField**PC** generates a specific error message and sets StackID**ST**.FieldUpdated**BL** = **F**; so also when the field index is out of scope.

e) The Process of Record Update

The *update record* process of Record**ST**, UpdateRecord**PC**, is formally modeled as shown in Figure 32, which writes a set of values onto each field of the record. The input arguments of the process are the target record ID, number of fields, and the data for each given field. Its output is the status of the record update operation. UpdateRecord**PC** is an inverse operation of RetrieveRecord**PC**. Before the operation is carried out, the number of the filed must match with that of the record. When the given record is empty or does not exist, UpdateRecord**PC** generates a specific error message and sets Stack-ID**ST**.RecordUpdated**BL** = **F**; so also when the total number of fields does not match that of the record.

The Dynamic Behavior Model of Record

On the basis of the work products, Record**ST**.StaticBehaviors**PC**, developed in the preceding subsection as a set of static behavioral processes, this subsection describes the dynamic behaviors of RecordRecord**ST** at run-time using the RTPA process dispatching methodology. Record**ST**.DynamicBehaviorsPC as shown in Figure 33 models the event-driven behaviors of Record**ST**, which establishes the relations between system events and the stack behavioral processes. The event-driven dispatching mechanisms also put RecordST into the context of applications.

Figures 26 through 33 describe a typical ADT model, Record **ST**, in a coherent design and using a unified formal notation. With the RTPA specification and refinement methodology, the mechanisms, architectures, and behaviors of Record**ST** are rigorously and precisely modeled.

The practical formal engineering methodology of RTPA for system modeling and specification

Figure 33. The dynamic behavioral model of the record ADT

$$
\begin{aligned}
&\text{Record}\mathbf{ST}.\text{DynamicBehaviors}\mathbf{PC} \triangleq \\
&\{ \S \rightarrow \\
&\quad (\ @\text{CreateRecord}\mathbf{S} \quad \hookrightarrow \text{CreateRecord}\mathbf{PC}(<\mathbf{I}:: \text{RecordID}\mathbf{S}, \#\text{Fields}\mathbf{N}, \underset{i\mathbf{N}=0}{\overset{\#\text{Fields}\mathbf{N}-1}{\mathbf{R}}} \text{Field}(i\mathbf{N})\mathbf{RT}>; \\
&\qquad\qquad\qquad\qquad\qquad\qquad <\mathbf{0}:: \text{RecordID}\mathbf{ST}.\text{Created}\mathbf{BL}>; <\mathbf{UDM}:: \text{Record}\mathbf{ST}>) \\
&\quad | \ @\text{InitialRecord}\mathbf{S} \quad \hookrightarrow \text{InitializeRecord}\mathbf{PC}(<\mathbf{I}:: \text{RecordID}\mathbf{S}, \text{InitialValue}\mathbf{RT}>; <\mathbf{0}:: \text{RecordID}\mathbf{ST}.\text{Initialized}\mathbf{BL}>; \\
&\qquad\qquad\qquad\qquad\qquad\qquad <\mathbf{UDM}:: \text{Record}\mathbf{ST}>) \\
&\quad | \ @\text{RetrieveField}\mathbf{S} \quad \hookrightarrow \text{RetrieveField}\mathbf{PC}(<\mathbf{I}:: \text{RecordID}\mathbf{S}, i\mathbf{N}>; <\mathbf{0}:: \text{RecordID}\mathbf{ST}.\text{FieldRetrieved}\mathbf{BL}, \text{Field}(i\mathbf{N})\mathbf{RT}>; \\
&\qquad\qquad\qquad\qquad\qquad\qquad <\mathbf{UDM}:: \text{Record}\mathbf{ST}>) \\
&\quad | \ @\text{RetrieveRecord}\mathbf{S} \quad \hookrightarrow \text{RetrieveRecord}\mathbf{PC}(<\mathbf{I}:: \text{RecordID}\mathbf{S}>; <\mathbf{0}:: \text{RecordID}\mathbf{ST}.\text{RecordRetrieved}\mathbf{BL}, \\
&\qquad\qquad\qquad\qquad\qquad\qquad \underset{i\mathbf{N}=0}{\overset{\#\text{Fields}\mathbf{N}-1}{\mathbf{R}}} \text{Field}(i\mathbf{N})\mathbf{RT}>; <\mathbf{UDM}:: \text{Record}\mathbf{ST}>) \\
&\quad | \ @\text{UpdateField}\mathbf{S} \quad \hookrightarrow \text{UpdateField}\mathbf{PC}(<\mathbf{I}:: \text{RecordID}\mathbf{S}, \text{Field}(i\mathbf{N})\mathbf{RT}>; <\mathbf{0}:: \text{RecordID}\mathbf{ST}.\text{FieldUpdated}\mathbf{BL}>; \\
&\qquad\qquad\qquad\qquad\qquad\qquad <\mathbf{UDM}:: \text{Record}\mathbf{ST}>) \\
&\quad | \ @\text{UpdateRecord}\mathbf{S} \quad \hookrightarrow \text{UpdateRecord}\mathbf{PC}(<\mathbf{I}:: \text{RecordID}\mathbf{S}, \#\text{Fields}\mathbf{N}, \underset{i\mathbf{N}=0}{\overset{\#\text{Fields}\mathbf{N}-1}{\mathbf{R}}} \text{Field}(i\mathbf{N})\mathbf{RT}>; \\
&\qquad\qquad\qquad\qquad\qquad\qquad <\mathbf{0}:: \text{RecordID}\mathbf{ST}.\text{RecordUpdated}\mathbf{BL}>; <\mathbf{UDM}:: \text{Record}\mathbf{ST}>) \\
&\quad | \ @\text{ReleaseQueue}\mathbf{S} \quad \hookrightarrow \text{ReleaseRecord}\mathbf{PC}(<\mathbf{I}:: \text{RecordID}\mathbf{S}>; <\mathbf{0}:: \text{RecordID}\mathbf{ST}.\text{Released}\mathbf{BL}>; <\mathbf{UDM}:: \text{Record}\mathbf{ST}>) \\
&\quad) \rightarrow \S \\
&\}
\end{aligned}
$$

provides a coherent notation system and systematic approach for large-scale software and hybrid system design and implementation. A series of formal design models of real-world and real-time applications in RTPA have been developed using RTPA notations and methodologies (Wang, 2002, 2007, 2008a, 2008b, 2009b; Wang & Huang, 2008) in the formal design engineering approach, such as the Telephone Switching System (TSS) (Wang, 2009b), the Lift Dispatching System (LDS) (Wang et al., 2009), the Automated Teller Machine (ATM) (Wang et al., 2010b), the Real-Time Operating System (RTOS+) (Wang et al., 2010c, 2010d), and the Air Traffic Control System (ATCS, to be reported). Further studies have demonstrated that RTPA is not only useful as a generic notation and methodology for software engineering, but also good at modeling human cognitive processes in cognitive informatics and computational intelligence as reported in (Wang, 2008d, 2009a; Wang & Ruhe, 2007; Wang & Chiew, 2010).

CONCLUSION

Abstract Data Types (ADTs) have been recognized as an important set of rigorously modelled complex data structures with pre-specified behaviors. This paper has introduced the formal RTPA modeling methodology for ADT architectures and behavioral specification and refinement in a top-down approach. The architectures, static behaviors, and dynamic behaviors of a set of typical ADTs such as stack, queue, sequence, and record, have been comparatively studied. Two generic methodologies of RTPA known as the Unified Data Models (UDMs) for system architectural modeling and the Unified Process Models (UPMs) for behavioral modeling have been elaborated. On the basis of the formal and rigorous models of the ADT system, code can be automatically generated or be manually transferred from the formal models.

The RTPA models of more complex ADTs such as universal arrays, lists, binary trees, files, and digraphs will be reported in related future work in the

Series of Formal Software Design Models, Patterns, and Frameworks in IJSSCI. This work have been applied in a number of real-time and nonreal-time system designs and modeling such as a Real-Time Operating System (RTOS+), an Air Traffic Control System (ATCS), as well as the developments of the ADT library of an RTPA support tool and the anonymous automatic code generator (RTPA-CG) (Wang et al., 2010a; Ngolah & Wang, 2009) based on RTPA.

ACKNOWLEDGMENT

The authors would like to acknowledge both the Natural Science and Engineering Council of Canada (NSERC) and the International Institute for Software Technology at the United Nations University (IIST/UNU) for their partial support to this work. We would like to thank the reviewers for their valuable comments and suggestions.

REFERENCES

Broy, M., Pair, C., & Wirsing, M. (1984). A Systematic Study of Models of Abstract Data Types. *Theoretical Computer Science, 33*, 139–1274. doi:10.1016/0304-3975(84)90086-0

Cardelli, L., & Wegner, P. (1985). On Understanding Types, Data Abstraction and Polymorphism. *ACM Computing Surveys, 17*(4), 471–522. doi:10.1145/6041.6042

Guttag, J. V. (1977). Abstract Data Types and the Development of Data Structures. *Communications of the ACM, 20*(6), 396–404. doi:10.1145/359605.359618

Lipschutz, S., & Lipson, M. (1997). *Schaum's Outline of Theories and Problems of Discrete Mathematics* (2nd ed.). New York: McGraw-Hill Inc.

Louden, K. C. (1993). *Programming Languages: Principles and Practice*. Boston: PWS-Kent Publishing Co.

McDermid, J. (Ed.). (1991). *Software Engineer's Reference Book*. Oxford, UK: Butterworth Heinemann Ltd.

Mitchell, J. C. (1990). Type systems for programming languages . In van Leeuwen, J. (Ed.), *Handbook of Theoretical Computer Science* (pp. 365–458). Amsterdam, The Netherlands: North Holland.

Ngolah, C. F., & Wang, Y. (2009). Tool Support for Software Development based on Formal Specifications in RTPA. *International Journal of Software Engineering and Its Applications, 3*(3), 71–88.

Russel, B. (1903). *The Principles of Mathematics*. London: George Allen & Unwin.

Stubbs, D. F., & Webre, N. W. (1985). *Data Structures with Abstract Data Types and Pascal*. Monterey, CA: Brooks/Cole Publishing Co.

Wang, Y. (2002). The Real-Time Process Algebra (RTPA). *Annals of Software Engineering: An International Journal, 14*, 235–274. doi:10.1023/A:1020561826073

Wang, Y. (2007). *Software Engineering Foundations: A Software Science Perspective*. Boca Raton, FL: CRC.

Wang, Y. (2008a). RTPA: A Denotational Mathematics for Manipulating Intelligent and Computational Behaviors. *International Journal of Cognitive Informatics and Natural Intelligence, 2*(2), 44–62.

Wang, Y. (2008b). Mathematical Laws of Software. *Transactions of Computational Science, 2*, 46–83. doi:10.1007/978-3-540-87563-5_4

Wang, Y. (2008c). Deductive Semantics of RTPA. *International Journal of Cognitive Informatics and Natural Intelligence*, 2(2), 95–121.

Wang, Y. (2008d). On Contemporary Denotational Mathematics for Computational Intelligence. *Transactions of Computational Science*, 2, 6–29. doi:10.1007/978-3-540-87563-5_2

Wang, Y. (2009a). Paradigms of Denotational Mathematics for Cognitive Informatics and Cognitive Computing. *Fundamenta Informatic.*, 90(3), 282–303.

Wang, Y. (2009b). The Formal Design Model of a Telephone Switching System (TSS). *International Journal of Software Science and Computational Intelligence*, 1(3), 92–116.

Wang, Y., & Chiew, V. (2010). On the Cognitive Process of Human Problem Solving. *Cognitive Systems Research: An International Journal*, 11(1), 81–92. doi:10.1016/j.cogsys.2008.08.003

Wang, Y., & Huang, J. (2008). Formal Modeling and Specification of Design Patterns using RTPA. *International Journal of Cognitive Informatics and Natural Intelligence*, 2(1), 100–111.

Wang, Y., Ngolah, C. F., Ahmadi, H., Sheu, P. C. Y., & Ying, S. (2009). The Formal Design Model of a Lift Dispatching System (LDS). *International Journal of Software Science and Computational Intelligence*, 1(4), 98–122.

Wang, Y., Ngolah, C. F., Zeng, G., Sheu, P. C. Y., Choy, C. P., & Tian, Y. (2010c). The Formal Design Models of a Real-Time Operating System (RTOS+): Conceptual and Architectural Frameworks. *International Journal of Software Science and Computational Intelligence*, 2(2), 105–122.

Wang, Y., Ngolah, C. F., Zeng, G., Sheu, P. C. Y., Choy, C. P., & Tian, Y. (2010d). The Formal Design Models of a Real-Time Operating System (RTOS+): Static and Dynamic Behavior Models. *International Journal of Software Science and Computational Intelligence*, 2(3), 79–105.

Wang, Y., & Ruhe, G. (2007). The Cognitive Process of Decision Making. *International Journal of Cognitive Informatics and Natural Intelligence*, 1(2), 73–85.

Wang, Y., Tan, X., & Ngolah, C. F. (2010a). Design and Implementation of an Autonomic Code Generator based on RTPA (RTPA-CG). *International Journal of Software Science and Computational Intelligence*, 2(2), 44–67.

Wang, Y., Zhang, Y., Sheu, P. C. Y., Li, X., & Guo, H. (2010b). The Formal Design Models of an Automatic Teller Machine (ATM). *International Journal of Software Science and Computational Intelligence*, 2(1), 102–131.

This work was previously published in International Journal of Software Science and Computational Intelligence, Volume 2, Issue 4, edited by Yingxu Wang, pp. 72-100, copyright 2010 by IGI Publishing (an imprint of IGI Global).

Chapter 17
A Least–Laxity–First Scheduling Algorithm of Variable Time Slice for Periodic Tasks

Shaohua Teng
Guangdong University of Technology, China

Xiufen Fu
Guangdong University of Technology, China

Wei Zhang
Guangdong University of Technology, China

Jiangyi Su
Guangdong University of Technology, China

Haibin Zhu
Nipissing University, Canada

Baoliang Cui
Guangdong University of Technology, China

ABSTRACT

The LLF (Least Laxity First) scheduling algorithm assigns a priority to a task according to its executing urgency. The smaller the laxity value of a task is, the sooner it needs to be executed. When two or more tasks have same or approximate laxity values, LLF scheduling algorithm leads to frequent switches among tasks, causes extra overhead in a system, and therefore, restricts its application. The least switch and laxity first scheduling algorithm is proposed in this paper by searching out an appropriate common divisor in order to improve the LLF algorithm for periodic tasks.

INTRODUCTION

There are many procedures and jobs with cyclical characteristics in the real world, as well as in the batch production of products. Every batch is a production cycle and there are many processes in the production cycle. For example, automobile manufacturing, production of milk, computer manufacturing, clothing making, and crops pro-

duction all have cyclical characteristics. They all are composed of periodic tasks. The cycle of crops production is once or twice per year from sowing to harvesting and that of fruit production is once a year.

After analyzing the production process of these periodic tasks carefully, it is not difficult to find out the following common characteristics of them:

- There exist parallel actions among processes. For example, parallelism occurs

DOI: 10.4018/978-1-4666-0264-9.ch017

in an assembly line. The second process of the first product making action and the first process of the second product making action are in parallel. When one product is being assembled in a process, the other might be in the next process. In general, all of the batch productions are the same, which all are parallel actions.

- The system with periodic tasks is not usually fully loaded. It might become idle in some intervals, such as the winter in agricultural production. All the batch productions have the same or similar property. Their differences are long or short in idle intervals.
- Each task is independent and has possibly different production cycles.
- There are not strict sequences among some processes.

If we extract the essential features and ignore the specific production procedure for every production task which has the periodic characteristics, we can discuss the production scheduling with the help of computer simulation. Production details of a task is not important for scheduling, but the start time of periodic task, the length of a cycle and the time of real production in a cycle are essential. In order to make full use of the production resources and make the greatest benefit, an efficient scheduling is necessary. Efficient scheduling schemes could use the least scheduling time and make a system to gain the most execution time. For instance, rural workers can take in hand more part time when his major task, i.e., crop production is idle. A production system could be used to take on other jobs in free times. This kind of scheduling is quite useful and can make an enterprise to gain more benefit. Hence, real-time task scheduling is an important topic. A computer simulation could give an exact solution for the production task scheduling in the real world.

Real-time task scheduling has been studied widely in computer science. Many scholars and experts have paid much attention to studying on the real-time task scheduling and they have achieved a lot of research results. The real-time scheduling is a fundamental problem of operating systems. When a computer is multi-programmed, it frequently has multiple processes competing for the CPU (Central Process Unit) at the same time. This situation occurs whenever two or more processes are simultaneously in the ready state. If only one CPU is available, a choice has to be made, i.e., which process runs first. The part of an operating system that makes the choice is called scheduler and the used algorithms is called scheduling algorithms. These topics form the subject matter of the process scheduling (Tanenbaum, 2002). The process is basically a program in execution. Then the real-time scheduling of tasks is very important. Scheduling is also a daily human cognitive activity, people need to think of the schedules everyday to make their work more efficient. It is a common problem in every field related with cognitive informatics (Wang, 2003, 2007; Ngolah, Wang, & Tan, 2004), such as, software development, knowledge management, natural intelligence and artificial intelligence.

In fact, the real-time task scheduling comes from the production practice in nature. Therefore, it has wide applications in many fields, such as, agile manufacturing, E-commerce, subway, air traffic control, aeronautics and astronautics, adaptive fault-tolerance, and robotics. Among real-time scheduling algorithms, the dynamic-priority scheduling algorithms have widespread applications in many real-time systems (Tang, Liang, Zhe, & Tang, 2007; Wang, Xu, Wang, Wang, & Dai, 2004). The Rate-Monotonic algorithm (Liu & Layland, 1973; Naghibzadeh & Kim, 2002), the Earliest Deadline First algorithm (Liu & Layland, 1973; Naghibzadeh & Kim, 2002; Tang, Liang, Zhe, & Tang, 2007; Wang, Lin, Wang, Han, & Zhao, 2004; Wang, Xu, Wang, Wang, & Dai, 2004), the Highest Value First algorithm (Jensen, Locke, & Toduda, 1985), and the Least Laxity First algorithm (Tang, Liang, Zhe, & Tang, 2007) or called Least Slack First algorithm (Abbott & Garcia-Molina, 1992; Dertouzos & Mok, 1989; Jin, Wang, Wang, & Dai, 2004) are examples of such kinds of algorithms.

Usually, this type of algorithm has only considered one common scheduling strategy that neglects the inherent features of tasks. In this kind of strategy, a task is scheduled and executed always by using time slices of an operating system (more exactly CPU). This often leads to a low utilization rate of the system. Specially, when the number of periodic tasks is invariable, a good scheduling algorithm could obtain more execution time of the CPU and make the CPU more efficient. Moreover, when the laxity values of tasks are close, the situation occurs that tasks switch frequently. It is inappropriate, because the production task switch in the real world takes a long time. Sometimes, a switch among tasks in real world may spend hours, or even days. For example, in the production process of molds, a switch between different molds will consume a mass of adjusting time of skilled workers. The skilled workers have to repeatedly adjust the molds according to the temperature, humidity, wind power, time, plastic, shape and size of the product and other factors, so that they can determine each appropriate parameter value. Therefore, in an actual production procedure, it is extremely useful to find a scheduling strategy that leads to the least switches and more working time for fixed periodic tasks. A real-time scheduling is a simulation of production task scheduling in the real world. In order to get more benefit, we must have a good real-time task scheduling plan.

This paper is based on the following premises:

(1) There is only one processor in the system;
(2) All parts of each task in the system may be preempted from the processor.
(3) All of the tasks are independent and they have no ordered.
(4) Any task cannot be suspended by itself.

RELATED WORK

Task-based priority scheduling means to choose among the tasks by their priorities. The priorities of tasks are set by calculating some feature parameters of the tasks, such as the deadline, maximum value, least laxity value, least idle time, importance, etc. Wang et al. apply the Genetic Algorithm to the scheduling of a real-time system (Wang, Lin, Wang, Han, & Zhao, 2004). Their method improves the scheduling ability and enhances the performance of a real-time system. Jensen, Locke, and Toduda (1985) propose the Highest Value First Algorithm, which obviously prevents the system from running more low reward tasks at an idle period. Abbott (1992) and Dertouzos et al. (1989) suggest the Least Laxity First algorithm (Abbott, & Garcia-Molina, 1992; Dertouzos, & Mok, 1989), which assigns a priority to each task according to its urgent degree. The less the idle time of a task is, the sooner it should be executed. Hence, the most urgent tasks (the tasks that may not be the earliest deadline) have the highest priorities to be executed. Along with the system action, the idle time of a task in the executing state is not altered, but the idle times of the tasks in the ready queue or waiting queue are significantly decreased. The urgent degree of a waiting task becomes higher when time elapses. Therefore, during the action period of the system, these tasks which wait long have more opportunities to get the resource of CPU. But the algorithm has one evident drawback. If the values of many laxities are near zero, a thrashing phenomenon (i.e., serious frequent switches among the tasks) happens. It expends much executing time of a system and leads to the low efficiency of the LSF algorithm. In order to improve the efficiency of the Least Laxity First Algorithm, Hildebrandt, Oh et al. propose a complex algorithm to choose among the tasks with the same least idle time (Hildebrandt, Golatowski, & Timmermann, 1999; Oh & Yang, 1998). Although this algorithm reduces switch times among the tasks, it needs to manage those tasks respectively which have the same least idle time. As a result, it increases the complexity of the task scheduling and the cost of the algorithm and does not achieve goal of obtaining the least switch times. Wang and Saksena (1999) describe a scheduling model based on preemption with an assumption that the task set and the number of the tasks are known before scheduling. The premise of this method is: the priorities of these tasks are different, and each task's priority and preemption threshold value are fixed integers. Hence, it is a static scheduling strategy. However, in the Least Laxity First (LLF) Algorithm, the idle times of the waiting tasks are rigidly decreased and the priority levels of the tasks continuously change (i.e., higher and higher), so this method is useless in the LLF algorithm. Jin et al. (2004) propose an Improved Least Laxity First Scheduling Algorithm based on the decreasing idle times of the tasks. It does not restrict to the number of the tasks and the integer attribute of the preemption threshold values. It is shown by the experiments that the Improved Least Laxity First Scheduling Algorithm can reduce the switch times of the tasks and decrease the number of the thrashing phenomenon, but it cannot ultimately deracinate the thrashing phenomenon.

In order to solve these problems, Zhang and Fu (2006) describe a periodic task scheduling algorithm which has a better performance of scheduling. This paper improves the periodic task scheduling algorithm from another point of view by bringing in some terminologies and symbols. It proposes the ILLF (Improved Least Laxity First) Scheduling algorithm, which has the least times of task scheduling and the least number of switches among tasks. The ILLF scheduling algorithm makes full use of the intrinsic features of periodic tasks of the real-time system.

THE PROBLEM AND THE SCHEDULING ALGORITHM

The Problem

The following example is used to show that tasks with the shortest deadline or the least laxity value can also wait.

Example 1: There are two periodic tasks A and B. Suppose that they arrive at a one-processor system at the same time. The cycle time of Task A is 10 milliseconds (ms) and that of Task B is 50 ms. Task A is executed once every 10 ms and uses 5 ms of CPU time. Task B is executed once every 50 ms and uses 25 ms of CPU. According to the Earliest Deadline First Algorithm or the Least Laxity First Algorithm, the running sequence should be first sequence in Figure 1:

```
A(5ms)  B(5ms)  A(5ms)  B(5ms)  A(5ms)
B(5ms)  A(5ms)  B(10ms)  A(5ms)  ...
```

But this example can also be executed in the second sequence shown in Figure 1:

```
A(5 ms)  B(10 ms)  A(10 ms)  B(10 ms)
A(10 ms)  B(5 ms)  ...
```

As for this example, the two methods are both valid. But it is obviously seen from Figure 1 that the number of task switches of the latter is 3 times less than that of the former. Moreover, the scheduling units of the two sequences are both 5 ms that are not necessarily the time slice of the operating system.

Generally, there is the following scheduling problem:

In a one-processor system, there are N hard real-time tasks waiting to be executed concurrently. The executed time of each task is C_i and the cycle time is P_i, $1 \leq i \leq N$. A scheduling algorithm should be composed to accomplish the scheduling of the tasks.

The Schedulability of a System

The resources of every system are limited, hence the load of the system is inevitably limited. For example, in a one-processor system, there are 8 hard real-time tasks. The cycle time of each task is 30 ms and the processing time of each task is 10 ms.

Figure 1. The comparison of two executing sequences

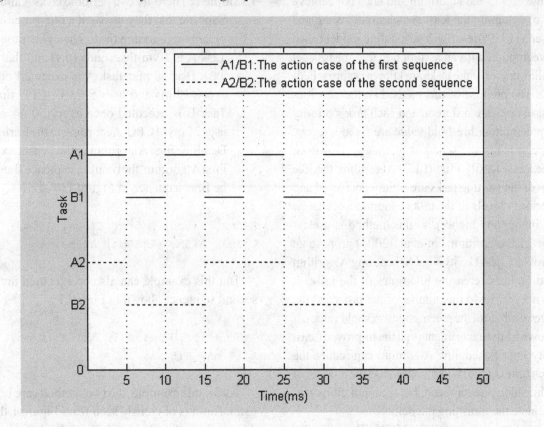

Then the system cannot process these tasks. But, if there is only one hard real-time task like this, then the system can afford to process it. If there are 3 similar hard real-time tasks, then the system needs to schedule these tasks properly in order to execute them. In the following discussions, all the times are in ms except the special statements.

Therefore, there are the following definitions:

Definition 1: Task Cycle (TC). The real-time task cycle of a system is defined as the time difference between two consecutive beginning times of the task.

Definition 2: Processing Time (PT). The processing time of a task is the time it needs to occupy the CPU to complete it in TC.

Definition 3: The schedulability of a system (Naghibzadeh & Kim, 2002; Tang, Liang,

Zhe, & Tang, 2007; Zhang & Fu, 2006). Suppose there are M periodic hard real-time tasks in the system, the processing time of each task is C_i, the task cycle is P_i, $1 \leq i \leq$ M. Then in a one-processor system, the following condition must be satisfied to make sure that the tasks can be scheduled.

$$\sum_{i=1}^{M} \frac{C_i}{P_i} \leq 1 \qquad (1)$$

The Least Laxity First Scheduling Algorithm

The laxity value of a task is the longest waiting time before it can normally finishes its job. The calculation of the laxity value is related to the system time and TC. For example, if we do not take into account of the cycles of the tasks, in Example 1, before task B is executed, task A can be executed three times continuously. But this situation will not be compatible with the cycle of the real problem. Thus, we have the following definition:

Definition 4: The laxity value. The laxity value of periodic task A is calculated by the following expression:

Laxity value of A = the deadline of A – (PT of A + the current time of the system)

or

Laxity value of A = TC - PT

Definition 5: The least laxity value first principle. A task is assigned with the highest priority if it has the least laxity value. The higher the priority of the task is, the sooner the task is executed.

In Example 1, the laxity value of Task A is 5 ms and the laxity value of Task B is 25 ms. Hence, if they are executed according to the least laxity value first algorithm, the real executing situation will be that Task A is executed first because its laxity value is 5 ms. After Task A executes 5 ms, Task A will normally end periodic running. Then Task B obtains the opportunity to execute. After Task B runs for 5 ms, Task A will grab CPU from Task B because the laxity value of Task A is less than Task B. Hence, the executing sequence is the first sequence in Figure 1. That is:

```
A(5ms)  B(5ms)  A(5ms)  B(5ms)  A(5ms)
B(5ms)  A(5ms)  B(10ms) A(5ms)  ...
```

TERMS AND SYMBOLS

Terms

If a system with N real-time tasks satisfies the condition in Definition 3, then these tasks are schedulable. In such a system, the definition of Scheduling Cycle and Scheduling Unit are as follows:

Definition 6: Scheduling Cycle. Suppose there are N real-time tasks in a system and they satisfy the condition in Definition 3, then the Scheduling Cycle of the system denoted as LCM_sch is defined as the least common multiple (LCM) of all the task cycles (TCs).

Definition 7: Running Time (RT). The running time of a task is the CPU time occupied by a task in one scheduling.

PT differs from RT. A PT is often divided into many RTs.

Definition 8: Scheduling Unit. Suppose there are N real-time tasks in a system and they satisfy the condition in Definition 3, then the Scheduling Unit of the system denoted as GCD_sch is defined as the greatest common divisor (GCD) of TCs and PTs of all the tasks.

GCD_sch is existed. 1 is common divisor.

In a scheduling cycle, the number of the cycles of each hard real-time task T_i may be different. In Example 1, the LCM_sch is 50 ms. In this scheduling cycle, Task A has five TCs and Task B has only one. In this example, the GCD_sch is 5 ms.

Symbols

For convenience, this paper supposes that the task cycles and the running time of the real-time tasks are all integers. If they are not integers, they can be easily converted into integers by being multiplied with 10^n (n>=1).

The following symbols are used in this paper:

```
class task {
int ID; //task ID
int TC; //cycle of the real-time task
```

int PT; //running time of the real-time task in one cycle

int r_lax; //remaining laxity value of the real-time task

int r_run; //remaining processing time of the real-time task

... //methods
}

(1) N stands for the number of the tasks in a real-time task set;

(2) T[i] denotes the identification of a real-time task i, (i = 1, 2, ..., N), that is:

class task T[N];

Theorem 1: Let T[i] (i=1, 2, ..., N) be a group of the real-time tasks, then we have:

(1) $\forall i$ {T[i].TC | LCM_sch}

(2) $\forall i$ {(GCD_sch | T[i].TC) and (GCD_sch | T[i].PT)}

THE IMPROVED LLF SCHEDULING ALGORITHM

Process of System Scheduling

The issue in Section 3.1 belongs to a one-processor periodic real-time task scheduling. When the scheduling conditions are satisfied, this kind of problem is solvable. The scheduling of these problems needs two queues. One is RQ (least laxity first Ready Queue), which is used to store the ready periodic tasks waiting CPU. The other is a WQ (Waiting Queue), which is used to store the tasks whose next cycle time has not yet arrived. The system's scheduling policy is showed by Figure 2:

According to Definition 6, we only need to consider the scheduling problems of N tasks T_i in a scheduling cycle. The next scheduling cycle can be scheduled as the scheduling of the previous cycle done. The detailed scheduling algorithms are given below.

Scheduling program choices T_i: Scheduling program choices a Task T_i from the least laxity value first ready queue into the execution in CPU according to the LLF scheduling algorithm.

Task T_i insert into queue: When time slice of Task T_i is over, it interrupts executing and enters the least laxity value first ready queue.

T_i ends, waits for next cycle: When Task T_i finishes its PT and waits for the next cycle, it will enter waiting queue and stay here until the next cycle.

Task T_i begins next cycle and enters queue: When Task T_i begins next task cycle, it will transfers from WQ to RQ.

Preparation of the Scheduling Algorithm

Before the algorithm begins, firstly we need to decide if these tasks are schedulable or not, then calculate LCM_sch, GCD_sch and other initial values. The following operations are executed in sequence.

Initialization

The modules and operations which include in the work of initialization are shown in Figure 3.

Initialize real-time task: Let *T[i]* (i = 1, 2, ..., N) be a group of real-time tasks. Initialize the values of *r_lax* and *r_run* of each task.

Figure 2. System scheduling chart

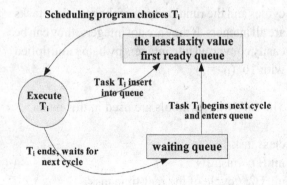

322

Figure 3. Initialization

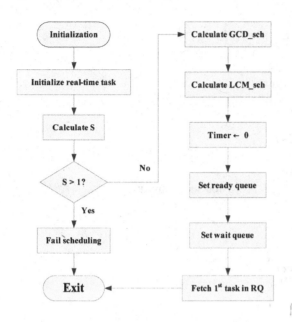

$\forall i \{T[i].r\_lax = T[i].TC - T[i].PT, T[i].r\_run = T[i].PT\}$

(2) **Calculate S**: $S = \sum_{i=1}^{N} \dfrac{T[i].PT}{T[i].TC}$

(3) **Judging frame**: Determine whether the task is schedulable. Based on Definition 3, if S > 1, then these tasks are not schedulable in a single processor and need to quit the system; otherwise jump to next step.

(4) **Calculating GCD_sch:** $\forall i \{(GCD\_sch \mid T[i].TC)$ and $(GCD\_sch \mid T[i].PT)\}$;

(5) **Calculating LCM_sch:** $\forall i \{T[i].TC \mid LCM\_sch\}$;

(6) **Timer ← 0**: Initialize the system timer, let Timer = 0.

(7) **Set ready queue**: Create the least laxity first ready queue. The tasks which do not complete PT are stored in this queue. These tasks are sorted by the values of the laxities from small to large (Ascending). The data structure of the queue node is defined below.
class ReadyQueue: public task
{

ReadyQueue * pt; //a pointer,pt is a pointer to the next node
… // some methods
}

(8) **Set wait queue**: Create the waiting queue. The tasks, which have completed PT and waiting for the next cycle, are stored in this queue and they are ordered by the values of the remaining laxity from small to large (Ascending). The data structure of the node in the queue is defined below.
class WaitQueue: public task
{

int WQr_lax; //remaining laxity,present how long the next cycle will start
WaitQueue *pt; //a pointer,pt is a pointer to the next node
… //some methods
}

(9) **Fetch 1st task in RQ**: Get the first task T[1] of RQ. Load it into the CPU and execute it.

Calculating the Scheduling Unit

Using the each task *T[i].TC* and processing time *T[i].PT(1 ≤ i ≤ N)* to calculate the scheduling unit *GCD_sch. GCD_sch* meets the condition:

$\forall i \{ (GCD\_sch \mid T[i].TC)$ and $(GCD\_sch \mid T[i].PT) \}$

The flowchart of calculating GCD_sch is shown in Figure 4.

Calculating the Scheduling Cycle

Using each task *T[i].TC(1 ≤ i ≤ N)* to calculate the scheduling cycle *LCM_sch. LCM_sch* meets the condition:

$\forall i \{T[i].TC \mid LCM\_sch \}$

The flowchart of the calculating LCM_sch is shown in Figure 5.

Figure 4. Calculating the scheduling unit GCD_sch

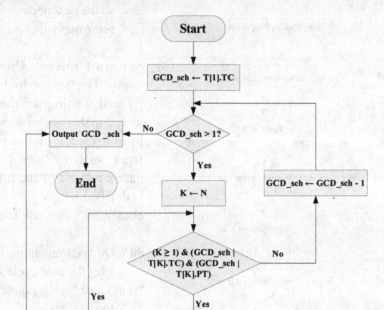

Figure 5. Calculating the scheduling cycle LCM_sch

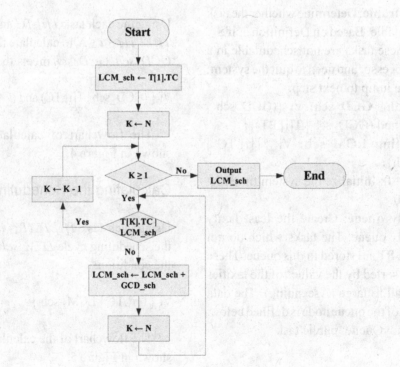

The Scheduling Algorithm

Generally speaking, when the task T completes, the system will choose the next task according to the scheduling algorithm. This paper presents a scheduling algorithm which is based on the improved least-laxity-first scheduling algorithm.

The Architecture

The modules of this algorithm and their relationship are listed in Figure 6.

The ILLF scheduling algorithm is divided into 7 modules:

(1) Let T1 = T.
(2) Fetch the first task of the least-laxity-first ready queue and enter T.
(3) Check safe state.
(4) Calculate the length of the running time of the task chosen currently.
(5) Calculate the laxity of each task.
(6) Adjust the ready queue and waiting queue.
(7) Insert the task T1 into the corresponding queue (ready queue or waiting queue).
(8) Execute task T.

Checking Safe State

Whenever the real-time scheduling begins, it is required that the system is always under a safe state (Tang, Liang, Zhe, & Tang, 2007). The concept of safe state is defined as below.

Definition 9: Safe state (Tang, Liang, Zhe, & Tang, 2007). It indicates that all the tasks (including all task cycles in a scheduling cycle) in the system can be scheduled in a sequence $(T_{i1}^{(1)}, T_{i2}^{(1)}, ..., T_{ij}^{(1)}, T_{i1}^{(2)}, T_{i2}^{(2)}, ..., T_{ik}^{(2)}, ..., T_{ir}^{(S)})$ $(1 \leq i, j, k, r \leq N; 1 \leq s \leq N)$. All of the tasks can normally be completed in a scheduling cycle. Otherwise, if the system cannot find such a sequence, then the system is in an unsafe state.

Calculating the Running Time

In order to have the least scheduling times, the system must keep in the safe state after each scheduling and the running time of each scheduling must be maximum. Thus, before each scheduling, the running time of the task should be calculated to update the laxity value of each task in RQ and WQ and determine the priority of the candidate tasks.

In the paper, let Req_Exec stand for the length of current scheduling requirement, T[i] stand for the ith task in RQ, and WT[j] stand for the jth task in WQ $(1 \leq i, j \leq N)$. The candidate running time is initialed as:

Req_Exec = min (T[1].r_run, T[2].r_lax)

Where we have the following reasons:

① The first node of RQ has the highest priority.
② Because each scheduling adopts the longest running time and is based on the least-laxity-

Figure 6. The modules of ILLF scheduling algorithm and their relationship

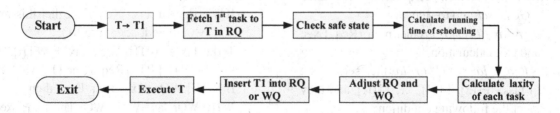

first scheduling algorithm, the priority of the task T completed currently is lower than the first task in RQ.

③ Because each scheduling adopts the longest running time, the running time of the current scheduling task is related with the laxity of each task in RQ and WQ. Moreover, the laxity value of the second task in RQ is larger than that of the first task in RQ and is smaller than others.

The running time of the current task is related with the laxity of each task. It not only relates to the laxity of RQ but also WQ. Therefore, they are uniformly known as super-laxity in this text. The super-laxity of RQ is remaining laxity T[i].r_lax, and that of WQ includes two parts: one is WT[i].WQr_lax, and the other is the next laxity value of the task. The details of the calculation are listed below:

(1) When the task T[i] is in RQ, its super-laxity is T[i].r_lax.

When the task WT[i] is in WQ, its super-laxity is

$$WT[i].WQr_lax + WT[i].TC - WT[i].PT$$

The module of calculating the running time of the scheduling is as follows:

①Let Req_Temp = Req_Temp + T1[i].r_run, i = i + 1;
②Sort all the tasks (include RQ and WQ) by the super-laxity from small to large, suppose the sorted sequence is T1[1], T1[2], …, T1[N].
③Let Req_r_lax=T1[2].Super-laxity−Req_Exec;
④If *Req_r_lax < 0* then *{ Req_Exec = Req_Exec – GCD_sch;* go to step ③; }
⑤If *Req_r_lax≥T1[1].r_lax* then return Req_Exec and exit calculation;
⑥If *0 ≤ Req_r_lax < T1[1].r_lax* then select a set of tasks T1[2], T1[3], …, T1[K], and they meet the following condition:

$$0 \le T1[i].super\text{-}laxity - Req_Exec \le T1[1].r_lax$$

⑦ Calculate the deadline of T1[2], T1[3], …, T1[K],
- If T1[i] is in RQ, T1[i].deadline = T1[i].r_run + T1[i].r_lax;
- If T1[i] is in WQ, T1[i].deadline = T1[i].TC + T1[i].WQr_lax;
- ⑧In the T1[2], T1[3], …, T1[K], select the tasks which meet the condition:

$$T1[i].deadline < T1[1].r_run + T1[1].r_lax$$

Suppose that the result of selection is T11[1], T11[2], …, T11[M], and suppose that the sequence is sorted by laxity from small to large and least deadline first.

⑨Let i=2, Req_Temp = Req_Eexc;
⑩If T11[i].super-laxity − Req_Temp < 0 then Req_Exec=Req_Exec−GCD_sch, go to ⑦;
⑪ Let Req_Temp = Req_Temp + T11[i].r_run, i = i + 1;
⑫If i≤M then Req_Exec=Req_Exec−GCD_sch, go to ⑨;
⑬ Return Req_Exec;
⑭ Exit.

The algorithm flowchart of calculating the running time of the scheduling is shown in Figure 7.

Calculating the laxities

Definition 10: The calculation of the laxity value of each task.

(1) RQ: T[i].r_lax = T[i].r_lax − Req_Exec; $2 \le i \le N$

(2) WQ:
If WT[i].WQr_lax≤Req_Exec then this task would be loaded into RQ;
T[i].r_lax = WT[i].WQr_lax + WT[i].TC − WT[i].PT − Req_Exec ($1 \le i \le N$);
If WT[i].WQr_lax > Req_Exec then
WT[i].WQr_lax=WT[i].WQr_lax−Req_Exec.

Figure 7. Flowchart of calculating scheduling length

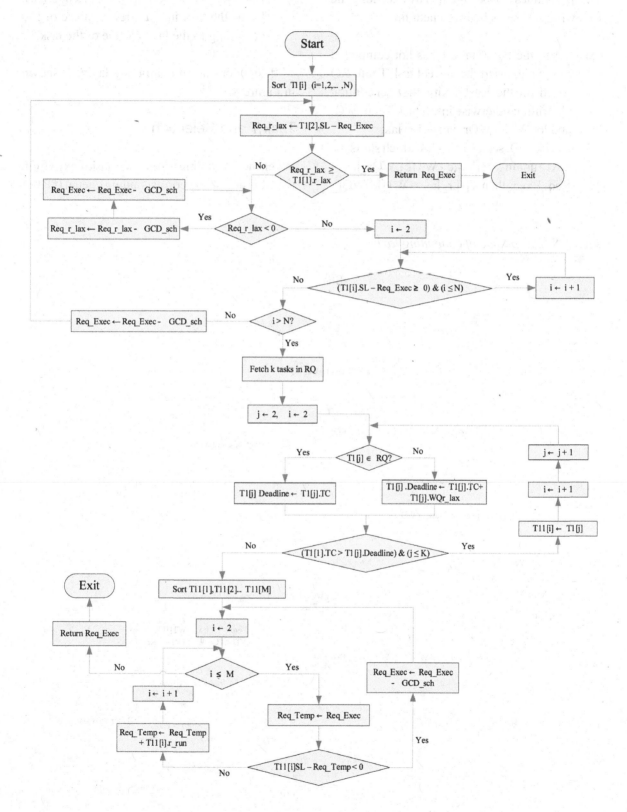

The next values can be obtained by executing the following two steps before scheduling:

(1) When the PT of task T has not completed in a cycle, insert the current task T into RQ based on the least laxity first scheduling algorithm; otherwise insert task T into WQ, and let WT[i].WQr_lax = T.r_lax;

(2) Check WQ, select the task *k* which starts the next running periodic (WT[k].WQr_lax ≤ Req_Exec, then T[i].r_lax − WT[k].WQr_ lax + WT[k].TC − WT[k].PT − Req_Exec). Insert the task into a relevant place of RQ according to the laxity value of the task.

The algorithm of computing laxity is shown in Figure 8.

Task T and Selection

When the scheduling takes place, task T exits from the CPU and enters corresponding queue. If PT of

Figure 8. The module of computing laxity

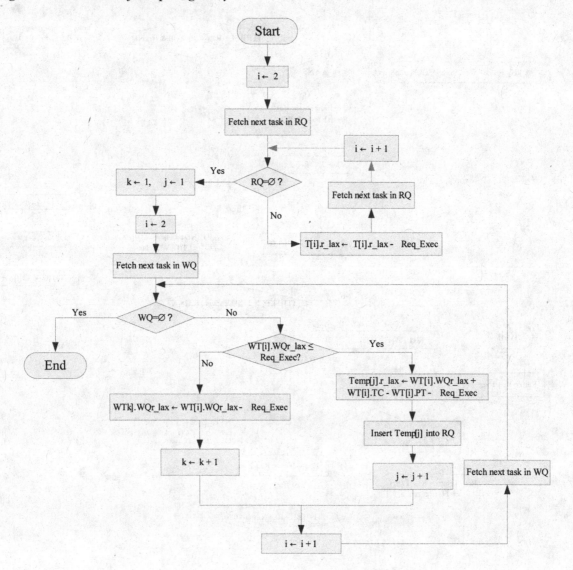

task T has not completed, task T is inserted into RQ. The laxity value of task T does not change. If PT of task T completes, task T is inserted into WQ, then

WT[k].WQr_lax = T.r_lax, WT[k].r_run = 0.

The procedure of task T is shown in Figure 9, and the detail of algorithm is listed below:

① if T.r_run = 0 then insert Task T into WQ; Otherwise insert Task T into RQ;
② Let Req_Exec ← T[1].r_run;

Figure 9. Improved least-laxity-first scheduling algorithm

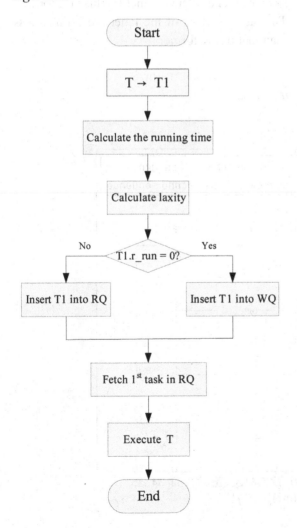

③ Call the module of calculating the running time of the scheduling ;
④ Call the module of calculating the laxity;
⑤ Fetch the first task in RQ;
⑥ Execute task T.

EXPERIMENTS

Analyzing the scheduling in Example 1, let A_1, A_2, A_3, A_4, A_5 to represent the action situations of task A in the first, second, third, fourth and fifth task cycle respectively. Use (5) to stand for running 5 ms, use (10) to stand for running 10 ms. According to the Least-Laxity-First scheduling algorithm, the executing sequence of Example 1 in a scheduling cycle is as follows. LCM_sch is 50 ms and GCD_sch is 5 ms.

$A_1B(5) A_2(5) B(5) A_3(5) B(5) A_4(5) B(5) B(5) A_5(5)$

According to the algorithm given in this paper, the scheduling sequence will be (refers to Figure 1):

$A_1B(10) A(10) [A_2(5) A_3(5)] B(10) A(10) [A_4(5) A_5(5)] B(5)$

In the above two scheduling sequences, the former needs to schedule 10 times and switch tasks 8 times, the latter only needs to schedule 6 times and switch tasks 5 times. The reason of more scheduling times is that the former follows LLF scheduling algorithm strictly and the latter uses ILLF scheduling algorithm in this paper.

Example 2: There are three periodic tasks A, B and C. Suppose that they arrive at the same time, task A is executed every 6 ms and PT is 2 ms, task B is executed every 12 ms and PT is 4 ms, task C is executed every 18 ms and PT is 6 ms.

The problem is described as follows:

A:$TC_1 = 6$, $PT_1 = 2$, $r\_lax_1 = 4$

B:$TC_2 = 12$, $PT_2 = 4$, $r\_lax_2 = 8$

C:$TC_3 = 18$, $PT_3 = 6$, $r\_lax_3 = 12$

Because $S = \dfrac{PT_1}{TC_1} + \dfrac{PT_2}{TC_2} + \dfrac{PT_3}{TC_3} = 1$, these tasks can be scheduled.

After computing LCM_sch and GCD_sch, we have:

LCM_sch = 36 ms; GCD_sch = 2 ms

If the earliest deadline first or the least laxity value first scheduling algorithm is used, the scheduling sequence will be:

$A_1 B_1(2)\ B_1(2)\ A_2(2)\ C_1(2)\ C_1(2)\ C_1(2)\ A_3(2)\ B_2(2)$
$B_2(2)\ A_4(2)\ C_2(2)\ A_5(2)\ B_3(2)\ C_2(2)\ C_2(2)\ B_6(2)\ A_3(2)$

If the ILLF scheduling algorithm is applied, the scheduling sequence will be:

$A_1(2)\ B_1 A_2(2)\ C_1(6)\ A_3(2)\ B_2(4)\ A_4(2)\ C_2(6)$
$A(4)\ [A_5(2)\ A_6(2)]\ B_3(4)$

In which A_i stands for the ith task cycle of task A in scheduling cycle; B_j stands for the jth task cycle of task B; C_k stands for the kth task cycle of task C.

The executing case of the two algorithms is shown in Figure 10.

There are 13 scheduling times in the first sequence and 10 scheduling times in the second sequence. The latter is 3 times less than the former. The task switches of the latter are 3 times less than that of the former.

Figure 10. The comparison of two action sequences with 3 tasks

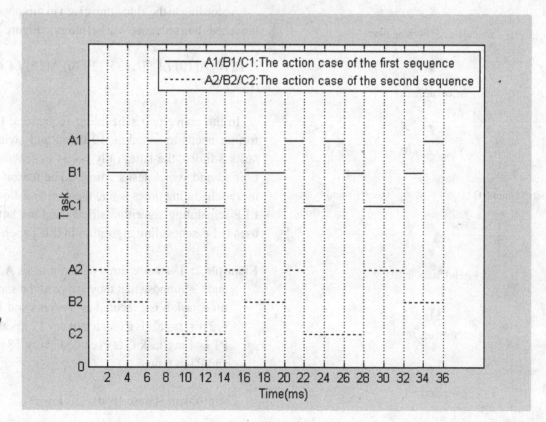

Example 3: There are four periodic tasks A, B, C and D. Suppose their cycles and running times are as follows.

A:$TC_1 = 4$, $PT_1 = 1$, $r\_lax_1 = 3$

B:$TC_2 = 6$, $PT_2 = 1$, $r\_lax_2 = 5$

C:$TC_3 = 12$, $PT_3 = 1$, $r\_lax_3 = 11$

D:$TC_4 = 16$, $PT_4 = 8$, $r\_lax_4 = 8$

Because $S = \dfrac{PT_1}{TC_1} + \dfrac{PT_2}{TC_2} + \dfrac{PT_3}{TC_3} + \dfrac{PT_4}{TC_4} = 1$, these tasks can be scheduled.

After computing LCM_sch and GCD_sch, we have:

LCM_sch = 48 ms; GCD_sch = 1 ms

The executing case of the two algorithms is shown in Figure 11.

There are 34 switch times in the first sequence and 24 in the second sequence. This demonstrates that the latter is much better than the former.

THE ANALYSIS AND THE EXPANSION OF THE ALGORITHM

The scheduling algorithm proposed in this paper is based on the intrinsic features of tasks, the task cycles and the processing time. ILLF scheduling algorithm makes that the running time of every scheduling is as long as possible. Then it overcomes the thrashing problem existing in the current algorithms. Finally a scheduling plan with the least scheduling times and the least switching times is achieved.

Figure 11. The comparison of two action sequences with 4 tasks

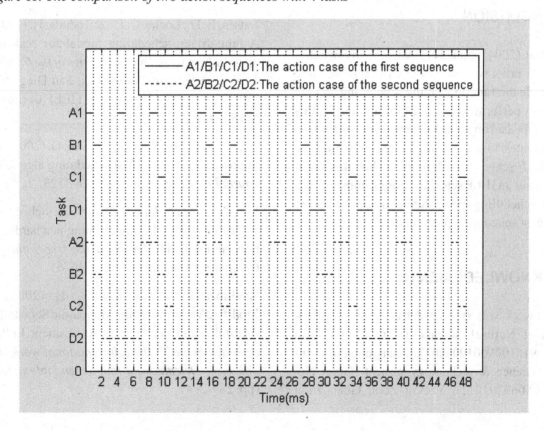

The larger the GCD of all the task cycle TC_i and all the processing time PT_i ($1 \leq i \leq N$), the smaller the number of switches is and the better the system performs in real applications.

Based on fixed periodic real-time tasks, this paper proposes an ILLF scheduling algorithm. Generally speaking, the industrial scheduling is unsure. The productions of the most products are fixed but some temporary manufactured tasks may be accepted occasionally. Therefore, it is necessary to modify the scheduling algorithm proposed in this paper to form a suitable scheduling strategy according to the problem. For instance, when the workload of the system is not full, it is possible to take in some temporary manufactured tasks. If the temporary manufactured task needs much time to run, in order not to affect the execution of real-time tasks, it is better to divide the temporary manufactured task into many pieces and run them in different scheduling cycles.

CONCLUSION

Jin et al. (2004) pointed out that too many switches among tasks will waste the CPU resource and degrade the functions of the scheduling and the system performance. Based on this result, this paper focuses on the tasks themselves and find out the greatest task executing time slice to improve the LLF scheduling algorithm. Then this paper proposes an ILLF scheduling algorithm with the least scheduling and switching times so as to get the best scheduling performance.

ACKNOWLEDGMENTS

This work was supported by Guangdong Provincial Natural Science Foundation (Grant No. 9151009001000007), Guangdong Provincial science & technology project (Grant No. 2008A060201011), Yuexiu Zone Guangzhou city science & technology project (Grant No. 2007-GX-075).

REFERENCES

Abbott, R. K., & Garcia-Molina, H. (1992). Scheduling real-time transactions: A performance evaluation. *ACM Transactions on Database Systems, 17*(3), 513–560. doi:10.1145/132271.132276

Dertouzos, M. L., & Mok, A. K. (1989). Multiprocessor online scheduling of hard-real-time tasks. *IEEE Transactions on Software Engineering, 15*(12), 1497–1506. doi:10.1109/32.58762

Hildebrandt, J., Golatowski, F., & Timmermann, D. (1999). Scheduling coprocessor for enhanced least-laxity-first scheduling in hard real-time systems. In *Proceedings of the 11ᵗʰ Euromicro Conference on Real-Time Systems* (pp. 208-215). Washington, DC: IEEE Computer Society Press.

Jensen, E. D., Locke, C. D., & Toduda, H. (1985). A time-driven scheduling model for real-time operating systems. In *Proceedings of the 6ᵗʰ IEEE Real-Time Systems Symposium*, San Diego, CA (pp. 112-122). Washington, DC: IEEE Computer Society Press.

Jin, H., Wang, H., Wang, Q., & Dai, G. (2004). An improved least-slack first scheduling algorithm. *Journal of software, 15*(8), 1116-1123.

Liu, C. L., & Layland, J. W. (1973). Scheduling algorithms for multiprogramming in a hard real-time environment. *Journal of the Association for Computing Machinery, 20*(1), 46–61.

Naghibzadeh, M., & Kim, K. H. (2002). A Modified Version of Rate-Monotonic Scheduling Algorithm and its Efficiency Assessment. In *Proceedings of the 7ᵗʰ IEEE international workshop on Object-Oriented real-time dependable systems* (pp. 289-294).

Ngolah, C. F., Wang, Y., & Tan, X. (2004). The Real-Time Task Scheduling Algorithm of RTOS+. *IEEE Canadian Journal of Electrical and Computer Engineering, 29*(4), 237–243.

Oh, S., & Yang, S. (1998). *A modified least-laxity-first scheduling algorithm for real-time tasks.* In *Proceedings of the 5th International Conference on Real-Time Computing Systems and Applications* (pp. 31-36). Washington, DC: IEEE Computer Society Press.

Tanenbaum, A. S. (2002). *Modern operating systems* (2nd ed.). Zurich, Switzerland: China Machine Press.

Tang, X., Liang, H., Zhe, F., & Tang, Z. (2007, May). *Computer Operating System* (3rd edition). Shaanxi, China: Xidian University Press.

Wang, J., Lin, T., Wang, J., Han, G., & Zhao, H. (2004). Research on preemptions of preemptive EDF and improvement on its performance. *Acta Electronica Sinica, 32*(1), 64–68.

Wang, Q., Xu, J., Wang, H., Wang, H., & Dai, G. (2004). A new Priority Table based Real-time Scheduling Algorithm. *Acta Electronica Sinica, 2*, 310–313.

Wang, Y. (2003). On Cognitive Informatics. *Brain and Mind: A Transdisciplinary Journal of Neuroscience and Neurophilosophy, 4*(2), 151-167.

Wang, Y. (2007). The Theoretical Framework of Cognitive Informatics. *International Journal of Cognitive Informatics and Natural Intelligence, 1*(1), 1–27.

Wang, Y., & Saksena, M. (1999). Scheduling fixed-priority tasks with preemption threshold. In *Proceedings of the 6th International Conference On Real-Time Computing Systems and Applications* (pp. 328-335). Washington, DC: IEEE Computer Society Press.

Zhang, W., & Fu, X. (2006). An Improved Least-Laxity-First Scheduling Algorithm for periodic tasks. *Journal of Jiangxi normal university, 30*(4), 365-368

This work was previously published in International Journal of Software Science and Computational Intelligence, Volume 2, Issue 2, edited by Yingxu Wang, pp. 88-105, copyright 2010 by IGI Publishing (an imprint of IGI Global).

Section 4
Applications of Computational Intelligence and Cognitive Computing

Chapter 18
Cognitive Location–Aware Information Retrieval by Agent–Based Semantic Matching

Eddie C. L. Chan
The Hong Kong Polytechnic University, China

George Baciu
The Hong Kong Polytechnic University, China

S. C. Mak
The Hong Kong Polytechnic University, China

ABSTRACT

This paper proposes semantic TFIDF, an agent-based system for retrieving location-aware information that makes use of semantic information in the data to develop smaller training sets, thereby improving the speed of retrieval while maintaining or even improving accuracy. This proposed method first assigns intelligent agents to gathering location-aware data, which they then classify, match, and organize to find a best match for a user query. This is done using semantic graphs in the WordNet English dictionary. Experiments will compare the proposed system with three other commonly used systems and show that it is significantly faster and more accurate.

INTRODUCTION

One of the most challenging problems in retrieving the location-aware information is to understand the behavior of users and how it suits the current location. Wireless tracking applications are popular ways to help user navigate that may make use of current location-aware information.

However, very often, the information retrieved in common search engines is both excessive and unstructured from the user's point of view. The basic requirement of an effective location-aware retrieval system is that it should match user queries and provides accurate information where users access location-aware (e.g., pervasive computing-enabled) applications and services. The retrieval system should do this in an organized and efficient way.

DOI: 10.4018/978-1-4666-0264-9.ch018

In recent years, researchers have focused on how to provide higher accuracy and faster retrieval by making use of keywords and textual semantics. However, the results so far have been unsatisfactory. First, the truth-conditional semantics that are often applied provide only a very limited account of meaning. Second, information is derived from few sources and the information from those sources is not structured. In these circumstances, the value of the information that can be extracted is very limited. Third, information collection is an expensive, time-consuming process that is often carried out manually. This makes it very difficult to build, maintain and grow comprehensive databases. Forth, some approaches, such as Naïve-Bayes (Danesh et al., 2007) and K-Nearest Neighbors (K-NN) classifiers (Weiss et al., 1996) machine learning approaches ignore the semantic meaning in text classification. This leads to inadequate search results. Finally, location-aware information is distributed in different locations and some information, traffic information for example, they will quickly become out-of-date so location-aware information must be updated frequently.

This paper proposes an agent-based semantics retrieval system for location-aware information. The proposed system uses the WordNet (WordNet, 2004) dictionary to construct the semantics graph structure of a location. This graph structure sets the weight values between edges and nodes (words) of the semantics and the classic information retrieval, term-frequency-time-inverse-document-frequency (TFIDF) technique is modified with semantics weight values. As the location-aware information is distributed in different locations, the approach also implement agents using the IBM Aglets Agent Software Development Kit (IBM, 2004). These mobile network agents are programs that can be dispatched from one computer and transported to a remote computer for execution. Arriving at the remote computer, they present their credentials and obtain access to local services and data. The remote computer may also serve as a broker by bringing together agents with similar interests and compatible goals, thus providing a meeting place at which agents can interact. The proposed system uses four types of agents: one each to gather, classify, match, and organize information.

The proposed system offers a number of benefits. First, the proposed semantics graph structure provides a hierarchical structure for the location-aware information. Second, the proposed agent system obviates the need for extensive manual information grasping. Third, the modified TFIDF with semantics weights improves the accuracy of matching keywords and provides a more meaningful result from the point of view of semantics. Forth, the agent can update information directly by communicating with its neighbor agents. Finally, it is fast and cost-effective.

The rest of paper is organized as follows: Section 1 presents the related work of information retrieval techniques and agent-based information systems. Section 2 describes cognitive semantics TFIDF technique in our system. Section 3 presents the system implementation and architecture of agent-based cognitive semantics retrieval system. Section 4 describes the experiment setup and result. Section 5 presents the case study. Finally, Sections 6 offers our conclusion and future work.

1. RELATED WORK

In this section, we summarize current research works of the information retrieval techniques, agent-based information retrieval systems and positioning system in the area of cognitive informatics and cognitive computing (Baciu et al., 2009; Wang, 2003, 2007, 2009).

1.1 Information Retrieval Techniques

There are a number of information retrieval techniques. These include, Naïve Bayes classifier (Lewis & Ringutte, 1994), linear or quadratic discriminated analysis (LDA or QDA) (Hull et al.,

1996), artificial neural network (Tan et al., 2006), back-propagation-based technique (Nawi et al., 2008) and C4.5 (Ruggieri, 2002) rule learning technique. Naïve Bayes classifier (Lewis & Ringutte, 1994) suffers from its assumption that words are independent of each other and are, therefore, less accurate than a more complex model. While standard parametric methods such as LDA, QDA (Hull et al., 1996) and regression are mostly criticized as being dependent on strong assumptions about the distribution of the underlying data, classification and pattern recognition methods require large number of training points. Artificial neural network-based (Tan et al., 2006) approaches are blamed to be black-box models thus not being able to provide insight into the complex interactions of the ecosystem processes, although they are able to overcome the difficulties associated with traditional statistical models. Back-propagation-based techniques (Nawi et al., 2008) are inherently off-line, that is iterative, methods using all the available data at once. This techniques need to retrain the entire database again in order to get each new observation, thus requiring a significant amount of computational resources and time. The motivation in C4.5 (Ruggieri, 2002) is to optimize rules locally by dropping conditions, as the initial rule set, being generated from a decision tree, is unduly large and redundant. But the process itself is rather complex and heuristic.

1.2 Agent-Based Information Retrieval Systems

Agents such as Harvest (Brown & Danzig, 2004), FAQ-Finder (Doorenbos et al., 1997), Information Manifold (Levy et al., 2005), OCCAM (Kwok & Weld, 1996), and Parasite (Spertus, 1997) rely either on pre-specified domain specific information about particular types of documents, or on hard-coded models of the information sources to retrieve and interpret documents. The Harvest system (Doorenbos et al., 1997) relies on semi-structured documents to improve its ability to extract information.

For example, it knows how to find author and title information in Latex documents and how to strip position information from postscript files. Harvest neither discovers new documents nor learns new models of document structure. Similarly, FAQ-Finder (Doorenbos et al., 1997) extracts answers to frequently asked questions (FAQs) from FAQ files available on the web. In a conclusion, the performance of current agent-based information retrieval systems is not satisfied.

1.3 Positioning Systems

The Global Positioning System (GPS) (Taheri et al., 2004) is currently the standard for location sensing in outdoor wireless environments. Many GPS tracking applications has been developed and launched to the market to help users to locate themselves, such as a car navigation system and GPS in iPhone devices. Over the last several years, wireless local area network (WLAN) has evolved rapidly. Positioning systems for indoor areas (Prasithsangaree et al., 2002; Jan & Lee, 2003) using the existing wireless local area network infrastructure have been suggested. Although we have a full positioning coverage application across topologically varied landscape, recent applications ignores the importance of information driven by a location and it seems to be lack of research to study the location-aware information. The application should allow users to access or even proactively provide location-aware information where users trigger positioning function. A location-aware information is usually very useful for the user to know and understand a particular region, such that user could know where to access facilities.

2. COGNITIVE SEMANTICS TFIDF TECHNIQUE

Normally, a location-aware application receives a keyword query from users. This section begins by describing how to use the keyword feature selection technique. It then introduces the TFIDF technique for forming a space vector model. The WordNet (WordNet, 2004) English dictionary is then used to form a graph of the semantic structure of a term/word and to set weight values to each edge of the graph. Instead of using Euclidean distance directly, the approach calculates the distance including the weight value of each vector. Finally, the information is clustered using K-NN algorithm.

2.1 Feature Selection Technique

Feature selection is a common information retrieval technique. Usually, there are three feature selection criteria: 1) pruning of infrequent features, 2) pruning of high frequency features and 3) Choosing features, which have high mutual information with the target concept.

The first step is to prune the infrequent words from my training sets of data. This removes most spelling errors and speeds up the later stages of feature selection. The nest step is to prune the most frequent words. This technique should eliminate non-content words like "the", "and", or "for". Finally, the remaining words are ranked using the TFIDF technique according to their mutual information with reference to the target concept/category.

2.2 TFIDF Technique

TFIDF (Wen et al., 2001; Lo et al., 2008) is an information retrieval technique commonly used in query searching. This technique formulates the significance of a term/word according to its frequency in a document or a collection of documents. This work uses TFIDF to determine the weights that are assigned to individual terms. If a term t occurs in document d,

$$w_{di} = tf_{di} \times \log(N / idf_{di}) \qquad (1)$$

where t_i is a word (or a term) in the document collection, w_{di} is the weight of t_i, tf_{di} is the term

frequency (term count of each word in a document) of t_i, N is the total number of documents in the collection and idf_{di} is the number of document in which t_i appears. The TFIDF technique learns a class model by combining document (vectors) into a vector space model.

2.3 Cognitive Semantics Graph Structure

The WordNet English dictionary provides a hierarchical representation of English words organized according to the strength of their associations in a number of defined domains, which I will refer to here as a semantics graph. WordNet defines a weight value for each relationship in a graph.

Figure 1 shows a graph for the word "taste". The words "tart" and "unpleasant" are at the same level of hierarchal and have relation with each other so they are very similar. Their distance in the tree structure can measure the similarity of two words. The ontology-based term frequency can be obtained by comparing the meanings of two terms,

$$otf_1 = tf_1 \times (1+(1/D(t_1,t_2))^{tf2} \qquad (2)$$

where t_1, t_2 are different terms; otf_1 is ontology-based term frequency of t_1; tf_1, tf_2 are the term frequency respectively to t_1 and t_2; $D(t_1,t_2)$ is the depth between t_1 and t_2. $D(t_1,t_2)$ can be calculated.

For example, assume the term frequencies of "tart" and "unpleasant" are 3 and 2 respectively and depth between "tart" and "unpleasant" is 3. The ontology-based term frequency of "tart" will be $otf_1 = 3 \times (1+(1/3))^2 = 5.33$. The ontology-based term frequency of "unpleasant" will be $otf_2 = 2 \times (1+(1/3))^3 = 4.67$. After adjustment of each term frequency, their term frequency value may increase. The two terms could thus become more significant after computing TFIDF.

Figure 1. The word graph example of "taste"

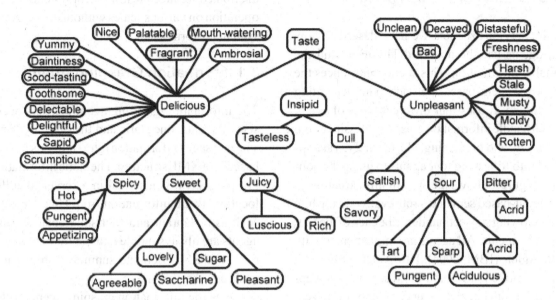

2.4 Term Document Matrix

A term document matrix (Sudarsun et al., 2006; Jaber et al., 2007) is widely used in natural language processing and information retrieval as a way to reduce space requirements and speed up searching. A term document matrix is a large grid representing every document and content word in a collection. A term document matrix is generated to store my data. (2) is used to get a new (ontology-based) TFIDF value for each term and then a document vector denoted by $A = \{a_1, a_2 ..., a_n\}$ where n is the total number of documents. A document vector contains three elements, a term, an ontology-based TFIDF, and a term frequency. These elements allow each document vector to be formed as a matrix in which each row stands for a term and each column stands for a document. Each cell will contain the ontology-based TFIDF weight of a particular document. If a given term appears in a given document, it can be seen at the intersection of the appropriate row and column. Finally, each document matrix is normalized and scaled down to prevent large documents with many keywords from overwhelming smaller documents. Smaller documents are considered to be more im-

portant and larger document are penalized, making every document equally significant. Once a normalized term document matrix has been created, singular value decomposition is run to allow faster operations on the matrix.

2.5 K-NN Algorithm

After developing a set of term document martices, the K-NN algorithm is applied to a document w and a set of document clusters $C = .$ D $= \{d_1, d_2 ... d_j\}$ is a set of distance between w and c_i. It is possible to estimate the simiarlity between a document and a set of document clusters by calculating the Euclidean distance $|w - c_i|$. In a hierarchical clustering, two clusters c_i and c_j are randomly chosen and their similarity $sim(c_i, c_j)$ is calculated. They are merged if the similarity value is greater than the threshold value. Otherwise, this step repeats until reaching the termination condition with K clusters.

$$d = \frac{\sum_{i=1}^{n} \dfrac{d_i}{|w - c_i|}}{\sum_{i=1}^{n} \dfrac{1}{|w - c_i|}} \tag{3}$$

3. SYSTEM IMPLEMENTATION

In the previous section, we have described how our agents use the modified TFIDF to find the suitable information. This section introduces the proposed agent-based approach to implementing the system. It uses four different types of agent, which handle information grasping, classification, matching, and organizing. (1), (2) and (3) are applied into following four agents to grasp the content. Figure 2 shows the system infrastructure of the agent-based semantics retrieval system while the following subsections describe each of the four types of agents. All agents are implemented with IBMAglets (IBM, 2004). IBMAglets provides a collaborative platform to build sophisticated application with interactive services among different modules. It also provides an asynchronous runtime environment in an agent server enables parallel processing to increase system performance, while

distributed architecture in an agent system supports operation on various scales without damaging the system performance.

3.1 Information Grasping Agent

The information-grasping agent consists of two sets of agents, one static and the other dynamic. The message (information) stored in this agent is based on a XML structure. The static information-grasping agent is installed in a server to collect location-aware information from URL websites, such as restaurant and tourism websites. Static agents are always online and maintain a 24-hour record of RSS (rich site summary) information from popular websites.

Dynamic information grasping agents collect information in a mobile environment. In most of cases, they collect location-aware information through information exchanges between users or

Figure 2. System Architecture of Agent-based cognitive semantics retrieval system in our system

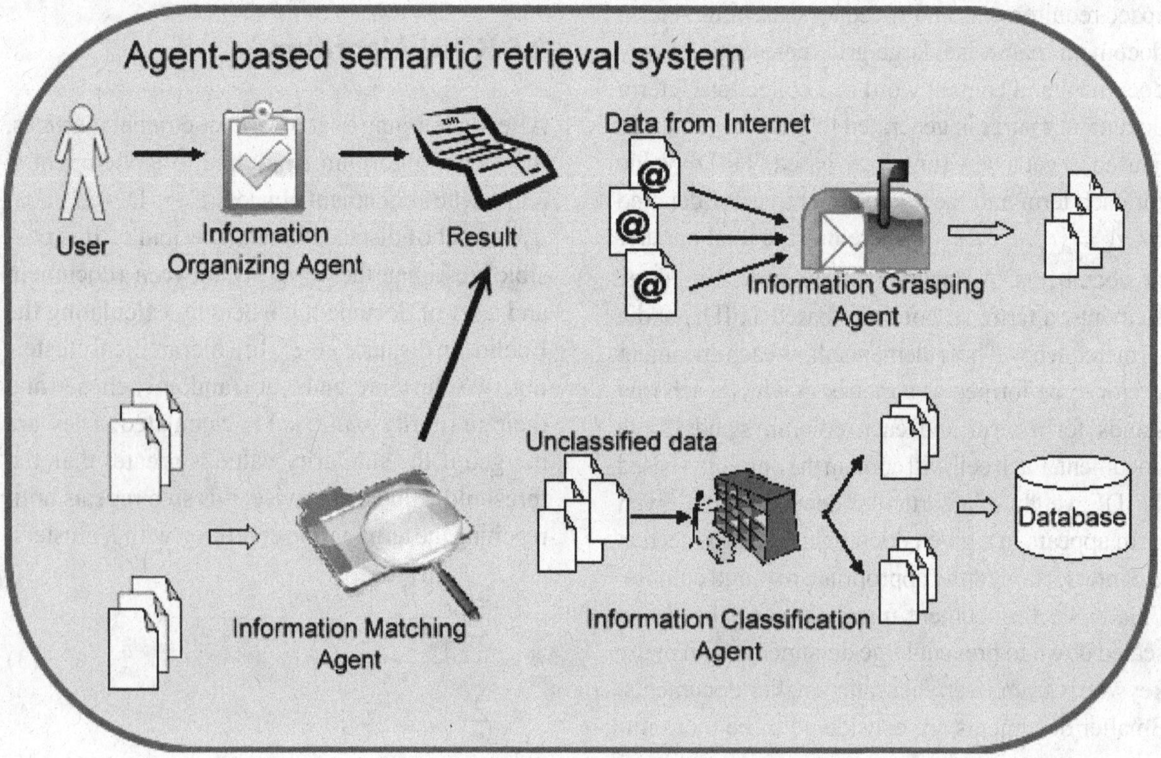

sometimes collect data invoked by other real-time systems such as surveillance systems or supply chain RFID tracking systems. Increasing the number of dynamic information agents will help keep information more up-to-date but on the other hand puts an added burden on network traffic. A user-driven process will allow only the dynamic information-grasping agent to be triggered. When the agent is invoked at a user's request, it gathers different sources of information automatically and then updates the information with neighbors or other systems. It thus contributes to and receives the latest information through the system.

Dynamic information grasping agents has following properties: (1) Autonomous: it collects the information according to user's preference and is not required constant human guidance. (2) Proactive: it has the ability to sense the new location and respond to collect new information stimulation appropriately. (3) Mobile: it is able to migrate itself from one host to another and bring data across different mobile platform. (4) Collaborative: it is able to make conversation with following (other) agents to achieve sociability.

3.2 Information Classification Agent

The information classification agent classifies output information into suitable categories and calculates the Euclidean distance between the words to form a word graph, which expresses relationships between words (Figure 1). It is a core part in the system because word classification directly affects the accuracy of searching.

3.3 Information Matching Agent

The information-matching agent matches user queries and categorizes information. According to the users' preferences, the agent analyzes and searches for information in the categorized information. The best match for the user's requirements is found using (2) and (3).

3.4 Information Organizing Agent

The information-organizing agent organizes the search result. It provides a user-friendly interface, receiving user preferences and change the display and organization of the content.

4. EXPERIMENT SETUP AND RESULTS

This section makes use of the Chinese Learner English Corpus (CLEC) (PolyU, 2004) and in particular 500 location-related articles subdivided into six categories. There are 83 articles each for the domains Hotel, Restaurant, Traffic and Shopping mall and 84 for the domain of College and Clinic. Figure 3 illustrates the number of articles in each category.

Two sets of experiment are conducted to compare three types of techniques, the three-layer neural-network (NN), TFIDF with hierarchical clustering, and the proposed semantics TFIDF techniques. The first experiment tests the precision of categorization/clustering. The second experiment measures the computation time required to cluster using three techniques. An additional three test sets of 100 user queries is input to find out suitable information from the system. Each user query consists of at most ten words. All the experiments are conducted on a common desktop computer with a CPU of Intel Pentium 4.3 GHz, 2GB DDR2 SDRAM and physical storage of 200GB with 7200 rpm.

In subsection 4.1, we discuss the precision rate in three different techniques. Subsection 4.2 measures the computational time during information retrieval, and discuss the effectiveness of using different techniques.

4.1 Precision Rate

Table 1 and Figure 4 show the result of the precision when using the three different information

Figure 3. The precision rate for the classification with 3 different information retrieval techniques

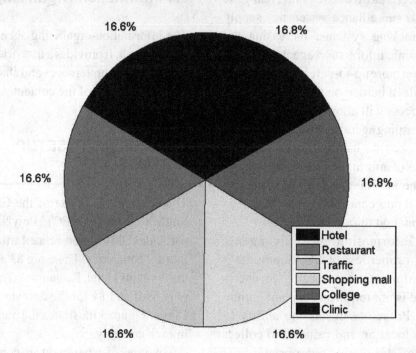

retrieval techniques. The average precision across different categories of semantics TFIDF is 95.68% which is the highest of the three techniques.

4.2 Speed

Figure 5 shows the computational time required to find suitable information when using three dif-

ferent information retrieval techniques. The NN technique takes 5295 seconds for clustering, which is approximately five times longer than the other two methods. The shortest time required finding suitable information is TFIDF with hierarchical clustering technique, at only 1138 seconds to finish clustering. The semantics TFIDF technique requires 1185 seconds.

5. CASE STUDY

In this section, we discuss our proposed system with our tourist guide application in iPhone 3GS. The system will identify the user current location with positioning technologies such as Differential Global Positioning System (DGPS) and return the favorable dinning place search result according to the user's preference. Figure 6 shows the user interface of our application in iPhone 3GS.

There are three main layers in our iPhone application. The first layer is the positioning

Table 1. Comparison of the precision rate (%)

Category	Method		
	NN (3-Layer)	*TFIDF with hierarchical clustering*	*Cognitive semantics TFIDF*
Hotel	68.40%	90.30%	95.13%
Restaurant	58.45%	93.37%	96.72%
Traffic	73.43%	93.88%	95.14%
Shopping mall	67.00%	94.33%	97.44%
College	70.22%	93.78%	94.38%
Clinic	50.23%	91.67%	95.24%
Average	64.62%	93.72%	95.68%

Figure 4. Proposed Location-aware Application using Apple's iPhone

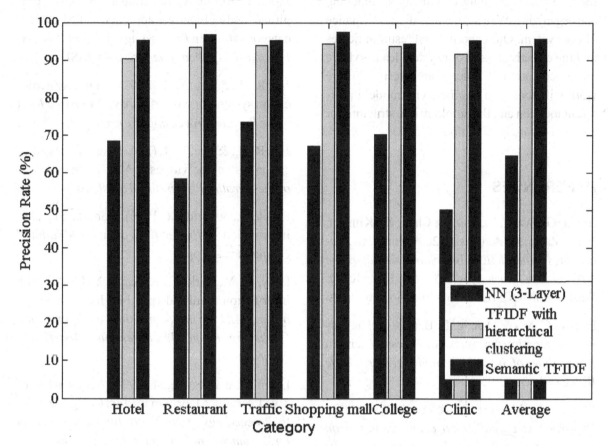

layer. DGPS would be used to estimate the user's location. iPhone 3GS has already included the features of DGPS.

The second layer is the user input layer which reads users' query, displays the restaurant information and identify the location in the Google map. We implement our system using iPhone as front-end user interface. iPhone is a touch device that it can easily control the zooming function of the map.

The third layer is our proposed agent system layer. This layer includes a location-aware database server which stores the name, address, price, type and global co-ordinate of 17,000 restaurants. We make use of the proposed system to help the user to find suitable dinning places (Table 2).

6. CONCLUSION AND FUTURE WORK

In this paper, our agent-based cognitive semantics retrieval system for location-aware information is introduced. We illustrate our cognitive semantics TFIDF technique and implement intelligent agents

Table 2. Comparison of time taken for clustering

Category	Method		
	NN (3-Layer)	*TFIDF with hierarchical clustering*	*Cognitive semantics TFIDF*
Set 1	5277 seconds	1114 seconds	1175 seconds
Set 2	5432 seconds	1123 seconds	1186 seconds
Set 3	5175 seconds	1176 seconds	1195 seconds
Average	5295 seconds	1138 seconds	1185 seconds

for information grasping, classification, matching and organizing. We also evaluate the performance of our system. Our experimental result indicates that the effectiveness of our system leads to have more accurate and faster search result. Future work will consist in user behavior model in different location and the ontology tree structure for location-aware information.

REFERENCES

Baciu, G., Wang, Y., Yao, Y., Chan, K., Kinsner, W., & Zadeh, L. A. (Eds.). (2009, June). In *Proceedings of the 8th IEEE International Conference on Cognitive Informatics (ICCI'09),* Hong Kong. Washington, DC: IEEE Computer Society Press.

Brown, C. M., & Danzig, B. B. (2004). The harvest information discovery and access system. In *Proceedings of the 2nd International World Wide Web Conference.*

Danesh, A., Moshiri, B., & Fatemi, O. (2007). *Improve text classification accuracy based on classifier fusion methods.* In *Proceedings of the Information Fusion, 2007 10th International Conference* (pp. 1-6).

Davis, J., & Goadrich, M. (2006). The Relationship Between Precision-Recall and ROC Curves. In *Proceedings of the ACM 23rd International Conference on Machine learning* (pp. 233-240).

Doorenbos, R. B., Etzioni, O., & Weld, D. S. (1997). *A scalable comparison shopping agent for the world wide web (Tech. Rep. No. TR 97-027).* Minneapolis, MN: University of Minnesota.

Hull, D., Pedersen, J., & Schutze, H. (1996). Document Routing as Statistical Classification. In *Proceedings of the AAAI Spring Symposium on Machine Learning in Information Access Technical Papers,* Palo Alto, CA.

IBM. (2004). *IBM Aglets.* Retrieved June 10, 2004, from http://www.trl.ibm.com/aglets/

Jaber, T., Amira, A., & Milligan, P. (2007). Empirical study of a novel approach to LSI for text categorisation. In *Proceedings of Signal Processing and Its Applications* (pp. 1–4). ISSPA.

Jan, R. H., & Lee, Y. R. (2003). An indoor geolocation system for wireless LANs. In *Proceedings of the Parallel Processing Workshops* (pp. 29-34).

Jan, R. H., & Lee, Y. R. (2003). An indoor geolocation system for wireless LANs. In *Proceedings of the Parallel Processing Workshops.*

Kwok, C., & Weld, D. (1996). Planning to gather information. In *Proceedings of the 14th National Conference AI* (pp. 15).

Levy, A. Y., Kirk, T., & Sagiv, Y. (2005). The information manifold (pp. 14). In *Proceedings of the AAAI Spring Symposium on Information Gathering From Heterogeneous Distributed Environments.*

Lewis, D., & Ringutte, M. (1994). A comparison of Two Learning Algorithm for Text Categorization. In *Proceedings of the Third Annual Symposium on Document Analysis and Information Retrieval* (pp. 81-93).

Lo, C.-C., Cheng, D.-Y., Chen, C.-H., & Yan, Y.-S. (2008). Design and Implementation of Situation-Aware Medical Tourism Service Search System (pp. 1-5). In *Proceedings of the Wireless Communications, Networking and Mobile Computing (WiCOM '08), the 4th International Conference.*

Nawi, N. M., Ransing, R. S., & Ransing, M. R. (2008). A New Method to Improve the Gradient Based Search Direction to Enhance the Computational Efficiency of Back Propagation Based Neural Network Algorithms. In *Proceedings of the Modeling & Simulation, the Second Asia International Conference* (pp. 546-552).

Poly, U. (2004). *Chinese Learner English Corpus (CLEC).* Retrieved June 10, 2004, from http://langbank.engl.polyu.edu.hk/corpus/clec.html

Prasithsangaree, P., Krishnamurthy, P., & Chrysanthis, P. K. (2002). On indoor position location with wireless LANs. In *Proceedings of the 13th IEEE International Symposium on Personal, Indoor and Mobile Radio Communications* (Vol. 2).

Ruggieri, S. (2002). Efficient C4.5 [classification algorithm]. *Knowledge and Data Engineering . IEEE Transactions, 14*(2), 438–444.

Spertus, E. (1997). Parasite: Mining structural information on the web. In *Proceedings of the 6th WWW Conference* (pp. 16).

Sudarsun, S., Kalaivendhan, D., & Venkateswarlu. (2006). Unsupervised Contextual Keyword Relevance Learning and Measurement using PLSA. In *Proceedings of the Annual India Conference* (pp. 1-6).

Taheri, A., Singh, A., & Emmanuel, A. (2004). Location fingerprinting on infrastructure 802.11 wireless local area networks (WLANs) using locus. In *Proceedings of the Local Computer Networks, 2004, 29th Annual IEEE International Conference* (pp. 676-683).

Tan, C. O., Ozesmi, U., Beklioglu, M., Per, E., & Kurt, B. (2006). Predictive Models in Ecology: Comparison of Performances and Assessment of Applicability. *Ecological Informatics*, 195–211. doi:10.1016/j.ecoinf.2006.03.002

Wang, Y. (2003). On Cognitive Informatics. *Brain and Mind: A Transdisciplinary Journal of Neuroscience and Neurophilosophy, 4*(2), 151-167.

Wang, Y. (2007). The Theoretical Framework of Cognitive Informatics. *International Journal of Cognitive Informatics and Natural Intelligence, 1*(1), 1–27.

Wang, Y. (2009). On Cognitive Computing. *International Journal of Software Science and Computational Intelligence, 1*(3), 1–15.

Weiss, S., Kasif, S., & Brill, E. (1996). Text Classification in USENET Newsgroup: A Progress Report. In *Proceedings of the AAAI Spring Symposium on Machine Learning in Information Access Technical Papers*, Palo Alto, CA.

Wen, W. C., Liu, H., Wen, W. X., & Zheng, J. (2001). A Distributed Hierarchical Clustering System for Web Mining. In *Proceedings of the WAIM2002* (LNCS 2118, pp. 103-113). Berlin: Springer Verlag.

WordNet. (2004). *WordNet*. Retrieved June 10, 2004, from http://www.wordnet.com

This work was previously published in International Journal of Software Science and Computational Intelligence, Volume 2, Issue 3, edited by Yingxu Wang, pp. 21-31, copyright 2010 by IGI Publishing (an imprint of IGI Global).

Chapter 19
Perceiving the Social:
A Multi-Agent System to Support Human Navigation in Foreign Communities

Victor V. Kryssanov
Ritsumeikan University, Japan

Shizuka Kumokawa
Ritsumeikan University, Japan

Igor Goncharenko
3D Incorporated, Japan

Hitoshi Ogawa
Ritsumeikan University, Japan

ABSTRACT

This paper describes a system developed to help people explore local communities by providing navigation services in social spaces created by the community members via communication and knowledge sharing. The proposed system utilizes data of a community's social network to reconstruct the social space, which is otherwise not physically perceptible but imaginary, experiential, yet learnable. The social space is modeled with an agent network, where each agent stands for a member of the community and has knowledge about expertise and personal characteristics of some other members. An agent can gather information, using its social "connections," to find community members most suitable to communicate to in a specific situation defined by the system's user. The system then deploys its multimodal interface, which "maps" the social space onto a representation of the relevant physical space, to locate the potential interlocutors and advise the user on an efficient communication strategy for the given community.

DOI: 10.4018/978-1-4666-0264-9.ch019

MOTIVATION

Since the advent of computer age several decades ago, the role of various information systems in human knowledge sharing and proliferation has been increasing continuously. At the same time, however, the bulk of information learned by people in their lifetimes still never appears in a database or on the Internet but is readily available to members of various local communities, such as families, school students and alumni, indigenous people, company employee, and the like. This information is typically conveyed via word-of-mouth in conversations on an individual, person-to-person basis. While the modern information technologies traditionally focus on asynchronous mass-communication and deliver a vast array of tools (e.g. electronic libraries and search engines) supporting this form of information exchange, little has been done to assist the essentially personified and synchronous communication occurring daily, as we quire a teacher at a school, ask a local for directions, or seek advice from a friend or the "best" expert in a field (e.g. a doctor or lawyer). Even though existing computer systems do provide for person-to-person information exchange, their support does not go far beyond, say, a postal service that promotes communication among people who are already socially connected in one or another way. Whether we walk on a street or chat using an instant messenger, or else write to a forum of a social network system, our chances of obtaining information of interest are roughly the same. It is then our abilities to navigate social spaces (which are, at best, partly known) and to initiate and maintain communication at a level of synchronicity optimal for given time constraints that determine the success or otherwise of an information quest.

None of the present-day information systems and "e-services" known to the authors targets supporting this essentially "interhuman" navigation process. The very concepts of social space and communication synchronicity, although not totally alien in computer sciences, are presently discussed as quite theoretical and speculative rather than as something that would be practically used in and strongly affect information system design and development (Derene, 2008; Kalman & Rafaeli, 2007). While there is a growing interest to modeling social aspects of human communication and knowledge production processes in the relatively new fields of cognitive informatics and symbiotic computing, the community's present efforts are, however, mainly directed at the theory rather than at the development (see Wang & Kinsner, 2006).

Our study aims at the creation of an information service to facilitate human navigation in (unknown) social environments by enabling people to "perceive" and explore the corresponding social spaces. The envisaged service is also to help the users locate "carriers" of specific information (i.e. advisers) that would be approached in a particular situation. This paper describes a multi-agent information system "SoNa" (*So*cial *Na*vigator) developed to provide the social navigation service.

In line with the most common understanding of the social space concept (see Lefebvre, 1994; Monge & Contractor, 2003), the proposed system reproduces in a 3D virtual reality (a relevant fragment of) the physical space together with members of the local community present in the space at the moment. Unlike the physical proximity, social relationships (e.g. "trust" or "friendship") are usually not directly perceived in real life, but are inferred and "felt" from (collective and individual) communicative experiences. A haptic environment including a force display is then used to convey important parts of the community's communication practices – the "social knowledge" – to the user via the subconscious tactile communication channel. An agent network is created and used by the system to deal with the social knowledge. This network represents a real social network of the community, and the agents exchange information by communicating with their "socially connected" counterparts in the same way as people do it in the real world. Each agent in the network has parameters indicating whether the corresponding member is sociable, can be trusted, can afford to communicate (e.g. in terms of time), and is currently reachable (e.g. physically or via e-mail). Apart from exploration of the social space in various modalities and under different contexts, the user can use the system as a navigator in her or his search of a community member who would be approached with a specific information request.

In the next section, the design of the proposed system is presented. Section 3 describes a working prototype of the system implemented in the study. Section 4 elaborates on the developed multimodal user interface and user-system interactions. Section 5 then presents the haptic model of the social space. Section 6 gives an account of a case study of applying the proposed system's prototype in practice. Finally, Section 7 discusses related work and concludes the paper.

SYSTEM DESIGN

Overall Functionality and Architecture

Navigation in an environment, whether physical or virtual, can generally be defined as a four-stage iterative process (Spence, 1999): 1) perception of the environment, 2) reconciliation of the perception and cognition, 3) deciding on whether the goal has been reached, and 4) selecting the next action. Among these stages, only the first two directly depend on information about the environment and can thus be supported with an information system (Kryssanov et al., 2002). To provide for navigation in a social space, the proposed system has five functions: 1) creating individual profiles of members of the community in focus and constructing a network of agents that reflects the community's communication and knowledge-sharing experiences, 2) displaying the social space as relevant fragments of the agent network together with established communication practices in 3D graphics and haptic virtual environments, 3) receiving the user's request and gathering the agents' knowledge, 4) extracting information that meets the user's needs, and 5) updating the states of the agents.

Figure 1 depicts the architecture of the system. The multimodal interface provides for the interaction of the user with other parts of the system and delivers information for the navigation process. The agent manager creates the agent network using data stored in the database. When the recommender system receives a request through the multimodal interface, it selects an appropriate agent and sends a query to this agent to gather relevant information in the network. For information gathering, an efficient agent-based communication algorithm proposed by F.E. Walter with co-authors is implemented (Walter et al., 2008). Once the recommender system receives responses from all the agents in the network, it analyzes the obtained data and sends results of the analysis to the multimodal interface. The multimodal interface shows carriers of information sought by the users (who are thus the potential advisers) in the related segments of the social and physical spaces. The interface also assists the user in selecting among the advisers and in finding the "best approaching / communication strategy" for a given adviser.

Agent Network

The agent network is composed of the same number of agents as the number of members in the community in focus, and the agents are connected to their "acquaintance agents" just as the corresponding people are socially connected in the real world. To assemble the agents into a network, the following information is required: profiles with individual characteristics of the community members, personal network data of the community members, and each member's communicative experiences in respect to other members.

Figure 1. System architecture

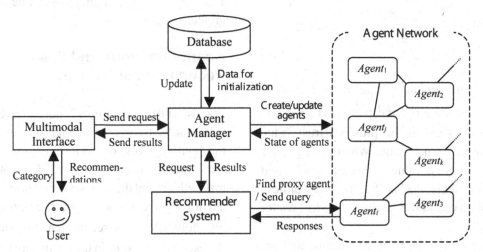

First, the agent manager creates N_A agents, denoted $A = \{a_1, a_2, ..., a_{N_A}\}$ (it is understood that N_A is equal to the number of members in the community). Each agent's profile, which is registered in the database, initially includes only static data, such as member's name, gender, and usual ("permanent") location/address in the physical space. This static data is set as the agent's parameters. Next, the agent manager informs agents (by attaching relevant descriptions – keywords) about the expertise of the corresponding members in the real world. Members with expertise are specified as $O = \{o_1, o_2, ..., o_{N_O}\}$, $N_O \leq N_A$. With O, we will thus denote members who have been evaluated by other members of the community in respect to a specific category of knowledge c_k. The evaluation is performed by rating the members as "relevant" or "irrelevant" when information sought falls into the category c_k. Totally, there are N_C pre-defined knowledge categories denoted $C = \{c_1, c_2, ..., c_{N_C}\}$. The rate of o_j, $j \in [1, N_O]$, is represented as r_j. In the current implementation of the agent model, we assume the binary rate: $r_j = 1$ for the positive evaluation, and $r_j = -1$ otherwise.

Each agent is connected to its "acquaintance agents," using the members' personal network data. This data has the structure of an undirected graph, and the state of linkage between the nodes (i.e. agents) is represented, using an adjacency matrix. The matrix is constructed via mutual certification of pairs of agents. Each agent then receives two dynamic attributes: agents-acquaintances called "neighbors" and "trust" (that can also be thought of as "practical usefulness") values for the neighbors. A trust value between agents a_i and a_j is expressed as T_{a_i, a_j}, which is a real number fluctuating between 0 (no information / low trust) and 1 (full trust; if $i = j$, then generally $T_{a_i, a_j} = 1$). The dynamics of T_{a_i, a_j} is specified with the following equations ($t = 0$ corresponds to the moment when the agent network is initialized, and each discrete time-instant $t > 0$ – to a consecutive update of the rating data in the member profiles; initialization by setting $T_{a_i, a_j}(t = 0) = 0$):

$$\tilde{T}_{a_i, a_j}(t = 0) \equiv 0, \tag{1a}$$

$$\tilde{T}_{a_i, a_j}(t + 1) = \begin{cases} \gamma \tilde{T}_{a_i, a_j}(t) + (1 - \gamma) r_k, & r_k > 0 \\ (1 - \gamma) \tilde{T}_{a_i, a_j}(t) + \gamma r_k, & r_k < 0, \end{cases} \tag{1b}$$

$$T_{a_i,a_j}(t+1) = \frac{1 + \tilde{T}_{a_i,a_j}(t+1)}{2}, \quad t = 1, 2, \ldots ,$$

$$(1c)$$

where r_k is the product of rates by a_i and a_j in respect to member o_k, and parameter γ determines to what extent the previous trust value affects the new trust value. When γ is greater than 0.5, the trust value increases slowly, and decreases quickly that is the "trust dynamics" usually observed in real social networks (Walter *et al.*, 2008).

The trust value between two agents that are not directly connected (i.e. are not neighbors) is calculated as the product of all of the trust values in the query path connecting the two agents. At any time, members can add new rates for other community members into the knowledge of their respective agents. The calculated trust values are used by the recommender system when there are more than one person to recommend under the same conditions. The data of a member recommended by a_j is sent to the user interface with a weight ω calculated for the user's agent a_i as follows:

$$\omega = \frac{e^{\beta \hat{T}_{a_i,a_j}}}{\sum_{k=1}^{N_R} e^{\beta \hat{T}_{a_i,a_k}}}, \quad (2)$$

where

$$\hat{T}_{a_i,a_j} = \frac{1}{2} \ln\left(\frac{1 + 2(T_{a_i,a_j} - 0.5)}{1 - 2(T_{a_i,a_j} - 0.5)}\right). \quad (3)$$

In formula (2), N_R is the number of responses to the specific request made by a_i, and parameter β determines to what degree the weight ω accounts for the trust value T_{a_i,a_j}: when β is 0, all weights are the same, and when β is close to 1, a member with a higher trust value receives a greater weight.

Agent Functions and the Recommender System

Whenever the system user is not a member of the community, the recommender system accesses the agent network to find an agent with a profile most similar to the user's self-description, and makes this agent the user's proxy. The user, whose agent (or proxy) is a_i, inputs a category of her/his enquiry, c_k. The recommender system sends the user's query to a_i in the agent network, where it is relayed by a_i to its neighbors as $query\,(a_i, c_k)$. When a neighbor of the agent receives the query, it checks if it has knowledge about members rated in category c_k. If the neighbor agent finds a rated member, it sends a response to the agent a_i. The response is formed as $response\,(a_i, a_j, c_k, (o_l, r_l), T_{a_i,a_j})$, where a_j stands for the agent, which sent the response, and o_l is the member, which is rated with r_l by a_j in category c_k; T_{a_i,a_j} is the trust value between a_i and a_j. If the neighbor does not have knowledge about relevant members for the given category of expertise, it further transmits the query to its neighbors. These latter neighbor-agents process the query in the same way as described above. To prevent unnecessary communications, every agent, which has once processed a query, ignores this query when it is received repeatedly. Usually, there are many paths between agents a_i and a_j in the agent network, but the generated responses always pass through the same path as the query does.

When the information-gathering algorithm terminates, the agent, which originally sent the query, has a set of responses from the community members. The next step is selecting members, which meet the user's criteria, to recommend from the available set. In the set, there may be people impossible to approach at the given moment, regardless of how strongly other community members would recommend them. For example, when the user needs to meet an adviser immediately, if the system recommends a person who is currently not reachable or who can only speak a foreign language not mastered by the user, such a recommendation would have little practical value. The system filters the responses to remove any potentially useless recommendations and, while doing so, attempts to balance the synchronicity of the expected communication.

DEVELOPED PROTOTYPE

In our study, we reconstructed the social network of the Intelligent Communication Laboratory, College of Information Science and Engineering, Ritsumeikan University. For a typical application of the system, we considered situations where a student having troubles with studying particular subjects, such as networking or programming, seeks an advice for her/his study. She/he thus needs to find out who would be the best candidate—a member of the laboratory—to be requested for help.

The modeled community is composed of 43 members. Each member created a profile containing the member's name, gender, grade, and certain dynamic characteristics, such as personal network data, availability, and trust values calculated via rating other students in the laboratory. The rating data has been collected from the laboratory members in regard to some 19 categories about classes (e.g. Math), specialized knowledge topics (e.g. Java programming), and the campus life (e.g. Events). The members were asked to select and rate maximum three other members, whom they previously requested for help in the given category. By implementing the information-gathering algorithm described in the previous section, the system's developed prototype can then choose the "best" adviser in the category, as it is socially recognized in the community.

MULTIMODAL INTERFACE AND USER-SYSTEM INTERACTIONS

The proposed system has a multimodal interface to facilitate the system-user interaction and increase the efficiency of the navigation process. In SoNa, the user receives information about the community not only in a visual form, but also from physically sensing objects and areas in the virtualized social space. For the latter, the user manipulates a haptic device–force display PHANToM (see http://www.sensable.com/; last accessed on March 9, 2009). As the force display reproduces the reaction force, the user receives additional information about the friendliness and socializability "structure" of the community. In addition to representing the community's physical disposition in the "traditional" 3D virtual reality, the interface then delivers relevant social and personal information via the tactile channel by imposing force fields on the 3D graphics space. Figure 2 illustrates modalities of the user-system interactions for the developed prototype (in the figure, gray blocks indicate active channels).

Figure 3 is a screen-shot of the prototype's interface, where the members of the community are represented with cone and sphere polygons. The members are placed in a virtual space partly reconstructing the laboratory settings with relevant photographic images interactively displayed for locations currently under exploration. In the screen-shot, the "active" area around the cursor is the two lines—the 3rd and 4th from the right—of students highlighted with the photographic image window in the background. The shape of the displayed member representation depends on the member's gender, and the color—on the grade. When the user "touches" a member in the virtual reality with the haptic interface pointer (HIP), the corresponding user profile appears. If the user touches the "Search" button on the screen, new 19 buttons pop up and are used to specify a category of the user's request. Once a category is selected, the agent of the user attempts to find the best advisers, utilizing the agent network. The potential advisers are proposed by the recommender system, and the

Figure 2. Exploration of the social space with the multimodal interface

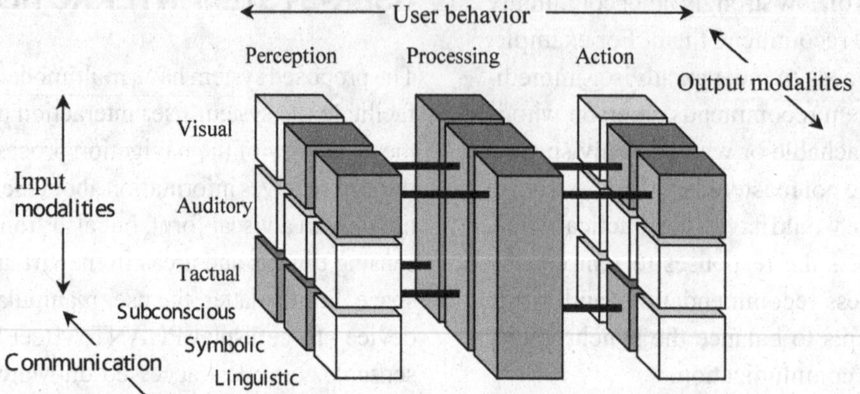

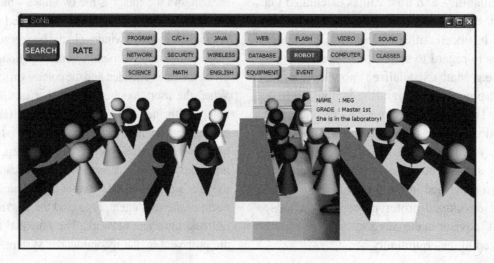

best 3 chosen members are indicated with brighter color tones, while scalar force-fields are reproduced with the haptic device to assist the user's navigation in the social space created by the members currently present in the displayed physical space.

HAPTIC ENVIRONMENT

Social Space Model

The social space is composed of the community members, where each member is represented in the tactile space as a solid object. Tactile characteristics of the represented members are set to reflect their social qualities. An underlying assumption of the proposed model is that different social qualities can be associated with and evoke different emotions which, it turn, can be associated with tactile perceptions. The model assumes the following very general associations: "friendliness" → "pleasant emotions," "socializability" → "anxiety/ elevated emotional states," and "trustability" → "pleasant or neutral emotions." To extend these associations to tactile representations, an experiment was conducted, in which subjects were asked

Figure 3. Screen-shot of the prototype interface

to try to describe their communicative emotional experiences (emotions) in terms of the following tactile perceptions: "hard or soft," "sticky or slick," "rough or smooth," and "attracting or repulsing."

Totally, 224 subjects participated in the experiment, with 47% females and 53% males, all Japanese adults aged from 19 to 45 years old. The collected emotional experiences were classified into 5 general, non-orthogonal emotion classes, as it is shown in Table 1, using the emotional state model proposed in (Desmet, 2002). Table 2 shows results of the experiment.

No statistically significant difference was detected for the answers by males and females; the data also appeared statistically homogeneous in respect to the respondent's age. Among the

statistically significant results (p<0.05), we would like to point to the following. The pleasant/unpleasant dimension is, apparently, well associated with an attracting/repulsing force filed. Pleasant emotions are also associated with softness, while unpleasant with stickiness (i.e. high viscosity). For the anxiety/boredom dimension, roughness (as opposite to smoothness) appears the dominant association.

Based on the experimental results, the following social space model was implemented in the system prototype. All the laboratory members (as well as other objects of the physical environment, e.g. furniture, etc.) are represented as solid, by default hard objects. The stiffness coefficient is adjusted in proportion to the member's friendliness

Table 1. Human emotions classified in regard to their "value" (pleasant/unpleasant) and psychological arousal (anxiety/boredom)

Class	Emotions
Unpleasant emotions	Disgusted, frightened, annoyed, hostile, despise, indignant, alarmed, irritated, frustrated, bewildered, nervous, contemptuous, disturbed, flabbergast, jealous, aversive, irked, moody, grouchy, ashamed, cynical, embarrassed, disappointed, dissatisfied, disapproving, confused, gloomy, melancholy, isolated, sad, guilty, disillusioned, bored
Pleasant emotions	Loving, jubilant, excited, desiring, inspired, enthusiastic, entertained, admiring, joyful, fascinated, yearning pleasantly, proud, surprised, happy, appreciated, amused, cheerful, sociable, attracted, fulfilled, intimate, satisfied, cozy, comfortable, softened, relayed
Anxiety	Disgusted, frightened, annoyed, hostile, despise, indignant, alarmed, irritated, frustrated, bewildered, nervous, loving, jubilant, excited, desiring, inspired, enthusiastic, surprised, concentrated, eager, astonished, amazed, aroused, longing, avaricious, curious
Boredom	Gloomy, melancholy, isolated, sad, guilty, disillusioned, bored, fulfilled, intimate, satisfied, cozy, comfortable, softened, relayed, composed, awaiting, deferent, passive
Neutral emotions	Surprised, concentrated, eager, astonished, amazed, aroused, longing, avaricious, curious, composed, awaiting, deferent, passive

Table 2. Human emotions and the associated tactile perceptions (for each perception, the number in the table indicates the number of subjects with the given association)

Emotion class	Hard	Soft	Sticky	Slick	Smooth	Rough	Attracting	Repulsing
Unpleasant	89	0	162	53	33	191	10	153
Pleasant	4	193	11	103	101	2	152	22
Anxiety	64	20	73	17	9	97	112	62
Boredom	124	156	11	117	156	28	11	55
Neutral	104	4	24	41	63	4	35	22

so that members called by the other members as "friends" appear softer. At the same time, a viscosity field is generated around an object representing an "unfriendly" (i.e. declared by few or none as friend) member who is, nevertheless, chosen as adviser by the recommender system. The roughness of the represented object surface is set to a high value for members with high socializability. Attraction/repulsion haptic force fields are generated around objects representing members selected by SoNa as advisers in the given situation, where the driving force is adjusted in proportion to the trust value between the user's agent and the agent of the adviser closest (in the physical space) to the position of the HIP. With a threshold set for the trust parameter at 0.5, the lower trust values trigger generation of repulsion, and the higher values – of attraction fields.

Haptic Force Modeling

The described prototype was implemented in C++ programming language with its haptic environment built on top of the SmartCollision Studio™ commercial software package (Tamura *et al.*, 2007). The latter package provides penetration depth calculation in real-time with realistic friction and elastic force modeling during collisions of the HIP and (visualized) geometrical objects. The stiffness (or "solidness") coefficient was associated with personal "friendliness" of displayed members who are not among the 3 best advisers (e.g. "hard" stands for an "unfriendly" subject). After a short training, the participants of our case study (see Section 6) could easily discriminate "soft", "average," and "hard" virtual objects for the stiffness coefficient set at 75, 200, and 350 N/m, respectively. The friction (i.e. "roughness") coefficient was associated with the member's socializability (higher friction—better socializability—easier to perceive/harder to miss or overlook). Usually, the feedback force is set to zero when there is no collision of the HIP with objects. However, this method does not allow for discriminating between intuitive, distant perceptions

of various members and of the empty (i.e. "member-free") space. For the exploration of the entire social space, we introduced a new approach based on scalar viscosity fields set around recommended but "unfriendly" members, and attracting/repulsing force fields – around "trustable/untrustable" recommended members, as it is stipulated by the social space model described in the previous section.

The dynamic model of the method is described as follows. Let us first consider a point of mass m in a viscosity field λ. We will assume that the point is loaded by external "attraction" and driving forces, F_a and $-F_h$, respectively. The point dynamics is then defined with the following differential equations:

$$m \frac{d^2\rho}{dt^2} + \lambda(\rho - \rho_1) \frac{d\rho}{dt} = F_a(\rho - \rho_0) - F_h(t),$$

(4a)

$$F_h(t) = k_h \, \Delta\rho(t) + b_h \Delta \frac{d\rho(t)}{dt},$$ (4b)

where $\rho = (x, y, z)^{\mathrm{T}}$, T is the transposition operator, is the point radius-vector. The driving force is opposite to the haptic feedback force F_h, which is calculated in real-time by the standard "spring-damper" model (Goncharenko *et al.*, 2006, 2007), using the PHANToM coordinate input. In equations (4), $\Delta\rho(t)$ is a vector from the current HIP position to the mass point, and k_h and b_h are coefficients of the spring-damper model. For simplicity, we used only one "attraction/repulsion" pole at position ρ_0, and calculated F_a as the force in the direction to (or from, in the case of repulsion) ρ_0 and proportional to the distance between ρ and ρ_0. Likewise, we selected only one focus of "unfriendliness" at ρ_1 and calculated an isotropic scalar viscosity field λ, which depends on the distance to the focus of "unfriendliness" as

$$\lambda(\rho - \rho_1) = \frac{c_a}{1 + d_a(\rho - \rho_1)^2}, \text{ where } c_a \text{ and } d_a$$

are some constants.

In the beginning of haptic interaction, it is assumed that the HIP and the mass point coincide. The corresponding differential equation (4a) is numerically solved by a fourth-order Runge-Kutta method, using the real-time control function $F_h(t)$. In our study, the model parameters c_a and d_a were set to provide the viscosity from 1 kg/s to 15 kg/s inside the working PHANToM space.

The physical values of the haptic model coefficients were set as linearly proportional to the social characteristics obtained from profiles of the members. The proportionality constants were adjusted to yield subjectively smooth haptic feedback, which obviously makes it difficult to move around an "unfriendliness" pole, and which "guides" in the direction to the focus of attraction but (weakly) drives from the focus of repulsion. The personal friendliness was set proportional to the total number of people declaring the member as "friend," and the socializability – to the number of contacts in the member's personal network. In all cases, the pole location is defined by the nearest (in respect to the HIP) recommended member's position in the physical space. The dynamic model parameters were adjusted to yield negligible forces and viscosity when the physical distance to the nearest recommended member exceeds the "social distance" of 2 meters (Hall, 1966). Model (4) with one attracting (or repulsing) pole and a central radial viscosity field provides for subjectively good intuitive reinforcement guidance in the social space. It was found experimentally that haptic guidance becomes ambiguous when the number of poles is more than two. Therefore, only the recommended members nearest to the HIP are visualized in the tactile space with the force fields (the latter, however, results in some "tactile discretization" effects when perceiving the social space with the haptic device).

CASE STUDY

The developed prototype was installed on an ordinary desktop computer (with the haptic device connected) in the Intelligent Communication Laboratory. The laboratory members were asked to review and possibly update their profiles in the system database at least once a week during the spring semester when the case study took place. The laboratory is also equipped with a semi-automatic system monitoring the current location of each member – this data was used to automatically update the location dynamic parameter of the agents in the prototype's agent network.

Thirty students who are not members of the laboratory and are generally unfamiliar with the community were selected as subjects, which were then divided into two groups: A and B. The subjects were asked to name a member of the laboratory who, in their opinion, would be the best adviser in three knowledge categories. The categories were randomly assigned from the 19 categories supported by the developed prototype. The subjects in group A were given 10 minutes to decide on the best adviser in each category, based solely on their own communicative experience. The subjects in group B were asked to first use only their own experience and then the system, and name the best advisers in both cases. To reduce the possible bias, the B-group subjects were told that the system does not always recommend the best adviser, and that they should rather rely on own communicative experience in choosing a candidate for the contact. The total (communication, user-system interaction, and decision-making) time for every subject in group B was limited by 6 minutes. Prior to the experiment, group B was familiarized with the user interface of the prototype but received no explanations about the specific "meaning" of the reaction force feedback in the haptic environment. Subjects in both groups were encouraged to communicate any member of the laboratory at any moment within the given time frames. Tables 3 and 4 show results of the evaluation of the members (with private information removed), where the number in the parentheses is the number

Table 3. Advisers selected by group A

Category	1st adviser	2nd adviser	3rd adviser
C1	Aaron (6)	Bill (6)	Carl (3)
C2	Eddy (9)	Aaron (3)	Bill (3)
C3	George (12)	Dave (3)	--

Table 4. Advisers selected by group B

Category	Before using the system			After using the system		
	1st	2nd	3rd	1st	2nd	3rd
C1	Bill (9)	Carl (3)	Frank (3)	Bill (9)	Carl (6)	--
C2	Eddy (12)	Aaron (3)	--	Aaron (12)	Eddy (3)	--
C3	George (6)	Aaron (6)	Dave (3)	George (15)	--	--

of subjects who contemplated the given member as a useful adviser.

Based on the presented results, two points can be discussed: the effectiveness and the efficiency of SoNa. After using the system, all the subjects belonging to group B changed their answers in one or two categories. All the changes made were related to higher-ranked members. Although all the subjects in both groups were given almost the same time (10 and 6 minutes) to think about the questions, the members who used the system chose statistically "better" ($p<0.05$) advisers, as it can be inferred by comparing the individual answers with the entire community's knowledge shown in Table 5. It can, therefore, be said that the system is effective and efficient, as it indeed provides the user with the best information available and, at the same time, does not increase the decision-making time.

CONCLUSION

The experimental results obtained in the case study suggest that the proposed system can be a useful tool for assisting human navigation in unknown social environments, and for increasing the efficiency of information search in such environments. It is understood, however, that while the developed system is a working prototype that can be used in practice "as is," at least some of the design solutions implemented in the multimodal interface are rather arbitrary. Larger scale and more elaborated experiments need to be conducted to justify the choice of specific parameters of the social network, which are used to reconstruct the social space in the virtual reality. Although the presented system has, to the authors' best knowledge, no direct analogs, some of the recently reported design solutions would be used to enhance the proposed service concept

Table 5. Ranking obtained using questionnaires filled in by all the laboratory members

Category	The best adviser	2nd adviser	3rd adviser	4th adviser
C1	Carl	Bill	Aaron	Frank
C2	Aaron	Eddy	Henry	Ian
C3	George	Dave	Aaron	Jack

and facilitate the social space reconstruction. Specifically, to improve the currently deployed profile-based model of the community's social network, a human activity tracking mechanism, as it was proposed in other work (Wojek *et al.*, 2006; Danninger *et al.*, 2005), would be used to assess communication practices of the community in a closed (laboratory-like) environment. Besides, the development of the community's knowledge model, e.g. an ontology as was proposed in (Giménez-Lugo *et al.*, 2005), would allow us to improve the recommender function of the system and extend its potential applicability to the domain of organizational management.

A deficiency in the authors' current understanding of the developed system utility is the role of the subconscious tactile interaction channel. As an audio interaction channel would naturally be added to the multimodal interface (that is, in fact, part of the authors' plans for future work), separate experiments should be conducted to analyze how the interactions in different modalities affect the navigation process. Although there have been earlier attempts to convey human emotions via the tactile channel (Picard, 1995; Smith & MacLean, 2007), the immediate communicative effect of the reproduced tactile perceptions as well as the place of "tactile" emotions in the social space remains an open research question (Haans & Ijsselsteijn, 2006).

The main contributions of the presented work, as seen by the authors, are the original concept of the social navigation support service, the haptic model of the social space, and the developed information system that realizes the envisaged theoretical concepts. Specific design solutions may and will be changed, however. In the next version of the prototype, we plan to significantly increase the size of the agent network and the number of knowledge categories supported. Attempts will also be made to improve the scenes reproduced in the 3D graphics virtual reality along with the haptic image of the social space.

ACKNOWLEDGMENT

The authors would like to thank all the members of the Intelligent Communication Laboratory for their participation in the case study. The contribution of Izumi Kurose, who collected the emotional association data for the social space model, is gratefully acknowledged. Discussions of the social space model with Eric W. Cooper are also appreciated.

REFERENCES

Danninger, M., Flaherty, G., Bernardin, K., Ekenel, H., Köhler, T., Malkin, R., et al. (2005). The connector: Facilitating context-aware communication. In *Proceedings of the 7th International Conference on Multimodal Interfaces, ICMI'05* (pp. 69-75). New York: ACM Publishing.

Derene, G. (2008). How social networking could kill web search as we know it. *Popular Mechanics*. Retrieved March 9, 2009, from http://www.popularmechanics.com/technology/industry/4259135.html

Desmet, P. M. A. (2002). *Designing emotions.* Unpublished doctoral dissertation, TU Delft.

Giménez-Lugo, G. A., Sichman, J. S., & Hübner, J. F. (2005). Addressing the social components of knowledge to foster communitary exchanges. *International Journal of Web Based Communities*, *1*(2), 176–194. doi:10.1504/IJWBC.2005.006062

Goncharenko, I., Svinin, M., Kanou, Y., & Hosoe, S. (2006). Predictability of rest-to-rest movements in haptic environments with 3D constraints. *Robotics and Mechatronics*, *18*(4), 458–466.

Goncharenko, I., Svinin, M., Kanou, Y., & Hosoe, S. (2007). Skilful motion planning with self- and reinforcement learning in dynamic virtual environments. In *Proceedings of the 4th INTUITION International Conference,* Athens, Greece (pp. 237-238).

Haans, A., & Ijsselsteijn, W. A. (2006). Mediated social touch: A review of current research and future directions. *Virtual Reality (Waltham Cross)*, *9*(2), 149–159. doi:10.1007/s10055-005-0014-2

Hall, E. T. (1966). *The hidden dimension*. New York: Doubleday.

Kalman, Y. M., & Rafaeli, S. (2007). Modulating synchronicity in computer mediated communication. In *Proceedings of the 2007 Conference of the International Communication Association*, San-Francisco. Retrieved on March 9, 2009, from http://www.kalmans.com/synchasynchI-CAsubmit.pdf

Kryssanov, V. V., Kumokawa, S., Goncharenko, I., & Ogawa, H. (2008). A system for multimodal exploration of social spaces. In A. Pirhonen & S. Brewster (Eds.), *Haptic and audio interaction design* (LNCS 5270, pp. 40-49).

Kryssanov, V. V., Okabe, M., Kakusho, K., & Minoh, M. (2002). Communication of social agents and the digital city – a semiotic perspective. In M. Tanabe, P.V. den Besselaar, & T. Ishida (Eds.), *Digital cities II, computational and sociological approaches* (LNCS 2362, pp. 56-70).

Lefebvre, H. (1994). *The production of space* (Donald Nicholson-Smith, Trans.). Oxford, UK: Blackwell

Monge, P., & Contractor, N. (2003). *Theories of communication in networks*. Oxford, UK: Oxford University Press.

Picard, R. W. (1995). *Affective computing MIT* (Media Laboratory Perceptual Computing Section Tech. Rep. No. 321). Cambridge, MA: MIT Press.

Smith, J., & MacLean, K. (2007). Communicating emotions through a haptic link: Design space and methodology. *International Journal of Human-Computer Studies*, *65*, 376–387. doi:10.1016/j.ijhcs.2006.11.006

Spence, R. (1999). A framework for navigation. *International Journal of Human-Computer Studies*, *51*(5), 919–945. doi:10.1006/ijhc.1999.0265

Tamura, Y., Matsumoto, S., Ueki, H., & Mizuguchi, N. (2007). Constuction of design support system with interference detection in the immersive projection display. *The IEICE Transactions on Information and Systems, J90-D*(10), 2927-2931.

Walter, F. E., Battiston, S., & Schweitzer, F. (2008). A model of a trust-based recommender system on a social network. *Autonomous Agents and Multi-Agent Systems*, *16*(1), 57–74. doi:10.1007/s10458-007-9021-x

Wang, Y., & Kinsner, W. (2006). Recent advances in cognitive informatics. *IEEE Transactions on Systems, Man and Cybernetics. Part C, Applications and Reviews*, *36*(2), 121–123. doi:10.1109/TSMCC.2006.871120

Wojek, C., Nickel, K., & Stiefelhagen, R. (2006). Activity recognition and room-level tracking in an office environment. In *Proceedings of the IEEE Conference on Multisensor Fusion and Integration for Intelligent Systems, MFI'06*, Heidelberg, Germany (pp. 25-30).

This work was previously published in International Journal of Software Science and Computational Intelligence, Volume 2, Issue 1, edited by Yingxu Wang, pp. 24-37, copyright 2010 by IGI Publishing (an imprint of IGI Global).

Chapter 20
Symbiotic Aspects in e–Government Application Development

Claude Moulin
Compiègne University of Technology, France

Marco Luca Sbodio
Hewlett Packard – Italy Innovation Center, Italy

ABSTRACT

For e-Government applications, the symbiotic aspect must be taken into account at three stages: at design time in order to integrate the end-user, at delivery time when civil servants have to discover and interact with new services, at run time when ambient intelligence could help the interaction of citizens with specific services. In this paper, we focus on the first two steps. We show how interoperability issues must concern application designers. We also present how semantics can help civil servants when they have to deal with e-government service frameworks. We then describe an actual application developed during the European Terregov project where semantics is the key point for simplifying the role of citizens when requesting for health care services.

SYMBIOTIC ASPECTS IN E-GOVERNMENT APPLICATION DEVELOPMENT

According to the definition given in the Symbiotic Computing website[1], "Symbiotic computing is a basic idea that achieves an information processing environment, which autonomously supports hu-man activities, by understanding human behavior and sociality in the real world."

Initiatives occurring inside the e-Government domain can contribute to some aspects of this definition. Research in the area of e-Government combines the information and communication technology in public administrations with or-ganizational changes and new skills in order to improve public services and democratic processes, and to strengthen support to public policies. The

DOI: 10.4018/978-1-4666-0264-9.ch020

potential of e-Government goes far beyond the early achievements of online public services. New public services are user-centered and aim to support the interaction between citizens and administrations. They generally take into account the social profile of people, and try to deliver the most accurate information that citizen is looking for, or the most appropriate services that the citizen can benefit from. This is particularly true in the social and health care domains.

When dealing with public services, two levels have to be considered: (i) the discovery of the services that citizens can benefit from, and (ii) the enactment of such services. The first level deals with the selection of services, based on capabilities and/or constraints; it is an area of on-going research, and for example, travelers who are confronted with foreign Public Administrations could benefit of results in this domain. The second level deals with the execution of selected services. New technologies like ubiquitous middleware technology could be effectively employed for simplifying the access to some service functionalities. For example, physically impaired people can highly benefit from the use of intelligent mobile devices capable of seamlessly interacting with distributed computational units embedded in the environment (ubiquitous computing). At both levels human society and digital space interact with each other using different kind of technologies.

Developing user-centered applications and frameworks requires symbiosis among several actors at design times: project managers, domain experts, human-machine interaction experts, design experts and end-users. Particularly in the e-Government domain a better symbiosis between civil servants and systems actually delivering services is highly desirable. Civil servants can be considered as a Community where usual hierarchy disappears. One issue is the emergence of new roles based on new knowledge and has been identified with the so-called "social-ware" technologies (Hattori et al., 1999).

From the perspective of cognitive informatics, delivering new e-Government services requires the convergence of several research domains. The socio-economic research studies many cases in Europe and all over the world to determine the criteria of their success or failure. It produces guidelines useful to follow. A new e-Government also requires the definition of new processes and a better integration of citizens' and civil servants' behaviors. Finally, knowledge representation (ontologies) is the core of new semantic technologies and allows systems to perform symbolic reasoning.

The work presented in this paper is based on the results of the Terregov research project: "Impact of e-Government on Territorial Government Services" (Terregov, 2008). A platform has been developed in which semantics combines with more traditional technologies in order to enable new capabilities and to overcome technical and cultural challenges. The design and development of this e-Government Semantic Platform has been conducted with the financial support of the European Commission. The goal of this platform is to let local government and government agencies offer online access to their services in an interoperable way, and to allow them to participate in orchestrated processes involving services provided by multiple agencies.

IMPLEMENTED SCENARIO

For a better understanding of the concepts analyzed in this paper, we first present a scenario that was implemented with the collaboration public administration of the Venice Region in northern Italy. Public Administrations (PA) offer a number of services for citizens in the area of social-care and health assistance for elderly and physically/mentally impaired people. The main use case is the following. A citizen asks for some assistance service; a civil servant receives the request and assembles the citizen profile (a set of relevant information about the citizen making the request);

domain experts meet and decide if the citizen is eligible for any service.

The Terregov platform supports the creation of the citizen profile, and the automation of service selection. Domain experts have defined the eligibility criteria of each service, and have identified the relevant information in the citizen profile to evaluate the eligibility criteria. With their collaboration, ontology experts have translated the eligible criteria in rule-like expressions, that can be evaluated to assess the citizens eligibility for services (see section 7).

In the Terregov project, the semantics used by different software modules is based on a core ontology, which has been developed within the Terregov project itself (see section 3). The core ontology defines a set of important concepts and relations in the e-Government domain, but it does not aim at being exhaustive. The core ontology is intended to be used as a common basis, and to be extended incorporating domain-specific knowledge useful for describing services or other relevant entities. We have in fact extended the Terregov core ontology to incorporate some concepts specific of the Venice Region use case presented above. For example, we have extended the concept of Service with a subclass hierarchy that defines the various services available in the Venice Region.

REQUIREMENTS FOR A SYMBIOTIC E-GOVERNMENT

Design Time

The concept of interoperability is crucial for understanding the on-going changes in the e-Government domain. We analyze the different dimensions that influence the implementation of an interoperable electronic administration (namely the political, organizational and technical dimensions). The political and organizational dimensions are at the same time the main driving forces for the management of innovation, and a major obstacle that sometime prevents a full introduction of innovative approaches. Analysis of good practices is necessary to build models for guiding the development of electronic administration. Such analysis must be based on concepts and on a theoretical framework able to describe and classify the various initiatives and to identify the organizational problems which are the main barriers against adoption of innovation. Such a theoretical framework also provides local governments with methodologies and guidelines to implement business process re-engineering and change management.

Busson et al. (2004) define the concepts of Information-sharing, Information-exchange and Organizational coordination, as the main relevant features when planning for e-Government. Information-sharing is the provision of information anytime and anywhere, and it is a major benefit of modern web-based systems. Of course Information-sharing must take into account the high fragmentation of information sources, which often belong to different entities. It is desirable that information-sharing crosses organizational boundaries without affecting internal organizational structures.

Information-exchange affects the mobility of data for building value-added services. A service supports a bidirectional flow and requires actions of both involved parties: the information supplier and recipient.

Organizational coordination deals with the willingness of organizations for building or adapting services. On-line service delivery on a large scale increases the complexity due to the fact that it involves several actors, which are often both geographically distributed (national or local administrations), and heterogeneous (public agencies, nonprofit organizations, private service providers, etc.). If service provision is a mix of different services, the civil servant in charge of the citizen's request has to know enough information about the different involved organizations. This has several consequences. The involved actors have not only to cooperate, i.e. to exchange useful information, but also to coordinate their actions.

Delivery

We analyze requirements for Symbiotic e-Government Delivery along three dimensions: technical, semantic and cultural interoperability.

Technical Interoperability

Local administrations often act as a front office to the citizens. One of the main challenges of e-government is that local administrations become the channel for online delivery of a large variety of services, often covering heterogeneous domains and having different providers.

The reorganization and modernization of government does not remove the current legacy systems, but wrap them for allowing the exchange of information. Interoperability is the capability of systems to export and import data toward and from other systems (Garcia et al., 2005). Interoperability between heterogeneous systems enables the sharing of information and creates knowledge. This allows the elaboration of new procedures involving several departments and institutions.

Security is highlighted as an important issue to take into account when deploying new frameworks. They must ensure both data integrity and privacy of people. They also require security procedures for identification and certification.

Semantic Interoperability

Semantic technologies provide an innovative approach for the implementation of e-Government solutions addressing the ever increasing need for seamless interoperability among e-Government services provided by different agencies. Semantics add the key feature to standardize the information as concepts and to enable automatic service discovery.

In the Semantic Web (Berners-Lee et al., 2001) information is given explicit meaning, making it easier for machines to automatically process and integrate information available on the Web. The difficulty in ensuring flexible discovery and service initiation, as well as operational use of information exchanged with Web services, has led to incorporate semantic technologies to the traditional Web services, thus leading to the Semantic Web services vision introduced by McIlraith et al. (2001). We propose to extend such a vision to social and health assistance services provided by Public Administration: an assistance service becomes a precise entity with a formal semantic description defining its preconditions and effects. The availability of semantic descriptions of assistance services enables the use of intelligent techniques for matching a citizen case with the set of potentially useful services. Such an intelligent matchmaking symbiotically supports the civil servants in their daily task of answering citizens' requests for assistance services.

Cultural Interoperability

The goal of a symbiotic aware e-Government platform is primarily to support civil servants in extricating the increasingly complex bundle of on-line and assistance services provided by local and regional government agencies. Additionally, such a platform can simplify the creation of interoperable and collaborative processes involving multiple agencies, by supporting processes designers and engineers in identifying and combining existing and new services.

While the implementation of electronic processes across organizations is a well-studied domain, technical solutions based on traditional workflows and business process automation become unpractical due to the increasing number of actors and services. For instance the French Districts are responsible for Social Care and they allocate between 50% and 80% of their budget and staff to this end. Each District manages several types of social allowances, and cooperates with a huge number of local agencies that use heterogeneous IT systems. In such a complex scenario the civil servants are in great difficulty, and would highly benefit from a symbiotic approach that actively supports them, lowering the cultural barriers among agencies and organizations.

BUILDING THE ONTOLOGY

Semantics is a crucial factor for the elaboration of new e-Government services. In the Terregov project we proposed a methodology for ontology building involving different experts and end-users. A summary of the main methodologies for building ontologies can also be found in (Fernández-López, 1999). We followed well known methodologies like those presented in (Fernández-López et al., 1997; Uschold et al., 1996). However, we adapted some recommended methods and added some

steps in the ontology building in order to fulfill all the ontology objectives.

We integrated a step on document analysis (Aussenac-Gilles et al., 2000), and we took into account end user comments to refine the ontology. We worked with domain experts in several countries in Europe and particularly in collaboration with experts responsible of the health care services in the Venice Region. In designing our core ontology we also took into account the research on Government Enterprise Architecture presented in (Peristeras et al., 2004).

The method adopted (see Figure 1) for building the core ontology has five steps. The fifth step deals with the ontology extensions needed for implementing service descriptions and service eligibility criteria. Several actors and information sources contribute of the creation of the first basic ontology, and to its progressive refinement and extension. This process yields the final core ontology.

Figure 1.

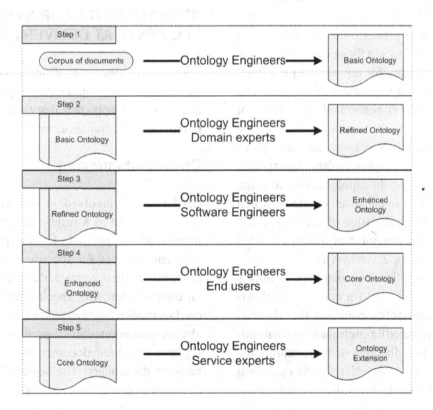

In the first step we collect and process a set of administrative, legal and general documents related to the government domain, and we extract the most important terms and expressions from this corpus using natural language processing tools. These tools can extract a set of terms from the analyzed documents, and classify them using a morphologic and a syntactic analysis of texts. In the Terregov project we used Nomino[2] to analyze documents written in French and English. Ontology engineers use their experience to derive concepts and relations from candidate terms thus creating a basic taxonomy expressing the semantics of the most relevant elements found in the corpus of documents.

The second step yields a refined ontology, which is built by ontology engineers taking into account the comments of domain experts. Although the refined ontology is adequate for providing a shared formal vocabulary of the domain, or to be used in enhanced collaborative tools and in information retrieval systems, it does not effectively support the definition of formal semantics for services.

The third step further enhances the refined ontology, in order to add those concepts and relationships necessary for representing the input and output types of semantic web services. The enhancement step is performed by a team of software engineers and ontology engineers: the former bring the necessary knowledge about web services data structures, and the latter incorporate such knowledge into the ontology. The outcome of the third step is an enhanced ontology, which map not only the knowledge of the domain experts, but also the general data structure needed to model the semantic web services.

The fourth step involves ontology engineers and a group of end users (in our case, civil servants). The analysis of the content of the enhanced ontology is performed through questions that end-users can ask to a dialog system integrating the ontology. Answers proposed by the dialog system allow the ontology engineers to iteratively improve the ontology. Here, we follow the methodology advocated by (Grüninger et al., 1995). The output of the fourth step is the core ontology. It contains the core of general concepts and relationships that are needed to describe the domain knowledge and the domain web services.

Finally, the fifth step is performed by ontology experts when the core ontology is extended to incorporate knowledge from specific application domain. The outcome of such a step is an ontology extension, which can both specialize and augment the concepts and relations of the core ontology. The fifth step of ontology engineering process is required in the scenario presented in section 5, in order to allow a precise description of assistance services offered by public administrations.

The iterative, user-centered, and multidisciplinary approach followed in the construction of the core ontology yields an effective representation of a shared and operational vocabulary of the e-Government domain.

REQUIREMENTS FOR SYMBIOTIC ELEMENTS AT DELIVERY TIME

We present requirements of three major application areas in the e-Government, highlighting the need of a symbiotic approach that facilitates the support of human activities by intelligent interaction.

Document Indexing

Civil servants involved in e-Government processes often act as a front-end to citizens: they provide advice, and help in identifying the most adequate services for specific citizen needs. It is useful for them to track the documents based on their relation with specific problems. When civil servants recognize a situation that they have already encountered, they need tools for searching/browsing their document base, and finding relevant documents. The searchable document base should contain not only official documents, but also any kind of relevant documents that civil servants think should be indexed for subsequent use (for example e-mails or notes).

We consider two ways of indexing documents: key word indexing and semantic indexing. Keyword indexing allows identifying a document by its vocabulary. Semantic indexing allows identifying a document by its meaning rather than by its vocabulary. Unlike standard keyword indexing technologies, which are designed to generate inverted indexes containing every word occurring in a document, semantic indexing techniques associate documents only with items from a predefined vocabulary (the so-called controlled vocabulary). When the vocabulary is an ontology, we can properly speak of semantic indexing: in this case, a concept label is a textual representation of a concept (semantic unit) which is formally defined in the underlying ontology. The concept label provides a technical way to associate a document with that a semantic unit.

Semantic indexing provides powerful capabilities when searching for documents. The relations defined in the ontology define connections among concepts, ant such connection can be exploited to refine and/or enlarge the search results. For example, starting from documents associated with the concept "Law" it is possible to look for related documents, such as those associated with concepts having some ontological relations with "Law" or those edited by the same "Organization", etc.

Starting with concept labels extracted from an ontology, semantic indexing must then attempt to match such labels with the text in a document. Techniques derived from natural language processing (NLP) overcome the difficulties related to the matching. Particularly, NLP deals with morphological and syntactical issues, such as singular and plural forms, verbs, nouns, etc. The core ontology provides the semantics required for a controlled vocabulary. However, this is not sufficient with respect to the difficulties encountered in the matching process. For this reason, an additional, auxiliary ontology must be developed and provided with a semantic indexing tool. The auxiliary ontology encapsulates the lexical, semantic and grammatical knowledge necessary to correctly detect items from that controlled vocabulary in the documents. See the work from (Moulin et al., 2006) for more details about semantic indexing.

Searching Supporting Tool

The user interface design is very important when a civil servant has to use complex frameworks such as those developed for e-Government services. The user interface should allow querying not only the document base or the registry of services. Civil servants should be able to send questions to the system. The auxiliary ontology developed specifically for semantic indexing provides also an effective mean for querying, using natural language. As mentioned previously, semantic indexing transforms the ontology into an inverted index. The proposed approach essentially consists in treating a query just as any other natural language input, i.e. as a very short document.

The same methodological approach applied to the semantic indexing of documents is thus also applied to the queries. Consequently, the same concept labels that were successfully detected in the indexed documents will be successfully detected in the queries. This approach ensures a complete consistency between the query processing results, and the indexing of the documents that are targeted by the query. According to the nature of queries, a civil servant can receive information from the ontology itself (e.g. the definition of a concept), or references to documents or services associated with specific related concepts. The Terregov platform contains a module allowing the semantic indexing of documents and a module supporting free queries in user interfaces.

SCENARIO

In this section we describe in more detail the original scenario presented in section 1 (that is without technological support), and we show how semantics-based technology can simplify and automate some of the processes involved.

The scenario begins with a citizen asking to a civil servant for some service offered by the Public Administration. The citizens may or may not know in advance which are the services offered by the Public Administration, and therefore their request may be specific (citizens would like to benefit from a specific service) or generic (citizens would like to know if there is any service for which they are eligible). Similarly the civil servant does not necessarily know all the services provided by the Public Administration.

The citizen's request triggers an e-Government process, whose first step usually consists in a data collection activity: information on the citizen is collected in a citizen profile. The profile may contain a number of heterogeneous data related to the citizen, ranging from home address and contact information to social or economical status. Such data are usually scattered among a number of different systems within the Public Administration, and they are not always accessible (for example because of interoperability, security, or privacy issues).

When some information is not directly available, the civil servant may ask the citizen to provide it. Some sections of the citizen profile may require intervention of domain experts (for example physicians), who have to interview or visit the citizen to assess her/his health or social status. The data collection activity may require some time to be completed. Finally, the outcome of such activity may be a partial citizen profile, where some information is missing because it was either unavailable or inaccessible.

The second step of the e-Government process in our scenario is the selection of services for the citizen. This activity is performed by a group of domain experts (human actors), who assess the citizen profile, and select the services for which the citizen is eligible. The service selection activity is based on the knowledge of the domain experts, who evaluate the information collected in the citizen profile and check if the eligibility criteria for the various services are satisfied.

Since the evaluation of the citizen profile against the eligibility criteria of services is a human activity, it is not necessarily systematic: it may not be totally accurate (incomplete evaluation of eligibility criteria of a given service), and it may be partial (not all possible services are taken into account). The service selection activity is largely based on the experience of the domain experts, who usually try to compare some relevant information of the current citizen profile with previous cases that they examined. If such information matches, then they decide that the citizen is eligible for an already established set of services. This approach essentially reduces a citizen case to some established standard case, where the set of services for which the citizen is eligible is already known. The domain experts perform a detailed evaluation only when the citizen case does not fall in any known standard case.

Interviewing domain experts who participated to the Italian pilot of the project Terregov, we discovered two interesting facts: about 60% of the citizen cases are reduced to a standard case, and the reduction is often based on the evaluation of eligibility criteria that involve a specific subset of the information contained in the citizen profile. We therefore worked on the problem of automating the service selection activity, with the goal of automatically identifying citizen cases that can be reduced to a standard case.

SEMANTIC DESCRIPTION OF SERVICES FOR CITIZENS

Automatic Service Selection

For automating the selection of services for citizen according to their profiles it is necessary to semantically describe available services. We worked with the domain experts to: a) assess the services for citizens, and their characteristics; b) understand the eligibility criteria of each service; c) identify the relevant information in citizen profile to evaluate the eligibility criteria.

We then formalized in an OWL (OWL, 2004) ontology extending the Terregov core ontology some concepts that allowed us to describe the various kind of services and the relevant information of the citizen profile. The eligibility criteria have been originally formalized as simple rules that specify: a) the logical expressions specifying the eligibility criteria; such expressions are based on the information from the citizen profile (precondition); b) the set of services for which the citizen is eligible if a logical expression is met (postconditions).

Our scenario does not involve web services, but simply assistance services for citizens provided by a Public Administration. A major difference between web services and services for citizen is that the former usually require some input message and may produce an output message, whereas the latter do not necessarily require any input or produce any output. In the semantic description of web services, input and output messages are usually defined by classes in some ontology.

However there is a common aspect between web services and services for citizens: the full denotation of a service (either web service or service for citizens) requires the specification of preconditions and postconditions. Preconditions and postconditions are usually defined by logical expressions; preconditions define a set of constraints that must be satisfied to successfully use the service; postconditions describe the effects of the service usage that is the state of the world after the service usage.

In the case of web services, preconditions and postconditions are essential to disambiguate the operations of different web services that have the same input and output messages. Consider for example the two web services: a) [WS1]: given a

citizen's passport, the service returns the details of her/his social security card; WS1 input is defined by the ontological class Passport, and its output is defined by the ontological class SocialSecurityCard; b) [WS2]: given a citizen's passport, the service creates a new social security card for the citizen; WS2 input is defined by the ontological class Passport, and its output is defined by the ontological class SocialSecurityCard.

Although the meaning of the service operations is different, their input and output are defined by the same ontological classes. Despite its simplicity, the example shows that the definition of input/output messages of web services through ontological classes is not sufficient to express the full semantics of a web service operation (Sbodio et al., 2006). Preconditions and postconditions fill in this gap in the semantic description, and allow for a full denotation of a web service operation.

In the case of semantic description of services for citizen it is evident that preconditions play a crucial role. Similarly to what happen for web services, which cannot be invoked if their preconditions are not satisfied, we can say that a citizen cannot benefit from a service if its preconditions are not satisfied. Postconditions play also an important role in the formal definition of the effects of the service: they allow an unambiguous specification of the state of the world after the service usage. In the case of services for citizens, postconditions help in specifying the kind of service that a citizen may benefit from.

From our analysis preconditions and postconditions are therefore essential to provide semantic descriptions of services for citizens. Among the various emerging formalisms for semantic web services, we use OWL-S (OWL-S, 2008). There are several reasons for this choice. First of all, OWL-S was originally selected in the Terregov project for semantic web services descriptions, because at that time it was the most mature formalism. Besides this, OWL-S actually fits very well with our goal to build semantic descriptions of services that are not web services. OWL-S is itself an OWL ontology that defines concepts for describing services and it allows for the definition of a service model (that is the semantic specification of what the service does) independently of the definition of other details. Such an approach is very useful for describing services for citizens. The OWL-S service model also incorporates the preconditions and postconditions, which can be expressed using a variety of expression languages, among which we chose SPARQL (Prud'hommeaux, 2007).

Example

The problem of automatic selection of services for citizens can be reduced to the problem of semantic web services matchmaking. We developed a software agent performing such task. The agent goal is to find all services for which the citizen is potentially eligible for.

Concepts and relation from the core (or extended) ontology are used to build the goal and

the knowledge base of the agent that perform the automatic service selection. Such a knowledge base provides a representation of some relevant portions of the citizen profile. The agent's task is to fulfill its assigned goal. The OWL-S service descriptions are stored in a repository, which allows can be searched by our software agents. The agent checks the preconditions of services against the citizen profile: if the preconditions are fulfilled, then the citizen is eligible for that service. Figure 2 shows the interactions among the civil servants, the software agent, and the repository of semantic descriptions of services for citizens. Note that the interaction between the civil servant and the software agent is totally transparent, because the civil servants needs only to provide the citizen profile and the agent will autonomously search for services that the citizen is potentially eligible for.

The agent may also partial matching: it may select some services even if their preconditions

Figure 2.

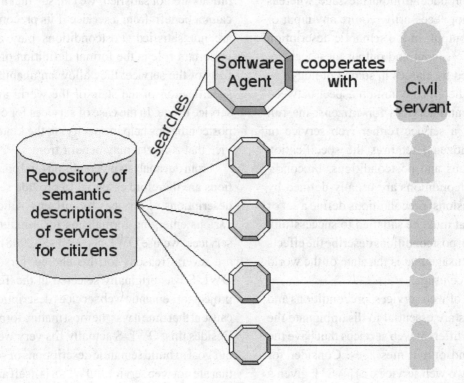

are not fully satisfied. This feature is quite useful when the citizen profile is incomplete: the eligibility criteria for a certain service may in fact require some piece of information that is not available in the current version of the citizen profile. In such a situation the agent may select the service as a partial match, and outline the eligibility criteria that were not evaluated due to the lack of information. Figure 3 shows a high-level definition of eligibility criteria for assistance services.

The example shows how we use ontological concepts in the definition of eligibility criteria: "Independence Level" is a concept representing the level of autonomy of an elderly person, and "Strong Need of Medical Assistance" and "High Reliance" are specializations representing respectively the fact that the citizen strongly requires some kind of medical assistance, and that the citizen highly rely on other persons for her/his daily needs. If the citizen profile matches the criteria shown in the example, then she/he is eli-

gible either for a service of type "Economical Benefit" or for a service of type "Part-time Home Medical Assistance" (both are defined by concepts in our ontology).

The use of semantic web services technologies such as OWL-S allows us to formally define the eligibility criteria, thus enabling the use of software agents that can automatically discover the most appropriate services for matching a citizen profile. In real-world use cases it is quite common that services are highly heterogeneous, changing over time, different from one administrative area to another, and often constrained by various eligibility criteria. In such a complex scenario the civil servants may not know in advance all the various services or their respective eligibility criteria, and therefore they need help in order to efficiently answer citizens' requests. Our software agent autonomously supports the civil servants in their tasks, effectively helping them in identifying the most appropriate services for a specific citizen profile. This is an example of symbiotic computing

Figure 3.

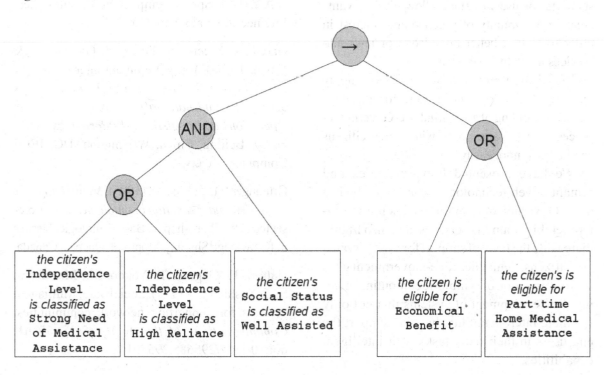

made possible by the adoption of semantic web services technologies.

CONCLUSION

We have considered three important phases where e-Government applications may or should deal with symbiotic aspects: design time, delivery time and running time. The last phase is more linked to ambient intelligence or ubiquitous computing and is not covered by our study.

We have shown that interoperability issues must be taken into account by application designers in order to integrate several heterogeneous systems. We also proved that semantics is a solution for designers when they have to model domain knowledge. Information systems able to semantically maintain citizens' profile are important modules for having frameworks taking into account knowledge about people.

The evolution of e-Government frameworks involves more and more civil servants. They act as a knowledgeable front-end to citizens. Semantic supports for user interface allow civil servants creating community of practice and interest in order to have a better knowledge of laws and services available to citizens.

During the Terregov project we tried to apply the concepts developed in this paper for contributing to the building of a new kind of e-Government processes and frameworks with which citizens can interact more easily.

We have presented how semantics and semantic web technologies can be applied to the e-Government domain, enhancing the interoperability among services, and also highly increasing the level of support for civil servants and citizens. Semantics for e-Government goes into the direction of symbiotic computing, helping the development of systems that not only facilitate interoperability, but also support the end users in their daily tasks with intelligent capabilities.

REFERENCES

Aussenac-Gilles, N., Biébow, B., & Szulman, S. (2000). *Revisiting ontology design: A methodology based on corpus analysis*. Paper presented at the 12th International Conference in Knowledge Engineering and Knowledge Management (EKAW), Juan-Les-Pins, France.

Berners-Lee, T., Hendler, J., & Lassila, O. (2001). The semantic web. *Scientific American*.

Busson, A., & Keravel, A. (2004). *Strategies used to reach e-government interoperability: A first evaluation*. Paper presented at e-Challenge, Vienna, Austria.

Fernández-López, M. (1999). Overview of methodologies for building ontologies. In V. R. Benjamins, B. Chandrasekaran, A. Gómez-Pérez, N. Guarino, & M. Uschold (Eds.), *Proceedings of the IJCAI-99 Workshop on Ontologies and Problem-Solving Methods (KRR5),* Stockholm, Sweden.

Fernández-López, M., Gómez-Pérez, A., & Juriso, N. (1997). *Methontology: From ontological art towards ontological engineering*. Paper presented at AAAI-97, Spring Symposium on Ontological Engineering, Palo Alto, CA.

Garcia, X., Vicente, S., Pérez, M., Gimeno, A., & Naval, J. (2005). E-government interoperability in a semantically driven world. In *Proceedings of the IEEE International Conference on Service, Operations and Logistic and Informatics (SOLI 2005),* Beijing, China. Washington, DC: IEEE Computer Society.

Grüninger, M., & Fox, M. (1995). *Methodology for the design and evaluation of ontologies*. Paper presented at the Workshop on Basic Ontological Issues in Knowledge Sharing, Montreal, Quebec, Canada.

Hattori, F., Ohguro, T., Yokoo, M., Matsubara, S., & Yoshida, S. (1999). Socialware: Multiagent systems for supporting network communities. *Communications of the ACM, 42*(3), 55–61. doi:10.1145/295685.295701

McIlraith, S. A., Son, T. C., & Zeng, H. (2001). Semantic web services. *IEEE Intelligent Systems, 16*(2), 46–53. doi:10.1109/5254.920599

Moulin, C., Bettahar, F., Barthès, J.-P., Sbodio, M., & Korda, N. (2006). Adding support to user interaction in e-government environment. In *Advances in web intelligence and data mining* (pp. 151-160).

OWL. (2004). *OWL web ontology language overview*. Retrieved from http://www.w3.org/TR/owl-features/

OWL-S. (2008). *OWL-S 1.2 pre-release*. Retrieved from http://www.ai.sri.com/daml/services/owl-s/1.2/

Peristeras, V., & Tarabanis, K. (2004). Advancing the government enterprise architecture gea: The service execution object model. In *Database and expert systems applications*, Zaragoza, Spain: DEXA.

Prud'hommeaux, E. S. A. (2007). *SPARQL query language for RDF*. Retrieved from http://www.w3.org/TR/rdf-sparql-query/

Sbodio, M., & Moulin, C. (2006). Denotation of semantic web services operations through OWL-S. In *Proceedings of the Workshop on Semantics for Web Services (SemWS'06) in conjunction with the 4th European Conference on Web Services (ECOWS'06)* (pp. 17-24).

Terregov. (2008). *TERREGOV project: Impact of e-government on territorial government service* (IST-2002-507749). Retrieved from http://www.terregov.eupm.net

Uschold, M., & Grüninger, M. (1996). Ontologies principles, methods and applications. *The Knowledge Engineering Review, 11*(2). doi:10.1017/S0269888900007797

ENDNOTES

[1] http://symbiotic.agent-town.com/
[2] http://www.nominotechnologies.com

This work was previously published in International Journal of Software Science and Computational Intelligence, Volume 2, Issue 1, edited by Yingxu Wang, pp. 38-51, copyright 2010 by IGI Publishing (an imprint of IGI Global).

Chapter 21
CoPBoard:
A Catalyst for Distributed Communities of Practice

Gilson Yukio Sato
Université de Technologie de Compiègne, France

Jean-Paul A. Barthès
Université de Technologie de Compiègne, France

ABSTRACT

Symbiotic computing leads to a proliferation of computing devices that allow linking people, favoring the development of distributed Communities of Practice (CoPs). Their members, being dispersed geographically, have to rely strongly on technological means to interact. In this context, coordinating distributed CoPs is more challenging than coordinating their collocated counterparts. Hence, the increasing role of the coordination should be supported by an adequate set of coordination tools. In this paper, we present an approach based on multi-agent systems for coordinating distributed CoPs. It includes analyzing the exchanges among members and translating this information into a graphical format to help the coordinators to follow the evolution of the participation and the domain of the community.

The notion of Communities of Practice (CoP) has interested academics, managers and consultants in the last few years. This interest is justified by the usefulness of the notion in helping to study and understand learning and collaborative work in education and management (Barton & Tusting, 2005; Cox, 2005; Gherardi, 2006; Hughes, Jewson, & Unwin, 2007; Kimble, 2006; Roberts, 2006; Soulier, 2004; Wenger, McDermott, & Snyder, 2002).

Such notion has been used in knowledge management initiatives by several organizations (for example: Brown & Duguid, 1998; Raybourn, Kings, & Davies, 2003; von Krogh, Nonaka, & Aben, 2001; Wenger et al., 2002). At the same time, the emergence of Internet based tools, rang-

DOI: 10.4018/978-1-4666-0264-9.ch021

ing from email to virtual environments, facilitated the creation of distributed CoPs. Distributed CoPs use such tools to interact because they cannot rely exclusively on face-to-face interactions. The distance between members, the lack of awareness of other members, the higher number of members, the different cultural mindsets make coordinating distributed CoPs more demanding and challenging than coordinating a collocated/local one (Wenger et al., 2002). In this context, we think that the availability of coordination systems is highly desirable. A question is how to do it? Multi-Agent Systems could provide the adequate technology for supporting such an approach. Intelligent agents, being cooperative, proactive and adaptable, could perform tasks to decrease the additional workload of the coordination of a distributed CoP.

In this paper we present an approach for improving the coordination of distributed CoPs. The basic idea is to propose a tool that works as a catalyst for CoP by helping coordinators to follow the evolution of the participation in the community and the evolution of its domain (topics of interest). We first we introduce some definitions used in our research work. Then we present some requirements for supporting the coordination of CoP. Then we present the system that we developed following the requirements. Finally, we discuss the results of our research.

DEFINITIONS

We first give some definitions for the main concepts under consideration.

SYMBIOTIC COMPUTING

The concept comes from the view expressed by Licklider (1960) of man-computer symbiosis. In this view a person is tightly coupled with the digital space through traditional and new types of devices. In the neo-symbiosis approach (Griffith & Greiter,

2007) the relation between a person and the digital space can then be defined in terms of partnership, e.g. through a partner agent who has knowledge about the person and the community. Sugawara, Fujita, Kinoshita, and Shiratori (2008, p. 278) define Symbiotic Computing as "a methodology to realize human/society oriented functions". They consider that developing such functions requires integrating three types of functions: Ubiquitous/Network Functions, Web Functions and Symbiotic Functions. Suganuma, Takahashi, and Shiratori (2008) propose to consider the Symbiotic Functions as a function space that includes Perceptual Functions, Social Functions and Mutual Cognition Functions.

Although our research and the tool presented in this paper were not developed in the Symbiotic Computing framework, we consider that they are closely related. Distributed CoP can only exist because a group of people in different locations are able to come together using Ubiquitous/Network Functions and Web Functions. On the other hand, a CoP helps to motivate people to connect using these functions. Furthermore, our tool, CoPBoard, can be considered to fulfill a Social Function. A function to acquire social information and heuristics related to communities is considered a Social Function (Suganuma et al., 2008) and it is exactly what CoPBoard does.

COMMUNITIES OF PRACTICE

Considering the development of the concept Communities of Practice, it is possible to observe three phases. In each phase, the concept undergoes important changes (Cox, 2005; Kimble, 2006). For our work, we adopted the concept presented in the third phase discussed mainly in Wenger et al. (2002) in which a CoP is defined "a group of people who share a concern, a set of problems, or a passion about a topic, and who deepen their knowledge and expertise in the corresponding area by interacting on an ongoing basis." A CoP is an informal structure that exists in any organization, whether acknowledged or not. CoPs cannot be established (like a multifunctional team), but can be cultivated. It is possible to create an environment where CoPs can thrive.

The structural model of a CoP combines three elements: (i) a *domain* of knowledge; (ii) a *community* of people; and (iii) a shared *practice*. The domain defines a set of issues and legitimizes the community by affirming its purpose and value to its members. The *domain* motivates members´ participation and contribution and helps them to define what activities should be performed. The *community* creates the social fabric of learning and fosters interactions and relationships based on mutual respect and trust. This kind of relationship creates an environment encouraging people to share ideas, to expose their ignorance, to ask questions and to listen carefully. The *practice* is a set of frameworks, ideas, tools, information, styles, languages, stories and documents that community members share. It represents the knowledge that the community creates shares and maintains.

A distributed CoP is a CoP whose members are geographically distributed. They have to rely on technological means instead of face-to face meetings in order to interact.

MULTI-AGENT SYSTEMS

In our work we considered that a multi-agent system (MAS) is a system composed of a group of possibly heterogeneous and autonomous agents sharing a common goal and working cooperatively to achieve this goal (Tacla & Barthès, 2003).

MAS have been deployed in various domains, like concurrent engineering, manufacturing (Shen, Norrie, & Barthès, 2001), knowledge management (Tacla & Barthès, 2004), computer communications (Manvi & Venkataram, 2004), CSCW (Gräther & Prinz, 2001) or e-commerce. They can be used to intelligently assist users in specialized and generic tasks. Specialized tasks

include, among others, network management (Manvi & Venkataram, 2004) or operation of CAE tools (Miyoshi, Yagawa, & Sasaki, 1999). Generic tasks can also be supported by agents and by MAS. For example: handling information (e.g. retrieving, filtering, synthesizing), making decisions (decision support systems) (Klusch, 2001) or capturing lessons learned by a project team (Tacla & Barthès, 2003).

COORDINATING A DISTRIBUTED COMMUNITY OF PRACTICE

Requirements

Coordinating a local community can be done informally since members are more visible. Even if a member does not give her opinion in a meeting, other members can observe her passive participation. Newcomers can speak in private when they run into other members in the cafeteria to network informally. In a distributed community, it is difficult to know who is reading the messages posted on the discussion board. Informal networking is also difficult in teleconferences. The most obvious obstacle is the distance.

Distributed CoPs have more potential members than local ones, so they tend to be larger. When the number of members is large, it is difficult to know everybody personally and establish relationships based on trust and mutual respect. The number of members can also affect the way the community is structured. For example, a large distributed community can be divided into sub-communities coordinated locally. Distributed CoPs can also encounter cultural issues, as they can have members distributed all over the world. Language is also an important factor (Wenger et al., 2002).

CoPs can differ from one another. For example, some communities can privilege the use of asynchronous tools like email or blogs while others will prefer using synchronous tools like chats. In such cases a good application for a community may not be so useful for the other one (e.g. a meeting scheduler). Therefore, flexibility is an important factor. Flexibility can be more important for distributed communities. They can be formed by sub-communities that have different needs. For larger sub-communities, the use of information technology could be inevitable, but small ones can always count on face-to-face interactions. So, a distributed community would need services that are more flexible than the ones required by a local community. Another factor requiring flexibility from the technology is the evolution of communities. A CoP has a life cycle: it starts, grows, matures and disappears. We think that in this context the tools used in the community should follow its evolution.

In a CoP, members can participate as peripheral members, active members and core members, depending on the pertinence of their participation to the community domain. Usually, the coordination of a CoP is entrusted to a core member or a group of core members. If a distributed CoP is structured as a community of local sub-communities, the local coordinators can form the coordination of the distributed community (Wenger et al., 2002).

MULTI-AGENT SYSTEM FOR COORDINATING CoP

MAS technology is adequate for developing applications for CoPs, distributed or not, because it has the flexibility to build complex applications. Moreover, an MAS offer the possibility to:

- adapt by the addition or suppression of agents,
- include proactive services that run in the background,
- interface to legacy software,
- run several options for the same service in parallel.

The activities of the CoP coordination and members are performed in parallel with other activities like the activities of a project team. In this context, members do not have much time to dedicate to community tasks. A MAS can help them to decrease their workload by performing tasks that can be automated.

USE CASE

In this section, we describe a hypothetical situation in which a MAS is used for supporting distributed CoPs. It concerns a person, John, who belongs to two communities, one of managers, and one of software developers.

John is living a transition phase in his career: he is managing his first big project, after a long time doing hands-on job in software development, and, at the same time, he is giving a hand to the new developers that have just arrived.

As a project manager, at first, he was feeling uncomfortable and dissatisfied with his own performance. So he decided to join a community of managers who discuss practical problems in project management. He feels comfortable asking questions and sharing his experiences inside the group. His participation in the community has taught him a lot about handling practical questions and about the company policy. He should not be surprised to see how the participation in the community has boosted his performance as a project manager. He has seen the same thing happen in the study group he and some colleagues created some years ago about software development.

John activates his personal assistant agent Stevens that, after greeting him, informs that he received 26 email messages in the last 24 hours. Stevens identified six from the project managers' community, eight from the software developers' community and another eight from his project team. Stevens reminds John that he should chat on-line with Paul at 10:00AM about how to account for the part-time members of the team in the budget.

He also remembers John that at 4:00PM he should attend the monthly meeting about the community of developers. Stevens suggests that John should look Bill's blog because he posted a new entry about the new components he is working on.

At the 10:00AM on-line chat, John and Paul think that the content of the chat can be useful to other members of the managers' community. So they agree to ask Stevens to save a transcription of the session.

At the 4:00PM meeting, John meets Bill and other members who coordinate informally the developers' community. John asks Stevens to make the information about the community available. Stevens shows some graphics with information like the number of messages exchanged, the number of entries in the members' blogs, the number of on line chats among members. Analyzing this information, the community coordinators can observe the steady growth in the exchanges among members, indicating that the community is doing quite well. The coordination group also notices that a sub community is forming and discussing the issue, they consider the possibility to create a new more focused community.

Then, John is back to his desk and asks Stevens to show the information about his own participation in both developers' and managers' communities. He notices that his participation in the managers' community is increasing in the same degree that his participation in the developers' community is decreasing. The number of developers with whom he interacts is each time smaller and the number of managers is larger than ever.

John is wondering about the latest developments in his career when Stevens reminds him that a meeting with the project team is scheduled first thing next morning.

RELATED WORK

Hattori, Ohguro, Yokoo, Matsubara, and Yoshida (1999) argue that a MAS is attractive to support networked communities. The distributed character of this kind of community fits in a distributed architecture like the multi-agent architecture. The argument can be used to support the use of MAS for distributed CoP as well. They also mention that the support system should handle the dynamic nature of the community in which members change the way they participate, meaning that the individuality of the members is preserved. They suggest that a personal agent should be used to preserve such individuality.

Case, Azarmi, Thint, and Ohtani (2001), although not referring to CoPs, also argue that intelligent agents are the ideal technological platform to provide services and solutions for building electronic communities because an intelligent agent is cooperative, proactive and adaptable.

Hattori et al. (1999) describe a system called Community Organizer that facilitates the formation of new communities by providing a virtual space where people with similar interests can meet and interact. They also describe CommunityBoard that classifies messages from a discussion board according three dimensions: the author, the subject and the author's reputation. The result is presented graphically. Analyzing such a graph, the user can choose to participate or not in the discussion.

The Forum system, discussed in Raybourn, Kings, and Davies (2003), was specifically designed for CoPs. This web-based collaborative virtual environment deploys agents to support chance meetings, informal communication and information sharing among community members. The Forum system helps to handle one of the problems presented by distributed CoP: the lack of opportunities to connect informally. It "introduces" people with similar profiles putting their avatars together to facilitate informal networking.

The eLogbook aims at supporting the management of explicit and tacit knowledge in a CoP (Gillet, El Helou, Yu, & Salzmann, 2008). This system puts together tools to manage assets (resources) and tasks and a discussion board. Each user can build her own work environment with her activities, the community members with whom she interacts and the resources she uses.

KEEx (Knowledge Enhancement and Exchange) is a virtual environment for organizational learning based in a peer-to-peer architecture. In this environment, users can search and share artifacts using a hierarchy of concepts instead of an ontology. To improve the research results, KEEx uses the hierarchy of concepts as the artifact context and a user's profile. The system can also produce a graph with the relevance of retrieved documents and recommend documents (Soller, Guizzardi, Molani, & Perini, 2004).

The works developed by Hattori et al. (1999), Raybourn et al. (2003) and Soller et al. (2004) are based in Multi-Agent Systems and Intelligent Agents like the CoPBoard. But, they are virtual environments, like the eLogbook (Gillet et al., 2008), where communities can be formed or can develop their activities. For CoPBoard we used a different approach. CoPBoard aims at extracting information from the environments where communities gather. We organize the information around some social indicators in an approach similar to the one elaborated by Ackerman and Starr (1995).

EXPECTATIONS

Our work was aimed at improving the coordination of distributed CoP by providing indicators about the participation of the community members and the evolution of its domain. The idea was to provide graphs that could help the coordination observe the evolution of the community domain, the fluctuation in the members' participation and the emergence of sub-communities.

CoPBOARD

Our approach to improve the coordination of CoP is inspired by the concept of control panel. We call it CoPBoard. As a car control panel (dashboard)

that shows indicators to help the user decide when to accelerate, change gears, or refuel the car, the CoPBoard shows to the community coordinators when they should act to keep the community in good health.

SOCIAL FUNCTION

The role of the CoPBoard is thus to facilitate the coordination of a distributed CoP by gathering information about the participation of the members and also to collect information about the domain of the community. It aims at being a lightweight assistant helping the community coordinators.

STRUCTURE

We assume in our work that members of a CoP are linked through a Multi-Agent System. Each member has a personal assistant agent (PA) to interface with the system and with other members. Each PA has a Trajectory Agent (TA) that saves, organizes and displays information about her participation in various communities. For each community using the system, a Community Agent (CA) is created. In this organization, the CA should extract, organize, analyze and present information from the exchanges (e.g. email messages, blogs, chats) among community members (e.g. email messages, blogs, chats). It should be able to present the information in a flexible way, allowing the user to change visualization parameters easily. The CA can also count on Service Agents (SA) to perform specific tasks like analyzing a post in a blog or accessing a mailbox (Figure 1).

THE COMMUNITY AGENT

In this section, we describe a Community Agent (CA) that is part of the CoPBoard structure that we presented above. As a research prototype it imple-

Figure 1. MAS organization for CoPs

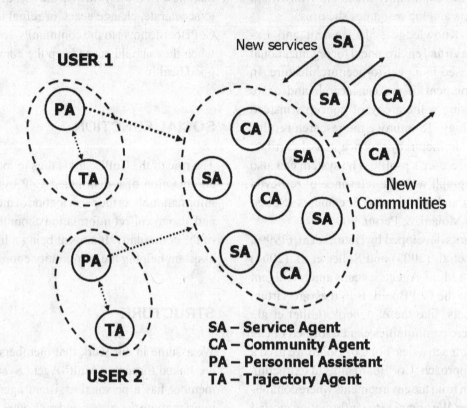

USER 1

New services

New Communities

SA – Service Agent
CA – Community Agent
PA – Personnel Assistant
TA – Trajectory Agent

USER 2

ments only some of the features that we described in our hypothetical use case. So, currently, the CA can only analyze messages exchanged through a discussion board. Furthermore, the presentation of information is not as flexible as it should be. We also concentrated all functionalities into a single agent instead of using Service Agents. In doing so, we tried to simplify the implementation in order to test the idea of an agent supporting the coordination of a CoP.

The CA is intended to support the coordination of distributed CoPs, graphically showing information about the evolution of some of the community aspects: the members' participation and the domain of the community. It analyses exchanges among members in the community discussion list and creates some graphical representations of the contents of the exchanges and of the members' participation. The following figures

have been established by analyzing the contents of the *com-prac* list messages. The *com-prac* list is a discussion list about CoPs from the Yahoo Groups.

We monitor:

- the number of messages exchanged daily (Figure 3),
- the number of participants that send messages daily (similar to the number of messages),
- the level of participation of each member in the last 30 days, classified into 3 levels: low, medium and high (Figure 4),
- the number of messages of the past seven days classified in pre-established categories of messages (Figure 5),
- the dispersion of messages after computing a distance value explained thereafter (Figure 6),

- the frequency of *macro-concepts* grouping a particular set of concepts (Figure 7),
- the dispersion of *macro-concepts* (Figure 8).

All representations are accessed through a main window shown in Figure 2.

NUMBER OF MESSAGES AND OF PARTICIPANTS

The *number of messages and of participants* give an idea of the level of activity of the CoP during the last seven days (Figure 3).

Figure 2. Main window (the slide bar shows the number of messages received since the last access to the mailbox)

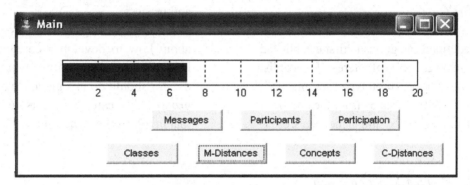

Figure 3. Number of messages graph

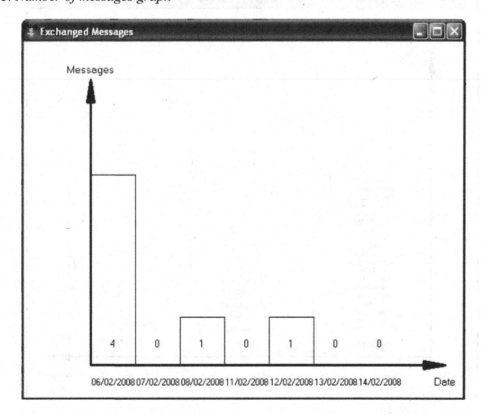

LEVELS OF PARTICIPATION

The *level of participation* singles out the members that were active and less active. One computes the number of participations of each member during the last 30 days and classifies the participation into three levels: low, medium and high participation (Figure 4), using the Fisher Algorithm (Hartigan, 1975).

NUMBER OF MESSAGES PER CATEGORY

A set of predefined categories is first established, corresponding to concepts of interest. To establish the categories for our prototype, we manually analyzed about 300 messages from the *com-prac* discussion list. We grouped similar messages, estab-

lished a category for each group and we chose some messages as examples to represent the categories. Then, the messages from the last seven days were considered and classified into one of the categories. Of course the number and nature of categories depend on the particular CoP being monitored. In the *com-prac* case, we established six categories:

- *concepts*: this category refers to messages that discuss concepts, e.g. what is a CoP or what is the difference between practice and process;
- *develop*: this category refers to messages about how to develop a community, e.g. how to start a community or what the coordinator should do in a given situation;
- *groups*: this category refers to messages that involve other types of groups, e.g. how

Figure 4. Level of participation graph

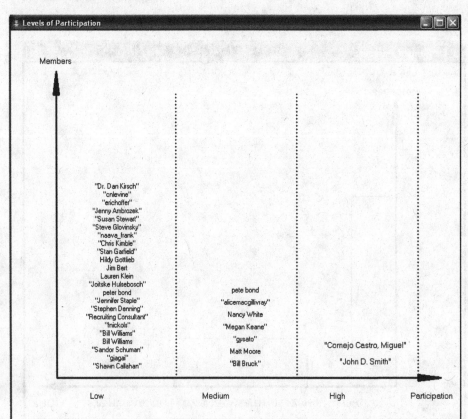

communities and teams compare or what is the difference between different types of community;

- *participation*: this category refers to messages about membership and participation, e.g. why people participate or how to consider lurkers;
- *tools*: this category refers to messages that discuss tools and technology, e.g. how a tool fit in a community or what this technology is about;
- *value*: this category refers to messages that discuss evaluation of the community, results and the relation with the organization in which the community operates, e.g. how to measure the effectiveness of the community or how to align it with the strategy of the organization. The result is shown Figure 5.

To classify messages we used a technique developed by Enembreck to classify documents (Enembreck & Barthès, 2007). This technique associates the idea of centroid and the discriminating power of each term (Gini index). Each category is represented by the centroid of a set of example-messages. In the case of this prototype, we have six centroids for six sets of example-messages, each one corresponding to one of the six categories. For each example-message a TF-IDF (Term Frequency - Inverse Document Frequency) vector is calculated and the centroid is calculated from these vectors. To classify a new message, CA calculates the new message vector and compares it with the centroid vector of each category. In this comparison the discriminating power of each term is also considered.

DISPERSION OF MESSAGES

The idea behind the concept of message dispersion is to compute a distance between the messages proportional to the similarity of their content in the message space, then to project onto a 2-dimensional plane (Figure 6). In addition, one can size the circle representing a message proportionally to the number of terms relevant to the community. If two messages are near, then it means that their content is similar.

However, when projecting from an n-dimensional space onto a 2-dimensional one, the perception of distance between two points can vary significantly. To re-establish true distance, we introduced a scroll-bar at the right hand side of the picture. The user can choose a message as a reference (anchor) and then use the scroll bar to change the reference distance. As the user changes the reference distance, messages for which the distance to the anchor is smaller than the reference distance change their color from blue to red (Figure 6).

To calculate the distance among messages, we use a normalized vector with the frequency of terms (t) to represent each message (M). So, messages a and b can be represented as:

$$M_a = (t_{1a}, t_{2a}, ..., t_{na}), M_b = (t_{1b}, t_{2b}, ..., t_{nb})$$

Using these vectors we calculate a matrix (message X message) with the Euclidean distances (d) between every pair of messages (e.g. dab for the distance between a and b) defined by:

$$d_{ab} = \sqrt{\sum_{i=1}^{n} |t_{ia} - t_{ib}|^2}$$

We apply in this matrix the Multi Dimensional Positioning (MDS) method (Cox & Cox, 1994; Young, 2002) that gives us the coordinates of each message.

FREQUENCY OF MACRO-CONCEPTS

It is interesting to visualize the main topics that have been addressed by showing the concepts that were inserted in the exchanged messages. However, this

Figure 5. Number of messages in each category

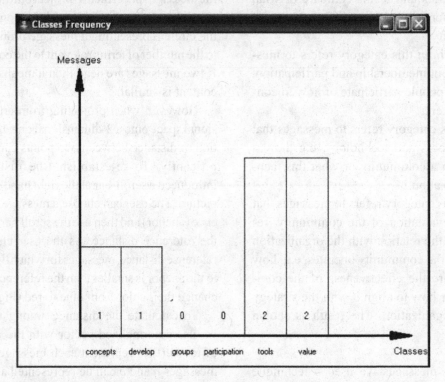

Figure 6. Dispersion of messages

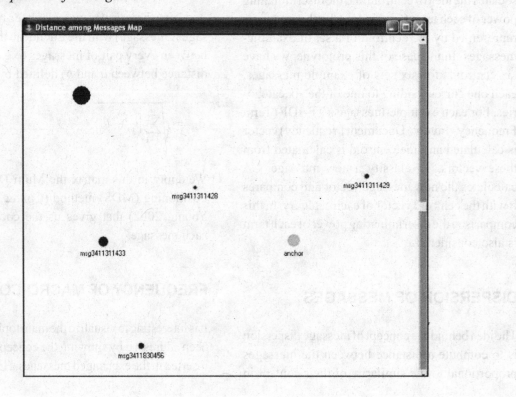

may lead to very crowded pictures. To make a graph of concepts more legible by reducing its dimension, we introduce the notion of *macro-concept*.

A *macro-concept* groups the occurrences of a set of terms under a unique term. For example, the occurrences of *communities of practice*, *CoP*, or *CP* are grouped into the *community of practice macro-concept*.

Or, the terms *effectiveness, added-value, evaluate* are considered under the *macro-concept evaluation*. The CA has an ontology that allows grouping synonyms and related terms under a unique *macro-concept*. In our test, we established the *macro-concepts* (as well as their synonyms and related terms) by analyzing the older messages exchanged in the *com-prac* discussion list (Figure 7).

DISPERSION OF MACRO-CONCEPTS

The idea behind representing the dispersion of macro-concept is the same as the one for representing dispersion of messages. It represents how the *macro-concepts* appear or not in the same context (Figure 8).

Macro-concepts are represented as circles and the size of the circles are proportional to the number of occurrences of the *macro-concept* in the messages of the last seven days. *Macro-concepts* that are used in similar contexts are probably located near each other. For example, the *macro-concepts knowledge management* and *organization* tend to appear in messages discussing organizational issues more often than the *macro-concept participation* or *practice*. So probably *knowledge management* and *organization* are nearer each other than to *participation*. But sometimes *macro-concepts* expected to be near one another are distant or vice-versa. We think that analyzing this kind of discrepancy can help the coordination of the community to discuss its domain. Like in the dispersion of messages, the visualization can be improved by using an anchor and the scroll bar.

To calculate the distance among *macro-concepts*, we start by calculating a vector for each *macro-concept*. Each coordinate in the vectors corresponds to the number of occurrences (*no*) of

Figure 7. Frequency of macro-concepts from the last seven days

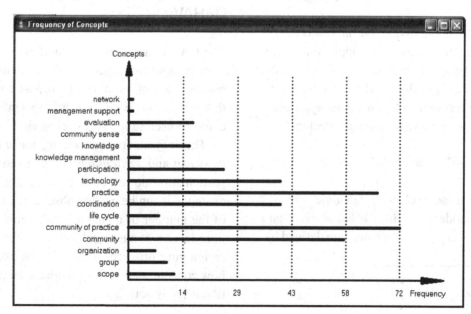

Figure 8. Dispersion of macro-concepts from the last seven days

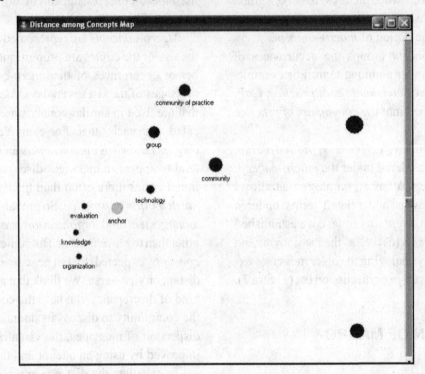

the *macro-concept* (*MC*) in the messages of the seven last days. So *macro-concepts a* and *b* can be represented as:

$$MC_a = (no_{1a}, no_{2a}, ..., no_{na}), MC_b = (no_{1b}, no_{2b}, ..., no_{nb})$$

To try to approximate the *macro-concepts* used in similar contexts, we apply the Latent Semantic Analysis method (Landauer, Foltz, & Laham, 1998) to the matrix formed with the *macro-concepts* vectors. From the resultant matrix we obtain the new *macro-concepts* vectors:

$$MC'_a = (no'_{1a}, no'_{2a}, ..., no'_{na}), MC'_b = (no'_{1b}, no'_{2b}, ..., no'_{nb})$$

We use these vectors to calculate a matrix with the Euclidean distances between every pair of *macro-concepts*. The distances are defined by:

$$d_{ab} = \sqrt{\sum_{i=1}^{n} \left| no'_{ia} - no'_{ib} \right|^2}$$

As we did for the dispersion of messages, we apply the MDS method to obtain the coordinates of each *macro-concept*.

BEHAVIOR

The CA captures, processes and presents information about two aspects of the community: the participation of its members and its domain. In this sub-section, we discuss how this information could be used to follow the evolution of a CoP.

The information concerning the *number of messages* and *participants* is used to analyze the participation during different time periods. For example, it can be used to observe the evolution of the number of members or the effects of the introduction of a new subject or artifact into the community practice. It can also be used to see how concentrated in few members the participation is (or is not).

The *levels of participation* graph helps to observe how a member changes her participation level. Observed in time, the graph gives a clue about the trajectory of a community member. Associated with other graphs, it can help to understand what makes some members engage or disengage. For example, if a member who used to participate at a high level is suddenly participating less, maybe it is correlated with the sudden increase in the number of new members.

The *categorization of messages* can be used to observe how the domain of the community behaves. More messages in a given category usually indicate more concern about a subject. Analyzed in time, this graph indicates how some subjects evolve inside the community.

The *dispersion of messages* is used to discern the various foci of the community and help to redefine the categories in which the messages are classified. It helps in the identification of sub-communities.

The *frequency of the macro-concepts* and *dispersion of macro-concepts* are useful to indicate trends in the community domain. But they also help to understand the relationships among *macro-concepts* in a specific community. For example, if the use of technology is an important issue, the number of messages in the category *tools* should be high. If in the *dispersion of messages*, the *macro-concept technology* is near the other *macro-concepts*, it probably indicates that the use of technology is an issue for the whole community. But if the *macro-concept technology* is distant from other important concepts, it could indicate the emergence of sub-community interested just in the technological aspect.

EXAMPLE OF THE USE OF THE DISPERSION OF MACRO-CONCEPTS

To illustrate the use of the CA, we analyze two graphs showing the dispersion of *macro-concepts* (Figures 9 and 10).

We observe that:

- the *macro-concepts* that are not used frequently (smaller circles) in the represented discussion are grouped;
- the *macro-concepts community of practice*, *community* and *practice* could be considered as a reference for the analysis;
- it is possible to observe the relation among subjects in a discussion.

The *macro-concepts* that are not used frequently form a group. As they do not appear in most messages, the distances among them are smaller. We tried to minimize the effect of these infrequent *macro-concepts* by eliminating some of them (they do not appear in the figure) but it seems that it was not enough. We could use the TF-IDF index to improve these results. Another idea is to create other more encompassing *macro-concepts* from the not frequent used ones.

As most messages use the *macro-concepts community of practice*, *community* and *practice* (used as the anchor in the figures), we analyzed the figures using them as a reference. In the first case (Figure 9), we can observe that the *macro-concept coordination* is nearer to the reference than the *macro-concepts technology* or *participation*. Analyzing the messages represented in this discussion, we notice that most messages refer to the substitution of coordinators in communities, which explains the proximity of *coordination*.

Such messages refer also to other members, their reactions and the community development, so participation is not so far from the reference. The discussion also contains messages concerning back-channeling. This subject is much less discussed than the substitution of the coordinator, so the *macro-concept technology* appears further from the reference.

In the second case, the distances between *technology* and the reference and between *coordination* and the reference are similar. Analyzing the messages from this discussion, we observe that two subjects are discussed with an equal intensity. The first subject concerns religion/church as a

Figure 9. Case 1. Dispersion of macro-concepts from the last seven days

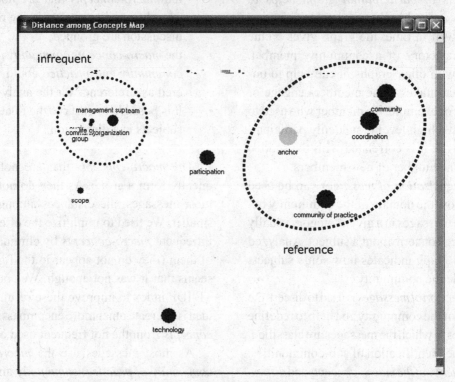

Figure 10. Case 2. Dispersion of macro-concepts from the last seven days

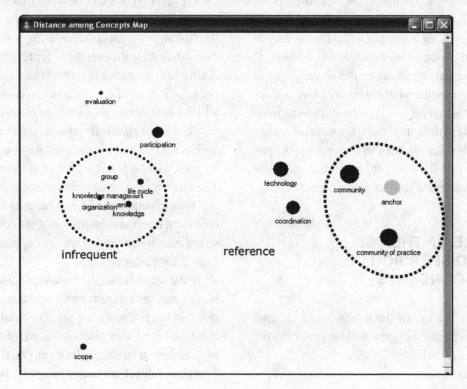

CoP (from the perspective of the engagement, the leadership, etc.), the second concerns the Wikipedia entry about communities of practice and the Wikipedia itself. The first subject justifies the proximity of *coordination* and the second the proximity of *technology*.

Using the *dispersion of macro-concepts*, we can observe the behavior of the community domain. We can observe how the subjects alternate and determine the more important ones for the community (*coordination* and *technology*). We used the *dispersion of macro-concepts* to exemplify how the agent CA can be used to follow the community domain. The other graphs (or a combination of them) are useful to observe other aspects of the community. For example, the *number of messages* and *of participants* let us observe if some people monopolize the discussions. The *levels of participation* picture lets us observe if there are participants changing their status inside the community.

RESULTS AND DISCUSSION

Results

The coordination of distributed CoPs is even more challenging that the coordination of the local ones because the problems caused or correlated with the geographical distance, the potentially greater number of members and the cultural differences. We think that an adequate set of tools could decrease the workload of community coordination. In this context, we presented the prototype of a Community Agent. The presented prototype analyzes the messages exchanged through a discussion list and displays graphs giving information about the evolution of two important aspects of a community: the participation of the members and the domain of the community. We think that by analyzing such graphs the coordinator(s) of the community will be able to observe how members participate, and how this participation is altered by other changes in the community.

When developing the CoPBoard and the Community Agent, we aimed at helping coordinators to develop distributed CoPs by elaborating a tool to support them. The idea behind such a tool is to provide information that could induce coordinators to reflect about the community domain and the participation of its members. To reflect about the domain and the participation can help them to better understand what is happening in the community and consequently to make better decisions about how to keep it active, productive and in continuous development. In this sense, the CoPBoard aims at acting like a catalyst, helping coordinators to accelerate the community development.

We do not have yet concrete examples of the validity of our approach, but we are willing to test it in real conditions. Using the *com-prac* discussion list was useful to evaluate the CA in a real context (actual domain, messages, discussions and problems). It was useful to observe the technical problems to handle message formats, signatures, abbreviations, spurious messages and so forth. But this evaluation was partial, since the *com-prac* list is not the discussion list of an actual distributed CoP and we were not able to have our graphs analyzed by a significant number of community members (Sato, 2008).

The major adaptation required for testing our approach in another community is the elaboration of a practical specific ontology. As long as we are able to build such an ontology, the system will be able to analyze the messages of the community discussion list. So the domain in which the community operates is not as important as its attitude toward reflection about its activities. To apply the CA prototype to another community, it is also necessary to create the categories used to classify the messages. Although it is a manual process, it consumes an acceptable amount of time. Establishing the categories for the CA prototype took us about 12 hours.

We tested the CA message classification technique by comparing the automatic classification with a manual classification. We observed that the

CA was able to classify correctly just 48% of the messages. But analyzing the messages that were incorrectly classified, we estimate that the CA can reach 70% of correctness with small improvements in the ontology and in the definition of the message categories. Considering that the technique we used achieves in ideal conditions (i.e. longer texts for examples, more examples) about 82% of correctness, we estimate that for a first approach the technique is applicable to the CA (Sato, 2008). The tests of the *level of participation* graph showed that the Fisher algorithm is applicable to the CA. We compared the CA classification with our manual classification and we could observe that in 12 analyzed data sets, both classifications agreed in nine situations. One data set was not suitable for the algorithm (there were just two groups) and in the other two, our classification was more subjective (we were influenced by the member's participation as a whole, instead of considering just the analyzed period of time) (Sato, 2008).

Although the *dispersion of macro-concepts* could be improved, we observed that it can be used to monitor the evolution of the community domain. In the presented example, we could observe that the *macro-concepts coordination* and *technology* were the most discussed. It reflects the profile of most discussion list members. As practitioners, they prefer to discuss ways to improve the community instead of discussing basic concepts or the role of a CoP in the organization. In addition, the fact that the community around the discussion list is mature, *macro-concepts* as *concepts* and *scope* were less discussed, because they were already considered as "black boxes." This kind of transition in the most used *macro-concepts* can help the coordinators to observe the evolution on the community domain.

UNEXPECTED BENEFITS

Although the CoPBoard and the Community Agent aim at helping the coordinators of distributed communities, we think that they could be also used as a tool to study them. We think that the same reasons that make the coordination of such groups challenging, apply to their study. It is more difficult to observe a distributed group in action because the distance among members and the number of potential members. As members can live in different regions and countries, the difference among their cultural backgrounds can be more significant that the ones found in collocated communities. We think that tools like the CoPBoard could help researchers to study some aspects of distributed communities and, consequently, contribute to the understanding of such groups.

In our research we are able to observe that to find CoP as they are described in the adopted theoretical framework present some difficulties. Some groups present characteristics of CoP as a common domain but they do not develop a practice (Sato, 2008). It seems that to make a community thrive demands a high coordination effort. We think that it is a matter of further investigation.

REFERENCES

Ackerman, M. S., & Starr, B. (1995). *Social activity indicators: interface components for CSCW systems*. Paper presented at the 8th annual ACM symposium on User Interface and Software Technology, Pittsburgh, PA.

Barton, D., & Tusting, K. (Eds.). (2005). *Beyond communities of practice* (1st ed.). Cambridge, UK: Cambridge University Press.

Brown, J. S., & Duguid, P. (1998). Organizing knowledge. *California Management Review, 40*(3), 90–111.

Case, S., Azarmi, N., Thint, M., & Ohtani, T. (2001). Enhancing e-communities with agent-based systems. *Computer, 34*(7), 64–69. doi:10.1109/2.933505

Cox, A. (2005). What are communities of practice? A comparative review of four seminal works. *Journal of Information Science, 31*(6), 527–540. doi:10.1177/0165551505057016

Cox, T. F., & Cox, M. A. A. (1994). *Multidimensional scaling* (Vol. 59). London: Chapman & Hall.

Enembreck, F. C., & Barthès, J. P. (2007). Multiagent based Internet search. *International Journal Product Lifecycle Management, 2*(2), 135–156. doi:10.1504/IJPLM.2007.014276

Gherardy, S. (2005). *Organizational knowledge: The texture of workplace learning* (1st ed.). London: Blackwell.

Gillet, D., El Helou, S., Yu, C. M., & Salzmann, C. A.-S. C. (2008). *Turning Web 2.0 social software into versatile collaborative learning solutions.* Paper presented at the First International Conference on Advances in Computer-Human Interaction.

Gräther, W., & Prinz, W. (2001). *The social web cockpit: Support for virtual communities.* Paper presented at the 2001 International ACM SIG-GROUP Conference on Supporting Group Work, Boulder, CO.

Griffith, D., & Greiter, F. L. (2007). Neo-symbiosis: The next stage in the evolution of human information interaction. *International Journal of Cognitive Informatics and Natural Intelligence, 1*(1), 39–52.

Hartigan, J. A. (1975). *Clustering algorithms.* New York: John Wiley & Sons.

Hattori, F., Ohguro, T., Yokoo, M., Matsubara, S., & Yoshida, S. (1999). Socialware: Multiagent systems for supporting network communities. *Communications of the ACM, 42*(3), 55–61. doi:10.1145/295685.295701

Hughes, J., Jewson, N., & Unwin, L. (Eds.). (2007). *Communities of pratice: Critical perspectives.* London: Routledge.

Kimble, C. (2006). *Communities of practice: Never knowingly undersold.* Paper presented at the Innovative Approaches for Learning and Knowledge Sharing: EC-TEL 2006 Workshops, Crete, Greece.

Klusch, M. (2001). Information agent technology for the Internet: A survey. *Data & Knowledge Engineering, 36*(3), 337–372. doi:10.1016/S0169-023X(00)00049-5

Landauer, T. K., Foltz, P. W., & Laham, D. (1998). Introduction to latent semantic analysis. *Discourse Processes, 25,* 259–284.

Licklider, J. C. R. (1960, March). Man-computer symbiosis. *IRE Transactions on Human Factors in Electronics, HFE-1,* 4–11. doi:10.1109/THFE2.1960.4503259

Manvi, S. S., & Venkataram, P. (2004). Applications of agent technology in communications: A review. *Computer Communications, 27*(15), 1493–1508. doi:10.1016/j.comcom.2004.05.011

Miyoshi, A., Yagawa, G., & Sasaki, S. (1999). An interface agent that actively supports CAE beginner users in performing analyses. *Advances in Engineering Software, 30*(8), 575–579. doi:10.1016/S0965-9978(99)00010-1

Raybourn, E. M., Kings, N., & Davies, J. (2003). Adding cultural signposts in adaptive community-based virtual environments. *Interacting with Computers, 15*(1), 91–107. doi:10.1016/S0953-5438(02)00056-5

Roberts, J. (2006). Limits to communities of practice. *Journal of Management Studies, 43*(3), 623–639. doi:10.1111/j.1467-6486.2006.00618.x

Sato, G. Y. (2008). *Contribution à l'amélioration de la coordination de communautés de pratique distribuées.* Unpublished PhD thesis, Université de Technologie de Compiègne, Compiègne.

Shen, W., Norrie, D. H., & Barthès, J. P. (2001). *Multi-agent systems for concurrent intelligent design and manufacturing*. London: Taylor and Francis.

Soller, A., Guizzardi, R., Molani, A., & Perini, A. (2004). *SCALE: Supporting community awareness, learning, and evolvement in an organizational learning environment*. Paper presented at the 6th International Conference on Learning Sciences, Santa Monica, CA.

Soulier, E. (2004). Les communautés de pratique au coeur de l'Organisation Réelle des Entreprises. *Systèmes d'Information et Management*, 9(1), 3–23.

Suganuma, T., Takahashi, H., & Shiratori, N. (2008). *Agent-based middleware for advanced ubiquitous communication services based on symbiotic comput*ing. Paper presented at the 7th IEEE International Conference on Cognitive Informatics, Palo Alto, CA.

Sugawara, K., Fujita, S., Kinoshita, T., & Shiratori, N. (2008). *A design of cognitive agents for recognizing real space - towards symbiotic computing*. Paper presented at the 7th IEEE International Conference on Cognitive Informatics, Palo Alto, CA.

Tacla, C. A., & Barthès, J.-P. (2003). A multi-agent system for acquiring and sharing lessons learned. *Computers in Industry*, 52(1), 5–16. doi:10.1016/S0166-3615(03)00065-4

Tacla, C. A., & Barthès, J. P. (2004). A multi-agent architecture for evolving memories. In *Agent-Mediated Knowledge Management* (LNAI 2926, pp. 388-404).

von Krogh, G., Nonaka, I., & Aben, M. (2001). Making the most of your company's knowledge: A strategic framework. *Long Range Planning*, 34(4), 421–439. doi:10.1016/S0024-6301(01)00059-0

Wenger, E., McDermott, R., & Snyder, W. M. (2002). *Cultivating communities of practice: A guide to managing knowledge, vol. 1* (1st ed.). Boston: Harvard Business School Press.

Young, F. W. (1985). Multidimensional scaling. In S. Kotz & N. L. Johnson (Eds.), *Encyclopedia of statistical sciences* (Vol. 5, pp. 649-659). New York: John Wiley & Sons.

This work was previously published in International Journal of Software Science and Computational Intelligence, Volume 2, Issue 1, edited by Yingxu Wang, pp. 52-71, copyright 2010 by IGI Publishing (an imprint of IGI Global).

Chapter 22
Remote Conversation Support for People with Aphasia

Nilar Aye
Myanmar Info-Tech Corporation Ltd., Myanmar

Takuro Ito
Brother Industries Ltd., Japan

Fumio Hattori
Ritsumeikan University, Japan

Kazuhiro Kuwabara
Ritsumeikan University, Japan

Kiyoshi Yasuda
Chiba Rosai Hospital, Japan

ABSTRACT

This paper proposes a remote conversation support system for people with aphasia. The aim of our system is to improve the quality of lives (QoL) of people suffering cognitive disabilities. In this framework, a topic list is used as a conversation assistant in addition to the video phone. The important feature is sharing the focus of attention on the topic list between a patient and the communication partner over the network to facilitate distant communication. The results of two preliminary experiments indicate the potential of the system.

INTRODUCTION

Recently, the concept of cognitive informatics is attracting attention as a new discipline of new generation computing paradigm (Wang & Kinsner, 2006; Wang, 2006, 2007). It studies the natural intelligence and internal information processing

mechanisms of the brain, as well as processes involved in perception and cognition. It is natural to extend the concept of the cognitive intelligence from the individual natural intelligence to the plural intelligence of group or community.

Symbiotic computing is one of the important applications of the extended cognitive informatics. It is developed to achieve an information processing environment as an interaction between humans

DOI: 10.4018/978-1-4666-0264-9.ch022

and computers as well as fundamental issues in human perception and cognition. Sugawara et al. (2008) mentioned that it is a methodology that can be realized by integrating three functions such as Ubiquitous/Network functions, the Web Functions and the Symbiotic Functions. Symbiotic computing is formal to bridge an e-Gap between Real Space (RS) and Digital Space (DS) as bringing the social heuristics and cognitive functions into DS (Sugawara et al., 2007). Based on the "basic principle of symbiosis", human society and digital space mutually interacts each other and various communication systems become widespread to help people's daily lives. Socialware is one of the core technologies of symbiotic computing together with perceptualware and networkware. It is introduced (Hattori et al., 1999) to assist in various social activities as well as to resolve limitations on network communities. Hattori et al. (2007) have proposed a framework of socialware especially to support people with cognitive disabilities.

One of the typical cognitive disabilities is aphasia. Aphasic people have difficulty in communication results from damage to the language centers of the brain. Aphasia is not only a speech disorder anymore, but also a handicap that hinders people from participating in social interaction [3]. Family members and caretakers are required to simplify language by using short, uncomplicated sentences, repeating key words or writing meaning of the words as needed while communicating with them.

In order to assist people with aphasia, a vocabulary data file is proposed to improve the quality of lives (QoL) of people suffering cognitive disabilities (Yasuda et al., 2007). Quality of life of aphasic people may be understood in terms of their participation of social affairs, emotional health, and psychological well-being (Cruice et al., 2003). The patients would like to make daily conversation with their family members, relatives or friends beyond their basic needs and wants. Enjoying conversation itself would be a basic

requirements or necessary condition of anyone's happiness to maintain their QoL. In this system, called "Rakuraku Jiyu Kaiwa (Easy, Natural Conversation)", the topic list taken from the vocabulary file is shown on a PC monitor. By pointing at the word on a PC monitor, aphasic patients enjoy daily communication with their partners.

This system is, in a sense, intended to be used for helping face to face conversation. That is, a person with aphasia and a therapist (conversation partner) talk each other in front of a PC monitor that displays the word list. In that situation, both users are required to be at the same place to conduct a conversation. This is the limitation when the patient wants to talk with other people who are not near to his/her place. From the viewpoint of increasing his/her quality of life, it is desirable for a patient to have as many opportunities as possible for a conversation. In order to achieve this objective, we have extended the concept of "Rakuraku Jiyu Kaiwa" to facilitate remote (distance) conversation over the network.

There are many conversation support systems for people with aphasia and their communication partners. Similar to our proposed framework, Spaniol et al. (2004) introduced a system to make use of distant communication in specially designed chat boards that focuses on input assistance as well as automatic prediction of the user input or adaptive content presentation. It is implemented the community initiated repair strategies in digital media. Regarding conventional chat board communication, aphasic are able to guess the word and take over the word or sentence by clicking on it. Thus, the words that aphasic desire to talk is posted on the chat board. However, the utilization of touch pads as an input assistance is still bound to costly and sensitive equipment. Besides, aphasics face problems in spelling and word finding while communicating via an asynchronous chat-board. The advantage of using our system is that aphasic people do not need to feel stress to find an appropriate word and its spelling as most of the topic list or words are displayed on the screen. Words can be added, if they are not enough to describe during conversation.

In this paper, we present the overall framework of remote conversation support for people with aphasia along with preliminary experimental results. The paper is organized as follows. Section 2 introduces aphasia and a conversation support system ("Rakuraku Jiyu Kaiwa"). Motivation of the current work and the difference between two conversation support systems are presented in Section 3. System implementation is expressed in Section 4. Methodology, results and discussions of two experiments are described in Section 5. Finally, Section 6 presents conclusion and further developments.

CONVERSATION SUPPORT FOR PEOPLE WITH APHASIA

Cognitive Ability of Aphasia

Aphasia is a cognitive disorder, usually acquired as a result of damage to the language centers of the brain due to a stroke, lack of blood supply, brain tumor or other brain injury. It involves impairment of the expression as well as understanding of language. Some types of aphasia (normal aphasia) can perceive and express language but can not name the objects correctly. The symptoms generally include disturbances in naming, reading out loud and/or comprehension of speech (Kohn & Smith, 1992). One of the most serious consequences of having moderate-to-severe aphasia is exclusion from conversation (Davidson et al., 2003).

There are different multidimensional classifications schemes fall into the categories of fluent, non fluent and other aphasias. Chapey and Hallowell (2001) describes that each category has various types of aphasia based primarily on the location of lesion or on the person's behavior as "Wernicke's aphasia", "Broca's aphasia", "Anomic aphasia" or others.

Language therapy is an essential treatment and it should be tailored to the requirements of the individual patient. Rehabilitation with a speech pathologist involves extensive exercises in which patients read, write, follow directions, and repeat what they hear.

Conversation Support for Aphasia

Recently, various prostheses have been developed to assist people with physical impairments or cognitive disabilities. One of the example applications is a conversation support system for people with aphasia proposed by Yasuda et al. (2007). This system consists of three electronic resources: a vocabulary data file named "Rakuraku Jiyu Kaiwa (Easy, Natural Conversation)", an encyclopedia, and homepages on the Internet. The data file is used as a kind of conversation assistant during conversation. The detailed information on the topic can be accessed through the encyclopedia. The presence of homepages on the Internet is vital for accessing information about recent, highly specific items of personal and professional interest during the conversation. The data file contains approximately 50,000 words; mainly 70% are proper names. Most of the words are written in Kanji. They are classified in various categories such as entertainment, sports, home and living and so on. Each of which has a tree structure consisting of four levels. These category names are listed on a PC screen and used as a tool in a conversation (Figure 1).

A typical scenario goes like this: A person with aphasia and his or her communication partner sit in front of a PC. First, they decide on a topic of a conversation, for example, "Sports". The partner clicks the category "Sports" on the first level page, and then a list of keywords of various sport names appear on the screen such as "Baseball", "Soccer", "Tennis" and "Judo". If the person points the word "Baseball" that he/she likes, the partner clicks on this word to make the names of baseball team appear. If the person points at the

Figure 1. "Rakuraku Jiyu Kaiwa"

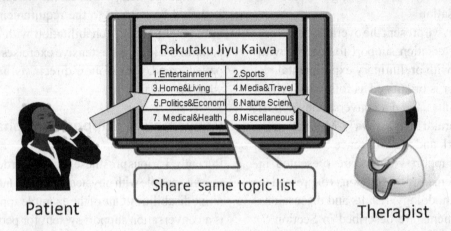

"Boston Red Sox" from the third level page, the partner opens that page to display the names of players of this team. The partner asks the aphasic's favorite or most interesting player's name. If the person points to "Daisuke Matsuzaka", the partner might complete the conversation by saying "he is a famous baseball player in Japan". In this way, a conversation continues until it reaches the lowest level of category (Figure 2) or they satisfy the conversation.

The current version of Rakuraku Jiyu Kaiwa includes more than 50,000 topics. An experiment demonstrated that the topic list is useful to improve communication between patient and therapist (Yasuda et al., 2007).

REMOTE CONVERSATION SUPPORT FOR APHACIA

We have implemented a system to support aphasic people who have difficulties in speaking. They often have problems choosing the appropriate word to express their thoughts or they may feel stress communicating verbally. We have extended the mechanism of distant communication creating more chances to partake in daily conversation along the lines of non-aphasic people to improve their QoL.

Motivating Scenario

The motivation of our system is displaying keywords that represent the topics of aphasic people's desires to talk about such things as the places where they visited, names of sports they like or songs they want to listen and so on. The objective is to increase casual conversation of the patient; not only to talk with a therapist but also with family members or friends or any others.

A therapist initiates a conversation by asking a question verbally via a real time communication tool, For example; "Which places have you visited before?" and clicks "Area and Places" button. The patient hears the question and sees two keywords such as "Overseas" and "Domestic". Next, the therapist continues questioning: "Is it inside or outside Japan?" The selected word "Domestic" is highlighted on both PC screens as the patient chose the domestic one. The therapist knows the patient's choice (place in this case) which is highlighted. Then, he clicks the same button to show the name of various places such as Hokkaido, Okinawa, Kyushu and so on (these are the names of places in Japan). The patient selects one among the list by pointing at the word on the touched screen. The conversation is carried out similar to answering a multiple choice question. It continues by asking one question after another

Figure 2. Example of a topic list category

based on the topic list although the patient has difficulties communicating verbally.

System Design

The system helps the partner to encourage aphasic people to participate a conversation by using a touch panel display. It facilitates a patient's conversation without consideration of their cognitive disabilities. To use this system, the patient's PC and the therapist's PC must be connected to each other. We use an online communication tool such as Windows NetMeeting or Skype for video and audio messaging.

In this system, we create a topic list based on the categories that would be included in conversation. The same topic list is displayed on both PC monitors where they are located separately. The word/icon that is currently being talked about is highlighted on the list of both displays. The topic a patient pays attention to is transferred to a therapist and vice versa (Figure 3). As a result,

Figure 3. Proposed system to support remote conversation

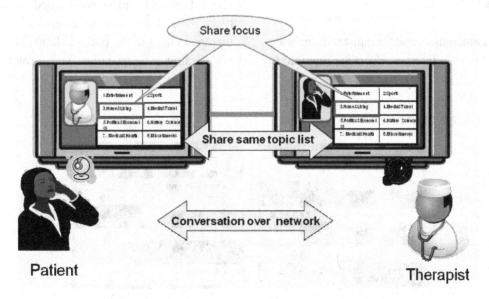

the patient can see focused topic on his/her display and select easily.

If a word or place that the patient wants to express is not included in the topic list (Figure 4), the patient may remain silent. The system allows a therapist to add new words under the current category. The topic list displayed on the patient terminal would be controlled remotely by a therapist. Currently, topic lists are collected and categorized manually. They are compiled into a set of HTML files and used during conversation. The topic list is created according to the hierarchy of categories. On the display, a list of words that belong to the selected category is shown. The system includes about one thousand words under various categories to show the effectiveness of the system such as entertainment, sports, home and living, place names, etc. Word list updating can be done during conversation.

The important feature of this system is sharing attention(focus) between patient and communication partner. The patient does not need to feel stress in speaking and finding appropriate words. In this way, our system helps the aphasic person to enjoy communication with their partners without taking into account their locations as well as their cognitive impairments.

Implementation

In this system, patient and therapist terminals are connected via the Internet. Users are required to log in the system. Depending on the type of user, patient or therapist, the display menu and functions are different. The additional functions of topic list management such as "addword", "wordlist", "clear", and "undo" are included in the therapist display to update the words during conversation. We used XMPP (Extensible Messaging and Presence Protocol) which is the base technology of Jabber, Internet standard protocol for instant messaging and presence communication (Jabber Software Foundation., 2004-a,b). Installing Jabber (OPENFIRE) (Ignite Realtime, n.d.) server (a leading Open Source, cross-platform IM server) that provides comprehensive group chat and instant messaging (IM) services together with Smack API, client library for IM and presence, based on the XMPP protocol. The advantage of this protocol is to send chat message and the topic list simultaneously. Skype is installed for audio and video messages. However, it is used independently of the current conversation system. Jabber sever receives focus information from one client and transports it to another client to share choices between a patient and a therapist (Figure 5). In addition, it keeps user's login information.

We have implemented a system to process the messages. The steps for sending and receiving messages are different from patient to therapist client (Figures 6 and 7). We defined two message types. One is for sending a topic list from the therapist client to the patient client. The other is for sending a focus point. The former type of

Figure 4. A sample of topic list

Figure 5. Overview of the system

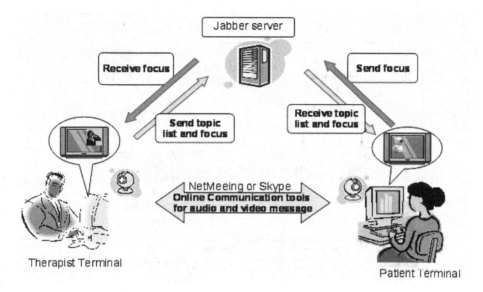

Therapist Terminal

Patient Terminal

message is unidirectional (from the therapist to the patient), and the latter is bidirectional in the sense that it is used for sending the focus point from the patient to the therapist as well as from the therapist to the patient.

The general flow of message processing is as follows. For a therapist client, the message of signaling the focus point is received, the designated word is highlighted on the display. In addition, an additional procedure is needed to select the appropriate topic list from a database that stores several topics used in conversation. After the topic list is constructed, it is sent to a patient client to display. For a patient client, when the topic list message is received, the display is updated to show the newly received topic list. Besides, when the patient touches the word on the display, the touched word is sent as the focus point to the therapist client.

EXPERIMENT

We conducted two preliminary experiments to investigate the merits of the proposed system for people with aphasia in distant communication.

Experiment 1

Method

The first experiment is carried out to see the effects of exchanging focus information, that is, attention word in the topic list. We call the attention word which is currently talking about is highlighted on the lists of both PC monitors. This experiment is conducted with people without a handicap. However, they were limited not to speak for expressing their idea. Two different implementations are used: one including the focus information (type 1) (Figure 8) and the other without focus information (type 2) (Figure 9). Participants of this study are remotely allocated and in order to simulate the speech handicap, they are instructed not to use verbal communication other than simple "yes" or "no" for a question asked. Windows NetMeeting is used for audio and video message exchange in this experiment.

Initially, the system displays the same topic list on both users' screen. The conversation is started by a partner (who acts as a therapist) by asking a question about Japanese baseball. For example: the partner asks "Let me know the name

Figure 6. Patient client's message processing

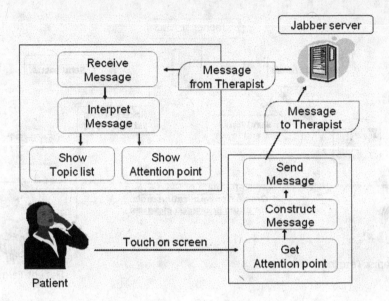

of the players you know?" A participant (who acts as a person with aphasia) chooses the player name that he/she likes by pointing at the word displayed on the touch-screen. Or, they do not reply at all that indicates thinking of something which is not included in the topic list.

In this experiment we set two sequences of questions. One is regarding the topic of sports

(Figure 10) and the other is area or place related. We tested with eight participants. Four of them were required to conduct with focus function and the other four are without focus function. During the experiment, we counted the number of times that participants answered the question by pointing to a word from the list. The question that is asked repeatedly (looped question) is marked with '*'

Figure 7. Therapist client's message processing

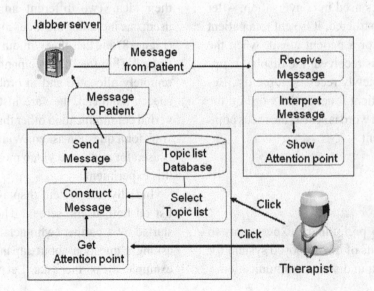

Figure 8. Display topic list including focused word

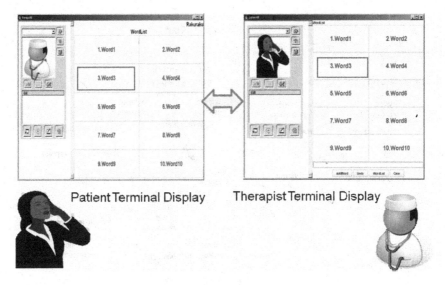

in the flowchart (Figure 10). Different questions are set for (type 1) and (type 2) to compare the results of two experiments.

Evaluation Results and Discussion

The conversation goes smoothly during experiments. But in the (type 2) experiment, as the participants could not see the attention word on his/her screen they faced difficulty responding to a question. Just displaying the plain text without highlighting a current topic makes them confused. Comparison between two functions (Figure 11) shows that the number of times required to ask a loop question is higher in those functioning without focusing. The values in this table are calculated based on the numbers of question asked per total number of respondents. Result demonstrates that

Figure 9. Display topic list excluding focused word

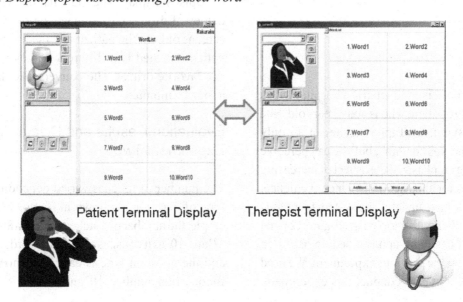

Figure 10. Sample sequence of questions

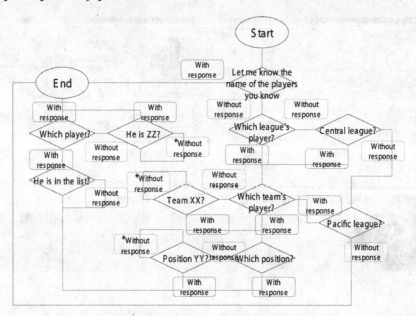

the (type 1) with focused information is easier to understand and communicate than the (type 2). Participants respond that they do not need to feel stress to find a correct word to express their thought when they see the focus word. Besides, they replied, the system is easy to use. However, it is suggested that it would be more convenient if the system display both the topic list and related image together instead of showing only the text.

Experiment 2

Method

The experiment 2 is conducted at a hospital with a female aphasic patient who is sixty years old. She have typical symptom of aphasia; She can talk only simple words "yes" or "no", but she can perceive language. We emphasized the aspect of increasing opportunities for aphasics and their convenience. Therefore, we have updated the system to include pictures together with a topic list (Figure 12) that is to be used easily by aphasic people based on responses from the previous experiment. We used two separate rooms to conduct this experiment.

Each room has a PC connected with a local area network. We used Skype, an online communication tool, to enhance the quality of audio and video messaging.

In this experiment, a therapist asked several questions (Figure 13) and the patient replied by using a touch panel display. For example, a therapist asked a question "What is your favorite drink?" and then clicked "Drinks" button on the therapist's display. The topic list that consists of names of drink and its images appeared on the screens of both the patient and the therapist. The patient touched two different names to express her favorite drinks. The conversation lasted for about 15 minutes.

Evaluation Results and Discussion of Experiment Two

The number of touches varied depending on the type of question as shown in Figure 13. For example, the number of touches for question number '7' are '10' as it consists of various words to choose and the question type is easy. But, no response for question number '10' and '4' as it is either too

Figure 11. Average times of asking looped questions

	Q.1	Q.2	Q.3	Q.4	Q.5	Average
Without focusing function	2.8	2.5	4.1	4.5	4.4	3.7
With focusing function	1.5	1.4	1.6	1.3	1.1	1.4
Difference	1.3	1.1	2.5	3.2	3.3	2.3

Figure 12. Snapshot of screen in the experiment 2

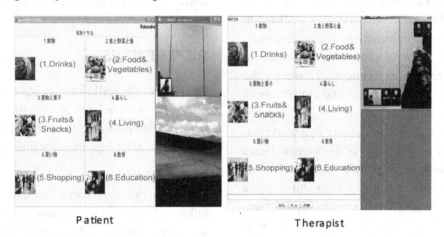

Patient   Therapist

Figure 13. Number of times of a patient's touch to the question

Number	Question	Times of Patient's touch
No.1	Where are you from?	2
No.2	What is your hobby?	3
No.3	Have you visited a hot spring resort?	4
No.4	What sports do you like?	0
No.5	Do you like Rakugo?	2
No.6	What is your favorite drink?	2
No.7	What is your favorite fruit?	10
No.8	Where do you go shopping?	1
No.9	Do you know the name of the prime minister?	1
No.10	What are you interested in?	0

difficult to answer or the scope is too broad or not interesting at all. The patient answered eight questions out of ten in this experiment. It shows that conversation went well and the patient could convey her feelings/thoughts easily to a partner in a different room. This experiment result indicates that the system can help the conversation between a patient and a therapist in distant places.

CONCLUSION

We proposed a remote conversation support system for people with aphasia which has extended the concept of "Rakuraku Jiyu Kaiwa". A mechanism of sharing focused information between two users is introduced. We have shown the usefulness of the system through experiments. However, the system is limited as a one to one conversation. Sharing attention word among group of users or allowing many people to include in a conversation would be an extension of the system. Since language therapy is one of the essential treatments of aphasic people, it is useful both showing the topic list and playing audio (pronunciation of this word) at the same time. By doing so, patients would have a chance to say or repeat what they hear as speech rehabilitation.

For future studies it would be advantageous to expand upon the current research by taking consideration on some facts. Fruitfulness of a conversation depends on the number of topics (words). To get into deep conversation, a lot of words which might appear in the conversation are necessary. Creation of a topic list that covers a wide range of conversation topics is essential to become an effective conversation support system. We are trying to develop topic lists automatically from Web resources. Not only the word but also a sentence or phrases or interesting pictures to be displayed according to the severity of patients or difference of patient's cognitive abilities would be a future work (Nilar Aye et al., 2008). In addition, it is desirable to implement bi-directional conversation:

people with aphasia can ask a question by selecting a possible generated question from a template with the help of ontology definitions. We will introduce a semantic conversion mechanism to bridge the knowledge gap between conversation users.

ACKNOWLEDGMENTS

The authors would like to thank Ms. Mika Masuyama of Kusatsu General Hospital for her support of the experiments at the hospital. The authors would also like to thank Mr. Tasuku Koyama for constructing the topic list and conducting the second experiment.

REFERENCES

Chapey, R., & Hallowell, B. (2001). *Language intervention strategies in aphasia and related neurogenic communication disorders* (4th ed.). Baltimore, MD: Lippincott Williams & Wilkins.

Cruice, M., Worrall, L., Hickson, L., & Murison, R. (2003). Finding a focus for quality of life with aphasia: Social and emotional health, and psychological well-being. *Aphasiology*, *17*(4), 333–353. doi:10.1080/02687030244000707

Davidson, B., Worrall, L., & Hickson, L. (2003). Identifying the communication activities of older people with aphasia: Evidence from naturalistic observation. *Aphasiology*, *17*(3), 243–264. doi:10.1080/729255457

Hattori, F., Kuwabara, K., Kuwahara, N., Abe, S., & Yasuda, K. (2007). Socialware for people with disabilities. In *Proceedings of the 6th International Conference on Cognitive Informatics (ICCI'07)* (pp. 321-326).

Hattori, F., Ohguro, T., Yokoo, M., Matsubara, S., & Yoshida, S. (1999). Socialware: Multiagent systems for supporting network communities. *Communications of the ACM*, *42*(3), 55–61. doi:10.1145/295685.295701

Jabber Software Foundation. (2004a). *Extensible messaging and presence protocol (XMPP): Core* (Tech. Rep.). Retrieved November 17, 2008, from http://www.ietf.org/rfc/rfc3920.txt

Jabber Software Foundation. (2004b). *Extensible messaging and presence protocol (XMPP): Instant messaging and presence* (Tech. Rep.). Retrieved November 17, 2008, from http://www.ietf.org/rfc/rfc3921.txt

Kohn, S. E., & Smith, K. L. (1992). On the notion of "aphasia syndrome". In S. E. Kohn (Ed.), *Conduction aphasia* (pp. 1-18). London: Lawrence Erlbaum Associates.

Nilar, A., Hattori, F., & Kuwabara, K. (2008). Bridging semantic gap in distant communication: Ontology-based approach. In *Agent and multi-agent systems: Technologies and applications: Second KES International Symposium, KES-AMSTA 2008* (LNAI 4953, pp. 252-260).

Realtime, I. (n.d.). *Openfire*. Retrieved November 17, 2009, from http://www.igniterealtime.org/projects/openfire/index.jsp

Sorin-Peters, R., & Behrmann, M. (1995). Change in perception of communication abilities of aphasic patients and their families. *Aphasiology, 9*(6), 565–575. doi:10.1080/02687039508248715

Spaniol, M., Springer, L., Klamma, R., & Jarke, M. (2004). SOCRATES: Barrier free communities of aphasics on the internet. In K. Miesenberger et al. (Eds.), *ICCHP 2004* (LNCS 3118, pp. 1024-1031).

Sugawara, K., Fujita, S., & Hara, H. (2007). A concept of symbiotic computing and its application to telework. In *Proceedings of the 6th International Conference on Cognitive Informatics (ICCI'07)* (pp. 302-311).

Sugawara, K., Fujita, S., & Hara, H. (2007). A concept of symbiotic computing and its application to telework. In *Proceedings of the 6th International Conference on Cognitive Informatics (ICCI'07)* (pp. 302-311).

Sugawara, K., Fujita, S., Kinoshta, T., & Shiratori, N. (2008). A design of cognitive agents for recognizing real space towards symbiotic computing. In *Proceedings of the 7th International Conference on Cognitive Informatics (ICCI'08)* (pp. 277-285).

Wang, Y. (2006). Cognitive informatics: Towards future generation computers that think and feel. In *Proceedings of the IEEE 5th International Conference on Cognitive Informatics* (pp. 3-7).

Wang, Y. (2007). The theoretical framework of cognitive informatics. *International Journal of Cognitive Informatics and Natural Intelligence, 1*(1), 1–27.

Wang, Y., & Kinsner, W. (2006). Recent advances in cognitive informatics. *IEEE Transactions on Systems, Man and Cybernetics. Part C, Applications and Reviews, 36*(2), 121–123. doi:10.1109/TSMCC.2006.871120

Yasuda, K., Nemoto, T., Takenaka, K., Mitachi, M., & Kuwabara, K. (2007). Effectiveness of vocabulary data file, encyclopedia, and Internet homepages in a conversation-support system for people with moderate-to-severe aphasia. *Aphasiology, 21*(9), 867–882. doi:10.1080/02687030600783024

This work was previously published in International Journal of Software Science and Computational Intelligence, Volume 2, Issue 1, edited by Yingxu Wang, pp. 72-85, copyright 2010 by IGI Publishing (an imprint of IGI Global).

Chapter 23
Estimating which Object Type a Sensor Node is Attached to in Ubiquitous Sensor Environment

Takuya Maekawa
NTT Communication Science Laboratories, Japan

Yutaka Yanagisawa
NTT Communication Science Laboratories, Japan

Takeshi Okadome
NTT Communication Science Laboratories, Japan

ABSTRACT

By simply attaching sensor nodes to physical objects with no information about the objects, the method proposed in this paper infers the type of the physical indoor objects and the states they are in. Assuming that an object has its own states that have transitions represented by a state transition diagram, we prepare the state transition diagrams for such indoor objects as a door, a drawer, a chair, and a locker. The method determines the presumed state transition diagram from prepared diagrams that matches sensor data collected from people's daily living for a certain period. A 2 week experiment shows that the method achieves high accuracy of inferring objects to which sensor nodes are attached. The method allows us to introduce ubiquitous sensor environments by simply attaching sensor nodes to physical objects around us.

INTRODUCTION

In ubiquitous sensor environments, we can effectively manage behaviors of applications by using information about the type of object a sensor node is attached to. In fact, many studies focus on

DOI: 10.4018/978-1-4666-0264-9.ch023

context-aware services that depend on the types, states, and state changes of physical objects in a home where sensor nodes are attached to the objects. An example service is one that issues a caution when a door is left open at midnight. However, when hundreds of sensor nodes are attached to objects, we cannot manually tell the nodes what types of objects they are attached to.

The advances that have been made in wireless communication, sensing, and power-saving technologies mean it will not be long before we can employ many small and cheap sensor nodes. In anticipation of such a development, we propose a system framework named *Tag and Think* (TnT).

With this approach we can automatically infer the types of objects and the states they are in simply by attaching general-purpose sensor nodes to indoor objects about which we have no information. In TnT, after collecting sensor data from a general-purpose sensor node that has been attached to a physical object for a certain period of time, the method determines the presumed model of the object type from prepared models that matches the sensor data. Also, the method estimates the state changes that occurred in the object throughout the period. For example, if a sensor node is attached to a door, our method infers the type of object to which the node is attached and detects state changes of the door, e.g., 'door open' and 'door close.' Converting raw sensor data into human understandable symbols such as 'door open' is important in human-machine symbiosis. General-purpose sensor nodes equipped with such widely used sensors as accelerometers and illuminometers have an advantage over object-specific nodes in terms of deployment cost. They can reduce the time and effort spent on introducing sensor network environments because the sensor nodes are simply attached to objects. On the other hand, most object-specific sensors such as magnetic door sensors and window sensors are required to be installed in appropriate position and direction. Accelerometers and illuminometers are most common in entertainment, security, and maintenance purposes, have been growing in importance. This means we can expect both their cost and size to decrease. As ubiquitous and sensor environments become more common, object-specific nodes will be embedded in many objects during the manufacturing process. However, before the environments will become common, our framework may be useful as the first step to the ubiquitous computing deployment. We introduce and evaluate a method designed to infer object type and state changes by using knowledge constructed based on a person's common knowledge.

BACKGROUND AND GOAL

Obtaining states and state changes of objects is becoming possible by attaching cheap sensor nodes to indoor objects (Intille et al., 2003). This has triggered surveillance studies concerned with end-user sensor installation. The following comments on end-user installation can be found in Beckmann (2004): "the monetary and time cost of professional installation is prohibitive for non-critical applications" and "leveraging the fact that an end-user is a domain expert for his own home can lead to an application better tailored to his needs or preferences." However, some problems have arisen as regards end-user installation. For example, Beckmann et al. (2004) revealed that some end-users could not understand the meaning of the association itself in the experiment, where a bar-code reader and bar-codes attached to sensor nodes were used to associate a sensor node and the type of object to which the node is attached. Also, it takes an average of 84 minutes for participants to deploy ten sensor nodes in an experiment (this is not only the time needed for the association). If there are dozens of nodes, manual association will become a burden for end-users. Tapia et al. (2004) also mention that installation without association would dramatically reduce the installation time when engineers install the sensors in a home.

Our goal is to infer what type of object a sensor node is attached to simply by attaching the sensor node to the object. To achieve this, we prepare models of object types that can be used in every end-user's home throughout the world. By comparing the models with sensor data obtained from a sensor node for a certain period and by estimating a presumed model that matches the sensor data, we infer the type of object. However, object type inference is insufficient to achieve context-aware applications. In general, the services provided by activity based context-aware applications are classified into two kinds: (1) those triggered by states and state changes of objects (Kidd et al., 1999) and (2) those triggered by the users' Activity of Daily Living (ADL), which is inferred from sensor outputs and teacher signals. To achieve the latter services, in most cases, we need not add semantics to the type and states of an object to which a sensor node is attached. Tapia et al. (2004), for example, adopt a supervised learning approach to infer ADL by using a sensor that detects state changes of an object, where users construct teacher signals by labeling their daily living, e.g., 7:45 to 8:00 in the lavatory. To achieve the former services, we add semantics to states and state changes of objects, i.e., we infer the states and state changes of objects in this paper. By achieving the goal, we can provide services triggered by semantics added to the states and state changes of an object, e.g., turning on a light when a user *opens* a *door*.

APPROACH

The ways in which an object is used have their own characteristics. When a person brushes his/her teeth, for example, the acceleration obtained from a sensor node attached to the brush exhibits its own frequency components. Also, when a person opens a door, a sensor node attached to the door may detect a rotation and an illuminance change simultaneously. With TnT, we infer the type and state changes of an object by detecting 'the ways in which the object is used' and by comparing them with the models of objects. Note that the state changes of an object occur while the object is being used. We can divide object types into three categories according to their characteristics of usage.

C1: Such object types as toothbrushes and shoes that move repetitively.

C2: Such object types as doors and chairs whose characteristics are represented by a combination of characteristic sensor outputs.

C3: Such object types as tables and rulers that have no characteristic motion or whose characteristic phenomena cannot be detected by generic sensors.

We can determine the characteristics of the repetitive motion of such C1 objects as toothbrushes by calculating sensor signals. We can use research that detects such repetitive movements as "walking" and "bike riding" in the ADL estimation (Bao, 2004) to detect the characteristic repetitive motion of C1 objects. That is, we can infer the types and state changes of C1 objects by modeling the object types using the Fourier components of acceleration obtained when a person uses the objects. On the other hand, we build the models of C2 objects based on a person's basic knowledge by abstracting sensor outputs. We can roughly imagine what kind of sensor outputs are produced when such C2 objects as doors are used. When a person opens a door, for example, a sensor node attached to the door may detect a 'rotation' and an 'illuminance change' simultaneously. This paper focuses on how to build models of C2 objects and infer object types in C2.

Let us explain how to model object types in C2. We add semantics to states and state changes of the objects in addition to inferring the types of objects. For each object type, we prepare a model, which has the states and state changes with their semantics. Although we can build the models by using supervised learning as a simple approach, it requires the preparation of teacher signals corresponding to the sensor data obtained in the end-user's home for each home because end-users' home environments differ. Many ADL estimation studies use teacher signals that end-users generate by labeling their daily living. The Experience Sampling Method (ESM) has been proposed to support teacher signal generation by end-users (Intille, Rondoni, Kukla, Anacona, & Bao, 2003).

With ESM, a handheld device is employed to label end-users' activities. Unlike the labeling of ADLs, however, end-users cannot easily label the sensor data obtained from a huge number of sensor nodes attached to objects. Also, the models generated by an end-user can be used only in the end-user's home environment. We also have experience in labeling the state changes of objects by using a video annotation tool (Anvil, http://www.dfki. de/~kipp/anvil/) in an environment where video cameras and forty-four sensor nodes are installed. We have found that it takes up to seven hours for us to label ten minutes of sensor data. Labeling by end-users in homes is not practical.

Some studies generate models of physical phenomena without end-user labeling. Philipose, et al. (2004), for example, model an activity as a sequence of used objects when a user performs an activity by extracting knowledge from the web. Tea making is modeled as a sequence: using a kettle; and using sugar, lemon, or milk. The model can be used in any environment. Let us imagine how we should model C2 objects, which can also be used in any environment. For example, a door has two states; "Opened" and "Closed." When the door state transits from "Opened" to "Closed," the accelerator and illuminometer on a sensor node attached to the door simultaneously detect a rotation and an illumination change, respectively. The model, which anyone can imagine based on his/her general knowledge, can be shared by most doors in the world and has semantics added to its states. In actual environments, some phenomena must occur that do not exactly match the above model constructed based on general knowledge. However, we can cope with the problem by adopting a robust method to infer the type and state changes of an object. We can easily build such models which can be used in many environments by using general knowledge but they would include noises. On the other hand, we can build accurate models by using supervised learning but these are costly and environment specific. An approach that uses a robust method and noisy models, which we

can easily build based on general knowledge, is more practical than ML approaches using a teacher signal constructed by end-users.

This paper uses the models that we constructed based on experience and general knowledge to infer the type and state changes of an object. Then, we examine how effective the models constructed by participants in an experiment are. In the next section, we propose a model description method that anyone can use. In the section of inference method, we propose a method for inferring the types and state changes of objects to cope with manually built noisy models. The contributions of this work are outlined above.

MODEL FOR OBJECT TYPE

We selected a state transition diagram to model object types in C2. Diagrams can enable us to model the states and state changes of C2 objects intuitively. Henceforth, we refer to a 'state change' as a 'transition.'

DIAGRAMS FOR OBJECT TYPES

Figure 1 shows an example of a door state transition diagram obtained in the experiment described below. The diagram has "Opened" and "Closed" states, and these states transit to each other when a person "Opens" and "Closes" the door. The balloon from the transition "Open" shows three groups of events (hereafter called *event groups*) that can be detected by a sensor node attached to the door when the transition (Open) occurs. Formally, a transition is defined by a set of event groups. The first and second groups represent cases where a person walks through a door. The third represents a case where a person walks to the door, opens it, and then walks away from or through the door. That is, we can describe multiple event groups to cope with various situations. 'Acc. rotate,' 'illumi.bright,' and 'illumi.dark' denote

Figure 1. Diagram for a door obtained in an experiment

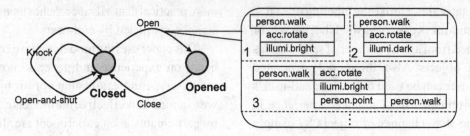

'a rotate motion' detected by an accelerometer on the node, 'an illuminance increase' detected by an illuminometer on the node, and 'an illuminance decrease' detected by the illuminometer, respectively. 'Person.walk' and 'person.point' respectively denote 'a person walking' and 'some motion that the person performs in a location' detected by other devices such as shoe mounted sensors and floor pressure sensors. An event group consists of events that have temporal relationships. In the first event group of "Open," 'acc. rotate' and 'illumi.bright' occur simultaneously with 'person.walk.'

SENSOR DATA AND DIAGRAMS

Here we explain the relationship between sensor data and the diagrams. A transition in the diagram corresponds to a time interval during which the attached sensor node detects some activity (a segment where a signal has large amplitude). A state in a diagram corresponds to a time interval during which the sensor node attached to the object detects no activity. Let us explain the sensor signal terms with respect to Figure 2, which shows the signals produced by a sensor node attached to a door when the door is twice "Opened," twice "Closed," and twice "Opened-and-shut," where ax_i and az_i $(i = 1, ..., 6)$ are activities obtained by the x- and z-axis accelerometers and ai_i is an activity obtained by the illuminometer (we omitted the y-axis from Figure 2). An acceleration activity aa_i $(i = 1, ..., 6)$ is a union of ax_i, ay_i, and az_i. We call a set of activities that occur almost simultaneously an *activity group*. In Figure 2, each ag_i $(i = 1, ..., 6)$ is an activity group, e.g., ag_1 is an event group consisting of aa_1 and ai_1. For simplicity, we omit events involving people walking from Figure 2. Activity groups correspond to the transitions (event groups) of the diagram. For example, ag_1 and ag_4 correspond to the door transition "Open." When inferring a type of object, we compare the activity groups with the event groups in the diagram. However, because event groups are described in symbols, e.g., 'acc.rotate' and 'illumi. bright,' we abstract activities into symbols for the comparison, e.g., aa_1 is abstracted into 'acc. rotate.' By ordering all activity groups in time, we obtain a sequence such as ag_1, ag_2, ag_3, $\cdots$. The inference method proposed in the next section (1) extracts activities from sensor data, (2) abstracts the activities, (3) groups the activities, (4) orders the activity groups, and (5) selects a presumed diagram that matches the activity group sequence.

Let us consider "Open-and-shut" as one activity group in Figure 2. "Open-and-shut" denotes a phenomenon where a person closes a door just after opening it. Naturally, we can divide "Open-and-shut" into "Open" and "Close." However, it is difficult for a simple signal processing technique to recognize ax_3 and az_3 in Figure 2 as two phenomena. We thus simply regard one activity group as one phenomenon.

Figure 2. Signals from a sensor node attached to a door

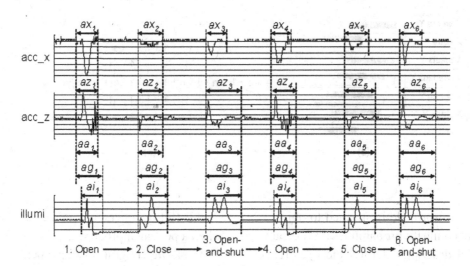

EVENT GROUPS

Here we explain how to represent event groups. First, we describe the events that we prepared, namely the events 'illumi.bright,' 'illumi.dark,' 'illumi.bright_dark,' and 'illumi.dark_bright' that an illuminometer can detect. For example, we describe 'illuminance increases' and 'illuminance decreases' as 'illumi.bright' and 'illumi.dark.'

An 'illumi.bright_dark' event represents the illuminance returning to its initial level after it had increased. We prepare motion events; 'acc. slide_horizontal,' 'acc.rotate,' 'acc.drop,' 'acc. fall,' 'acc.raise,' 'acc.vibrate,' and 'acc.other' that represent the 'horizontal slide of the object,' 'horizontal rotation of the object,' 'free fall of the object,' 'falling over of the object,' 'vertical movement from a lower to a higher place,' 'minute vibration of the object,' and 'other motion.' We selected these events because we can detect them with a high degree of accuracy from acceleration signals. Also, we can accurately detect only an early part of a movement because of the accumulated error.

For example, "Open-and-shut" in Figure 2 includes rotations of the door in two directions where the first occurs just before the second.

However, because the above restriction makes accurate detection of the second rotation difficult, we use only the first (acc.rotate) to represent these rotations. We can use events related to people walking detected by other devices. We prepare events "person.walk" and "person.point."

The events in an event group have temporal relationships. For example, the first event group of "Open" in Figure 1 includes 'acc.rotate' and 'illumi.bright,' which occur simultaneously while 'person.walk' is occurring. We represent such temporal relationships between events using Allen's interval logic (Allen, 1983). Allen defined the thirteen relationships between temporal intervals in Figure 3 (a) considering the inverses. For example, the relationship "X before Y" indicates that event X occurs before event Y. We use the interval logic to describe temporal relationships between events.

The event groups have occurrence probabilities that are important in terms of object type inference. For example, let us assume that a characteristic of an event group eg_A that often occurs in object type A is similar to that of an event group eg_B that rarely occurs in object type B. If only eg_A occurs many times in object A to which a sensor node is attached, we cannot easily judge

Figure 3. (a) Allen's interval logic and (b) distances between interval relations

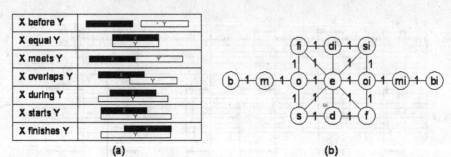

whether the sensor node is attached to object A or B without taking the probabilities into account. So, a model descriptor defines the occurrence probabilities as binary, 'low' or 'high,' based on his/her experience for easy description. For example, in the diagram of a door constructed in the following experiment, the probability of an event group in an 'Open' transition, which corresponds to a situation where a person opens a door after chatting in front of the door, is defined as 'low.' As above, in the following experiment, the participants describe occurrence probabilities of event groups taking their situations into consideration.

COMMON TRANSITIONS

All object types have common transitions, e.g., illuminance around an object changes when a person approaches the object. Portable or mobile object types also have common transitions. A cup and an alarm clock, for example, are portable objects that have such transitions as "a person carries it" and "it drops from a higher place." A chair is a mobile object that has such transitions as "a person moves it" and "it falls over." In a diagram, if an object is specified as portable or mobile, all the states of that object have corresponding transitions. Therefore, a descriptor need not actually describe many common transitions in a diagram. All, portable, and mobile objects have the following transitions:

All {hit by a person, changes its illuminance when a person approaches}

Portable {migrates (with a person walking), migrates (without a person walking), falls, falls over}

Mobile {migrates (with a person walking), falls over}

A model descriptor can define these transitions as event groups that do not change the state in the diagrams. That is, they are loop-back transitions. Also, a descriptor can set the occurrence probabilities of event groups for each object.

INFERENCE METHOD

Activity Detection

Many speech recognition studies extract voice activities from voice signals (Sohn, 1999). These studies use voice and noise models generated by supervised learning to determine the model that matches the test data. We adopt the same approach. However, end-users cannot easily prepare sensor data segments that correspond to activities. Instead of preparing these segments, we judge whether a test data segment includes an activity by comparing the data with a model generated from noise sensor data obtained while the inhabitants are away from home. We generate a model as a Gaussian Mixture Model (GMM) by using the Fourier components of a certain period of a sensor data segment for each sensor type (Bilmes, 1998). We judge whether a data segment includes an activity by computing the log likelihood between the model and the Fourier components of the segment.

Activity Abstraction

Activities extracted from acceleration data are abstracted into the events described above. To detect 'acc.rotate' and 'acc.slide_horizontal,' we calculate the trajectories of the sensor node by integration using the Runge-Kutta method. We can know the vertical direction from DC components of x-, y-, and z-axis acceleration data. Thus, we can know direction of a trajectory by comparing it to the vertical direction. We determine 'acc.drop,' 'acc.fall,' and 'acc. raise' by calculating trajectories together with the vertical acceleration. We also determine 'acc.vibrate' by judging whether the activity interval consists almost only of high frequency components. In this implementation, we use the heuristic method to detect 'acc.vibrate.' However, we can model general vibration by using the same method as the noise sensor data modeling in the activity detection. Activities extracted from the illuminometer are also abstracted into the events described above. The illuminometer we use produces integer values from 0 to 1024 as illuminance. When the illuminance increases (decreases) by more than twenty during an activity, we recognize the activity as 'illumi.bright' ('illumi.dark'). The twenty is the average amplitude of noise sensor data times ten. To recognize 'illumi.bright_dark' and 'illumi.dark_bright,' we determine whether the illuminance returns or not.

We combined the abstracted acceleration and illuminance activities that overlap in time into an activity group, where the relations among the abstracted activities are represented by Allen's interval logic. After that, we obtain an activity group sequence by ordering activity groups in time.

Object Type Inference

We used the Viterbi algorithm, which is fast and robust, to bridge sensor data, and manually built state transition diagrams, which may include noises. The Viterbi algorithm uses the dynamic programming technique to find the most likely state sequence from an observed sequence when a Hidden Markov Model (HMM) is given. In our method, an HMM corresponds to a state transition diagram and an observed sequence to an abstracted activity group sequence. Also, a state sequence corresponds to an event group sequence (transition sequence) because a state transition diagram outputs symbols (an event group) when a state transits. The method calculates the likelihood $P(D, AG)$ of an activity group sequence $AG = ag_1, ag_2, \cdots, ag_T$ against each diagram $D = (A, ST)$ and outputs an object type whose diagram has the largest likelihood as an inference result, where

$A = \{a_i\}$, where $a_i = 1 / N$ is the initial state probability of a state s_i $(1 \leq i \leq N)$,

$ST = \{t_{n,m}\}$, where $t_{n,m}$ is a transition from state s_n to s_m $(1 \leq n \leq N, 1 \leq m \leq N)$, and

$t_{n,m} = \{eg_i\}$, where eg_i is an event group involved in $t_{n,m}$ $(i \geq 0)$.

We explain above symbols by using the example diagram (HMM) in Figure 1. The HMM has two states s_1 and s_2 (*Closed* and *Opened*). Thus, N is 2 in the HMM. The HMM also has four transitions $t_{1,2}$, $t_{2,1}$, $t_{1,1}$, and $t_{1,1}$ (*Open, Close, Open-and-shut,* and *Knock*). Each transition has some event groups. In Figure 1, only three event groups eg_0, eg_1, and eg_2 included in $t_{1,2}$ (*Open*) are shown.

The likelihood $P(D, AG)$ is calculated in the Viterbi algorithm:

$$P(D, AG) = \max_{1 \leq i \leq N}(p_{i,T+1}),$$

$$p_{i,j} = \max_{1 \leq k \leq N}(p_{k,j-1} + Sim(t_{k,i}, ag_{j-1}, Th)),$$
$$(1 \leq i \leq N, 2 \leq j \leq T+1),$$

$$Sim(t_{n,m}, ag_i, Th) = \max_{j, e_j > Th}(sim(ag_i, eg_j) \cdot e_j),$$

where Th is a threshold, and $p_{i,0}$ is a_i when j is 1, $sim(ag_i, eg_j)$ is a similarity function between ag_i and eg_j, and e_i is the occurrence probability of eg_i. We define the similarity function $sim(ag_i, eg_j)$ as the inverse number of the conversion cost from ag_i to eg_j. Freksa (1991) defines the distance between interval relations, which is used for similarity scene search in video search studies. Figure 3 (b) shows the distances between the 13 interval relations ('b' means 'before' and 'bi' means the 'inverse of before'). Distance between two nodes in the graph represents distance between their corresponding interval relations. For example, distance between 'before' and 'meets' relations is one. As shown in Figure 3 (a), 'before' is very similar with 'meets.' On the other hand, distance between 'before' and 'equal' relations is three. Thus, 'before' is not similar with 'equal' as shown in Figure 3 (a). We use the distance between interval relations as the conversion cost, and we set the cost of adding or deleting an event at twenty and that of converting a sensor event to another at five. We selected values that yielded a good inference result in a preliminary test. Let us show an example of conversion. The cost of conversion from an activity group (illumi.dark meets acc. rotate) to an event group (illumi.dark equal acc. raise) is seven: the conversion cost rom 'meets' to 'equal' is two and that from 'acc.rotate' to 'acc. raise' is five. If an event group includes a person's walking event, we must select a corresponding walking event that occurs in the environment. When using sensor nodes that cannot detect their locations, we cannot determine the corresponding walking event detected by other sensors. In that case, we select the walking event that maximizes $sim(ag, eg)$. We ignore event groups whose occurrence probabilities are lower than

Th because many diagrams are applied to the above procedure. After calculating $D_{\max}$, which has the largest $P(D, AG)$, the method outputs the transition sequence with the largest likelihood as an inference result by applying the procedure to $D_{\max}$ again where Th is 0. Here, occurrence probabilities are represented as 'low' or 'high' in manually constructed diagrams. We set Th at a value between $e_{(low)}$ and $e_{(high)}$.

EVALUATION

This section clarifies the effectiveness and weakness of models constructed by participants in experiments and verifies what kinds of object types are suited to the diagram.

EXPERIMENTAL ENVIRONMENT

The sensor nodes that we have developed are equipped with an illuminometer and a three-axis accelerometer. The nodes also have communication modules that send observed sensor data to a storage server. A sensor node sends sensor data values every 60 milliseconds. Figure 4 (a) shows a sensor node. We implemented a sensor network system in an office as illustrated in Figure 4 (b). To enable people to continue working, we included desks, chairs, and lockers. In this room, one to four workers (not researchers) maintain the sensor network system and undertake their work from 9 a.m. to 5 p.m. every weekday. We installed a sensor floor system to cover the room, which enabled us to leverage a person walking by detecting floor pressure. Although floor pressure sensors are not widely used and may be an obstacle to the introduction of ubiquitous environments, we used a sensor floor system in this experiment because it permits us to collect sensor data naturally without imposing a burden on workers and thus adequately evaluate the

Figure 4. (a) Sensor node (b) Sensing room

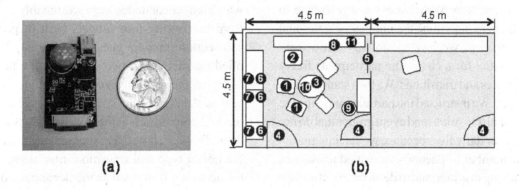

(a)   **(b)**

method. However, we can construct TnT with only sensor nodes by detecting a person walking via sensor nodes attached to slippers or shoes. That is, after inferring that the sensor nodes are attached to the slippers, we leverage the person's walking obtained from the nodes. We have already implemented a walking detection system that uses a walking model constructed by supervised learning. We can infer that a node is attached to a slipper by using the model.

Figure 4 (b) also depicts the positions of objects with sensor nodes. The workers attached sensor nodes to indoor objects categorized as C2 and C3. Objects categorized as C2 are the backs of straight chairs (Figure 4-b-1), the back of a swivel chair on casters (Figure 4-b-2), the inside of a trash can lid (Figure 4-b-3), interior doors (Figure 4-b-4), an interior sliding door (Figure 4-b-5), the outside of locker doors (Figure 4-b-6), locker interiors (Figure 4-b-7), and the outside of a drawer (Figure 4-b-8). Objects categorized as C3 are a cup (Figure 4-b-9), a table (Figure 4-b-10), and an alarm clock (Figure 4-b-11). The categorizations as C2 and C3 are simply our predictions. Also, the one door is the different type of product from the other two doors and the two straight chairs are the same type of product. This experiment simulates performance of our method in home environments because C2 objects in this experiment are also common in home environments.

MODEL PREPARATION

Three experimental participants built graphic models such as that shown in Figure 1 by using drawing software (Microsoft PowerPoint) after reading a document that explains how to build the models. We then manually converted the models into an XML like format. Participants A and B have worked in an IT company. Participant C has only limited experience in using computers, and so we explained to her how to use PowerPoint. Each participant built thirteen models (the inside of a locker door, a drawer interior, the seat of swivel chair with casters, the seat of a straight chair, the back of a swivel chair without casters, the seat of a swivel chair without casters, the seat of a rocking chair, the back of a rocking chair, a dressing table mirror, the outside of a locker door that opens downward, the inside of a locker door that opens downward, a window frame, and a mirror mounted on a cabinet that opens upward) in addition to the eleven models seen in Figure 4 (b) and the common transitions. We selected object types whose instances have characteristic movements that occur when a user employs them from about four thousands products stocked by an on-line furniture shop KAGOO (http://www.kokugai.com/kagoo). Note that, we did not distinguish object types whose instances have similar movements and roles, e.g., a desk drawer and a cabinet drawer. We provided the participants the top ten verbs related to each noun (object) extracted from 1.4 G bytes of textual corpora (the New York Times) as a reference to allow them to determine the number of states and transitions, e.g., we gave 'sit down,' 'take a seat,' 'get up,' etc., for a chair. The participants freely named states and transitions. We then standardized the names. We instructed the participants to ignore exceptional transitions and event groups that do not occur in our daily lives because we can imagine an infinite number of phenomena related to objects, e.g., kicking in a door, and to describe event groups taking various situations into consideration. The latter instruction enabled the participants to note a variety of situations in a state transition. We explained that with examples. For example, 'acc. rotate' and 'illumi.bright' occur simultaneously in the first event group of "Open" in Figure 1, while 'acc.rotate' and 'illumi.dark' occur simultaneously in the second event group. The illuminance around a node attached to a door increases or decreases depending on the environment when the door is opened. Both situations should be included in the transition to build models that can be used in any environment.

It took seven, four, and ten days, respectively, for participants A, B and C to build the twenty four models. The average numbers of event groups per transition were 5.8, 3.4, and 3.6. We confirmed that, for an object type, almost all of the models constructed by the participants were the same as regards their diagram shape. We show one exception; the diagram of a trash can built by participant B includes two states: "Opened" and "Closed," while the diagram of a trash can built by participant A includes a state and a loop-back transition of 'Throw out the garbage.'

EXPERIMENT

Settings

We collected sensor data for successive five days from the eighteen sensor nodes depicted in Figure

4(b). By using the data, we inferred the model to which the sensor nodes were presumably attached from the twenty-four models built in previous sub-section (random guess ratio is 0.04). We applied the method to two cases. For the first, we executed the method five times using one day's sensor data. For the second, we executed the method four times using two successive day's data. Table 1 shows the average accuracies for the object type and transition inferences, where the accuracy is defined as the percentage of correctly classified instances. For the objects whose types we successfully inferred, we also inferred their state transitions. By checking a recorded video, the workers evaluated the 1,244 inference results individually for the transitions. Although an inference result (transition sequence) includes such common transitions as "hit by a person" and "changes its illuminance" described above, we ignored them in the evaluation because most are not important for ubicomp applications.

Model Segregation

Basically, the inference accuracy of types and transitions increases with the amount of data (# of days). The type inference accuracies were high for doors, chairs, trash cans, and locker doors whose models the participants said they could easily describe. However, the accuracy of the result obtained from participant B for the locker door was low because the locker doors were wrongly estimated as being doors. This is caused by *model segregation*. That is, because participants A and C knew that the models are used for the type inference, they described models that are distinguishable from each other considering their characteristics, e.g., a user often stops in front of a locker before opening it, while a user often opens a door while walking. Although participant B also knew that the models are used for the type inference, she did not care for them. We found that model segregation greatly affects type inference accuracy.

Table 1. Accuracies of object type (o) and transition (t) inferences (%)

parti-cipant	o/t	#days	straight chair	swivel chair on casters	trashcan lid	door	sliding door	locker door	locker interior	drawer	cup	table	alarm clock
A	o	1	80	100	100	93.33	80	80	0	60	40	0	0
A	o	2	87.5	100	100	100	100	91.67	0	50	50	0	0
A	t	1	76.92	47.83	97.5	92.31	79.07	92.31	-	87.5	81.25	-	-
A	t	2	82.06	50.34	97.01	97.4	68.37	92.93	-	71.43	78.95	-	-
B	o	1	80	100	80	93.33	100	0	0	20	60	0	0
B	o	2	87.5	100	100	100	100	0	0	25	50	0	0
B	t	1	84	34.78	96.97	90.38	66.07	-	-	100	81.82	-	-
B	t	2	84.02	36.05	94.03	95.17	64.29	-	-	85.71	78.95	-	-
C	o	1	60	100	60	86.67	80	80	0	60	60	0	0
C	o	2	62.5	100	100	100	100	91.67	0	75	75	0	0
C	t	1	81.82	41.3	96.67	93.1	53.33	93.84	-	78.57	60.61	-	-
C	t	2	81.31	42.86	97.01	97.03	52.08	93.27	-	70.83	79.59	-	-

Where to Attach

For the objects whose types we inferred with high accuracy, we could successfully infer their state transitions except for the sliding door and the swivel chair. Because the sensor node attached to the sliding door could not detect illuminance changes when it was dark, we could not recognize the event groups as "Open" and "Close" that included illuminance changes. For the back of the swivel chair on casters, we were unable to recognize some "Get up" transitions because a worker sometimes stood up from the chair without moving it. If it becomes possible to attach a node on the seat of a chair due to the miniaturization and thin technology of nodes, we will easily detect "Get up" phenomena. Also, two participants commented that they had trouble in modeling the outside of a drawer because there are various patterns of illuminance changes around a drawer caused by a person when opening and shutting the drawer. The type inference accuracies of the drawer were actually low. If the workers had attached a sensor node to the drawer interior, the accuracy would have been higher because the node would detect a sliding motion and an increase in

illumination with high probability when the drawer was opened. (An additional experiment proved the hypothesis.) Furthermore, the type inference accuracies of the locker interior were low. This is because the event groups were confused with the common transition of 'changes its illuminance when a person approaches,' which includes the same event groups. (When a locker is opened, a node which is attached to the locker interior does not move but vibrate.) As above, we found that the inference accuracies differ depending on where the sensor node is attached to an object.

C3 Objects

We failed to infer the table, cup, and alarm clock types, which clearly belong to C3, and the participants commented that they could not construct these models well. These types are not suitable for description in a state transition diagram. Note that it is very difficult to determine which object is classified into which category (C1, C2, or C3). We consider that we have to experimentally confirm whether an object is categorized into which category. That is, if the object is successfully modeled by using acceleration features (or state transition diagram), we can say that the object is categorized into C1 (or C2).

Model Making

As with the above results, we found that the participants easily modeled the types of objects that have simple and/or non-confusing movements, and which achieved high inference accuracies. In an environment where there were four thousand kinds of products, we would successfully infer object types whose accuracies were high in the experiment if they care for the model segregation. In the experiment, we found some activity groups that did not completely match the event groups in the models, e.g., 51% of the activity groups obtained from a sensor node attached to a locker door did not completely match the event groups in the model of the locker door built by participant A. However, the Viterbi algorithm, which considers the consistency of the activity group sequence, could connect most activity groups to correct transitions. A combination of the algorithm and the state transition diagrams of the object types achieved high inference accuracy using the manually constructed noisy models. In addition to three participants, a kind of professional model descriptor (the first author of this paper) also made the object models. However, we could not find significant difference between the models of the author and those of three participants in the object type inference accuracy with the exception of the 'locker interior.' (The inference accuracy was high by using the author's model because the model has acc.vibrate in the 'Open' transition.)

This finding indicates that there are two ways to make object models. (1) Trained model descriptor makes models. The models can achieve slightly higher accuracies than those of this experiment. However, it is expensive. (2) End users make models and share them. The inference accuracies of the models is about the same as those of this experiment. However, it is inexpensive.

We confirmed that it takes a lot of time to construct all the models. If we had not explained the concept of a state transition diagram to participant C, she would not have built any models. Also, there were transitions and event groups that a participant could not follow. Thus, it would be better for multiple model descriptors (end users) to construct the models collaboratively. Building models collaboratively would reduce the burden per descriptor, and they could construct models considering various situations. Also because we assume that we use models of object types that can be used in every end-user's home throughout the world, end users in the world can share the models via the Internet. Thus, the cost per end user is very low. Note that if anyone in the world cannot/don't build a model of an object type, of course, each end user should manually associate a sensor node and the type of object in his/her environment. This is a shortcoming of this approach.

CONCLUSION

This paper proposed a *Tag and Think* framework in which, by simply attaching sensor nodes to indoor objects, we infer the types of objects and the states they are in. Specifically, this paper proposed a way to infer type and state changes by using models constructed by end-users. The experimental result shows that a combination of our algorithm and state transition diagrams is robust for manually built models. In the future, we will try to infer object types that cannot be inferred by the methods and also to improve the descriptive power of the models. Also, we will try to achieve token identity of objects, that is, we will try to infer names of objects, e.g., Mary's chair and bedroom door. This may be achieved by estimating attributes of an object, e.g., owner of the object, location of the object, and role of the object.

REFERENCES

Allen, J. F. (1983). Maintaining knowledge about temporal intervals. *Communications of the ACM, 26*(11), 832–843. doi:10.1145/182.358434

Bao, L., & Intille, S. S. (2004). Activity recognition from user-annotated acceleration data. In . *Proceedings of PERVASIVE, 2004*, 1–17.

Beckmann, C., Consolvo, S., & LaMarca, A. (2004). Some assembly required: Supporting end-user sensor installation in domestic ubiquitous computing environments. In . *Proceedings of Ubicomp, 2004*, 107–124.

Bilmes, J. A. (1998). *A gentle tutorial of the EM algorithm and its application to parameter estimation for gaussian mixture and hidden markov models* (Tech. Rep. TR-97-021). Berkeley, CA: International Computer Science Institute and Computer Science Division, University of California Berkeley.

Freksa, C. (1991). Conceptual neighborhood and its role in temporal and spatial reasoning. In *Proceedings of the IMACS Workshop on Decision Support Systems and Qualitative Reasoning* (pp. 181-187).

Intille, S. S., Rondoni, J., Kukla, C., Anacona, I., & Bao, L. (2003). A context-aware experience sampling tool. In *Proceedings of CHI2003: Extended Abstracts*. ACM Publishing.

Intille, S. S., Tapia, E. M., Rondoni, J., Beaudin, J., Kukla, C., & Agarwal, S. (2003). Tools for studying behavior and technology in natural settings. In . *Proceedings of UbiComp, 2003*, 157–174.

Kidd, C., Orr, R., Abowd, G. D., Atkeson, C. G., Essa, I. A., MacIntyre, B., et al. (1999). The aware home: A living laboratory for ubiquitous computing research. In *CoBuild99* (LNCS 1670, pp. 191-198).

Philipose, M., Fishkin, K. P., & Perkowitz, M. (2004). Inferring activities from interactions with objects. *IEEE Pervasive Computing / IEEE Computer Society [and] IEEE Communications Society, 3*, 50–57. doi:10.1109/MPRV.2004.7

Sohn, J., Kim, N.-S., & Sung, W. (1999). A statistical model-based voice activity detection. *IEEE Signal Processing Letters, 6*, 1–3. doi:10.1109/97.736233

Tapia, E. M., Intille, S. S., & Larson, K. (2004). Activity recognition in the home using simple and ubiquitous sensors. In . *Proceedings of Pervasive, 2004*, 158–175.

This work was previously published in International Journal of Software Science and Computational Intelligence, Volume 2, Issue 1, edited by Yingxu Wang, pp. 86-101, copyright 2010 by IGI Publishing (an imprint of IGI Global).

Chapter 24
Delay–Range–Dependent Robust Stability for Uncertain Stochastic Neural Networks with Time–Varying Delays

Wei Feng
Chongqing University and Chongqing Education College, China

Haixia Wu
Chongqing University and Chongqing Education College, China

ABSTRACT

This paper is concerned with the robust stability analysis problem for uncertain stochastic neural networks with interval time-varying delays. By utilizing a Lyapunov-Krasovskii functional and conducting stochastic analysis, the authors show that the addressed neural networks are globally, robustly, and asymptotically stable if a convex optimization problem is feasible. Some stability criteria are derived for all admissible uncertainties, and these stability criteria are formulated by means of the feasibility of a linear matrix inequality (LMI), which can be effectively solved by some standard numerical packages. Five numerical examples are given to demonstrate the usefulness of the proposed robust stability criteria.

INTRODUCTION

The dynamics of neural networks has been extensively investigated in the past two decades because of their great significance for both practical and theoretical purposes. At the same time, neural networks have been successfully applied in many areas such as combinatorial optimization, signal processing, pattern recognition and many other fields (Wang, 2009, pp. 41-48; Chen, 2010, pp. 345-351; Mingo, 2009, pp. 67-80). However, all successful applications are greatly dependent on the dynamic behaviors of neural networks. As is well known now, stability is one of the main

DOI: 10.4018/978-1-4666-0264-9.ch024

properties of neural networks, which is a crucial feature in the design of neural networks. On the other hand, axonal signal transmission delays often occur in various neural networks, and may cause undesirable dynamic network behaviors such as oscillation and instability. Up to now, the stability analysis problem of neural networks with time-delays has been attracted a large amount of research interest and many sufficient conditions have been proposed to guarantee the asymptotic or exponential stability for the neural networks with various type of time delays such as constant, time-varying, or distributed. (Forti, 1994, pp. 491-494; Arik, 2000, pp. 1089-1092; Liao, 2002, pp. 855-866; Mou, 2008, pp. 532-535; Liu, 2008, pp. 823-833; Feng, 2009, pp. 414-424; Feng, 2009, pp. 2095-2104).

It is worth noting that the synaptic transmission is a noisy process brought on by random fluctuations from the release of neurotransmitters and other probabilistic causes in real nervous systems. It has also been known that a neural network could be stabilized or destabilized by certain stochastic inputs (Blythe, 2001, pp. 481-495). Hence, the stability analysis problem for stochastic neural networks becomes increasingly significant, and meantime some results related to this problem have recently been published (Liao, 1996, pp. 165-185; Wan, 2005, pp. 306-318; Wang, 2007, pp. 62-72; Zhang, 2007, pp. 1349-1357). On the other hand, the connection weights of the neurons depend on certain resistance and capacitance values that include uncertainties. When modeling neural networks, the parameter uncertainties (also called variations or fluctuations) should be taken into account, and therefore the problem of stability analysis for neural networks emerges as a research topic of primary importance (Kim, 2005, pp. 306-318; Huang, 2007, pp. 93-103; Liu, 2007, pp. 455-459).

Recently, a special type of time delays in practical engineering systems, i.e., interval time-varying delays, is identified and investigated (He, 2006, pp. 1235-1239; Jiang, 2006, pp. 1059-1065; Yue,

2005, pp. 999-1007; Yue, 2006, pp. 658-664). Interval time-varying delay is a time delay that varies in an interval in which the lower bound is not restricted to be zero. A typical example of dynamical systems with interval time-varying delays is networked control systems (NCSs) (Yue, 2006, pp. 658-664; Tian, 2007, pp. 103-107). As far as we know, there are systems which are stable with some nonzero delays, but they are unstable without delays (Gu, 2001, pp. 479-504; Zhao, 2004, pp. 399-407; Gu, 2001, pp. 737-744). Therefore, it is important to perform the stability analysis of systems with nonzero delays (Yue, 2005, pp. 999-1007; Tian, 2001, pp. 544-559; Jiang, 2005, pp. 2099-2106), and the nonzero delays can be placed into a given interval. This paper will address uncertain stochastic neural networks with interval time-varying delays.

In most published papers, the stochastic analysis problems and the robust stability analysis problems have been treated separately. There are few results considering the global stability analysis problem for uncertain stochastic neural networks with interval time-varying delays, a well-known inequality was used repetitively, which may lead some conservative results. Therefore, to the best of the authors' knowledge, the robust stability analysis problem for uncertain stochastic neural networks with interval time-varying delays has not been fully investigated, which still remains important and challenging.

Based on the above discussion, a class of uncertain stochastic neural networks with interval time-varying delays is considered in this paper. The main purpose of this paper is to study the global robust stability in the mean square for uncertain stochastic neural networks with interval time-varying delays. The parameter uncertainties are assumed to be norm bounded. A stability criterion is developed by using the Lyapunov stability theory and the LMI technique. The LMI condition can be efficiently solved by Matlab LMI Control Toolbox, and no tuning of parameters is required (Boyd, 1994). Numerical examples are given to illustrate the effectiveness and less conservativeness of the proposed techniques.

Notations: The notations are quite standard. Throughout this paper, $\mathbb{R}^n$ and $\mathbb{R}^{n \times n}$ denote, respectively, the n-dimensional Euclidean space and the set of all $n \times n$ real matrices. The superscript "T" denotes matrix transposition and the notation $X \geq Y$ (respectively, $X > Y$) where X and Y are symmetric matrices, means that $X - Y$ is positive semi-definite (respectively, positive definite). I_n is the $n \times n$ identity matrix. $|\cdot|$ is the Euclidean norm in $\mathbb{R}^n$. Moreover, let $(\Omega, \mathcal{F}, \{\mathcal{F}_t\}_{t \geq 0}, \mathcal{P})$ be a complete probability space with a filtration $\{\mathcal{F}_t\}_{t \geq 0}$ satisfying the usual conditions (i.e., the filtration contains all P-null sets and is right continuous). Denote by $L_{\mathcal{F}_0}^P([-h, 0]; \mathbb{R}^n)$ the family of all $\mathcal{F}_0$ – measurable $C([-h, 0]; \mathbb{R}^n)$ – valued random variables $\xi = \{\xi(\theta): -h \leq \theta \leq 0\}$ such that $\sup_{-h \leq \theta \leq 0} \mathbb{E} |\xi(\theta)|^P < \infty$ where $\mathbb{E}\{\cdot\}$ stands for the mathematical expectation operator with respect to the given probability measure P. The shorthand $diag\{M_1, M_2, ..., M_n\}$ denotes a block diagonal matrix with diagonal blocks being the matrices $M_1, M_2, ..., M_n$. The notation $\star$ always denotes the symmetric block in one symmetric matrix. Sometimes, the arguments of a function or a matrix will be omitted in the analysis when no confusion can arise.

Problem Formulation

In this section, we consider the following stochastic neural networks with interval time-varying delays:

$$dx(t) = \begin{bmatrix} (-A(t)x(t)) + W_0(t)f(x(t)) \\ +W_1(t)f(x(t-\tau(t))) \end{bmatrix} dt + [H_0(t)x(t) + H_1(t)x(t-\tau(t))]d\omega(t) \tag{1}$$

where $x(t) = [x_1(t), x_2(t), ..., x_t(t)]^T \in \mathbb{R}^n$ is the neural state vector, The matrices

$$A(t) = A + \Delta A(t), \quad W_0(t) = W_0 + \Delta W_0(t),$$
$$W_1(t) = W_1 + \Delta W_1(t), \quad H_0(t) = H_0 + \Delta H_0(t)$$
and $H_1(t) = H_1 + \Delta H_1(t)$,

where

$$A = diag[a_1, a_2, ..., a_n] > 0, \quad W_0, W_1 \in \mathbb{R}^{n \times n}$$

is the connection weight matrices, $H_0 \in \mathbb{R}^{n \times n}$ and $H_1 \in \mathbb{R}^{n \times n}$ are known real constant matrices, $\Delta A_1(t), \Delta W_0(t), \Delta W_1(t), \Delta H_0(t)$ and $\Delta H_1(t)$ represent the time-varying parameter uncertainties.

$$f(x(t)) = [f_1(x_1(t)), f_2(x_2(t)), ..., f_n(x_n(t))]^T \in \mathbb{R}^n$$

is the neuron activation function vector with $f(0) = 0$, $\omega(t) = [\omega_1(t), \omega_2(t), ..., \omega_m(t)]^T \in \mathbb{R}^m$ is an m-dimensional Brownian motion defined on a complete probability space $(\Omega, \mathcal{F}, \mathcal{P})$.

In order to obtain our main results, the assumptions are always made throughout this paper.

Assumption 1. The neuron activation function $f(\cdot)$ is bounded, and satisfies the following Lipschitz condition

$$|f(x) - f(y)| \leq |G(x-y)| \quad \forall x, y \in \mathbb{R}, \tag{2}$$

where $G \in \mathbb{R}^{n \times n}$ is a known constant matrix.

Assumption 2. The time-varying delays $\tau(t)$ satisfy

$$0 \leq h_1 \leq \tau(t) \leq h_2, \quad \dot{\tau}(t) \leq \tau_d < 1, \tag{3}$$

where h_1, h_2, τ_d are positive constants.

Assumption 3. The parameter uncertainties $\Delta A(t), \Delta W_0(t), \Delta W_1(t), \Delta H_0(t), \Delta H_1(t)$ are of the form:

$$\begin{bmatrix} \Delta A(t) & \Delta W_0(t) & \Delta W_1(t) & \Delta H_0(t) & \Delta H_1(t) \end{bmatrix}$$
$$= DF(t)\begin{bmatrix} E_1 & E_2 & E_3 & E_4 & E_5 \end{bmatrix}$$

$$(4)$$

in which H, E, E_0, E_1 are known constant matrices with appropriate dimensions. The uncertain matrix $F(t)$ satisfies

$$F^T(t)F(t) \le I \quad \text{for} \quad \forall_t \in \mathbb{R}. \tag{5}$$

Remark 1. Obviously, when $\tau_d = 0$ i.e., $h_1 = h_2$, then $\tau(t)$ denotes a constant delays, which is investigated in Zhang (2007); the case when $h_1 = 0$, it implies that $0 \le \tau(t) \le h_2$, which is investigated in Huang (2007).

Remark 2. In system (1), the stochastic disturbance term, $[H_0(t)x(t) + H_1(t)x(t - \tau(t))]d\omega(t)$ can be viewed as stochastic perturbations on the neuron states and delayed neuron states. It has been used in recent papers dealing with stochastic neural networks (Rakkiyappan, 2008, pp. 526-533; Huang, 2007, pp. 646-653; Wang, 2007, pp. 62-72; Wang, 2006, pp. 1119-1128).

Itô's differential formula (or generalized Itô's formula) (Mao, 1997) plays an important role in the analysis of stochastic systems. For a general stochastic system $dx(t) = g(x(t),t)dt + h(x(t),t)d\omega(t)$ on $t \ge 0$ with initial condition $x(t_0) = x_0 \in \mathbb{R}^n$, where $\omega(t)$ is m-dimensional Brownian motion defined on $(\Omega, \mathcal{F}, \mathcal{P})$, $g : \mathbb{R}^n \times \mathbb{R}^+ \to \mathbb{R}^n$ and $h : \mathbb{R}^n \times \mathbb{R}^+ \to \mathbb{R}^{n \times m}$.

Let $V \in \mathcal{C}^{2,1}(\mathbb{R}^n \times \mathbb{R}^+; \mathbb{R}^+)$, an operator $\mathcal{L}V$ is defined from $\mathbb{R}^n \times \mathbb{R}^+$ to $\mathbb{R}$ by

$$\mathcal{L}V(x,t) = V_t(x,t) + V_x(x,t)g(x,t)$$
$$+ \frac{1}{2} trace[h^T(x,t)V_{xx}(x,t)h(x,t)],$$

where

$$V_t(x,t) = \frac{\partial V(x,t)}{\partial t},$$

$$V_x(x,t) = \left(\frac{\partial V(x,t)}{\partial x_1}, ..., \frac{\partial V(x,t)}{\partial x_n} \right),$$

$$V_{xx}(x,t) = \left(\frac{\partial^2 V(x,t)}{\partial x_i \partial x_j} \right)_{n \times n},$$

and $i, j = 1, 2, ..., n$.

Now, we give the following definition of robust asymptotically stability for the uncertain stochastic neural networks (1).

Definition 1. The equilibrium point of the delayed neural networks (1) is said to be globally robustly asymptotically stable for all admissible uncertainties satisfying (4) and (5) in the mean square if t the following condition holds:

$$\lim_{t \to \infty} \mathbb{E}|x(t;\xi)|^2 = 0, \quad \forall t > 0. \tag{6}$$

Before ending this section, we give the following lemmas that are useful in deriving our LMI-based stability criteria in the next section.

Lemma 1. [Schur complement] *Given constant symmetric matrices* $\Sigma_1, \Sigma_2, \Sigma_3$ *where* $\Sigma_1 = \Sigma_1^T$ *and* $0 < \Sigma_2 = \Sigma_2^T$, *then* $\Sigma_1 + \Sigma_3^T \Sigma_2^{-1} \Sigma_3 < 0$ *if and only if*

$$\begin{bmatrix} \Sigma_1 & \Sigma_3^T \\ \Sigma_3 & -\Sigma_2 \end{bmatrix} < 0, \quad or \quad \begin{bmatrix} -\Sigma_2 & \Sigma_3 \\ \Sigma_3^T & \Sigma_1 \end{bmatrix} < 0.$$

Lemma 2. *For given matrices* D, E, F *with* $F^T F \le I$ *and a positive scalar* ε, *the following inequality holds:*

$$DFE + E^T F^T D^T \le \varepsilon D^T D + \varepsilon^{-1} E^T E.$$

Lemma 3. *For any constant matrix* $M \in \mathbb{R}^{n \times n}$, $M = M^T > 0$, *a scalar* $\rho > 0$, *vector function* $\omega : [0, \rho] \to \mathbb{R}^n$ *such that the integrations are well defined, the following inequality holds:*

$$\left[\int_0^\rho \omega(s)ds \right]^T M \left[\int_0^\rho \omega(s)ds \right] \le \rho \int_0^\rho \omega^T(s) M \omega(s) ds.$$

Main Results and Proofs

Theorem 1. *System (1) is globally robustly asymptotically stable in mean square if there exist symmetric positive definite matrices* Q, M_1, M_2 *and* Z, *and positive scalars* $\varepsilon_1, \varepsilon_2, \delta$ *and* λ *such that the LMI holds:*

$$\Xi = \begin{bmatrix} \Xi_{11} & \varepsilon_2 E_4^T E_5 & P^*W_0 - \varepsilon_1 E_1^T E_2 & P^*W_1 - \varepsilon_1 E_1^T E_3 & 0 & 0 & 0 & H_0^T P & PD & 0 \\ \star & \Xi_{22} & 0 & 0 & 0 & 0 & 0 & H_1^T P & 0 & 0 \\ \star & \star & -\delta I + \varepsilon_1 E_2^T E_2 & \varepsilon_1 E_2^T E_3 & 0 & 0 & 0 & 0 & 0 & 0 \\ \star & \star & \star & -\lambda I + \varepsilon_1 E_3^T E_3 & 0 & 0 & 0 & 0 & 0 & 0 \\ \star & \star & \star & \star & -M_1 & 0 & 0 & 0 & 0 & 0 \\ \star & \star & \star & \star & \star & -M_2 & 0 & 0 & 0 & 0 \\ \star & \star & \star & \star & \star & \star & -(h_2-h_1)^{-1}Z & 0 & 0 & 0 \\ \star & \star & \star & \star & \star & \star & \star & -P & 0 & PD \\ \star & \star & \star & \star & \star & \star & \star & \star & -\varepsilon_1 I & 0 \\ \star & \star & \star & \star & \star & \star & \star & \star & \star & -\varepsilon_2 I \end{bmatrix} < 0, \quad (7)$$

where

$$\Xi_{11} = -PA(t) - A^T(t)P + M_1 + M_2 + Q + (h_2 - h_1)Z + \delta G^T G + \varepsilon_1 E_1^T E_1 + \varepsilon_2 E_4^T E_4,$$

$$\Xi_{22} = -(1 - \tau_d)Q + \lambda G^T G + \varepsilon_2 E_5^T E_5.$$

Proof. Using Lemma 1(Schur complement), $\Xi < 0$ implies that

$$\Xi = \begin{bmatrix} \Gamma_{11} & 0 & PW_0 & PW_1 & 0 & 0 & 0 & H_0^T P \\ \star & \Gamma_{22} & 0 & 0 & 0 & 0 & 0 & H_1^T P \\ \star & \star & -\delta I & 0 & 0 & 0 & 0 & 0 \\ \star & \star & \star & -\lambda I & 0 & 0 & 0 & 0 \\ \star & \star & \star & \star & -M_1 & 0 & 0 & 0 \\ \star & \star & \star & \star & \star & -M_2 & 0 & 0 \\ \star & \star & \star & \star & \star & \star & -(h_2-h_1)^{-1}Z & 0 \\ \star & \star & \star & \star & \star & \star & \star & -P^{-1} \end{bmatrix}$$

$$+ \varepsilon_1 \begin{bmatrix} -E_1^T \\ 0 \\ E_2^T \\ E_3^T \\ 0 \\ 0 \\ 0 \\ 0 \end{bmatrix} \begin{bmatrix} -E_1^T \\ 0 \\ E_2^T \\ E_3^T \\ 0 \\ 0 \\ 0 \\ 0 \end{bmatrix}^T + \varepsilon_1^{-1} \begin{bmatrix} PD \\ 0 \\ 0 \\ 0 \\ 0 \\ 0 \\ 0 \\ 0 \end{bmatrix} \begin{bmatrix} PD \\ 0 \\ 0 \\ 0 \\ 0 \\ 0 \\ 0 \\ 0 \end{bmatrix}^T + \varepsilon_2 \begin{bmatrix} E_4^T \\ E_5^T \\ 0 \\ 0 \\ 0 \\ 0 \\ 0 \\ 0 \end{bmatrix} \begin{bmatrix} E_4^T \\ E_5^T \\ 0 \\ 0 \\ 0 \\ 0 \\ 0 \\ 0 \end{bmatrix}^T + \varepsilon_2^{-1} \begin{bmatrix} 0 \\ 0 \\ 0 \\ 0 \\ 0 \\ 0 \\ 0 \\ PD \end{bmatrix} \begin{bmatrix} 0 \\ 0 \\ 0 \\ 0 \\ 0 \\ 0 \\ 0 \\ PD \end{bmatrix}^T < 0, \quad (8)$$

where

$$\Gamma_{11} = -PA - A^T P + M_1 + M_2 + Q + (h_2 - h_1)Z + \delta G^T G,$$

$$\Gamma_{22} = -(1 - \tau_d)Q + \lambda G^T G.$$

Then, noting that (4) and (5), using Lemma 2, we get

$$\begin{bmatrix} -P\Delta A(t) - \Delta A^T(t)P & 0 & P\Delta W_0(t) & P\Delta W_1(t) & 0 & 0 & 0 & \Delta H_0^T(t)P \\ \star & 0 & 0 & 0 & 0 & 0 & 0 & \Delta H_1^T(t)P \\ \star & \star & 0 & 0 & 0 & 0 & 0 & 0 \\ \star & \star & \star & 0 & 0 & 0 & 0 & 0 \\ \star & \star & \star & \star & 0 & 0 & 0 & 0 \\ \star & \star & \star & \star & \star & 0 & 0 & 0 \\ \star & \star & \star & \star & \star & \star & 0 & 0 \\ \star & \star & \star & \star & \star & \star & \star & 0 \end{bmatrix}$$

$$= \begin{bmatrix} -E_1^T \\ 0 \\ E_2^T \\ E_3^T \\ 0 \\ 0 \\ 0 \\ 0 \end{bmatrix} F^T(t) \begin{bmatrix} PD \\ 0 \\ 0 \\ 0 \\ 0 \\ 0 \\ 0 \\ 0 \end{bmatrix}^T + \begin{bmatrix} PD \\ 0 \\ 0 \\ 0 \\ 0 \\ 0 \\ 0 \\ 0 \end{bmatrix} F(t) \begin{bmatrix} -E_1^T \\ 0 \\ E_2^T \\ E_3^T \\ 0 \\ 0 \\ 0 \\ 0 \end{bmatrix}^T + \begin{bmatrix} E_4^T \\ E_5^T \\ 0 \\ 0 \\ 0 \\ 0 \\ 0 \\ 0 \end{bmatrix} F(t) \begin{bmatrix} 0 \\ 0 \\ 0 \\ 0 \\ 0 \\ 0 \\ 0 \\ PD \end{bmatrix}^T + \begin{bmatrix} 0 \\ 0 \\ 0 \\ 0 \\ 0 \\ 0 \\ 0 \\ PD \end{bmatrix} F(t) \begin{bmatrix} E_4^T \\ E_5^T \\ 0 \\ 0 \\ 0 \\ 0 \\ 0 \\ 0 \end{bmatrix}^T$$

$$\le \varepsilon_1 \begin{bmatrix} -E_1^T \\ 0 \\ E_2^T \\ E_3^T \\ 0 \\ 0 \\ 0 \\ 0 \end{bmatrix} \begin{bmatrix} -E_1^T \\ 0 \\ E_2^T \\ E_3^T \\ 0 \\ 0 \\ 0 \\ 0 \end{bmatrix}^T + \varepsilon_1^{-1} \begin{bmatrix} PD \\ 0 \\ 0 \\ 0 \\ 0 \\ 0 \\ 0 \\ 0 \end{bmatrix} \begin{bmatrix} PD \\ 0 \\ 0 \\ 0 \\ 0 \\ 0 \\ 0 \\ 0 \end{bmatrix}^T + \varepsilon_2 \begin{bmatrix} E_4^T \\ E_5^T \\ 0 \\ 0 \\ 0 \\ 0 \\ 0 \\ 0 \end{bmatrix} \begin{bmatrix} E_4^T \\ E_5^T \\ 0 \\ 0 \\ 0 \\ 0 \\ 0 \\ 0 \end{bmatrix}^T + \varepsilon_2^{-1} \begin{bmatrix} 0 \\ 0 \\ 0 \\ 0 \\ 0 \\ 0 \\ 0 \\ PD \end{bmatrix} \begin{bmatrix} 0 \\ 0 \\ 0 \\ 0 \\ 0 \\ 0 \\ 0 \\ PD \end{bmatrix}^T.$$

Therefore, we have

$$\begin{bmatrix} \Sigma_{11} & 0 & PW_0(t) & PW_1(t) & 0 & 0 & 0 & H_0^T(t)P \\ \star & \Sigma_{22} & 0 & 0 & 0 & 0 & 0 & H_1^T(t)P \\ \star & \star & -\delta I & 0 & 0 & 0 & 0 & 0 \\ \star & \star & \star & -\lambda I & 0 & 0 & 0 & 0 \\ \star & \star & \star & \star & -M_1 & 0 & 0 & 0 \\ \star & \star & \star & \star & \star & -M_2 & 0 & 0 \\ \star & \star & \star & \star & \star & \star & -(h_2-h_1)^{-1}Z & 0 \\ \star & \star & \star & \star & \star & \star & \star & -P \end{bmatrix} < 0. \tag{9}$$

Utilizing Schur complement again, we obtain

$$\Sigma = \begin{bmatrix} \Sigma_{11} & 0 & PW_0(t) & PW_1(t) & 0 & 0 & 0 \\ \star & \Sigma_{22} & 0 & 0 & 0 & 0 & 0 \\ \star & \star & -\delta I & 0 & 0 & 0 & 0 \\ \star & \star & \star & -\lambda I & 0 & 0 & 0 \\ \star & \star & \star & \star & -M_1 & 0 & 0 \\ \star & \star & \star & \star & \star & -M_2 & 0 \\ \star & \star & \star & \star & \star & \star & -(h_2-h_1)^{-1}Z \end{bmatrix} + \varkappa(t)P\varkappa(t)^T < 0 \tag{10}$$

where

$$\Sigma_{11} = -PA(t) - A^T(t)P + M_1 + M_2 + Q + (h_2 - h_1)Z + \delta G^T G,$$

$$\Sigma_{22} = -(1-\tau_d)Q + \lambda G^T G,$$

$$\dot{\varkappa}(t) = \begin{bmatrix} H_0(t) & H_1(t) & 0 & 0 & 0 \end{bmatrix}^T.$$

To obtain the result, the Lyapunov-Krasovskii functional of system (1) is defined by:

$$V(x(t)) = V_1(x(t)) + V_2(x(t)) + V_3(x(t)), \tag{11}$$

$$V_1(x(t)) = x^T(t)Px(t),$$

$$V_2(x(t)) = \int_{t-\tau(t)}^t x^T(s)Qx(s)ds + \int_{t-h_1}^t x^T(s)M_1 x(s)ds$$
$$+ \int_{t-h_2}^t x^T(s)M_2 x(s)ds,$$

$$V_3(x(t)) = \int_{-h_2}^{-h_1} \int_{t+\theta}^t x^T(s)Zx(s)dsd\theta.$$

By Itô's differential formula, the stochastic derivative of $V(x(t), t)$ along the trajectories of the system (1), and then we have

$$dV(x(t), t) =$$
$$\mathcal{L}V(x(t), t) +$$
$$\left\{ 2x^T(t)P \begin{bmatrix} H_0(t)x(t) + \\ H_1(t)x(t-\tau(t)) \end{bmatrix} \right\} d\omega(t)$$

$$= \mathcal{L}V_1(x(t), t) +$$
$$\mathcal{L}V_2(x(t), t) + \mathcal{L}V_3(x(t), t) + \tag{12}$$
$$\left\{ 2x^T(t)P \begin{bmatrix} H_0(t)x(t) + \\ H_1(t)x(t-\tau(t)) \end{bmatrix} \right\} d\omega(t)$$

$$\mathcal{L}V_1(x(t), t) =$$
$$\left\{ 2x^T(t)P \begin{bmatrix} -A(t)x(t) + W_0(t)f(x(t)) \\ +W_1(t)f(x(t-\tau(t))) \end{bmatrix} \right.$$

$$+ \begin{bmatrix} H_0(t)x(t) + \\ H_1(t)x(t-\tau(t)) \end{bmatrix}^T P \begin{bmatrix} H_0(t)x(t) + \\ H_1(t)x(t-\tau(t)) \end{bmatrix} \right\} dt \tag{13}$$

$$\mathcal{L}V_2(x(t), t) =$$
$$x^T(t)Qx(t) -$$
$$(1-\dot{\tau}(t))x^T(t-\tau(t))Qx(t-\tau(t))$$

$$+ x^T(t)M_1 x(t) - x^T(t-h_1)M_1 x(t-h_1) + \\ x^T(t)M_2 x(t) - x^T(t-h_2)M_2 x(t-h_2) \tag{14}$$

$$\mathcal{L}V_3(x(t), t) =$$
$$(h_2-h_1)x^T(t)Zx(t) - \int_{t-h_2}^{t-h_1} x^T(s)Zx(s)ds$$

$$\leq (h_2-h_1)x^T(t)Zx(t)$$
$$- \frac{1}{h_2-h_1}\left(\int_{t-h_2}^{t-h_1} x^T(s)ds \right)^T Z\left(\int_{t-h_2}^{t-h_1} x^T(s)ds \right). \tag{15}$$

Combining (13)-(15), we have

$$\mathcal{L}V(x(t),t) \leq x^T(t) \begin{bmatrix} -2PA(t) + Q + M_1 + M_2 \\ +(h_2 - h_1)Z \end{bmatrix} x(t)$$
$$+ 2x^T(t)PW_0(t)f(x(t))$$

$$+ 2x^T(t)PW_1(t)f(x(t-\tau(t)))$$
$$-(1-\tau_d)x^T(t-\tau(t))Qx(t-\tau(t))$$

$$-x^T(t-h_1)M_1x(t-h_1) - x^T(t-h_2)M_2x(t-h_2)$$
$$-\frac{1}{h_2-h_1}\left(\int_{t-h_2}^{t-h_1} x^T(s)ds\right)^T Z\left(\int_{t-h_2}^{t-h_1} x^T(s)ds\right)$$

$$+\begin{bmatrix} H_0(t)x(t) + \\ H_1(t)x(t-\tau(t)) \end{bmatrix}^T P \begin{bmatrix} H_0(t)x(t) + \\ H_1(t)x(t-\tau(t)) \end{bmatrix}.$$
(16)

From (2), we obtain the follow inequality easily,

$$f^T(x(t))f(x(t)) -$$
$$x^T(t)G^TGx(t) \leq 0,$$

$$f^T(x(t-\tau(t)))f(x(t-\tau(t))) -$$
$$x^T(t-\tau(t))G^TGx(t-\tau(t)) \leq 0.$$

Noticing that, for any scalars $\delta > 0$ and $\lambda > 0$, there exist

$$-\delta[f^T(x(t))f(x(t)) -$$
$$x^T(t)G^TGx(t)] \geq 0,$$
(17)

$$-\lambda[f^T(x(t-\tau(t)))f(x(t-\tau(t))) -$$
$$x^T(t-\tau(t))G^TGx(t-\tau(t))] \geq 0.$$
(18)

Substituting (17), (18) into $dV(x(t),t)$ and utilizing Lemma 3, there exists

$$dV(x(t),t) \leq \left\{\xi^T(t)\Sigma\xi(t)\right\}dt +$$
$$\left\{2x^T(t)P\left[H_0(t)x(t) + H_1(t)x(t-\tau(t))\right]\right\}d\omega(t)'$$

where Σ is given in (10) and

$$\xi^T(t) = \begin{bmatrix} x^T(t)\,x^T\left(t-\tau(t)\right)f^T\left(x(t)\right) \\ \bullet f^T\left(x\left(t-\tau(t)\right)\right)x^T\left(t-h_1\right)x^T\left(t-h_2\right) \\ \bullet\left(\int_{t-h_2}^{t-h_1} x(s)\,ds\right)^T \end{bmatrix}$$

It is obvious that for $\Sigma < 0$, and there exists a scalar $\gamma > 0$ such that $\Sigma + \text{diag}\{\gamma I, 0, 0, 0, 0, 0, 0, 0\} < 0$, which indicates that

$$dV(x(t),t) \leq \gamma\|x(t)\|^2 dt$$
$$+ \left\{2x^T(t)P\begin{bmatrix} H_0(t)x(t) \\ +H_1(t)x(t-\tau(t)) \end{bmatrix}\right\}d\omega(t)$$
(19)

Taking the mathematical expectation of both sides of (19), there exists

$$\frac{d\mathbb{E}V(x(t),t)}{dt} \leq -\gamma\mathbb{E}\|x(t)\|^2,$$
(20)

this indicates from the Lyapunov stability theory that the dynamics of the neural network (1) is globally robustly asymptotically stable in the mean square.

Remark 3. It is shown in Theorem 1 that the global robust asymptotical stability of addressed stochastic delayed neural networks can be ensured if the matrix inequality (7) is feasible. It should be noted that the condition (7) is given as linear matrix inequality LMIs. Therefore, by using the Matlab LMI Toolbox, it is straightforward to check the feasibility of (7) without tuning any parameters.

Remark 4. It is worth pointing out that, following the similar line of the proof of Theorem 1, it is not difficult to prove the exponential stability of the neural network (1) under the same conditions in Theorem 1.

Based on the proof of Theorem 1, we show that our main results can be easily specialized to two cases that have been studied in the literature.

Case 1. We first consider the case without external stochastic perturbations. That is, there are no parameter stochastic perturbations, and the neural network is described by

$$
\dot{x}(t) = -(A + \Delta A)x(t) + (W_0 + \Delta W_0)f(x(t)) + (W_1 + \Delta W_1)f(x(t - \tau(t)))
$$

(21)

where the parameters are as same as the ones in Eq. (1). The parameter uncertainties ΔA, ΔW_0, ΔW_1 are satisfies Assumption 3. Then we have the following Corollary 1.

Corollary 1. *The system (21) is globally, robustly, asymptotically stable, if there exist symmetric positive definite matrices Q, M_1, M_2 and Z, and positive scalars ε_1, δ and λ such that the LMI holds:*

$$
\begin{bmatrix}
(1,1) & 0 & P*W0 - \varepsilon_1 E_1^T E_2 & P*W1 - \varepsilon_1 E_1^T E_3 & 0 & 0 & 0 & PD \\
\star & (2,2) & 0 & 0 & 0 & 0 & 0 & 0 \\
\star & \star & -\delta I + \varepsilon_1 E_2^T E_2 & \varepsilon_1 E_2^T E_3 & 0 & 0 & 0 & 0 \\
\star & \star & \star & -\lambda I + \varepsilon_1 E_3^T E_3 & 0 & 0 & 0 & 0 \\
\star & \star & \star & \star & -M_1 & 0 & 0 & 0 \\
\star & \star & \star & \star & \star & -M_2 & 0 & 0 \\
\star & \star & \star & \star & \star & \star & -(h_2 - h_1)^{-1}Z & 0 \\
\star & \star & \star & \star & \star & \star & \star & -\varepsilon_1 I
\end{bmatrix} < 0,
$$

(22)

where

$$
(1,1) = -PA(t) - A^T(t)P + M_1 + M_2 + Q + (h_2 - h_1)Z + \delta G^T G + \varepsilon_1 E_1^T E_1,
$$

$$
(2,2) = -(1 - \tau_d)Q + \lambda G^T G.
$$

Case 2. In the case, we consider the case have no parameter uncertainties in A, W_0 and W_1. The neural network can be described by

$$
dx(t) = \left[(-Ax(t)) + W_0 f(x(t)) + W_1 f(x(t - \tau(t))) \right] dt + \left[H_0(t)x(t) + H_1(t)x(t - \tau(t)) \right] d\omega(t)
$$

(23)

where the parameters are as same as the ones in Eq. (1). Then we have the following Corollary 2.

Corollary 2. *The system (23) is globally, robustly, asymptotically stable, if there exist symmetric positive definite matrices P, Q, M_1, M_2 and Z, and positive scalars ε_2, δ and λ such that the LMI holds:*

$$
\begin{bmatrix}
(1,1) & \varepsilon_2 E_4^T E_5 & P*W0 & P*W1 & 0 & 0 & 0 & H_0^T P & PD \\
\star & (2,2) & 0 & 0 & 0 & 0 & 0 & H_1^T P & 0 \\
\star & \star & -\delta I & 0 & 0 & 0 & 0 & 0 & 0 \\
\star & \star & \star & -\lambda I & 0 & 0 & 0 & 0 & 0 \\
\star & \star & \star & \star & -M_1 & 0 & 0 & 0 & 0 \\
\star & \star & \star & \star & \star & -M_2 & 0 & 0 & 0 \\
\star & \star & \star & \star & \star & \star & -(h_2 - h_1)^{-1}Z & 0 & 0 \\
\star & \star & \star & \star & \star & \star & \star & -P & 0 \\
\star & \star & \star & \star & \star & \star & \star & \star & -\varepsilon_2 I
\end{bmatrix} < 0
$$

(24)

where

$$
(1,1) = -PA - A^T P + M_1 + M_2 + Q + (h_2 - h_1)Z + \delta G^T G + \varepsilon_2 E_4^T E_4,
$$

$$
(2,2) = -(1 - \tau_d)Q + \lambda G^T G + \varepsilon_2 E_5^T E_5.
$$

Case 3. In the case, we consider the case have no parameter uncertainties in A, W_0 and W_1 and no parameter stochastic perturbations. The neural network can be described by

$$
\dot{x}(t) = -Ax(t)) + W_0 f(x(t)) + W_1 f(x(t - \tau(t)))
$$

(25)

where the parameters are as same as the ones in Eq. (1). Then we have the following Corollary 3.

Corollary 3. *The system (25) is globally, asymptotically stable, if there exist symmetric positive definite matrices* P, Q, M_1, M_2 *and* Z, *and positive scalars* δ *and* λ *such that the LMI holds:*

$$\begin{bmatrix} (1,1) & 0 & P*W0 & P*W1 & 0 & 0 & 0 \\ \star & (2,2) & 0 & 0 & 0 & 0 & 0 \\ \star & \star & -\delta I & 0 & 0 & 0 & 0 \\ \star & \star & \star & -\lambda I & 0 & 0 & 0 \\ \star & \star & \star & \star & -M_1 & 0 & 0 \\ \star & \star & \star & \star & \star & -M_2 & 0 \\ \star & \star & \star & \star & \star & \star & -(h_2 - h_1)^{-1}Z \end{bmatrix} < 0 \quad (26)$$

where

$$(1,1) = -PA - A^T P + M_1 + M_2 + Q + (h_2 - h_1)Z + \delta G^T G,$$

$$(2,2) = -(1 - \tau_d)Q + \lambda G^T G.$$

Numerical Examples

To illustrate the usefulness of our results, this section will provide five numerical examples. It will be shown that the proposed results can provide less conservative results than the recent ones given in (Wang, 2007, pp. 62-72; Wang, 2006, pp. 1119-1128; Zhang, 2007, pp. 1349-1357)... The LMI involved in this section is solved by the LMI-Toolbox in Matlab.

Example 1. In this example, we consider the following two-neuron uncertain neural network with time-varying delays:

$$dx(t) = \begin{bmatrix} (-(A + DF(t)E_1)x(t)) \\ +(W_0 + DF(t)E_2)f(x(t)) \\ +(W_1 + DF(t)E_3)f(x(t - \tau(t))) \end{bmatrix} dt . \quad (27)$$

The parametric coefficients are given as follows:

$$A = \begin{bmatrix} 1.2 & 0 \\ 0 & 1.15 \end{bmatrix}, \ W_0 = 0, \ W_1 = \begin{bmatrix} 0.4 & -1 \\ -1.4 & 0.4 \end{bmatrix},$$

$$D = \begin{bmatrix} 1.2 & 0 \\ 0 & 1.2 \end{bmatrix}, \ E_1 = \begin{bmatrix} 0.2 & 0 \\ 0 & 0.2 \end{bmatrix}, \ E_2 = 0,$$

$$E_3 = \begin{bmatrix} 0.2 & 0 \\ 0 & 0.2 \end{bmatrix},$$

$$G = \begin{bmatrix} 0.5 & 0 \\ 0 & 0.5 \end{bmatrix} \tau_d = 0, \ h_1 = 0, \ h_2 = 0.8,$$

$$F^T(t)F(t) \le I .$$

Using Matlab LMI Control Toolbox, by our Corollary 1, we can find that the system (27) described by Example 1 is globally, robustly, asymptotically stable in the mean square and the feasible solution of LMI (22) is obtained as

$$P = \begin{bmatrix} 647.0508 & 147.4803 \\ 147.4803 & 464.9835 \end{bmatrix},$$

$$Q = \begin{bmatrix} 367.5690 & 28.7569 \\ 28.7569 & 316.5836 \end{bmatrix},$$

$$M_1 = \begin{bmatrix} 125.8507 & 46.4949 \\ 46.4949 & 42.9066 \end{bmatrix},$$

$$M_2 = \begin{bmatrix} 125.8507 & 46.4949 \\ 46.4949 & 42.9066 \end{bmatrix},$$

$$Z = \begin{bmatrix} 141.3326 & 51.2410 \\ 51.2410 & 49.9180 \end{bmatrix},$$

$$\varepsilon_1 = 1.9381e+003, \ \delta = 104.3976,$$

$$\lambda = 1.1677e+003.$$

It should be point out that; the conditions in (Wang, 2006, pp. 1119-1128) are not feasible, which implies that the stability conditions fail to conclude whether the genetic networks are robust stable or not. Therefore, our method is less conservative in some degree than that in (Wang, 2006, pp. 1119-1128).

Example 2. In this example, we consider the following three-neuron uncertain stochastic neural network with time-varying delays:

$$dx(t) = \begin{bmatrix} (-(A + DF(t)E_1)x(t)) \\ +(W_0 + DF(t)E_2)f(x(t)) \\ +(W_1 + DF(t)E_3)f(x(t - \tau(t))) \end{bmatrix} dt$$

$$+ \begin{bmatrix} (DF(t)E_4)x(t) \\ +(DF(t)E_5)x(t - \tau(t))) \end{bmatrix} d\omega(t). \quad (28)$$

The parametric coefficients are given as follows:

$$A = \begin{bmatrix} 2.2 & 0 & 0 \\ 0 & 2.4 & 0 \\ 0 & 0 & 2.6 \end{bmatrix}, W_0 = 0,$$

$$W_1 = \begin{bmatrix} 0.3 & -1.8 & 0.5 \\ -1.1 & 1.6 & 1.1 \\ 0.6 & 0.4 & -0.3 \end{bmatrix},$$

$$D = \begin{bmatrix} 0.1 & 0 & 0 \\ 0 & 0.5 & 0 \\ 0 & 0 & 0.3 \end{bmatrix}, G = \begin{bmatrix} 0.5 & 0 & 0 \\ 0 & 0.5 & 0 \\ 0 & 0 & 0.5 \end{bmatrix},$$

$$E_1 = \begin{bmatrix} 0.6 & 0 & 0 \\ 0 & 0.6 & 0 \\ 0 & 0 & 0.6 \end{bmatrix}, E_2 = 0,$$

$$E_3 = E_4 = E_5 = \begin{bmatrix} 0.2 & 0 & 0 \\ 0 & 0.2 & 0 \\ 0 & 0 & 0.2 \end{bmatrix},$$

$$H_0 = H_1 = 0, \tau_d = 0, h_1 = 0, h_2 = 0.8,$$

$$F^T(t)F(t) \le 1.$$

Using Matlab LMI Control Toolbox, by our Theorem 1, we can find that the system (28) described by Example 2 is globally, robustly, asymptotically stable in the mean square and the feasible solution of LMI (7) as following:

$$P = \begin{bmatrix} 2.4593 & 0.3383 & 0.0176 \\ 0.3383 & 2.0609 & -0.0189 \\ 0.0176 & -0.0189 & 2.3740 \end{bmatrix},$$

$$Q = \begin{bmatrix} 2.6145 & 0.4060 & 0.1464 \\ 0.4060 & 2.3737 & 0.0786 \\ 0.1464 & 0.0786 & 3.2180 \end{bmatrix},$$

$$M_1 = \begin{bmatrix} 1.2430 & 0.5557 & 0.1646 \\ 0.5557 & 0.9201 & 0.0838 \\ 0.1646 & 0.0838 & 1.9978 \end{bmatrix},$$

$$M_2 = \begin{bmatrix} 1.2430 & 0.5557 & 0.1646 \\ 0.5557 & 0.9201 & 0.0838 \\ 0.1646 & 0.0838 & 1.9978 \end{bmatrix},$$

$$Z = \begin{bmatrix} 1.2171 & 0.4941 & 0.1173 \\ 0.4941 & 0.9314 & 0.0547 \\ 0.1173 & 0.0547 & 1.8238 \end{bmatrix},$$

$$\varepsilon_1 = 1.8892, \varepsilon_2 = 2.0307, \delta = 1.4530,$$

$$\lambda = 6.6978.$$

Furthermore, by the result of (Wang, 2006, pp. 1119-1128) and (Zhang, 2007, pp. 1349-1357), the stability of the system depends on the size of delay τ. It was reported in (Wang, 2006, pp. 1119-1128) that the above system is asymptotically stable in the mean square when $\tau = 0.8$. However, by our Theorem 1 and using LMI toolbox, it is found that the system described by Example 2 is asymptotically stable in the mean square for any constant delay τ.

Example 3. Consider the following three-neuron uncertain stochastic neural network with time-varying delays:

$$dx(t) = \begin{bmatrix} (-(A + DF(t)E_1)x(t)) \\ +(W_0 + DF(t)E_2)f(x(t)) \\ +(W_1 + DF(t)E_3)f(x(t - \tau(t))) \end{bmatrix} dt$$
$$+ \begin{bmatrix} (DF(t)E_4)x(t) \\ +(DF(t)E_5)x(t - \tau(t))) \end{bmatrix} d\omega(t). \quad (29)$$

The parametric coefficients are given as follows:

$$A = \begin{bmatrix} 2.2 & 0 & 0 \\ 0 & 2.4 & 0 \\ 0 & 0 & 2.6 \end{bmatrix},$$

$$W_0 = \begin{bmatrix} -0.2 & -1 & 0.1 \\ -0.4 & 0.4 & 0.2 \\ 0.3 & 0.3 & -0.1 \end{bmatrix},$$

$$W_1 = \begin{bmatrix} 0.3 & -1.8 & 0.5 \\ -1.1 & 1.6 & 1.1 \\ 0.6 & 0.4 & -0.3 \end{bmatrix},$$

$$D = \begin{bmatrix} 0.1 & 0 & 0 \\ 0 & 0.5 & 0 \\ 0 & 0 & 0.3 \end{bmatrix}, G = \begin{bmatrix} 0.5 & 0 & 0 \\ 0 & 0.5 & 0 \\ 0 & 0 & 0.5 \end{bmatrix},$$

$E_1 = 0.6I$, $E_2 = E_3 = E_4 = E_5 = 0.2I$,

$H_0 = H_1 = 0.1I$, $\tau_d = 0.2$, $h_1 = 0.6$,

$h_2 = 2.2$, $F^T(t)F(t) \le 1$.

Again, using Matlab LMI Control Toolbox, by our Theorem 1, the feasible solution is obtained as

$$P = \begin{bmatrix} 18.8303 & 3.7692 & 1.3029 \\ 3.7692 & 16.8954 & -0.0204 \\ 1.3029 & -0.0204 & 21.9255 \end{bmatrix},$$

$$Q = \begin{bmatrix} 23.1985 & 2.6038 & 2.1214 \\ 2.6038 & 23.3196 & 0.8689 \\ 2.1214 & 0.8689 & 29.7855 \end{bmatrix},$$

$$M_1 = \begin{bmatrix} 4.7590 & 4.0485 & 2.6036 \\ 4.0485 & 4.6726 & 0.8500 \\ 2.6036 & 0.8500 & 13.4320 \end{bmatrix},$$

$$M_2 = \begin{bmatrix} 4.7590 & 4.0485 & 2.6036 \\ 4.0485 & 4.6726 & 0.8500 \\ 2.6036 & 0.8500 & 13.4320 \end{bmatrix},$$

$$Z = \begin{bmatrix} 4.2834 & 3.5861 & 3.3546 \\ 3.5861 & 3.9490 & 1.4915 \\ 3.3546 & 1.4915 & 14.2905 \end{bmatrix},$$

$\varepsilon_1 = 10.9220$, $\varepsilon_2 = 7.5188$, $\delta = 27.4836$,

$\lambda = 61.3745$,

which indicates from Theorem 1 that the system (29) is indeed globally, robustly, asymptotically stable in the mean square. Since the time delays are variant with time t, the stability criteria in (Wang, 2007, pp. 62-72; Wang, 2006, pp. 1119-1128) cannot be applicable to the example.

Example 4. Consider the following three-neuron stochastic neural network with time-varying delays:

$$dx(t) = \begin{bmatrix} (-Ax(t)) + W_0 f(x(t)) \\ +W_1 f(x(t - \tau(t))) \end{bmatrix} dt$$
$$+ \begin{bmatrix} H_0(t)x(t) \\ +H_1(t)x(t - \tau(t)) \end{bmatrix} d\omega(t) \quad (30)$$

The parametric coefficients are given as follows:

$$A = \begin{bmatrix} 2.2 & 0 & 0 \\ 0 & 2.6 & 0 \\ 0 & 0 & 1.5 \end{bmatrix},$$

$$W_0 = \begin{bmatrix} 0.5 & -1.3 & 0 \\ -1.1 & 0.1 & 0.5 \\ 0.2 & 0 & 0.5 \end{bmatrix},$$

$$W_1 = \begin{bmatrix} -0.6 & 0.5 & 0.1 \\ -0.9 & -0.7 & 0 \\ 0 & 0.4 & -0.2 \end{bmatrix},$$

$$D = \begin{bmatrix} 0.2 & 0.3 & 0.3 \\ 0.7 & 0.1 & 0 \\ 0.3 & 0 & 0.2 \end{bmatrix},$$

$$G = \begin{bmatrix} 0.5 & 0 & 0 \\ 0 & 0.5 & 0 \\ 0 & 0 & 0.5 \end{bmatrix}, \quad E_4 = E_5 = 0.1I,$$

$$H_0 = H_1 = 0.1I, \quad \tau_d = 0.4, \quad h_1 = 0.8,$$

$$h_2 = 2.0, \quad F^T(t)F(t) \le 1.$$

In this case, according to our Corollary 2, by solving the LMI (24), we obtain

$$P = \begin{bmatrix} 6.3840 & 0.3826 & -1.2645 \\ 0.3826 & 5.7970 & 0.0287 \\ -1.2645 & 0.0287 & 13.2257 \end{bmatrix},$$

$$Q = \begin{bmatrix} 22.2868 & 0.6498 & -1.6553 \\ 0.6498 & 23.0138 & 0.0417 \\ -1.6553 & 0.0417 & 26.3864 \end{bmatrix},$$

$$M_1 = \begin{bmatrix} 12.6828 & 0.2339 & -0.5959 \\ 0.2339 & 12.9445 & 0.0150 \\ -0.5959 & 0.0150 & 14.1586 \end{bmatrix},$$

$$M_2 = \begin{bmatrix} 12.6828 & 0.2339 & -0.5959 \\ 0.2339 & 12.9445 & 0.0150 \\ -0.5959 & 0.0150 & 14.1586 \end{bmatrix},$$

$$Z = \begin{bmatrix} 30.5075 & -0.4042 & 1.0297 \\ -0.4042 & 30.0553 & -0.0259 \\ 1.0297 & -0.0259 & 27.9573 \end{bmatrix},$$

$$\varepsilon_2 = 17.7768, \quad \delta = 16.7436, \quad \lambda = 15.9699,$$

which indicates from Corollary 2 that the system (30) is indeed globally, robustly, asymptotically stable in the mean square.

Example 5. Consider the following three-neuron neural network with time-varying delays:

$$\dot{x}(t) = -Ax(t)) + W_0 f(x(t)) + W_1 f(x(t - \tau(t))) \tag{31}$$

The parametric coefficients are given as follows:

$$A = \begin{bmatrix} 3.2 & 0 & 0 \\ 0 & 1.6 & 0 \\ 0 & 0 & 2.5 \end{bmatrix}, \quad W_0 = \begin{bmatrix} 2.5 & 1.2 & 0 \\ 0.8 & 1.1 & 2.5 \\ 2.2 & 0.8 & 1.5 \end{bmatrix},$$

$$W_1 = \begin{bmatrix} -1.6 & 0.5 & 1.1 \\ -2.9 & 2.7 & 0.4 \\ 0.6 & 0.4 & -2.2 \end{bmatrix},$$

$$\tau_d = 1.6, \quad h_1 = 1.2, \quad h_2 = 2.8.$$

Using our Corollary 3 and LMI Control Toolbox in Matlab, we find that the neural networks (31) is indeed globally, asymptotically stable and the feasible solution of LMI (26) is given as follows:

$$P = \begin{bmatrix} -2.6946 & 0.8887 & 0.2956 \\ 0.8887 & -0.9301 & 0.1671 \\ 0.2956 & 0.1671 & -1.5883 \end{bmatrix},$$

$$Q = \begin{bmatrix} -159.7638 & 0.9609 & 0.3795 \\ 0.9609 & -156.5495 & 0.1543 \\ 0.3795 & 0.1543 & -157.6680 \end{bmatrix},$$

$$M_1 = \begin{bmatrix} 75.3780 & 0.3459 & 0.1366 \\ 0.3459 & 76.5351 & 0.0555 \\ 0.1366 & 0.0555 & 76.1325 \end{bmatrix},$$

$$M_2 = \begin{bmatrix} 75.3780 & 0.3459 & 0.1366 \\ 0.3459 & 76.5351 & 0.0555 \\ 0.1366 & 0.0555 & 76.1325 \end{bmatrix},$$

$$Z = \begin{bmatrix} 81.5876 & -1.4169 & -0.5596 \\ -1.4169 & 76.8480 & -0.2275 \\ -0.5596 & -0.2275 & 78.4972 \end{bmatrix},$$

$\delta = 73.3198$, $\lambda = 60.5418$.

CONCLUSION

In this paper, we have dealt with the problem of robust stability analysis for a class of uncertain stochastic delayed neural networks with interval time-varying delays. Some new stability criteria have been presented to guarantee that these delayed neural networks are globally, robustly, asymptotically stable in the mean square for all admissible parameter uncertainties, and the stability criteria have been given in terms of linear matrix inequality (LMIs). Numerical examples have also been used to demonstrate the usefulness and less conservative of the main results.

ACKNOWLEDGMENT

This work described in this paper was partially supported by National Natural Science Foundation of China (No. 60973114, 60903213), Natural Science Foundation Project of Chongqing of China (Grant No. CSTC, 2009BB2378, 2008BB2189, 2007BB2386).

REFERENCES

Arik, S. (2000). Stability analysis of delayed neural networks. *IEEE Transactions on Circuits and Systems. I, Fundamental Theory and Applications*, *47*(7), 1089–1092. doi:10.1109/81.855465

Blythe, S., Mao, X., & Liao, X. (2001). Stability of stochastic delay neural networks. *Journal of the Franklin Institute*, *338*(4), 481–495. doi:10.1016/S0016-0032(01)00016-3

Boyd, S., El Ghaoui, L., Feron, E., & Balakrishnan, V. (1994). *Linear matrix inequalities in system and control theory*. Philadelphia: SIAM.

Chen, W., & Jiao, L. (2010). Adaptive tracking for periodically time-varying and nonlinearly parameterized systems using multilayer neural networks. *IEEE Transactions on Neural Networks*, *21*(2), 345–351. doi:10.1109/TNN.2009.2038999

Feng, W., Yang, S. X., Fu, W., & Wu, H. (2009). Robust stability analysis of uncertain stochastic neural networks with interval time-varying delay. *Chaos, Solitons, and Fractals*, *41*(1), 414–424. doi:10.1016/j.chaos.2008.01.024

Feng, W., Yang, S. X., & Wu, H. (2009). On robust stability of uncertain stochastic neural networks with distributed and interval time-varying delays. *Chaos, Solitons, and Fractals*, *42*(4), 2095–2104. doi:10.1016/j.chaos.2009.03.141

Forti, M., Manetti, S., & Marini, M. (1994). Necessary and sufficient condition for absolute stability of neural networks. *IEEE Transactions on Circuits and Systems. I, Fundamental Theory and Applications*, *41*(7), 491–494. doi:10.1109/81.298364

Gu, K. (2001). Discretization schemes for Lyapunov-Krasovskii functionals in time-delay systems. *Kybernetika*, *37*(4), 479–504.

Gu, K., Han, Q. L., Luo, A. C. J., & Niculescu, S. I. (2001). Discretized Lyapunov functional for systems with distributed delay and piecewise constant coefficients. *International Journal of Control*, *74*(7), 737–744. doi:10.1080/00207170010031486

He, Y., Wang, Q. G., & Lin, C. (2006). An improved H_∞ filter design for systems with time-varying interval delay. *IEEE Transactions on Circuits and Wystems. II, Express Briefs, 53*(11), 1235–1239. doi:10.1109/TCSII.2006.883209

Huang, H., & Cao, J. (2007). Exponential stability analysis of uncertain stochastic neural networks with multiple delays. *Nonlinear Analysis Real World Applications, 8*(2), 646–653. doi:10.1016/j.nonrwa.2006.02.003

Huang, H., & Feng, G. (2007). Delay-dependent stability for uncertain stochastic neural networks with time-varying delay. *Physica A: Statistical Mechanics and its Applications, 381*, 93-103.

Jiang, X., & Han, Q. L. (2005). On H_∞ control for linear systems with interval time-varying delay. *Automatica, 41*(12), 2099–2106. doi:10.1016/j.automatica.2005.06.012

Jiang, X., & Han, Q. L. (2006). Delay-dependent robust stability for uncertain linear systems with interval time-varying delay. *Automatica, 42*(6), 1059–1065. doi:10.1016/j.automatica.2006.02.019

Kim, J. H. (2001). Delay and its time-derivative dependent robust stability of time-delayed linear systems with uncertainty. *IEEE Transactions on Automatic Control, 46*(5), 789–792. doi:10.1109/9.920802

Liao, X., Chen, G., & Sanchez, E. N. (2002). Delay-dependent exponential stability analysis of delayed neural networks: an LMI approach. *Neural Networks, 15*(7), 855–866. doi:10.1016/S0893-6080(02)00041-2

Liao, X. X., & Mao, X. (1996). Exponential stability and instability of stochastic neural networks. *Stochastic Analysis and Applications, 14*(2), 165–185. doi:10.1080/07362999608809432

Liu, B., & Liu, X. (2007). Robust stability of uncertain discrete impulsive systems. *IEEE Transactions on Circuits and Wystems. II, Express Briefs, 54*(4), 455–459. doi:10.1109/TCSII.2007.892395

Liu, Y., Wang, Z., & Liu, X. (2008). Robust stability of discrete-time stochastic neural networks with time-varying delays. *Neurocomputing, 71*(4-6), Mao, X. (1997). *Stochastic differential equations and their applications.* Chichester, UK: Horwood. 823-833.

Mingo, L., Gómez, N., Arroyo, F., & Castellanos, J. (2009). Hierarchical function approximation with a neural network model. *International Journal of Software Science and Computational Intelligence, 1*(3), 67–80.

Mou, S., Gao, H., Lam, J., & Qiang, W. (2008). A new criterion of delay-dependent asymptotic stability for Hopfield neural networks with time delay. *IEEE Transactions on Neural Networks, 19*(3), 532–535. doi:10.1109/TNN.2007.912593

Rakkiyappan, R., & Balasubramaniam, P. (2008). Delay-dependent asymptotic stability for stochastic delayed recurrent neural networks with time varying delays. *Applied Mathematics and Computation, 198*(2), 526–533. doi:10.1016/j.amc.2007.08.053

Tian, E., & Peng, C. (2001). Delay-dependent stability analysis and synthesis of uncertain T-S fuzzy systems with time-varying delay. *Fuzzy Sets and Systems, 157*(4), 544–559. doi:10.1016/j.fss.2005.06.022

Tian, Y. C., Yu, Z. G., & Fidge, C. (2007). Multifractal nature of network induced time delay in networked control systems. *Physics Letters. [Part A], 361*(1/2), 103–107. doi:10.1016/j.physleta.2006.09.046

Wan, L., & Sun, J. (2005). Mean square exponential stability of stochastic delayed Hopfield neural networks. *Physics Letters. [Part A]*, *343*(4), 306–318. doi:10.1016/j.physleta.2005.06.024

Wang, Z., Lauria, S., Fang, J., & Liu, X. (2007). Exponential stability of uncertain stochastic neural networks with mixed time-delays. *Chaos, Solitons, and Fractals*, *32*(1), 62–72. doi:10.1016/j.chaos.2005.10.061

Wang, Z., Liu, Y., & Liu, X. (2009). State estimation for jumping recurrent neural networks with discrete and distributed delays. *Neural Networks*, *22*(1), 41–48. doi:10.1016/j.neunet.2008.09.015

Wang, Z., Shu, H., Fang, J., & Liu, X. (2006). Robust stability for stochastic Hopfield neural networks with time delays. *Nonlinear Analysis Real World Applications*, *7*(5), 1119–1128. doi:10.1016/j.nonrwa.2005.10.004

Yue, D., Han, Q. L., & Lam, J. (2005). Network-based robust H_∞ control of systems with uncertainty. *Automatica*, *41*(6), 999–1007. doi:10.1016/j.automatica.2004.12.011

Yue, D., Peng, C., & Tang, G. Y. (2006). Guaranteed cost control of linear systems over networks with state and input quantisations. *IEE Proceedings. Control Theory and Applications*, *153*(6), 658–664. doi:10.1049/ip-cta:20050294

Zhang, J., Shi, P., & Qiu, J. (2007). Novel robust stability criteria for uncertain stochastic Hopfield neural networks with time-varying delays. *Nonlinear Analysis Real World Applications*, *8*(4), 1349–1357. doi:10.1016/j.nonrwa.2006.06.010

Zhang, Q., & Xu, X. W. J. (2007). Delay-dependent global stability results for delayed Hopfield neural networks. *Chaos, Solitons, and Fractals*, *34*(2), 662–668. doi:10.1016/j.chaos.2006.03.073

Zhao, H., & Wang, G. (2004). Delay-independent exponential stability of recurrent neural networks. *Physics Letters. [Part A]*, *333*(5/6), 399–407. doi:10.1016/j.physleta.2004.10.040

This work was previously published in International Journal of Software Science and Computational Intelligence, Volume 2, Issue 4, edited by Yingxu Wang, pp. 45-69, copyright 2010 by IGI Publishing (an imprint of IGI Global).

Chapter 25
Classifier Ensemble Based Analysis of a Genome–Wide SNP Dataset Concerning Late-Onset Alzheimer Disease

Lúcio Coelho
Biomind LLC, USA

Ben Goertzel
Biomind LLC, USA, and Xiamen University, China

Cassio Pennachin
Biomind LLC, USA

Chris Heward
Kronos Science Laboratory, USA

ABSTRACT

In this paper, the OpenBiomind toolkit is used to apply GA, GP, and local search methods to analyze a large SNP dataset concerning Late-Onset Alzheimer's Disease (LOAD). Classification models identifying LOAD with statistically significant accuracy are identified as well as using ensemble-based important features analysis in order to identify brain genes related to LOAD, most notably the solute carrier gene SLC6A15. Ensemble analysis is used to identify potentially significant interactions between genes in the context of LOAD.

INTRODUCTION

We report results obtained by using the OpenBio-mind machine learning based bioinformatics data analysis toolkit (see http://code.google.com/p/openbiomind/) for the analysis of a dataset of

DOI: 10.4018/978-1-4666-0264-9.ch025

Single-Nucleotide Polymorphisms (SNPs) concerning late-onset Alzheimer's Disease (LOAD) (Reiman et al., 2007). Putting it simply, SNPs are genomic variations of a single DNA base observed in the population under study. Although they not necessarily have a direct relation with a given phenotype (say, a medical condition with some potential genetic background), they often serve as markers commonly associated with those phenotypes. Hence the interest in studying SNPs for the development of diagnosis tools or for collecting clues that might point to genes interesting for shedding light into the problem at hand.

We used the OpenBiomind functions which provide Genetic Algorithms (GA), Genetic Programming (GP) and local search methods for supervised categorization; and also functions which enable several forms of ensemble-based analysis, including important features analysis, Model Utilization-Based Clustering (MUTIC) and Model Based Role Analysis (MOBRA). In this way we

- Obtained classification rules that can distinguish LOAD from Control via SNP combinations
- Identified a number of potentially LOAD related SNPs and genes.

Classification results were tested with permutation analysis and the accuracy results are described here. While the results are highly statistically significant, the accuracy is not sufficient to serve as the basis of a practical diagnostic test. Further, it is our tentative, subjective opinion based on this work that no analytic method is going to be able to figure out a practical diagnostic test based on the SNPs in this study.

However, regarding the identification of genes potentially related to Alzheimer's Disease (AD), our results are more promising. The metatask classification method used by OpenBiomind provided a set of most important (in the context of LOAD) SNPs, and their related genes. The relations of these genes to LOAD were assessed by clustering and with biological analyses. Visualization for clustering results and SNP inter-relations are shown in order to ease the interpretation. Results show a few brain genes that we believe have a high chance of being related to LOAD, especially the solute carrier gene, SLC6A15.

The results presented here constitute another piece of evidence in favor of the power of the unorthodox OpenBiomind methods to yield statistically meaningful analytical results and novel, suggestive biological hypotheses.

DATA

Original Data

The dataset used in this study comprises the genome-wide SNP mapping of 1411 samples. 859 of them are case for late-onset Alzheimer Disease (LOAD), while the remaining 552 are control. Each sample is characterized by 312,316 single-nucleotide polymorphisms (SNPs). A more thorough description is given in Reiman et al. (2007).

The samples in the dataset are divided into three different cohorts representing different sources: a "Neuropathological Discovery Cohort" of 736 brain donors, a "Neuropathological Replication Cohort" of 311 brain donors and an additional "Clinical Replication Cohort" of 364 living subjects.

Sample Partition and SNP Selection

Machine learning experiments reported here were executed over the following sample partitions:

- All samples
- Neuropathological discovery cohort
- Neuropathological replication cohort
- Clinical replication cohort

Each of the sample partitions above was by its turn divided in three pairs of train-test sets, in a 3-fold cross-validation. All classification results reported here were obtained by applying classification methods to those folds divisions.

Finally, for each of those sample partitions, the following kinds of SNP selection were performed:

- **Homozygosis-based selection:** selection of the top 100 SNPs with highest positive difference of homozygosis frequency in case and control samples. In other words, selected SNPs are those with high homo-zygosis incidence in case samples and low in control samples.
- **Gene-based selection:** Selection of 1054 SNPs associated to 64 genes suspected to have some relation to Alzheimer Disease, compiled from literature on the condition.

PRELIMINARY ANALYSIS

Since the volume of data in this study is very large and leads to very long execution times, some preliminary experimentation was performed in order to choose the following constraints for the main sequence of experiments:

- The data partition(s) to be used.
- The type of SNP selection to be used.
- The supervised machine learning (or simply classification) method to be used.

All Machine Learning experimentation reported here was performed using the OpenBio-mind toolkit, which contains support for SNP data alongside microarray gene expression data. The OpenBiomind framework is conceptually similar to the earlier, proprietary Biomind Analyzer data analysis framework described in Goertzel et al. (2007). The OpenBiomind classification methods available for SNPs are:

- Genetic Programming (GP): evolves Boolean (logical) expressions that have as input variables telling whether a given SNP matches a given value in a sample.
- Genetic Algorithm (GA): evolves pattern-strength classifiers. A pattern strength classifier is simply a list of SNPs that classifies a given sample as Case if the number of

SNPs in the list that is in homozygosis is greater than the number of SNPs in the list that is in heterozygosis.
- Local search: evolves pattern-strength classifiers using simple local search.

The above methodologies for analyzing SNP data are described in more detail in Go-ertzel et al. (2006), where they were applied to analyzing data regarding Chronic Fatigue Syndrome.

For each of the six combinations of classification method/feature selection, a short sequence (or metatask, using OpenBiomind lingo) of 100 classification tasks was executed. (A classification task is the application of the method at hand to the three train-test validation folds described in the previous Dataset section. Also, it may be useful to stress that all three classification methods above are non-deterministic, and therefore different classification tasks over the same data will not produce exactly the same results.) The validation folding used was that for all samples, from all cohorts. Average train and test accuracies for all classification tasks for the resulting combinations are shown in Table 1.

It can be noticed in this table that the two simplest methods - GA and Local Search - are the ones reaching the highest in and out of sample accuracies in homozygosis selection. Also, the purely numerical method of homozygosis-based selection is clearly superior to the gene-based

Table 1. Accuracies by method

Method	Average Accuracies			
	Homozygosis-based selection		Gene-based selection	
	Train	Test	Train	Test
GP	64.5%	59.3%	62.2%	60.6%
GA	78.9%	57.1%	62.2%	60.2%
Local search	77.7%	61.0%	62.5%	61.1%

method, which relies on previous literature about Alzheimer Disease.

One can see from the results above that this dataset poses a very difficult generalization problem, meaning that a classifier can reach reasonably high accuracies in the training set and nevertheless get near-random accuracies in the test set. However, it will be shown through permutation analysis in the following sections that nevertheless the out-of-sample accuracies are still highly statistically significant, and therefore the feature analysis executed over the models generated during classification experiments is likely to represent real patterns regarding LOAD.

Weighting in and out-of-sample accuracies, the chosen combination of classification method and feature selection was local search over homozygosis-based selection. Next, we applied this combination separately to the three existing cohorts in order to see if there was some suspicious deviance from the results above obtained using all samples from all cohorts. The numbers thus obtained are shown in Table 2.

Oddly, it can be clearly seen that the two neuropathological cohorts have a strong tendency to overfit, getting out-of-sample accuracies well below random. On the other hand, the clinical replication cohort seems more promising in terms of generalization, capturing LOAD patterns that present some applicability to out-of-sample classifications.

Due to that quality disparity between the sample sets composing the data, the main experimentation described in the next section will deal separately with all samples and with the clinical replication cohort.

MAIN ANALYSIS RESULTS

Classification Quality

Our main run of analytical experiments involved a meta-task of 1000 classification tasks, each one using local search applied over homozygosis-selected data. These were run separately for two data partitions: all samples and just Clinical

replication samples, for reasons explained above. Table 3 shows the metatask accuracies from our main analytic experiments.

Mirroring preliminary results, experimentation on all samples yielded out-of-sample accuracies that are basically random, and therefore it seemed suspicious at first that this experiment sequence was detecting any real pattern at all. In order to test that hypothesis, we further conducted a permutation analysis: it consisted of 10 metatasks of 100 tasks, each one running on a version of the all-samples dataset were category labels for case/control were randomly shuffled among shuffles. In Table 4 we see the comparison of average and standard deviation of in and out of sample categories for all 1,000 tasks for both experiment sequences (shuffled and non-shuffled) for the all-samples partition.

Table 2. Accuracies by cohort

Cohort	Average Accuracies	
	Train	**Test**
Neuropathological discovery	83.5%	56.8%
Neuropathological replication	93.2%	54.4%
Clinical replication	88.6%	64.8%

Table 3. Main Experimentation accuracies

Sample partition	Average accuracy	
	Train	**Test**
All samples	76.7%	59.4%
Clinical replication cohort	88.7%	64.9%

Table 4. Comparing shuffled and real accuracies

Experiment Sequence	Average accuracies (%)			
	Train		**Test**	
	Average	**Standard Deviation**	**Average**	**Standard Deviation**
Non-shuffled	76.7	0.7	59.4	1.0
Shuffled	76.0	0.9	54.9	1.4

Assuming normal distributions, the numbers above for out-of-sample accuracies imply a p-value <0.001, implying that the differences between distributions for shuffled and non-shuffled sequences have high statistical significance. In particular, we can see that shuffled data has a stronger tendency for overfitting, achieving in-sample accuracies comparable to non-shuffled data, but lower out-of-sample ones; in other words, non-shuffled data generalizes better, indicating that the detected patterns are likely to be real ones.

Furthermore, another interesting distribution is that of sizes of models produced by the two sequences. Table 5 shows the average and standard deviation of the distributions of sizes of models for shuffled and non-shuffled data.

Although visually the numbers look very similar, due to the large number of cases the p-value for the distribution above is also <0.001. Also, it is interesting to see that non-shuffled models are on average a bit smaller, which is a good sign: in Machine Learning, smaller models are considered better, in terms of being more parsimonious and less prone to overfitting.

Important Features

The metatask methodology, by generating a large ensemble of models through a non-deterministic classification algorithm, allows the computation of the importance, or utility, of features in the dataset, a technique described more fully in Looks et al. (2007); Goertzel et al. (2006b). The importance of a given feature f is computed as the frequency of occurrence of f through all generated models.

According to that metric, Table 6 shows the top 5 most important SNPs found for the main test on all samples, in decreasing order of importance. The genes were those SNPs are located - which may potentially be of biological functional importance for the problem at hand - are also supplied. Importance is given as percent of models using the SNP. Further extended versions of this and the following tables may be found on the supplementary website for the paper.

Interestingly, it is also possible to compute importance for a given gene g, by simply computing the percent of models that use SNPs associated to g. Table 7 shows the top 5 most important genes under that view.

Table 8, by its turn, shows the most important SNPs obtained by computing importance values for the sequence using just the Clinical Replication Cohort.

Somehow surprisingly, the list above is disjoint from the corresponding list regarding all three cohorts. This disparity appears again in the gene-oriented list for the Clinical Replication sequence, shown in Table 9.

As pointed out by the out-of-sample and metatask accuracy results, the clinical replication cohort seemed to be more promising and we decided to look through the biological meanings of its top 10 important features. Unfortunately, there are a lot of badly characterized features

Table 5. Comparing model sizes

Experiment Sequence	Model size (# of SNPs)	
	Average	Standard Deviation
Non-shuffled	33.3	3.6
Shuffled	33.9	3.8

Table 6. Most important SNPs, Main Test

SNP	Importance (%)	Corresponding gene
SNP_A-2079203	40.3	TMEM51: Homo sapiens transmembrane protein 51 (TMEM51), mRNA.
SNP_A-1848074	39.7	CDH11: Homo sapiens cadherin 11, type 2, OB-cadherin (osteoblast) (CDH11), mRNA.
SNP_A-1987295	39.2	HS3ST5: Homo sapiens heparan sulfate (glucosamine) 3-O-sulfotransferase 5 (HS3ST5), mRNA.
SNP_A-2148765	38.7	RGS1: Homo sapiens regulator of G-protein signalling 1 (RGS1), mRNA.

(e.g., 'domain containing like') and even a chromosome open reading frame. The only feature that could have any relation to Alzheimer is SLC6A15 (the first in the rank in both sets). This feature is a neurotransmitter transport with unknown exact function. Previous works from the literature have showed that a protein from the same family (SLC11A2) has very weak relations to Alzheimer's (Jamieson et al., 2005). We believe that our results implicate SLC6A15 somehow in the disease. The following two features found in the brain are: NBEA: Homo sapiens neurobeachin (NBEA), mRNA, implicated in neuronal trafficking and BAI3: Homo sapiens brain-specific angiogenesis inhibitor 3 (BAI3), mRNA, implicated in angiogenesis in brain. Both have no reported relations to Alzheimer yet. All other features are brain unrelated and/or not characterized.

Clustering Analysis

Traditional techniques of clustering applied to gene expression can be adapted to work with

Table 7. Most important genes, main test

Gene	Importance (%)	Description
SLCO3A1	80.8	Homo sapiens solute carrier organic anion transporter family, member 3A1 (SLCO3A1), mRNA.
CDH11	64.3	Homo sapiens cadherin 11, type 2, OB-cadherin (osteoblast) (CDH11), mRNA.
ELP2	56.1	Homo sapiens elongation protein 2 homolog (S. cerevisiae) (ELP2), mRNA.
HS3ST5	46.6	Homo sapiens heparan sulfate (glucosamine) 3-O-sulfotransferase 5 (HS3ST5), mRNA.
CHORDC1	45.2	Homo sapiens cysteine and histidine-rich domain (CHORD)-containing 1 (CHORDC1), mRNA.

Table 8. Most important SNPs, clinical replication

SNP	Importance	Associated gene
SNP_A-2074605	34.7	SLC6A15: Homo sapiens solute carrier family 6, member 15 (SLC6A15), transcript variant 1, mRNA.
SNP_A-2216245	29.5	TANC1: Homo sapiens tetratricopeptide repeat, ankyrin repeat and coiled-coil containing 1 (TANC1), mRNA.
SNP_A-4227539	27.9	NBEA: Homo sapiens neurobeachin (NBEA), mRNA.
SNP_A-4295379	26.2	
SNP_A-2301218	24.3	

Table 9. Most important genes, clinical replication

Gene	Importance (%)	Description
SLC6A15	65.8	Homo sapiens solute carrier family 6, member 15 (SLC6A15), transcript variant 1, mRNA.
BAI3	56.6	Homo sapiens brain-specific angiogenesis inhibitor 3 (BAI3), mRNA.
LRFN5	34.5	Homo sapiens leucine rich repeat and fibronectin type III domain containing 5 (LRFN5), mRNA.
TYRP1	31.6	Homo sapiens tyrosinase-related protein 1 (TYRP1), mRNA.
TANC1	29.5	Homo sapiens tetratricopeptide repeat, ankyrin repeat and coiled-coil containing 1 (TANC1), mRNA.

SNP data in a meaningful way, provided that a distance metric suitable for working with SNPs is supplied. Here, we developed a metric, informally called "co-zygosis", which compares two different SNPs by checking matches of homozygosis and heterozygosis for corresponding samples. Let s_1 and s_2 be two SNPs and S a sample. $match(s_1, s_2, S)$ is a function that returns 1 if s_1 and s_2 are both in homozygosis (or heterozygosis), 0 otherwise. Considering the set of all samples $\{S_1, S_2, S_3, ..., S_n\}$, the similarity metric between two SNPs is defined as $sim(s_1, s_2) = (match(s_1, s_2, S_1) + match(s_1, s_2, S_2) + match(s_1, s_2, S_3) + ... + match(s_1, s_2, S_n)) / n$.

Omniclust, OpenBiomind's clustering algorithm, was then applied over the selected SNPs (the ones used in the classification experiments) for both all samples and clinical replication samples using "co-zygosis" as a similarity metric. Omniclust is almost non-parametric (the similarity metric is the only parameter used) and tends to break up the data into tightly coupled "clustlets" containing a handful of elements. Those clusters can be ranked by quality metrics based on homogeneity/separation or combined utility, therefore allowing to one analyzing the data to focus on a few small sets of genes that apparently are more relevant to the problem under study.

Clusters obtained using the "co-zygosis" metric where quite uninteresting, in the sense that clusters tended to just gather together SNPs located in the same gene. For instance, the cluster with highest geometric quality (product homogeneity x separation) for the dataset corresponding to all samples, contained only SNPs from gene AFF1 (Homo sapiens AF4/FMR2 family, member 1).

An approach potentially able to provide more insight into LOAD-relevant relationships between SNPs involves clustering of SNP-related information extracted from ensembles of classification models, instead of using SNP allelic data directly. It is possible to extract utilization vectors from the ensemble of models for each SNP and then apply the clustering algorithm over those transformed SNP-associated vectors.

OpenBiomind provides two types of such model-based clustering transformations, described more fully in Looks et al. (2007) and Goertzel et al. (2006b). The first one, MUTIC, associates each dimension of the SNP-related vector to a classification task, and sets as the value for each dimension the utility/importance of the SNP in that particular task. Another transformation, MOBRA, associates to each vector dimension a SNP used by the ensemble of models, and sets the value of the dimension as the degree of co-occurrence between the corresponding SNP and the SNP associated to the vector. For instance a SNP s_i will have a transformed vector $mobra(s_i) = \{c(s_i, s_1), c(s_i, s_2), c(s_i, s_3), ..., c(s_i, s_n)\}$, where $c(s_i, s_j)$ is the co-occurrence between s_i and s_j - that is, the percent of models using both s_i and s_j - and $\{s_1, s_2, s_3, ..., s_n\}$ is the set of all SNPs used by the ensemble of models.

Both types of transformation were tried. Unfortunately, MUTIC has a strong tendency for "overclustering" in datasets with relatively few features (such as the one used, containing just selected SNPs), and therefore grouped all SNPs into a single cluster, which is not interesting. On the other hand, MOBRA produced rich clusterings. In Table 10, the top two clusters (according to geometric quality) are shown for Omniclust applied over MOBRA transforms using the classification models generated for all samples. Potentially, the clusters shown in Table 10 (and the others shown on the supplementary website) may reveal some LOAD-related inter-relationship between clustered SNPs/genes.

Table 11 by its turn displays the results of the same type of clustering applied over the Clinical Replication sequence.

Finally, as in the case of conventional gene-expression clustering, MOBRA clustering can also be visualized. Figure 1 and Figure 2 at the supplementary website show the visualization of all clusters for the all-samples and clinical replication partitions, respectively.

The top 5 clusters found by MOBRA over the clinical replication cohort were analyzed via in-

Table 10. SNP clustering, all samples

Quality	SNP	Gene
0.56516	SNP_A-1899703	GRM3: Homo sapiens glutamate receptor, metabotropic 3 (GRM3), mRNA.
	SNP_A-2312908	SLCO3A1: Homo sapiens solute carrier organic anion transporter family, member 3A1 (SLCO3A1), mRNA.
	SNP_A-4213249	-
0.54796	SNP_A-2298547	CHORDC1: Homo sapiens cysteine and histidine-rich domain (CHORD)-containing 1 (CHORDC1), mRNA.
	SNP_A-2105091	-
	SNP_A-2079203	TMEM51: Homo sapiens transmembrane protein 51 (TMEM51), mRNA.
	SNP_A-4250072	NRCAM: Homo sapiens neuronal cell adhesion molecule (NRCAM), transcript variant 3, mRNA.

Table 11. SNP clustering, clinical replication

Quality	SNP	Gene
0.50941	SNP_A-4209746	SLC9A9: Homo sapiens solute carrier family 9 (sodium/hydrogen exchanger), member 9 (SLC9A9), mRNA.
	SNP_A-2241000	SLC6A15 Homo sapiens solute carrier family 6, member 15 (SLC6A15), transcript variant 1, mRNA.
	SNP_A-4209817	-
	SNP_A-2025707	LOC92345: Homo sapiens hypothetical protein BC008207 (LOC92345), mRNA.
	SNP_A-1994538	ZFPM2: Homo sapiens zinc finger protein, multitype 2 (ZFPM2), mRNA.
	SNP_A-2058147	SLC6A15: Homo sapiens solute carrier family 6, member 15 (SLC6A15), transcript variant 1, mRNA.
	SNP_A-2114323	C5orf21: Homo sapiens chromosome 5 open reading frame 21 (C5orf21), mRNA.
	SNP_A-4232317	PPP1R3A: Homo sapiens protein phosphatase 1, regulatory (inhibitor) subunit 3A (glycogen and sarcoplasmic reticulum binding subunit, skeletal muscle)
	SNP_A-2313882	-
	SNP_A-2014521	CNTN5: Homo sapiens contactin 5 (CNTN5), transcript variant 1, mRNA.
0.50372	SNP_A-4295379	-
	SNP_A-2216245	TANC1: Homo sapiens tetratricopeptide repeat, ankyrin repeat and coiled-coil containing 1 (TANC1), mRNA.
	SNP_A-2074605	SLC6A15: Homo sapiens solute carrier family 6, member 15 (SLC6A15), transcript variant 1, mRNA.
	SNP_A-4227539	NBEA: Homo sapiens neurobeachin (NBEA), mRNA.
	SNP_A-4201456	POSTN: Homo sapiens periostin, osteoblast specific factor (POSTN), mRNA.
	SNP_A-4228152	-

spection of the relevant biological literature. The majority of the clusters show brain related features, two from a neurotransmitter carrier family of proteins, found in clusters 1 and 2, which have a not-present member (SLC11A1) related poorly to AD, as discussed later. The others are neuro-beachin (NBEA), found in cluster 2, which may be involved in trafficking events and BAI3, found in cluster 4, which is a brain specific angiogen-esis inhibitor. We believe biological experimentations are needed in order to reveal probable relations to AD.

Graph Analysis

While clustering is already a means of detecting potential LOAD-relevant SNP inter-relationships, OpenBiomind contains yet another feature - graph visualization - able to integrate different types of information in a diagram with SNPs as nodes interconnected by edges showing inter-relatedness metrics.

A given graph shows the top n most important SNPs and their strongest relations of co-occurrence (solid lines) and "co-zygosis" (dashed lines).

Each SNP node still has information on the corresponding gene and a row of numbers representing importance degree, importance rank, differentiation rank and SAM rank. (SAM is a significance analysis originally developed for micro arrays, but the numerical method can also be adapted to SNPs.) Figure 1 and Figure 2 show such graphs for all samples and clinical replication samples only, respectively.

It can be seen that the graph for all samples has a "centralizing SNP" - SNP_A-4287142, from gene PRKG1 - were seven co-zygosis edges converge. Another centralizing SNP - SNP_A-2148765, from gene RGS1 - operates on the co-occurrence level.

Figure 1. Graph visualization of main SNP interrelations for all samples. For each node, the SNP code is given in the first row and the corresponding gene (if any) in the second row. The third row shows importance, importance rank, differentiation rank and SAM rank, in that order. Solid edges show co-occurrence values, while dashed edges show "co-zygosis".

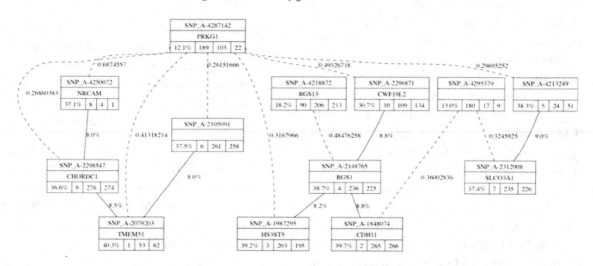

Figure 2. Graph visualization of main SNP interrelations for Clinical Replication samples. Visualization conventions are the same ones used in Fig. 2.

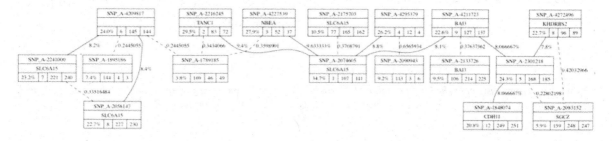

As for the graph concerning clinical replication samples, there seems to be only one centralizing SNP based on co-occurrence: SNP_A-2074605, from gene SLC6A15. Curiously, as seen in our biological analysis of the most important features and MOBRA clustering, this gene is related to a family of genes (solute carrier family) which have shown small relations to AD.

CONCLUSION

As a methodological exercise, the results reported here demonstrate the value of the OpenBiomind tools for analyzing a large and complex SNP dataset which is also a difficult dataset, in the sense of lacking highly obvious patterns related to the biological phenomenon under study. The capability to find statistically significant classification rules in difficult data is demonstrated, as is the ability to identify potentially interesting, promising-looking data patterns via several forms of classifier ensemble analysis.

As a biological study, there is one clear negative result and one clear positive result. The negative result is that this dataset does not appear to support the learning of a useful diagnostic rule for LOAD. It is of course possible that some more powerful machine learning algorithm could identify such a diagnostic from this dataset, but our intuition is that this is unlikely. The positive result is that the solute carrier gene SLC6A15 appears to have a high chance of playing a major role in LOAD. To explore this hypothesis further, however, will require additional lab experiments.

REFERENCES

Goertzel, B., Coelho, L., Pennachin, C., & Mudado, M. (2006b). Identifying Complex Biological Interactions based on Categorical Gene Expression Data. In *Proceedings of the Conference on Evolutionary Computing 2006 (CEC 2006)*, Vancouver, Canada.

Goertzel, B., Pennachin, C., Coelho, L., Gurbaxani, B., Maloney, E. B., & Jones, J. F. (2006). Combinations of single nucleotide polymorphisms in neuroendocrine effector and receptor genes are predictive of chronic fatigue syndrome. *Pharmacogenomics*, 7(3), 475–483. doi:10.2217/14622416.7.3.475

Goertzel, B., Pennachin, C., Coelho, L., Shikida, L., & Queiroz, M. (2007). Biomind ArrayGenius and GeneGenius: Web Services Offering Microarray and SNP Data Analysis via Novel Machine Learning Methods. In *Proceedings of IAAI 2007*, Vancouver, Canada (pp. 1700-1706).

Jamieson, S. E., White, J. K., Howson, J. M., Pask, R., Smith, A. N., & Brayne, C. (2005, February). Candidate gene association study of solute carrier family 11a members 1 (SLC11A1) and 2 (SLC11A2) genes in Alzheimer's disease. *Neuroscience Letters*, 374(2), 124–128. doi:10.1016/j.neulet.2004.10.038

Looks, M., Goertzel, B., Coelho, L., Mudado, M., & Pennachin, C. (2007). Clustering Gene Expression Data via Mining Ensembles of Classification Rules Evolved Using MOSES. In *Proceedings of the Genetic and Evolutionary Computation Conference (GECCO)* (pp. 407-414).

Reiman, E. M., Webster, J. A., Myers, A. J., Hardy, J., Dunckley, T., & Zismann, V. L. (2007). GAB2 Alleles Modify Alzheimer's Risk in APOE e4 Carriers. *Neuron*, 54(5), 713–720. doi:10.1016/j.neuron.2007.05.022

This work was previously published in International Journal of Software Science and Computational Intelligence, Volume 2, Issue 4, edited by Yingxu Wang, pp. 60-71, copyright 2010 by IGI Publishing (an imprint of IGI Global).

Compilation of References

Abbott, R. K., & Garcia-Molina, H. (1992). Scheduling real-time transactions: A performance evaluation. *ACM Transactions on Database Systems*, *17*(3), 513–560. doi:10.1145/132271.132276

Ackerman, M. S., & Starr, B. (1995). *Social activity indicators: interface components for CSCW systems.* Paper presented at the 8th annual ACM symposium on User Interface and Software Technology, Pittsburgh, PA.

Aho, A. V., Sethi, R., & Ullman, J. D. (1985). *Compilers: Principles, Techniques, and Tools*. Reading, MA: Addison-Wesley.

Aiber, S., Gilat, D., Landau, A., Razinkov, N., Sela, A., & Wasserkrug, S. (2004, May). Autonomic self-optimization according to business objectives. In *Proceedings of the International Conference on Autonomic Computing*, New York (pp. 206- 213).

Albert, D., Hockemeyer, C., Mayer, B., & Steiner, C. M. (2007). Cognitive Structural Modeling of Skills for Technology-Enhanced Learning. In *Proceedings of the Seventh IEEE International Conference on Advanced Learning Technologies (ICALT 2007)*.

Aleksander, I., & Dummall, B. (2003). Axioms and Tests for the Presence of Minimal Consciousness in Agents. *Journal of Consciousness Studies*, *10*(4-5).

Allen, J. F. (1983). Maintaining knowledge about temporal intervals. *Communications of the ACM*, *26*(11), 832–843. doi:10.1145/182.358434

Alligood, K. T., Sauer, T. D., & Yorke, J. A. (1996). *Chaos: An Introduction to Dynamical Systems*. New York: Springer Verlag.

Altschul, S. F., Boguski, M. S., Gish, W., & Wootton, J. C. (1994). Issues in Searching Molecular Sequence Databases. *Nature Genetics*, *6*, 119–129. doi:10.1038/ng0294-119

Altschul, S. F., Gish, W., Miller, W., Myers, E., & Lipman, D. J. (1990). Basic Local Alignment Search Tool. *Journal of Molecular Biology*, *215*, 403–410.

Anderson, J. R. (1990). *The Adaptive Character of Thought (Studies in Cognition Series)* (p. 304). London: Psychology Press.

Anderson, M., Bothell, M., Byrne, D., Douglass, S., Lebiere, C., & Qin, Y. (2004). An integrated theory of the mind. *Psychological Review*, *111*(4), 1036–1060. doi:10.1037/0033-295X.111.4.1036

Anderson, T. E., Lazowska, E. D., & Levy, H. M. (1989). The Performance Implications of Thread Management Alternatives for Shared-Memory Multiprocessors. *IEEE Transactions on Computers*, *38*(12), 1631–1644. doi:10.1109/12.40843

Angelov, P., Lughofer, E., & Zhou, X. (2008). Evolving fuzzy classifiers using different model architectures. *Fuzzy Sets and Systems*, *159*(23), 3160–3182. doi:10.1016/j.fss.2008.06.019

Anil, K., Jain, A., Ross, A., & Flynn, P. (2007). *Handbook of Biometrics*. Berlin: Springer Verlag.

Arbib, M. A. (2005). The Mirror System Hypothesis: How did protolanguage evolve? In Tallerman, M. (Ed.), *Language Origins: Perspectives on Evolution*. Oxford, UK: Oxford University Press.

Arik, S. (2000). Stability analysis of delayed neural networks. *IEEE Transactions on Circuits and Systems. I, Fundamental Theory and Applications*, *47*(7), 1089–1092. doi:10.1109/81.855465

Arneodo, A., Audit, B., Decoster, N., Muzy, J.-F., & Vaillant, C. (2002). Wavelet based multifractal formalism: Applications to DNA sequences, satellite images of the cloud structure, and stock market data. In Bunde, A., Kropp, J., & Schellnhuber, H. J. (Eds.), *The Science of Disasters: Climate Disruptions, Heart Attacks, and Market Crashes* (pp. 27–104). Berlin: Springer Verlag.

Arrigo, P., Giuliano, F., & Damiani, G. (1991). Identification of A New Motif on Nucleic Acid Sequence Data Using Kohonen's Self-Organising Map. *CABIOS, 7*, 353–357.

Atmuri, V., Martin, D. C., Hemming, R., Gutsol, A., Byers, S., & Sahebjam, S. (2008, October). Hyaluronidase 3 (HYAL3) knockout mice do not display evidence of hyaluronan accumulation. *Matrix Biology, 27*(8), 653–660. doi:10.1016/j.matbio.2008.07.006

Audit, B., Thermes, C., Vaillant, C., d'Aubenton-Carafa, Y., Muzy, J.-F., & Arneodo, A. (2001). Long-range correlations in genomic DNA: A signature of the nuclosomal structure. *Physical Review Letters, 86*, 2471–2474. doi:10.1103/PhysRevLett.86.2471

Aussenac-Gilles, N., Biébow, B., & Szulman, S. (2000). *Revisiting ontology design: A methodology based on corpus analysis*. Paper presented at the 12th International Conference in Knowledge Engineering and Knowledge Management (EKAW), Juan-Les-Pins, France.

Baciu, G., Wang, Y., Yao, Y., Chan, K., Kinsner, W., & Zadeh, L. A. (Eds.). (2009, June). In *Proceedings of the 8th IEEE International Conference on Cognitive Informatics (ICCI'09)*, Hong Kong. Washington, DC: IEEE Computer Society Press.

Bains, W. (1993). Local self-similarity of sequence in mammalian nuclear DNA is modulated by a 180 bp periodicity. *Journal of Theoretical Biology, 161*, 137–143. doi:10.1006/jtbi.1993.1046

Baldi, P., & Brunak, S. (1998). *Bioinformatics: The Machine Learning Approach*. Cambridge, MA: MIT Press.

Baldi, P., Pollastri, G., Anderson, C. A., & Brunak, S. (1995). Matching Protein Beta-Sheet Partners by Feedforward and Recurrent Neural Networks. In [ISMB]. *Proceedings of the International Conference on Intelligent Systems for Molecular Biology, 8*, 25–36.

Bao, L., & Intille, S. S. (2004). Activity recognition from user-annotated acceleration data. In. *Proceedings of PERVASIVE, 2004*, 1–17.

Bargiela, A., & Pedrycz, W. (2002). *Granular Computing: An Introduction*. Boston: Kluwer Academic Publishers.

Bargiela, A., & Pedrycz, W. (2008). Toward a theory of Granular Computing for human-centered information processing. *IEEE Transactions on Fuzzy Systems, 16*(2), 320–330. doi:10.1109/TFUZZ.2007.905912

Bartolini, C., Preist, C., & Jennings, N. R. (2002). Architecting for reuse: A software framework for automated negotiation. In. *Proceedings, AOSE-02*, 87–98.

Barton, D., & Tusting, K. (Eds.). (2005). *Beyond communities of practice* (1st ed.). Cambridge, UK: Cambridge University Press.

Beckmann, C., Consolvo, S., & LaMarca, A. (2004). Some assembly required: Supporting end-user sensor installation in domestic ubiquitous computing environments. In. *Proceedings of Ubicomp, 2004*, 107–124.

Bellavista, P., Corradi, A., Montanari, R., & Stefanelli, C. (2003). Context-Aware Middleware for Resource Management in the Wireless Internet. *IEEE Transactions on Software Engineering, 29*(12), 1086–1099. doi:10.1109/TSE.2003.1265523

Bellazzi, R., Larizza, C., Magni, P., Montani, S., & Stefanelli, M. (2000). Intelligent analysis of clinical time series: an application in the diabetes mellitus domain. *Artificial Intelligence in Medicine, 20*(1), 37–57. doi:10.1016/S0933-3657(00)00052-X

Bell, B. I., & Marr, T. G. (Eds.). (1990). *Computers and DNA*. Redwood City, CA: Addison-Wesley.

Benyoucef, M., Alj, H., & Keller, R. K. (2001). An infrastructure for rule-driven negotiating software agents. In *Proceedings of the 12th International Workshop on Database and Expert Systems Applications*, Montreal, Canada (pp. 737-741).

Bernaola-Galvan, P., Roman-Roldan, R., & Oliver, J. L. (1996). Compositional segmentation and long-range fractal correlations in DNA sequences. *Physical Review E: Statistical Physics, Plasmas, Fluids, and Related Interdisciplinary Topics, 53*, 5181–5189. doi:10.1103/PhysRevE.53.5181

Berners-Lee, T., Hendler, J., & Lassila, O. (2001). The semantic web. *Scientific American*.

Berry, E. A., Dalby, A. R., & Yang, Z. R. (2004). Reduced Bio-Basis Function Neural Network for Identification of Protein Phosphorylation Sites: Comparison with Pattern Recognition Algorithms. *Computational Biology and Chemistry*, *28*, 75–85. doi:10.1016/j.compbiolchem.2003.11.005

Bertino, E., Terzi, E., Kamra, A., & Vakali, A. (2005, December). Intrusion detection in RBAC-administered databases. In *Proceedings of the 21st Annual Computer Security Applications Conference*, Tucson, AZ (pp. 170-182).

Bertino, E., Bonatti, P. A., & Ferrari, E. (2001, August). TRBAC: A Temporal Role-Based Access Control Model. *ACM Transactions on Information and System Security*, *4*(3), 191–223. doi:10.1145/501978.501979

Beynon, M. (2001). Reducts within the variable precision rough sets model: A further investigation. *European Journal of Operational Research*, *134*(3), 592–605. doi:10.1016/S0377-2217(00)00280-0

Bezdek, J. C. (1981). *Pattern Recognition with Fuzzy Objective Function Algorithms*. New York: Plenum Press.

Bilmes, J. A. (1998). *A gentle tutorial of the EM algorithm and its application to parameter estimation for gaussian mixture and hidden markov models* (Tech. Rep. TR-97-021). Berkeley, CA: International Computer Science Institute and Computer Science Division, University of California Berkeley.

Bjorner, D., & Jones, C. B. (1982). *Formal specification and software development*. Upper Saddle River, NJ: Prentice Hall.

Blake, E. K. C., & Merz, C. J. (1998). *UCI Repository of machine learning databases* (Tech. Rep.). Irvine, California: University of California, Irvine, Dept. of Information and Computer Sciences. Retrieved from http://www.ics.uci.edu/$\sim$mlearn/MLRepository.html

Blanz, V., & Vetter, T. (2002). Reconstructing the complete 3D shape of faces from partial information. *Informationsetechnik und Technische Informatik*, *44*(6), 295–302.

Blanz, V., & Vetter, T. (2003). Face recognition based on fitting a 3D morphable model. *IEEE Transactions on Pattern Analysis and Machine Intelligence*, *25*(9), 1063–1074. doi:10.1109/TPAMI.2003.1227983

Bloom, B. (1956). *Taxonomy of Educational Objectives, Handbook I: The Cognitive Domain*. New York: David McKay Co Inc.

Blum, M., Williams, R., Juba, B., & Humphrey, M. (2005, June). Toward a High-level Definition of Consciousness. In *Proceedings of the Annual IEEE Computational Complexity Conference*, San Jose, CA.

Blythe, S., Mao, X., & Liao, X. (2001). Stability of stochastic delay neural networks. *Journal of the Franklin Institute*, *338*(4), 481–495. doi:10.1016/S0016-0032(01)00016-3

Bollella, G. (2002). *The Real-Time Specification for Java*. Reading, MA: Addison Wesley.

Bollella, G., & Brosgol, B. (2002). *The Real-Time Specification for Java*. Reading: Addison Wesley.

Bollella, G., Brosgol, B., Dibble, P., Furr, S., Gosling, J., & Hardin, D. (2002). *The Real-Time Specification for Java*. Reading, MA: Addison-Wesley.

Borovik, A. S., Grosberg, A. Y., & Frank-Kamenetskii, M. D. (1994). Fractality of DNA texts. *Journal of Biomolecular Structure & Dynamics*, *12*, 655–669.

Boyd, S., El Ghaoui, L., Feron, E., & Balakrishnan, V. (1994). *Linear matrix inequalities in system and control theory*. Philadelphia: SIAM.

Branden, C., & Tooze, J. (1991). *Introduction to Protein Structure*. New York: Garland Publishing.

Breault, J. L., Goodall, C. R., & Fos, P. J. (2002). Data mining a diabetic data warehouse. *Artificial Intelligence in Medicine*, *26*(1-2), 37–54. doi:10.1016/S0933-3657(02)00051-9

Brinch-Hansen, P. (1971, October). Short-Term Scheduling in Multiprogramming Systems. In *Proceedings of the Third ACM Symposium on Operating Systems Principles* (pp. 103-105).

Brooks, R. A. (1991). Intelligence without reason. In *Proceedings of the 12th Intl. Conference on Artificial Intelligence (IJCAI-91)*.

Brooks, L. R. (1978). Nonanalytic concept formtaion and memory for instances. In Rosch, E., & Loyd, B. B. (Eds.), *Cognition and Categorization* (pp. 169–215). Hillsdale, NJ: Erlbaum Associates.

Brown, C. M., & Danzig, B. B. (2004). The harvest information discovery and access system. In *Proceedings of the 2nd International World Wide Web Conference.*

Brown, J. S., & Duguid, P. (1998). Organizing knowledge. *California Management Review, 40*(3), 90–111.

Broy, M., Pair, C., & Wirsing, M. (1984). A Systematic Study of Models of Abstract Data Types. *Theoretical Computer Science, 33,* 139–1274. doi:10.1016/0304-3975(84)90086-0

Brusilovsky, P. (2001). Adaptive Hypermedia. *User Modeling and User-Adapted Interaction, 11,* 87–110. doi:10.1023/A:1011143116306

Bulusu, N., Heidemann, J., Estrin, D., & Tran, T. (2004, February). Self-configuring localization systems: Design and Experimental Evaluation. [TECS]. *ACM Transactions on Embedded Computing Systems, 3*(1), 24–60. doi:10.1145/972627.972630

Burset, M., & Guigo, R. (1996). Evaluation of gene structure prediction programs. *Genomics, 34,* 353–367. doi:10.1006/geno.1996.0298

Busson, A., & Keravel, A. (2004). *Strategies used to reach e-government interoperability: A first evaluation.* Paper presented at e-Challenge, Vienna, Austria.

Caire, G. (2003). *Jade Turorial: Jade Programming for Beginners.*

Cai, Y. D., & Chou, K. C. (1998). Artificial Neural Network Model for Predicting HIV Protease Cleavage Sites in Protein. *Advances in Engineering Software, 29*(2), 119–128. doi:10.1016/S0965-9978(98)00046-5

Cai, Y. D., Liu, X. J., Xu, X. B., & Chou, K. C. (2002). Support Vector Machines for Predicting the Specificity of GalNAc-transferase. *Peptides, 23,* 205–208. doi:10.1016/S0196-9781(01)00597-6

Calegari, S., & Farina, F. (2006). Fuzzy Ontologies and Scale-free Networks Analysis. *International Journal of Computer Science & Applications, 4,* 125–144.

Campbell, N. A., & Reece, J. B. (2002). *Biology* (6th ed.). San Francisco, CA: Benjamin Cummings.

Cardelli, L., & Wegner, P. (1985). On Understanding Types, Data Abstraction and Polymorphism. *ACM Computing Surveys, 17*(4), 471–522. doi:10.1145/6041.6042

Carey, S. (1985). *Conceptual Change in Childhood.* Cambridge, MA: MIT Press.

Case, S., Azarmi, N., Thint, M., & Ohtani, T. (2001). Enhancing e-communities with agent-based systems. *Computer, 34*(7), 64–69. doi:10.1109/2.933505

Chan, C. L., Baciu, G., & Mak, S. (2009b). Using Wi-Fi Signal Strength to Localize in Wireless Sensor Networks. In *Proceedings of the IEEE International Conference on Communications and Mobile Computing (CMC)* (pp. 538-542).

Chan, C. L., Baciu, G., & Mak, S. C. (2008). Wireless Tracking Analysis in Location Fingerprint. In *Proceedings of the 4th IEEE Wireless and Mobile Computing, Networking and Communications (WiMOB)* (pp. 214-220).

Chan, C. L., Baciu, G., & Mak, S. C. (2009a). Using the Newton Trust-Region Method to Localize in WLAN Environment. In *Proceedings of the 5th IEEE Wireless and Mobile Computing, Networking and Communications (WiMOB)* (pp. 363-369).

Chapey, R., & Hallowell, B. (2001). *Language intervention strategies in aphasia and related neurogenic communication disorders* (4th ed.). Baltimore, MD: Lippincott Williams & Wilkins.

Chen, P., Ding, W., Bowes, C., & Brown, D. (2009). *A Fully Unsupervised Word Sense Disambiguation Method and Its Evaluation on Coarse-grained All-words Task.* NAACL.

Chen, W., & Jiao, L. (2010). Adaptive tracking for periodically time-varying and nonlinearly parameterized systems using multilayer neural networks. *IEEE Transactions on Neural Networks, 21*(2), 345–351. doi:10.1109/TNN.2009.2038999

Chiew, V. (2002). A Software Engineering Cognitive Knowledge Discovery Framework. *Proceedings of the IEEE, ICCI,* 163–174.

Chou, K. C. (1993). A Vectorised Sequence-Coupling Model for Predicting HIV Protease Cleavage Sites in Proteins. *The Journal of Biological Chemistry, 268*(23), 16938–16948.

Chou, K. C. (1996). Prediction of Human Immunodeficiency Virus Protease Cleavage Sites in Proteins. *Analytical Biochemistry, 233*(1), 1–14. doi:10.1006/abio.1996.0001

Cios, K. J., & Kurgan, L. A. (2004). CLIP4: Hybrid inductive machine learning algorithm that generates inequality rules. *Inf. Sci, 163*(1-3), 37–83. doi:10.1016/j.ins.2003.03.015

Clayton, J., & Dennis, C. (2003). *50 Years of DNA*. New York: Nature/Palgrave Macmillan.

Colman, A., & Han, J. (2007). Using role-based coordination to achieve software adaptability. *Science of Computer Programming, 64*, 223–245. doi:10.1016/j.scico.2006.06.006

Corballis, M. C. (2002). *From Hand to Mouth: the origins of language*. Princeton, NJ: Princeton University Press.

Cornelis, C., & Jensen, R. (n.d.). *A Noise-tolerant Approach to Fuzzy-Rough Feature Selection*. Retrieved from http://hdl.handle.net/2160/581

Corsetti, E., Montanari, A., & Ratto, E. (1991). Dealing with different time granularities in formal specifications of real-time systems. *Journal of Real-Time Systems, 3*(2), 191–215. doi:10.1007/BF00365335

Covington, M. J., Moyer, M. J., & Ahamad, M. (2000). Generalized Role-Based Access Control for Securing Future Applications. In *Proceedings of the 23rd National Information Systems Security Conference*. Retrieved October 20, 2008, from http://smartech.gatech.edu/dspace/bitstream/1853/6580/1/GIT-CC-00-02.pdf

Cox, T. F., & Cox, M. A. A. (1994). *Multidimensional scaling* (Vol. 59). London: Chapman & Hall.

Cox, A. (2005). What are communities of practice? A comparative review of four seminal works. *Journal of Information Science, 31*(6), 527–540. doi:10.1177/0165551505057016

Crespo, F., & Weber, R. (2005). A methodology for dynamic data mining based on fuzzy clustering. *Fuzzy Sets and Systems, 150*, 267–284. doi:10.1016/j.fss.2004.03.028

Cruice, M., Worrall, L., Hickson, L., & Murison, R. (2003). Finding a focus for quality of life with aphasia: Social and emotional health, and psychological well-being. *Aphasiology, 17*(4), 333–353. doi:10.1080/02687030244000707

Cruse, H. (2003). The evolution of cognition—a hypothesis. *Cognitive Science, 27*(1).

Csikszentmihalyi, M. (1991). *Flow: The Psychology of Optimal Experience*. New York: Harper Perennial. Retrieved from http://www.amazon.com/Flow-Psychology-Experience-Mihaly-Csikszentmihalyi/dp/0060920432

Dale, J. W., & von Schantz, M. (2002). *From Genes to Genomes: Concepts and Applications of DNA Technology*. New York: Wiley. doi:10.1002/0470856912

Danesh, A., Moshiri, B., & Fatemi, O. (2007). *Improve text classification accuracy based on classifier fusion methods*. In *Proceedings of the Information Fusion, 2007 10th International Conference* (pp. 1-6).

Danninger, M., Flaherty, G., Bernardin, K., Ekenel, H., Köhler, T., Malkin, R., et al. (2005). The connector: Facilitating context-aware communication. In *Proceedings of the 7th International Conference on Multimodal Interfaces, ICMI'05* (pp. 69-75). New York: ACM Publishing.

Darnell, J., Lodish, H., & Baltimore, D. (1990). *Molecular Cell Biology* (2nd ed.). New York: W. H. Freeman.

Datta, A., & Dougherty, E. R. (2006). *Introduction to Genomic Signal Processing with Control*. Boca Raton, FL: CRC. doi:10.1201/9781420006674

Davidson, B., Worrall, L., & Hickson, L. (2003). Identifying the communication activities of older people with aphasia: Evidence from naturalistic observation. *Aphasiology, 17*(3), 243–264. doi:10.1080/729255457

Davis, J., & Goadrich, M. (2006). The Relationship Between Precision-Recall and ROC Curves. In *Proceedings of the ACM 23rd International Conference on Machine learning* (pp. 233-240).

Dayhoff, M. O., Schwartz, R. M., & Orcutt, B. C. (1978). A Model of Evolutionary Change in Proteins. Matrices for Detecting Distant Relationships. *Atlas of Protein Sequence and Structure, 5*, 345-358.

Defense TechBriefs. (2009, February 1). *DNA sequencing technique can produce a genome in less than a minute*. Retrieved December 10, 2009, from http://www.defensetechbriefs.com/component/content/article/4967

Deitel, H. M., & Kogan, M. S. (1992). *The Design of OS/2*. Reading, MA: Addison-Wesley.

Dennett, D. (1991). *Consciousness Explained*. New York: The Penguin Press.

Derene, G. (2008). How social networking could kill web search as we know it. *Popular Mechanics*. Retrieved March 9, 2009, from http://www.popularmechanics.com/technology/industry/4259135.html

Dertouzos, M. L., & Mok, A. K. (1989). Multiprocessor online scheduling of hard-real-time tasks. *IEEE Transactions on Software Engineering*, *15*(12), 1497–1506. doi:10.1109/32.58762

Desmet, P. M. A. (2002). *Designing emotions*. Unpublished doctoral dissertation, TU Delft.

DeVries, R. (2002). *What Is Constructivist about Constructivist Education? (Freeburg Early Childhood Program)* (pp. 1–20). Iowa City, Iowa: University of Iowa.

Dijkstra, E. W. (1968). The Structure of the Multiprogramming System. *Communications of the ACM*, *11*(5), 341–346. doi:10.1145/363095.363143

Dillenbourg, P., Schneider, D., Synteta, P., Dillenbourg, P., Schneider, D., Synteta, P., et al. (2002). Virtual Learning Environments. *Communication*, 3-18.

DOE Human Genome Program. (1992, June). *Primer on Molecular Genetics*. Washington, DC: US Department of Energy, Office of Health and Environmental Research.

Doorenbos, R. B., Etzioni, O., & Weld, D. S. (1997). *A scalable comparison shopping agent for the world wide web (Tech. Rep. No. TR 97-027)*. Minneapolis, MN: University of Minnesota.

Downes, S. M. (2010). *Evolutionary Psychology, Stanford Encyclopedia of Philosophy*. Retrieved from http://plato.stanford.edu/entries/evolutionary-psychology/

Duda, R. O., Hart, P. E., & Stork, D. G. (2001). *Pattern Classification*. New York: John Wiley & Sons.

Ebeling, W., Molgedey, L., Kurths, J., & Schwarz, U. (2002). Entropy, complexity, predictability and data analysis of time series and letter sequences. In Bunde, A., Kropp, J., & Schellnhuber, H. J. (Eds.), *The Science of Disasters: Climate Disruptions, Heart Attacks, and Market Crashes* (pp. 2–25). Berlin: Springer Verlag.

Eddie, C. L., Chan, G. B., & Mak, S. C. (2009). Using a Cell-based WLAN Infrastructure Design for Resource-effective and Accurate Positioning. *IEEE Journal of Communications Software and Systems*, *5*(4).

Eddie, C. L., Chan, G. B., & Mak, S. C. (2010b). Cognitive Location-Aware Information Retrieval by Agent-based Semantic Matching. *International Journal of Cognitive Informatics & Natural Intelligence*.

Eddie, C. L., Chan, G. B., & Mak, S. C. (2010a). *Newton Trust Region Method for Wi-Fi Tracking*. IEEE Transactions on Systems, Man and Cybernetics - Part A.

Enembreck, F. C., & Barthès, J. P. (2007). Multi-agent based Internet search. *International Journal Product Lifecycle Management*, *2*(2), 135–156. doi:10.1504/IJPLM.2007.014276

ETTX. (2009, February). In *Proceedings of the First Eueopean TinyOS Technology Exchange*, Cork, Ireland.

Fairbanks, D. J., & Andersen, W. R. (1999). *Genetics: The Continuity of Life*. Pacific Grove, CA: Brooks/Cole.

Fecher, H. (2001). A Real-Time Process Algebra with Open Intervals and Maximal Progress. *Nordic Journal of Computing*, *8*(3), 346–360.

Feldman, J. (2006). *From Molecule to Metaphor*. Cambridge, MA: MIT Press.

Feng, W., Yang, S. X., Fu, W., & Wu, H. (2009). Robust stability analysis of uncertain stochastic neural networks with interval time-varying delay. *Chaos, Solitons, and Fractals*, *41*(1), 414–424. doi:10.1016/j.chaos.2008.01.024

Feng, W., Yang, S. X., & Wu, H. (2009). On robust stability of uncertain stochastic neural networks with distributed and interval time-varying delays. *Chaos, Solitons, and Fractals*, *42*(4), 2095–2104. doi:10.1016/j.chaos.2009.03.141

Fernández-López, M. (1999). Overview of methodologies for building ontologies. In V. R. Benjamins, B. Chandrasekaran, A. Gómez-Pérez, N. Guarino, & M. Uschold (Eds.), *Proceedings of the IJCAI-99 Workshop on Ontologies and Problem-Solving Methods (KRR5)*, Stockholm, Sweden.

Fernández-López, M., Gómez-Pérez, A., & Juriso, N. (1997). *Methontology: From ontological art towards ontological engineering*. Paper presented at AAAI-97, Spring Symposium on Ontological Engineering, Palo Alto, CA.

Ferraiolo, D. F., Sandhu, R., Gavrila, S., Kuhn, D. R., & Chandramouli, R. (2001, August). Proposed NIST Standard: Role-Based Access Control. *ACM Transactions on Information and System Security, 4*(2), 224–274. doi:10.1145/501978.501980

Ferran, E. A., & Ferrara, P. (1991). Topological Maps of Protein Sequences. *Biological Cybernetics, 65*, 451–458. doi:10.1007/BF00204658

FIPA. (2000). *FIPA SL Content Language Specification.*

FIPA. (2002, December 6). *Contract Net Interaction Protocol Specification.* Retrieved from http://www.fipa.org/specs/fipa00029/SC00029H.pdf

FIPA. (2002, December 6). *Iterated Contract Net Interaction Protocol Specification.* Retrieved from http://www.fipa.org/specs/fipa00030/SC00030H.pdf

Fodors, J. A. (1975). *The Language of Thought* (p. 214). Cambridge, MA: Harvard University Press.

Ford, B., Back, G., Benson, G., Lepreau, J., Lin, A., & Shivers, O. (1997). The Flux OSKit: a Substrate for OS and Language Research. In *Proceedings of the 16th ACM Symposium on Operating Systems Principles*, Saint Malo, France.

Forti, M., Manetti, S., & Marini, M. (1994). Necessary and sufficient condition for absolute stability of neural networks. *IEEE Transactions on Circuits and Systems. I, Fundamental Theory and Applications, 41*(7), 491–494. doi:10.1109/81.298364

França, L. T. C., Carrilho, E., & Kist, T. B. L. (2002). A review of DNA sequencing techniques. *Quarterly Reviews of Biophysics, 35*(2), 169–200. doi:10.1017/S0033583502003797

Freksa, C. (1991). Conceptual neighborhood and its role in temporal and spatial reasoning. In *Proceedings of the IMACS Workshop on Decision Support Systems and Qualitative Reasoning* (pp. 181-187).

Fujita, S., Hara, H., Sugawara, K., Kinoshita, T., & Shiratori, N. (1998). Agent-based design model of adaptive distributed systems. *The International Journal of Artificial Intelligence. Neural Networks and Complex Problem-Solving Technologies, 9*(1), 57–70.

Gallese, V., Eagle, M. E., & Migone, P. (2007). Intentional attunement: mirror neurons and the neural underpinnings of interpersonal relations. *Journal of the American Psychoanalytic Association, 55*, 131–176.

Garcia, X., Vicente, S., Pérez, M., Gimeno, A., & Naval, J. (2005). E-government interoperability in a semantically driven world. In *Proceedings of the IEEE International Conference on Service, Operations and Logistic and Informatics (SOLI 2005)*, Beijing, China. Washington, DC: IEEE Computer Society.

GeneCards. (2009). Database of Human Genes. *Crown Human Genome Center & Weizmann Institute of Science.* Retrieved December 2009, from http://www.genecards.org/cgi-bin/carddisp.pl?gene=Hyal1

Gherardy, S. (2005). *Organizational knowledge: The texture of workplace learning* (1st ed.). London: Blackwell.

Giardina, M., Azuaje, F., McCullagh, P. J., & Harper, R. (2006). A Supervised Learning Approach to Predicting Coronary Heart Disease Complications in Type 2 Diabetes Mellitus Patients. In *Proceedings of BIBE* (pp. 325-331).

Gibas, C., & Jambeck, P. (2001). *Bioinformatics: Computer Skills.* Sebastopol, CA: O'Reilly and Associates.

Gillet, D., El Helou, S., Yu, C. M., & Salzmann, C. A.-S. C. (2008). *Turning Web 2.0 social software into versatile collaborative learning solutions.* Paper presented at the First International Conference on Advances in Computer-Human Interaction.

Giménez-Lugo, G. A., Sichman, J. S., & Hübner, J. F. (2005). Addressing the social components of knowledge to foster communitary exchanges. *International Journal of Web Based Communities, 1*(2), 176–194. doi:10.1504/IJWBC.2005.006062

Goertzel, B., Coelho, L., Pennachin, C., & Mudado, M. (2006b). Identifying Complex Biological Interactions based on Categorical Gene Expression Data. In *Proceedings of the Conference on Evolutionary Computing 2006 (CEC 2006)*, Vancouver, Canada.

Goertzel, B., Pennachin, C., Coelho, L., Shikida, L., & Queiroz, M. (2007). Biomind ArrayGenius and Gene-Genius: Web Services Offering Microarray and SNP Data Analysis via Novel Machine Learning Methods. In *Proceedings of IAAI 2007*, Vancouver, Canada (pp. 1700-1706).

Goertzel, B., Pennachin, C., Coelho, L., Gurbaxani, B., Maloney, E. B., & Jones, J. F. (2006). Combinations of single nucleotide polymorphisms in neuroendocrine effector and receptor genes are predictive of chronic fatigue syndrome. *Pharmacogenomics*, 7(3), 475–483. doi:10.2217/14622416.7.3.475

Goncharenko, I., Svinin, M., Kanou, Y., & Hosoe, S. (2007). Skilful motion planning with self- and reinforcement learning in dynamic virtual environments. In *Proceedings of the 4th INTUITION International Conference*, Athens, Greece (pp. 237-238).

Goncharenko, I., Svinin, M., Kanou, Y., & Hosoe, S. (2006). Predictability of rest-to-rest movements in haptic environments with 3D constraints. *Robotics and Mechatronics*, 18(4), 458–466.

Gong, X., & Wang, G. (2009). 3D Face Deformable Model Based on Feature Points. *Journal of Software*, 20(3), 724–733. doi:10.3724/SP.J.1001.2009.03317

Gräther, W., & Prinz, W. (2001). *The social web cockpit: Support for virtual communities*. Paper presented at the 2001 International ACM SIGGROUP Conference on Supporting Group Work, Boulder, CO.

Greco, S., Slowinski, R., & Yao, Y. Y. (2007). Bayesian decision theory for dominance-based rough set approach. In *Proceedings of the Second International Conference on Rough Sets and Knowledge Technology (RSKT'07)* (pp. 134-141).

Gregory, T. R., & Hebert, P. D. (1999). The modulation of DNA content: Proximate causes and ultimate consequences. *Genome Research*, 9, 317–324.

Gribble, S., Welsh, M., Behren, R., Brewer, E., Culler, D., Borisov, N., et al. (2001). The Ninja architecture for robust Internet-scale systems and services. *Special Issue of Computer Networks on Pervasive Computing, 35*(4). InterSense. (n.d.). *IS600: IS-600 Mark 2 Precision Motion Tracker*. Retrieved from http://www.isense.com/

Griffith, D., & Greiter, F. L. (2007). Neo-symbiosis: The next stage in the evolution of human information interaction. *International Journal of Cognitive Informatics and Natural Intelligence, 1*(1), 39–52.

Grosof, B. N., & Poon, T. C. (2004). SweetDeal: Representing Agent Contracts with Exceptions using Semantic Web Rules, Ontologies, and Process Descriptions. *International Journal of Electronic Commerce, 8*(4).

Grosse, I., Herzel, H., Buldyrev, S. V., & Stanley, H. E. (2000). Species independence of mutual information in coding and noncoding DNA. *Physical Review E: Statistical Physics, Plasmas, Fluids, and Related Interdisciplinary Topics, 61*, 5624–5629. doi:10.1103/PhysRevE.61.5624

Gruber, T. R. (1993). Toward Principles for the Design of Ontologies Used for Knowledge Sharing. *International Journal of Human-Computer Studies, 43*, 907–928. doi:10.1006/ijhc.1995.1081

Grune, D., Bal, H. E., Jacobs, C. J. H., & Langendoen, K. G. (2000). *Modern Compiler Design*. New York: John Wiley & Sons.

Grüninger, M., & Fox, M. (1995). *Methodology for the design and evaluation of ontologies*. Paper presented at the Workshop on Basic Ontological Issues in Knowledge Sharing, Montreal, Quebec, Canada.

Grzymala-Busse, J. W. (2002). MLEM2: A new algorithm for rule induction from imperfect data. In *Proceedings of the 9th International Conference on Information Processing and Management of Uncertainty in Knowledge-Based Systems (IPMU 2002)*, Annecy, France (pp. 243-250).

Grzymala-Busse, J. W., & Lakshmanan, A. (1996). LEM2 with interval extension: An induction algorithm for numerical attributes. In *Proceedings of the Fourth International Workshop on Rough Sets, Fuzzy Sets, and Machine Discovery*, Tokyo (pp. 67 - 73).

Grzymala-Busse, P., Grzymala-Busse, J. W., & Hippe, Z. S. (2001). Melanoma prediction using data mining system LERS. In *Proceedings of the 25th Annual International Computer Software and Applications Conference (COMPSAC 2001)* (pp. 615-620).

Grzymala-Busse, J. W. (1988). Knowledge Acquisition under Uncertainty - A Rough Set Approach. *J. Intel. Rob. Syst.*, *1*, 3–16. doi:10.1007/BF00437317

Grzymala-Busse, J. W. (1992). LERS - A system for learning from examples based on rough sets. In Slowinski, R. (Ed.), *Intelligent Decision Support: Handbook of Applications and Advances of the Rough Sets Theory* (pp. 3–18). Dordrecht, The Netherlands: Kluwer Academic Publishers.

Grzymala-Busse, J. W. (2004). Data with missing attribute values: Generalization of idiscernibility relation and rule induction. *Transactions on Rough Sets*, *1*, 78–95.

Guigo, R., Knudsen, S., Drake, N., & Smith, T. (1992). Prediction of gene structure. *Journal of Molecular Biology*, *226*, 141–157. doi:10.1016/0022-2836(92)90130-C

Gu, K. (2001). Discretization schemes for Lyapunov-Krasovskii functionals in time-delay systems. *Kybernetika*, *37*(4), 479–504.

Gu, K., Han, Q. L., Luo, A. C. J., & Niculescu, S. I. (2001). Discretized Lyapunov functional for systems with distributed delay and piecewise constant coefficients. *International Journal of Control*, *74*(7), 737–744. doi:10.1080/00207170010031486

Guttag, J. V. (1977). Abstract Data Types and the Development of Data Structures. *Communications of the ACM*, *20*(6), 396–404. doi:10.1145/359605.359618

Guyon, I., & Elisseeff, A. (2003). An Introduction to Variable and Feature Selection. *Journal of Machine Learning Research*, *3*, 1157–1182. doi:10.1162/153244303322753616

Haans, A., & Ijsselsteijn, W. A. (2006). Mediated social touch: A review of current research and future directions. *Virtual Reality (Waltham Cross)*, *9*(2), 149–159. doi:10.1007/s10055-005-0014-2

Hall, E. T. (1966). *The hidden dimension*. New York: Doubleday.

Hamori, E. (1985). Novel DNA sequence representations. *Nature*, *314*, 585–586. doi:10.1038/314585a0

Hansmann, U., Merk, L., Nicklous, M. S., & Stober, T. (2003). *Pervasive Computing: The Mobile World* (Springer Professional Computing). New York: Springer. Retrieved from http://www.amazon.com/Pervasive-Computing-Mobile-Springer-Professional/dp/3540002189

Harnad, S. (1990). The Symbol Grounding Problem. *Physica D. Nonlinear Phenomena*, *42*, 335–346. doi:10.1016/0167-2789(90)90087-6

Harnad, S. (1991). Other bodies, other minds: a machine incarnation of an old philosophical problem. *Minds and Machines*, (1): 43–54.

Hartigan, J. A. (1975). *Clustering algorithms*. New York: John Wiley & Sons.

Hattori, F., Kuwabara, K., Kuwahara, N., Abe, S., & Yasuda, K. (2007). Socialware for people with disabilities. In *Proceedings of the 6th International Conference on Cognitive Informatics (ICCI '07)* (pp. 321-326).

Hattori, F., Ohguro, T., Yokoo, M., Matsubara, S., & Yoshida, S. (1999). Socialware: Multiagent systems for supporting network communities. *Communications of the ACM*, *42*(3), 55–61. doi:10.1145/295685.295701

Hawkins, J., & Blakeslee, S. (2004). *On Intelligence*. New York: Henry Holt and Company.

Hayes, I. (1985). Applying formal specifications to software development in industry. *IEEE Transactions on Software Engineering*, *11*(2), 169–178. doi:10.1109/TSE.1985.232191

Henderson, J., Salzberg, S., & Fasman, K. H. (1997). Finding genes in DNA with a hidden Markov model. *Journal of Computational Biology*, *4*, 127–141. doi:10.1089/cmb.1997.4.127

Henikoff, S., & Henikoff, J. G. (1992). Amino Acid Substitution Matrices from Protein Blocks. *PNSA*, *89*, 10915–10919. doi:10.1073/pnas.89.22.10915

Hernández, P., & Yasmín, M. (2007). *Modelo de Comportamiento Afectivo para Sistemas Tutores Inteligentes (Tech. Rep.)*. Cuernavaca, Mexico: Instituto Tecnológico y de Estudios Superiores de Monterrey Campus Cuernavaca.

He, Y., Wang, Q. G., & Lin, C. (2006). An improved H_∞ filter design for systems with time-varying interval delay. *IEEE Transactions on Circuits and Wystems. II, Express Briefs, 53*(11), 1235–1239. doi:10.1109/TCSII.2006.883209

Higman, B. (1977). *A Comparative Study of Programming Languages* (2nd ed.). Westfield, NJ: MacDonald.

Hildebrandt, J., Golatowski, F., & Timmermann, D. (1999). Scheduling coprocessor for enhanced least-laxity-first scheduling in hard real-time systems. In *Proceedings of the 11th Euromicro Conference on Real-Time Systems* (pp. 208-215). Washington, DC: IEEE Computer Society Press.

Hoare, C. A. R. (1985). *Communicating sequential processes.* Upper Saddle River, NJ: Prentice-Hall.

Hoare, C. A. R. (1978). Communicating Sequential Processes. *Communications of the ACM, 21*(8), 666–677. doi:10.1145/359576.359585

Hobbes, T. (1969). *Elements of Law, Natural and Political* (p. 186). New York: Routledge. Retrieved from http://www.amazon.com/Elements-Natural-Political-Thomas-Hobbes/dp/071462540X

Holland, O. (Ed.). (2003)... *Journal of Consciousness Studies, 10*(4-5).

Holland, O., & Goodman, R. (2003). Robots With Internal Models: A Route to Machine Consciousness? *Journal of Consciousness Studies, 10*(4-5).

Horn, P. (2001, October). *Autonomic Computing: IBM's perspective on the State of Information Technology.* IBM. Retrieved October 20, 2008, from http://www.research.ibm.com/autonomic/

Huang, H., & Feng, G. (2007). Delay-dependent stability for uncertain stochastic neural networks with time-varying delay. *Physica A: Statistical Mechanics and its Applications, 381*, 93-103.

Huang, H., & Cao, J. (2007). Exponential stability analysis of uncertain stochastic neural networks with multiple delays. *Nonlinear Analysis Real World Applications, 8*(2), 646–653. doi:10.1016/j.nonrwa.2006.02.003

Huang, Y., McCullagh, P. J., Black, N. D., & Harper, R. (2007). Feature selection and classification model construction on type 2 diabetic patients' data. *Artificial Intelligence in Medicine, 41*(3), 251–262. doi:10.1016/j.artmed.2007.07.002

Hughes, J., Jewson, N., & Unwin, L. (Eds.). (2007). *Communities of pratice: Critical perspectives.* London: Routledge.

Hull, D., Pedersen, J., & Schutze, H. (1996). Document Routing as Statistical Classification. In *Proceedings of the AAAI Spring Symposium on Machine Learning in Information Access Technical Papers*, Palo Alto, CA.

Hume, D. (1975). Enquiry Concerning Human Understanding. In L. A. Selby-Bigge (Ed.), *Enquiries concerning Human Understanding and concerning the Principles of Morals* (3rd ed., revised by P. H. Nidditch). Oxford, UK: Clarendon Press.

Hu, Q., Liu, J., & Yu, D. (2008). Mixed feature selection based on granulation and approximation. *Knowledge-Based Systems, 21*(4), 294–304. doi:10.1016/j.knosys.2007.07.001

Hu, Q., Xie, Z., & Yu, D. (2007). Hybrid attribute reduction based on a novel fuzzy-rough model and information granulation. *Pattern Recognition, 40*(12), 3509–3521. doi:10.1016/j.patcog.2007.03.017

Hu, Q., Yu, D., Liu, J., & Wu, C. (2008). Neighborhood rough set based heterogeneous feature subset selection. *Inf. Sci., 178*(18), 3577–3594. doi:10.1016/j.ins.2008.05.024

Hu, Q., Yu, D., & Xie, Z. (2006). Information-preserving hybrid data reduction based on fuzzy-rough techniques. *Pattern Recognition Letters, 27*(5), 414–423. doi:10.1016/j.patrec.2005.09.004

Hurford, J. R. (2002). Language beyond our grasp: what mirror neurons can, and cannot, do for language evolution. In Kimbrough, O., Griebel, U., & Plunkett, K. (Eds.), *The Evolution of Communication systems: A Comparative Approach.* Cambridge, MA: MIT Press.

Hutchinson, G., & Hayden, M. (1992). The prediction of exons through an analysis of spliceable open reading frames. *Nucleic Acids Research, 20*, 3453–3462. doi:10.1093/nar/20.13.3453

Hu, X., & Cercone, N. (1999). Data Mining via Discretization, Generalization and Rough Set Feature Selection. *Knowledge and Information Systems, 1*(1), 33–60.

IBM. (2004). *IBM Aglets*. Retrieved June 10, 2004, from http://www.trl.ibm.com/aglets/

Intille, S. S., Rondoni, J., Kukla, C., Anacona, I., & Bao, L. (2003). A context-aware experience sampling tool. In *Proceedings of CHI2003: Extended Abstracts*. ACM Publishing.

Intille, S. S., Tapia, E. M., Rondoni, J., Beaudin, J., Kukla, C., & Agarwal, S. (2003). Tools for studying behavior and technology in natural settings. In. *Proceedings of UbiComp, 2003*, 157–174.

ISO/IEC 9945-1. (1996). *ISO/IEC Standard 9945-1: Information Technology-Portable Operating System Interface (POSIX) - Part 1: System Application Program Interface (API) [C Language]*. Geneva, Switzerland: ISO/IEC.

Itao, T., Nakamura, T., Matsuo, M., Suda, T., & Aoyama, T. (2002). Adaptive creation of network applications in the jack-in-the-net architecture. In *Proceedings of IFIP Networking* (pp. 129-140).

Itoh, M., Goto, S., Akutsu, T., & Kanehisa, M. (2005). Fast and Accurate Database Homology Search Using Upper Bounds of Local Alignment Scores. *Bioinformatics (Oxford, England)*, *21*(7), 912–921. doi:10.1093/bioinformatics/bti076

Iwamoto, T., & Tokuda, H. (2003). PMAA: Media access architecture for ubiquitous computing. *Journal of IPSJ*, *44*(3), 848–856.

Jabber Software Foundation. (2004a). *Extensible messaging and presence protocol (XMPP): Core* (Tech. Rep.). Retrieved November 17, 2008, from http://www.ietf.org/rfc/rfc3920.txt

Jabber Software Foundation. (2004b). *Extensible messaging and presence protocol (XMPP): Instant messaging and presence* (Tech. Rep.). Retrieved November 17, 2008, from http://www.ietf.org/rfc/rfc3921.txt

Jaber, T., Amira, A., & Milligan, P. (2007). Empirical study of a novel approach to LSI for text categorisation. In *Proceedings of Signal Processing and Its Applications* (pp. 1–4). ISSPA.

JADE. *(Java Agent DEvelopment Framework)*. (2004). Retrieved from http://jade.cselt.it/

Jamieson, S. E., White, J. K., Howson, J. M., Pask, R., Smith, A. N., & Brayne, C. (2005, February). Candidate gene association study of solute carrier family 11a members 1 (SLC11A1) and 2 (SLC11A2) genes in Alzheimer's disease. *Neuroscience Letters*, *374*(2), 124–128. doi:10.1016/j.neulet.2004.10.038

Jan, R. H., & Lee, Y. R. (2003). An indoor geolocation system for wireless LANs. In *Proceedings of the Parallel Processing Workshops* (pp. 29-34).

Jeffry, H. J. (1990). Chaos game representation of gene structure. *Nucleic Acids Research*, *18*, 2163–2170. doi:10.1093/nar/18.8.2163

Jensen, E. D., Locke, C. D., & Toduda, H. (1985). A time-driven scheduling model for real-time operating systems. In *Proceedings of the 6th IEEE Real-Time Systems Symposium*, San Diego, CA (pp. 112-122). Washington, DC: IEEE Computer Society Press.

Jiang, X., & Han, Q. L. (2005). On H_∞ control for linear systems with interval time-varying delay. *Automatica*, *41*(12), 2099–2106. doi:10.1016/j.automatica.2005.06.012

Jiang, X., & Han, Q. L. (2006). Delay-dependent robust stability for uncertain linear systems with interval time-varying delay. *Automatica*, *42*(6), 1059–1065. doi:10.1016/j.automatica.2006.02.019

Jin, H., Wang, H., Wang, Q., & Dai, G. (2004). An improved least-slack first scheduling algorithm. *Journal of software, 15*(8), 1116-1123.

Johnson, M. S., & Overington, J. P. (1993). A Structural Basis for Sequence Comparisons. An Evaluation of Scoring Methodologies. *Journal of Molecular Biology*, *233*, 716–738. doi:10.1006/jmbi.1993.1548

Joshi, J. B. D., Bertino, E., Latif, U., & Ghafoor, A. (2005, January). Generalized Temporal Role Based Access Control Model. *IEEE Transactions on Knowledge and Data Engineering*, *7*(1), 4–23. doi:10.1109/TKDE.2005.1

Julesz, B. (1971, December). *Foundations of cyclopean perception*. Chicago: University of Chicago Press.

Kacprzyk, J., & Zadrozny, S. (2005). Linguistic database summaries and their protoforms: towards natural language based knowledge discovery tools. *Information Sciences*, *173*(4), 281–304. doi:10.1016/j.ins.2005.03.002

Kagan, S. (2008). *Rethinking Thinking Does Bloom's Taxonomy Align with Brain Science?* Spencers Thinkpad.

Kalman, Y. M., & Rafaeli, S. (2007). Modulating synchronicity in computer mediated communication. In *Proceedings of the 2007 Conference of the International Communication Association,* San-Francisco. Retrieved on March 9, 2009, from http://www.kalmans.com/synchasynchICAsubmit.pdf

Karlin, S., & Brendel, V. (1993). Patchiness and correlations in DNA sequences. *Science, 259*(5095), 677–680. doi:10.1126/science.8430316

Keil, F. C. (1979). *Semantic and Conceptual development: An Ontological perspective.* Cambridge, MA: Harvard University Press.

Kephart, J. O. (2005, May). Research Challenges of Autonomic Computing. In *Proceedings of the International Conference on Software Engineering (ICSE '05),* St. Louis, MO (pp. 15-22).

Kidd, C., Orr, R., Abowd, G. D., Atkeson, C. G., Essa, I. A., MacIntyre, B., et al. (1999). The aware home: A living laboratory for ubiquitous computing research. In *CoBuild99* (LNCS 1670, pp. 191-198).

Kieleczawa, J. (Ed.). (2008). *DNA Sequencing III: Dealing with Difficult Templates.* Boston, MA: Jones & Bartlett.

Kiliç, K., Uncu, O., & Türksen, I. B. (2007). Comparison of different strategies of utilizing fuzzy clustering in structure identification. *Information Sciences, 177*(23), 5153–5162. doi:10.1016/j.ins.2007.06.030

Kilpatrick, W. H. (1925). Syllabus in the philosophy of education; questions for discussion, with reading references and topics for papers. *Education,* 203–204.

Kimble, C. (2006). *Communities of practice: Never knowingly undersold.* Paper presented at the Innovative Approaches for Learning and Knowledge Sharing: EC-TEL 2006 Workshops, Crete, Greece.

Kim, J. H. (2001). Delay and its time-derivative dependent robust stability of time-delayed linear systems with uncertainty. *IEEE Transactions on Automatic Control, 46*(5), 789–792. doi:10.1109/9.920802

Kinsner, W. (1994, May). *Fractal dimensions: Morphological, entropy, spectra, and variance classes* (Tech. Rep. No. DEL94-4). Winnipeg, Manitoba, Canada: University of Manitoba, Department of Electrical & Computer Engineering.

Kinsner, W. (2008, August 14-16). Complexity and its measures in cognitive and other complex systems. In *Proceedings of the IEEE 7th Intern. Conf. Cognitive Informatics (ICCI08),* Stanford University, Palo Alto, CA (pp. 13-29).

Kinsner, W., & Zhang, H. (2009, June 15-17). Multifractal analysis and feature extraction of DNA sequences. In *Proceedings of the IEEE 8th Intern. Conf. Cognitive Informatics (ICCI09),* Hong Kong, China (pp. 29-37). ISBN 1-4244-4642-1

Kinsner, W. (2007, October-December). A unified approach to fractal dimensions. *International Journal of Cognitive Informatics and Natural Intelligence, 1*(4), 26–46.

Klusch, M. (2001). Information agent technology for the Internet: A survey. *Data & Knowledge Engineering, 36*(3), 337–372. doi:10.1016/S0169-023X(00)00049-5

Kohn, S. E., & Smith, K. L. (1992). On the notion of "aphasia syndrome". In S. E. Kohn (Ed.), *Conduction aphasia* (pp. 1-18). London: Lawrence Erlbaum Associates.

Kreuzinger, J., Brinkschult, U. S., & Ungerer, T. (2002). *Real-Time Event Handling and Scheduling on a Multithread Java Microntroller.* Dordrecht, The Netherlands: Elsvier Science Publications.

Kryssanov, V. V., Kumokawa, S., Goncharenko, I., & Ogawa, H. (2008). A system for multimodal exploration of social spaces. In A. Pirhonen & S. Brewster (Eds.), *Haptic and audio interaction design* (LNCS 5270, pp. 40-49).

Kryssanov, V. V., Okabe, M., Kakusho, K., & Minoh, M. (2002). Communication of social agents and the digital city – a semiotic perspective. In M. Tanabe, P.V. den Besselaar, & T. Ishida (Eds.), *Digital cities II, computational and sociological approaches* (LNCS 2362, pp. 56-70).

Kurgan, L. A. (2004). Reducing Complexity of Rule Based Models via Meta Mining. In *Proceedings of the International Conference on Machine Learning and Applications* (pp. 242- 249).

Kurgan, L. A., & Cios, K. J. (2004). CAIM Discretization Algorithm. *IEEE Transactions on Data and Knowldge Engineering, 16*(2), 145–153. doi:10.1109/TKDE.2004.1269594

Kurgan, L. A., Cios, K. J., & Dick, S. (2006). Highly scalable and robust rule learner: Performance evaluation and comparison. *IEEE Transactions on Systems, Man, and Cybernetics, 36,* 32–53. doi:10.1109/TSMCB.2005.852983

Kurgan, L. A., & Musilek, P. (2006). A survey of Knowledge Discovery and Data Mining process models. *The Knowledge Engineering Review, 21*(1), 1–24. doi:10.1017/S0269888906000737

Kwok, C., & Weld, D. (1996). Planning to gather information. In *Proceedings of the 14th National Conference AI* (pp. 15).

Labrosse, J. J. (1999). *MicroController/OS-II, The Real-Time Kernel* (2nd ed.). Gilroy, CA: R&D Books.

Lamie, E. L. (2008). *Real-Time Embedded Multithreading using ThreadX and MIPS*. Newnes.

Landauer, T. K., Foltz, P. W., & Laham, D. (1998). Introduction to latent semantic analysis. *Discourse Processes, 25,* 259–284.

Lander, E. S., Linton, L. M., Birren, B., & Nusbaoum, C. (2001). Initial sequencing and analysis of the human genome. *Nature, 409,* 860–921. doi:10.1038/35057062

Langley, P. (2005). An adaptive architecture for physical agents. In *Proceedings of the 2005 IEEE/WIC/ACM International Conference on Intelligent Agent Technology,* Compiegne, France (pp. 18-25). Washington, DC: IEEE.

Laplante, P. A. (1977). *Real-time systems design and analysis* (2nd ed.). Washington, DC: IEEE Press.

Lapouchnian, A., Yu, Y., Liaskos, S., & Mylopoulos, J. (2006, October). Requirements-Driven Design of Autonomic Application Software. In *Proceedings of the conference of the Center for Advanced Studies on Collaborative Research,* Toronto, Canada.

Larhammar, D., & Chatzidimitriou-Dreismann, C. A. (1993). Biological origins of long-range correlations and compositional variations in DNA. *Nucleic Acids Research, 21,* 5167–5170. doi:10.1093/nar/21.22.5167

Lave, & Wenge. (1990). *Situated Learning: Legitimate Periperal Participation.* Cambridge, UK: Cambridge University Press.

Lefebvre, H. (1994). *The production of space* (Donald Nicholson-Smith, Trans.). Oxford, UK: Blackwell

Levy, A. Y., Kirk, T., & Sagiv, Y. (2005). The information manifold (pp. 14). In *Proceedings of the AAAI Spring Symposium on Information Gathering From Heterogeneous Distributed Environments.*

Lewis, D., & Ringutte, M. (1994). A comparison of Two Learning Algorithm for Text Categorization. In *Proceedings of the Third Annual Symposium on Document Analysis and Information Retrieval* (pp. 81-93).

Lewis, B., & Berg, D. (1998). *Multithreaded Programming with Pthreads.* Upper Saddle River, NJ: Sun Microsystems Press.

Lewis, H. R., & Papadimitriou, C. H. (1998). *Elements of the Theory of Computation* (2nd ed.). Upper Saddle River, NJ: Prentice-Hall.

Liao, X. X., & Mao, X. (1996). Exponential stability and instability of stochastic neural networks. *Stochastic Analysis and Applications, 14*(2), 165–185. doi:10.1080/07362999608809432

Liao, X., Chen, G., & Sanchez, E. N. (2002). Delay-dependent exponential stability analysis of delayed neural networks: an LMI approach. *Neural Networks, 15*(7), 855–866. doi:10.1016/S0893-6080(02)00041-2

Licklider, J. C. R. (1960, March). Man-computer symbiosis. *IRE Transactions on Human Factors in Electronics, HFE-1,* 4–11. doi:10.1109/THFE2.1960.4503259

Lightstone, S. (2007, March). Foundations of Autonomic Computing Development. In *Proceedings of the 4th IEEE International Workshop on Engineering of Autonomic and Autonomous Systems (EASe '07),* Tucson, AZ (pp. 163-171).

Lin, T. Y. (1988). Neighborhood systems and relational databases. In *Proceedings of the 1988 ACM sixteenth annual conference on Computer science (CSC '88)* (p. 725). New York: ACM. Retrieved from http://doi.acm.org/10.1145/322609.323183

Lindsay, P. H., & Norman, D. A. (1997). *An Introduction to Psychology* (2nd ed.). New York: Academic Press.

Lipschutz, S., & Lipson, M. (1997). *Schaum's Outline of Theories and Problems of Discrete Mathematics* (2nd ed.). New York: McGraw-Hill Inc.

Lipton, R. J., & Baum, E. B. (Eds.). (1995). *DNA Based Computers*. Providence, RI: American Mathematical Society.

Liu, J. (2000). *Real-time systems*. Upper Saddle River, NJ: Prentice-Hall.

Liu, Y., Bai, G., & Feng, B. (2008a). On Mining Rules that Involve Inequalities from Decision Table. In D. Zhang, Y. Wang, & W. Kinsner (Eds.), *Proceedings of the 7th IEEE International Conference on Cognitive Informatics (ICCI 2008)* (pp. 255–260). doi: 10.1109/COGINF.2008.4639176

Liu, Y., Bai, G., & Feng, B. (2008b, August 14-16). CompactLEM2: A Scalable Rough Set based Knowledge Acquisition Method that Generates Small Number of Short Rules. In D. Zhang, Y. Wang, & W. Kinsner (Eds.), *Proceedings of the Seven IEEE International Conference on Cognitive Informatics (ICCI 2008),* Stanford University, CA (pp. 215-223). Washington, DC: IEEE.

Liu, Y., Wang, Z., & Liu, X. (2008). Robust stability of discrete-time stochastic neural networks with time-varying delays. *Neurocomputing, 71*(4-6), Mao, X. (1997). *Stochastic differential equations and their applications*. Chichester, UK: Horwood. 823-833.

Liu, B., & Liu, X. (2007). Robust stability of uncertain discrete impulsive systems. *IEEE Transactions on Circuits and Wystems. II, Express Briefs, 54*(4), 455–459. doi:10.1109/TCSII.2007.892395

Liu, C., & Layland, J. (1973). Scheduling Algorithms for Multiprogramming in Hard-Real-Time Environments. *Journal of the Association for Computing Machinery, 20*(1), 46–56.

Lo, C.-C., Cheng, D.-Y., Chen, C.-H., & Yan, Y.-S. (2008). Design and Implementation of Situation-Aware Medical Tourism Service Search System (pp. 1-5). In *Proceedings of the Wireless Communications, Networking and Mobile Computing (WiCOM '08), the 4th International Conference*.

Lodish, H., Berk, A., Matsudaira, P., Kaiser, C.A., Krieger, M., & Scott, M. P. (2004). *Molecular Cell Biology* (5th ed.). New York: W. H. Freeman and Company.

Looks, M., Goertzel, B., Coelho, L., Mudado, M., & Pennachin, C. (2007). Clustering Gene Expression Data via Mining Ensembles of Classification Rules Evolved Using MOSES. In *Proceedings of the Genetic and Evolutionary Computation Conference (GECCO)* (pp. 407-414).

Louden, K. C. (1993). *Programming Languages: Principles and Practice*. Boston: PWS-Kent Publishing Co.

Lum, W. Y., & Lau, F. C. M. (2003). User-centric content negotiation for effective adaptation service in mobile computing. *IEEE Transactions on Software Engineering, 29*(12), 1100–1111. doi:10.1109/TSE.2003.1265524

Lutes, K. D., & Baggili, I. M. (2006). Diabetic e-Management System (DEMS). In *Proceedings of ITNG* (p. 619-624). Washington, DC: IEEE Computer Society. Retrieved from http://doi.ieeecomputersociety.org/10.1109/ITNG.2006.53

Mandelbrot, B. B. (1977). *The Fractal Geometry of Nature*. New York: W. H. Freeman and Company.

Manvi, S. S., & Venkataram, P. (2004). Applications of agent technology in communications: A review. *Computer Communications, 27*(15), 1493–1508. doi:10.1016/j.comcom.2004.05.011

Martin-Lof, P. (1975). An Intuitionistic Theory of Types: Predicative Part. In Rose, H., & Shepherdson, J. C. (Eds.), *Logic Colloquium 1973*. Amsterdam, The Netherlands: North Holland. doi:10.1016/S0049-237X(08)71945-1

Marwell, G., & Hage, J. (1970). The Organization of Role-Relationships: A Systematic Description. *American Sociological Review, 35*(5), 884–900. doi:10.2307/2093299

Maturana, H. R., & Varela, F. J. (1980). *Autopoiesis and Cognition the realization of living*. London: D. Reidel pub.

McDermid, J. (Ed.). (1991). *Software Engineer's Reference Book*. Oxford, UK: Butterworth Heinemann Ltd.

McIlraith, S. A., Son, T. C., & Zeng, H. (2001). Semantic web services. *IEEE Intelligent Systems, 16*(2), 46–53. doi:10.1109/5254.920599

Mezirow, J. (1981). A Critical Theory of Adult Learning and Education. *Adult Education Quarterly, 32*(1), 3–24. doi:10.1177/074171368103200101

Michael, H. C., & Butler, R. W. (1996). Impediments to Industrial Use of Formal Method. *IEEE Computer, 24*(9), 25–26.

Michalski, R. S. (1983). A Theory and Methodology of Inductive Learning. *Artificial Intelligence, 20*(2), 111–161. doi:10.1016/0004-3702(83)90016-4

Mi, J., Wu, W., & Zhang, W. (2004). Approaches to knowledge reduction based on variable precision rough set model. *Inf. Sci, 159*(2), 255–272. doi:10.1016/j.ins.2003.07.004

Miller, G. A. (1956). The magical number seven, plus or minus two: some limits on our capacity for processing information. *Psychological Review, 63*, 81–97. doi:10.1037/h0043158

Miller, M., Schneider, J., Sathayanarayana, B. K., Toth, M. V., Marshall, G. R., & Clawson, L. (1989). Structure of Complex of Synthetic HIV-1 Protease with Substrate-Based Inhibitor at at 2.3 Resolution. *Science, 246*, 1149–1152. doi:10.1126/science.2686029

Milner, R. (1980). *A Calculus of Communicating Systems* (LNCS 92). New York: Springer.

Minakuchi, Y., Satou, K., & Konagaya, A. (2002). Prediction of Protein-Protein Interaction Sites Using Support Vector Machines. *Genome Informatics, 13*, 322–323.

Minami, M., Morikawa, H., & Aoyama, T. (2003). The design and evaluation of an interface-based naming system for supporting service synthesis in ubiquitous computing environment. *IEICE Transactions, J86-B*(5), 777–789.

Mingo, L., Gómez, N., Arroyo, F., & Castellanos, J. (2009). Hierarchical function approximation with a neural network model. *International Journal of Software Science and Computational Intelligence, 1*(3), 67–80.

Minoh, M., & Kamae, T. (2001). Networked appliance and their peer-to-peer srchitecture AMIDEN. *IEEE Communications Magazine, 39*(10), 80–84. doi:10.1109/35.956117

Minsky, M. (1998). Consciousness is a big suitcase. *EDGE*. Retrieved from http://www.edge.org/3rd/culture/minsky/minsky/p2.html

Minsky, M. (2007). *The Emotion Machine: Commonsense Thinking, Artificial Intelligence, and the Future of the Human Mind*. New York: Simon & Schuster Paperbacks.

Mitchell, J. C. (1990). Type Systems for Programming Languages. In van Leeuwen, J. (Ed.), *Handbook of Theoretical Computer Science* (pp. 365–458). Amsterdam, The Netherlands: North Holland.

Mitchelson, K. R. (Ed.). (2007). *New High Throughput Technologies for DNA Sequencing and Genomics*. Maryland Heights, MO: Elsevier.

Miyoshi, A., Yagawa, G., & Sasaki, S. (1999). An interface agent that actively supports CAE beginner users in performing analyses. *Advances in Engineering Software, 30*(8), 575–579. doi:10.1016/S0965-9978(99)00010-1

Molina, C., Rodríguez-Ariza, L., Sánchez, D., & Amparo Vila, M. (2006). A new fuzzy multidimensional model. *IEEE Transactions on Fuzzy Systems, 14*(6), 897–912. doi:10.1109/TFUZZ.2006.879984

Monge, P., & Contractor, N. (2003). *Theories of communication in networks*. Oxford, UK: Oxford University Press.

Morton, J., & Johnson, M. (1991). CONSPEC and CONLERN: A Two-Process Theory of Infant Face Recognition. *Psychological Review, 98*(2), 164–181. doi:10.1037/0033-295X.98.2.164

Moulin, C., Bettahar, F., Barthès, J.-P., Sbodio, M., & Korda, N. (2006). Adding support to user interaction in e-government environment. In *Advances in web intelligence and data mining* (pp. 151-160).

Mou, S., Gao, H., Lam, J., & Qiang, W. (2008). A new criterion of delay-dependent asymptotic stability for Hopfield neural networks with time delay. *IEEE Transactions on Neural Networks, 19*(3), 532–535. doi:10.1109/TNN.2007.912593

Müller, H., O'Brien, L., Klein, M., & Wood, B. (2006). *Autonomic Computing* (Technical Note CMU/SEI-2006-TN-006). Pittsburgh, PA: Carnegie Mellon University. Retrieved October 20, 2008, from http://www.sei.cmu.edu/pub/documents/06.reports/pdf/06tn006.pdf

Murphy, G. L., & Medin, D. L. (1985). The role of Theories in conceptual coherence. *Psychological Review, 92*, 289–316. doi:10.1037/0033-295X.92.3.289

Murray, J. D. (2002). *Mathematical Biology: An Introduction* (3rd ed.). New York: Springer Verlag.

Murray, J. D. (2002). *Mathematical Biology: Spatial Models and Biomedical Applications* (3rd ed.). New York: Springer Verlag.

Naghibzadeh, M., & Kim, K. H. (2002). A Modified Version of Rate-Monotonic Scheduling Algorithm and its Efficiency Assessment. In *Proceedings of the 7th IEEE international workshop on Object-Oriented real-time dependable systems* (pp. 289-294).

Nakazawa, J., Tobe, Y., & Tokuda, H. (2001). On dynamic service integration in VNA architecture. *IEICE Transactions. E (Norwalk, Conn.), 84-A*(7), 1624–1635.

Narayanan, A., Wu, X. K., & Yang, Z. R. (2002). Mining Viral Protease Data to Extract Cleavage Knowledge. *Bioinformatics (Oxford, England), 18*, 5–13.

Nawi, N. M., Ransing, R. S., & Ransing, M. R. (2008). A New Method to Improve the Gradient Based Search Direction to Enhance the Computational Efficiency of Back Propagation Based Neural Network Algorithms. In *Proceedings of the Modeling & Simulation, the Second Asia International Conference* (pp. 546-552).

Neumann, J., Schnörr, C., & Steidl, G. (2005). Combined SVM-Based Feature Selection and Classification. *Machine Learning, 61*(1-3), 129–150. doi:10.1007/s10994-005-1505-9

Newell, A. (1994). *Unified Theories of Cognition.* Cambridge, MA: Harvard University Press.

Ngolah, C. F., & Wang, Y. (2009). Tool Support for Software Development based on Formal Specifications in RTPA. *International Journal of Software Engineering and Its Applications, 3*(3), 71–88.

Ngolah, C. F., & Wang, Y. (2010). The Formal Design Model of a Real-Time Operating System (RTOS+). *International Journal of Software Science and Computational Intelligence, 2*(2).

Ngolah, C. F., Wang, Y., & Tan, X. (2004). The Real-Time Task Scheduling Algorithm of RTOS+. *IEEE Canadian Journal of Electrical and Computer Engineering, 29*(4), 237–243.

Nicollin, X., & Sifakis, J. (1991). An Overview and Synthesis on Timed Process Algebras. In *Proceedings of the 3rd International Computer Aided Verification Conference* (pp. 376-398).

Nilar, A., Hattori, F., & Kuwabara, K. (2008). Bridging semantic gap in distant communication: Ontology-based approach. In *Agent and multi-agent systems: Technologies and applications: Second KES International Symposium, KES-AMSTA 2008* (LNAI 4953, pp. 252-260).

Nunnally, B. K. (Ed.). (2005). *Analytical Techniques in DNA Sequencing.* Boca Raton, FL: CRC. doi:10.1201/9781420029086

Nyanchama, M., & Osborn, S. (1999). The Role Graph Model and Conflict of Interest. *ACM Transactions on Information and System Security, 2*(1), 3–33. doi:10.1145/300830.300832

Odell, J., Nodine, M., & Levy, R. (2005). A Metamodel for Agents, Roles, and Groups. In J. Odell, P. Giorgini, & J. Müller (Eds.), *Agent-Oriented Software Engineering (AOSE)* (LNCS 3382, pp. 78-92). Berlin: Springer.

Ogawa, A., Kobayashi, K., Sugiura, K., Nakamura, O., & Murai, J. (2000). *Design and implementation of DV based video over RTP.* Paper presented at the Packet Video Workshop 2000.

Oh, S., & Yang, S. (1998). *A modified least-laxity-first scheduling algorithm for real-time tasks.* In *Proceedings of the 5th International Conference on Real-Time Computing Systems and Applications* (pp. 31-36). Washington, DC: IEEE Computer Society Press.

Olarnsakul, M., & Batanov, D. N. (2004). Customizing Component-Based Software Using Component Coordination Model. *International Journal of Software Engineering and Knowledge Engineering, 14*(2), 103–140. doi:10.1142/S0218194004001622

Osherson, D., & Smith, E. (1981). On the adequacy of prototype theory as a theory of concepts. *Cognition, 9*(1), 35–58. Retrieved from http://www.mendeley.com/research/on-the-adequacy-of-prototype-theory-as-a-theory-of-concepts/. doi:10.1016/0010-0277(81)90013-5

OWL. (2004). *OWL web ontology language overview.* Retrieved from http://www.w3.org/TR/owl-features/

OWL-S. (2008). *OWL-S 1.2 pre-release.* Retrieved from http://www.ai.sri.com/daml/services/owl-s/1.2/

Paquette, G. (2007). Graphical Ontology Modeling Language for Learning Environments. *Technology, Instruction., Cognition and Learning, 5*, 133-168. Retrieved from http://ares.licef.teluq.uqam.ca/Portals/29/docs/pub/modelisation/TICL 133-168pp. Paquette.pdf

Paquette, G. (2007). An Ontology and a Software Framework for Competency Modeling and Management Competency in an Instructional Engineering Method (MISA). *Journal of Educational Technology & Society, 10*, 1–21.

Parashar, M., & Hariri, S. (2005). Autonomic Computing: An Overview. In J. P. Banâtre (Eds.), *Proceedings of UPP 2004* (LNCS 3566, pp. 247-259). Berlin: Springer Verlag.

Parr, T. (2000). *ANTLR Reference Manual*. Retrieved from http://www.antlr.org/doc/

Parr, T. J., & Quong, R. W. (1995). ANTLR: A Predicated-LL(k) Parser Generator. *Software, Practice & Experience, 25*(7), 789–810. doi:10.1002/spe.4380250705

Paum, G., Rozenberg, G., & Salomaa, A. (1998). *DNA Computing: New Computing Paradigm*. New York: Springer.

Pawlak, Z. (1982). Rough Sets. *International Journal of Computer and Information Sciences*, 341-356.

Pawlak, Z., & Skowron, A. (2007). Rudiments of rough sets. *Inf. Sci, 177*(1), 3–27. doi:10.1016/j.ins.2006.06.003

Pazzani, M., & Kibler, D. (1992). The Utility of Knowledge in Inductive Learning. *Machine Learning, 9*, 57–94. doi:10.1007/BF00993254

Pearl, L. H., & Taylor, W. R. (1987). A Structural Model for the Retroviral Proteases. *Nature, 329*, 351–354. doi:10.1038/329351a0

Pedrycz, W. (2005). *Knowledge-Based Clustering: From Data to Information Granules*. New York: John Wiley. doi:10.1002/0471708607

Pedrycz, W., & Gomide, F. (1998). *An Introduction to Fuzzy Sets: Analysis and Design*. Cambridge, MA: MIT Press.

Pedrycz, W., & Rai, P. (2008). Collaborative clustering with the use of Fuzzy C-Means and its quantification. *Fuzzy Sets and Systems, 159*(18), 2399–2427. doi:10.1016/j.fss.2007.12.030

Pedrycz, W., Skowron, A., & Kreinovich, V. (Eds.). (2008). *Handbook of Granular Computing*. West Sussex, UK: John Wiley & Sons. doi:10.1002/9780470724163

Peitgen, H.-O., Jürgens, H., & Saupe, D. (2004). *Chaos and Fractals* (2nd ed.). New York: Springer Verlag.

Peng, C.-K., Buldyrev, S. V., Goldberger, A. L., Havlin, S., Sciortino, F., Simmons, M., & Stanley, H. E. (1992). Long-range correlations in nucleotide sequences. *Nature, 356*, 168–170. doi:10.1038/356168a0

Peristeras, V., & Tarabanis, K. (2004). Advancing the government enterprise architecture gea: The service execution object model. In *Database and expert systems applications*, Zaragoza, Spain: DEXA.

Peterson, J. L., & Silberschantz, A. (1985). *Operating System Concepts*. Reading, MA: Addison-Wesley.

Pezzulo, G., & Castelfranchi, C. (2007). The symbol detachment problem. *Cognitive Processing, 8*, 115–131. doi:10.1007/s10339-007-0164-0

Pfeifer, R., & Bongard, J. (2006). *How the body shapes the way we think: a new view of intelligence*. Cambridge, MA: MIT Press.

Pfeifer, R., & Scheier, C. (1999). *Understanding Intelligence*. Cambridge, MA: MIT Press.

Pham, D. T., & Castellani, M. (2006). Evolutionary learning of fuzzy models. *Engineering Applications of Artificial Intelligence, 19*(6), 583–592. doi:10.1016/j.engappai.2006.01.007

Philipose, M., Fishkin, K. P., & Perkowitz, M. (2004). Inferring activities from interactions with objects. *IEEE Pervasive Computing / IEEE Computer Society [and] IEEE Communications Society, 3*, 50–57. doi:10.1109/MPRV.2004.7

Piaget, J., & Inhelder, B. (1958). *The Growth of Logical Thinking from Childhood to Adolescence*. New York: Basic Books.

Picard, R. W. (1995). *Affective computing MIT* (Media Laboratory Perceptual Computing Section Tech. Rep. No. 321). Cambridge, MA: MIT Press.

Pokraev, S., Zlatev, Z., Brussee, R., & Eck, P. V. (2004). Semantic Support for Automated Negotiation with Alliances. In *Proceedings of the ICEIS 2004: 6th International conference on enterprise information systems*, Portugal (Vol. 5, No. 3, pp. 244-249).

Poly, U. (2004). *Chinese Learner English Corpus (CLEC)*. Retrieved June 10, 2004, from http://langbank.engl.polyu.edu.hk/corpus/clec.html

Potter, M., & Kinsner, W. (2007, April 15-20). Direct calculation of the f(α) fractal dimension spectrum from high-dimensional correlation-integral partitions. In Proceedings of the IEEE 2007 Intern. Conf. Acoustics, Speech, Signal Processing (ICASSP07), Honolulu, USA (vol. III, pp. 989-992). ISBN 1-4244-0728-1

Prasithsangaree, P., Krishnamurthy, P., & Chrysanthis, P. K. (2002). On indoor position location with wireless LANs. In *Proceedings of the 13th IEEE International Symposium on Personal, Indoor and Mobile Radio Communications* (Vol. 2).

Prud'hommeaux, E. S. A. (2007). *SPARQL query language for RDF*. Retrieved from http://www.w3.org/TR/rdf-sparql-query/

Qian, N., & Sejnowski, T. J. (1988). Predicting the Secondary Structure of Globular Proteins Using Neural Network Models. *Journal of Molecular Biology, 202*, 865–884. doi:10.1016/0022-2836(88)90564-5

Quinlan, J. R. (1993). C4.5: Programs for Machine Learning.

Quinlan, J. (1986). Induction of Decision Trees. *Machine Learning, 1*, 81–106. doi:10.1007/BF00116251

RAISE. (1995). *The RAISE Specification Language (BCS Practitioner Series)*. London: Prentice Hall, London.

Rakkiyappan, R., & Balasubramaniam, P. (2008). Delay-dependent asymptotic stability for stochastic delayed recurrent neural networks with time varying delays. *Applied Mathematics and Computation, 198*(2), 526–533. doi:10.1016/j.amc.2007.08.053

Ramachandran, V. S. (2000). Mirror neurons and imitation as the driving force behind "the great leap forward" in human evolution. *EDGE: The third culture*. Retrieved from http://www.edge.org/3rd_culture/ramachandran/ramachandran_p1.html

Ramírez, C., & Cooley, R. (1997). A Theory of the Acquisition of Episodic Memory. In *Proceedings of the ECML-97: Case-Based Reasoning Workshop*, Prague, Czech Republic (pp. 48-55). New York: Springer Verlag.

Ramirez, C., Concha, C., & Valdes, B. (2010). Cardiac Pulse Detection in BCG Signals Implemented on a Regular Classroom Chair Integrated to an Emotional and Learning Model for Personalization of Learning Resources. In L. G. Richards & K. Curry, *Proceedings of the 40th Annual Frontiers in Education (FIE) Conference*, Arlington, VA. Washington, DC: IEEE.

Raybourn, E. M., Kings, N., & Davies, J. (2003). Adding cultural signposts in adaptive community-based virtual environments. *Interacting with Computers, 15*(1), 91–107. doi:10.1016/S0953-5438(02)00056-5

Realtime, I. (n.d.). *Openfire*. Retrieved November 17, 2009, from http://www.igniterealtime.org/projects/openfire/index.jsp

Reiman, E. M., Webster, J. A., Myers, A. J., Hardy, J., Dunckley, T., & Zismann, V. L. (2007). GAB2 Alleles Modify Alzheimer's Risk in APOE e4 Carriers. *Neuron, 54*(5), 713–720. doi:10.1016/j.neuron.2007.05.022

Ren, S., Yu, Y., Chen, N., Tsai, J. J.-P., & Kwiat, K. (2007, September). The role of roles in supporting re-configurability and fault localizations for open distributed and embedded systems. *ACM Trans. Autonomic & Adaptive Sys., 2*(3), 1–27.

Rifaat, R., & Kinsner, W. (1999, May 10-12). Multi-fractal analysis of DNA sequences. In *Proceedings of the IEEE Can. Conf. Electrical and Computer Eng. (CCECE'99)*, Edmonton, AB (pp. 801-804).

Riley, E. P., Lochry, E. A., & Shapiro, N. R. (1979). *Lack of response inhibition in rats*.

Rivas, M. A., & Harbour, M. G. (2001, May). MaRTE OS: An Ada Kernel for Real-Time Embedded Applications. In Proceedings of Ada-Europe 2001, Leuven, Belgium.

Rizzolatti, G., Fadiga, L., Gallese, V., & Fogassi, I. (1996). Premotor cortex and the recognition of motor actions. *Brain Research. Cognitive Brain Research, 3*, 131–141. doi:10.1016/0926-6410(95)00038-0

Roberts, J. (2006). Limits to communities of practice. *Journal of Management Studies, 43*(3), 623–639. doi:10.1111/j.1467-6486.2006.00618.x

Rohn, T. T., Cusack, S. M., Kessinger, S. R., & Oxford, J. T. (2004). Caspase Activaion Independent of Cell Death is Required for Proper Cell Dispersal and Correct Morphology in PC12 Cells. *Experimental Cell Research, 293*, 215–225. doi:10.1016/j.yexcr.2003.12.029

Ruggieri, S. (2002). Efficient C4.5 [classification algorithm]. *Knowledge and Data Engineering. IEEE Transactions, 14*(2), 438–444.

Rumelhart, D. E., & Norman, D. A. (1981). *Cognitive Skills and their acquisition*. New York: Lawrence Earlbaum.

Russel, B. (1903). *The Principles of Mathematics*. London: George Allen & Unwin.

Salzsieder, E., Fischer, U., Hierle, A., Oppel, U., Rutscher, A., & Sell, C. (1995). Knowledge-Based Education Tool to Improve Quality in Diabetes Care. In *Proceedings of the AIME* (pp. 417-418).

Samimi, F. A., McKinley, P. K., & Masoud Sadjadi, S. M. (2006). Mobile Service Clouds: A Self-managing Infrastructure for Autonomic Mobile Computing Services. In A. Keller & J.-P. Martin-Flatin (Eds.), *Proceedings of SelfMan 2006* (LNCS 3996, pp. 130-141). Berlin: Springer Verlag.

Samuel, A. L. (1959). Some studies in machine learning using the game of checkers. *IBM Journal of Research and Development*, *3*(3), 210–229. doi:10.1147/rd.33.0210

Sandhu, R., Bhamidipati, V., & Munawer, O. (1999, February). The ARBAC97 Model for Role-Based Administration of Roles. *ACM Transactions on Information and System Security*, *2*(1), 105–135. doi:10.1145/300830.300839

Sanz, R., López, I., Rodriguez, M., & Hernández, C. (2007). Principles for consciousness in integrated cognitive control. *Neural Networks*, *20*, 938–946. doi:10.1016/j.neunet.2007.09.012

Sato, G. Y. (2008). *Contribution à l'amélioration de la coordination de communautés de pratique distribuées*. Unpublished PhD thesis, Université de Technologie de Compiègne, Compiègne.

Sbodio, M., & Moulin, C. (2006). Denotation of semantic web services operations through OWL-S. In *Proceedings of the Workshop on Semantics for Web Services (SemWS'06) in conjunction with the 4th European Conference on Web Services (ECOWS'06)* (pp. 17-24).

Schroeder, M. (1991). *Fractals, Chaos, Power Laws: Minutes from an Infinite Paradise*. New York: W. H. Freeman.

Searle, J. R. (1980). Minds, brains, and programs. *The Behavioral and Brain Sciences*, *3*(3), 169–225. doi:10.1017/S0140525X00005756

Selfridge, O. G. (1959). Pandemonium: a paradigm for learning. In *Proceedings of the Symposium on Mechanisation of Thought Processes*, London (pp. 511-529).

Sha, L., Rajkumar, R., & Lehoczky, J. P. (1990, September). Priority Inheritance Protocols: An Approach to Real-Time Synchronization. *IEEE Transactions on Computers*, 1175. doi:10.1109/12.57058

Shanahan, M. P. (2005). Consciousness, emotion, and imagination: a brain-inspired architecture for cognitive robotics. In *Proceedings AISB 2005 Symposium on Next Generation Approaches to Machine Consciousness* (pp. 26-35).

Shannon, C., & Weaver, W. (1964). *The Mathematical Theory of Communication*. Chicago: University of Illinois Press.

Shen, W., Norrie, D. H., & Barthès, J. P. (2001). *Multi-agent systems for concurrent intelligent design and manufacturing*. London: Taylor and Francis.

Sheng, L. (1999). *The Java Native Interface: Programmers Guide and Specification*. Reading, MA: Addison-Wesley.

Shen, Q., & Chouchoulas, A. (2002). A rough-fuzzy approach for generating classification rules. *Pattern Recognition*, *35*(11), 2425–2438. doi:10.1016/S0031-3203(01)00229-1

Silberschatz, A., Galvin, P., & Gagne, G. (2003). *Applied Operating System Concepts* (1st ed.). New York: John Wiley & Sons, Inc.

Silverman, D. D., & Linsker, R. (1986). A measure of DNA periodicity. *Journal of Theoretical Biology*, *118*, 295–300. doi:10.1016/S0022-5193(86)80060-1

Simon, R., & Zurko, M. E. (1997, June). Separation of duty in role based access control environments. In *Proceedings of the 10th IEEE Workshop on Computer Security Foundations*, Rockport, MA (pp. 183-194).

Skarmeas, N. (1995, January). Organizations through Roles and Agents. In *Proceedings of the Int'l Workshop on the Design of Cooperative Systems*, Antibes-Juan-Les-Pins, France. Retrieved October 20, 2008, from http://citeseer.ist.psu.edu/174774.html

Skiena, S. (1990). *Implementing Discrete Mathematics: Combinatorics and Graph Theory with Mathematica*. Reading, MA: Addison-Wesley.

Sloman, A. (2007). *Why symbol-grounding is both impossible and unnecessary, and why theory-tethering is more powerful anyway*. Retrieved from http://www.cs.bham.ac.uk/research/projects/cogaff/talks/models.pdf

Smee, A. (1849). *Principles of the Human Mind Deduced from Physical Laws.*

Smith, J., & MacLean, K. (2007). Communicating emotions through a haptic link: Design space and methodology. *International Journal of Human-Computer Studies, 65,* 376–387. doi:10.1016/j.ijhcs.2006.11.006

Smith, R. G. (1980). The contract net protocol high-level communication and control in a distributed problem solver. *IEEE Transactions on Computers, 29*(12), 1104–1113. doi:10.1109/TC.1980.1675516

Snyder, E. E., & Stormo, G. D. (1993). Identification of coding regions in genomic DNA sequences: An application of dynamic programming and neural networks. *Nucleic Acids Research, 21,* 607–613. doi:10.1093/nar/21.3.607

Sohn, J., Kim, N.-S., & Sung, W. (1999). A statistical model-based voice activity detection. *IEEE Signal Processing Letters, 6,* 1–3. doi:10.1109/97.736233

Soller, A., Guizzardi, R., Molani, A., & Perini, A. (2004). *SCALE: Supporting community awareness, learning, and evolvement in an organizational learning environment.* Paper presented at the 6th International Conference on Learning Sciences, Santa Monica, CA.

Solovyev, V., Salamov, A., & Lawrence, C. (1994). Predicting internal exons by oligonucleotide composition and discriminant analysis of spliceable open reading frames. *Nucleic Acids Research, 22,* 5156–5163. doi:10.1093/nar/22.24.5156

Sorin-Peters, R., & Behrmann, M. (1995). Change in perception of communication abilities of aphasic patients and their families. *Aphasiology, 9*(6), 565–575. doi:10.1080/02687039508248715

Soulier, E. (2004). Les communautés de pratique au coeur de l'Organisation Réelle des Entreprises. *Systèmes d'Information et Management, 9*(1), 3–23.

Spaniol, M., Springer, L., Klamma, R., & Jarke, M. (2004). SOCRATES: Barrier free communities of aphasics on the internet. In K. Miesenberger et al. (Eds.), *ICCHP 2004* (LNCS 3118, pp. 1024-1031).

Spence, R. (1999). A framework for navigation. *International Journal of Human-Computer Studies, 51*(5), 919–945. doi:10.1006/ijhc.1999.0265

Spertus, E. (1997). Parasite: Mining structural information on the web. In *Proceedings of the 6th WWW Conference* (pp. 16).

Steels, L., Loetzsch, M., & Spranger, M. S. (2007). *Semiotic dynamics solves the symbol grounding problem.* Retrieved from http://hdl.nature.com/10101/npre.2007.1234.1

Stepaniuk. (1999). Rough Set Data Mining of Diabetes Data. In *Proceedings of the 11th International Symposium on Foundations of Intelligent Systems (ISMIS '99)* (pp. 457–465). London: Springer Verlag.

Stephens, L. M., & Huhns, M. N. (2001). Consensus Ontologies. Reconciling The Semantics of Web Pages and Agents. *IEEE Internet Computing, 5*(5), 92–95. doi:10.1109/4236.957901

Sterritt, R., & Hinchey, M. (2004, April). Apoptosis and Self-Destruct: A Contribution to Autonomic Agents? In *Proceedings of the 3rd NASA/IEEE Workshop on Formal Approaches to Agent-Based Systems,* Greenbelt, MD (pp. 262-270).

Sterritt, R., & Hinchey, M. (2005, April). Engineering ultimate self-protection in autonomic agents for space exploration missions. In *Proceedings of the 12th IEEE International Conference and Workshops on the Engineering of Computer-Based Systems,* Greenbelt, MD (pp. 506-511).

Stojmirovic, A. (2004). Quasi-Metric Spaces With Measure. *Topology Proceedings, 28*(2), 655–671.

Strachan, T., & Read, A. P. (1996). *Human Molecular Genetics.* New York: Wiley-Liss.

Strogatz, S. H. (2000). *Nonlinear Dynamics and Chaos.* Cambridge, MA: Westview/Perseus.

Stubbs, D. F., & Webre, N. W. (1985). *Data Structures with Abstract Data Types and Pascal.* Monterey, CA: Brooks/Cole Publishing Co.

Sudarsun, S., Kalaivendhan, D., & Venkateswarlu. (2006). Unsupervised Contextual Keyword Relevance Learning and Measurement using PLSA. In *Proceedings of the Annual India Conference* (pp. 1-6).

Suganuma, T., Takahashi, H., & Shiratori, N. (2008). *Agent-based middleware for advanced ubiquitous communication services based on symbiotic computing.* Paper presented at the 7th IEEE International Conference on Cognitive Informatics, Palo Alto, CA.

Sugawara, K., Fujita, S., & Hara, H. (2007). A concept of symbiotic computing and its application to telework. In *Proceedings of the 6th International Conference on Cognitive Informatics (ICCI'07)* (pp. 302-311).

Sugawara, K., Fujita, S., Kinoshita, T., & Shiratori, N. (2008). *A design of cognitive agents for recognizing real space - towards symbiotic computing*. Paper presented at the 7th IEEE International Conference on Cognitive Informatics, Palo Alto, CA.

Sugawara, K., Hara, H., Kinoshita, T., & Uchiya, T. (2002). Flexible distributed agent system programmed by a rule-based language. In *Proceedings of the Sixth IASTED International Conference of Artificial Intelligence and Soft Computing* (pp. 7-12).

Sugawara, K., Shiratori, N., & Kinoshita, T. (2003). Toward post ubiquitous computing – symbiotic computing. *IEICE Technical Report, 103*(244), 43–46.

Sun Developer Network. (n.d.). *JMF: Java media framework*. Retrieved from http://java.sun.com/products/java-media/jmf/

Sun, Wang, Lu, Zhang, Zhang, Kinsner, & Zedah. (Eds.). (2010). In *Proceedings of the 9th IEEE International Conference on Cognitive Informatics (ICCI'10)*, Tsinghua University, Beijing, China. Washington, DC: IEEE.

Sysomos. (2010). *Twitter and the Nine-Month Bounce*. Retrieved from http://techcrunch.com/2010/03/29/twitter-nine-month-bounce/

Tacla, C. A., & Barthès, J. P. (2004). A multi-agent architecture for evolving memories. In *Agent-Mediated Knowledge Management* (LNAI 2926, pp. 388-404).

Tacla, C. A., & Barthès, J.-P. (2003). A multi-agent system for acquiring and sharing lessons learned. *Computers in Industry, 52*(1), 5–16. doi:10.1016/S0166-3615(03)00065-4

Taheri, A., Singh, A., & Emmanuel, A. (2004). Location fingerprinting on infrastructure 802.11 wireless local area networks (WLANs) using locus. In *Proceedings of the Local Computer Networks, 2004, 29th Annual IEEE International Conference* (pp. 676-683).

Takagaki, A., Uchiya, T., Hara, H., Abe, T., & Kinoshita, T. (2003). Interactive development support environment for agent systems. *Information Technology Letters, 2*, 143–144.

Tamai, T., Ubayashi, N., & Ichiyama, R. (2005, May). An Adaptive Object Model with Dynamic Role Binding. In *Proceedings of the Int'l Conf. of Software Engineering*, St. Louis, MO (pp. 166-175).

Tamma, V., Wooldridge, M., & Dickinson, I. (2002). An ontology for automated negotiation. In *Proceedings of the Workshop on Ontologies in Agent Systems*, Bologna, Italy (pp. 267-273).

Tamma, V., Phelps, S., Dickinson, I., & Wooldridge, M. (2005). Ontologies for Supporting Negotiation in E-Commerce. *Engineering Applications of Artificial Intelligence, 18*(2), 223–236. doi:10.1016/j.engappai.2004.11.011

Tamura, Y., Matsumoto, S., Ueki, H., & Mizuguchi, N. (2007). Constuction of design support system with interference detection in the immersive projection display. *The IEICE Transactions on Information and Systems, J90-D*(10), 2927-2931.

Tan, X., Wang, Y., & Ngolah, C. F. (2004). Specification of the RTPA Grammar and Its Recognition. In *Proceedings of the 2004 IEEE International Conference on Cognitive Informatics (ICCI'04)*, Victoria, Canada (pp. 54-63). Washington, DC: IEEE CS Press.

Tan, X., Wang, Y., & Ngolah, C. F. (2006, May). Design and Implementation of an Automatic RTPA Code Generator. In *Proceedings of the 19th Canadian Conference on Electrical and Computer Engineering (CCECE'06)*, Ottawa, ON, Canada (pp. 1605-1608).

Tan, C. O., Ozesmi, U., Beklioglu, M., Per, E., & Kurt, B. (2006). Predictive Models in Ecology: Comparison of Performances and Assessment of Applicability. *Ecological Informatics*, 195–211. doi:10.1016/j.ecoinf.2006.03.002

Tanenbaum, A. S. (1994). *Distributed Operating Systems*. Upper Saddle River, NJ: Prentice Hall Inc.

Tanenbaum, A. S. (2002). *Modern operating systems* (2nd ed.). Zurich, Switzerland: China Machine Press.

Tang, X., Liang, H., Zhe, F., & Tang, Z. (2007, May). *Computer Operating System* (3rd edition). Shaanxi, China: Xidian University Press.

Tan, X., & Wang, Y. (2008). A Denotational Semantics of Real-Time Process Algebra (RTPA). *International Journal of Cognitive Informatics and Natural Intelligence, 2*(3), 57–70.

Tapia, E. M., Intille, S. S., & Larson, K. (2004). Activity recognition in the home using simple and ubiquitous sensors. In *Proceedings of Pervasive, 2004*, 158–175.

TCGARN: The Cancer Genome Atlas Research Network. (2008, October 23). Comprehensive genomic characterization defines human glioblastoma genes and core pathways. *Nature, 455*, 1061–1068. doi:10.1038/nature07385

Tennyson, R., & Rasch, M. (1988). Linking cognitive learning theory to instructional prescriptions. *Instructional Science, 17*(167), 369–385. doi:10.1007/BF00056222

Terregov. (2008). *TERREGOV project: Impact of e-government on territorial government service* (IST-2002-507749). Retrieved from http://www.terregov.eupm.net

Tesauro, G., Chess, D. M., Walsh, W. E., Das, R., Segal, A., Whalley, I., et al. (2004, July). A Multi-Agent Systems Approach to Autonomic Computing. In *Proceedings of the Third Int'l Joint Conf. on Autonomous Agents and Multiagent Systems,* New York (Vol. 1, pp. 464-471).

Thomson, J. N. Jr, Hellack, J. J., Braver, G., & Durica, D. S. (1997). *Primer of Genetic Analysis: A Problem Approach* (2nd ed.). Cambridge, UK: Cambridge University Press.

Thomson, R., Hodgman, C., Yang, Z. R., & Doyle, A. K. (2003). Characterising Proteolytic Cleavage Site Activity Using Bio-Basis Function Neural Network. *Bioinformatics (Oxford, England), 19*(14), 1741–1747. doi:10.1093/bioinformatics/btg237

Tian, E., & Peng, C. (2001). Delay-dependent stability analysis and synthesis of uncertain T-S fuzzy systems with time-varying delay. *Fuzzy Sets and Systems, 157*(4), 544–559. doi:10.1016/j.fss.2005.06.022

Tian, Y. C., Yu, Z. G., & Fidge, C. (2007). Multifractal nature of network induced time delay in networked control systems. *Physics Letters. [Part A], 361*(1/2), 103–107. doi:10.1016/j.physleta.2006.09.046

Tollinger, I., Lewis, R. L., McCurdy, M., Tollinger, P., Vera, A., Howes, A., & Pelton, L. J. (2005). *Supporting Efficient Development of Cognitive Models at Multiple Skill Levels: Exploring Recent Advances in Constraint-based Modeling.*

Torres, J., Juarez, E., Dodero, J. M., & Aedo, I. (2009). Advanced Transactional Models for Complex Learning Processes. In U.A de Yucatan (Ed.), *Recursos Digitales para el Aprendizaje* (pp. 360-368). Mérida, Mexico: U. A. de Yucatan.

Torres, J., Doredo, J. M., Ramírez, C., Valdes, B., & Lugo, A. (2009). Adaptive Learning Scenarios Based on Student Profile. In de Yucatan, U. A. (Ed.), *Recursos Digitales para el Aprendizaje* (pp. 348–359). Mérida, Mexico: U. A. de Yucatan.

Triggs-Raine, B., Salo, T. J., Zhang, H., Wicklow, B. A., & Natowicz, M. R. (1999, May 25). Mutations in HYAL1, a member of a tandemly distributed multigene family encoding disparate hyaluronidase activities, cause a newly described lysosomal disorder, Mucopolysaccharidosis IX. *Proceedings of the National Academy of Sciences of the United States of America, 96*(11), 6296–6300. doi:10.1073/pnas.96.11.6296

Tsumoto, S. (2004). Mining diagnostic rules from clinical databases using rough sets and medical diagnostic model. *Inf. Sci., 162*(2), 65–80. Retrieved from http://dx.doi.org/10.1016/j.ins.2004.03.002. doi:10.1016/j.ins.2004.03.002

Tu, M. T., Kunze, C., & Lamersdorf, W. (2000). A rule management framework for negotiating mobile agents. In *Proceedings of the 4th International Enterprise Distributed Object Computing Conference*, Makuhari, Japan (pp. 135-143).

Turcotte, D. L. (1997). *Fractals and Chaos in Geology and Geophysics* (2nd ed.). New York: Springer Verlag.

Turing, A. (1950). Computing Machinery and Intelligence. *Mind, 9*(236), 433–460. doi:10.1093/mind/LIX.236.433

Uberbacher, E., & Mural, R. (1991). Locating protein-coding regions in human DNA sequences by a multiple sensor-neural network approach. *Proceedings of the National Academy of Sciences of the United States of America, 88*, 11261–11265. doi:10.1073/pnas.88.24.11261

Univan, A., & Chris, G. (2000). C++ Translator for RAISE Specifications (Tech. Rep. No. 220). Macau: UNU-IIST.

Uschold, M., & Grüninger, M. (1996). Ontologies principles, methods and applications. *The Knowledge Engineering Review, 11*(2). doi:10.1017/S0269888900007797

Valiant, L. G. (1994). *Circuits of the Mind*. New York: Oxford University Press.

Vapnik, V. (1995). *The Nature of Statistical Learning Theory*. New York: Springer Verlag.

Venter, C. J., Adams, M. D., Myers, E. W., & Li, P. W. (2001, February 16). The sequence of the human genome. *Science*, *291*(5507), 1304–1351. doi:10.1126/science.1058040

Verma, R., & Chen, P. (2007, April). Integrating Ontology Knowledge into a Query-based Information Summarization System. In *Proceedings of the DUC 2007*, Rochester, NY.

Viscarola, P. G., & Mason, W. A. (2001). *Windows NT Device Driver Development*. Indianapolis, IN: Macmillan Technical Publishing.

von Krogh, G., Nonaka, I., & Aben, M. (2001). Making the most of your company's knowledge: A strategic framework. *Long Range Planning*, *34*(4), 421–439. doi:10.1016/S0024-6301(01)00059-0

Voss, R. F. (1992). Evolution of long-range fractal correlations and 1/f noise in DNA base sequences. *Physical Review Letters*, *68*, 3805–3808. doi:10.1103/PhysRevLett.68.3805

Voss, R. F. (1993). 1/f noise and fractals in DNA base sequences. In Crilly, A. J., Earnshaw, R. A., & Jones, H. (Eds.), *Applications of Fractals and Chaos: The Shape of Things* (pp. 7–20). New York: Springer Verlag.

Voss, R. F., & Clarke, J. (1975). 1/f noise in music and speech. *Nature*, *258*, 317–318. doi:10.1038/258317a0

Vygotsky, L. (1986). *Thought and Language*. Cambridge, MA: MIT Press.

W3C. (2004). *Owl Web Ontology Language Use Cases and Requirements*.

Walter, F. E., Battiston, S., & Schweitzer, F. (2008). A model of a trust-based recommender system on a social network. *Autonomous Agents and Multi-Agent Systems*, *16*(1), 57–74. doi:10.1007/s10458-007-9021-x

Wang, F. (2005). On acquiring classification knowledge from noisy data based on rough set. Expert Systems with Applications, 29(1), 49–64. doi:10.1016/j.eswa.2005.01.005

Wang, J. F. (2003). Cell Biology. Beijing, China: Science Press.

Wang, J., Lin, T., Wang, J., Han, G., & Zhao, H. (2004). Research on preemptions of preemptive EDF and improvement on its performance. Acta Electronica Sinica, 32(1), 64–68.

Wang, Q., Xu, J., Wang, H., Wang, H., & Dai, G. (2004). A new Priority Table based Real-time Scheduling Algorithm. Acta Electronica Sinica, 2, 310–313.

Wang, Y. (2002). Keynote: On Cognitive Informatics. In Proceedings of the 1st IEEE International Conference on Cognitive Informatics (ICCI'02), Calgary, Canada (pp. 34-42). Washington, DC: IEEE.

Wang, Y. (2002). The Real-Time Process Algebra (RTPA). Annals of Software Engineering: An International Journal, 14, 235–274. doi:10.1023/A:1020561826073

Wang, Y. (2003). On Cognitive Informatics. Brain and Mind: A Transdisciplinary Journal of Neuroscience and Neurophilosophy, 4(2), 151-167.

Wang, Y. (2003). Using process algebra to describe human and software system behaviors. Brain and Mind, 4(2), 199–213. doi:10.1023/A:1025457612549

Wang, Y. (2004). Operating Systems. In Dorf, R. (Ed.), The Engineering Handbook (2nd ed.). Boca Raton, FL: CRC Press.

Wang, Y. (2006). Keynote: Cognitive Informatics - Towards the Future Generation Computers that Think and Feel. In Proceedings of the 5th IEEE International Conference on Cognitive Informatics (ICCI'06), Beijing, China (pp. 3-7). Washington, DC: IEEE.

Wang, Y. (2006). On Concept Algebra and Knowledge Representation. In Proceedings of the 5th IEEE International Conference on Cognitive Informatic (pp. 320-331).

Wang, Y. (2006). On the Informatics Laws and Deductive Semantics of Software. [Part C]. IEEE Transactions on Systems, Man, and Cybernetics, 36(2), 161–171. doi:10.1109/TSMCC.2006.871138

Wang, Y. (2007). Software Engineering Foundations: A Software Science Perspective. Boca Raton, FL: CRC.

Wang, Y. (2007). The OAR Model of Neural Informatics for Internal Knowledge Representation in the Brain. International Journal of Cognitive Informatics and Natural Intelligence, 1(3), 66–77.

Wang, Y. (2007). The Theoretical Framework and Cognitive Process of Learning. In Proceedings of the 6th IEEE ICCI (pp. 470-479). Washington, DC: IEEE.

Wang, Y. (2007). The theoretical framework of cognitive informatics. International Journal of Cognitive Informatics and Natural Intelligence, 1(1), 1–27.

Wang, Y. (2007, July). Toward Theoretical Foundations of Autonomic Computing. International Journal of Cognitive Informatics and Natural Intelligence, 1(3), 1–16.

Wang, Y. (2008). Deductive Semantics of RTPA. International Journal of Cognitive Informatics and Natural Intelligence, 2(2), 95–121.

Wang, Y. (2008). Mathematical Laws of Software. Transactions of Computational Science, 2, 46–83. doi:10.1007/978-3-540-87563-5_4

Wang, Y. (2008). On Concept Algebra: A Denotational Mathematical Structure for Knowledge and Software Modeling. International Journal of Cognitive Informatics and Natural Intelligence, 2(2), 1–19.

Wang, Y. (2008). On contemporary denotational mathematics for computational intelligence. Transactions of Computational Science, 2, 6–29. doi:10.1007/978-3-540-87563-5_2

Wang, Y. (2008). On System Algebra: A Denotational Mathematical Structure for Abstract System Modeling. International Journal of Cognitive Informatics and Natural Intelligence, 2(2), 20–42.

Wang, Y. (2008). RTPA: A Denotational Mathematics for Manipulating Intelligent and Computational Behaviors. International Journal of Cognitive Informatics and Natural Intelligence, 2(2), 44–62.

Wang, Y. (2009). A cognitive informatics reference model of autonomous agent systems. International Journal of Cognitive Informatics and Natural Intelligence, 3(1), 1–16.

Wang, Y. (2009). On Abstract Intelligence: Toward a Unifying Theory of Natural, Artificial, Machinable, and Computational Intelligence. International Journal of Software Science and Computational Intelligence, 1(1), 1–17.

Wang, Y. (2009). On Cognitive Computing. International Journal of Software Science and Computational Intelligence, 1(3), 1–15.

Wang, Y. (2009). On Visual Semantic Algebra (VSA): A Denotational Mathematical Structure for Modeling and Manipulating Visual Objects and Patterns. International Journal of Software Science and Computational Intelligence, 1(4), 1–15.

Wang, Y. (2009). Paradigms of Denotational Mathematics for Cognitive Informatics and Cognitive Computing. Fundamenta Informaticae, 90(3), 282–303.

Wang, Y. (2009). The Formal Design Model of a Telephone Switching System (TSS). International Journal of Software Science and Computational Intelligence, 1(3), 92–116.

Wang, Y. (2009, January). A Cognitive Informatics Reference Model of Autonomous Agent Systems (AAS). International Journal of Cognitive Informatics and Natural Intelligence, 3(1), 1–16.

Wang, Y. (2010). A Sociopsychological Perspective on Collective Intelligence in Metaheuristic Computing. International Journal of Applied Metaheuristic Computing, 1(1), 110–128.

Wang, Y. (2010). Abstract Intelligence and Cognitive Robots. Journal of Behavioral Robotics, 1(1), 66–72.

Wang, Y. (2010). Cognitive Robots: A Reference Model towards Intelligent Authentication. IEEE Robotics and Automation, 17(4), 54-62.

Wang, Y. (2010). On Formal and Cognitive Semantics for Semantic Computing. International Journal of Semantic Computing, 4(2), 83–118. doi:10.1142/S1793351X10000833

Wang, Y. (2011). Cognitive Informatics: Foundations of Natural, Abstract, and Computational Intelligence. Cambridge, MA: MIT Press.

Wang, Y. (2012). Toward a Cognitive Behavioral Reference Model of Artificial Brains. *Journal of Computational and Theoretical Nanoscience, 9*(2), 178-188.

Wang, Y. L. (Ed.). (2009). Special Issue on Cognitive Computing, On Abstract Intelligence. *International Journal of Software Science and Computational Intelligence, 1*(3).

Wang, Y. L., Zadeh, A., & Yao, Y. (2009). On the System Algebra Foundations for Granular Computing. *International Journal of Software Science and Computational Intelligence, 1*(1), 1–17.

Wang, Y., & Chiew, V. (in press). On the cognitive process of human problem solving. *Cognitive Systems Research: An International Journal, 11*(1), 81-92.

Wang, Y., & Huang, J. (2008). Formal Modeling and Specification of Design Patterns using RTPA. *International Journal of Cognitive Informatics and Natural Intelligence, 2*(1), 100–111.

Wang, Y., & King, G. (2000). Software engineering processes: Principles and applications. In *CRC series in software engineering* (Vol. I). Boca Raton, FL: CRC Press.

Wang, Y., & Kinsner, W. (2006). Recent Advances in Cognitive Informatics. *IEEE Transactions on Systems, Man, and Cybernetics. Part C, 36*(2), 121–123.

Wang, Y., & Ngolah, C. F. (2008). An Operational Semantics of Real-Time Process Algebra (RTPA). *International Journal of Cognitive Informatics and Natural Intelligence, 2*(3), 71–89.

Wang, Y., & Ruhe, G. (2007). The Cognitive Process of Decision Making. *International Journal of Cognitive Informatics and Natural Intelligence, 1*(2), 73–85.

Wang, Y., & Saksena, M. (1999). Scheduling fixed-priority tasks with preemption threshold. In *Proceedings of the 6th International Conference On Real-Time Computing Systems and Applications* (pp. 328-335). Washington, DC: IEEE Computer Society Press.

Wang, Y., & Wang, Y. (2006). Cognitive Informatics Models of the Brain. *IEEE Transactions on Systems, Man, and Cybernetics. Part C, 36*(2), 203–207.

Wang, Y., Baciu, G., Yao, Y., Kinsner, W., Chan, K., & Zhang, B. (2010). Perspectives on Cognitive Informatics and Cognitive Computing. *International Journal of Cognitive Informatics and Natural Intelligence, 4*(1), 1–29.

Wang, Y., King, G., Fayad, M., Patel, D., Court, I., & Staples, G. (2000). On built-in tests reuse in object-oriented framework design. *ACM Journal on Computing Surveys, 32*(1), 7–12. doi:10.1145/351936.351943

Wang, Y., Kinsner, W., & Zhang, D. (2009). Contemporary Cybernetics and its faces of Cognitive Informatics and Computational Intelligence. *IEEE Trans. on System, Man, and Cybernetics–Part B, 39*(4), 1–11.

Wang, Y., Kinsner, W., Anderson, J. A., Zhang, D., Yao, Y., & Sheu, P. (2009). A Doctrine of Cognitive Informatics. *Fundamenta Informaticae, 90*(3), 203–228.

Wang, Y., Ngolah, C. F., Ahmadi, H., Sheu, P. C. Y., & Ying, S. (2009). The Formal Design Model of a Lift Dispatching System (LDS). *International Journal of Software Science and Computational Intelligence, 1*(4), 98–122.

Wang, Y., Ngolah, C. F., Zeng, G., Sheu, P. C. Y., Choy, C. P., & Tian, Y. (2010). The Formal Design Model of a Real-Time Operating System (RTOS+): Conceptual and Architectural Frameworks. *International Journal of Software Science and Computational Intelligence, 2*(2), 107–124.

Wang, Y., Ngolah, C. F., Zeng, G., Sheu, P. C. Y., Choy, C. P., & Tian, Y. (2010). The Formal Design Models of a Real-Time Operating System (RTOS+): Static and Dynamic Behavior Models. *International Journal of Software Science and Computational Intelligence, 2*(3), 79–105.

Wang, Y., Tan, X., & Ngolah, C. F. (2010). Design and Implementation of an Autonomic Code Generator based on RTPA (RTPA-CG). *International Journal of Software Science and Computational Intelligence, 2*(2), 44–67.

Wang, Y., Wang, Y., Patel, S., & Patel, D. (2006). A Layered Reference Model of the Brain (LRMB). *IEEE Transactions on Systems, Man and Cybernetics. Part C, Applications and Reviews, 36*(2), 124–133. doi:10.1109/TSMCC.2006.871126

Wang, Y., Zadeh, L. A., & Yao, Y. (2008). On the System Algebra Foundation for Granular Computing. *International Journal of Software Science and Computational Intelligence*, 1(1), 64–86.

Wang, Y., Zhang, D., & Tsumoto, S. (2009). Cognitive Informatics, Cognitive Computing, and Their Denotational Mathematical Foundations (I). *Fundamenta Informaticae*, 90(3), 1–7.

Wang, Y., Zhang, Y., Sheu, P. C. Y., Li, X., & Guo, H. (2010). The Formal Design Models of an Automatic Teller Machine (ATM). *International Journal of Software Science and Computational Intelligence*, 2(1), 102–131.

Wang, Z., Lauria, S., Fang, J., & Liu, X. (2007). Exponential stability of uncertain stochastic neural networks with mixed time-delays. *Chaos, Solitons, and Fractals*, 32(1), 62–72. doi:10.1016/j.chaos.2005.10.061

Wang, Z., Liu, Y., & Liu, X. (2009). State estimation for jumping recurrent neural networks with discrete and distributed delays. *Neural Networks*, 22(1), 41–48. doi:10.1016/j.neunet.2008.09.015

Wang, Z., Shu, H., Fang, J., & Liu, X. (2006). Robust stability for stochastic Hopfield neural networks with time delays. *Nonlinear Analysis Real World Applications*, 7(5), 1119–1128. doi:10.1016/j.nonrwa.2005.10.004

Wan, L., & Sun, J. (2005). Mean square exponential stability of stochastic delayed Hopfield neural networks. *Physics Letters. [Part A]*, 343(4), 306–318. doi:10.1016/j.physleta.2005.06.024

Weiser, M. (1991). The computer for the twenty-first century. *Scientific American*, 265(3), 94–104.

Weiss, S., Kasif, S., & Brill, E. (1996). Text Classification in USENET Newsgroup: A Progress Report. In *Proceedings of the AAAI Spring Symposium on Machine Learning in Information Access Technical Papers*, Palo Alto, CA.

Wen, W. C., Liu, H., Wen, W. X., & Zheng, J. (2001). A Distributed Hierarchical Clustering System for Web Mining. In *Proceedings of the WAIM2002* (LNCS 2118, pp. 103-113). Berlin: Springer Verlag.

Wenger, E., McDermott, R., & Snyder, W. M. (2002). *Cultivating communities of practice: A guide to managing knowledge, vol. 1* (1st ed.). Boston: Harvard Business School Press.

Werbos, P. J. (1974, August). *Beyond Regression: New Tools for Prediction and Analysis in the Behavioral Sciences*. Unpublished doctoral dissertation, Harvard University, Cambridge, MA.

Widrow, B., & Winter, R. (1988). Neural nets for adaptive filtering and adaptive pattern recognition. *Computer*, 21(3), 25–39. doi:10.1109/2.29

Wiedermann, J. (1998). Towards Algorithmic Explanation of Mind Evolution and Functioning (Invited Talk). In L. Brim, J. Gruska, & J. Zlatuška (Eds.), *Proceedings of the 23rd International Symposium on Mathematical Foundations of Computer Science (MFCS'98)* (LNCS 1450). Berlin: Springer Verlag.

Wiedermann, J. (2003). Mirror Neurons, Embodied Cognitive Agents and Imitation Learning. In *Computing and Informatics, 22*(6).

Wilson, D. R., & Martinez, T. R. (1997). Improved Heterogeneous Distance Functions. [JAIR]. *Journal of Artificial Intelligence Research*, 6, 1–34.

Wilson, L. B., & Clark, R. G. (1988). *Comparative Programming Language*. Reading, MA: Addison-Wesley Publishing Co.

Winograd, T., & Flores, F. (1987). *Understanding Computers and Cognition*. Norwood, NJ: Ablex Publishing.

Wojek, C., Nickel, K., & Stiefelhagen, R. (2006). Activity recognition and room-level tracking in an office environment. In *Proceedings of the IEEE Conference on Multisensor Fusion and Integration for Intelligent Systems, MFI'06*, Heidelberg, Germany (pp. 25-30).

Wolfe, S. L. (1993). *Molecular and Cellular Biology*. Belmont, CA: Wadsworth Publishing.

Woodcock, J., & Davies, J. (1996). *Using Z: Specification, Refinement, and Proof*. Upper Saddle River, NJ: Prentice Hall International.

WordNet. (2004). *WordNet*. Retrieved June 10, 2004, from http://www.wordnet.com

Wu, Q., & Bell, D. (2003). Multi-knowledge extraction and application (LNCS 2639, pp. 274-278).

Xiao, Y., Chen, R., Shen, R., Sun, J., & Xu, J. (1995). Fractal dimension of exon and intron sequences. *Journal of Theoretical Biology, 175*, 23–26. doi:10.1006/jtbi.1995.0117

Yang, Z. R. (2004). Biological Application of Support Vector Machines. *Briefings in Bioinformatics, 5*(4), 328–338. doi:10.1093/bib/5.4.328

Yang, Z. R. (2005). Orthogonal Kernel Machine for the Prediction of Functional Sites in Proteins. *IEEE Transactions on Systems, Man, and Cybernetics. Part B, Cybernetics, 35*(1), 100–106. doi:10.1109/TSMCB.2004.840723

Yang, Z. R. (2005). Prediction of Caspase Cleavage Sites Using Bayesian Bio-Basis Function Neural Networks. *Bioinformatics (Oxford, England), 21*(9), 1831–1837. doi:10.1093/bioinformatics/bti281

Yang, Z. R., & Chou, K. C. (2004). Predicting the Linkage Sites in Glycoproteins Using Bio-Basis Function Neural Networks. *Bioinformatics (Oxford, England), 20*(6), 903–908. doi:10.1093/bioinformatics/bth001

Yang, Z. R., & Thomson, R. (2005). Bio-Basis Function Neural Network for Prediction of Protease Cleavage Sites in Proteins. *IEEE Transactions on Neural Networks, 16*(1), 263–274. doi:10.1109/TNN.2004.836196

Yang, Z. R., Thomson, R., McNeil, P., & Esnouf, R. (2005). RONN: Use of the Bio-Basis Function Neural Network Technique for the Detection of Natively Disordered Regions in Proteins. *Bioinformatics (Oxford, England), 21*(16), 3369–3376. doi:10.1093/bioinformatics/bti534

Yao, Y. (2008b). Granular computing: past, present and future. In *Proceedings of the 2008 IEEE International Conference on Granular Computing* (pp. 80-85).

Yao, Y. Y. (1999). Granular computing using neighborhood systems. In *Proceedings of the Advances in Soft Computing: Engineering Design and Manufacturing* (pp. 539-553). New York: Springer-Verlag.

Yao, Y. Y. (2004). Concept formation and learning: a cognitive informatics perspective. In *Proceedings of the Third IEEE International Conference on Cognitive Informatics, 2004* (pp. 42-51). doi: 10.1109/COGINF.2004.1327458.

Yao, Y. (2006). Three perspectives of granular computing. *Journal of Nanchang Institute of Technology, 25*, 16–21.

Yao, Y. (2008a). A unified framework of granular computing. In Pedrycz, W., Skowron, A., & Kreinovich, V. (Eds.), *Handbook of Granular Computing* (pp. 401–410). New York: Wiley. doi:10.1002/9780470724163.ch17

Yasuda, K., Nemoto, T., Takenaka, K., Mitachi, M., & Kuwabara, K. (2007). Effectiveness of vocabulary data file, encyclopedia, and Internet homepages in a conversation-support system for people with moderate-to-severe aphasia. *Aphasiology, 21*(9), 867–882. doi:10.1080/02687030600783024

Yodaiken, V. (1999, May). An RT-Linux Manifesto. In *Proceedings of the 5th Linux Expo*, Raleigh, NC.

Young, F. W. (1985). Multidimensional scaling. In S. Kotz & N. L. Johnson (Eds.), *Encyclopedia of statistical sciences* (Vol. 5, pp. 649-659). New York: John Wiley & Sons.

Yue, D., Han, Q. L., & Lam, J. (2005). Network-based robust H_∞ control of systems with uncertainty. *Automatica, 41*(6), 999–1007. doi:10.1016/j.automatica.2004.12.011

Yue, D., Peng, C., & Tang, G. Y. (2006). Guaranteed cost control of linear systems over networks with state and input quantisations. *IEE Proceedings. Control Theory and Applications, 153*(6), 658–664. doi:10.1049/ip-cta:20050294

Yu, L., & Liu, H. (2004). Efficient Feature Selection via Analysis of Relevance and Redundancy. *Journal of Machine Learning Research, 5*, 1205–1224.

Yu, Z., & Anh, V. V. (2001). Time series model based on global structure of the complete genome. *Chaos, Solitons, and Fractals, 12*, 1827–1834. doi:10.1016/S0960-0779(00)00147-8

Yu, Z., Anh, V. V., & Wang, B. (2001). Correlation property of length sequences based on global structure of the complete genome. *Physical Review E: Statistical, Nonlinear, and Soft Matter Physics, 63*, 1–8.

Zadeh, L. A. (1975). Fuzzy Logic and Approximate Reasoning. *Syntheses, 30*, 407–428. doi:10.1007/BF00485052

Zadeh, L. A. (1997). Towards a theory of fuzzy information granulation and its centrality in human reasoning and fuzzy logic. *Fuzzy Sets and Systems, 90*, 111–117. doi:10.1016/S0165-0114(97)00077-8

Zadeh, L. A. (1999). From Computing with Numbers to Computing with Words – from Manipulation of Measurements to Manipulation of Perception. *IEEE Trans. on Circuits and Systems I, 45*(1), 105–119. doi:10.1109/81.739259

Zadeh, L. A. (2005). Toward a generalized theory of uncertainty (GTU)—an outline. *Information Sciences, 172*, 1–40. doi:10.1016/j.ins.2005.01.017

Zhang, H. (2001). *Compositional Complexity Measures of DNA Sequence Using Multi-fractal Techniques*. Master's thesis, Winnipeg, Manitoba, Canada, University of Manitoba.

Zhang, W., & Fu, X. (2006). An Improved Least-Laxity-First Scheduling Algorithm for periodic tasks. *Journal of Jiangxi normal university, 30*(4), 365-368

Zhang, B., & Zhang, L. (1992). *Theory and Applications of Problem Solving*. Amsterdam: North-Holland.

Zhang, J., Shi, P., & Qiu, J. (2007). Novel robust stability criteria for uncertain stochastic Hopfield neural networks with time-varying delays. *Nonlinear Analysis Real World Applications, 8*(4), 1349–1357. doi:10.1016/j.nonrwa.2006.06.010

Zhang, Q., & Xu, X. W. J. (2007). Delay-dependent global stability results for delayed Hopfield neural networks. *Chaos, Solitons, and Fractals, 34*(2), 662–668. doi:10.1016/j.chaos.2006.03.073

Zhao, H., & Wang, G. (2004). Delay-independent exponential stability of recurrent neural networks. *Physics Letters. [Part A], 333*(5/6), 399–407. doi:10.1016/j.physleta.2004.10.040

Zhu, H. (2008, May). Fundamental Issues in the Design of a Role Engine. In *Proceedings of the 5th Int'l Symp. on Collaborative. Systems and Technologies*, San Diego, CA (pp. 399-407).

Zhu, H., & Zhou, M. C. (2003, October). Methodology First and Language Second: A Way to Teach Object-Oriented Programming. In *Proceedings of the 2003 Educator's Symposium on Object-Oriented Programming, Systems, Languages and Applications (OOPSLA '03)* (pp. 140-147).

Zhu, H., Grenier, M., Alkins, R., Lacarte, J., & Hoskins, J. (2008, May). A Visualized Tool for Role Transfer. In *Proceedings of the 6th Int'l Conf. on Infor. Sys. for Crisis Response and Management*, Washington, DC (pp. 2225-2230).

Zhu, H. (2007, July). Role as Dynamics of Agents in Multi-Agent Systems. *System and Informatics Science Notes, 1*(2), 165–171.

Zhu, H., & Zhou, M. C. (2006, July). Role-Based Collaboration and its Kernel Mechanisms. *IEEE Trans. on Systems, Man and Cybernetics, Part C, 36*(4), 578-589.
Zhu, H., & Zhou, M. C. (2008, June). New Java Mechanism for Role-Based Information System Development. *International Journal of Intelligent Control and Systems, 13*(2), 97–108.

Zhu, H., & Zhou, M. C. (2008, May). Role Mechanisms in Information Systems - A Survey. *IEEE Trans. on Systems, Man and Cybernetics. Part C, 38*(6), 377–396.

Zhu, H., & Zhou, M. C. (2008, November). Role Transfer Problems and their Algorithms. *IEEE Trans. on Systems, Man and Cybernetics. Part A, 38*(6), 1442–1450.

Ziarko, W. (1993). Variable Precision Rough Set Model. *Journal of Computer and System Sciences, 46*(1), 39–59. doi:10.1016/0022-0000(93)90048-2

About the Contributors

Yingxu Wang is professor of cognitive informatics, cognitive computing, and software engineering, President of International Institute of Cognitive Informatics and Cognitive Computing (IICICC), and Director of the Cognitive Informatics and Cognitive Computing Lab at the University of Calgary. He is a Fellow of WIF, a P.Eng of Canada, a Senior Member of IEEE and ACM, and a member of ISO/IEC JTC1 and the Canadian Advisory Committee (CAC) for ISO. He received a PhD in Software Engineering from the Nottingham Trent University, UK, and a BSc in Electrical Engineering from Shanghai Tiedao University. He has industrial experience since 1972 and has been a full professor since 1994. He was a visiting professor on sabbatical leaves in the Computing Laboratory at Oxford University in 1995, Dept. of Computer Science at Stanford University in 2008, and the Berkeley Initiative in Soft Computing (BISC) Lab at University of California, Berkeley in 2008, respectively. He is the founder and steering committee chair of the annual IEEE International Conference on Cognitive Informatics and Cognitive Computing (ICCI*CC). He is founding Editor-in-Chief of *International Journal of Cognitive Informatics and Natural Intelligence* (IJCINI), founding Editor-in-Chief of *International Journal of Software Science and Computational Intelligence* (IJSSCI), Associate Editor of *IEEE Trans on System, Man, and Cybernetics* (Part A), associate Editor-in-Chief of *Journal of Advanced Mathematics and Applications*, and Editor-in-Chief of *CRC Book Series in Software Engineering*. Dr. Wang is the initiator of several cutting-edge research fields or subject areas such as cognitive informatics, abstract intelligence, cognitive computing, cognitive computers, denotational mathematics (i.e., concept algebra, inference algebra, real-time process algebra, system algebra, granular algebra, and visual semantic algebra), software science (on unified mathematical models and laws of software, cognitive complexity of software, and automatic code generators, coordinative work organization theory, built-in tests (BITs), and deductive semantics of languages), the layered reference model of the brain (LRMB), the mathematical model of consciousness, and the reference model of cognitive robots. He has published over 120 peer reviewed journal papers, 220+ peer reviewed full conference papers, and 16 books in cognitive informatics, software engineering, and computational intelligence. He is the recipient of dozens international awards on academic leadership, outstanding contributions, research achievement, best papers, and teaching in the last three decades. He can be reached at: yingxu@ucalgary.ca.

* * *

Juan Carlos Aragon received the Bachelor degree in electronic engineering from the Pontifical Catholic University of Peru and the Master of Science and PhD degrees in Electrical Engineering from Stanford University, Stanford, CA, in April 2010. He was a Teaching Fellow at Stanford between 2007 and 2009. His current research interests include human memory, human-like memory for computers, pattern recognition, problem solvers and artificial reasoning.

Nilar Aye received BS and MS degrees in computer science from the University of Computer Studies, Yangon (UCSY) in 1995 and 1998 respectively. She joined (UCSY) as a teaching staff from 1998 to 2004. In 2005, she moved to Non- governmental organization named Myanmar Computer Federation (MCF) and became a Project Manager of Myanmar ICT Development Master Plan Project. She got MS in engineering from Ritsumeikan University in 2008.

Guohua Bai is a docent, PhD professor at the School of Engineering, Blekinge Institute of Technology, in Sweden. He is the chairperson of sections for several international conferences, such as the 10th International Congress of Systems and Cybernetics, in Bucharest, the International Conference on Information Systems Analysis and Synthesis, Orlando, in USA.

George Baciu holds a PhD degree in Engineering and a B.Math degree in Computer Science and Applied Mathematics from the University of Waterloo. He has been a member of the Computer Graphics Laboratory and the Pattern Analysis and Machine Intelligence Laboratory at the University of Waterloo and subsequently Director of the Graphics And Music Experimentation Laboratory at The Hong Kong University of Science and Technology in Hong Kong. Currently, Professor George Baciu is Director of the Graphics And Multimedia Applications (GAMA) Laboratory in the Department of Computing at The Hong Kong Polytechnic University. His research interests are primarily in mobile augmented reality systems, user interfaces, physically-based illumination, rendering, image processing, motion tracking and synthesis for both outdoor and indoor location aware systems.

Jean-Paul Barthès obtained his engineering degree from Ecole Centrale de Paris (France) and his PhD from Stanford University. Currently, he is a professor in the Department of Computer Science at the University of Technology of Compiègne (UTC) in France. His main research interests are related to knowledge representation and mixed societies of cognitive artificial and human agents.

Eddie Chan received his BSc Degree in Computing and MSc Degree in E-commerce in the Department of Computing from The Hong Kong Polytechnic University in 2005 and 2007, respectively. Currently, he is a PhD student in the same university. His research interests include wireless communication, localization, fuzzy logic, 3D visualization of tracking system, agent technology and data mining. He is a member of the Graphics and Multimedia Applications (GAMA) Laboratory at The Hong Kong Polytechnic University.

Philip Choy is a PhD candidate in Software Engineering with the Theoretical and Empirical Software Engineering Research Center (TESERC) at the University of Calgary. He received his BSc (Hon.) in Computer and Information Science from Queen's University, Kingston., Canada in 1985. He is a member of the IEEE and has served on the Canadian Board of the IEEE for over a decade. He has also held a number of executive positions with the IEEE Southern Alberta Section (SAS) including the Chairmanship during 2007 and 2008. He has over two decades of experience in the IT, software, and telecommunications industries, where he has held various executive positions. His research interests are in software engineering, cognitive informatics, and real-time systems as well as their industrial applications.

Lúcio Coelho is a researcher and engineer working at Biomind LLC. He has conducted research on the fields of Artificial Intelligence and Bioinformatics over the past decade. He is also the main contributor of the OpenBiomind Project, the ongoing development of OpenBiomind, Biomind's open-source tool for machine learning-based analysis of biological datasets.

Chandra Das received BSc (Hons) in Computer Science in 1999, MSc in Computer and Information Science in 2001, and M.Tech in Computer Science and Engineering in 2003, all from the University of Calcutta, India. Currently, she is a Senior Lecturer at the Department of Computer Science and Engineering, Netaji Subhash Engineering College, Kolkata, India. She has a number of publications in international journals and conferences. Her research interests include pattern recognition, bioinformatics, machine learning, neural networks, cellular automata, etc.

Boqin Feng is a professor at the Department of Computer Science and Technology, Xi'an Jiaotong University, in P. R. China. He is the National Award for Distinguished Teacher (The Ministry of Education, 2003), the dean of Xi'an Jiaotong University Computer Teaching & Experiment Center. He is a specialist in teaching methods of the fundamental computer technology. He has also authored and co-authored many SCI/EI indexed papers.

Wei Feng was born in Sichuan province, China in 1978. He received his B.S. degree in Mechanical Engineering from Harbin Institute of Technology, Harbin, China, in 2000, his M.S. degree in Computer Applied Technology from Southwest Agricultural University, Chongqing, China, in 2004, and Ph.D. degree in Control Theory and Control Engineering from Chongqing University, Chongqing, China, in 2009. His research interests include stability theory, nonlinear systems, and control theory.

Ben Goertzel is a researcher in the field of artificial intelligence. He currently leads Novamente LLC, a privately held software company that attempts to develop a form of strong AI they call "Artificial General Intelligence". He is also the CEO of Biomind LLC, a company that markets a software product for the AI-supported analysis of biological microarray data; and he is a Research Professor in the Fujian Key Lab for Brain-Like Intelligent Systems in the Cognitive Science Department at Xiamen University in China.

Igor Goncharenko holds an MS in control systems from the Moscow Institute of Physics and Technology (1984) and a PhD in computer science from the Russian Academy of Sciences (1994). He is currently a Chief Research Officer of 3D Incorporated, Yokohama, Japan.

Hong Guo is a Senior Lecturer in Software Engineering and a member of the Biomedical Computing and Engineering Technologies Applied Research Group (BIOCORE) at Coventry University. She received her PhD from Nottingham Trent University in 2001. She has published many papers in journals and conferences on software quality management, object oriented software engineering, the application of software process assessment improvement in healthcare applications and in Teleworking environments. She is a Visiting Professor at Beijing Technology and Business University, Beijing, China.

Fumio Hattori received the B.E. and the M.E. degree from Waseda University in 1973 and 1975 respectively. He also received PhD in informatics from Kyoto University in 2000. In 1975, he joined Nippon Telegraph and Telephone public corporation (currently NTT Corporation). At NTT Laboratories, he engaged in the research and development of database systems, knowledge engineering, expert systems, agent-based communication, and so on. Since 2004, he is Professor at Department of Information and Communication Science, College of Information Science and Engineering, Ritsumeikan University.

Chris Heward passed away in January 11th, 2009. He was the president of Kronos Science Laboratory and was actively engaged in all of its research projects. Dr. Heward's research interests included healthy aging, endocrinology, oxidative stress, Alzheimer's disease, prion disease (TSE) and menopause.

Takuro Ito received BS and MS degrees in engineering from Ritsumeikan University in 2007 and 2009 respectively. He is currently working at Brother Industries Ltd.

Luyang Jiao is a doctor, associate professor at the Clinical Laboratory, First Affiliated Hospital of Xinxiang Medical College, in P. R. China. In 2007, he has participated in collecting a set of patients' measurements among different types of groups within the district of Henan province. He has authored and co-authored many papers related to medical diagnosis and testament.

Witold Kinsner is Professor and Associate Head of the Department of Electrical and Computer Engineering, University of Manitoba, Winnipeg, Canada. He is also Affiliate Professor at the Institute of Industrial Mathematical Sciences, Winnipeg, and Adjunct Scientist at the Telecommunications Research Laboratories (TRLabs), Winnipeg. He obtained his PhD in electrical and computer engineering from McMaster University, Hamilton in 1974. He has authored and co-authored over 620 publications in his research areas of computing engines, digital signal processing, and computational intelligence. Dr. Kinsner is a senior member of the Institute of Electrical & Electronics Engineers (IEEE), a member of the Association of Computing Machinery (ACM), a member of Sigma Xi, a Fellow of the Engineering Institute of Canada (EIC), and a life member of the Radio Amateur of Canada (RAC).

Victor V. Kryssanov received his MS in physics from the Far-Eastern National University, Russia, and PhD in biophysics from the Russian Academy of Sciences in 1991 and 1994, respectively. He currently serves as Professor at the College of Information Science and Engineering, Ritsumeikan University, Japan.

Shizuka Kumokawa received her BS in engineering from Ritsumeikan University in 2008, and she is currently pursuing an MS degree in information science at Graduate School of Science and Engineering, Ritsumeikan University.

Kazuhiro Kuwabara received B. Eng., M. Eng., and Dr. Eng. degrees from the University of Tokyo, in 1982, 1984, and 1997 respectively. In 1984, he joined Nippon Telegraph and Telephone Public

Corporation (NTT), and was engaged in research and development on knowledge-based systems, multi-agent systems and socialware. He was with ATR Intelligent Robotics and Communication Laboratories in 2003 - 2006. Currently he is a professor at Department of Information and Communication Science, College of Information Science and Engineering, Ritsumeikan University.

Xuhui Li is Xuhui Li received the BS degree in information science and the MS and the PhD degrees in computer science from Wuhan University in 1996, 1999, and 2003, respectively. He is currently an associate professor in the State Key Laboratory of Software Engineering, Wuhan University in China. His research interests are programming languages, formal theory, data management and parallel and distributed computing. He is a member of ACM, a member of IEEE and a member of IEEE Computer Society.

Yang Liu is a PhD candidate at the Department of Computer Science and Technology, Xi'an Jiaotong University, in P. R. China. During 2007 to 2009, he is a joint PhD candidate with School of Engineering, Blekinge Institute of Technology, in Sweden. He is doing research on machine learning, knowledge discovery, and the extensions of rough set model and its applications.

Takuya Maekawa is a researcher at NTT Communication Science Laboratories in Japan. His research interests include Web content engineering in mobile and ubiquitous environment. He received his Ph.D. in information science and technology from Osaka University in 2006.

Pradipta Maji received the BSc (Hons) degree in physics, the MSc degree in electronics science, and the PhD degree in the area of computer science from Jadavpur University, Kolkata, India, in 1998, 2000, and 2005, respectively. Currently, he is the assistant professor in the Machine Intelligence Unit, Indian Statistical Institute, Kolkata, India. His research interests include pattern recognition, computational biology and bioinformatics, medical image processing, cellular automata, soft computing, and so forth. He has published around 60 papers in international journals and conferences. He is also a reviewer of many international journals. He has received the 2006 Best Paper Award of the International Conference on Visual Information Engineering from The Institution of Engineering and Technology, U.K., the 2008 Microsoft Young Faculty Award from Microsoft Research Laboratory India Pvt. and the 2009 Young Scientist Award from the National Academy of Sciences, India, and has been selected as the 2009 Associate of the Indian Academy of Sciences, India.

S.C. Mak received his BSc Degree in Computing in the Department of Computing from The Hong Kong Polytechnic University in 2008. His research interests include wireless communication, localization, agent technology and data mining. Currently, He is a member of the Graphics and Multimedia Applications (GAMA) Laboratory at The Hong Kong Polytechnic University.

Claude Moulin: PhD in Computer Sciences since 1998, Claude Moulin has been working for four years in research centers in Italy. He is now Assistant Professor at the University of Technology of Compiègne (France) and member of the laboratory HeuDiaSyc (Information Knowledge and Interaction team). This laboratory is a research unit associated with the French CNRS (National Center for Scientific Research). He has a background in Computer Sciences: Virtual Documents, Knowledge Engineering,

Multi-Agent systems, Adaptive and multi-modal Interfaces. He published several papers in journals and conference proceedings in these domains. His current research interests include Knowledge Base System, web service semantic description, ontology design and formalisms in the fields of eLearning, eGovernment and Semantic Web. He is involved in several national and European projects with e-Government and e-Learning as application domains.

Cyprian F. Ngolah received a PhD in Software Engineering from the University of Calgary, Canada in 2006, an MSc in Control Engineering from the University of Bradford, England in 1989, and a BSc in Mathematics and Computer Science from the University of Essex, England in 1988. He taught several computer science and software engineering courses at both the graduate and undergraduate levels for thirteen years at University of Buea, Cameroon. He is currently a senior software engineer in the Research and Development Department of Sentinel Trending & Diagnostics Ltd, Calgary, carrying out research on the development of a neural network for machine condition monitoring and predictive maintenance using vibration analysis. His main research interests are in real-time process algebra and its applications, tool support for formal specification languages, real-time operating systems, formal methods in software engineering and real-time software systems, and artificial neural networks.

Hitoshi Ogawa received his Dr.Eng. from Osaka University in 1977. He is currently Professor at the Department of Information and Communication Science, College of Information Science and Engineering, Ritsumeikan University.

Takeshi Okadome is a project leader of Ambient Semantics Research Group in NTT Communication Science Laboratories, Nippon Telegraph and Telephone Corporation. His current interest is the study of creating contents of the real-world events using sensors. He received the Doctor of Science degree in Computer Science from the University of Tokyo in 1988.

Witold Pedrycz (M'88, SM'90, F'99) is a Professor and Canada Research Chair (CRC - Computational Intelligence) in the Department of Electrical and Computer Engineering, University of Alberta, Edmonton, Canada. He is also with the Systems Research Institute of the Polish Academy of Sciences, Warsaw, Poland. He also holds an appointment of special professorship in the School of Computer Science, University of Nottingham, UK. In 2009 Dr. Pedrycz was elected a foreign member of the Polish Academy of Sciences. He main research directions involve Computational Intelligence, fuzzy modeling and Granular Computing, knowledge discovery and data mining, fuzzy control, pattern recognition, knowledge-based neural networks, relational computing, and Software Engineering. He has published numerous papers in this area. He is also an author of 14 research monographs covering various aspects of Computational Intelligence and Software Engineering. Witold Pedrycz has been a member of numerous program committees of IEEE conferences in the area of fuzzy sets and neurocomputing. Dr. Pedrycz is intensively involved in editorial activities. He is an Editor-in-Chief of *Information Sciences* and Editor-in-Chief of *IEEE Transactions on Systems, Man, and Cybernetics - part A*. He currently serves as an Associate Editor of *IEEE Transactions on Fuzzy Systems* and a number of other international journals. He has edited a number of volumes; the most recent one is entitled "Handbook of Granular Computing" (J. Wiley, 2008). In 2007 he received a prestigious Norbert Wiener award from the IEEE Systems, Man, and Cybernetics Council. He is a recipient of the IEEE Canada Computer Engineering Medal 2008. In

2009 he has received a Cajastur Prize for Soft Computing from the European Centre for Soft Computing for "*pioneering and multifaceted contributions to Granular Computing*".

Cassio Pennachin has developed quality work over a great variety of subfields and applications of Artificial Intelligence, including but not limited to bioinformatics, financial market prediction, natural language and intelligent virtual agents, among others. He has also been leading software development projects in those areas since the mid-1990's.

Qiumei Pu (pu_qiumei@163.com) is lecturer of MINZU University of China. She received a PhD in Computer Application technology from Wuhan University of Technology, China, in 2007.

Carlos Ramirez is full professor of artificial intelligence and theory of computation at the Tecnologico de Monterrey, México; member of DASL4LTD research group at ITESM Campus Queretaro. He received a PhD in computer science from The University of Kent at Canterbury, UK (1998), and a BSc in Computer Science from the Tecnologico de Monterrey (1984). He has published more than 20 papers in artificial intelligence, cognitive science and control, won best paper, and several academic awards, and has supervised dozens of projects on those fields. His interests are on Adaptive Virtual Learning Environments, Pattern Recognition and Optimization through Artificial Intelligence.

Gilson Yukio Sato is a lecturer at Federal University of Technology - Paraná (UTFPR - Brazil). He received his electronic engineering degree (1992) and his MSc (2001) from UTFPR. He obtained his PhD from the University of Technology of Compiègne (UTC - France) in 2008. His main research involves agents in the support of communities of practice.

Marco Luca Sbodio works at Hewlett-Packard Italy Innovation Center. He has a M.S. in Computer Science from Politecnico di Torino, and he is currently a PhD candidate in Computer Science at Politecnico di Torino (Italy) and Université de Technologie de Compiègne (France). His research interests are in the area of Semantic Web, Semantic Web Services and Artificial Intelligence.

Phillip C-Y. Sheu is currently a professor of Computer Engineering, Information and Computer Science, and Biomedical Engineering at the University of California, Irvine. He received his Ph.D. and M.S. degrees from the University of California at Berkeley in Electrical Engineering and Computer Science in 1986 and 1982, respectively, and his B.S. degree from National Taiwan University in Electrical Engineering in 1978. Between 1982 and 1986, he also worked as a computer scientist at Systems Control Technology, Inc., Palo Alto, CA., where he designed and implemented aircraft expert control systems, and he worked as a product planning engineer at Advanced Micro Devices Inc., Sunnyvale, CA, where he designed and integrated CAD systems. From 1986 to 1988, he was an assistant professor at School of Electrical Engineering, Purdue University. From 1989 to 1993, he was an associate professor of Electrical and Computer Engineering at Rutgers University. He has published two books: (1) Intelligent Robotic Planning Systems and (2) Software Engineering and Environment - An Object-Oriented Perspective, and more than 100 papers in object-relational data and knowledge engineering and their applications, and biomedical computations. He is currently active in research related to complex biological systems, knowledge-based medicine, semantic software engineering, proactive web technologies, and large real-time knowledge systems for defense and homeland security. His current research projects are sponsored by the National Science Foundation, National Institute of Health, and Department of Defense. Dr. Sheu is a Fellow of IEEE.

Norio Shiratori received his doctoral degree from Tohoku University, Japan in 1977. Presently he is a Professor of the Research Institute of Electrical Communication, Tohoku University. He has been engaged in research related to symbiotic computing paradigms between human and information technology. He was the recipient of the IPSJ Memorial Prize Winning Paper Award in 1985, the Telecommunication Advancement Foundation Incorporation Award in 1991, the Best Paper Award of ICOIN-9 in 1994, the IPSJ Best Paper Award in 1997, the IPSJ Contribution Award in 2007, and many others. He was the vice president of IPSJ in 2002 and now is the president of IPSJ. He is also a fellow of IEEE and IEICE.

Takuo Suganuma is an associate professor of Research Institute of Electrical Communication of Tohoku University, Japan. He received a Dr.Eng. degree from Chiba Institute of Technology. He received UIC-07 Outstanding Paper Award in 2007, etc. His research interests include agent-based computing, flexible network, and symbiotic computing. He is a member of IEICE, IPSJ and IEEE.

Kenji Sugawara is a professor of the Department of Information and Network Science, and a dean of Faculty of Information and Computer Science, Chiba Institute of Technology, Chiba, Japan. He received BS (1972), his doctorate degree in Engineering (1983) from Tohoku University, Japan. His research interests include Multi-agent System, Artificial Intelligence, Ubiquitous Computing and Symbiotic Computing. Prof. Sugawara is a Fellow of IEICE Japan and a member of IEEE, ACM, and IPSJ.

Hideyuki Takahashi is a research fellow of Research Institute of Electrical Communication of Tohoku University, Japan. He received his doctoral degree in Information Sciences from Tohoku University in 2008. His research interests include ubiquitous computing and agent-based computing. He is a member of IPSJ.

Xinming Tan is a professor in the School of Computer Science and Technology at Wuhan University of Technology, China. He is the head of the Department of Computer Science. He received a BSc and an MSc in Computer Science at Wuhan University of Technology, and a PhD in Software Engineering at University of Calgary, Canada in 2007. His major research interests are in formal methods, real-time systems, and cognitive informatics.

Yousheng Tian is a PhD candidate in cognitive computing and software engineering with the International Center for Cognitive Informatics and Cognitive Computing (ICCICC) as well as Theoretical and Empirical Software Engineering Center (TESERC) in Dept. of Electrical and Computer Engineering at the University of Calgary, Canada. He received a PhD from Xian Jiantong University, China, in Computer Science in 2002 and was a Post Doctoral Fellow at ICCICC during 2006 to 2007. His research interests are in cognitive informatics, cognitive computing, software engineering, machine learning, and denotational mathematics.

Benjamín Valdés is a research assistant member of the DASL4LTD at ITESM Campus Queretaro; He received a BSc in Computer Science from the Tecnologico de Monterrey (2007) and is currently a postgraduate candidate on Information technology with publications on the fields of: adaptive technologies, cognitive informatics, and e-learning software tools. His interests are on Knowledge Representation, Cognitive Informatics, Adaptive Systems and Virtual Learning Environments.

Bernard Widrow received the Bachelor's, Master's, and Doctor of science degrees from the Massachusetts Institute of Technology (MIT), Cambridge. He served on the MIT faculty before coming to Stanford in 1959. He has published three textbooks and numerous journal articles. He is a pioneer in the field of adaptive filters and neural networks and a long-time Professor of Electrical Engineering at Stanford who concentrates his research on adaptive signal processing, adaptive control systems, adaptive neural networks, human memory, and human-like memory for computers. He was inducted into the National Academy of Engineering in 1995.

Jiří Wiedermann is a professor and one of the first generation of computer scientists graduating in former Czechoslovakia. His research interests include ad-hoc networks, algorithms (design and analysis), algorithmic systems, applied algorithmics, artificial intelligence, artificial life, cognitive systems, computational complexity theory (incl. non-uniform complexity theory), datastructures, distributed computing, embodied robotics, information technology, intelligent algorithms, languages and automata, machine learning, non-standard computational models (amorphous computing, molecular computing, nano-computing, super-Turing computability, etc.), networks and network modeling, network algorithms, neurocomputing, parallel computing, theoretical computer science, and more. In these fields he published two monographs and more than 150 papers in scientific journals and conference proceedings. Some of his results have entered the monographs and textbooks in computer science. By his invited talks, publications and activities in organization of important European and national computer science conferences he contributed to the development of informatics both at national and international level. In nineteen nineties he acted as the vice-president of the European Association for Theoretical Computer Science (EATCS). In 2000 he became the director of the Institute of Computer Science of Academy of Sciences of the Czech Republic. Professor Wiedermann is a member of Academia Europaea (London) and of the Czech Learned Society.

Haixia Wu was born in Shandong province, China in 1979. She received her B.S. and M.S. degree in Computer Applied Technology from Southwest Agricultural University, Chongqing, China, in 2001 and 2004, respectively. In 2009, she received her Ph.D. degree in Computer Science and Engineering from Chongqing University, Chongqing, China. Her research interests include stability theory, nonlinear systems, neural networks, and genetic regulatory networks.

Yutaka Yanagisawa is a member of the Ambient Semantics Research Group at the NTT Communication Science Laboratories. His research interests include localization systems for mobile computing environment, programming languages to develop middleware and operating systems on small mobile devices, and augmented reality systems to support people using mobile devices. Yanagisawa received PhD in engineering from Osaka University.

Kiyoshi Yasuda received BA from Ritsumeikan University in 1983. He also got a license of Speech/language therapist in 1983. He received PhD from Chiba University in 2003. Since 1983, he is working as a Speech/language therapist at Speech pathology services in the Rehabilitation department, Chiba Rosai Hospital. From 2003 to 2007, he is a visiting researcher at Intelligent Robotics and Communications Laboratories, Advanced Telecommunications Research International. He is currently Project Professor, Holistic Prosthetics Center, Kyoto Institute of Technology.

Guangping Zeng is a professor of computer science and Director of School of Information Engineering at the University of Science and Technology, Beijing (USTB), China. He received a PhD and MSc in computer science from USTB in 2005 and 1995, respectively, and a BSc in Petroleum Engineering from the Chinese Petrol University in 1984. He was a postdoctoral fellow in EECS at University of California, Berkeley during 2008 to 2009. He was the former head of Department of Computer Science and Technology at USTB in 2003-2005. He is a senior member and a steering committee member of the Chinese Association of AI. He has published over 70 peer-reviewed papers and two books. His research interests are in artificial intelligence, intelligent software, soft-man, virtual robots, embedded networks, and Internet-based computing.

Hong Zhang is a senior software engineer and a product manager of Nuctech Ltd. in Beijing, China. He obtained his two Master's degrees from the Department of Human Anatomy & Cell Sciences (1998) and the Department of Electrical & Computer Engineering (2002), both at the University of Manitoba, Winnipeg, Canada. He has published in the bioscience area.

Yanan Zhang is an MSc candidate in Software Engineering from at University of Calgary, Canada. She received a BSc degree in Computer Science from the North Jiaotong University, Beijing, China in 1989. Her main research interests are in software engineering, Internet-based and distributed systems, and real-time process algebra and its applications.

Haibin Zhu is a Professor of the Department of Computer Science and Mathematics, Nipissing University, Canada and has published about 100 research papers, four books and two book chapters on object-oriented programming, distributed systems, collaborative systems, agent systems and computer architecture. He is a senior member of IEEE, a member of ACM, and a life member of the Chinese Association for Science and Technology, USA. He is serving and served as co-chair of the technical committee of Distributed Intelligent Systems of IEEE SMC Society, guest (co-)editor for 3 special issues of prestigious journals, PC vice chair, poster co-chair, and publicity co-chair for many IEEE conferences. He is the recipient of the 2006-2007 research award from Nipissing University, the 2004 and 2005 IBM Eclipse Innovation Grant Awards, the Best Paper Award from the 11th ISPE Int'l Conf. on Concurrent Engineering (ISPE/CE2004), the Educator's Fellowship of OOPSLA'03, a 2nd Class National Award of Excellent Textbook from the Ministry of Education of China (2002), a 2nd class National Award for Education Achievement(1997), and three 1st Class Ministerial Research Achievement Awards from The Commission of Science Technology and Industry for National Defense of China (1997, 1994, and 1991).

Index

A

B

C

C (continued)

D

E